The Boatowner's Guide to Corrosion

A COMPLETE REFERENCE FOR BOATOWNERS AND MARINE PROFESSIONALS

Everett Collier

International Marine / McGraw-Hill

Camden, Maine • New York • San Francisco • Washington, D.C. • Auckland
Bogotá • Caracas • Lisbon • London • Madrid • Mexico City • Milan • Montreal
New Delhi • San Juan • Singapore • Sydney • Tokyo • Toronto

Of all those who have contributed to the writing of this book, there are those who—bound by ties of family and friendship—had no choice but nonetheless made their contributions cheerfully. Their contributions were made in terms of nights, weekends, and vacations shared with "the book." Betty, Scott, and Greg—wife and sons, in that order—friends, partners, boatbuilding and sailing buddies in any order. It is to these contributors that this book is dedicated with thanks.

International Marine

A Division of The McGraw-Hill Companies

10 9 8 7 6 5 4 3 2 1

Copyright © 2001 International Marine

All rights reserved. The publisher takes no responsibility for the use of any of the materials or methods described in this book, nor for the products thereof. The name "International Marine" and the International Marine logo are trademarks of The McGraw-Hill Companies. Printed in the United States of America.

Library of Congress Cataloging-in-Publication Data
Collier, Everett.
    The boatowner's guide to corrosion : a complete reference for boatowners and marine professionals / Everett Collier.
            p.   cm.
    Includes bibliographical references and index.
    ISBN 0-07-155019-4
    1. Boats and boating—Corrosion. 2. Ships—Cathodic protection. I. Title.
VM951.C585 2000
623.8'48—dc21   00-033488

Questions regarding the content of this book should be addressed to
    International Marine
    P.O. Box 220, Camden, ME 04843
    www.internationalmarine.com

Questions regarding the ordering of this book should be addressed to
    The McGraw-Hill Companies
    Customer Service Department
    P.O. Box 547, Blacklick, OH 43004
    Retail customers: 1-800-262-4729
    Bookstores: 1-800-722-4726

This book is printed on 60 lb. Finch by
    R. R. Donnelley & Sons, Crawfordsville, IN
Design by Joyce C. Weston
Production by Dan Kirchoff
Edited by Jonathan Eaton, Don Casey, and Jane M.
    Curran

3M, Acrilan, Anchorfast, Aquamet, BoatLIFE, Boeshield T-9, Corrosion Block, Corrosion X, Cor-Ten, Cuprinol, Dacron, Delrin, Divinycell, Ferralium, Forespar, Hastelloy, Incoloy, Inconel, Jack Nut, Kapton, Kevlar, LanoCote, Lexan, Loctite, Marelon, Mer-Cathode, Monel, Multimet, Mylar, Nitronic, Nomex, Orlon, Phillips, Pop (rivet), Porta Potti, Sikaflex, Spectra, Stronghold, Technora, Tedlar, Tefgel, Teflon, Terylene, Tobin bronze, Torx, Vectran, Viny-Lux, Well-Nut, Zamak, and Zytel are registered trademarks.

WARNING: Repairing and maintaining your boat can expose you, your boat, and your equipment to potentially dangerous situations and substances. Reference to brand names does not indicate endorsement of or guarantee the safety of using these products. In using this book, the reader releases the author, publisher, and distributor from liability for any loss or injury, including death, allegedly caused, in whole or in part, by relying on information contained in this book.

Contents

Tables

Introduction

Countless excellent articles on various aspects of marine corrosion, written by knowledgeable and experienced professionals, have appeared in marine periodicals and trade magazines. Much valuable information on the subject is contained in the many fine books that have been published on the broader subjects of boatbuilding, maintenance, and repair. A wealth of valuable information, current with the present state of technology in metals and alloys, coatings and barriers, exists in the literature of other related industrial communities such as the chemical process and the petrochemical industries.

However, nowhere in the current marine literature is there one place where all this useful information is brought together for ready reference by the weekend boaters who can't use their boats, or the boatyard operators to whom they turn for help, or the boatbuilders—backyard or professional—who would like very much to head off corrosion problems before they occur.

This book is written and organized principally for three groups within the marine community. First are the recreational boaters, weekend sailors, sportfishers, and commercial fishers who either don't have or can't afford to spend the time and must solve their corrosion problems quickly and as simply as possible. They are not corrosion or chemical engineers and are not interested in the underlying chemistry and physics of corrosion science. They simply have a problem and want to solve it as quickly as possible. These readers can safely skip over the first five chapters, which are devoted to the underlying physics and chemistry and the various types of corrosion. Depending on the nature of the problem, readers can go directly to chapters 16 through 21, each of which deals with a specific

vessel system, the corrosion problems that typically occur in these systems, and some solutions.

The second group is composed of boatyard and marina owners and operators, repairers, and surveyors to whom the folks in the first group turn when they have a problem they can't solve. This group must therefore take a more thorough and analytical approach to problem solving based on a more in-depth understanding of the corrosion process. These readers may find the basic foundational information in chapters 1 through 7 helpful before going on to the later chapters.

The third group consists of designers, builders, and restorers who may not only have to solve existing problems but also have the opportunity to take steps to prevent or mitigate corrosion problems and extend the trouble-free life of the boat. This group will also find much useful information in chapters 8 through 15, which cover in some depth the various marine metals and coatings, including the more recent alloys and formulations that are currently available. This group will also find much useful information in the appendices.

There are (at least) two schools of thought on the broad, generic definition of corrosion. One of these would limit the definition to metals; the other would include any and all materials of construction. The latter group would define corrosion as the deterioration of a material of construction or of its properties as a result of exposure to an environment. This group seems to have history on its side, and it is this definition that has been followed in this book.

Finally, I would leave you with the following bit of humorous doggerel written by a former president of the National Association of Corrosion Engineers (NACE). I recommend this little verse not only for its humor but for the truth that lies buried in it, just below the humor.

Mighty ships upon the ocean
Suffer from severe corrosion.
Even those that stay at dockside
Are rapidly becoming oxide.
Alas, that piling in the sea
Is mostly Fe_2O_3.
And when the ocean meets the shore,
You'll find there's Fe_2O_4
Cause when the wind is salt and gusty,
Things are getting awfully rusty.

We can measure it. We can test it.
We can halt it or arrest it.
We can gather it and weigh it.
We can coat it. We can spray it.
We examine and dissect it.
We cathodically protect it.
We can pick it up and drop it,
But heaven knows we'll never stop it.
So here's to rust! No doubt about it.
Most of us would starve without it.

T. R. B. Watson

Acknowledgments

One of the more difficult tasks in writing a book such as this is the need and the desire to acknowledge those who have contributed to the project. There are those who contributed from their technical and scientific knowledge and experience, others from their vast store of experience in the marine industry, and still others from their unique and proprietary knowledge of their products and service. Finally, there are those whose contributions were made over the years through informal teaching and training in boatyards, boatshops, magazine articles, and books too numerous to count but too valuable to ignore. In order to avoid the risk of offending by omission, I'll not attempt to identify them here—the list would be too long in any case—but they know who they are and they have here, again, my thanks.

CHAPTER 1

Basic Molecular Theory

Corrosion is a chemical reaction, or more precisely, an electrochemical reaction. The chemical properties of matter are largely determined by the electrons around the nucleus of its atoms, particularly the outer or valence electrons. Understanding corrosion requires an elementary grasp of the structure of materials.

MATTER

Matter is the stuff that everything is made of—metals, woods, plastics, petunias, soda pop, and even people. Matter can exist as a solid, a liquid, or a gas. (It can also exist in the plasma form, but that's not our problem.) We will be dealing with matter in all these forms, but primarily with solids (the metals that are corroding) and liquids (the seawater in which the corrosion is taking place). The gases, mostly hydrogen and oxygen, help us explain what happens to all the matter involved in the corrosion process. Matter can also be classified according to its composition: whether it's an *element*, a *compound*, or a *mixture*.

This is going to sound a little like "the foot-bone's connected to the shin-bone, the shin-bone's connected to the knee-bone," but a basic understanding of the skeletal structure of matter is necessary if we're going to be able to deal effectively with corrosion problems encountered on a boat.

Matter consists of molecules. Molecules consist of atoms. Atoms consist of protons, neutrons, and, alas, electrons. It is those rascally electrons that are at the bottom of it all. So let's focus on atoms since that is where electrons hang out.

ATOMS AND MOLECULES

The atom is electrically neutral; it has no electrical charge. That's because the electrical charges of the particles that comprise the atom balance each other. The core of the atom is the nucleus. It consists of two types of particles—protons carrying a positive charge and neutrons carrying no charge. Thus, the net charge on the nucleus is positive.

This positive charge is balanced by negatively charged electrons, the atom's remaining particles. It helps to think of electrons as orbiting around the nucleus in "shells" something like the layers of an onion, each increasingly farther out from the core or nucleus. Each shell can hold only a specific number of electrons—a maximum of 2 electrons in the first or lowest energy shell, 8 for the second shell, 18 for the third, 32 for the fourth. Because it requires the least energy to orbit a nucleus that is close, the innermost shell is filled first, then the second innermost, and so on.

The number of electrons actually present in the shells of an atom depends upon the specific element, and a shell may be empty or may be occupied but not filled. Let's take a look at the simplest atom of them all, the hydrogen atom (fig. 1-1).

Hydrogen has only one electron, and it is in the first shell as shown. Since the first shell can hold a maximum of two electrons, we might logically expect to find an atom with two electrons in its first shell. Indeed, the helium atom, shown in figure 1-2, has two electrons in its innermost shell.

Were we to look for an atom with three electrons, we would expect to find two of these in

1

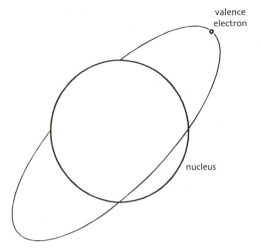

Fig. 1-1. The hydrogen atom, with a single valence electron.

the first shell and one in the second. Lithium is just such an atom. Additional electrons would go into this second shell until it held a maximum of 8 electrons, giving us an atom with a total of 10 electrons. An atom with 11 electrons would have 2 electrons in the first shell, 8 in the second shell, and 1 in the third shell—and so on. OK so far?

Now let's consider the tendency of an atom to gain or lose electrons and, amounting to the same thing, its tendency to participate in chem-

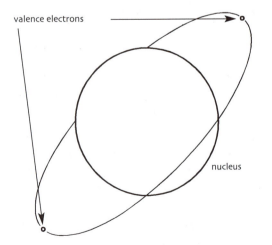

Fig. 1-2. The helium atom, with its two valence electrons.

ical (or electrochemical) reactions. This is called *valence*. The valence of an atom is determined by the number of electrons in its outermost, or valence, shell. When the outermost shell is completely filled, the atom is in its most stable state and least inclined to enter into chemical reactions. In combining with other atoms, it will tend to gain or lose valence electrons in order to attain a stable configuration.

Molecules are made up of two or more atoms. The atoms may be of the same element or of two or more different elements. There are 110 known elements, fundamental substances that consist of atoms of only one kind. These, singly or in combination, constitute all matter.

Molecules, like atoms, carry no electrical charge.

IONIZATION

There are a couple more fundamental concepts we should talk about. The first, *ionization*, is the process by which an atom or molecule acquires a charge. Atoms or molecules that have either gained or lost one or more electrons are known as ions. Ions consequently bear positive or negative charges, and significantly for us, the flow of ions constitutes an electrical current. Ionization is fundamental to the corrosion process. We'll talk more about it in chapter 2.

CHEMICAL BONDING

The second concept is *chemical bonding*. Chemical bonds are links that join the atoms of matter together. The forces that cause the bonding between atoms result from the interactions between charged particles—the positive protons and the negative electrons. The atoms of some elements become more stable when they acquire one or more electrons; others become more stable when they give up electrons.

Due to their compelling tendency to maintain electrical neutrality, atoms can't simply take on or give up electrons. In forming chemical bonds, they try to attain increased stability without giving up their electrical neutrality. There are a number of different types of chemical bonds, but for our purposes we can consider two basic types—*covalent bonds* and *ionic bonds*. The specific nature of the bonds formed depends upon the nature of the elements involved. This is an important consideration in corrosion.

Covalent Bonding

Atoms of elements that become more stable by gaining electrons can maintain electrical neutrality by sharing electrons with other atoms of the *same or similar* elements. When atoms form chemical bonds by sharing electrons, this is called *covalent bonding*. The molecules formed by covalent bonding are designated with a subscript showing the number of atoms. For example, when two hydrogen (H) atoms combine by sharing electrons, the resulting molecule is designated H_2. Similarly, oxygen atoms combine into O_2, nitrogen atoms into N_2.

Ionic Bonding

Atoms of elements that become more stable by losing electrons can give up electrons to atoms of elements that become more stable by gaining them. However, the atom giving up the electron becomes a positive ion while the atom gaining an electron becomes a negative ion. Since oppositely charged bodies are attracted to each other, the two atoms are now bound together by what

is called an *ionic bond*, and the overall electrical charge of the molecule is neutral. An example of relevant elements that form ionic bonds are sodium (Na) and chlorine (Cl), which combine to form sodium chloride (Na^+Cl^-), or salt.

SUMMARY

To sum up what we've covered so far, *atoms* are tiny energy systems bound together by the force of attraction between the positive nucleus and the negative electrons. There are 110 known *elements*, fundamental substances that consist of atoms of only one kind and, singly or in various combinations, constitute all matter. Atoms link together to form various compounds through chemical bonding. An atom is in its most stable (lowest energy) state and least inclined to gain or lose electrons when its outermost shell is filled. An atom becomes a *positive* ion when it loses a valence electron and a *negative* ion when it gains an electron. Ions and electrons are the charge carriers that constitute electrical current flow, and ionization is a critical part of the corrosion process.

In chapter 2 we examine the chemical processes by which atoms and molecules combine to form various materials.

Basic Chemical Theory

Now that we have defined all the pieces and parts and their peculiarities, let's see how they go together. This requires a light review of a few basics in chemical theory.

SYMBOLS

In chemistry, an abbreviation—called a *symbol*—is used to designate a particular chemical element. The symbol is usually the first letter or the first letter and another letter of the English name of the element. For example, O is the symbol for oxygen, H is the symbol for hydrogen, and Cl is the symbol for chlorine. In some cases, however, the symbol is derived from the Latin name of the element. We see this in the symbol for sodium, Na, which comes from *natrium*, sodium's Latin name.

Each symbol also represents a definite quantity of the element—the *gram-atomic weight*, or *mole*. The mole is an important concept in chemistry. In dealing with chemical reactions we must be able to account for all of the materials involved in the reaction. That is, all of the atoms that we start with before the reaction takes place must be present or accounted for in the materials resulting from the reaction. We do this by keeping track of the atoms using their atomic weights and the mole.

The term *mole* can be confusing. Its meanings range from a small pointy-nosed animal to a stone breakwater that encloses a harbor, and in between we have international spies, tunneling machines, and a spicy Mexican sauce. Let's be clear as to what we mean when we use the term here. A mole is a quantity, like a dozen. A dozen is 12 anythings. A mole is 6.02×10^{23} anythings. The term *mole* is used because it's a whole lot easier to work with than 6.02×10^{23}.

The symbol of an element represents 1 atomic weight or mole of that element. So, the gram-atomic weight of an element is a quantity equal to the atomic weight of the element expressed in grams. For example, the atomic weight of sodium is 23. This means that 23 grams represents 1 atomic weight of sodium—or to put it differently, 1 mole of sodium weighs 23 grams.

Table 2-1 gives the symbols and the approximate atomic weights for some of the common elements that we may encounter in the marine environment.

FORMULAS

As we discussed in chapter 1, atoms combine to form molecules. Molecules are made up of two or more atoms, either of the same element or of different elements. The formula for a given mol-

Table 2-1

Atomic Symbols and Weights of Common Elements

Chemical Element	Atomic Symbol	Atomic Weight (grams)
hydrogen	H	1
carbon	C	12
nitrogen	N	14
oxygen	O	16
sodium	Na	23
aluminum	Al	27
silicon	Si	28
chlorine	Cl	35.5
titanium	Ti	47.9
manganese	Mn	54.9
iron	Fe	55.8
nickel	Ni	58.7
copper	Cu	63.5
zinc	Zn	65.4
molybdenum	Mo	95.9
tin	Sn	118.7

ecule consists of the symbols for all the included elements, and if the molecule contains more than one atom of any element, the formula incorporates a subscript following that element to indicate the number of atoms.

A chemical formula also represents 1 gram-molecular weight, or mole. For example, the formula for a hydrogen molecule is H_2, and its gram-molecular weight is 2 grams. We know this because hydrogen atoms (H) have a 1 gram-atomic weight each, and there are two such atoms in H_2.

The formula for water is H_2O, and its gram-molecular weight is 18 grams. Two hydrogen atoms at 1 gram each plus one oxygen atom at 16 grams give us a total of 18 grams. Similarly, a sodium chloride (salt) molecule, represented by the formula NaCl, consists of one atom of sodium (Na) and one of chlorine (Cl). The atomic weight of the sodium atom is 23 and the atomic weight of the chlorine atom is 35.5, so the total molecular weight of sodium chloride is 58.5.

Use of the mole is not limited to atoms. We also use this term to express the quantity of molecules. Where a mole of atoms represents the number of atoms in a gram-atom, a mole of molecules represents the number of molecules in a gram-molecule. We can use the term *mole* to refer to the gram-atomic weight of a single atom (*monatomic*) element, such as Na, or to the gram-molecular weight of a *polyatomic* (more than one atom) element, such as H_2, or to the gram-molecular weight of a compound such as NaCl. Notice that in H_2, we would have 2 moles of hydrogen atoms or 1 mole of hydrogen molecules.

Table 2-2 gives some of the common chemical formulas and molecular weights that will be of interest to us in the marine environment.

ATOMIC STRUCTURE

We said earlier that an atom is composed of three basic particles—electrons, protons, and neutrons. Protons and neutrons are of roughly equal size and make up the nucleus. The total of the number of protons and neutrons is referred to as the *mass number*. Neutrons are electrically

Table 2-2

Common Chemical Formulas and Molecular Weights

Compound	Formula	Molecular Weight
sodium chloride	NaCl	58.5
water	H_2O	18
hydrogen peroxide	H_2O_2	34
sodium hydroxide	NaOH	40
copper oxide	CuO	79.5
aluminum oxide (alumina)	Al_2O_3	102
ferric oxide (rust)	Fe_2O_3	159.6

neutral, having no electrical charge. Protons have a unit positive electrical charge ($+1.602 \times 10^{-19}$). Electrons, 1/1837 the mass of a proton, have a unit negative electrical charge (-1.602×10^{-19}). The electrons are located outside the nucleus, arranged in increasingly distant orbits, called shells. Shell number 1 is the innermost shell.

Atoms are electrically neutral since they contain an equal number of protons (positive charge) and electrons (negative charge). The number of protons or the number of electrons is referred to as the *atomic number*. Notice that as the atomic numbers of the atoms increase, electrons fill the shells in a prescribed fashion. The first or innermost shell is filled first and is filled when it has 2 electrons. The second shell can hold a maximum of 8 electrons. The third shell can hold a maximum of 18. There are exceptions to this (for example, as in argon, potassium, calcium, and iron) having to do with subshells and energy levels. However, that is more detail than is necessary for our purpose. What is significant here for us is that it is the electrons in the outer or valence shell that are involved in the corrosion process and whether the particular atom involved considers that shell to be full.

There is no truly satisfactory way to show the shells pictorially; figure 2-1 is a greatly simplified representation of the concept. The tendency of an atom to participate readily in chemical reactions or changes is related to the number of electrons in its outermost shell.

Table 2-3 gives the properties of the elements

valence number = +3
atomic number = 13

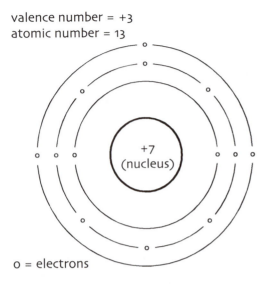

o = electrons

Fig. 2-1. Electron shell structure of an aluminum atom.

in order of their atomic and mass numbers. The mass number is the total number of protons and neutrons in the nucleus.

Note that the outermost electron shells for helium, neon, and argon are all "filled"—with 2, 8, and 8 electrons, respectively. These elements belong to a group called the *noble* or *inert gases*. Noble gases are extremely stable and show little tendency to enter into chemical reactions. They are very seldom found in compounds. Since everything in nature seeks to attain a more stable state, we can conclude from the noble gases that when elements combine, they seek to fill their outermost electron shells, thus attaining greater stability.

COMBINING CAPACITY

The combining capacity of an atom is the number of electrons it can gain, lose, or share in the

Table 2-3

Elements and Their Properties

Element	Symbol	Atomic Number	Mass Number	Nucleus p = protons n = neutrons	Number of Electrons in Shells			
					1	2	3	4
hydrogen	H	1	1	1p	1			
helium	He	2	4	2p + 2n	2			
lithium	Li	3	7	3p + 4n	2	1		
beryllium	Be	4	9	4p + 5n	2	2		
boron	B	5	11	5p + 6n	2	3		
carbon	C	6	12	6p + 6n	2	4		
nitrogen	N	7	14	7p + 7n	2	5		
oxygen	O	8	16	8p + 8n	2	6		
fluorine	F	9	19	9p + 10n	2	7		
neon	Ne	10	20	10p + 10n	2	8		
sodium	Na	11	23	11p + 12n	2	8	1	
magnesium	Mg	12	24	12p + 12n	2	8	2	
aluminum	Al	13	27	13p + 14n	2	8	3	
silicon	Si	14	28	14p + 14n	2	8	4	
phosphorus	P	15	31	15p + 16n	2	8	5	
sulfur	S	16	32	16p + 16n	2	8	6	
chlorine	Cl	17	35	17p + 18n	2	8	7	
argon	Ar	18	40	18p + 22n	2	8	8	
potassium	K	19	39	19p + 20n	2	8	8	1
calcium	Ca	20	40	20p + 20n	2	8	8	2
iron	Fe	26	56	26p + 30n	2	8	14	2
copper	Cu	29	64	29p + 35n	2	8	18	1
zinc	Zn	30	65	30p + 35n	2	8	18	2

Table 2-4

Elements and Their Valence Numbers

Element	Symbol	Valence Number
aluminum	Al	+3
calcium	Ca	+2
chlorine	Cl	−1
copper	Cu	+1, +2
fluorine	F	−1
iron	Fe	+2, +3
lithium	Li	+1
magnesium	Mg	+2
oxygen	O	−2
potassium	K	+1
sodium	Na	+1
sulfur	S	−2
zinc	Zn	+2

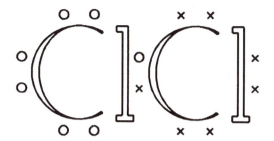

Fig. 2-2. Lewis dot diagram of a chlorine molecule depicting covalent bonding.

forming of chemical bonds. This is the *valence number*. The atom that loses electrons has a positive combining capacity, or positive valence number. The atom that gains electrons has a negative combining capacity, or negative valence number. *Electron transfer* refers to both the donating and the receiving of electrons since both processes occur simultaneously. An electron transfer forms oppositely charged ions—the so-called *ionic bond*. Atoms may also combine by electron *sharing*. When atoms share electrons, the result is referred to as a *covalent bond*.

Chemists are able to predict valence numbers from the electronic structure of the atoms, as given in table 2-4.

COVALENT, IONIC, AND POLAR BONDS

Chemical bonds are the means by which atoms and molecules are held together to form the compounds and mixtures we'll be dealing with. More to the point, corrosion is the breaking of some bonds and the formation of new ones. Since the nature of the bonds, along with the specific atoms and molecules involved, determines the nature and the rate of the reaction, we should spend a little more time on chemical bonds and the bonding process.

Atoms may attain a more stable structure by *sharing* electrons. This is called *covalent bonding*. Each atom exerts the same amount of attractive force on the bonding electrons, so there is no strong tendency for one atom to lose an electron or for another to gain an electron. Figure 2-2 depicts covalent bonding in the chlorine molecule. The *o*'s represent the valence electrons—those in the outermost shell—of one chlorine atom, and the *x*'s represent the valence electrons of the other chlorine atom.

An atom that gives up an electron becomes a positively charged particle called a positive ion. An atom that gains an electron has a negative charge and is called a negative ion. The attraction between oppositely charged ions constitutes an *ionic bond* or *polar bond*.

Elements whose atoms give up electrons readily are said to be *metallic*. Those whose atoms gain electrons readily are said to be *nonmetallic*. An ionic bond results from the *transfer* of electrons from an atom of a metallic element to an atom of a nonmetallic element. In general, atoms with 1 or 2 electrons in their outermost shells are metals and have a tendency to give up electrons. Those with 6 or 7 electrons in their outermost shells are nonmetals and have a tendency to gain electrons.

One more clarifying concept is necessary. Ionic and covalent bonds represent the two extremes in bond formation. Pure ionic or pure covalent bonds rarely exist in nature. All bonds are covalent in the sense that electrons are being shared. The degree to which the bond is also ionic depends on the relative attractions the atoms have for the electrons. If one atom exerts a greater attractive force, shared electrons will spend more time nearer the nucleus of that atom, giving it a relatively negative charge. Its partner atom assumes a relatively positive charge. Thus, the bond will have a definite ionic character.

Consider the bonding between the oxygen atom and the hydrogen atoms in the water molecule, H_2O—or more precisely, H–O–H, where the dashes represent the bonds. Oxygen has a greater attraction for electrons than hydrogen so the shared electrons are displaced toward the oxygen and away from the hydrogen, and the bonds are ionic.

Since the electrons in an ionic bond are closer to the atom with the greater attractive force, the molecule has a nonsymmetrical shape that allows one end to be relatively positive and the other end to be relatively negative. The molecule is said to be a polar or dipole molecule. This is illustrated in figure 2-3.

When bonds are formed, the products resulting from the change are more stable than the starting material. The increased stability is accompanied by decreased potential energy, so energy has been released. Conversely, energy is consumed when bonds are broken.

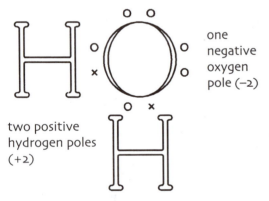

two positive hydrogen poles (+2)

one negative oxygen pole (–2)

Fig. 2-3. Lewis dot diagram of a water molecule depicting its nonsymmetrical shape. Because the oxygen atom has a greater attraction for electrons, the shared electrons are displaced toward the oxygen atom and away from the hydrogen atoms. This gives the water molecule its angular, nonsymmetrical shape, allowing the hydrogen ends to be positive and the oxygen atom at the apex to be negative —a polar or dipole molecule. This shape gives water its exceptional qualities as a solvent.

EQUATIONS

A chemical equation is a graphic means of displaying what happens in a chemical reaction, just as a mathematical equation shows what happens in a numerical reaction. In both equations, the starting quantities are shown on the left-hand side and the resulting quantities are shown on the right. The two sides of a numerical equation are separated by an equal (=) sign. In the chemical equation, they are separated by a reaction arrow ($\rightarrow$) that means "yields" or "forms." In both types, all of the quantities on the left side of the equation must be accounted for on the right side of the equation.

The quantities on the left side of a chemical equation are referred to as the *reactants*. Those on the right side are referred to as the *products* of the reaction. Since atoms and other particles present in the reactants are neither created nor destroyed in the reaction, they must be present and accounted for in the products, or results, of the reaction. They may however, change their form or state, so it is common practice to indicate parenthetically the phase or state of the materials in the equation. The following letters are used to indicate each phase:

(s)	solid
(l)	liquid
(g)	gas
(aq)	aqueous (dissolved in water)

Let's consider a generalized reaction:

$$A + B_2 \rightarrow AB$$

This equation says that element A and element B combine to form the compound AB. Notice, however, that we have two B atoms on the left side of the equation and only one atom on the right. For the equation to be most useful, it must be balanced; that is, it must account for all of the atoms and other particles on both sides of the equation. This is done by using numerical coefficients before the symbols and formulas. Thus, the equation becomes

$$2A + B_2 \rightarrow 2AB$$

Let's see how this would look in the case of rusting of iron (Fe). Both water and oxygen are required for the formation of iron rust. Rust is what the chemists refer to as a hydrated (chemically combined with water) ferric oxide in which the amount of water is variable, so we will use an x as the coefficient for the water component. The formula would look like this:

$$2\ Fe\ (s)\ +\ 1\tfrac{1}{2}\ O_2(g)\ +\ x\ H_2O\ \rightarrow\ Fe_2O_3(s)$$

The equation reads that 2 atomic weights of solid Fe react with $1\tfrac{1}{2}$ atomic weights of gaseous O to form 1 molecular weight of solid rust, Fe_2O_3 (ferric oxide). In this reaction, Fe is in a +3 valence state, and the bonding is predominantly ionic.

For chemical analysis of a reaction to be most meaningful, we must account for energy on both sides of the equation as well. Energy levels can change in a chemical reaction. Energy is released when bonds are formed because the elements attain more stable configurations at lower energy levels. Energy is consumed when bonds are broken and elements attain higher-energy, less stable arrangements. Because the liquid and gas states are progressively less stable than the solid state, energy is absorbed in the change from solid to liquid to gas. Conversely, energy is liberated in the shift from gas to liquid to solid, which is what happened to the O_2 in our chemical reaction. We show this in the above equation as follows:

$$2\ Fe\ (s)\ +\ 1\tfrac{1}{2}\ O_2(g)\ +\ x\ H_2O\ \rightarrow\ Fe_2O_3(s)\ +\ Heat$$

Typically, the process proceeds more rapidly at higher temperatures. You need not write or balance chemical equations to combat corrosion, but the fundamentals we have covered here will enable you to understand the equations that will describe the corrosion process in later chapters.

WATER AS AN ELECTROLYTE

Water is a solvent. It is sometimes referred to as the universal solvent. This is an overstatement, but water is the most widely used of all solvents. Under the right conditions, there are few substances that will not dissolve in water to some degree. Water plays an important part in many chemical reactions, particularly those we're interested in.

Water molecules are *polar*. Each consists of a relatively large oxygen molecule and two small hydrogen atoms. There are two H–O bonds that form an angle of about 105°. The result is a V-shaped molecule. The oxygen end, at the apex, carries a negative charge while the hydrogen ends carry positive charges. It is this polar nature of the water molecule that makes it a good solvent.

When an ionic substance like sodium chloride (salt) is immersed in water, it undergoes dissociation, dissolving into positive and negative ions, which are then surrounded by water molecules. This solution is called an *electrolyte*. Electrolytes are electrical conductors in which current is carried by ions rather than by free electrons, as in a metal. Dissolved gases, especially oxygen, are important factors in the corrosion process and also occur in the electrolyte. Seawater, the medium in which most marine corrosion occurs, is an electrolyte.

SUMMARY

Chemical symbols are used to designate a particular chemical element. The symbol also represents a definite quantity of the element. Two or more atoms of the same or different elements combine to form molecules. Formulas show the elements and amounts of each element present in a molecule.

The combining capacity of an atom is the number of electrons it can gain, lose, or share in forming chemical bonds. This is called the *valence number*. Chemical bonds are the means by which atoms and molecules are held together to form compounds and mixtures. Chemical reactions, including corrosion, involve the breaking of these bonds and the formation of new bonds to form new compounds. The nature of these bonds as well as the specific atoms and molecules involved determine the nature and the rate of these chemical reactions. Chemical equations are graphic ways of describing what happens in a chemical reaction.

When an ionic substance is dissolved in water, ions are released from the substance, and the solution becomes an electrolyte. Seawater is an electrolyte, and this is the medium in which most marine corrosion occurs.

Chapter 3

Basic Electrical Theory

Knowledge of the fundamentals of electricity is essential to understanding marine corrosion and how to deal with it. Adequate comprehension of this subject does not involve advanced mathematics or physics, and we have already covered the necessary chemistry. It really boils down to a little further study of our friend and nemesis, the electron.

ELECTROSTATICS

We have already discussed the structure of the atom and the nature of protons (positive charge) and electrons (negative charge). We said that an atom contained the same number of electrons and protons; therefore the charges are balanced, and the atom is neutral or without an overall electrical charge. Protons and electrons having opposite charges attract each other. This attraction holds the electrons around the nucleus. Thus we saw that there exists a force of attraction between particles of opposite charge and a force of repulsion between particles of like charge. Like charges repel and unlike charges attract. This is the fundamental principle of electricity.

If an object (for example, an atom) has more electrons than protons, it is said to be negatively charged. An object with fewer electrons than protons has a positive charge. In proximity, these two objects will be attracted to each other. Conversely, if both objects have an excess of electrons (or protons), they have like charges, and the force between them is repulsion.

The magnitude of this force is directly proportional to the difference in the magnitudes of the electrical charges and proportional to the distance between the two objects. To be more precise on the latter, the magnitude of the force *varies inversely as the square of the distance.*

This simply means that if you increase the distance between the bodies by a factor of 2, the force decreases by a factor of 4.

Suppose we have two objects of different sizes, each with the same magnitude of negative charge (see fig. 3-1). The individual charges (electrons) on each body will be evenly distributed over its surface because of the mutual force of repulsion among those charges. Because A is smaller, the distance between the charges must be smaller, making the aggregate force of repulsion on A greater than on B. If we connect a wire between the two spheres, the greater repulsive force of A would cause a flow of electrons from A to B. This flow would continue until the repulsive forces are the same. The flow of electrons is called an *electric current.*

DIFFERENCE OF POTENTIAL: VOLTAGE

Both bodies in figure 3-1 have excess *electrons;* that is, both are negatively charged. One, however, has a greater negative charge than the other. This difference in charge level is referred to as the difference in potential, or *voltage.* Potential is measured relative to the potential of earth, which is considered to be neutral or zero. Positively charged bodies have a higher potential than that of earth; the potential of negatively charged bodies is lower than earth. Difference of potential is of great importance—there must be a difference in potential for current to continue.

Notice that between two bodies it is the difference in potential *relative to each other* that determines current flow. The force that exists between two bodies having different levels of charge is referred to as the *voltage,* and the unit of measurement is the *volt,* represented by the letter "V."

A   B

Fig. 3-1. Charged bodies.

Table 3-1	
Resistivity of Selected Common Metals	
Material	Ohms per Circular Mil-foot
aluminum	17
brass	45
copper	10.4
iron	59
phosphor bronze	70
silver	9.8
tin	69
tungsten	33
zinc	36

CURRENT

The flow of electrons between two bodies is called the *current*. For current to flow there must be a difference in potential between the two bodies and a *metallic* conductor connected between them to carry the electrons. If the conductor connects a negative body to a positive body—relative to earth—electrons will flow from the negative body to the positive body. If both bodies are positive, but with different levels (magnitudes) of potential, electrons will flow from the *lower* positive potential to the *higher* positive potential. Likewise, if both bodies have negative potential but of different magnitudes, electrons will flow from the *higher* negative potential to the *lower* negative potential.

The electrons that make up the flow of current are the *free electrons* in the valence or outermost shell of the atoms. The unit of measurement for current is the *ampere*, signifying a flow of 6.28×10^{18} electrons (one *coulomb*) per second. Current is represented by the letter "I."

RESISTANCE

We saw in chapter 2 that some elements release free electrons more easily than others. Because such elements present little resistance to the flow of electrons, they are good conductors of electric current. In contrast, elements that release few free electrons greatly oppose the flow of electrons. These elements are poor conductors, or insulators.

Even the best conductor exhibits some resistance to current flow. The magnitude of that resistance depends on the element or elements in the conductor. Resistance varies *directly* with length of the conductor and *inversely* with its cross section. The resistance of most of the materials of interest to us also increases with an increase in temperature.

Electrical resistance is designated with the letter "R", and the unit of measurement is the *ohm*. Typical resistivity values of some common metals at 68°F (20°C) are listed in table 3-1 (see also appendix 6, Wire Table).

OHM'S LAW

The plumbing system in a house is in many ways similar to an electrical circuit. Because water flow through pipes is easier to visualize than electrons through wires, let's take advantage of this analogy. In the plumbing system we are primarily interested in three factors: pressure, water flow, and resistance to water flow.

If the pressure on the system is increased, the amount of water flowing per unit time will increase. If the pressure is decreased, water flow will decrease. If the pressure on the system is removed, the flow of water will stop. We can correctly conclude that the rate of water flow is directly proportional to the magnitude of pressure.

If resistance to the flow of water is increased (smaller pipes, clogs, closing the tap), the flow of water will decrease. If the resistance is decreased, water flow will increase. Thus, the rate of water flow is inversely proportional to the resistance in the system.

We can expresses the relationship of these three factors with the mathematical equation

$$\text{rate of water flow} = \frac{\text{water pressure}}{\text{resistance}}$$

This equation makes it easy to see that doubling the pressure doubles the rate of flow, while doubling the resistance cuts the flow in half.

In an electrical circuit the rate of flow is called *current*, the pressure is called *voltage*, and resistance to the flow is called *resistance*. So the equation would look like

$$\text{current} = \frac{\text{voltage}}{\text{resistance}} \quad \text{or} \quad I = \frac{V}{R}$$

Stated verbally, this relationship says that the current in amperes is equal to the voltage in volts divided by the resistance in ohms. The symbols for amperes (amps), volts, and ohms are A, V, and Ω, respectively.

Let's plug some sample values into the equation to see how it works. If we know the voltage is 12 volts and the resistance is 6 ohms, we can calculate the current flow as 2 amperes:

$$I = \frac{12\,V}{6\,\Omega} = 2\,A$$

But perhaps we already know the current flow and the resistance and we want to compute the voltage. We simplify that calculation by rearranging the equation to

$$\text{voltage} = \text{current} \times \text{resistance} \quad \text{or} \quad V = I \times R$$

Verbally, voltage in volts is equal to current in amperes multiplied by resistance in ohms. Using the same values but solving for voltage, the calculation becomes

$$V = 2\,A \times 6\,\Omega = 12\,V$$

If we want to solve for resistance, we can again restate the equation as

$$\text{resistance} = \frac{\text{voltage}}{\text{current}} \quad \text{or} \quad R = \frac{V}{I}$$

Our example becomes

$$R = \frac{12\,V}{2\,A} = 6\,\Omega$$

This mathematical expression (in all three forms) is called Ohm's law and is the basis for

our understanding of electricity. A convenient mnemonic device for remembering these relationships is the Ohm's law triangle:

Putting your finger over the variable you want to compute reveals the arithmetic required,

$$I \times R \quad \text{or} \quad \frac{V}{I} \quad \text{or} \quad \frac{V}{R}$$

When a current flows through a resistance, a couple of things take place. The first is that a portion of the total potential difference is used up in forcing the current through the resistance. This voltage is lost to the rest of the circuit. This is called *voltage drop*, and we use Ohm's law to calculate it. As an example, pushing a 2-ampere current through a 6-ohm resistance will use up 12 volts of potential difference:

$$\begin{aligned} \text{voltage drop (V)} &= I \times R \\ &= 2\,A \times 6\,\Omega \\ &= 12\,V \end{aligned}$$

The second thing that happens is that work is done in pushing the electrons through the resistance. When work is done, power is dissipated. When electrical power is dissipated, heat is generated; that is, the resistance heats up. These are referred to as IR losses, typically expressed in *watts*. Power losses have a direct relationship to resistance and to current squared. It is expressed with the mathematical equation

$$\text{watts} = \text{current squared} \times \text{resistance} \quad \textbf{or} \quad P = I^2 \times R$$

Using our sample current and resistance values, the computation is

$$\begin{aligned} P &= (2\text{ amperes})^2 \times 6\text{ ohms} \\ P &= 4\text{ amperes} \times 6\text{ ohms} \\ &= 24\text{ watts} \end{aligned}$$

BASIC DIRECT CURRENT (DC) CIRCUITS

Up to this point we have described current flow as the movement of electrons from a negative

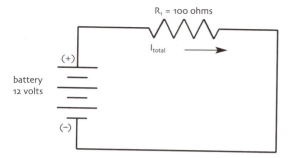

Fig. 3-2A. Basic series circuit with one resistor. All the voltage (12 volts) is dropped across resistor R_1.

body toward a positive body. This is based on electron theory and is, in fact, what actually takes place. However, before the development of electron theory, scientists made an arbitrary decision to postulate current flow from positive to negative. By the time the true nature of electron flow was understood, this erroneous expedient had been published in countless texts, handbooks, and manuals and was shown on all kinds of machinery. So despite the later science, we continue to assume that electric current flows from positive to negative. Our discussion of electric circuits will follow this long-standing convention.

Let's see how circuits work. Figure 3-2A depicts a basic electrical circuit composed of a 100-ohm resistance and a 12-volt battery connected in series. Using Ohm's law, we can determine the magnitude of the current flowing in this circuit:

$$I = \frac{V}{R}$$

$$= \frac{12\ V}{100\ \Omega}$$

$$= 0.12\ A$$

Since this is a series circuit, the current has only one possible path, so the current flow is the same in all parts of the circuit. If we add additional resistance to this circuit, in series with resistor R_1, we would expect the current to decrease (fig. 3-2B). We can calculate the new current by using the sum of all the resistors as R_t in the Ohm's law equation:

$$I = \frac{V}{R_t}\ \text{where}\ R_t = R_1 + R_2 + R_n$$

$$= \frac{12\ V}{150\ \Omega}$$

$$= 0.08\ A$$

Now let's see what happens if the additional resistance is in parallel with R_1 (see fig. 3-3).

Adding a resistor in parallel—like opening an additional check-out lane—actually lowers resistance. The total resistance (R_t) presented to the battery will be less than that of either of the parallel resistors alone. The rule for parallel circuits is *the total resistance is the reciprocal of the sum of the reciprocals of each of the resistances in the circuit*. The reciprocal just means the

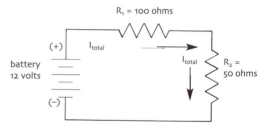

Fig. 3-2B. Basic series circuit with two resistors. Part of the voltage is dropped across R_1 and part is dropped across resistor R_2.

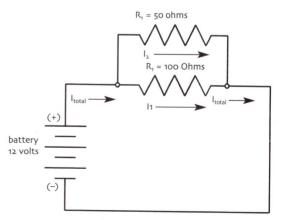

Fig. 3-3. Basic parallel circuit. Current split between the two branches in proportion to the resistance in the branches and all the voltage (12 volts) is dropped across the two resistors.

number 1 divided by the resistance, so the equation for parallel resistance looks like this:

$$\frac{1}{R_t} = \frac{1}{R_1} + \frac{1}{R_2} + \frac{1}{R_n}$$

If R_1 is 100 ohms and R_2 is 50 ohms, we get

$$\frac{1}{R_t} = \frac{1}{100} + \frac{1}{50}$$

$$1 = R_t\left(\frac{1}{100} + \frac{1}{50}\right)$$

$$1 = R_t\left(\frac{3}{100}\right)$$

$$\frac{100}{3} = R_t$$

$$R_t = 33.33 \text{ ohms}$$

Now we can use Ohm's law to solve for the total current flowing from the battery:

$$I_t = \frac{V}{R}$$

$$= \frac{12 \text{ V}}{33.33 \text{ }\Omega}$$

$$= 0.36 \text{ A}$$

Since this is a parallel circuit, the current from the battery splits, part traveling through R_1 and part through R_2. We know that more current will flow through the smaller resistor. We can calculate these currents by first determining the voltage drop across the resistors as

voltage drop = current (I_t) × resistance (R_t)
$$= 0.36 \text{ amperes} \times 33.33 \text{ ohms} = 12 \text{ volts}$$

Since this is the voltage across each resistor, we can compute the current through each resistor using Ohm's law as

$$I_1 = \frac{V}{R_1} \qquad\qquad I_2 = \frac{V}{R_2}$$

$$= \frac{12 \text{ V}}{100 \text{ }\Omega} \qquad\qquad = \frac{12 \text{ V}}{50 \text{ }\Omega}$$

$$= 0.12 \text{ A} \qquad\qquad = 0.24 \text{ A}$$

Notice that the sum of the two currents equals the total current of 0.36 amperes.

Real-world circuits may have resistances in series and in parallel. An example of a series-

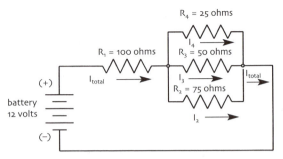

Fig. 3-4. Series-parallel circuit. Total current passes through resistor R_1 and then splits in proportion to the resistance of the individual branches, resulting in part of the total voltage (12 volts) being dropped across resistor R_1 and the remainder dropped across the parallel branch.

parallel circuit is shown in figure 3-4. To determine the total resistance of this circuit, we resolve the parallel branch first and then add that to the other resistance in series.

$$\frac{1}{R_p} = \frac{1}{75} + \frac{1}{50} + \frac{1}{25}$$

$$1 = R_p\left(\frac{1}{75} + \frac{1}{50} + \frac{1}{25}\right)$$

$$1 = R_p\left(\frac{11}{150}\right)$$

$$\frac{150}{11} = R_p$$

$$R_p = 13.64 \text{ ohms}$$

The total resistance of the circuit is

$$R_t = R_1 + R_p = 100 + 13.64 = 113.64 \text{ ohms}$$

If total circuit resistance (R_t) is 113.64 ohms, and the applied voltage is 12 volts, the total circuit current is

$$I_c = \frac{12}{113.64} = 0.106 \text{ A}$$

and the voltage drop across R_1 is

$$V_{R_1} = I \times R = 0.106 \times 100 = 10.6 \text{ V}$$

If we then subtract the voltage dropped across R_1 from the applied voltage, we know the voltage across the parallel branch circuit:

$$V_{R_p} = V_{applied} - V_{R_1} = 12.0 \text{ V} - 10.6 \text{ V} = 1.4 \text{ V}_{R_p}$$

Now we can calculate the current in each of the legs of the parallel branch as

$$I_{R_4} = \frac{1.4}{25} = 0.056 \text{ A}$$

$$I_{R_3} = \frac{1.4}{50} = 0.028 \text{ A}$$

$$I_{R_2} = \frac{1.4}{75} = 0.019 \text{ A}$$

MEASUREMENTS

Inasmuch as we will normally be troubleshooting circuits already in place, we can make direct measurements of volts, amperes, and ohms if we have the proper equipment. A *multimeter*, also called a *multitester*, measures voltage, current, and resistance or continuity. If you don't have one, you should.

You can spend just about anything you want for one of these useful little tools, from $10 or $15 at your local marine or electronics supplier on up to several hundred dollars. The differences are in sensitivity, accuracy, range, and, of course, quality. Buy the best you can afford, and if you're going to keep it on the boat—a good idea—select one intended for marine use. These are a little more rugged and sealed to keep moisture out.

You have a choice between digital and analog. Analog multitesters are the ones with the needle and numbered scale. These are relatively inexpensive, but they lack the sensitivity of a digital multimeter and are inherently fragile. If you're going to use an analog multimeter for corrosion troubleshooting, it must have a sensitivity of at least 50,000 ohms/volt to read reliably the very low levels of currents involved. It should also measure voltage accurately in the millivolt (thousandths of a volt) range.

Digital multimeters cost a little more but have a number of attractive features. They are more accurate, particularly in the low DC voltage range of interest in corrosion testing, and they are more robust. Better models include internal protection against incorrect polarity and autoranging, meaning the meter automatically se-lects the appropriate range that gives the most accurate reading. If you are buying a meter, buy digital, preferably one designed and constructed for use in the marine environment.

Your new multimeter will come with two test cables (one red, one black) and an instruction book. There are many variations among these instruments, so it is essential to read the instruction book. With analog instruments, placing of the test probes and selection of appropriate ranges are critical. You must always select a range that is higher than the voltage or current you expect to find. It's a good idea to get in the habit of starting on the highest scale and switching down till you get a reading in the center of the scale.

Measuring Voltage

We measure voltage relative to the potential of some other point, usually *earth*, or *ground*. The potential of earth is the established zero potential. When we say that voltage is "+10 volts," we mean that it is 10 volts positive *with respect to earth's potential*. In this case, current will flow from the +10 volt point to the zero potential of ground. Similarly, "–10 volts," is 10 volts negative *with respect to earth's potential*. Current will flow from ground to the more negative point. We physically create an earth connection, or ground, by burying a copper conductor in the ground.

To measure voltage with a meter, we touch one test probe—the red one if we expect the voltage to be positive—to the point whose potential we want to measure. We touch the other to the reference point—most commonly ground.

Measuring Current

To measure the flow of current, we must insert the meter into the circuit. This means the circuit must be broken and the meter connected across the opening, so that the current flowing through the circuit has to pass through the meter. If the circuit lacks a convenient disconnect, it may be necessary to cut a conductor or unsolder a connection to test the current. Connect the red test probe to the positive side of the circuit, black to the negative side. Remember to remake the connection after taking the measurement.

Measuring Resistance

When measuring resistance (ohms) there can be no power on the circuit. If you connect an analog meter in the ohms mode to a live circuit, you will in all probability burn out the meter. Most digital ohmmeters have some degree of internal protection against this, but you should still get in the habit of making certain that there is *no* power on the circuit.

Power for the ohmmeter is from an internal battery. Because this battery discharges over time, analog ohmmeters must be calibrated each time the meter is used (and each time the scale is changed) by touching the test probes together and turning the *ohms adjust* knob until the meter indicates zero ohms. When using a digital meter, check the meter and lead resistance by crossing the probes. When measuring very small resistance, you may need to subtract this from the meter reading.

BASIC AC CIRCUITS

In DC circuits the current flows in one direction. Alternating current (AC) reverses direction at regular intervals. Standard AC in the United States switches from maximum flow in one direction to maximum flow in the opposite direction, then back to maximum flow in the original direction 60 times per second. This is shown graphically in figure 3-5.

Corrosion due to stray currents can involve the shoreside wiring as well as onboard AC circuitry. We'll talk more about this in chapters 9 and 18. Typically, our troubleshooting activities will be limited to the DC characteristics of AC circuitry. Because AC systems behave differently and involve considerably higher voltages, they can be dangerous. There is one universally accepted ground rule where AC circuits are involved: if you have any question about what you are doing, *don't do it!*

Mistakes in AC circuits can be fatal. Before doing anything on the boat that MAY involve AC circuits, disconnect the shore-power cord and turn off any onboard sources of AC power, including inverters, if present.

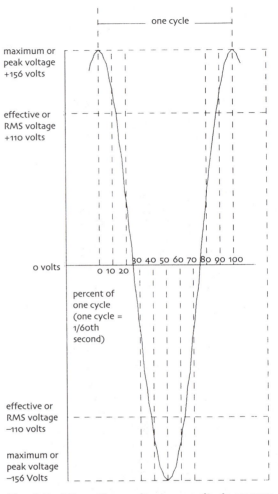

Fig. 3-5. Alternating voltage magnitude versus time. The graph shows the negative-positive cycle in an AC circuit.

SUMMARY

Voltage, or potential, is a relative term; that is, a body has a certain potential relative to ground or some other body. Electrons actually move from a negative body to the positive (less negative) body, but by convention we assume the flow of an electric current to be from positive to negative. The amount of current that will flow depends upon the magnitude of the difference in potential (voltage) and the resistance of the conducting path. Ohm's law describes this relationship mathematically.

CHAPTER 4

Basic Corrosion Processes

Corrosion ranks right up there with athlete's foot, fungi, and green hair mold. It is ugly, insidious, complex, and confusing. It thrives in dark, hard-to-get-at places, and just when you think you've got it licked, it flares up again and spreads like crazy. Its effects are often seriously damaging and even dangerous.

On a boat, signs of corrosion are everywhere—staining and deterioration of both wood (surprise, surprise) and metal, pitting of stainless steel, powdering on aluminum, flaking steel, and disintegrating brass screws (where someone has been foolish enough to use them below the waterline or where exposed to the weather). Corrosion shows up on propellers and shafts, rudders and stocks, struts, through-hulls and fastenings, and just about any other metallic fitting you're likely to find aboard.

Everyone who's ever owned a boat knows what corrosion is, but there is considerable confusion about the proper terms to describe it, and even greater confusion about preventing it. For example, some authoritative sources say you should bond everything. Others say don't bond at all. Still others say bond some components but not others. Given such divergent advice, it

should be no surprise that some recommended cures have the effect of causing more problems than they solve. Horror stories abound, and you've probably heard or had your share of them.

Corrosion of metals exposed to seawater or even a salt-air environment is all but inevitable, but corrosion can be prevented or controlled to the extent that it need not compromise the vessel's performance or seaworthiness. It *must* be controlled. The alternative is just too expensive in terms of repairs, lost fishing, sailing, or boating time, and even physical danger.

WHAT IS CORROSION?

Corrosion is a broad and complex subject. For our purposes, we limit our examination to three basic categories of corrosion and the particular forms that are important for us as owners, operators, builders, repairers, or restorers of boats. These three categories are simple electrochemical or single-metal corrosion; galvanic corrosion, sometimes referred to as two-metal or bimetallic corrosion; and electrolytic or stray-current corrosion.

A TROUBLESOME RESTORATION

For a particularly heart-rending story, get your hands on issue 41 (July–August 1981) of *Wooden-Boat* magazine and read about George Cadwalader's restoration of a 30-year-old mahogany-planked double-ender. The beautifully designed and heavily built 41-foot English cutter featured sawn oak and bent elm frames. The frames were tied together across the keel timber by massive wrought-iron floors, and the entire structure was tied together with iron and bronze straps. The boat was fastened with copper rivets on the bent frames and naval brass screws on the sawn frames. Four years later (*WoodenBoat* no. 70) Cadwalader completes his tale of the restoration, and he asks the question "Would I do it again?"

The answer is an emphatic "No!"

In all forms of corrosion, four components must be present—an *anode*, a *cathode*, a *metallic path* for the *electrons* to flow through, and an *electrolyte* (or electrolytic path) for the *ions* to flow through. Both the anode and the cathode must be in contact with the electrolyte. Oxygen and hydrogen also must be available, either directly or as a result of chemical action and the resultant dissociation of water into its two constituents.

Notice that I did not (and will not) use the term *electrolysis*. Electrolysis is what happens to the *electrolyte*, not to the *metals* involved. It is frequently used incorrectly to describe the corrosion process.

To help get the terms straight, let's take a look at one cell in a common storage battery. Figure 4-1 shows such a cell, known as a voltaic or galvanic cell.

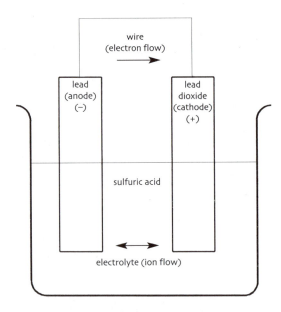

Fig. 4-1. Simple galvanic cell as in a common storage battery. The current is carried by electrons traveling from the anode to the cathode through the wire. In the electrolyte, the current is carried by ions, both positive and negative, traveling in opposite directions; positive ions move toward the negative anode, and negative ions toward the positive cathode.

The positive electrode is the cathode, and the negative electrode is the anode. When these two electrodes are connected by a wire, free electrons flow through the wire from the anode to cathode as an electrical current. (Don't be confused by the convention that direct currents flow from positive to negative. We are more concerned with the effects of the flow than the direction.) Current is also flowing through the electrolyte, carried by both positive and negative ions traveling in opposite directions—the positive ions toward the negative anode, and the negative ions toward the positive cathode. Thus, the circuit is complete. We talk more about this later. For now, let's define our three principal categories.

Simple Electrochemical Corrosion

Simple electrochemical corrosion involves a single piece of metal—either a pure metal (e.g., iron, tin, aluminum) or an alloy (e.g., stainless steel, bronze, brass)—in contact with an electrolyte. Electrochemical corrosion can occur in the atmosphere or under immersion. It normally proceeds continuously and at an extremely slow rate.

Galvanic Corrosion

Galvanic corrosion involves two or more dissimilar metals, by which I mean metals widely separated in the galvanic table—mild steel and bronze, for example. The metals must be connected by a metallic path—either by direct physical contact or by a conductor—and must be in contact with the same body of electrolyte. Notice that when galvanic corrosion occurs, it is in addition to the process of simple electrochemical corrosion, which is still taking place.

Electrolytic Corrosion

Electrolytic corrosion also involves two separate metals exposed to the same body of electrolyte, but in this case the corrosion is caused by an electrical current from an outside source flowing between the two metals. Electrolytic corrosion is also called *stray-current corrosion*.

In subsequent chapters we examine electrochemical, galvanic, and electrolytic corrosion in greater depth. For the moment we concentrate on the basic corrosion process.

THE CORROSION PROCESS

Someone described corrosion as nature's way of reclaiming the metals humans have taken from the earth. We mine iron ore, process it into steel, and make goods out of it. When those goods rust, the steel turns back into iron oxide, and the cycle is complete. How about that? Nature's been recycling since time began. We're just now getting with the program.

But rust is only one form of corrosion, a special case peculiar to iron and steel. Although the corrosion process is similar in all other metals, in those metals we don't call it rust. In fact, we have no one commonly accepted word for it except possibly *oxidation* since oxygen, either from the air or from the dissociation of water, is a necessary agent.

Interestingly, the metal oxides that are a product of corrosion can also become protective coatings. Take aluminum, for example. When aluminum is exposed to the atmosphere, a film of aluminum oxide (alumina) quickly forms on the surface. This film is so dense and so closely bonded to the metal surface that moisture and additional oxygen cannot penetrate it and cause further corrosion. Rust, on the other hand, is porous, flaky, and loosely bonded to the surface; it provides little or no protection to the base metal.

Corrosion can be defined as the destructive alteration of metal by reaction with its environment. For corrosion to take place, oxygen and hydrogen must be available, and the metal must be in contact with an electrolyte, that is, an electrically conductive medium. The rate at which corrosion takes place depends not only on the type of metal involved but also on the nature of the electrolyte. In our case, the electrolyte is usually seawater. How well seawater functions as an electrolyte is dependent on its temperature, its salinity, whether it is stagnant or fast moving, and the amount and nature of any pollution in the water. Simple electrochemical corrosion is an extremely slow process *in the absence of other influencing conditions*. A classic study by Francis LaQue shows that the surface metal loss in good quality marine bronze due to saltwater corrosion is about 0.0002 inches or less per year. That's definitely slow!

ELECTROCHEMICAL PROCESS

Electrochemistry deals with chemical reactions that produce electric currents and the chemical reactions that are caused by those currents *in an electrolyte*. The electrolyte conducts electric currents because its molecules have become *ionized*, that is, they have been changed into positively and negatively charged particles called *ions*, which have the property of conducting electric currents.

An old boatbuilding friend of mine recently had open-heart surgery. The first question he asked the doctor when he awoke was, "When you sawed through my rib cage, Doc, what happened to the sawdust?" I know what you're thinking: What happens to the ions and the electrons? Where do they go? We'll get to that, but to put some of this into perspective, an atom is roughly 2×10^{-8} inches in diameter and about 3.5×10^{-27} pounds. That's 3.5 with 27 zeros *in front*. We're talking about some pretty small stuff here.

What is of significance is that when the current flow is by metallic conduction, the electrons just move from one atom to the next and no mass is lost. However, when the current flow is ionic and an ion is lost from a piece of metal, essentially the mass of an atom is lost from the body of the metal. That's corrosion.

ELECTROMOTIVE POTENTIAL AND THE GALVANIC TABLE

Seawater, the electrolyte in our case, is essentially a solution of water and salt (and some other components as well). The salt is sodium chloride, NaCl, an electrically neutral molecule. When NaCl is dissolved in water, its molecules separate into ions (Na^+ and Cl^-) that can move about freely. Placing a piece of metal in this (or any) electrolyte sets up spontaneous voltage (or electromotive potential force, *emf*) between the metal and the electrolyte. The magnitude of this voltage is primarily a function of the type of metal and the temperature. This is shown, in simplified form, by the accumulation of negative chloride ions (Cl^-) on the surface of the metal in figure 4-2.

Since voltage is a relative term, the voltage of a single piece of metal must be measured with respect to some reference electrode. In classical chemistry the voltage is measured under laboratory conditions with respect to a hydrogen electrode (yielding the electromotive series). The marine industry takes comparative measurements under more realistic conditions. The resulting series, called the Galvanic Series of Metals in Seawater (see table 4-1) is based on a silver–silver chloride reference electrode. The electrolyte is seawater flowing at between 8 and 13 feet per second (4.7 to 7.7 knots) at a temperature between 50°F and 80°F (10°C and 26.7°C). In either series, the absolute numerical value of a single electrode potential is of little real significance. Their importance lies in the numerical difference between the potentials of any two metals.

The least noble metals—those at the top of the table—are the most active ones and corrode most easily. They are referred to as *anodic* and are electrically more negative (or less positive) when immersed in seawater. The most noble metals are those toward the bottom of the table. These are more passive, that is, less active chemically, and they are electrically less negative (or

Table 4-1

Galvanic Series of Metals in Seawater (ABYC Standard E-2)

Metals and Alloys	Corrosion Potential Range in Volts
Least Noble (Anodic) or Most Active	
magnesium and magnesium alloys	−1.60 to −1.63
zinc	−0.98 to −1.03
aluminum alloys*	−0.76 to −1.00
cadmium	−0.70 to −0.73
mild steel	−0.60 to −0.71
wrought iron	−0.60 to −0.71
cast iron	−0.60 to −0.71
13% chromium stainless steel, Type 410 (active in still water)	−0.46 to −0.58
18-8 stainless steel, Type 304 (active in still water)	−0.46 to −0.58
Ni-resist	−0.46 to −0.58
18-8, 3% Mo stainless steel, Type 316 (active in still water)	−0.43 to −0.54
Inconel (78% Ni, 14.5% Cr, 6% Fe) (active in still water)	−0.35 to −0.46
aluminum bronze (92% Cu, 8% Al)	−0.31 to −0.42
Nibral (81.2% Cu, 4% Fe, 4.5% Ni, 9% Al, 1.3% Mg)	−0.31 to −0.42
naval brass (60% Cu, 39% Zn)	−0.30 to −0.40
yellow brass (65% Cu, 35% Zn)	−0.30 to −0.40
red brass (85% Cu, 15% Zn)	−0.30 to −0.40
Muntz metal (60% Cu, 40% Zn)	−0.30 to −0.40
tin	−0.31 to −0.33
copper	−0.30 to −0.57
50–50 lead-tin solder	−0.28 to −0.37
admiralty brass (71% Cu, 28% Zn, 1% Sn)	−0.28 to −0.36
aluminum brass (76% Cu, 22% Zn, 2% Al)	−0.28 to −0.36
manganese bronze (58.5% Cu, 39% Zn, 1% Sn, 1% Fe, 0.3% Mn)	−0.27 to −0.34
silicon bronze (96% Cu max, 0.8% Fe, 1.5% Zn, 2% Si, 0.75% Mn, 1.6% Sn)	−0.26 to −0.29

more positive) in seawater. These metals are said to be *cathodic*, and they are more resistant to corrosion.

When two or more metals are immersed in the same body of seawater and connected together electrically—either by direct contact or wired together—electrons will flow from the least noble metal to the most noble metal, and in doing so the anodic metal corrodes, sacrificing itself to protect the more noble metal. The extra electrons collecting on the cathodic metal increase the negative charge on the protected metal, making it more negative than its characteristic potential as listed in the table.

The least noble metal, the *anode*, corrodes first. When the least noble metal is consumed, the next least noble metal will corrode, and so on. The farther apart the metals are in the table, the faster the rate of corrosion.

An *anode*, a *cathode*, a *metallic path* for the electrons, and an *electrolytic path* for the ions are the components of a *galvanic cell*. Note that the metals need not be immersed. Wood that is wet or damp with seawater will also act as an electrolyte and conduct ions.

A LITTLE TECHNICAL DETAIL

Two things happen during the corrosion process:

1. Metal atoms are lost by the anode. This is the corrosion.
2. Ions are formed in the seawater. These can either form a protective coating on the cathode or produce alkalis that attack wood.

Table 4-1 *(continued)*

Galvanic Series of Metals in Seawater (ABYC Standard E-2)

Metals and Alloys	Corrosion Potential Range in Volts
bronze-composition G (88% Cu, 2% Zn, 10% Sn)	−0.24 to −0.31
bronze ASTM B62 (through-hull) (85% Cu, 5% Pb, 5% Sn, 5% Zn)	−0.24 to −0.31
bronze-composition M (88% Cu, 3% Zn, 6.5% Sn, 1.5% Pb)	−0.24 to −0.31
13% chromium stainless steel, Type 401 (passive)	−0.26 to −0.35
copper nickel (90% Cu, 10% Ni)	−0.21 to −0.28
copper nickel (75% Cu, 20% Ni, 5% Zn)	−0.19 to −0.25
lead	−0.19 to −0.25
copper nickel (70% Cu, 30% Ni)	−0.18 to −0.23
Inconel (78% Ni, 13.5% Cr, 6% Fe) (passive)	−0.14 to −0.17
nickel 200	−0.10 to −0.20
18-8 stainless steel, type 304 (passive)	−0.05 to −0.10
Monel 400, K-500 (70% Ni, 30% Cu)	−0.04 to −0.14
stainless steel propeller shaft (UNS S17400–#17 & UNS S30452–#19)	−0.03 to −0.13
18-8 stainless steel, type 316 (passive) , 3% Mo	−0.00 to −0.10
titanium	−0.05 to +0.06
Hastelloy C	−0.03 to +0.08
stainless steel shafting (bar) (UNS S20910–#22)	−0.25 to +0.06
platinum	+0.19 to +0.25
graphite	+0.20 to +0.30

Most Noble (Cathodic) or Least Active

*The range shown does not include sacrificial aluminum anodes. Aluminum alloy sacrificial anodes are available that have a maximum corrosion potential of −1.100 volts.

Note: Values in table were measured in seawater flowing at 8 to 13 ft./sec. (4.7 to 7.7 kn.) and within a temperature range of 50°F to 80°F.

Source: American Boat and Yacht Council, "Recommended Standard E-2, Cathodic Protection of Boats."

metal

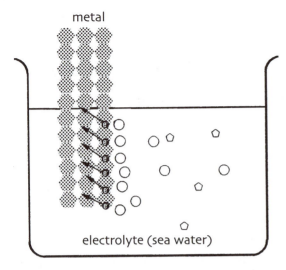

electrolyte (sea water)

- metal atom
- sodium ion (Na$^+$)
- chloride ion (Cl$^-$)
- electron

Fig. 4-2. Metal (iron) immersed in seawater electrolyte. Negatively charged chloride ions in the electrolyte at the surface of the metal push electrons from surface metal atoms deeper into the body of the metal. The surface metal atom dissolves into the electrolyte as a positively charged ion, leaving the remaining metal more negatively charged. The more chloride ions gather at the surface of the metal, the more negatively charged the (anodic) metal becomes.

The corrosion process involves three basic chemical reactions of significance for us. One takes place at the anode, one at the cathode, and one in the electrolyte. A look at some of the negative chemical details will be helpful in understanding some of the ill effects that can accompany corrosion.

The following chemical equation describes what happens at the anode:

$$2M \rightarrow 2M^{++} + 4e^-$$

Basically this says that at the anode an ionization reaction takes place in which, for most metals, two metal atoms (M) dissolve to form two double-positive charged metal ions in solution. This is the physical wastage of the metal—the corrosion. The remaining metal is left with some excess electrons (e$^-$) and therefore with a negative charge.

At the cathode, a dissolved oxygen molecule (O$_2$) in the seawater combines with the excess electrons and with hydrogen ions (H$^+$) to form hydroxyl ions (OH$^-$) in the seawater. This reaction restores the electrical neutrality of the cathode metal and of the electrolyte. For the scholars, the equation for the cathode reaction looks like

$$O_2 + 2H_2O + 4e^- \rightarrow 4(OH)^-$$

For every anode reaction, a cathode reaction takes place, and every anode reaction involves the loss of two atoms of the solid metal.

The chemical reaction that takes place in the electrolyte looks like

$$2M^{++} + 4(OH)^- \rightarrow 2M(OH)_2$$

The metal ions—2M^{++}—from the anode reactions combine with the hydroxyl ions from the cathode reactions—4(OH)$^-$—to form a metal hydroxide, which may precipitate out as a solid and deposit on the surface of the metal. This is the white, powder-like coating on aluminum and the pinkish coating on bronze. These coatings, except in the case of iron or mild steel, form a protective coating and inhibit further corrosion. However, where the hydroxyl ions are not captured or combined with the metal ions but are allowed to build up in the electrolyte, we have a different and not so happy result.

ALKALI DAMAGE

Water can be either *acidic* or *basic*. When water contains more hydroxyl ions (OH$^-$) than hydrogen ions (H$^+$), it is said to be *basic* or *alkaline*. Seawater is normally slightly alkaline. If hydroxyl ions produced at the cathode are not balanced by the reactions at the anode, and if they are able to concentrate, say in stagnant water, the water can become strongly alkaline. Strongly alkaline solutions can dissolve the lignin in wood. Lignin is what binds the cellulose fibers and hardens and strengthens the wood cells. This condition, called *alkali delignification,* is the cause of the deterioration of wood around rapidly corroding through-hulls and fasteners. We talk more about this in chapter 6.

OTHER FACTORS

In the absence of other influences, corrosion is an extremely slow process, especially in the case of high-quality copper alloys (such as bronze). The problems begin when we start introducing other influences. Some of these "other influences" are

- strength of the electrolyte
- temperature of the electrolyte
- whether the electrolyte is stagnant or moving
- pollutants and impurities in the electrolyte

- electrical contact between dissimilar metals
- stray electric currents
- installation of sacrificial anodes
- number and location of sacrificial anodes

Corrosion aboard boats is additionally influenced by

- whether the system is bonded
- whether a lightning protection system is installed

By performing some fairly simple and straightforward tests, you can determine the extent of your boat's corrosion potential. There are some equally simple and straightforward methods for preventing or controlling the situation so that serious problems do not occur. Before discussing these, we first need a better understanding of what we are up against.

CHAPTER 5

Electrochemical or Self-Corrosion

We talked in chapter 4 about the basic chemistry and physics of the corrosion processes. In this chapter we narrow our focus to simple electrochemical corrosion, also called single-metal corrosion or self-corrosion.

Basic electrochemical corrosion involves a single piece of metal—either a pure metal, such as iron, tin, or aluminum, or an alloy, such as stainless steel, bronze, or cast iron. Electrochemical corrosion is a very slow, almost imperceptible process unless affected by such other factors as dissimilar metals and stray currents. For now we're going to concentrate on components that are subject to simple electrochemical corrosion in the absence of other influencing conditions.

In this chapter we also touch on other straightforward degradation processes affecting single-metal systems in and around boats. These include metallurgically influenced decay, such as dealloying and intergranular corrosion, and some that are mechanically assisted, such as erosion, cavitation, and liquid metal embrittlement.

THE NECESSARY CONDITIONS

We always need an anode and a cathode for corrosion to occur, but there is no requirement that they be two different pieces of metal. In the case of an alloy, the different metals in the alloy can function as anodes and cathodes. In brass, for example—an alloy of copper and zinc—the zinc can function as the anode and the copper as the cathode.

But how does this occur when the metal isn't an alloy? In the case of a pure metal, the anodes and cathodes can be metallurgically dissimilar locations on the surface of the single piece. No metal is perfectly homogeneous throughout its structure. Differences in surface properties resulting from the manufacturing process,

stresses, heat treatment, impurities, and a variety of other factors can produce dissimilar surface sites. Such sites function as *local anodes* and *local cathodes* when the metal surface is in contact with an electrolyte (see fig. 5-1).

If we assume the presence of seawater, we have three of the four things necessary for corrosion to take place, namely an anode, a cathode, and an electrolytic path for ion flow— seawater. The final necessity, a metallic path for electron flow, is provided by the metal piece itself.

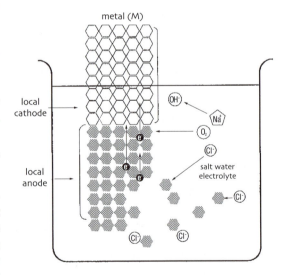

Fig. 5-1. Simple electrochemical corrosion. The local anode, the local cathode, the body of the metal for the conduction of electrons, and the saltwater electrolyte for the conduction of ions provide the four requirements for corrosion. Electrons move from the local anode toward the local cathode, causing metal atoms to ionize and dissolve into the electrolyte. Sodium ions and hydroxyl ions may combine near the cathode to form sodium hydroxide (caustic soda).

Described below are the various forms of single-metal corrosion, grouped by major distinctive features of the corrosion process.

ATMOSPHERIC CORROSION

Atmospheric corrosion is the more or less uniform, steady loss of surface metal. Rust is a good example. Rust is a scaly, reddish-brown hydrated (combined with water) ferric oxide that forms on iron and iron-containing materials by oxidation in the presence of moisture. Unlike oxide coatings formed by other metals, rust is brittle and easily flakes off the metal, thus offering little or no protection to the metal. Any and all carbon and alloy steels are subject to this form of corrosion. Under appropriate conditions, all metals exhibit atmospheric corrosion to some extent. It may also occur during galvanic or two-metal corrosion.

Prediction of a specific corrosion rate is extremely difficult. Average corrosion rates in arid areas can be as low as 0.18 mil/yr. (0.0046 mm/yr.), with 1 mil equaling 0.001 inch, while those in industrial areas may be nearly ten times as high at about 1.7 mil/yr. (0.043 mm/yr.). Those in marine environments can be higher still at some 12 mil/yr. (0.30 mm/yr.).

In any given geographical location it is helpful to consider five separate corrosion zones: atmospheric, splash zone, tidal, immersion, and bottom or mud zone. These zones together with their relative corrosion rates are shown in figure 5-2. However, it is somewhat misleading to talk about average corrosion rates since they are critically dependent on many factors. As mentioned above, in dry, salt-free air, corrosion is essentially negligible. In wet, salt-laden air in tropical climates, corrosion rates for carbon and low-alloy steels can be nearly as great as those for steel immersed in seawater, reaching rates of as much as 50 mil/yr. (1.27 mm/yr.). For example, in tests conducted at Cape Canaveral, Florida, at a location 60 yards from the ocean, the corrosion rate at ground level was 17.4 mil/yr. (0.43 mm/yr.), but it was only 6.5 mil/yr. (0.16 mm/yr.) at an elevation of 30 feet. Interestingly, at Daytona Beach, 65 miles to the

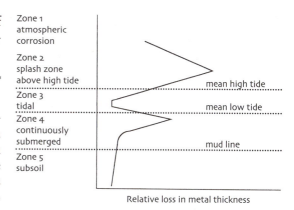

Relative loss in metal thickness

Fig. 5-2. Zones of corrosion for steel piling in seawater and relative loss of metal thickness. The most aggressive area for corrosive attack is the waterline area, the so-called *splash zone*. The corrosion rate in this area can be as much as two to three times the atmospheric corrosion rate because of the continuously fresh supply of oxygen-rich salt water washing over the metal in this area. Tests have shown that cycling through immersion and exposure to air produces more pitting than does continuous immersion.
ASM Handbook, vol. 13, *Corrosion*, 1987, p. 893.

north, the ground-level corrosion rate was more than twice as high at 42 mil/yr. (0.04 in./yr.).

IMMERSION CORROSION

Under immersion conditions, the corrosion rates of carbon and low-alloy steels are pretty much the same, ranging from less than 2 mil/yr. (0.05 mm/yr.) to more than 50 mil/yr. (1.25 mm/yr.). This is typically in the form of non-uniform attack and increased pitting. The specific nature of the attack is dependent on the following factors.

Salinity

While both freshwater and salt water are corrosive to metals, it is generally accepted that salt water is the more corrosive. What is not so commonly understood is just how much more corrosive (fig. 5-3). The presence of salt in the water does two important things—it increases the electrical conductivity of the water, and the chloride ions tend to break down protective films formed by the metal.

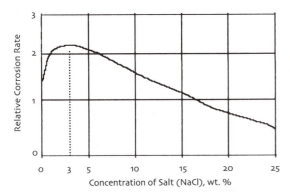

Fig. 5-3. Effect of NaCl concentration on corrosion rate of iron. Notice that the corrosion rate reaches a maximum at about 3.5 percent salt (NaCl) concentration, which is just about the salt concentration in seawater.
ASM Handbook, vol. 13, *Corrosion*, 1987, p .893, fig. 1.

Moving Water

The velocity of the seawater also has an effect on the corrosion rate. In slowly moving water, say 1 to 2 ft./sec. (0.304 to 0.609 m/sec.), a corrosion rate of about 40 mil/yr. (1.0 mm/yr.) may be expected. Doubling the velocity of the water would approximately double the corrosion rate. However, fouling by marine organisms may offset this effect. If these organisms, which attach themselves to the metal surface during slack periods in the tides, are not flushed off during the flow, then a growth can develop that, in effect, reduces the velocity at the surface of the metal.

Dissolved Oxygen and Temperature

The more dissolved oxygen in the water, the higher we would expect the rate of corrosion. An increase in the temperature of the water also increases its corrosivity. If the dissolved oxygen content were to be held constant, the corrosion rate would just about double for every 30°C (55°F) increase in temperature. The corrosion rate of mild steel in seawater increases directly with oxygen concentration, doubling for a doubling of oxygen concentration. In the marine environment, the doubling effect of dissolved oxygen concentration tends to dominate.

Mud Zone

Corrosion rates fall off to a minimum in clean mud (fig. 5-2). The reason is the lack of oxygen and the fact that the rust layer is not disturbed and does offer some protection to the metal. This should offer some small comfort to the operators of marinas and boatyards with steel pilings.

One last word of caution: *corrosion rates* can be misleading. Typically, they are determined by measuring the weight loss of metal over some period of time, then averaging this number over the area of the test sample and over the time period. However, the more serious damage is caused by pitting corrosion since areas of intense pitting constitute the potential failure sites of the metal. Corrosion rates tell us little about the density or depth of the pitting.

BIMETALLIC (GALVANIC) CORROSION

Carbon and low-alloy steels are susceptible to bimetallic corrosion when placed in contact with most other marine metals, especially brass, bronze, and stainless steels, unless the area ratios are favorable. A large surface area of steel relative to the area of the more noble metal would be a favorable ratio, for example, a bronze fastening in a large steel plate. If the area ratio is not favorable, the parts must be insulated from each other with some sort of barrier coating or material.

In proper welds, the weld metal is not sufficiently dissimilar to cause galvanic corrosion. However, if the weld is not ground smooth, protective paint coatings will tend to be thinner and less uniform over the weld bead, and rust will start to form here. Also, experience indicates that carbon steels should not be joined to weathering steels. These metals are sufficiently dissimilar to permit galvanic corrosion to occur.

STRAY-CURRENT CORROSION

Carbon and low-alloy steels are likewise susceptible to corrosion resulting from stray or leakage currents unintentionally caused by faulty electrical systems. Typically, the current from a bare wire or exposed connection immersed in the bilge water tries to find the lowest resistance path back to ground at the source. Like bimetallic corrosion, stray-current corrosion involves both anodic and cathodic sites. The point where the current leaves the metal and enters the electrolyte is the anodic site and suffers the deterioration. The point where the current leaves the electrolyte and reenters the metal is the cathode, which is protected. The anode and the cathode can be yards apart. The magnitude of the currents involved are considerably greater than those involved in bimetallic corrosion. Stray-current corrosion is essentially independent of such factors as oxygen concentration, acidity, or alkalinity. Prevention consists of designing, installing, and maintaining a proper electrical system.

CREVICE CORROSION

This type of corrosion occurs at or immediately adjacent to a crevice. For our purpose, a crevice is a narrow opening, space, or gap between two metal surfaces, or even between a metal and a nonmetal. Cracks, seams, flaws, or faults in the surface of the metal can qualify as crevice corrosion initiation sites. Fastenings and their washers, welded lap joints, and even sealants, coatings, and barnacles can cause crevice corrosion. A small volume of stagnant (oxygen-deficient) seawater becomes trapped in the crevice, and the crevice becomes anodic. The relatively small crevice area being anodic to the large surrounding cathodic area results in an unfavorable *cathode-to-anode ratio* (see chapter 6). Fortunately, this form of corrosion is usually readily apparent from the rust stains, and the source of the corrosion is easily traced.

Likely locations for crevice corrosion on steel vessels are places where stagnant moisture can collect, as in joints, narrow confined spaces around bolts, threaded fittings, vent trunks, hatch coamings, and other metal structure joints at the deck. Some of the critical points to check on sailboats are lower wire terminals, swaged fittings, chainplates, and closed-body turnbuck-

les. On all boats, metal structures like pulpits and tuna towers are particularly susceptible in the corners, at mounting flanges or where the structure is secured at the deck or house, and where they contact other metal fittings, fastenings, or deck machinery.

Crevice corrosion is best dealt with at the design and construction stage. The goal should be to avoid crevices wherever possible. If a crevice can't be avoided, it should be open and exposed to the surrounding seawater and no deeper than it has to be. In existing construction, crevice areas should be kept clean and free of debris. In some cases, it may be necessary to lay in a weld overlay to eliminate a crevice.

PITTING CORROSION

Pitting corrosion is an intense form of localized corrosion. It occurs where a surface irregularity or scratch causes a minute area to become more anodic than the surrounding surfaces. The intensity of pitting corrosion is due in large measure to the relatively small area of the anode (the pit) and the large area of the cathode (the surrounding area). Pits can develop and propagate very quickly. It is an insidious form of corrosion since it is not always readily apparent. Pits can occur under deposits, at defects or holidays in paint coatings, and around bits of weld spatter. Even when the metal cross section is not perforated, pits constitute stress concentration sites subject to catastrophic failure under stress.

Stainless steel is an alloy of iron and chromium (and some other metals). Where oxygen is present, the chromium oxidizes and forms a coating of chromium oxide, which is cathodic. The chromium oxide coating adheres tightly to the surface and protects the metal from corrosion. The stainless steel is then said to be "passive." However, if the steel is deprived of sufficient oxygen—as occurs anywhere stagnant water accumulates—the protective coating will begin to break down. Over time, pinholes develop in the coating. These points of exposed metal begin to function as anodes to the cathodic surfaces around them. The result is pitting. This kind of corrosion can be very intense since the corrosive action is concentrated in such a tiny area. Stainless steel hose clamps often exhibit pitting corrosion—a good reason for using double hose clamps on through-hulls.

Likely places for pitting corrosion to occur are inside stanchion bases, between shafts and bearings, in stern tubes, under barnacles, and on keel bolts. Other areas to watch are between propeller shafts and propellers, in the threads under propeller nuts, inside the lower terminals of wire rope fittings, and in turnbuckle threads. Also, if the plastic sheathing on lifelines is cracked or peeled back, moisture will inevitably be wicked up under the sheathing and cause pitting corrosion of the wire rope.

If pits are shallow, cleaning them thoroughly by sandblasting and then recoating (repainting) will be adequate, but once pitting has gotten well started, it must be ground out and the surface restored with weld metal. It is probably best to assume that a pit is at least as deep as it is wide.

POULTICE CORROSION

Poultice corrosion occurs where a soft, salt-water-saturated, typically organic mass is in contact with metal for long periods of time. Examples are damp insulation on pipes or exhaust system components, an accumulation of dirt and debris in the bilges or scuppers of a steel vessel, and even wood decking set on metal deck plates. Poultice corrosion is a risk wherever seawater can be absorbed, become stagnant, and lie against a metal surface for a long time.

MICROBIOLOGICALLY INDUCED CORROSION

When microorganisms form localized colonies on a metal surface they can facilitate corrosion. There are two basic groups of bacteria: anaerobic, which thrive in the absence of oxygen and which are the most common type, and aerobic, which require oxygen to live. Both cause corrosion, but of different kinds.

The formation and buildup of atomic hydrogen at the cathode will always limit the rate at which corrosion proceeds. Anaerobic bacteria, such as the sulfur-reducing bacteria (SRB), consume the hydrogen. This *depolarizes* the cathode, accelerating corrosion.

The aerobic counterpart of the SRB is the sulfur-oxidizing bacteria, which can create a sulfuric acid environment. The acid promotes corrosion, typically of the pitting type, beneath these colonies.

There have been reports of microbiologically induced corrosion (MIC) in steel hulls that bottom out on mud flats for extended times, but experts are reluctant to attribute such degradation to MIC. The corrosion damage in these instances could be simply localized corrosion (pitting and crevice corrosion) that results from oxygen depletion—similar to the corrosion that occurs under barnacles and other marine growth. A good, well-maintained coat of paint is the best preventive.

INTERGRANULAR ATTACK (WELD DECAY)

First of all, the term *weld decay* is misleading. It is the metal immediately adjacent to the weld and not the weld itself that deteriorates. Weld decay is a form of intergranular attack (IGA), a condition that gets its name from the individual crystalline particles that form the metal—called *grains*.

Austenitic stainless steels, such as those in the 300 series (Type 304, Type 316, etc.), contain moderate amounts of carbon. When they are welded, the dissolved carbon in the weld area migrates to the grain boundaries and forms chromium carbides. This leaves an area adjacent to the weld that is depleted of chrome and thus has a much lower resistance to corrosion in the grain boundaries. It is this area that is now susceptible to corrosive attack or *decay*.

Weld decay is a particularly treacherous form of corrosion since steel suffering intergranular corrosion may look sound but may actually be seriously weakened. Many think that only the austenitic stainless steels are susceptible to weld decay, but certain high-nickel alloys and some aluminum alloys can also experience this form of corrosion. However, stainless steel Types 304L and 316L—the *L* stands for low carbon—are not susceptible to weld decay.

DEALLOYING (DEZINCIFICATION)

Dealloying involves the preferential disintegration of one particular component of an alloy. Common yellow brass, an alloy of copper and zinc, offers an excellent example of this type of corrosion. Depending on the type of brass, the percentage of copper varies from 55 or 60 percent to 90 percent whereas the zinc content varies from 10 percent to 45 percent. The zinc, being higher in the galvanic series and therefore more anodic, functions as the anode. The copper, lower in the series and therefore more cathodic, functions as the cathode. The body of the brass object provides the metallic path for electrons. The seawater will carry the ion flow. We have everything we need for corrosion to occur.

The anode—that is, the zinc—will corrode away, leaving a soft, porous copper shell. This is popularly referred to as *dezincification*. Dealloying also occurs in alloys containing aluminum (*dealuminification*) and nickel (*denickelification*).

Brass is not a good choice for fastenings in exposed locations, especially below the waterline. Bronze, Monel, stainless steel, or even hot-dipped galvanized fastenings are vastly better. Incidentally, keep in mind that the popular manganese bronze is not really bronze. Composed of 58.5 percent copper, 39 percent zinc, some tin, some iron, and about 0.38 percent manganese, it's really a brass. Consequently, it is subject to dezincification, although not nearly as much so as common, or cartridge, brass.

Gray cast iron—deriving its name from its graphite content—is subject to a similar corrosion process. When dealloying takes place in gray cast iron, graphite is the constituent that is dissolved. The process is referred to as *degraphitization*.

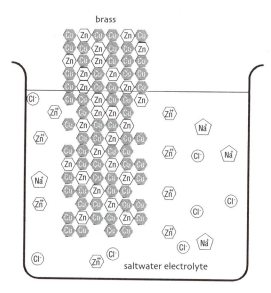

Fig. 5-4. Dezincification. The zinc is selectively dissolved from zinc-containing alloys. This occurs most commonly in copper-zinc alloys such as brasses that contain less than 85 percent copper.

EROSION CORROSION

Erosion corrosion is a mechanically assisted attack in which velocity or abrasion by a flowing medium is a major factor in the deterioration. The corrosion is caused or accelerated by the movement of the liquid medium over the surface of the metal. It may involve the removal of the protective coatings that form naturally on the surface of the metals. Turbulence or impingement may compound the problem.

Typical situations involve fast-moving water—for example, the flow of seawater through piping systems, valves, pumps, or heat exchangers, especially at bends or on surfaces that obstruct the flow. In severe cases, say a high-velocity stream of seawater with sand or other solid particles entrained, it can cause rapid thinning and eventual penetration of the metal. This can be a serious failure mode since the degradation is not visible, and failure can be sudden and catastrophic.

The flow rates in freshwater and fuel-system piping typically are not fast enough for erosion corrosion to be a problem. The practical significance of erosion corrosion for us as owners and operators of boats is in the engine cooling and exhaust systems. Here water velocities can be quite high, perhaps as much as 75 to 80 ft./sec. (23 to 24 m/sec.), and the raw water stream may well contain solid particles. Piping here is commonly steel or iron. The exhaust injection elbow, the most susceptible point in the system, eventually will corrode through and should be checked annually. Other places to keep an eye on are at elbows, tees, valves, and heat exchanger fittings. Preventive measures consist of the use of alloys with greater strength or corrosion resistance—such as stainless steel or Monel—or the use of larger diameter pipe and fittings. In one heat exchanger I took out of a 30-year-old boat, the bronze outside shell showed little evidence of corrosion, but a pressure test revealed terminal corrosion of the inside surfaces.

CAVITATION CORROSION

Cavitation is a particularly aggressive form of erosion corrosion that is caused by the formation and collapse of vapor bubbles in a liquid against a metal surface. These rapidly collapsing vapor bubbles produce explosive shock waves, and the high pressures this generates tend to enter microscopic cracks and pores on the metal's surface and cause damage. Cavitation damage is similar to pitting except that the surface in the pits tends to be much more coarse.

We normally think of cavitation only in connection with propellers, where it appears as severe pockmarking at the trailing edge of the blades. This results from the sudden formation and collapse of low-pressure bubbles due to the prop's high-speed rotation. However, cavitation also occurs on pump impellers and on many types of surfaces in contact with high-velocity liquids subject to change in pressure. In any water passage, when the stream flows through constrictions or abrupt changes in direction, or around immersed structures, the forceful reduction of pressure can lead to cavitation. Prevention consists primarily of avoiding these conditions wherever possible.

STRESS-CORROSION CRACKING

Stress-corrosion cracking (SCC) is the cracking of a metal resulting from the combined action of corrosion and tensile stress. This is a particularly troublesome form of attack since the part can fail suddenly without any warning after years of satisfactory service and under stress levels *below* the yield strength of the metal. Typically stress-corrosion cracking consists of a localized network of fine cracks with multiple branches, a sort of crazing at the surface of the metal. It is detectable visibly or with the help of a low-power magnifying glass. Penetrating dyes also are useful for detection.

The stress can either be applied—that is, during use—or be residual as a result of forming. Stress-corrosion cracking involves a chemical-mechanical interaction in which the electrochemical process is enhanced under the mechanical stress. Those areas in the part that are under stress become anodic with respect to surrounding areas. The electrochemical deterioration at the anodic areas combined with the tensile stress tends to pull the material apart. The result is cracking.

Stress-corrosion cracking frequently occurs in the crease in metal fittings that have been cold-formed by bending, in such items as angle brackets, chain plates, and braces. It is wise to keep an eye on bent fittings when they are used in critical applications.

When failure occurs due to *cyclical* stress as opposed to constant stress, this is referred to as *corrosion fatigue*, a mechanically assisted form of SCC.

CORROSION FATIGUE

Corrosion fatigue is the premature fracture of a metal under simultaneous conditions of an electrochemical corrosive action and recurring stress, happening sooner than would normally occur were there no corrosive activity taking place.

Steel is subject to corrosion fatigue in seawater environments. Boat components and fittings that are exposed to seawater and are subject to continual flexing or vibration, such as chainplates, uncoated wire rope, or hull plating in close proximity to the propeller and shaft are likely to suffer corrosion fatigue. Cracks tend to originate at surface or near-surface sites and frequently, although not always, at corrosion pits. In many cases the cracks are visible to the naked eye, but an inexpensive magnifying glass is helpful. The use of dye penetrants can also help reveal the extent of the cracking. Regular inspection, maintenance of protective coatings, prompt attention to the treatment of pitting and crevice corrosion damage, and, to the extent possible, elimination of stresses are principal preventive measures.

FRETTING CORROSION

Fretting corrosion occurs on the load-bearing surfaces between mating parts when they are subjected to vibration or motion consisting of very small amplitude oscillations. The constant abrasion between the metal surfaces causes minute particles to break away from the surfaces. These particles corrode and may cause seizing or galling. This is a frequent problem in pumps, valves, fastenings, and bearings where the mating surfaces rub together without the benefit of lubrication.

Not only does fretting damage the metal surfaces and consequently the integrity of the joint, but it also has a severe effect on the fatigue life of the metal. It can reduce its endurance limit by as much as 50 to 70 percent. In wire rope the wire strands rub against each other as the rope flexes, and fretting occurs at the wire-to-wire contacts. If the fretting occurs in an area that is subject to cyclic fatigue stresses, the wire rope can fail.

Fretting is not limited to ferrous metals, where it is accompanied by oxidation; it can also occur in the noble metals and even in nonmetals. Since vibration is the primary cause, its elimination is the first order of business in preventing fretting—properly tuned standing rigging, stiffeners to dampen movement of large plate areas, and proper tightening of fastenings.

Also avoid unfavorable material combinations—aluminum and stainless steel, brass or copper and cast iron. Increasing the clamping force (e.g., tightening of fastenings) to reduce relative movement seems logical and may help, but it can also make matters worse. Lubrication provides relief but only temporarily. Sometimes the use of sealants such as silicones or polysulfides are effective because they serve as insulators or separators.

HYDROGEN DAMAGE

Hydrogen damage is a general term that includes several different forms of attack, all involving hydrogen as a causative factor and, in most (but not all) cases, tensile stress. Hydrogen—in the atomic state (H), not the molecular state (H_2)—is a problem because the hydrogen atom is extremely small. It is so small that it readily diffuses into and through the structure of the metal, concentrating in microstructural voids and discontinuities. As the concentration increases, a high internal pressure is created. The result can be void growth, cracking, and a loss of strength and ductility.

So, where does the hydrogen come from and how does it come to be absorbed into the metal? Steel can absorb hydrogen in several different ways—during the manufacturing process, during heat treatment, during welding operations, through contact with cleaning and maintenance chemicals (acids and alkalis), as a result of corrosion reactions, or due to excess hydrogen generated by cathodic protection systems. The problem is greatest in the hardened alloy steels, including stainless steels and nickel-base alloys, but it has also been known to occur in naval bronze under the influence of impressed-current cathodic protection systems.

The tensile stresses can be either internal—that is, residual stresses that are inherent in most materials, especially hardened steels—or external, such as those that a structural component might be expected to undergo in its normal function. Cleats, chainplates, turnbuckles, and similar structural deck and rigging fittings are likely candidates for hydrogen damage.

The several forms of hydrogen damage are *hydrogen embrittlement*, *hydrogen-assisted cracking*, and *hydrogen blistering*. If no residual stress or external loading is present, hydrogen embrittlement can manifest itself as blistering, internal cracking, and reduced ductility. If stress is present, it can result in crack growth and eventual fracture. If no corrosion is taking place, this is called *hydrogen-assisted cracking* (HAC) or *hydrogen stress cracking* (HSC). If there is active corrosion taking place, typically crevice or pitting corrosion, it is called *stress-corrosion cracking*.

Fortunately for us, steels below about 140,000 psi (9,843 kg/cm^2) tensile strength, or 100,000 psi (7,031 kg/cm^2) yield strength, which includes carbon and low-alloy steels, are not susceptible to either stress-corrosion cracking or hydrogen-assisted cracking. However, hydrogen blistering and loss of ductility are frequently found in the low-strength steels commonly used in vessel construction. In low-strength steels—100,000 psi yield strength or less—hydrogen damage is predominantly in the form of blistering or increased brittleness.

LIQUID METAL CRACKING

Liquid metal cracking, while not strictly a corrosion phenomenon, is a potential problem for the boat owner and repairer. Also known as *liquid metal embrittlement*, this is the catastrophic brittle failure of a normally ductile metal. It results from the penetration of metals and alloys, including steels, by metals that have relatively low melting points, such as lead, zinc, copper, cadmium, and aluminum.

Liquid metal embrittlement occurs when the low-melting-point metal in the molten state—such as during brazing, soldering, or welding operations—is in intimate contact with a base metal that is under tensile stress. It also has been known to occur in galvanized steels that have been subjected to intense heat, as during a fire, and when welding steel has been coated with zinc-bearing paints. The result is a serious degradation of material properties, such as increased brittleness and loss of strength. The magnitude of the stress on the metal, the temperature, and the length of time of the exposure are factors that facilitate and accelerate the damage.

Great care should be taken in soldering, brazing, and welding to be sure the parts are clean and free of contamination (zinc-pigmented paint, scraps of zinc, lead, etc.), heating temperatures are no greater than necessary, joints are designed to minimize exposure, and the operation is carried out as quickly and as efficiently as possible.

HOT-SHORT CRACKING

At the risk of giving the novice welder one more thing to worry about, I must include another welding-related type of degradation that can lead to stress-corrosion cracking, corrosion fatigue, and crevice corrosion. Hot-short cracking can occur during manufacturing or when a metal is hot-worked or welded. It results from the presence of low-melting elements—such as copper—at the grain boundaries in the alloy being welded. When the metal solidifies, the low-melting elements separate, causing minute cracks. Typically, these cracks show up within a matter of hours and are detectable with a dye penetrant. However, they may not show up for months or even years.

Silicon bronze screws, bolts, and threaded rod are used widely in the marine industry. Silicon bronze, an alloy of copper and 1 to 3 percent silicon, is subject to hot-short cracking after welding, brazing, or hot-working.

CONCLUSIONS

All metal components, fittings, and machinery on your boat are undergoing corrosion of one form or another. Underwater fastenings and fittings such as bronze through-hulls and raw water strainers are undergoing simple self-corrosion. However, good-quality bronze is highly corrosion resistant, so corrosion is an extremely slow process—so slow, in fact, that you'd have trouble detecting any loss of metal in the fitting even after 25 or 30 years.

Isolated above-the-waterline fittings—isolated from each other and from metallic contact with other dissimilar metals—are also corrosion candidates when exposed to moisture-laden salt air, salt spray, or contact with a saltwater-saturated mass. Deck hardware such as wire rigging, stanchions and bases, and cleats are all undergoing basic electrochemical corrosion. Bronze deck fittings develop a corrosion-inhibiting coating and last for many years. Aluminum can deliver similar durability, especially if it is anodized. Stainless steel components develop a chromium oxide protective coating and also last very well, except for those areas where the coating fails and pitting takes place. Iron and mild steel parts will do as they always have done—rust.

Limiting self-corrosion basically comes down to two things—protective coatings and metal selection (both covered in later chapters). You can also slow self-corrosion by keeping the surface of the fitting clean and by drying out trapped water.

The most practical method of minimizing the *consequences* of corrosion is careful visual inspection. Use a bright light and a magnifying glass to take a good close look at all those places we discussed above. Wire rigging, lifelines, and chainplates fail suddenly and at the worst possible time. If there's any doubt about any piece of equipment, replace it.

Even metallic underwater components such as through-hull fittings, rudder blades and posts, and props and shafts will develop protective coatings if they are isolated. But when the prop and shaft are of different metals, as they often are, then something more than simple electrochemical corrosion is going on. We discuss this in chapter 16.

CHAPTER 6

Galvanic Corrosion

In chapter 4 we talked about the basic corrosion process—what actually happens to the metals involved and to the electrolyte in which they're immersed. Four things must be present for corrosion to take place: an anode, a cathode, a metallic path for the electrons, and a common electrolyte or electrolytic path for the ions. We talked about the chemical reactions that take place at the anode, where metal atoms ionize and dissolve into the electrolyte, and at the cathode, where the free electrons released by the anode combine with dissolved oxygen in the seawater to form hydroxyl ions. We see later how these hydroxyl ions *can*, under certain conditions, combine with other elements in the seawater to form alkalis that can be very damaging to wood. In chapter 5 our focus was self-corrosion, corrosion involving *local* anodes and *local* cathodes present in a single piece of metal, and we talked briefly about what we could do about that. All right! Now we're getting to the kind of corrosion that is the main kind you'll encounter.

WHAT IS GALVANIC CORROSION?

Galvanic corrosion is the most common form of corrosion in the marine environment and a major problem for boatowners. As in self-corrosion, galvanic corrosion involves an anode and a cathode connected to each other by a metallic path for electrons and an electrolytic path for ions. But galvanic corrosion differs from simple self-corrosion in some important ways.

First, galvanic corrosion involves two or more *different* metals. Each metal has a different electromotive potential, commonly referred to as its *corrosion potential*, and all are immersed in the same electrolyte. This is referred to as a *galvanic cell*.

Second, galvanic corrosion is more serious and proceeds at a much more rapid rate than simple self-corrosion.

Third, the chemical reactions that take place in a galvanic cell yield different results that can increase the probability of damage to wood in the area of the cathode.

In a galvanic cell, the difference in corrosion potentials of the two metals causes electrons to flow from the metal with the more negative potential (anode) toward the metal with the less negative potential (cathode). Electrons arriving at the cathode increase its negative potential. This continues until the two metals are at the same potential, that is, until there is no voltage difference between them. This occurs at a voltage level somewhere between their natural, or isolated, potentials.

Keep in mind that each of the metals was already undergoing simple self-corrosion as we saw in chapter 5. The reactions that take place at the local anodes of each metal, that is, the ionization of metal atoms into the seawater together with the release of free electrons into the body of the metal, are balanced by the reactions that take place at their local cathodes, where dissolved oxygen in the seawater combines the excess electrons and water molecules to form hydroxyl ions.

When the two metals are connected, the galvanic cell begins to function. Electrons flow from the anode through the wire to the cathode. These electrons are in addition to those already consumed in the cathode reactions in simple electrochemical corrosion. Therefore, more electrons must be produced by the anode, resulting in more rapid corrosion of the anode metal.

At the cathode the reaction rate must increase in order to accommodate the extra electrons arriving there. If the number of electrons arriving at the cathode is great enough, the self-corrosion rate of the cathode metal will decrease and may stop altogether. In other words, the rate of corrosion of the anode metal increases while the corrosion rate of the cathode metal may be even less than was taking place under simple self-corrosion (fig. 6-1).

However, and this is one of the problems, the increase in the production of hydroxyl ions at the cathode can result, depending on other conditions, in damage to the wood in contact with or close to the cathode. In self-corrosion, the reactions taking place at the local anodes and local cathodes are extremely close to each other physically. The hydroxyl ions formed at the local cathodes are close enough to the local anodes that they can combine with the metal ions released into the seawater there. This forms a metal oxide that attaches to the metal as a metal

hydroxide film. This is the protective film discussed previously.

In a galvanic cell, the anodic metal may be quite some distance from the cathodic metal, so the probability of metal ions released at the anode combining with the hydroxyl ions formed at the cathode is very small. Instead of combining into a protective film, the hydroxyl ions formed at the cathode stay in solution. If they are allowed to concentrate, the water becomes more alkaline and the wood in the area may be damaged. However, if the water is flowing and constantly changing, the hydroxyl ions are dispersed and the likelihood of alkali damage to the wood is lessened.

Any time a metal component is connected to or touching another metal and both are immersed in seawater or embedded in a saltwater-saturated medium—such as wood—they form a galvanic cell and are subject to galvanic corro-

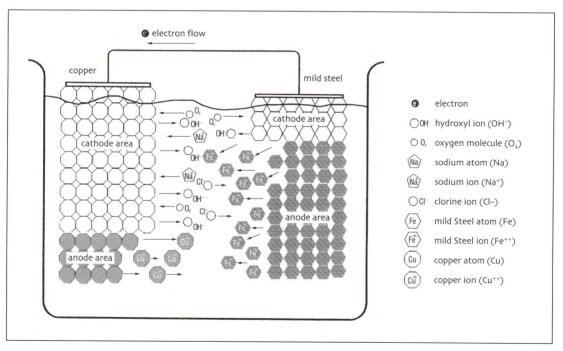

Fig. 6-1. Galvanic corrosion. The steel is predominantly anodic, whereas the copper is predominantly cathodic. Electrons move from the anode areas toward the cathode areas, leaving metallic ions that dissolve from the anode areas into the electrolyte. Sodium ions (Na^+) may combine with hydroxyl ions to form sodium hydroxide, or caustic soda, which is damaging to wood.

sion. The extent of the corrosion that takes place is a function of the following factors:

- the magnitude of the potential difference between the dissimilar metals and the nature of the electrical contact between them
- the relative areas of the two metal surfaces
- the *polarization* (see below) that takes place at each of the metals
- the nature of the environment in which the metals are immersed

POTENTIAL DIFFERENCE: THE GALVANIC SERIES

In chapter 4 we introduced the galvanic series, a list of metals and alloys ranked according to their *open-circuit* potentials (relative to a *silver–silver chloride* electrode). The farther apart the metals are in this list, the faster the rate of galvanic corrosion, so the galvanic series enables us to anticipate how two metals will react to each other when placed in contact. With this knowledge, we can try to avoid those combinations likely to result in severe corrosion.

Although the series is based on immersion in seawater, in a general way it is applicable to most natural waters and to the atmosphere, barring factors like acid rain or other contaminants that significantly alter the pH (acidity or alkalinity) of the water.

POLARIZATION

When two metals are electrically connected to form a galvanic cell, electron flow takes place between them, and they tend to come to a common potential somewhere between the isolated potentials of the individual metals as listed in the galvanic series. The potential of the anodic metal tends to move toward the potential of the cathode, whereas the potential of the cathode tends to move toward that of the anode. This shift in potentials is referred to as *polarization*. The resulting potential of the cell will depend on the relative surface areas of the two metals.

Once this equilibrium corrosion potential has been established, a rate at which electrons will

flow from the anode to the cathode has also been established. Since the magnitude of the current flow determines the amount of metal that will be removed from the anode, the rate at which corrosion will take place is also established—assuming that protective films are not formed.

CATHODE-TO-ANODE RATIO

The ratio of the area of the cathodic surface to that of the anodic surface is a critical factor in galvanic corrosion. Remember that we said electrons flow from the anodic surface area to the cathodic surface area through the metal contact or connection. The anodic metal supplies electrons by literally giving up pieces of itself (metal ions) to the electrolyte. The anode must supply enough electrons to maintain the cathode at its new, more negative potential. The greater the area of the cathode, the more electrons required.

When the area of cathodic surface (the one least likely to corrode) is significantly larger than that of the active or anodic surface (the most likely to corrode), an unfavorable cathode-to-anode ratio is said to exist. Since the magnitude of the current flow is determined by the area of the cathode, a larger cathodic surface can cause the current density at the anode to be excessively high (in amps per square inch). Because the amount of current determines the amount of anodic metal that will be dissolved, severe galvanic corrosion is likely. The opposite condition—where the anodic area is larger than the cathodic area—provides a favorable ratio.

Let's consider a practical example. Say we have a large, unpainted steel-hull vessel with a small, unpainted copper-alloy through-hull fitting. The large steel surface area is the anode and has no difficulty supplying the electrons demanded by the small surface area of the cathode—the copper-alloy through-hull—without experiencing significant deterioration.

Now suppose the hull is painted rather than bare, but the coating is not perfect, exhibiting tiny pinholes or chips. Here we have the opposite situation. The anodic surface is just the steel in contact with the electrolyte, that exposed by the pinhole or chip, so now the anodic surface area is tiny compared to the area of the copper-alloy fitting. The copper-alloy fitting is still the cathode and still requires the same number of electrons, but they must be supplied from an anode with a tiny surface area. This results in extremely high current densities and severe pitting corrosion.

Whenever possible it behooves us to maintain a favorable (low) cathode-to-anode ratio. We talk more about this when we discuss fastenings in chapter 16.

FORMS OF GALVANIC CORROSION

Galvanic corrosion takes place at the anodic member of the galvanic cell. It can occur uniformly over the anodic surface or at discrete sites on the anode, as pitting, crevice corrosion, and stress-corrosion cracking. Which form it takes will depend on the specific nature of the galvanic cell, whether films are present, what types of films are found, and what metals are involved.

Galvanic corrosion occurs most commonly where two or more dissimilar metals are in contact, such as prop and prop shaft, rudder and rudderpost, perhaps heat exchanger and engine. However, galvanic corrosion can also take place in situations where nonmetallic conductors act as cathodes in galvanic cells. An example is mill scale (magnetite, FeO), which forms on carbon steel. Mill scale is a conductive film that acts as a large area cathode to the anodic substrate, the steel.

A less commonly recognized nonmetallic conductor is carbon fiber composite used in masts and other spars and in rudders and rudderposts. Exposed carbon fibers are good conductors of electricity, and although the carbon fiber composite is not itself damaged by corrosion, it can function as the cathodic member of a galvanic cell when in contact with less noble components such as fastenings and fittings.

Another example of galvanic corrosion can occur when sacrificial metals are used as protective coatings on anodic metals, such as the zinc coating on carbon steel in galvanized steel fastenings and fittings. Corrosion of the steel can occur at pores, chips, scratches, and the edges of the protective coatings.

It is the process of galvanic corrosion that provides the basis for the cathodic protection schemes we use to combat the corrosion process. We discuss those schemes in greater depth in chapter 13.

GALVANIC CORROSION SUSCEPTIBILITY

The ease with which a specific metal is polarized has considerable influence on its role in a galvanic cell, so let's briefly review the concept of *polarization*. We said that polarization is the change in the metal's corrosion potential from its open-circuit value as the result of current flow between the metals in the galvanic couple. The potential of the anodic metal tends to become more noble and the potential of the cathodic metal tends to become more active. If the more noble metal is more easily polarized, its potential is shifted more toward the more active metal. The shift in potential of the more active metal in the direction of the cathode is therefore minimized so that accelerated galvanic corrosion is not as great as it would be otherwise. When the more noble metal is not readily polarized, the potential of the more active metal shifts farther toward the cathode, and significant accelerated galvanic corrosion results.

Although we discuss the specifics of the metals commonly used in the marine environment in greater detail later, now is a good time for some brief comments on common marine metals and their susceptibility to galvanic corrosion.

Aluminum and Its Alloys

Aluminum and its alloys are lightweight, fairly strong, and quite resistant both to atmospheric corrosion and, if of a suitable grade, to immersion in seawater—assuming that the atmosphere and the seawater are reasonably unpolluted.

Aluminum owes this resistance to its ability to quickly form a protective oxide surface film. Aluminum alloys, however, are very active metals, as can be seen from their position in the galvanic series (–0.76 to –1.00 volts; see table 4-1). In seawater, aluminum alloys are susceptible to localized galvanic corrosion such as pitting and crevice corrosion, and severe galvanic corrosion can result when aluminum alloys are coupled with more noble metals. In freshwater or water with low chloride concentrations, aluminum alloys are considerably less active because of the greater stability of the protective oxide film, hence galvanic effects are not as severe.

Certain aluminum alloys are used for sacrificial anodes in seawater. The aluminum alloys listed in the galvanic series table do not include these alloys. Aluminum alloys used as sacrificial anodes have a maximum corrosion potential of –1.100 volts.

Copper and Its Alloys

In this category we're talking about the bronzes and brasses. True bronzes are quite strong and ductile and are extremely resistant to corrosion, both atmospheric and immersed. Good-quality bronze is truly a superior marine metal. Nearly as strong as stainless steel, it is more ductile (an important safety feature) and is not subject to pitting corrosion. It is widely used in all manner of fittings, fastenings, and marine components. Silicon bronze (Everdur) is probably the most widely used and the most satisfactory metal for marine screws and bolts. It is, to all intents and purposes, immune to self-corrosion either in the atmosphere or immersed in seawater. However, it is subject to galvanic corrosion (as are all metals) when coupled with other more anodic metals.

The brasses, on the other hand, are frequently used for decorative fittings and trim in benign interior atmospheres, but they are not really satisfactory for outside use where they can be exposed to salt air or spray or immersed in seawater. Most brasses are only 58 to 60 percent copper and 39 percent zinc, and therein lies the rub. With the copper at –0.30 to –0.57 volts cor-

rosion potential and the zinc at –0.98 to –1.03 volts, we have a strong galvanic cell. The zinc, as zinc is wont to do, sacrifices itself (dezincifies), leaving a porous, spongy, brittle fitting. Brass gate valves used in place of proper bronze seacocks are a classic example of the dangerous misuse of brass fittings below the waterline. This is discussed further in chapter 16.

Broadly speaking, copper alloys occupy the corrosion potential range between –0.18 to –0.42 volts, which places them between the active and passive positions for the stainless steels. Because they are not easily polarized in seawater, they can cause severe corrosion of more active metals such as aluminum and steel.

Iron and Steel

Iron and carbon and low-alloy steels corrode readily when exposed to the atmosphere, immersed, or in seawater. Although they do develop oxide layers on the surface, these films are porous and loosely attached. They separate easily from the parent metal, re-exposing the surface and allowing the process to repeat. In other words, iron and steel rust. Even so, because of their low cost, ease of fabrication, and good strength, they are widely used as structural materials.

Iron and steel are quite active, with a range of corrosion potentials of –0.60 to –0.71 volts. Carbon steel, also called *mild* steel, corrodes at about the same rate in aerated freshwater as it does in aerated seawater, but the higher electrical conductivity of seawater can result in more severe pitting corrosion.

The so-called alloy steels were developed to provide added strength and toughness. Low-alloy steels typically contain the same basic constituent elements as the low-carbon grades but with small amounts of such alloying elements as niobium, vanadium, chrome, copper, or nickel added. Several grades offer enhanced atmospheric corrosion resistance and are referred to as *weathering steels* because they develop a unique protective oxide layer when exposed to atmospheric conditions. Cor-Ten is an example. These grades have found some use in steel vessel construction, but it should be noted that this protective layer does not occur when the metal is immersed. We talk more about this in chapter 8.

Stainless Steels

Stainless steels are high-alloy steels. They have better corrosion resistance than the carbon and low-alloy steels because they contain relatively large amounts of chromium. The three general classes of stainless steels are *austenitic*, *ferritic*, and *martensitic*. Of these three, the austenitic stainless steels have the greatest resistance to corrosion and are the most widely used in the marine environment for all manner of fittings, fastenings, and components. The basic composition of this group is commonly referred to as the *18-8* stainless steels, which refers to the percentages of chromium and nickel in the composition. The term *18-8* is imprecise and subject to various interpretations. I talk more about this in chapter 8.

Stainless steel is found in several different positions in the galvanic series, depending on the composition of the specific grade (that is, 304, 316, ASTM 564, ASTM 630) and on whether the steel is in the *passive* or the *active* state. The term *passive* here refers to a metal that has developed a protective oxide layer. The corrosion potentials of passive grades are much more noble than the same metal without its protective oxide layer. For example, Type 304 in the passive state has a corrosion potential range of –0.05 to –0.10 volts, whereas Type 304 in the active (nonpassive) state has a corrosion potential range of –0.46 to –0.58 volts. A similar difference is found for Type 316, which has a corrosion potential range of 0.00 to –0.10 volts in the passive state and –0.43 to –0.54 volts in the active state.

Stainless steels rely on the protective oxide coating for their resistance to corrosion. When in clean, flowing water containing plenty of oxygen, they are able to develop and maintain this oxide film. However, when they are deprived of this fresh supply of oxygen, they lose their protective film, become active, and are susceptible to serious corrosion. Oxygen deprivation frequently occurs under barnacles, in stern tubes, and under Cutless bearings. Galvanically induced corrosion can take place in stainless steels when they are in contact with more noble metals such as the copper alloys. Also, galvanic corrosion of carbon steels can be induced by stainless steel in seawater, especially with unfavorable cathode-to-anode ratios.

Lead and Its Alloys

Lead finds limited application in the marine environment; it is used primarily as ballast—external or internal—and as solder in electrical and plumbing joints. Lead is a fairly noble metal with a corrosion potential range of –0.19 to –0.23 volts. The protective film that forms on lead and its alloys is very effective, and atmospheric corrosion is essentially negligible. Even in seawater, corrosion is relatively slight. However, being more noble than steel, lead will accelerate corrosion in steel when in contact and immersed in seawater, hence the difficulty with steel keel bolts in lead ballast keels.

Soldering

Soldering utilizes lead-base or tin-base alloys with melting points below 800°F (426.7°C). Most solders in common use contain from 2 to 100 percent tin with the balance consisting of lead. The most common alloys are 50–50 and 40–60 tin–lead. These solders are close to copper and brass in the galvanic series.

Typically a flux is used in making the solder joint. The function of the flux is to remove oxides already present on the metal surface and to prevent the formation of new oxide films that might inhibit satisfactory wetting of the surfaces to be joined. Mild fluxes, such as the resin fluxes commonly used in electrical work, consist solely of natural resins. They are essentially inactive and leave a harmless residue. However, more powerful fluxes can contain chlorides and/or phosphoric acid to remove more stubborn oxides. Residues from these fluxes can be harmful and must be removed due to their corrosive effects.

Solder joints exposed to sea spray, trapped moisture, or flux residue can be susceptible to corrosion—depending upon the particular solder alloy used and the metals joined. When immersed in seawater, solder joints must be protected by coatings to prevent galvanic action.

Brazing

Brazing involves the use of hard solders, typically silver solders, which have silver, copper, or nickel bases and melting points above 800°F (426.7°C). These alloys make considerably stronger joints, and because they are higher in the galvanic series than the soft solders, they are more compatible with the bronzes and copper-nickel alloys.

Nickel and Its Alloys

Nickel and its alloys are even more noble (less active) than the copper-base alloys. They range in corrosion potential from −0.05 to −0.17 volts. They are very strong and highly resistant to corrosion, both in the atmosphere and immersed in seawater. However, most are not easily polarized and in galvanic couples will cause accelerated corrosion of more active metals like aluminum and steel. Nickel-base alloys are used extensively in the marine industry. Monel (−0.04 to −0.14 volts) is probably the best known.

Two other well-known nickel-base alloy trade names, Inconel (alloy 600) and Hastelloy (alloy C-276), offer an attractive combination of passive surface and the high corrosion resistance of nickel-chromium alloy. They occupy a very high position in the galvanic series: −0.14 to −0.17 volts and −0.03 to +0.08 volts, respectively. Both are easily polarized and therefore tend to minimize galvanic effects on less noble metals.

Zinc and Its Alloys

With a corrosion potential range of −0.98 to −1.03 volts, zinc is highly active, second only to magnesium in the galvanic series. It is highly susceptible to galvanic corrosion and is commonly used as sacrificial anodes, as a sacrificial coating (in galvanizing and electroplating, for example), and as a pigment in some paint coatings.

Referred to as *pot metal*, zinc is also used as an inexpensive metal for small castings—decorative hardware, small hinges, and the like. Unfortunately, it has also seen some use as a casting metal for cleats, chocks, stanchion bases, and other deck fittings. Such castings are not nearly as strong or corrosion resistant as steel, aluminum, or bronze and are unsuitable for high-load applications.

Precious Metals

Gold

Although not, strictly speaking, a marine metal (although the cost of some marine fittings might make you wonder), gold is included here because of its use as a plated coating on a wide variety of electrical and mechanical components. Gold is a good thermal and electrical conductor, and due to its very noble position in the galvanic series (0.00 to +0.200 volts), it is highly resistant to galvanic corrosion. Gold does not polarize readily and can therefore have a marked effect in galvanic couples with other metals or alloys.

Silver

Here again, silver is not a marine metal, but it is widely used in brazing alloys, electrical contacts, and printed circuit board fabrication. It is soft, ductile, and an excellent conductor of heat and electricity. Silver reacts with hydrogen sulfide in air to form a silver sulfide film (tarnish). Silver occupies a high position in the galvanic series (−0.15 to +0.05 volts), close to the passivated 18-8 stainless steels, and is therefore relatively immune to atmospheric corrosion. Silver is also resistant to galvanic corrosion, but it does not polarize readily and can therefore have a significant influence in galvanic couples with other metals or alloys.

Other Metals

Magnesium

With a corrosion potential range of −1.60 to −1.63 volts, magnesium is the most active of the metals listed in the galvanic series. It is used extensively in aerospace where its light weight offers real benefits, but with the exception of emergency flares, it has little application in the marine industry.

Titanium

With a corrosion potential range of −0.05 to +0.06 volts, titanium is highly noble and tends to polarize easily, minimizing its galvanic effects on other metals. It is susceptible to hydrogen embrittlement.

Titanium has the highest strength-to-weight ratio of any metal. It has long been used in airframe construction, but high cost has restricted marine applications to specialized fittings on high-performance racing sailboats such as America's Cup contenders, where light weight and high strength are critical.

Uranium

Depleted uranium is a waste by-product of the uranium-enrichment process. Because of its extremely high density, depleted uranium was used for a short time in the late 1980s for ballast keels on high-performance racing sailboats. It was subsequently realized that exposure to depleted uranium is harmful to both humans and the environment, and so marine use was soon discontinued.

CONTROLLING GALVANIC CORROSION

Galvanic corrosion can be annoying, seriously damaging (and expensive), and even dangerous for the vessel and the crew. It can and should be controlled or, better yet, eliminated. Fortunately there are a number of methods by which this may be accomplished.

One such method is the selection of *appropriate materials* according to their position in the galvanic series and their relative ease of polarization (see chapter 14). A related alternative is the use of metallic coatings to alter the differences in corrosion potentials of the members of the galvanic couple (see chapter 15).

Altering or controlling the environment surrounding the galvanic couple is another method. This involves the use of *corrosion-inhibiting chemicals*. An example of this method is the use of corrosion-resistant enhanced ethylene glycol engine coolant solutions (see chapter 17).

Applying organic *barrier coatings* (paint, plastic, etc.) to the surface of the anode and cathode to break the flow of current is an effective means of control. Great care must be taken with these coatings, however, since scratches or punctures in the anodic coatings can result in intensified corrosive attack at these sites. It is usually advisable to coat both the anode and the cathode members of the galvanic couple (see chapter 15).

Another commonly utilized method is the use of nonmetallic *insulators* at the contact surfaces of the dissimilar metals to prevent the flow of current between them (see chapter 14).

A method not commonly utilized in the marine community but worthy of mention is the use of a series of *transition metals* inserted between the contacting surfaces. In this method a metal insert similar galvanically to the anode metal but closer to the cathode in corrosion potential is inserted at the anode interface. Another metal insert, similar to this new metal but closer still to the cathode potential, is then placed in contact with the new metal, and so on. The objective is to form a gradual transition in corrosion potentials between the anode and the cathode so that no two metals are sufficiently far apart in corrosion potential to cause significant galvanic corrosion.

Cathodic protection (along with barrier coatings) is by far the most common method utilized in the marine industry. *Sacrificial anodes* made of zinc (and, less frequently in the marine industry, of aluminum or magnesium) are made a part of the galvanic circuit. The most active member of the circuit will corrode first, thus sacrificing itself to provide protection to the more noble members (see chapter 13).

Another cathodic protection method, similar to the use of sacrificial anodes, is the use of *impressed current systems*. Here an externally generated current is used to provide the flow of electrons to the cathode that the sacrificial anode provides in the sacrificial anode system (see chapter 13). Impressed current systems are not widely used in small craft because of their expense and their requirement for relatively complex control systems.

Finally, we can combat corrosion by paying attention to such design and construction considerations as the relative size of the members of the galvanic couple (area ratios); avoiding corners, cracks and crevices, and moist, stagnant pockets; and equipping limber holes with clearing chains (see chapter 14).

CHAPTER 7

Electrolytic Corrosion

Thus far we've seen that simple self-corrosion involves a single piece of metal—pure or alloy—in contact with an electrolyte. It proceeds continuously at an extremely slow rate, something like 0.0002 inch (0.005 mm) or less of surface loss per year for a high-quality bronze in seawater. The best practical method of reducing or controlling self-corrosion is through the use of a protective coating—such as paint, epoxy, anodizing—that bonds tightly to the metal's surface and prevents the penetration or entrapment of moisture.

In chapter 6 we saw that galvanic corrosion involves two or more dissimilar metals in electrical contact with one another and immersed in the same electrolyte. When galvanic corrosion occurs, it is in addition to simple electrochemical corrosion, which still takes place. Galvanic corrosion is more severe and can be very damaging. The usual way to deal with galvanic corrosion on a boat is through the use of sacrificial zinc anodes, which must be properly sized and positioned on the underbody of the boat. All fittings that need to be protected should be connected to the zinc anodes through a good, hefty bonding system (see chapter 18). However, sacrificial anodes will not prevent *electrolytic corrosion*. This is the most aggressive form of corrosion and the subject of this chapter.

Electrolytic corrosion is the result of electrical currents from within the boat, from a nearby boat, or from a shoreside outlet going to ground (in this case, the seawater surrounding the boat) through an underwater fitting. In other words, it is electrical current that has gone "astray," and it is commonly referred to as *stray current corrosion*. Electrolytic corrosion can be extremely serious, destroying a fitting in a matter of weeks—or in just hours in severe cases. The voltages involved in galvanic corro-

sion are in the millivolt (thousandths of a volt) range and produce currents measured in milliamps (thousandths of an amp). But the voltages involved in DC stray current corrosion can be as high as the battery voltage. In the case of AC stray currents, voltage can be as much as 120 volts, perhaps higher, so currents are likely to be orders of magnitude greater than in galvanic corrosion.

How does this happen? How does a current stray from its appointed rounds? Routes vary, but in all cases they result from faulty electrical wiring or equipment.

Remember, corrosion always requires an anode, a cathode, a metallic path for the electrons, and an electrolytic (or ionic) path for the ions. Let's take an example from my own checkered past. We had rewired a boat for dual batteries. There was no room in the main battery box for the second battery, so we installed it a couple of feet away under a berth in the cabin. When the second battery went ashore for charging, I separated the battery cables and tucked the terminal ends behind the bilge stringer well above the bilgewater. A few days later, preparing to reinstall the second battery back, we discovered that the positive battery cable had crawled out from behind the stringer and leaped into the bilgewater in a sort of suicidal frenzy. All that was left of the massive battery terminal clamp was a little dollop of green paste. Once submerged in the bilgewater, the clamp had become an anode, and a corrosion cell was in place. Electrons and ions (and people) always seek the path of least resistance, so the most probable electrolytic path was through the bilgewater to the saltwater saturated engine bed to the engine block and the common ground point. The metallic path for electrons was through the battery cable itself back to the positive battery post

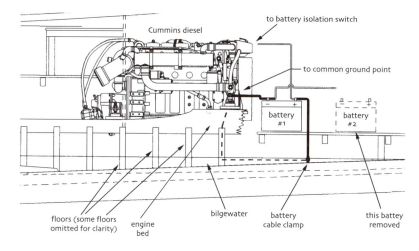

Fig. 7-1. Hot wire in the bilge. The lead battery cable clamp on the positive cable fell into the bilge and dissolved in a matter of days. The boat used in the chapter diagrams is a 38' Jonesport redrawn from plans by Arno Day in the collection of the Maine Maritime Museum, Bath, Maine; engine outline courtesy of Cummins Engine Company, Inc.

and from the negative battery post through the cable to the engine block (see fig. 7-1).

So a hot wire exposed in the bilge will corrode just as my battery cable terminal did. That's the bad news. The good news is that, just as in the case of the battery clamp, the corrosive action is self-limiting; when the anode is gone, the corrosion stops.

Now let's say that a piece of metal immersed in seawater—a through-hull, for example—comes in contact with an electrically positive wire from the electrical system. The through-hull becomes the anode of a battery cell. The

metallic path for electron flow consists of the through-hull and the wire to the positive side of the battery, and, from the negative side of the battery, the ground cable, engine block, shaft coupling, shaft, and prop. The prop becomes the cathode of the cell. The electrolytic path is from the prop through the seawater and back to the through-hull. Since we said that it is the anode of the cell that corrodes, the through-hull will suffer corrosion (see fig. 7-2).

In another possible scenario, a wire from the positive side of the DC electrical system falls into the bilgewater, close to but not touching a

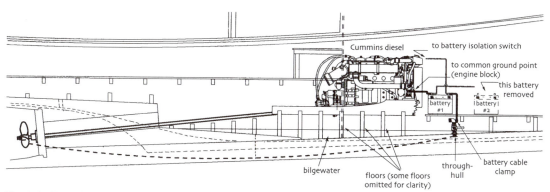

Fig. 7-2. Hot wire in bilge contacting through-hull. The through-hull becomes an anode, and an electrolytic path is established between the through-hull and the outside seawater to the prop and shaft.

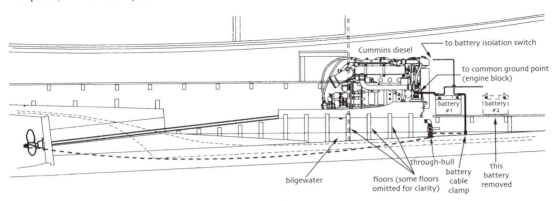

Fig. 7-3. Hot wire in bilge near but not touching a through-hull with two ionic paths. The cable clamp becomes an anode; an electrolytic path is established between the cable clamp and the through-hull. The inboard end of the through-hull becomes a cathode, and the outboard end becomes an anode. A secondary electrolytic path is established between the through-hull and the prop and shaft.

through-hull that is immersed in the bilgewater. Here the corrosion circuit becomes a little more complicated. The positive wire becomes an anode with an ionic path through the water to the inboard end of the through-hull, which becomes a cathode. But the circuit doesn't stop there. Because there is another ionic path through the seawater to the prop, the outboard end of the through-hull becomes an anode, and the prop becomes a cathode. The metallic path for electrons then goes from the prop through the shaft to the engine block and back to the battery (see fig. 7-3). The anodes—the end of the wire and the outside end of the through-hull—will corrode. But here again, once the end of the wire in the water has dissolved, the circuit is broken and the corrosion will cease.

DC SYSTEMS

The most common sources of DC stray current are faulty insulation, improper wiring, poor grounds, shorts, and equipment leaks. Let's take them one by one.

Faulty Insulation

Contrary to my own experience, loose wires don't often fall into the bilge. However, chafed wire insulation and poorly insulated splices in the bilge are a fairly common problem. You should avoid wire splices near the bilge like the plague, but if there is no alternative, take the time to do it right. Make up the splice in a dry place using a properly sized waterproof butt connector, and then encase it in a long piece of adhesive-lined heat-shrink tubing.

Submersible bilge pumps seem to be likely candidates for stray currents since they are electrical and sit in the bilge. However, I can't honestly say I've come across many situations in which the bilge pump was at fault. The manufacturer of a popular brand tells me stray currents can result if the shaft seal gets damaged by sand or grit, allowing water to get up into the armature. The armature itself is well insulated, so the pump could continue to function for some time. Once the armature or its connection becomes an anode, an ionic path is established through the seawater. Since the armature represents a fairly large mass, the stray current could continue for some time unless the wire connection to the armature dissolves, opening the circuit. Eventually the pump fails. You can avoid this by switching to a self-priming diaphragm pump mounted up out of the bilge, but the float switch might still be a source of the stray current if the wire seals fail.

Improper Wiring

Let's assume a submersible electric bilge pump and float switch wired as shown in the figure 7-4A. Notice that the float switch is in series with the "hot" or positive side of the power supply. This means that even if the shaft seal were damaged and water were to invade the motor, no voltage will be applied to the motor until the float switch closes.

If the float switch were wired into the negative side of the DC supply, the motor would be "hot," and stray current would flow regardless of the float switch position (see figure 7-4B). Always install switches, fuses, and circuit breakers in the "hot" or positive side of a circuit.

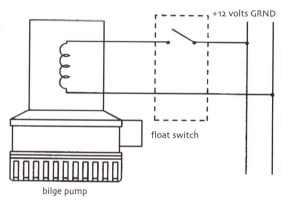

Fig. 7-4A. Proper wiring, with the On/Off switch in the positive side. When the switch is in the Off position, the circuit is open and there is no voltage at the load.

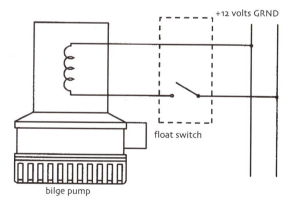

Fig. 7-4B. Improper wiring, with the On/Off switch in the negative side. The load is "hot" whether the switch is "On" or "Off."

Faulty Grounds

Anytime a voltage difference exists between two points, there will be a tendency for current to seek a path to the more negative point. Often this will be a leakage path through water. The greater the voltage difference, the stronger the tendency for stray current to flow.

A common example of faulty grounds is an SSB radio grounded to a groundplate on the outside of the hull. The groundplate will be at a different voltage than the common ground point on the engine block because of the resistance between the two. Current will flow through the seawater from the groundplate to any underwater fitting connected to the common ground point—the prop via the shaft or a through-hull fitting via a bonding wire. From the ground point the current passes through the battery cable to the negative battery terminal (see fig. 7-5).

Equipment Leaks

Electrical and electronic equipment contained in metal housings can be the source of stray currents. A frayed or bare wire touching the chassis energizes the housing, and if the housing is in contact with, for example, damp wood, a stray current flows to ground. This can be avoided by grounding all equipment cabinets and housings to a common ground point.

Salt-laden moisture on insulators or terminal strips can also provide a path for leakage currents.

BONDING

All electrical equipment housings should be connected to the same ground point by a heavy-gauge wire—at least #8 AWG—to ensure that no voltage differences exist. This includes all underwater metal fittings that come into contact with the bilgewater. This will enable stray currents reaching these fittings to flow directly to the common ground point instead of seeking other paths through metal fittings or fastenings to ground through the water. Bonding thus protects these fittings from internally generated DC

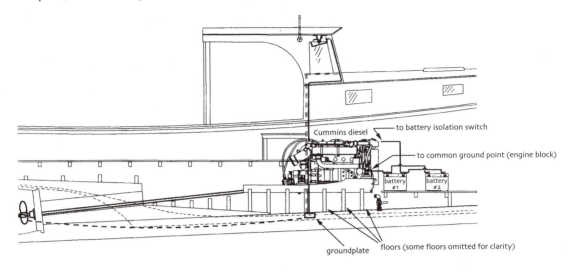

Fig. 7-5. Faulty grounds. The groundplate for the SSB radio is at a different potential than the common ground (engine block), creating potential for stray current. An electrolytic path is established between the groundplate and the prop and shaft, which are at common ground potential.

or AC stray-current corrosion. The following should all be connected to the common ground point:

- negative battery cable
- ground return cable from the main distribution panel
- main bonding conductor
- radio groundplate
- lightning groundplate
- grounding wire from shore power
- ground cable from the auxiliary generator

AC SYSTEMS

Now let's take a look at stray alternating current. There is a school of thought that says stray AC cannot cause corrosion. The logic is that since alternating currents are equal and opposite—that is, positive and negative half-cycles—any metal that was ionized during one half-cycle would be redeposited on the other half-cycle. This is a purely theoretical view and assumes 100 percent efficiency in the reactions during both half-cycles. In the real world, however, not

all the metallic particles dissolved into the electrolyte on the anodic half-cycle are recovered on the cathodic half-cycle. The result is a net loss of metal particles, or corrosion, due to AC stray currents.

There is not much factual data available in the current literature. The most recent is a 1984 paper titled "Corrosion by Alternating Current" by Der-Tau Chen, which concludes that corrosion rates of aluminum, tin-lead solder, mild steel, and copper increase spectacularly with increasing current density. Even stainless steel (304) suffered pitting. Protecting metals required more cathodic current (from zinc anodes) than in the absence of AC currents. Given the high currents that can be involved, stray AC can be very damaging. It may not be a big deal if you're going to be in the slip for just a couple of nights, but if this condition exists in your boat's regular berth, it could be a serious problem.

Some of the more common causes of AC stray-current corrosion are

- extension cords dropped into the bilge
- improper wiring on the boat

- improper wiring on the dock
- polarity indicators
- battery chargers

As for dropping extension cords into the bilge, the solution is simple—don't do that! For the rest of the causes, let's take them one by one.

Wiring on the Boat

First of all, let's assume for the moment that the shoreside electrics are properly wired and in good condition (it ain't necessarily so!). We'll come back to this.

To avoid stray current problems, AC wiring on the boat must be installed correctly and maintained in good condition. Leakage currents to ground can occur anywhere that bare wires or connections come into contact with a metal fitting or an electrolyte (bilgewater, saltwater-saturated wood, condensation, etc.). The resistance of this short-circuit path is often high enough to restrict the current to a level insufficient to activate circuit breakers or fuses, so the stray current condition can persist for some time. Most stray current conditions stem from some mistake made during installation.

OK, let's go a little slow here—this part can get confusing. The 120-volt AC shore-power system is typically a three-wire system. It consists of a hot (black) wire, a neutral (white) wire, and a grounding (green or bare) wire.

The black wire is an *ungrounded* current-carrying wire. It brings the current to the boat. It is referred to as the *ungrounded side*.

The white wire is also a current-carrying wire. Its purpose is to return the current to ground *at its power source*—where it wants very badly to go. *The white wire is only connected to ground at its power source.* So, the white wire is a *grounded* current-carrying wire and is referred to as the *grounded side*.

The green wire is also grounded *at the power source*, the shoreside outlet in this case. It does not normally carry current. It is referred to as the *grounding* (with an *i-n-g*) conductor. The green wire is there in case of an electrical short from the hot side of the circuit to a cabinet, frame, or housing of a piece of AC electrical equipment. Without the green wire, the housing or cabinet would be hot, that is, it would be at 120 volts and thus a potential source of some electrifying moments in the life of the unwary crew member. With the green, the short goes immediately to ground, probably tripping the breaker. In any case, it provides a lower resistance path to ground that protects the crew member. On the boat, the green wire is connected to outlet boxes, to equipment housings and cabinets, *and* to the boat's common ground point. Note that the AC electrical system on a boat should be totally isolated from the DC electrical system. The only connection they should have is where the green wire connects to the boat's common ground point.

AC is brought aboard the boat through a special marine-grade, three-wire shore power cable. One end of the cable is plugged into a shore power outlet on the dock, and the other is plugged into an onboard receptacle. The plugs and receptacles are polarized and configured according to their voltage and current carrying capacities. The pin and slot arrangements are physically different so that it is not possible to connect to a 50-amp service with 30-amp cord.

From the onboard receptacle, the black and white wires should be wired to an AC distribution panel through a double-pole main shore power disconnect circuit breaker. The green wire is connected to a common ground point through a galvanic isolator (more about this later). Note that in AC circuits, two-pole switches and circuit breakers should always be used, although the ABYC (American Boat and Yacht Council) does permit the use of single-pole devices in the branch circuits when a polarity-indicating device is installed. In other words, when the black hot wire is connected to a load, the white neutral must be available for the *return* path. Otherwise the current will seek alternative or "stray paths" to return to ground. Figure 7-6 shows our faithful old vessel all gussied up with shore power AC so we can watch the soaps while we're cleaning up the boat.

One of the more common mistakes made by residential electricians and home handymen in wiring boats for shore power is connecting both

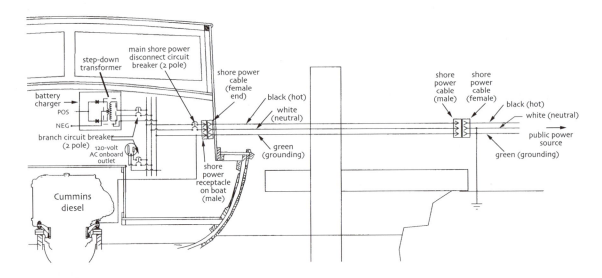

Fig. 7-6. Basic AC shore power circuit. Basic shore power systems generally have no provision for stray current protection.

the white neutral and the green grounding wire together on the boat. This is a very dangerous mistake. All of the current that comes aboard in the hot black wire *must* get back to the shoreside ground. In a properly wired system, the only return path is the white neutral wire, as shown by the heavy lines in figure 7-7. But when the white neutral wire and the green grounding wire are tied together *on the boat*, there are parallel return paths for this current. One is back to the shoreside ground through the white neutral wire. A second is back to shore side through the green grounding wire. However, because the green wire is connected to the boat's ground, which is in turn connected to metal fittings penetrating the hull to the water outside, there is a third return path through the seawater surrounding the boat. This is shown by the heavy lines in figure 7-8. Not only do we now have a complete galvanic cell making corrosion likely, but this is a dangerous situation for people in the water around the boat. What's worse, if the white wire should open for any reason, *all* of the return current could be through the seawater. The danger for anyone in the water near the boat cannot be overstated!

To sum up, in a properly wired system,

- The black wire will be connected to the hot side of the onboard circuit.
- The white wire will be grounded *only* at the source of power (such as at the shoreside outlet), at an onboard generator, at an onboard inverter, or at the secondary winding of an isolation transformer. More about this later, but I need to make the point here that improperly connecting the white and green wires can be lethal. If you not experienced with AC wiring systems—and perhaps even if you are—I strongly urge you to engage the services of a qualified expert marine electrical technician, preferably one that is ABYC certified.
- The green wire will be grounded at the source (as above) and connected to the common ground on the boat.
- Outlet boxes and equipment cabinets and housings will be connected to the boat's common ground.
- A *properly wired* bonding system will be in place.

Even when our own boat is properly wired, faulty shoreside wiring or improper wiring

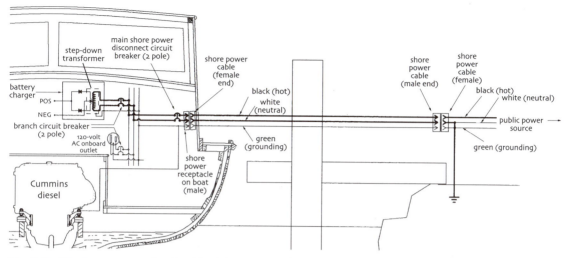

Fig. 7-7. AC shore power circuit. All of the current that flows to the loads in the hot black wire returns to ground at the source in the grounded white wire.

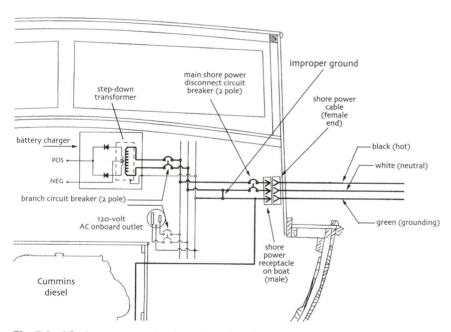

Fig. 7-8. AC shore power circuit. When the white wire in the AC shore power circuit is improperly grounded on the boat, a path for stray current is created, as shown by the heavy dark lines.

aboard boats nearby can cause us stray-current problems.

Shoreside Wiring

There is another concern when the white neutral is grounded on the boat. Should the black and white wires be reversed, either at the shoreside outlet or on the boat, then the white neutral wire becomes hot at 120 volts AC. If the white wire is grounded on the boat, everything on the boat that is also connected to ground will also be hot. This is an extremely dangerous condition and is, unfortunately, not as uncommon as you might think. There are some folks out there that are doing a good business with handy little devices whose purpose is to warn you when this situation exists.

These devices, called *reverse polarity indicators*, are basically a lamp or a buzzer wired into the incoming side of the onboard AC circuit from the white neutral wire to the green ground-ing wire. Figure 7-9 shows the AC circuit with the polarity indicator installed. If polarity has been reversed in the shoreside outlet, the neu-tral will be hot and the lamp will light or the buzzer will sound.

ABYC Standard E-8 recommends the instal-lation of a polarity-indicating device if any AC equipment on the boat requires proper polar-ization (i.e., black hot, white neutral) to func-tion properly *or* if any branch circuit in the AC system is protected by a single-pole circuit breaker or a fuse in the hot side only. However, if the device is not of sufficiently high resist-ance, it can provide a path for stray current. It should have an impedance (total AC resist-ance at 120 volts, 60 Hz) of at least 25,000 ohms to avoid contributing to stray current corrosion. The ABYC does not require a polarity indicator if the system has an isola-tion transformer installed. More about isolation transformers later. *(continued page 54)*

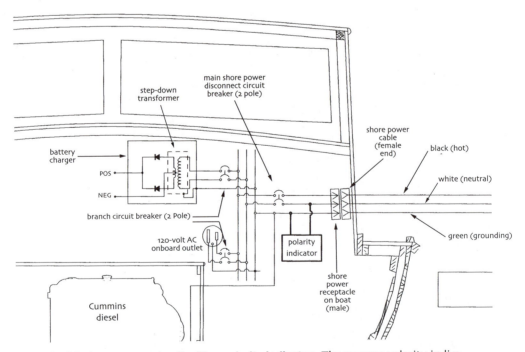

Fig. 7-9. AC shore power circuit with a polarity indicator. The reverse polarity indica-tor installed between the white neutral conductor and the green grounding conductor lights up or sounds an audible alarm when the hot and neutral wires are reversed in the shoreside outlet.

TESTING AND TROUBLESHOOTING

Every electrical circuit consists of a *source* of electric current that has a "hot" (ungrounded) side and a grounded side. A wire from the hot side of the source carries the current to the load. A second wire, the grounded return conductor, carries this same current back to the source. A third wire—the DC grounding conductor wire in DC circuits and the green grounding wire in AC circuits—is connected from non-current-carrying components (equipment cabinets, motor casings and frames, through-hulls, etc.) to the grounded side of the source. This wire carries no current except in the event of a short circuit or ground fault resulting in leakage or stray currents, so if there is current flowing in the bonding wire or the green grounding wire, we have a stray current problem. These currents can be appreciable, especially in the case of the 120-volt AC system; caution is required when taking measurements.

The figure below shows a simplified diagram of both an AC and a DC system. Remember, these are two separate systems. The only thing they have in common is that they share the same common ground point. Let's look at the DC system first.

DC Electrical System

The best way to find stray leakage currents is to measure the currents. However, these currents can be very high, high enough to damage the meter or even pose a serious threat to humans. So first we need to take some preliminary measurements to get an idea of how much current we may be dealing with.

Many digital multimeters use *autoscaling*, meaning they automatically select the appropriate scale. They also select the correct polarity automatically. As a result, digital multimeters are not that easy to damage. This is not the case with analog meters, so if that's what you're using, some additional steps are required to protect the meter.

Our first test is a voltage measurement to determine whether we have a leakage current problem. Make sure that all equipment in the DC system is switched off, using the On/Off switch on the equipment itself. (Don't forget lights.) Disconnect the positive cable from the battery and put the Battery Isolation Switch in the On position for that battery bank. Set your multimeter to read voltage and switch it to a scale greater than 12 volts. Place the positive (red) test probe from the meter on the positive terminal of the battery and the negative (black) test probe from the meter on the disconnected positive battery cable. The figure on page 52, top, shows this condition. Since all equipment On/Off switches are open, that is, in the Off position, there should be no complete circuit back to the negative terminal of the battery, and the voltmeter should read zero volts. If the meter reads 12 volts, then either some appliance is still on or there is a leakage path. Recheck to be sure that all equipment On/Off switches are Off.

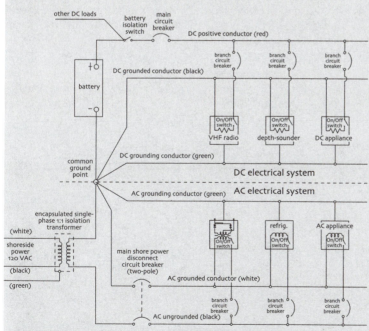

Simplified wiring diagram of AC and DC systems. The AC and DC systems are separate but share a common ground point on the engine block.

(continued)

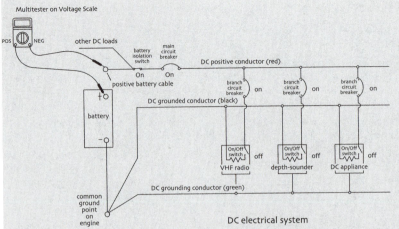

Preliminary voltage test to check for presence of leakage current.

Let's say the meter reads 12 volts, confirming that a leakage path exists. We don't know how much current is flowing through the leakage path; that depends on how much resistance there is in the path. The next thing to do is to measure the resistance of the path. With the positive battery cable still disconnected and all equipment switches set to the Off position, set the multimeter to read "Ohms" and switch it to the lowest scale, probably "X1." Put the red test probe on the disconnected positive battery cable and the black probe on the battery's *negative* terminal. (It doesn't matter which probe you use for resistance tests, but it's a good idea to get into the habit of observing polarity to avoid damaging the meter by mistake.) This is shown in the figure below. Notice that the battery is out of the circuit. The meter is measuring the resistance of the leakage path in ohms.

Since the current in amperes is equal to the voltage—12 volts when the battery is connected—divided by the resistance in ohms, we can estimate how much current is likely to be flowing through

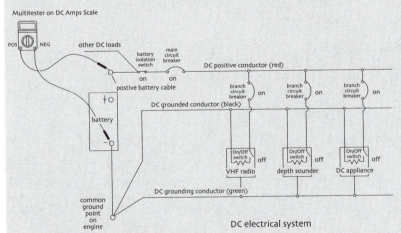

Resistance Check of Leakage Path. We measure the resistance of the leakage path to estimate how serious the problem is.

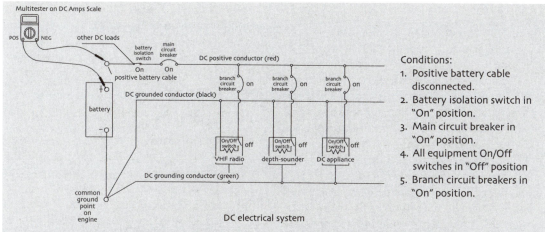

Multitester on DC Amps Scale

POS NEG

other DC loads

battery isolation switch

main circuit breaker

On   On
positive battery cable

DC positive conductor (red)

branch circuit breaker · on · branch circuit breaker · on · branch circuit breaker · on

battery

DC grounded conductor (black)

On/Off switch · off · On/Off switch · off · On/Off switch · off
VHF radio · depth-sounder · DC appliance

DC grounding conductor (green)

common ground point on engine

DC electrical system

Conditions:
1. Positive battery cable disconnected.
2. Battery isolation switch in "On" position.
3. Main circuit breaker in "On" position.
4. All equipment On/Off switches in "Off" position
5. Branch circuit breakers in "On" position.

Measuring current to isolate the leakage path. By monitoring the leakage current and systematically removing loads from the circuit we can isolate the faulty path.

the leakage path. Assuming your multimeter has a 10-amp scale (most do), a resistance measurement above 1.2 ohms means you can begin to isolate the leakage path using the multimeter to measure current directly.

First, place the Battery Isolation Switch in the Off position. Set the meter to measure DC amps and switch it to the highest amp scale on the meter, probably 10 amps. Fix the red test probe to the positive battery terminal and the black test probe to the disconnected positive battery cable. Close the Battery Isolation Switch and read the current on the meter, as shown in the above figure. If there is little or no deflection of the needle, switch the meter to a lower scale until the needle reads about in the middle of the scale. Leakage currents of less than 1 milliamp are not considered significant.

Now, open the Battery Isolation Switch. If the meter reading drops but still shows significant current flow, this indicates a leakage path on the battery side of the Isolation Switch—probably in one of the "other loads" connected directly to the battery, such as the

starter motor, bilge pump, or high-water alarm. Disconnect each of these loads one at a time. If the reading drops to zero, that is the offending load.

If, however, the reading dropped to zero when the Isolation Switch was opened, the leakage path is on the other side of the Isolation Switch. Leave the meter connected and close the Isolation Switch. At this point, all of the loads (appliances) on the side of the Isolation Switch away from the battery should have their On/Off switches in the Off position, but all circuit breakers should be closed or fuses in place. Now, one at a time, open the circuit breaker or remove the fuse protecting each branch circuit. When the current drops to zero, the fault is on this circuit. If there are any loads on this side of the Isolation Switch that don't have circuit breakers or fuses (shame on you— make a note to install protective devices on these circuits before putting the circuit back in service), disconnect their hot leads one at a time until the leakage path is found. Check the load on this circuit for internal shorts from the

positive supply side to the equipment housing. Depending on the type of load you have on this side, you may want to enlist the services of a qualified technician.

AC Electrical System

The AC electrical system is really not something that even talented amateurs should tackle. These AC voltages and currents can definitely be hazardous to your health, especially in the damp marine environment. Voltages can be 120 or maybe 240 volts, and currents are in the range of 15 to 50 amps, or more. A good marine electrician, if there happens to be one in your area, can run the checks for you and assist you in identifying the specific cause of the problem.

After all this talk about corrosion, I want to leave you with one thought. In a properly designed, installed, and maintained electrical system, stray-current corrosion is eliminated, galvanic corrosion is controlled, and electrochemical corrosion is not a problem. It's worth putting some effort and time into getting your electrical system right.

Nearby Boats

Figure 7-10 shows our boat in her slip plugged in to shore power. In an adjacent slip, another boat has also plugged in. The dockside wiring is fine. Both boats are properly wired for AC shore power and have good bonding systems. Our boat is properly fitted out with zincs (of course) to protect the underwater hardware, but our neighbor hasn't been as fastidious and has no zincs.

What happens? As soon as the other boat operator plugs in to shore power, a big galvanic cell is created, as shown by the heavy dark lines in figure 7-10. The zincs on our boat become the anode, while the bronze underwater hardware on the other boat becomes the cathode. The metallic path for electrons is from our zincs through the wires to the common ground point, through the green grounding wire of the AC system to the shoreside source, then through the other boat's green grounding wire to the common ground point on that boat to the bronze underwater hardware. The ionic path is from the zincs on our boat, through the seawater to the bronze fittings on the other boat. Our zincs (dedicated little devils) will sacrifice themselves to protect both boats' underwater hardware, so we'll be eating up zincs like peanuts! And the green grounding wire makes this possible.

So what do we do about it? Some people have been known to cut the green grounding wire to prevent this problem. *Don't do it!* The dangers of electrical shock we spoke of above are very real and very serious. This is where the galvanic isolator comes in.

Galvanic Isolators

A galvanic isolator is a device that is installed in series with the green grounding conductor. The isolator blocks stray direct current (DC) flow while permitting AC to pass, thus maintaining an unrestricted path for ground-fault currents. Galvanic isolators are available at most chandleries and through marine catalogs. To install a galvanic isolator, you simply mount it near the shore power receptacle on the boat, break the green ground wire, and connect the (now two) wires to the two terminals on the isolator. Figure 7-11 shows the AC wiring system with an isolator installed.

Isolation Transformers

A galvanic isolator will not block stray AC. To do that you'll need an isolation transformer.

A transformer transfers electrical energy from one circuit to another with no direct electrical connection between the two. It does this by elec-

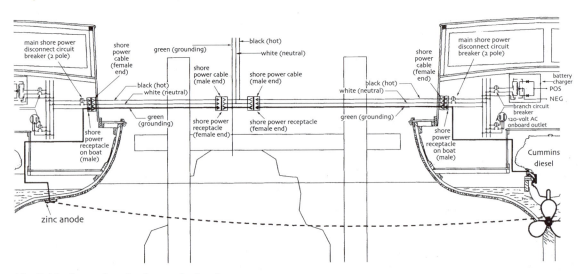

Fig. 7-10. Corrosion due to nearby boats.

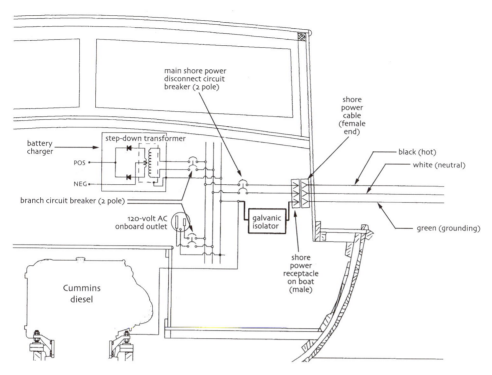

Fig. 7-11. AC shore power system with galvanic isolator. The galvanic isolator is installed in series with the green grounding wire to block DC galvanic current flow while allowing AC currents to flow as necessary.

tromagnetic induction: current flowing through the *primary winding* in the transformer induces a current to flow through the *secondary winding*.

Transformers are classified according to their use. Sometimes the transfer is made to effect a change in voltage or current—step-down or step-up transformers. The isolation transformer makes the transfer with no change to either voltage or current. Its function is simply to isolate the secondary side, that is, the wiring on the boat, from the primary side—in this case, the dockside wiring. This is shown in figure 7-12.

When an isolation transformer is used, the secondary side of the transformer becomes the boat's power source. Consequently, this means that both the white neutral wire and the green grounding conductor are grounded *on the boat*. This does a couple of good things for us. First, the AC current on the boat now finds a complete path from the appliance (load) through the

black hot wire to the secondary winding, through the winding to the white ground wire and to the boat's ground. The circuit is thus complete. Second, since there is now no DC path back to shoreside ground, there is no path for galvanic currents. With an isolation transformer installed, a galvanic isolator is unnecessary. Isolation transformers tend be somewhat bulky, heavy, and a bit pricey but—in this writer's opinion—worth the trouble.

Ground-Fault Circuit Interrupter

One other thing we should talk about is the ground-fault circuit interrupter, or GFCI. This is a device, often incorporated into a circuit breaker, that senses any difference in the amount of current flowing in the hot conductor and the neutral conductor. Remember that we said all of the current in the black hot conductor must be returned in the white neutral conductor, so they should be

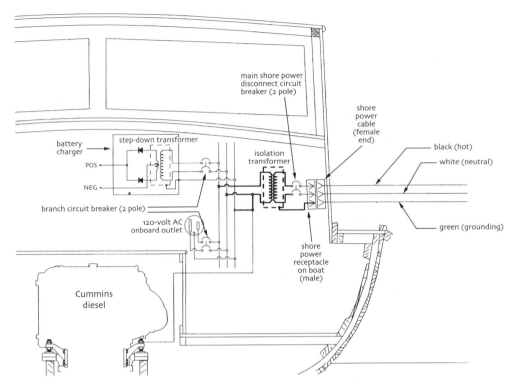

Fig. 7-12. AC shore power system with isolation transformer. The isolation transformer isolates the shoreside AC circuit from the onboard AC system.

the same. If there is a difference in the amount of current in the two wires, some current is going someplace we don't want it to go. It is either going through the green grounding wire, in which case it can cause stray current corrosion, or it is going through *someone*, which is not good either. When the GFCI senses a difference, it acts like a breaker and instantaneously opens the circuit.

Figure 7-13 shows the AC system with the GFCI included. In this instance, however, the GFCI provides ground-fault protection only for the primary side of the transformer. To provide protection to equipment and personnel on the secondary side of the transformer, that is, on the boat, a GFCI circuit breaker could be installed at the distribution panel. An alternative is the use of GFCI-type receptacles. ABYC recommends that if convenience outlets are installed in the head, in the galley, in machinery spaces, or on a weather deck, they should be of the GFCI

type. As long as the first receptacle on the circuit is a GFCI type, all downstream receptacles on that same circuit are protected.

Battery Chargers

Automotive battery chargers used aboard a boat are one of the more common causes of stray current corrosion. If you want a battery charger aboard, it must be designed for marine use. The one in your garage is not suitable for use aboard the boat.

Marine battery chargers are designed to have separate AC and DC ground points. All of the current brought to the charger from the AC source through the hot wire is returned to the source through the neutral wire. The cabinet is separately grounded through the green grounding wire. Most automotive chargers, however, use an *autotransformer* in which one side of the primary and of the secondary windings is com-

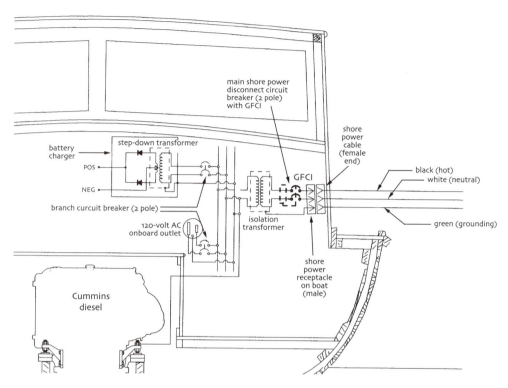

Fig. 7-13. AC shore power system with GFCI. The ground-fault circuit interrupter (GFCI) monitors the current in both the hot wire and the white neutral wire. These two currents should be equal. If the current in the white wire drops, indicating that some current has found an alternative path, the GFCI shuts off all current on the circuit in something like 0.02 seconds.

mon. If the charger has a two-prong appliance plug and it is inserted the wrong way, or if the incoming AC neutral and hot leads get crossed, the entire negative side of the boat's DC system can be at 120 volts AC. This constitutes a very severe shock hazard for people on the boat and for swimmers near the boat! This type of charger should never be used to charge batteries aboard the boat. If you have a dead battery in the boat, and you don't have a properly installed marine-grade battery charger, and you can't start the engine to charge the battery, don't bring a portable automotive-type charger aboard. The safest course to follow is to remove the battery and take it ashore for

charging. But keep an eye on those disconnected battery cables. Loose battery cables can't be trusted! They've been known to leap into the bilgewater.

SUMMARY

What can we conclude? If you're going to have AC aboard your boat, the circuit in figure 7-13 makes the most sense from all points of view— from a corrosion point of view, from a safety point of view, and, lest we forget, from an insurance point of view. Insurance companies aren't known for their willingness to pay off if the system isn't up to standard.

CHAPTER 8

Iron and Iron Alloys

Only a few metals, such as copper, gold, and platinum, occur naturally in their elemental forms. Most metals occur in nature as oxides in ores, combined with some worthless junk like clay and silica. The ores must be processed to get the pure metals out of them, and there are nearly as many different processes for this purpose as there are metals. The process, as well as the elements present, greatly influences the properties of the metal. An important characteristic of metals is the extremely significant effect that very small amounts of other elements can have upon their properties. The huge difference in properties resulting from a small amount of carbon alloyed with iron to make steel is an example of this.

After processing ores to reduce them to their elemental form, we then further process them to combine them with other substances to achieve the properties necessary or desirable for some particular application or class of applications. Then we go to great lengths to keep them from deteriorating—that is, corroding. In effect, we have converted oxides to usable metals, and now we're trying to keep them from reverting back to the oxide form.

Chemically, a metal is an element that tends to form positive ions in solution and whose oxides form hydroxides rather than acids with water. We saw the significance of this when we talked about basic corrosion in chapter 4. Physically, a metal is a material containing free electrons, which give it certain characteristic properties such as high thermal and electrical conductivity.

Alloys can be classified in a number of ways, but in this book we'll consider them according to their dominant elemental metal. Thus, this chapter is about alloys that are predominantly iron.

There are a wide variety of iron alloys, each produced from ore by various refinement processes. Pig iron is the least refined form and contains a high percentage of impurities. It may contain as much as 4 percent carbon and a similar percentage of other elements. It is very hard and brittle. Through a succession of refinement processes, pig iron can be converted into other more usable forms, such as iron and steel. The use of pure iron is very limited. Most is utilized in processed forms such as wrought iron, cast iron, and steel.

WROUGHT IRON

Wrought iron is purified iron with between 1 and 3 percent silica slag. It is tough, malleable, ductile, and easily welded and forged. It is used primarily to make ornamental ironwork, rivets, bolts, pipes, chains, and anchors. In its forged condition it has the reputation of being strong and surprisingly resistant to deep rust and corrosion. Wrought iron has been largely displaced in most of its applications by carbon steel, which is less expensive to produce and of more uniform quality.

CAST IRONS

Cast iron refers to a large family of ferrous alloys. They consist primarily of iron and contain 2 to 4.5 percent carbon, 0.5 to 3 percent silicon, and lesser amounts of sulfur, manganese, and phosphorus. By varying the relative percentages of carbon and silicon and by altering the melting, casting, and heat-treatment processes, a large group of materials with a broad range of properties can be produced. Adding various alloying elements in appropriate proportions extends this range of properties still further.

Cast irons, so-called because they are cast to shape while molten, are perhaps the least expensive of the structural engineering materials. They offer high strength, ease of manufacturing, and excellent corrosion resistance. A comprehensive discussion is beyond the scope of this book. However, we discuss some of the types of interest to mariners.

For our purposes, cast irons can be divided into two broad categories, unalloyed cast irons and alloy cast irons.

Unalloyed

Unalloyed cast irons are by far the largest category of cast irons. These typically have corrosion resistance equal to or slightly better than that of unalloyed steels, but they are not as corrosion resistant as the alloyed cast irons. There are four basic types of unalloyed cast irons: gray, white, malleable, and ductile.

Gray

Gray cast irons are the most common form of unalloyed cast iron. Because the casting is allowed to cool slowly, carbon precipitates out as flakes of graphite, which give the iron the grayish color seen in the fracture surfaces.

White

White cast iron is produced by rapidly cooling a low-silicon, high-manganese gray cast iron. Because the carbon is not allowed to precipitate as flakes but is retained in the form of iron carbides, white iron is hard, brittle, and extremely difficult to machine. It has extremely high compressive strength—typically greater than 200,000 psi. When fractured, the fracture surfaces have a silvery white appearance from which the iron gets its name. White iron is used primarily in the production of malleable iron castings by annealing or graphitization. It is also sometimes used in applications requiring high wear resistance.

Gray iron castings sometimes have a wear-resisting surface of white cast iron. These surfaces are produced in a mold that has provision for rapid cooling, which results in the formation of the white iron surface. Such surfaces are referred to as chilled cast iron.

Malleable

Malleable cast iron contains comparatively little carbon and is heat treated after casting, during which the carbon precipitates out as small rounded nodules rather than flakes. The result is a metal of great strength and toughness that is resistant to impact, ductile, machinable, and relatively corrosion resistant.

Ductile

Ductile cast irons are another widely used type of cast iron. The addition of small amounts of alloying elements together with some changes in the heat treatment process produces a ball-shaped graphite structure and results in a material with high strength, ductility, castability, machinability, and corrosion resistance. Its ability to withstand impact (toughness) is somewhere between that of most cast irons and steel, and it can be welded and brazed. Ductile cast irons are used in engine crankshafts, pistons, and cylinder heads.

Alloy

Alloy cast irons are cast irons to which alloying elements have been specifically added or increased to alter the properties of the material. The objective may be to increase strength, wear or abrasion resistance, heat resistance, or corrosion resistance. Typical alloying elements are silicon, nickel, chromium, copper, molybdenum, and manganese—and, less commonly, vanadium and titanium.

Silicon is used to increase corrosion resistance. When used specifically as an alloying element, the silicon content varies from 3 to 14 percent. This increases the corrosion resistance of the alloy substantially but reduces strength and ductility. The silicon facilitates the development of a tightly adherent protective surface film over the first several days of exposure. Initial corrosion rates can be quite high, in the range of 118 to 196 mil/yr. (3 to 5 mm/yr.), and then decreasing sharply to less than 39 mil/yr. (1 mm/yr.).

Nickel is used to improve strength and hardness and also contributes to improved corrosion resistance. Nickel forms a protective oxide film on the surface of the metal. Nickel is typically added in combination with chromium to increase both strength and corrosion resistance. The increase in hardness is particularly useful in increasing its resistance to erosion corrosion. Nickel content in these alloys is normally 12 percent or greater.

Chromium is added, either alone or in combination with nickel, primarily to improve corrosion resistance in seawater. The chromium also forms tightly adherent protective oxide film on the surface. Chromium content can vary from 15 to 30 percent, but high chromium content will cause a reduction in ductility of the alloy.

Copper may also be added in amounts up to 10 percent to increase corrosion resistance.

Molybdenum is added primarily to increase strength but also contributes to corrosion resistance. Molybdenum contents are typically less than 4 percent.

Most of the cast irons encountered on or around boats will be unalloyed, and most applications will be in the engine and its auxiliary components. You can find gray iron used for engine blocks and cylinder heads, transmission housings, oil pumps, and exhaust manifold, piping, and elbows. Malleable (nodular) or ductile cast iron is used in crankshafts and camshafts and for cleats and propeller- and ruddershaft flanges. Ductile iron is also used for pistons and piston rings, for tiller arms, oars, and oarlocks, and for engine-leveling shims. The usual material in cast iron ballast keels is gray iron.

Corrosion Resistance

Unalloyed cast irons are, in general, similar to ordinary steels in resistance to corrosion. They are subject to pitting and crevice corrosion in stagnant seawater and, of course, subject to galvanic corrosion when in contact with other metals such as passive stainless steels, bronze, and the nickel-copper alloys. While there have been a few instances of intergranular attack in some high-chromium cast irons, IGA is not commonly encountered in cast irons. Also, since iron-casting design specifically limits stresses in the casting, stress-corrosion cracking is also relatively rare.

Atmospheric

Atmospheric corrosion rates for the unalloyed cast irons are typically quite low—less than 5 mil/yr. (0.13 mm/yr.)—which is superior to steel under the same conditions. However, these rates are dependent on the nature of the atmosphere. High humidity, the presence of sulfur or other pollutants, and chlorides found in many industrial and marine atmospheres can significantly increase corrosion rates. When exposed to moist air, unalloyed cast iron, like mild steel, forms a flaky, reddish-brown hydrated ferric oxide called *rust*. This rusting process is accelerated in seawater. It proceeds even faster where rust is allowed to accumulate and the surface of the metal becomes pitted. Atmospheric corrosion is not a significant problem for the alloy cast irons.

Graphitic

Graphitic corrosion is unique to gray cast iron. It is similar to dezincification and is sometime referred to as *degraphitization*. In gray cast irons, the graphite that precipitates out as flakes are cathodic to the iron, thus forming a galvanic cell in which the iron is dissolved into the electrolyte. Just as with dezincification, graphitic corrosion can result in serious loss of strength, hardness, and ductility.

Cast irons require protection for satisfactory long-term service. Sacrificial zinc anodes can be and are used to protect many iron components, but the principal means of protecting most cast iron components is by the use of protective coatings. Four general types of coatings are commonly used: metallic, organic, conversion, and enamel. These are discussed in detail in chapter 15.

STEEL

Steel is a generic term that describes a large family of iron-carbon alloys. Raw iron ore is converted in a blast furnace into pig iron. The greatest bulk of pig iron produced, some 95 percent, is processed to make steel. The steel-making process consists of refining pig iron by removing undesirable elements from the melt and then adding other elements in specific amounts to obtain the desired properties in the final product. The wrought steel can then be cast to shape or reheated and hot-worked by rolling, forging, or extruding into what are called wrought mill shapes, such as plate, rod, and bar.

The percentage of carbon in the various steel grades varies from a few hundredths of a percent to about 1 percent. All steels also contain varying amounts of other elements, principally manganese, but silicon, phosphorus, and sulfur are also always present to some extent. The alloy may contain other elements, either as a result of their presence in the raw materials or added to achieve specific properties in the final product.

Carbon is the principal hardening and strengthening element in steel, but no single element controls the steel's characteristics. It is the combined effect of all the elements that determines how the final product behaves in terms of heat treatment, hardness, strength, microstructure, corrosion resistance, and formability. For our purposes, we consider three principal groups—carbon or mild steels, alloy steels, and high-alloy steels.

Carbon Steel

More than 90 percent of all steels are carbon steels, also called *mild steels*. Carbon steels contain varying amounts of carbon and not more than 1.65 percent manganese, 0.60 percent silicon, and 0.60 percent copper. Total alloy content is usually less than about 2 percent. The carbon percentage is varied to control the strength and optimize its use for various applications. No other alloying elements are added intentionally, but they may be present as trace elements. These steels are very ductile—they are easily drawn, molded, or shaped, not brittle. This is the type of steel generally used in ship and boat hulls.

The original numbering systems for steel were developed by the Society of Automotive Engineers (SAE) and the American Iron and Steel Institute (AISI). These systems have been incorporated into the Unified Numbering System (UNS). In this system each steel is assigned a unique alphanumeric designation consisting of a letter, usually "G" for carbon and low-alloy steels or "K" for miscellaneous steels and ferrous alloys, followed by a five-digit number. The first two digits denote the major alloy additions. The next two digits indicate the carbon content in hundredths of a percent. The last digit represents any special requirements. However, whenever possible, the numbers in the UNS system use numbering sequences taken directly from other existing systems to facilitate their identification. For example, a plain carbon steel of 0.20 percent carbon such as SAE (or AISI) 1020 would be designated G10200.

AISI-SAE grades 1005 through 1030 are commonly referred to as the low-carbon group. They are used where cold formability and weldability are primary considerations. As the carbon content is allowed to increase, strength and hardness also increase, but at the cost of formability—the ease of bending. Grades with a carbon content greater than about 0.25 percent are not favored for small vessel construction because of the greater difficulty in bending and forming.

Most steel vessels are built using ordinary low-carbon steels, the kind commonly available at any steel distribution center. Typically, these are general-purpose steels suitable for a wide variety of applications. AISI grades 1005 through 1023 are typical. Boatbuilders like these grades because of their bending capabilities and ease of welding (see table A7-1, page 281).

Slight variations in the carbon content cause significant changes in the basic microstructure of the steel. Varying the rate at which the steel is cooled also affects the microstructure. The mechanical properties of the steel—hardness, strength, toughness, etc.—all depend on the final microstructure of the steel. These properties may be further modified by heat treating, cold-working, or adding other alloying elements (see table A7-2, page 282). The difference between the tensile strength and the yield strength is a measure of the metal's ductility, that is, its tendency to stretch or dent rather than rupture.

Two specific types of carbon steel are favored for boat construction—ABS (American Bureau of Shipping) grade A steel and ASTM A36. These are preferred by many builders of steel boats because of their consistent quality and formability. Chemical properties are shown in table 8-1.

Obviously, boats can be built with just about any grade of steel. People have been known to build steel boats out of all kinds of raw steel stock, including plate of unknown pedigree at bargain prices from salvage yards. It's not a question of what will work, but the amount of work required in forming and welding and the longevity of the result.

The medium carbon content steels (AISI 1030 to 1053) have between 0.31 and 0.55 percent carbon. High-carbon steels (AISI 1055 to 1095) have between 0.56 percent and approximately 1 percent carbon. These have greater strength and hardness but are more difficult to form and weld and thus are not really suitable for use in small craft.

Steel is, of course, subject to corrosion, that is, rusting. However, the advent of advanced epoxy coatings has gone a long way toward eliminating the constant chipping, scraping, and painting necessary to avoid the seemingly ever-present rust streaks. We talk more about this in chapter 15.

Low-Alloy Steels

Alloy steels make up a class of steels that has a higher percentage of alloying elements than carbon steels, including elements not found in carbon steels purposely added to produce a formulation optimized for specific uses. They contain small amounts of such other elements as nickel, molybdenum, and chrome—and larger amounts of manganese than plain carbon steels. The combined percentage of alloying elements in low-alloy steels is limited to about 4 to 5 percent; for the most part thermal treatments are used to achieve specific mechanical properties. Steels containing more than 5 percent alloying elements are generally considered high-alloy steels. High-alloy steels contain more nickel, chrome, and molybdenum. These include the stainless steels, which we cover in a separate section.

Alloy steels are not typically used in hull fabrication. They may, however, find some use in high-strength fittings or for structures on the boat that carry heavy loads. Generally, these steels are supplied in the *annealed* condition but may be obtained in the *normalized* condition, in which tensile and yield strengths and hardness are considerably higher (see tables A7-3 and A7-4, page 282). This can have significance for us in certain types of corrosion.

High-Strength, Low-Alloy (HSLA) Steels

High-strength, low-alloy steels were developed to provide greater strength and toughness than the low-carbon grades. Typically they contain between 0.15 and 0.26 percent carbon, 1.0 to 1.65 percent manganese, 0.040 percent phosphorus, and small amounts of such other alloying elements as niobium, vanadium, and nitrogen. Several grades offer enhanced atmospheric corrosion resistance and are referred to as *weathering steels* (ASTM Standards A242 and A588).

One weathering steel that has found application in steel vessel construction is Cor-Ten steel, developed by U.S. Steel. Cor-Ten was and is referred to as a weathering steel because it develops a unique protective oxide layer when ex-

Table 8-1

Chemical Contents

Element	ABS Grade A	ASTM A36
carbon	0.21% (0.23 max.)	0.25%
manganese	2.5 times carbon min.	
phosphorus	0.035% max.	0.040
sulfur	0.035% max.	0.050
silicon	0.50% max.	0.40% max.
copper*	= or < 0.02%	0.20%
chrome	= or < 0.02%	
nickel	= or < 0.02%	

*Minimum percent when copper steel is specified
Source: American Bureau of Shipping, Houston, Texas.

posed to atmospheric conditions. This oxide layer (ferrous oxide), unlike the oxide layer formed by other carbon steels, is not crystalline in structure but amorphous—thus, it resists moisture penetration. A drop of water placed on ordinary rust will be quickly absorbed into the rust. On Cor-Ten's oxide layer it will stand up like a drop of water on the waxed hood of a car. Cor-Ten is used in bridge construction, light poles, guard rails, and some decorative architectural sculptures.

Cor-Ten is not popular with many boatbuilders because it is more difficult to bend and weld. Also, experts I have talked to do not recommend Cor-Ten for hull plate because the formation of the protective layer does not take place when the metal is immersed in water. So Cor-Ten used below the waterline will have to be coated just as with any other hull plate. It does offer some advantage if left exposed to the weather to form its coating over time, although pockets and crevices will have to be sealed. However, unless it is painted or otherwise coated, most people do not find its appearance aesthetically pleasing.

Notice the addition of chrome, nickel, and copper.

Corrosion Characteristics of Carbon and Low-Alloy Steels

The great disadvantage of carbon and low-alloy steels is their susceptibility to corrosion, primarily rust. The corrosion behavior of both groups is very much the same, so we treat them together. Besides rusting, they are susceptible to pitting corrosion, crevice corrosion, several

Table 8-2

Chemical Properties of Cor-Ten Steel

carbon	0.12%
manganese	0.2 to 0.5%
phosphorus	0.07 to 0.15%
sulfur	0.05% max.
silicon	0.25 to 0.75%
copper	0.25 to 0.55%
chrome	0.3 to 1.25%
nickel	0.65% max.

other types of corrosion described in chapter 5, and, of course, bimetallic and stray-current corrosion. Before we address this subject, let's first clarify a couple of terms—*mill scale* and *protective films*—as they apply to steel.

Mill Scale

As a result of the hot-rolling process, plate steel and bar stock frequently come from the mill with a surface coating of black scale, called mill scale. Steels that have been cold-rolled will have a comparatively bright surface. Mill scale forms a thin, flaky oxide film (magnetite, Fe_3O_4) in intimate contact with the steel substrate. Since the mill scale is more noble (–0.4 volts) than the steel substrate (–0.71 volts), when moisture is present a galvanic cell exists, and the steel will suffer pitting corrosion—as much as 0.030 in./yr. (0.76 mm). Protective coatings (paint) are not practical because mill scale is quite brittle and eventually flakes off, taking any protective coating with it and leaving the steel surface to rust and pit. Hence, it is important to remove the mill scale prior to applying a protective coating. This is usually done by allowing the plate to weather and then sandblasting it prior to use.

Protective Films

Steels, like most metals, form surface corrosion-product films. It is the specific nature of these films—their density, the degree to which they adhere to the surface of the metal, and their susceptibility to breakdown—that distinguishes the corrosion performance of these metals from one another.

When steel corrodes it is called rusting. Rusting is a complex chemical reaction in which the iron combines with oxygen and water to form a hydrated (water-bearing) oxide. Typically, atmospheric moisture condenses (dew) on the metal surface when the temperature drops during the night. This moisture absorbs contaminants in the air and forms a thin acidic film that dissolves the surface of the steel, thus beginning the rusting (oxidizing) process. During the day the sun and moving air dry the ferric oxide or rust. This wetting and drying cycle produces the layer of ferric oxide, or rust.

Several different oxides and hydroxides may be formed, depending on such factors as the acidity of the moisture, the availability of oxygen, the types of atmospheric pollutants present, and the chemical composition of the steel. In most cases, rust is flaky and porous and does not provide protection to the metal surface. However, some of these oxide films adhere more tightly to the surface of the metal. The more cohesive and less porous layer of rust that forms on weathering steels does protect the steel, reducing corrosion rates to perhaps only 25 or 30 percent of those for the mild steels. It should be noted that the wetting and drying cycle is critical to the formation of this protective film. When a weathering steel is subjected to constant immersion, the corrosion rate is the same as that for plain carbon steel, about 0.005 in./yr. (0.13 mm/yr.). Without the drying part of the cycle, the formation of the protective film is inhibited.

In dry, salt-free air, where relative humidity is below 60 percent, rusting is not a significant problem. Above 60 percent relative humidity, the rusting process increases rapidly. If the air is salt-laden, rusting begins at relative humidities as low as 20 percent and increases exponentially as the moisture content of the air increases. If the air also contains pollutants (e.g., acid rain), the deterioration can become appreciable, reaching rates of 0.05 in./yr. (1 mm/yr.) in tropical climates.

The only effective way to prevent the rusting of steel is to seal off the surface from contact with water. Proper preparation of the base metal before the application of protective coatings, reasonable care in the maintenance of the protective coatings, and the avoidance of crevices, joints, cracks, pockets, and seams that can trap water are fundamental to the elimination, minimization, and control of damaging corrosive activity. We talk more about this in later chapters.

HIGH-ALLOY STEELS

We have seen that small amounts of a limited number of alloying elements added to iron dramatically alter the mechanical, chemical, and physical properties of the steel. If we allow the total alloy content to exceed 5 percent and we broaden the number of alloying elements, we open up a whole new family of steels. Called high-alloy steels, these include many of the tool steels, but for us it is the stainless steels that are the most important members of this family.

In this section we discuss the chromium-nickel stainless steels, concentrating mainly on the austenitic class in general and the marine grades in particular. We also consider newer alloys that are finding considerable success in marine applications—the duplex and superaustenitic grades and the high-performance nickel-rich alloys. And finally, we discuss the forms of corrosion that like to attack these metals.

Stainless Steels

The development of low-alloy steels was largely motivated by the need to control their response to heat treatment in order to enhance and optimize their physical properties for various applications. Development efforts in the high-alloy steels were, in large measure, designed to improve their corrosion resistance in various environments.

Stainless steel has been around almost since the early 1900s. The boating industry, however, was not so quick to pick up on the new metal, with bronze being the material of choice. By the mid-1970s, stainless steel had found some applications in prop shafts, wire-rope rigging, and fittings, but Type 316 wood screws had to be made to order. With the fiberglass revolution of the late 1960s and early 1970s, the use of stainless steel increased sharply.

Strictly speaking, all that is required to produce a stainless steel is the addition of a little more than 10 percent chromium. The chromium reacts with oxygen in the air (or water) to form a thin layer of chromium oxide that protects the surface from corrosion. This is referred to as the *passive state*. If the protective film is scratched or otherwise damaged, it immediately heals itself by forming a new film over the exposed surface—as long as oxygen is available. In the absence of oxygen, the protective oxide film is not formed, and the steel is in the *active state*, during which it is susceptible to corrosive damage.

To further improve corrosion resistance or other mechanical and chemical properties, the following other elements can also be added to the steel.

Chromium

Chromium is *the* key alloying element in the formation of the protective passive film characteristic of the stainless steels. A minimum of 10.5 percent chromium content is necessary, but at this level the film formed is sufficient only to provide moderate protection in relatively clean, mild atmospheric conditions. Increasing the chromium content increases the effectiveness of the film—*up to a point*. However, chromium levels higher than about 29 percent can have a detrimental effect on mechanical properties, ease of fabrication (e.g., forming, machining, welding), and high-temperature performance. Difficulties in processing also tend to limit increases in chromium content. Thus, improved corrosion resistance is usually obtained by adding molybdenum.

Nickel

Nickel, another key alloying element, improves toughness as well as corrosion resistance. In concentrations of 8 to 10 percent, it has the undesirable effect of *increasing* the alloy's susceptibility to stress-corrosion cracking (SCC). However, at higher levels—up to 30 percent—resistance to SCC is restored. It is in this higher range that increases in yield strength and toughness are realized.

Manganese

In modest concentrations, and when nickel is present, manganese is also beneficial to corrosion resistance and toughness.

Molybdenum

In the presence of chromium, molybdenum has the effect of stabilizing the passive protective film and increasing the alloy's corrosion resistance.

Carbon

Carbon is a hardening agent and contributes to the high-temperature performance of the stainless steels. However, it is detrimental to corrosion resistance by virtue of its reaction with chromium. In the ferritic stainless steels (see below), carbon adversely affects toughness.

Nitrogen

Nitrogen improves strength and resistance to pitting corrosion in the austenitic stainless steels (see below). However, it is detrimental in the ferritic grades, adversely affecting mechanical properties.

Phosphorus

Phosphorous is an impurity that decreases ductility and toughness. A maximum of 0.04 percent is typically specified.

Sulfur

Sulfur is added to some grades to improve machinability, but in all other grades sulfur is undesirable. It leads to hot-short cracking of the austenitic grades during welding operations—and to the formation of sulfides, which facilitate pitting corrosion.

Copper

Copper is sometimes added to improve atmospheric corrosion resistance. However, copper content must be held to a minimum since it can also result in hot-short cracking.

The stainless steels are traditionally divided into three main groups—*martensitic, ferritic,* and *austenitic*—based on their different crystal structures (from which they derive their names) and that in turn depend on chromium content and heat treatment. We include here a fourth group, the *high-performance stainless steels*. Of these groups, only the austenitic and the high-performance groups include stainless steels that can be considered "marine grade." However, we cannot completely ignore the martensitic and ferritic groups since items made from these metals are used in the marine environment, most frequently as fasteners. A classical example is the screw on some lesser-quality hose clamps.

Martensitic Stainless Steels

Martensitic stainless steels contain from 12 to 18 percent chromium. Some grades have small additions of sulfur to improve machinability, whereas others may add nickel, molybdenum, or other elements to improve their mechanical properties. The standard grades are magnetic and can be hardened by tempering and quenching. Fabrication by welding is made difficult by the requirement for extensive pre- and postweld heat treatment.

Types 410 (UNS S41000) and 420 (UNS S42000) are typical of the martensitic grades (see table A7-5, page 282). They are commonly used for cutlery, turbine blades, high-temperature machinery, and a variety of fastenings, such as bolts, screws, clamps, and brackets. They are not suitable for use in severely corrosive environments such as seawater or salt-laden atmospheres. They are susceptible to hydrogen-assisted cracking and to intergranular corrosion.

Ferritic Stainless Steels

The standard ferritic stainless steels contain only iron and chromium (not counting residual elements). They are magnetic and have relatively high yield strengths but low ductility. Corrosion resistance is superior to the martensitic grades as a result of higher chromium content—standard grades range from 10 to 27 percent chromium. There are a number of proprietary and nonstandard grades that have higher chromium content—up to 30 percent—and also contain from less than 1 to 2.5 percent nickel. Type 430 is the basic ferritic grade (see table A7-6, page 283). The ferritic grades have good resistance to atmospheric corrosion, moderate mechanical properties, and an attractive finish.

Some ferritic grades can be quite susceptible to intergranular corrosion as a result of welding. Ductility also can be a limiting factor. Ferritic grades can change from relatively ductile to brittle over fairly *small changes in temperature*— even at or around room temperature. This is particularly true of ferritic stainless steel parts fabricated prior to the use of the argon-oxygen-decarburization (AOD) process in production.

The AOD process, along with other improved melting practices, was introduced in the early to mid-1970s. These innovations (now used to produce most, if not all, of the stainless steels) gave manufacturers precise control of the individual alloying elements. This resulted in the introduction of many new proprietary and nonstandard grades, including the so-called super-ferritic grades. These have higher chromium and molybdenum contents and thus have significantly improved corrosion resistance, mechanical properties, and weldability.

Nevertheless, even with this new generation of ferritic grades, they are still limited in impact resistance at low temperatures, weldability, and corrosion resistance and are not considered suitable for marine usage.

Austenitic Stainless Steels

The austenitic stainless steels are not magnetic. They cannot be hardened by heat treatment but can be hardened by cold-working. They are easily welded and have excellent resistance to both high and low temperatures. They have excellent corrosion resistance. Austenitic stainless steels are used in a wide variety of applications, such as heat exchangers, fastenings, rigging fittings and wire rope, and galley sinks.

There are more than 30 different grades of austenitic stainless steel, and not all of them are equally suitable for application in the marine environment. The basic grade in this group is commonly referred to as *18-8* (18% chromium, 8% nickel) and typified by Type 304 (S30400). The term *18-8* is a relic of an old classification convention, before the introduction of the more highly alloyed and improved grades, such as Types 316 and 317. Although 316 and 317 do contain 18 percent chromium and more than 8 percent nickel (typically 10 to 14), making them, technically, 18-8 stainless steels, they also contain nitrogen and molybdenum, and they have significantly better corrosion resistance. It's important to know the specific grade of the stainless steel with which you're working and to understand the applications for which it is suitable. In this book, the term *18-8* refers only to grades 301 to 304. Composition of these grades is given in table A7-7 (page 283).

Any of the austenitic stainless steels will serve indefinitely—with no significant deterioration either in appearance or in strength—in clean rural or urban atmospheres, even in areas where the average relative humidity is close to 100 percent. In industrial atmospheres they serve for many years with only slight rust staining that is readily washed off with regular household cleaners. Even in marine atmospheres, rust staining will range from light (Type 302) to slight (Type 316). All of the stains are easily cleaned and the bright surface finish restored.

The problem comes about when these alloys are immersed in water. There are a number of factors that influence the behavior of austenitic stainless steels in water, which are listed in table 8-3 in order of importance.

What is significant for us in this list is the importance of oxygen and chloride concentration. These factors have the greatest influence—by far—on the behavior of stainless steels in water. Table 8-4 gives approximate chloride concentrations in various types of water. Note that these are nominal figures; actual figures may vary widely.

It is worth noting, however, that not even seawater is aggressive enough to cause the protective passive film that forms on these steels to break down. The trouble comes when the film is scratched or otherwise damaged, or when there is insufficient oxygen present at the surface for the film to form.

Table 8-3

Factors That Affect Stainless Steels in Water

oxygen (and/or other oxidizing agents)
chloride ion concentration
conductivity of the electrolyte
crevices
sediment
scales and deposits
biological activity
surface condition
acidity (pH less than 5)
temperature

Table 8-4

Chloride Concentrations in Various Waters

Water Type	Chloride Concentration (ppm)
distilled and high-purity waters	1
freshwaters	50 to 250
freshwater in rivers	100 to 1,000
brackish water in rivers	2,000 to 4,000
brackish waters in sounds, harbors, and large estuaries	9,500 to 19,000
seawater	19,000
brines (deaerated)	57,000

There is a lot of unconsidered use of stainless steels in, on, and around boats that results in some unsightly fittings and fixtures at best and some potentially serious failures at worst. It is well to know the various marine grades and their limitations before putting them into use (see tables A7-8 and A7-9, page 283).

18-8 Grades

It has been estimated that 70 to 80 percent of the stainless fittings and hardware you'll find in marine stores and chandleries are 18-8 grades—either 302 (CF-20 in its cast form) or 304. The mechanical properties of 302 are equivalent to those of 304, but 302 is inferior in terms of corrosion resistance. It should be considered the minimum grade of stainless steel for marine use and limited to above-water or interior fittings.

I mention Type 303 here only because it can, and too often does, find its way aboard inadvertently. Type 303 is a "free-machining" version of Type 302. It is widely used for parts produced on screw machines such as threaded fastenings, screws, bolts, and nuts. It has less corrosion resistance than Type 302.

A knowledgeable expert has estimated that 95 percent of the 18-8 used worldwide is Type 304. It is one of the two most popular marine-grade stainless steels, the other being Type 316. It is used for fastenings, stainless steel fittings, prop shafts, rigging, and so on. Type 304 has been found to provide satisfactory service indefinitely in waters with less than 200 ppm chlorides and is marginally satisfactory—with some pitting and crevice corrosion—in waters with chloride contents up to 1,000 ppm. Usage of 304 immersed in waters with concentrations over 1,000 ppm is not recommended. From table 8-4, we see it is clear that 304 should *not* be used near or below the waterline in anything but unpolluted freshwaters. The situation becomes even worse if 304 is embedded in wet wood or fiberglass.

Having said this, I must also note that cast 304 (CF3) has been used successfully as a propeller material on *steel* workboats, including controllable pitch propellers and bow thrusters in situations where it has adequate cathodic protection. In these applications, the material has performed satisfactorily for up to 30 years with normal welded repairs to nicked blades, because the steel hull and its cathodic protection system protect the 304.

Molybdenum-Bearing Grades

Types 316 and 317 have 1 to 2 percent increased nickel content and 2 to 3 percent added molybdenum, both of which are beneficial in terms of improved resistance to pitting and crevice corrosion. The nickel improves strength and toughness and aids in the formation of the protective passivation film. This results in alloys with corrosion resistance that is distinctly superior to that of the 18-8 grades in general and Type 304 in particular.

On average, Type 316 is twice as resistant, in terms of pitting and crevice corrosion, as Type 304. For example, tests have shown that in water containing 10,000 ppm chlorides, 10 percent of the possible crevice sites in Type 304 and 5 percent of the sites in Type 316 showed evidence of corrosion. However, the use of these enhanced grades of stainless steel below the waterline or in the splash-zone is still not recommended. Some experts in the corrosion community go so far as to advise that we not even *think* about using them below the waterline.

Type 316 has become the workhorse of the marine industry and in many instances has been used successfully immersed in seawater. However, there are also many caveats. The seawater must be clean, unpolluted, free of mud and silt, continuously moving with a velocity of not less than 3 ft./sec. over the entire surface of the fitting, and the surface must be free of deposits (barnacles, growth) and crevices or occluded surfaces. Perhaps our experts' advice is not so far off. It would go a long way toward keeping us out of trouble.

Type 317 is the most highly alloyed of this group of stainless steels. It was developed primarily for use in the highly corrosive applications of the pulp and paper industry. It is, of course, more costly than the other grades. It has not achieved a high degree of usage in the boating industry, so there's not a lot of actual-use data available.

Stabilized Grades

There is a problem that occurs during welding of stainless steels. When the steel is heated during welding, the carbon in the steel reacts with the chromium to form chromium carbide. This leaves an area of the steel that is deficient in chromium and subject to corrosion and to failure under stress (see Intergranular Corrosion, chapter 5). The problem arises as a result of the availability of carbon in the steel, hence the development of the L grades—304L, 316L, and 317L. These grades have lower levels of carbon (see table A7-8, page 283) to combine with the chrome, and this minimizes the problem.

Another approach is to use Type 321 or Type 347. Type 321 is *titanium-stabilized*—the titanium combines with the carbon more readily than the chromium, leaving the chromium to perform its corrosion resistance function. In Type 347, *niobium* performs the carbon-combining function. The rule is, if an item is to be welded, it should be made of one of the L grades or of Type 321 or 347. One note of caution, though: Types 321 and 347 are not as resistant to rust staining as the others.

High-Performance Stainless Steels

For many years, it was commonly believed that the best available stainless steel was Type 316. This may have been true 15 or 20 years ago, but today there is a whole range of high-performance, duplex, superaustenitic, and nickel-rich stainless steel alloys that are superior to 316 in seawater applications, some of which are discussed below.

Austenitic Grades

These grades are higher in nickel and molybdenum content than the conventional 300 series stainless steels. Typical of this group is alloy 22-13-5 (UNS S20910), which has 22 percent chromium, 13 percent nickel, and 5 percent manganese. This is a nitrogen-strengthened stainless steel with a combination of good corrosion resistance, high strength, ductility, toughness, and fabricability. It has better corrosion resistance than 316 and approximately twice the strength. Resistance to pitting and crevice corrosion is excellent, whereas stress-corrosion-cracking resistance is equal to that of 316. It can be welded, machined, and cold-worked using the same tools, equipment, methods, and techniques used for conventional 300 series stainless steels. Alloy 22-13-5 has been used in boat shafting, fastenings, and marine hardware.

Nitronic 50 (S20910) and Aquamet 22 are high-performance stainless steels that have found wide usage in the marine industry—Nitronic 50 in sailboat rigging and Aquamet 22 in pleasure craft and workboat shafting. Nitronic 50 has also been used in chains, fasteners, pumps, and many other items. These two are really the same alloy (see tables A7-10 and A7-11, page 284), but the Aquamet 22 is hardened for prop shaft applications.

Aquamet actually refers to a family of propeller shafting alloys—Aquamet 17, 18, 19, and 22. Typically, they have high chromium and nickel content—14.5 to 23.5 percent chromium and 3.0 to 13.5 percent nickel—plus small amounts of manganese and, in the case of Aquamet 22, 1.5 to 3.0 percent molybdenum. Tensile strength ranges from 120,000 psi (827 MPa) to 145,000 psi (1000 MPa) with Aquamet 22 at the top of the line with 145,000 psi (1000 MPa). In terms of corrosion resistance, Aquamet 17 and 18 are similar to type 304 stainless steel, Aquamet 19 is superior to type 304, and Aquamet 22 is superior to type 316 stainless steel.

All require cathodic protection to inhibit pitting and crevice corrosion.

In corrosion tests of Aquamet 22 versus 316, after immersion for nine months in quiet seawater, both alloys were covered with barnacles and other marine organisms. After cleaning, the Aquamet 22 was completely unaffected, with no evidence of pitting or crevice corrosion, whereas the 316 suffered both random pitting and crevice corrosion. However, while corrosion resistance is markedly superior, cathodic protection of these metals is still recommended.

Duplex Grades

The duplex stainless steels get their name from their crystal structure, which is approximately 50 percent ferrite and 50 percent austenite. Typically, they contain substantial amounts of chromium, plus nickel and molybdenum (see tables A7-12 and A7-1, page 284). This, together with the duplex structure, gives them improved resistance to pitting, crevice corrosion, and stress-corrosion cracking. Many of the duplex grades exceed the corrosion resistance of the common austenitics.

The duplex stainless steels comprise a number of grades—some going back to the 1930s—with a wide range of corrosion resistance. The earliest grade (alloy 329, S32900) had excellent corrosion resistance, but welding upset the ferritic-austenitic balance. This resulted in greatly diminished corrosion resistance and mechanical properties, requiring postweld heat treatment to restore these properties.

The development of the argon-oxygen-decarburization (AOD) process provided the means to overcome these problems. This led to the development of a family of so-called second-generation duplex grades. These newer grades combine high strength, good toughness, high corrosion resistance, and good resistance to stress-corrosion cracking. Pitting and crevice corrosion resistance are superior to Type 317L in most environments and strength is more than twice that of Type 316 (see tables A7-12 and A7-13, page 284). The basic duplex grades today are alloy 2205 (S31803) and alloy 255 (S32550), also called Ferralium 255.

The largest application of the duplex grades is in the oil and gas offshore industry and in aggressive chloride environments such as brackish waters and seawater. Hundreds of miles of duplex grade pipelines are already in place, and their usage is expected to increase as design engineers become more familiar with their properties and performance.

High-Performance Nickel-Rich Alloys: Superaustenitics

According to convention, alloys are classified according to their major element. For example, an alloy with more than 50 percent iron (Fe) is classified as a steel alloy and given an alphanumeric designation beginning with "S" followed by five digits; an alloy with more than 50 percent copper is assigned a "C" plus five digits; and so on. However, by this convention, the superaustenitic alloys are neither steel-base nor nickel-base alloys since neither steel nor nickel is present in concentrations exceeding 50 percent. Characteristically they are austenitic and contain iron, nickel, chromium, and molybdenum, none of which is present in concentrations greater than 50 percent. This posed a problem for the designating authority (ASTM) that was subsequently resolved by arbitrarily assigning UNS (Unified Numbering System) "N" numbers to this group. I, equally arbitrarily, have chosen to discuss these alloys in this section on steel-base, high-performance alloys.

The superaustenitic grades have high concentrations of both chromium and nickel, each in the 20 to 30 percent range, and 6-plus percent molybdenum. The chromium makes its usual contribution to corrosion resistance. However, chromium much above 25 percent can have a detrimental effect on mechanical properties and ease of fabrication and workability. Thus, improved corrosion resistance must be obtained by the addition of other alloying elements, usually molybdenum. As we saw above, molybdenum, in combination with chromium, produces a more robust protective film and increases corrosion resistance. Nickel, in concentrations above 8 to 10 percent, not only improves corrosion resistance, it also increases yield strength,

toughness, and resistance to stress-corrosion cracking. So the superaustenitics come as close as we have come, so far, to optimizing the recipe for corrosion-resistant, high-performance alloys.

All of these grades are nitrogen-strengthened and are produced by the AOD process. This results in carbon concentrations of 0.02 maximum percent by weight, lower than those of the low-carbon L grades. See table A7-14 (page 284) for compositions of the superaustenitic grades.

Alloy 254 SMO

Superaustenitics with at least 6 percent molybdenum are often called *6 Mo* superaustenitic stainless steels. The first generation of these, for example, alloy 254 SMO, began to see actual service life in the field in the early 1980s. They have been used in a wide variety of brackish water and seawater applications—such as condenser tubing and piping, heat exchangers, pumps, valves, and fittings. Alloy 254 SMO performed exceedingly well, with no evidence of significant corrosion after 5 years in service, even in some applications where copper alloy and Type 316 stainless failed.

Alloy AL-6XN

Alloy AL-6XN was developed specifically for use in applications involving aggressive chloride environments where pitting, crevice corrosion, and stress-corrosion cracking are potential problems. It was developed by Allegheny Ludlum Corporation as a second generation of AL-6X, one of the first superaustenitic grades. It has excellent resistance to chloride pitting and crevice corrosion, superior to that of Type 316 and AL-6X. Alloy AL-6XN has been used extensively in both brackish and seawater applications. Millions of feet of AL-6X thin-wall tubing have shown more than 15 years of successful service in these environments.

Alloy 654 SMO

Alloy 654 SMO is one of the second generation of 6 Mo superaustenitics—except that this new member of the family has 7.3 percent molybdenum. In comparison testing with other stainless steels and nickel-base alloys in various kinds of seawater, 654 SMO was found to be superior to the 6 percent molybdenum steels and to compare favorably with nickel-base alloy C-276 (see chapter 10).

The superaustenitic stainless steels are truly outstanding marine metals. However, the unfortunate fact is that as boatowners, repairers, restorers, and, to a large extent, even builders, we have little to say about their use in our boats. When and whether we get to enjoy the benefits of these new metals depends upon the manufacturers who supply our fittings, fastenings, components, rigging equipment, deck gear, and ground tackle. Design engineers are slow to modify existing successful product designs for a new and unfamiliar material, especially if it is initially more costly, and since cost is a function of the degree of alloying and the complexity of the manufacturing process, these grades are typically more expensive. Also, since costs don't come down until usage increases, the result is that it takes years, perhaps 10 or 15 or more, for these new metals to become readily available. However, they're out there, and if they're as good as they seem to be, we'll have them on our boats eventually.

CORROSION CHARACTERISTICS OF STAINLESS STEELS

Atmospheric Corrosion

Some types of atmospheric exposures can be more aggressive than others. Atmospheric contaminants—sulfur compounds produced by the burning of fuels, nitrogen compounds that occur naturally during thunderstorms or from the use of ammonium-base fertilizers, marine salts (magnesium chlorides, sodium chlorides), and even dust particles—can contribute to the corrosion of stainless steels. Rural atmospheres are quite benign, with no industrial pollutants to contaminate the atmosphere and no salt-laden coastal air. Industrial and marine atmospheres are much more severe.

The nickel stainless steels are highly resistant to atmospheric corrosion—so much so that

metallic weight loss and corrosion rates are not meaningful measures of corrosive damage. Material weight loss also decreases as the chromium content of the alloy increases; at 18 percent chromium, weight loss is essentially nil. Consequently, the more significant measures of corrosive damage for stainless steels in atmospheric corrosion are *rust staining*, *actual rust*, and *pitting* damage.

Staining is basically a discoloration of the surface of the metal. Actual rusting is measurable buildup of corrosion product (rust). Pitting is highly localized corrosion that occurs on a metal surface with little or no general corrosion. Pitting occurs when a tiny local anode is created by some foreign material on the surface. It can be very intense since the anodic site is extremely small while the cathodic area is very large. It results in the actual penetration of the surface by small, even minute, pinholes, whose number and depth provide a measure of corrosive damage.

After 26 years exposure to the marine atmosphere at Kure Beach, North Carolina, at distances of 82 and 820 feet (25 and 250 meters) from the ocean, pitting corrosion was insignificant—less than 0.0004 inches (0.01 mm)—on the boldly exposed surface of all of the standard stainless steel grades. Still, some stainless steels are more resistant to pitting than others. Table 8-5 shows average pitting resistances.

Table 8-5

Resistance of Stainless Steels to Pitting Corrosion: Pitting Index*

Stainless Steel Categories	Pitting Index (nominal)
18-8 (Types 301 to 304)	20
molybdenum-bearing (316, 317)	32
high-performance: austenitics	35.7
high-performance: duplex	39
high-performance nickel-rich: austenitics	45.2
high-performance nickel-rich: superaustenitics	44.4

*Pitting index is a function of chromium, molybdenum, and nitrogen content.

The formula used to calculate this was devised by InterCorr International, Inc. (*www.clihouston.com* 15 May 1997).

Probably the best way to prevent pitting is to grind welds and rough edges off smoothly and to keep the surface clean. Proprietary cleaners are effective, but regular wash and wipe with freshwater works well also. Where serious pitting damage does occur, the only way to eliminate the pits is to grind them out and repair the surface with weld metal. If the pits are shallow, they can be cleaned thoroughly by sandblasting.

Immersion Corrosion

The waters in which boats operate range from relatively clean freshwater to brackish estuarine waters to highly aggressive seawater. These waters can be pure, or they can be contaminated by all manner of pollutants. The principal threat for us is not so much the contaminants but a natural constituent of the water—chlorides. Both freshwater and salt water contain chlorides to some degree. The chloride content of the water is the major determinant of its corrosive aggressiveness.

The chloride content of freshwater can be as high as 1,000 parts per million (ppm), whereas brackish waters can contain up to 13,000 to 14,000 ppm and seawater up to 19,000 ppm. The contaminants—industrial and agricultural pollutants—can significantly increase the corrosivity of these waters. Thus, corrosion damage is very much a function of the specific nature of the water in which the boat operates. Generally, the 300 series stainless steels are susceptible to pitting corrosion even in freshwater if the water is stagnant. If the water is moving and thus able to bring fresh supplies of dissolved oxygen to the metal surface, they can be used successfully.

In seawater, the stainless steels are susceptible to both pitting and crevice corrosion—again, depending on the velocity of the water. If the water is moving at less than 5 ft./sec. (1.5 m/sec.), severe corrosion can occur at crevices that result either from construction design or by fouling organisms.

The conclusion is that if we want to use stainless steel below the waterline, we must be sure that the surface of the metal is exposed to constantly flowing water, and we should take precautions to avoid crevices. Because we cannot eliminate all crevices, we should take steps to seal those we cannot eliminate. Finally, we should not use stainless steels as fastenings in wood or fiberglass underwater.

Galvanic Corrosion

Remember, galvanic corrosion occurs when any two metals, sufficiently far apart in the Galvanic Series of Metals in Seawater, are in electrical contact and immersed in the same electrolyte (seawater). The less noble (anodic) metal corrodes, protecting the more noble (cathodic) metal. All of the metals we've discussed in this section are more noble than any of the other metals you're likely to find on your boat. All of these alloys are in fairly close proximity in the galvanic series, and it is not likely that serious galvanic problems will occur when they are in contact with each other in seawater. When the galvanic separation is 200 mV or less, the probability of serious, aggressive corrosion is not great.

But although the stainless steel on your boat is unlikely to suffer galvanic damage, it can be the cause of such corrosion in other metals. It is always a good idea to follow a few basic rules where practical:

1. Select alloys that are close to each other in the galvanic series or have similar alloy content.
2. Have the surface area of the less noble metal (anode) be large relative to the more noble (cathode) metal. For example, a stainless steel rudder or prop should have little galvanic consequence on a steel or aluminum hull. However, an aluminum fastener (rivet) will have a short life in a stainless steel fitting.
3. Use coatings (paint, etc.) to limit the area of the cathodic metal.
4. Insulate between dissimilar metals.
5. Use adequate sacrificial zinc anodes for protection.

Corrosion Fatigue

Corrosion fatigue causes metal to fracture prematurely and at lower stress levels or fewer cycles than it would otherwise because of the simultaneous conditions of repeated cyclical loadings and a corrosive environment. It is similar to how a metal wire is broken by bending it back and forth repeatedly except that the process is accelerated by the corrosive environment. Corrosion fatigue cracks nearly always start at the surface of the metal and frequently, but not always, at corrosion pitting sites. Surface strains cause the formation of small cracks or crevices in the protective film. The metal surface thus exposed is anodic to the surrounding surface (small anode, large cathode) and corrodes at an accelerated rate, forming the corrosion pits.

The fatigue strength—that is, the magnitude of the stress that the part can withstand without failure—continues to decrease as the number of cycles (stress occurrences) increases. For example, Type 304 stainless, which has a yield strength of 35 ksi in air, has a corrosion fatigue strength of less than half that (15 ksi) in seawater after 10^8 (100,000,000) cycles. The figures are roughly the same for Type 316. Failures from corrosion fatigue are typically quite sudden with little or no warning.

The places to look for corrosion fatigue are in fittings and structural components whose mass and sections would allow them to be susceptible to vibrations caused by wind, the engine, or other sources. Chainplates, mast tangs, rigging fixtures, wire rope, and shaft struts are all examples of items subject to corrosion fatigue.

The amount of corrosion is frequently very small, and corrosion products—staining and rust on the surface—may not be present. They will, in any case, be very difficult to detect. It is a good idea to make frequent visual inspections with the aid of a magnifying glass and dye penetrants. This is particularly important with wire-rope rigging, especially where it enters the lower terminal.

Cathodic protection, when practical, is effective—zinc coatings on carbon steel components, for example. Nonanodic coatings, if they cover the entire surface completely, can provide protection. However, tiny defects, scratches, or holidays in a coating can cause intense pitting corrosion and can stimulate corrosion fatigue. Stainless steel props, bow thrusters, and prop shafts—all of which are subject to vibration—

are used successfully when they receive protection either from a steel or aluminum hull or from a cathodic protection system.

Intergranular Corrosion

When Type 300 series austenitic stainless steels with carbon contents of 0.08 percent or greater are heated to a temperature between 800° and 1650°F (426.7° and 898.9°C), the carbon dissolves and migrates to the grain boundaries. This can also occur in the high-nickel alloys. There the carbon combines with the chromium and precipitates out as chromium carbides, leaving a chromium-depleted zone around each grain. This chromium-depleted zone is highly susceptible to corrosion. This can happen during welding operations and is frequently referred to as *weld-decay*. Seawater and other high-chloride waters, such as brackish harbor and estuarine waters, will cause severe pitting corrosion in these heat-affected zones. Fresh, low-chloride waters are not a problem.

Intergranular corrosion led to the addition of certain stabilizing alloying elements such as titanium, as in Type 321, or niobium (sometimes called *columbium*), as in Type 347. In these grades the added alloying element combines with the carbon and precipitates as titanium or niobium carbides, leaving the chromium free to provide its protective chromium oxide film.

Another approach was the development of stainless steels with less than about 0.03 percent carbon, the low-carbon L grades—304L, 316L, 317L, etc. Some chromium carbide still precipitates but in such small amounts that no significant chromium depletion occurs. These grades are all but immune to weld-decay.

More recently, development of the argon-oxygen-decarburization (AOD) process, now used to produce most, if not all, of the stainless steels, routinely produces stainless steel with carbon content in the range below 0.03 percent. Such grades may be labeled *304/304L*, for example. The newer, high-performance stainless steels and also the nickel-rich alloys may utilize any or all of these approaches.

For us, it all comes down to two options. If

an item is to be welded, it must be made of an L or stabilized grade. Failing this, the item must be heat-treated. Postweld heat treatment consists of heating the item to about 1,920°F (1050°C) and then quenching it in water. Heating puts the carbide back into solution, and quenching cools the metal before the chromium and carbon have time to combine. However, this works only on items of low mass and thin cross sections; more massive items take too long to cool.

Stress-Corrosion Cracking

Stainless steels are susceptible to stress-corrosion cracking (SCC) in chloride (seawater) environments. Temperature and the availability of oxygen accelerate the process, as they do all corrosive processes. All of the austenitic grades are subject to stress-corrosion cracking to some extent, Types 304 and 316 especially so. In laboratory tests designed to accelerate the process, Types 304 and 316 failed—that is, cracking was observed in the test samples. Types 317 was marginal, with some samples passing and others failing. The 6 Mo superaustenitics all passed. Superaustenitic types AL-6X, AL-6XN, and 254 SMO are all currently performing satisfactorily in seawater applications.

Typical applications that are susceptible to stress-corrosion cracking are those where stainless steel is exposed to seawater at high temperatures—such as inside heat exchangers—especially if the temperatures get up to the boiling point. Another potential trouble spot is rigging fittings, where chlorides may concentrate in corners and crevices, and where the sun can cause extreme local heating.

There is actually little the boatowner can do to prevent stress-corrosion cracking. The most effective preventive measures are selection of appropriate materials and proper design of components. Keeping the temperatures as low as practical and flushing to avoid salt concentrations will also help.

Microbiologically Induced Corrosion

Stainless steels are susceptible to microbiologically induced corrosion (MIC). Seawater contains living microbial organisms that tend to form colonies on the surface of the metal. These areas are then depleted of the oxygen necessary for the formation of their protective films and susceptible to pitting and crevice corrosion attack. Rough or irregular surfaces, such as weld joints, are especially vulnerable. Here again we see the advisability of keeping metal surfaces clean.

CONCLUSIONS

The basic marine-grade stainless steels are Type 304 and Type 316—the workhorses of the industry. These are useful, versatile grades that give excellent service when used within their limitations. Type 317 is also an excellent marine grade and a good alternative to 316. These grades, indeed all grades, have their limitations. It's essential to understand these limitations and the conditions under which particular alloys may be used.

Since stainless steel alloys get their protective surface films from an adequate supply of oxygen, immersed stainless steels need a continuous flow of water over the surface. Another critical factor in the successful use of stainless steels is the importance of the anode-to-cathode area ratio. Also important is the use of the L grades (types 304L, 316L, 317L, etc.), the stabilized grades (types 321, 347), or AOD-processed low-carbon grades if the fitting is to be welded.

Technology has made available new families of marine-grade steels—the duplex super-austenitic alloys. These are excellent marine metals, superior to 304, 316, and 317 in corrosion resistance. They are currently a little costly for broad usage in recreational boating, but we can look forward to their eventual availability as industrial usage increases and costs come down.

CHAPTER 9

Aluminum and Aluminum Alloys

Aluminum is truly a most remarkable metal. It is light, tough, strong, and readily worked by all common processes, it has excellent resistance to corrosion in the marine environment, and it requires little maintenance. These are all attractive features for boat builders, owners, and repairers.

A quarter of a million aluminum boats are sold in the United States each year. The vast majority are outboard-powered boats in the 14- to 27-foot range, but a significant number of larger aluminum boats—both pleasure craft and commercial vessels—are built each year. I've seen some pretty radius-chined cruising sailboats in the 30- to 40-foot (9 to 12 m) range and a number of excellent aluminum commercial fishing vessels.

Aluminum has also achieved considerable popularity for small utility workboats subject to hard use. Aluminum boats are widely used as working platforms for gillnetters, urchin divers, clam diggers, seine boats, tenders, aquaculture, fisheries researchers, and many others. By some accounts, aluminum is the first choice of government agencies for boats in the 20- to 65-foot range. Most small- to medium-sized commercial fishing boats in the Pacific Northwest are aluminum. So are most of the crew and supply boats servicing the drilling rigs in the Gulf of Mexico.

Aluminum is available in number of different classes of alloys and a vast number of types. As you might expect, not all are suitable for saltwater applications. Of those that are, some are better than others for specific purposes. In this chapter we look at a variety of aluminum alloys used in the marine environment, their varying susceptibility to corrosion, and what we can do about that.

ALUMINUM GRADES AND COMPOSITIONS

High-purity aluminum is a soft, ductile metal of relatively low strength and not generally suitable for most commercial uses. Aluminum is strengthened by the addition of other elements and by the way the resulting alloy is processed.

Aluminum alloys can be broadly divided into two general groups, wrought alloys and cast alloys. The term *wrought* refers to products that have been worked (hammered, pressed, extruded, etc.) from the metal ingot. Wrought aluminum products include sheet, foil, plate, rod, bar, tubing, extrusions, and forgings. *Cast* describes products formed by remelting the ingot and pouring the molten metal into a cavity shaped to form the desired item. Cast aluminum products include cleats and chocks, plugs and end caps, and a variety of hardware items.

Whether wrought or cast, the various alloys have a numerical designation that enables us to select and specify the right alloy for the job.

Wrought and Cast Alloy Designations

There are nine wrought and nine cast alloy groups. Each is designated by a four-digit number—preceded in the UNS system by A9 for wrought alloys and by A0 for cast alloys. Alloys are grouped according to the *major* alloying element. The first digit indicates the alloy group as shown in table 9-1.

In the 1xxx series, the last two digits show the degree of purity above 99.00 percent, in hundredths. For example, alloy A91030 would be 99.30 percent aluminum. The last two digits have no significance in any of the other series (other than the 1xxx series) beyond distinguishing the various alloy types in that series, with

Table 9-1

Alloy Designations

Wrought Aluminum Alloys		Cast Aluminum Alloys	
Designation	Alloy Group	Designation	Alloy Group
A91xxx	aluminum, 99% or greater	A01xx.x	aluminum, 99% or greater
A92xxx	copper	A02xx.x	copper
A93xxx	manganese	A03xx.x	silicon, with copper and/or magnesium
A94xxx	silicon	A04xx.x	silicon
A95xxx	magnesium	A05xx.x	magnesium
A96xxx	magnesium and silicon	A06xx.x	unused series
A97xxx	zinc	A07xx.x	zinc
A98xxx	other elements	A08xx.x	tin
A99xxx	unused series	A09xx.x	other elements

higher numbers indicating more recent additions. If the second digit is zero, it indicates that there are no special controls on the amount of one or more of the impurities in that type. Notice that the cast series designations incorporate a decimal point.

Tempering Designations

Aluminum alloys in the annealed condition are sometimes strengthened or hardened by *tempering* (also called heat-treating) or *strain-hardening* (also called cold-working). The 2000, 6000, and 7000 series are heat-treatable alloys. The 3000 and 5000 series are not susceptible to heat treatment but can be strengthened by strain-hardening. The designation following the four-digit number, separated by a hyphen (for example, A95086-H32), indicates whether the alloy has been so processed and the nature of the processing. These tempering designations pertain to all forms of wrought and cast aluminum alloys. The basic letter designations are

- F: As fabricated. This applies to products that have acquired some temper from the shaping process with no specific control over the degree of strain-hardening or heat treatment. This designation is used with wrought products only.
- O: Annealed. This is the lowest-strength temper of an alloy.

- H: Strain-hardened. These products have had their strength increased by strain-hardening, which may or may not be followed by some form of thermal treatment. The letter H is always followed by two or more digits. The first digit indicates the combination of operations; H1x indicates strain-hardening only; H2x indicates strain-hardening followed by partial annealing; H3x indicates strain-hardening and then stabilizing. The second digit following the letter H indicates the degree, in eighths, to which the alloy has been hardened. For example, Hx2 would be "quarter hard" (two eighths); Hx4 would be "half hard," etc. This applies to wrought products only. A third digit indicates a slight variation from the processing of the two-digit version.
- T: Thermally treated. These products may or may not receive some supplementary strain-hardening. The number following the letter (1 through 10) indicates a specific combination of basic processes to which the alloy has been subjected, such as heat-treating, cold-working, and aging at room temperature.

Nonmarine Aluminum Alloys

The alloys of primary interest to us for marine use are the 5000 and 6000 series. The others are not commonly considered marine grades. However, since certain alloys of some of these other groups do find marine applications, a few brief comments may prove useful.

1000 series

The 1000 series alloys are essentially pure aluminum. They have excellent corrosion resistance, high thermal and electrical conductivity, and are easily worked. They are also quite soft. With relatively low mechanical properties, they have few direct marine applications. See table A7-15 (page 285) for the mechanical properties of these alloys.

2000 Series Wrought Alloys (A92xxx) and Casting Alloys (A02xx.x)

Copper is the major alloying element in the 2000 series. Corrosion resistance is not as good as most other aluminum alloys and tends to worsen over time as galvanic cells are created by the tiny copper particles deposited on the surface as a result of the corrosion process. Alloys of this group, including those clad with a more corrosion-resistant alloy—called *alclads*—are not suitable for marine applications. See table A7-15 (page 285) for the mechanical properties of these alloys.

3000 Series Wrought Alloys (A93xxx) and Casting Alloys (A03xx.x)

Manganese is the major alloying element in 3000 series wrought aluminum. These alloys have good resistance to corrosion, moderate strength, and good workability. The 3000 series alloys are frequently used for cooking and food-processing equipment and in architectural applications. See table A7-15 (page 285) for the mechanical properties of these wrought alloys.

Casting alloy 356, an aluminum-silicon-copper alloy, is sometimes used in the marine industry for cleats, end caps, and plugs. Almag 35, a 500 series casting alloy (A0535), is similar but also has chromium and is quite a bit stronger. Almag 35 is superior to 356 for such fittings as cleats, bow eyes, and traveler track.

The 300 series casting alloys have appreciable silicon content and tend to turn a dark gray. This makes them attractive for architectural applications, but some people don't consider this to be a desirable characteristic for marine fixtures. Almag does not exhibit this change of color.

4000 Series Wrought Alloys (A94xxx) and Casting Alloys (A04xx.x)

Silicon is the major alloying element in the 4000 series. Silicon substantially lowers the melting point without causing brittleness. These alloys are most widely used in welding wire and as brazing alloys.

2000 Series Wrought Alloys (A97000) and Casting Alloys (A07xx.x)

Zinc is the major alloying element in this group, and combining it with small percentages of magnesium and copper results in one of the strongest commercially available alloys. Probably the most prominent member of this group is alloy 7075, which, in the T4 condition, is used in applications subjected to high stress, most notably in airframe structures.

The 7000 series alloys are anodic (due to their zinc content) to many other aluminum alloys and are susceptible to stress-corrosion cracking. They are not used to any extent in the marine industry.

8000 Series Wrought Alloys (A98000) and Casting Alloys (A08xx.x)

There are only a few alloys in this group, typically containing less than 0.25 percent copper and only trace amounts of magnesium. They are of relatively low strength and not used in the marine industry.

Marine-Grade Aluminum Alloys

5000 Series Wrought Alloys (A95xxx) and Casting Alloys (A05xx.x)

In this series, magnesium is the principal alloying element. The 5000 series alloys have good welding characteristics and excellent corrosion resistance in the marine environment. They are as resistant to corrosion as pure aluminum and more resistant in salt water. The 5000 series are the most widely used alloys in marine applications.

The most popular marine alloys of this group are 5052, 5083, 5086, and a newer member of the family, 5456. For hull plate in boats less than about 20 feet in length, 5052 is most commonly used in 3/16-inch sheet. Since welding aluminum sheet of this thickness is difficult and time-consuming, these boats are usually riveted.

When length gets above 20 feet, aluminum boats built in the United States typically use 5086-H32 ¼-inch plate for the hull and 5052 for deck plate, consoles, and cabins. For plate thicker than ¼-inch, alloys with –H116 or –H117 tempers are used because they are easier to bend.

Europeans seem to prefer 5083 and 5454, respectively, for these applications. There's really not a great deal of difference between 5083 and 5086, but U.S. builders find 5086 a little easier to bend. The newer 5456 alloy is the one the U.S. Navy prefers, but it's about three times more expensive than 5086.

The cast alloys containing magnesium are very corrosion resistant, relatively strong, and ductile. A0514 (5 percent magnesium) and A0520 (10 percent magnesium) are both widely used marine-grade cast alloys. However, they are not as easily cast as those containing silicon.

Another attractive feature of Almag is that, unlike most castings, it does not fail catastrophically but tends to stretch or deform slightly, thus providing some advance warning before failure.

See table A7-16 (page 285) for the mechanical properties of these alloys.

6000 Series

These alloys contain both magnesium and silicon as major alloying elements. They have moderately high strength, good workability, and very good corrosion resistance. They are also capable of being heat-treated. Copper is used in some 6000 series alloys to increase strength, but copper content is kept very low because, as we saw in the 2000 series alloys, corrosion resistance decreases with increasing copper content. Also, 6000 series alloys can exhibit susceptibility to intergranular corrosion if the magnesium and silicon contents are not carefully balanced.

The most widely used and versatile 6000 series alloy is 6061-T6. It is used extensively in the boating industry, primarily for extruded components such spars, rails, and tubing. In the United Kingdom 6061 also finds some use in hull construction.

ANODIZING

Anodizing is not a coating. It is an electrochemical process that changes the outer surface layers of the metal. The aluminum part to be anodized is immersed in an acid electrolyte, and a direct current is passed through it. The aluminum part becomes an anode (hence the term "anodizing"), and a greatly thickened oxide layer forms on it. Prior to sealing the oxide layer—the final step in the anodizing process—the porous oxide may be colored by impregnation with dyes. Masts, spars, windshield and portlight frames, and deck fittings are typically of anodized aluminum.

There are three basic anodizing processes: chromic acid, sulfuric acid, and hard anodizing (sulfuric acid with additives). The first two typically produce oxide films ranging from 0.2 to 0.7 mil (0.005 to 0.018 mm). Aluminum components anodized by these processes are suitable for use inland or in freshwater environments. The hard anodizing process produces oxide films up to 2 mils (0.051 mm) in thickness. The amount of corrosion protection that anodizing provides depends on the thickness of the oxide film. Anodizing for marine application should be the thickest of the hard anodized type.

A few cautionary comments are needed. The oxide film is quite hard and resistant to abrasion, but it can be scratched or rubbed off. When this happens, the exposed bare aluminum is subject to pitting corrosion. Masts and spars are particularly susceptible from loose and flapping halyards. Aside from consideration of one's neighbors and getting a good night's sleep, it is well to take precautions against chafing halyards and the like. Washing aluminum spars with fresh water to remove dirt and deposits and waxing them at the annual haulout is also worthwhile.

CORROSION

Given the significant differences in the corrosion resistance of the various aluminum alloys, it is essential to use only the marine grades on boats. But even marine alloys can suffer surface pitting and other forms of corrosion. In the following sections we'll examine the usual corrosion suspects and how they work on the marine-grade aluminum alloys.

Atmospheric Corrosion

Aluminum alloys generally have excellent resistance to atmospheric corrosion, requiring no protective coatings or maintenance beyond cleaning, which aids greatly in preventing unsightly pitting where dirt or salt accumulates. When aluminum, like stainless steel, is exposed to oxygen, it forms an oxide surface film that protects it from corrosive attack. For the most part, damage due to atmospheric corrosion is pretty much limited to fairly slight pitting of the surface with no significant loss of material or strength. The extent of the damage depends on geographical location, wind, weather, temperature changes, pollutants involved, and the duration of exposure.

Duration of exposure is an important consideration in aluminum alloys. The rate of corrosion *decreases* with time to a low, steady rate, regardless of the type of alloy or the specific environment. Loss of tensile strength also decreases, but at a slower rate than that of corrosion. Table 9-2 is based on a comprehensive testing program conducted by the American Society for Testing and Materials (ASTM). The tests were conducted over a 7-year period at two seacoast locations. Data are shown for the marine grades in common use.

A couple of cautionary notes are in order. First, it is not a good idea to store aluminum sheets outdoors, even under cover. Moisture can collect on the surface, be absorbed by dust and dirt particles, and cause staining and pitting. If stored on edge, moisture may collect on the exposed edges and be drawn down between the sheets by capillary action, with the same consequences. If sheets must be stored in humid environments, they should be lightly oiled.

Second, alkalis will attack the protective aluminum oxide film and are thus corrosive to aluminum. Sodium hydroxide is one such alkali that is produced at the cathode of a galvanic cell during corrosion, and if it is concentrated, it will attack aluminum. Consider, for example, an aluminum lower unit immersed in stagnant brackish water with a magnesium sacrificial anode nearby. The aluminum lower unit is cathodic by some 800 millivolts to the magnesium anode. If alkali, produced at the cathode, are allowed to concentrate, they will attack the aluminum lower unit.

Table 9-2

Average Atmospheric Corrosion Rates and Loss in Tensile Strength after 7 Years of Exposure

Alloy	Corrosion Rates*		Maximum Depth of Attack in 7 Years		Average Depth of Attack in 7 Years		Loss in Tensile Strength in 7 Years
	mm/yr.	μin./yr.	μm	mils	μm	mils	%
Non-heat-treatable alloys							
5052-H34	362	14.3	62	2.4	43	1.7	0.8
5456-O	381	15.0	104	4.1	37	1.5	0.4
5083-O	469	18.5	102	4.0	52	2.0	1.8
5083-H34	375	14.8	88	3.5	56	2.2	2.2
5086-H34	436	17.2	105	4.1	76	3.0	1.9
Heat-treatable alloys							
6061-T6	422	16.6	98	3.9	42	1.7	0.7

* Based on weight change.
Excerpted from E. H. Hollingsworth and H. Y. Hunsicker, "Corrosion of Aluminum and Aluminum Alloys," *ASM Handbook*, vol. 13, *Corrosion*, ref. 89, p. 599.

Immersion Corrosion

Aluminum alloys in the 1000, 3000, 5000, and 6000 series all have good resistance to corrosion in freshwater. However, much depends on the specific nature of the water—its acidity, temperature, pollutants, and, especially, the presence or absence of such heavy metal contaminants as iron, copper, and lead. These metals may leach from shoreside industrial piping systems feeding into the freshwater body. Unfortunately, no reliable correlation has been established that would allow us to predict the corrosivity of aluminum in a particular body of freshwater.

In seawater we have an abundance of experience, particularly since the 1960s, when aluminum began to come into its own in the recreational boat and yacht industry. This experience shows clearly that 5000 and 6000 series aluminum alloys are the alloys of choice for saltwater applications. Many years of experience with these alloys in all kinds of seawater service—offshore structures, pipelines, ships and boats—have demonstrated their excellent corrosion resistance and long life under conditions of partial, intermittent, or total immersion in seawater.

The 6000 series alloys are somewhat less corrosion resistant than the 5000 series but are widely used for spars, pulpits, and railings because they are more easily extruded.

Among the casting alloys, alloys 356 (A0356) and 514 (A0514.0), together with Almag 35 (A0535), have shown high corrosion resistance in seawater. These three are commonly used for cast fittings, housings, deck cleats, and other marine hardware.

Table 9-3 gives the effects of seawater immersion on the marine-grade aluminum alloys over time at geographic locations. Protective paint coatings for the topsides are not required but are frequently used for aesthetic reasons. Antifouling bottom paint is required to discourage the attachment of marine organisms. When paint systems are applied to aluminum hulls, careful preparation of the surface is necessary to make the paint adhere properly to the metal. Primers containing red lead or copper must not be used, for galvanic corrosion will almost certainly damage the metal. The same applies for copper-base antifouling paints. We talk more about this in chapter 15 on coatings.

Galvanic Corrosion

Aluminum is extremely anodic; only zinc and magnesium are more anodic than aluminum. In contact with most other metals (except zinc and magnesium), the aluminum will corrode. When it is necessary for aluminum to be coupled with another metal, an insulating layer should be inserted between the two metals whenever possible; most plastics, sheet or liquid, work well.

Intergranular Corrosion: Exfoliation

Some wrought aluminum alloys in certain tempers are susceptible to a type of intergranular corrosion called *exfoliation*. The corrosion takes place along subsurface paths within the body of the metal parallel to the surface. The damage can appear as a swelling caused by the greater volume of the corrosion product within the body of the metal. The name comes from the leaf-like appearance of the surface when the corrosion occurs along the grain boundaries. Exfoliation does not cause sudden catastrophic failure. It is readily apparent and typically occurs close to the surface of the metal, giving plenty of warning of its presence.

The aluminum alloys most susceptible to exfoliation are the heat-treatable 2000 and 7000 series, but certain cold-worked 5000 series alloys, such as 5456-H321 (used for hull plating by the U.S. Navy), are also susceptible. A prominent aluminum boatbuilder reports hearing of this type of failure in some of the river patrol boats used in the Vietnam conflict. Such occurrences led to the development of the H116 and H117 tempers for 5083, 5086, and 5456 alloys when used for hull plating.

Manufacturers test exfoliation resistance by subjecting susceptible alloys to total immersion in aggressive acidified solutions or exposure to cyclical acidified salt spray. The samples are then etched, and the exposed microstructure is examined for telltale patterns.

Table 9-3

Average Weight Loss and Maximum Depth of Pitting for Aluminum Plate Specimens after Immersion in Seawater

Test Series	Alloy and Temper	Harbor Island, NC*				Halifax, NS				Esquimalt, BC*			
		1 yr.	2 yr.	5 yr.	10 yr.	1 yr.	2 yr.	5 yr.	10 yr.	1 yr.	2 yr.	5 yr.	10 yr.
Weight Loss (g)													
1	5052-H34	4.5	6.5	9.0	14.9	2.8	3.3		14.2	1.7	0.0	0.0	0.6
	6061-T4	4.8	6.6	12.4	18.6	4.4	6.0	8.0	15.6	0.9	2.3	28.2	62.0
	6061-T6	5.5	7.7	14.0	21.5	4.3	7.3	12.7	22.8	6.7	7.1	11.1	44.3
2	5083	2.5	3.7		7.3	2.8	0.0	6.1	8.5	1.3	1.9	2.7	3.3
	5083	4.7	3.4	5.7	8.1	2.6	3.2	5.2	7.5	15.3	16.3	36.3	31.1
	6061-T6	7.6	13.4	29.4	51.6	9.8	11.2	33.2	48.5	12.3	26.8	48.7	48.0
	6161-T6	5.5	6.5	15.4	34.2	10.0	9.4	19.1	54.1	7.3	7.0	21.3	18.6
3	5083	3.5	4.6	6.0		2.0	2.8	3.6		0.2	2.2	2.8	
Maximum depth of pitting (mils)													
1	5052-H34	0	0	0	0	5	20	6	12	16	6	0	5
	6061-T4	0	13	2	14	12	18	21	33	15	50	20	28
	6061-T6	36	24	60	95	36	43	43	54	30	25	80	116
2	5083	12	9	6	0	3	0	12	7	13	5	0	6
	5083	16	13	6	10	4	23	16	22	29	38	47	55
	6061-T6	67	100	144	130	50	67	90	122	60	100	125	125
	6161-T6	15	27	36	40	38	47	58	67	35	48	60	55
	5083	22	1	7		0	11	7		0	0	5	

* Harbor Island is near Wilmington, NC; Esquimalt is near Victoria, BC.

Specimens were 6.35 × 305 × 305 mm (0.250 × 12 × 12 in.) and weighed approximately 1.6 kg (3.5 lb.).

Source: E. H. Hollingsworth and H. Y. Hunsicker, "Corrosion of Aluminum and Aluminum Alloys," *ASM Handbook,* vol. 13, *Corrosion,* ref. 2, p. 603.

It is not likely that you'll experience this problem in a good-quality boat from a reputable manufacturer, but if you do encounter exfoliation in an older boat or one of questionable heritage, the problem should be readily recognizable. The fix is, as you might expect, replacement of the faulty plate.

Stress-Corrosion Cracking

Stress-corrosion cracking is primarily a problem in high-strength aluminum alloys such as the 2000 and 7000 series. It has not been a problem for marine grades properly manufactured and fabricated and used within their specifications. Tempers have been developed for most commercial alloys that provide a high degree of immunity to this form of corrosion. The 5000 series alloys with H116 or H117 tempers in particular are thermally processed to achieve a high degree of resistance to stress-corrosion cracking.

Poultice Corrosion

Even the best of the marine-grade alloys will corrode if denied access to a supply of fresh oxygen. This happens when damp organic materials such as insulation, wood decking (especially oak), or accumulations of dirt and debris in the bilge lie against the metal. Where this cannot be avoided, the metal surface should be protected with an anticorrosive paint coating. Aluminum fastenings in wet wood are definitely to be avoided.

Erosion Corrosion

The marine-grade alloys are susceptible to erosion corrosion from the impingement of cavitation or high-velocity water streams, especially those with entrained particles. Cathodic protection systems can help to minimize and sometimes eliminate this source of corrosive damage.

Contaminants

We discussed this briefly above, but it bears repeating. Aluminum is extremely susceptible to attack by certain heavy-metal ions, particularly copper and mercury. Concentrations of even a few parts per million will cause severe pitting. Copper tubing or tanks upstream of aluminum fittings can easily generate such concentrations. This situation is to be avoided.

I recently read of a 50-foot-tall, 10-foot-diameter water tower that was destroyed in six months as a result of pitting initiated by copper contamination. The source of the copper was a weld on an inlet waterline that had been made with a copper-bearing weld wire. Under the heading of tragedies of a more personal nature, a colleague tells of the destruction of a favorite aluminum coffeepot by water drawn from a copper line.

It is difficult to imagine how mercury would come into contact with aluminum surfaces on a boat, but of all the heavy metals, mercury can cause the most corrosion damage to aluminum. If some clumsy crew member (certainly the skipper would never be so careless) should drop a mercury thermometer on your aluminum vessel, it can be a very aggressive corrosive and should be cleaned up as quickly as possible.

However, mercury is toxic by skin contact or by inhalation of mercury vapors (which are odorless), so great care should be taken in dealing with it. The area should be *well ventilated*, and the droplets should be picked up with strips of adhesive tape and put into a sealed container. *Avoid skin contact*. Local health authorities should be contacted immediately for specific instructions.

SUMMARY

The basic marine-grade aluminum alloys are those of the 5000 and 6000 series. Alloys 5052, 5083, 5086, and 5456 in the H32, H116, and H117 tempers are the grades of choice for hull plate and structurals while 6061-T6 is favored for masts and spars. Of the cast grades, alloy 356 is most often used for applications that see little stress, decorative end caps and plugs, and cleats on some small craft. Almag 35 (A0535) is appreciably stronger and is used for cleats, bow eyes, and traveler track.

Aluminum, like stainless steel, forms an oxide coating as long as it has access to a supply of oxygen. In atmospheric exposures, the most prevalent form of corrosive damage is surface pitting due to dirt or particle deposits that prevent access to oxygen. Because aluminum is an extremely anodic metal and suffers from galvanic corrosion when in contact with most other common marine metals, such couplings must be insulated. When properly applied protective coatings are used where required, when adequate sacrificial anodes are fitted, when a proper electrical system is installed, and given a modest amount of housekeeping and maintenance, aluminum vessels can provide many years of satisfactory service.

CHAPTER 10

Nickel and Nickel Alloys

Nickel has two standout characteristics: it has a very high degree of corrosion resistance, and it is expensive. Nickel and its alloys are readily fabricated by conventional methods.

By judicious use of alloying elements, an extensive family of high-strength, high-temperature, wear-resistant, and corrosion-resistant alloys has been developed. These alloys have been optimized for service in some extremely demanding applications. Members of this large family of alloys have solved critical corrosion problems in aggressive seawater environments in the offshore oil and gas, chemical processing, pulp and paper, and marine industries.

Nickel is also commonly used as an alloying element in other metal alloys. In fact, more than 80 percent of all the primary nickel produced is used as an alloying element in some 3,000 different alloys, such as stainless steels, alloy steels, and nonferrous alloys. Nickel is also used as plating or cladding on steel. However, the nickel-base alloys are of principal interest to us.

NICKEL-BASE ALLOYS

In nickel-base alloys the nickel content is greater than that of any other element. In terms of their chemical compositions, they are commonly divided into two main classes:

1. Alloys that depend primarily on the inherent corrosion-resistant characteristics of nickel itself (with some help from alloying elements). These are the non-chromium-bearing alloys (e.g., Monel 400, Monel K-500).
2. Alloys that depend primarily on chromium as the passivating element, similar to the stainless steels. These are the chromium-bearing alloys (e.g., Inconel, Hastelloy).

In terms of their intended usage, some nickel-base alloys are formulated primarily for applications requiring strength at high temperatures, whereas others are intended for use where high corrosion resistance is essential. However, the high-temperature types frequently find application in corrosion service and vice versa.

As with most high-performance, highly alloyed alloys, nickel-base alloys have been developed for specific critical applications in offshore oil and gas, chemical processing, pharmaceutical, and pulp and paper industries. These are industries where longer service life and lowered maintenance can economically justify the high initial cost of the alloy. Eventually some of these superalloys find their way into relatively low-volume marine applications, but marine equipment represents only about 2 percent of the end-use market for nickel.

The nickel-base alloys that have found the most common use in the boating community are the Monels and, to a lesser extent, the Inconels and the Hastelloys. See table A7-17 (page 285) for the chemical and mechanical properties of marine nickel-base alloys. The age-hardened versions, Inconel X-750 (N07750) and Incoloy 901 (N09901), are also included, as well as Type 316 stainless steel (S31600) for purposes of comparison.

Monel

Monel is certainly the most well known of the nickel-base alloys in the boating community. Monel, however, is actually a proprietary trade name for a series of nickel-copper alloys.

Monel 400

Monel 400 is probably the most widely used of these alloys. It is very strong, ductile, tough, highly corrosion resistant, and . . . expensive. It is readily forged, worked, cast, and welded by common methods. However, when machining Monel, care should be taken to avoid exposure to sulfur, which may lead to liquid-metal-cracking susceptibility.

Monel 400 is used in prop shafts, fuel and water tanks, water pump parts, and fastenings, among other applications. Equivalent alloys to Monel 400 are commercially available. These are commonly referred to as *Alloy 400* (UNS N04400).

Monel K-500

More commonly referred to as *K-Monel*, Monel K-500 is also a nickel-copper alloy of much the same composition as Monel 400 but with the addition of small quantities of aluminum, silicon, and manganese. K-Monel is also hardened, which greatly increases its strength and abrasion resistance. K-500 (UNS N05500) is widely used for prop shafts, pump shafts and impellers, valve parts, and high-strength bolts.

Monel 505

Monel 505 has additional silicon added to improve its resistance to erosion corrosion and cavitation.

Hastelloy

Hastelloy is a proprietary trade name for a large family of nickel-base superalloys. These are divided into two basic groups according to their targeted application environment: high-temperature alloys and corrosion-resistant alloys.

The major user of the high-temperature Hastelloys is the aircraft gas turbine engine market. The earliest of this group was MULTI-MET. Hastelloy X (N06002) followed and is still the "workhorse" of the gas turbine industry. Other alloys in this group are Hastelloy alloys B (N10001), S (N06635), and W (N10004).

The corrosion-resistant Hastelloys are primarily used in the chemical processing industries, but they also find wide application in the oil and gas, pharmaceutical, pulp and paper, and other demanding industries.

Stellite: Alloy C

The original Hastelloy grade was Hastelloy C (N10002), first introduced in the 1930s. It was developed by a man named Haynes, who called it *Stellite* (meaning *star-like*). Haynes founded the Haynes Stellite Company, hence the trade name *Hastelloy*. Quite a remarkable metal, Stellite represented a breakthrough in corrosion resistance and pretty much set the standard for corrosion resistance at that time. A test sample has been on the beach (not in the water) at the LaQue Center for Corrosion Research in Wrightsville Beach, North Carolina, for the past 50 years and has yet to show any sign of corrosion.

However, Alloy C did exhibit a troubling weakness—a susceptibility to intergranular corrosion (weld decay). This led to the development of improved grades.

Advances in processing methods (such as argon-oxygen-decarburization) and more finely tuned alloy additions have resulted in some outstanding new alloys. Among these are Hastelloy C-22 (N06022) and C-276 (N10276). Both are nickel-chromium-molybdenum alloys and are markedly superior to Alloy C, which they have essentially replaced.

Hastelloy Alloy C-276 (N10276)

Alloy C-276 features high resistance to uniform/general corrosion, outstanding resistance to pitting and crevice corrosion, and excellent resistance to stress-corrosion cracking; it is easily welded and fabricated and is resistant to intergranular corrosive attack. Achieving a high degree of acceptance, this alloy has become a standard for overall corrosion resistance. Confusingly, C-276 is now commonly referred to as just Hastelloy C and is sometimes confused with the old Alloy C, which it has effectively replaced. It is a good idea to check the UNS designation to be sure which alloy is specified.

Hastelloy C-22 (N06022)

This is one of the more recent Hastelloy alloys, commercially introduced in the late 1970s to early 1980s. It has better overall corrosion resistance than C-276 and is readily welded by gas-tungsten-arc (GTAW), gas-metal-arc (GMAW), or shielded-metal-arc (SMAW).

C-22 has a higher chromium content to optimize its performance in highly oxidizing environments and hot acid, and it has better overall corrosion resistance than C-276. It has found wide application in a variety of industries. Of particular interest to us is the use of this alloy in heat exchangers, where it is without peer. (A frequent application of Hastelloy C-22 is in plate-type heat exchangers using seawater to cool hot acid fumes.)

Inconel and Incoloy

The Monels are nickel-copper alloys. The Hastelloys are nickel-chromium-iron-molybdenum alloys. There is another family of nickel-base alloys we should consider—the nickel-chromium-iron family. These alloys typically have some 44 percent iron which helps to reduce cost and improve high-temperature performance. These are high-strength, high-temperature alloys with excellent corrosion resistance in seawater environments and, like other nickel-base alloys, they're expensive.

Specific alloys in this group that are of interest to us are Inconel 600 (N06600) and 625 (N06625) and Incoloy 800 (N08800) and 825 (N08825). These alloys are excellent for use as exhaust system components, fastenings, and shaft seals.

CORROSION RESISTANCE

Atmospheric Corrosion

Nickel and nickel-base alloys generally exhibit excellent resistance to atmospheric corrosion in all types of atmospheres. Typical uniform and pitting corrosion rates are less than 0.1 mil/yr. (0.0025 mm/yr.)—for all practical purposes, negligible. Monel 400 (Alloy 400 or N04400) may develop a sort of thin greenish patina. The Inconels and Incoloys may tarnish after long exposures in some atmospheres. The Hastelloys also develop a thin protective oxide film similar to that of the other nickel-base alloys. These films are readily cleaned and the bright surfaces restored.

Immersion Corrosion

Nickel and the nickel-base alloys, in general, have very good corrosion resistance in freshwater. The nickel-copper alloys, such as Alloy 400, are sometimes used in higher-quality freshwater valves and fittings.

Alloy 400 and nickel-base alloys containing chromium and iron are highly corrosion resistant in *flowing* seawater. Where the water is stagnant or the velocity low, they are susceptible to pitting or crevice corrosion, particularly in places where they are denied access to oxygen (e.g., under marine organisms, inside cutless bearings). However, the rate of pitting starts out fairly fast but slows. Pit depths seldom exceed 50 mils (1.3 mm). In moderate- or fast-flowing seawater—more than 2 to 3 ft./sec. (0.6 to 0.9 m/sec.)—both Monel 400 and K-500 exhibit corrosion rates of less than 1 mil/yr. (0.025 mm/yr.). The nickel-chromium-molybdenum alloys are even superior to the Monels, and all of the nickel-base alloys are far superior to the marine-industry workhorse, Type 316 stainless steel.

Galvanic Corrosion

Nickel and the nickel-base alloys are quite noble (−0.1 to −0.2 V) with respect to aluminum (−0.76 to −1.00 V) and the mild steels (−0.6 to −0.71 V). Also, they are not readily polarized, so they will cause accelerated corrosion of these metals.

Nickel-base alloys are more noble than the bronzes (−0.24 to −0.31 V), so depending on such factors as salinity, conductivity, relative surface areas, and pollutants, galvanic activity can be a problem. Precautions should be taken. Typically, they are very close in the galvanic scale to the 18-8 (−0.05 to −0.10 V) and Type 316 (0.0 to −0.1 V) stainless steels, so the galvanic effects of contact will be minimal.

Intergranular Corrosion (Weld Decay)

At the temperatures involved in the welding process, the metals become molten, and when they cool, certain of the alloying elements can combine with other elements and precipitate out. Similar to the austenitic stainless steels, the nickel-chromium-molybdenum alloys—such as Hastelloy C, Inconel 625, and Incoloy 825—are susceptible to carbide precipitation in the heat-affected zone. Due to a high content of such alloying elements as chromium, molybdenum, tungsten, and niobium, nickel-base alloys are also prone to the precipitation of other intermetallic (compounds of two or more metallic elements) areas within the metal body called *phases*. Both the carbides and the intermetallics are rich in chromium, molybdenum, and tungsten, thus depriving adjacent areas of these elements necessary for corrosion resistance and leaving such areas susceptible to attack.

This is such a problem with Hastelloy C (N10002) that it requires the use of postweld annealing to prevent weld decay. In Hastelloy C-276 (N10276) the carbon and silicon contents were reduced significantly, retarding carbide precipitation and permitting the use of this alloy in the as-welded condition. In general, weld decay due to carbide precipitation is not a problem in alloys with carbon content less than about 0.05 percent.

Unfortunately C-276 still had the problem of intermetallic phase precipitation. Hastelloy C-4 (N06455)—with lower iron, cobalt, and tungsten levels—was developed to prevent this. But, and it seems there's always a but, because of the reduced tungsten level, C-4 is more susceptible to pitting and crevice corrosion than C-276. This led to the development of Hastelloy C-22 (N06022), which is superior to both C-276 and C-4 in corrosion resistance and thermal characteristics.

To counteract intergranular attack, there are basically three methods. First, carefully select alloys and welding filler materials that contain levels of carbon that are as low as possible to minimize carbide precipitation. Second, select alloys and welding consumables (electrodes, filler metals) that contain carbide-stabilizing elements such as titanium and niobium, which facilitate the formation of harmless titanium and niobium carbides instead of chromium carbides.

The third method is postweld heat treatment, which may be used if the part is small enough. This redissolves any precipitated carbides.

It is worth pointing out that high-nickel alloys require greater care than iron-base materials in precleaning and cleanliness to prevent contamination cracking. At the temperatures involved in welding, sulfur contamination (as from cutting oils)—even very small amounts—can result in liquid metal cracking.

Hydrogen Embrittlement

Hydrogen embrittlement has only recently (in the late 1980s) been recognized as an important form of corrosive damage in nickel-base alloys. In really severe cases, failure can occur suddenly, with no prior indication or visible evidence of damage.

For the most part, fully annealed nickel-base alloys are essentially immune, except when cold-working (or heat treatment) has increased the strength of the alloy. Also, only the alloys with less than 10 percent iron content (e.g., Monel 400, Hastelloys C-276 and C-22, Inconel 625) are affected to any significant degree unless they have been cold-worked or hardened. The precipitation-hardenable alloys, such as Inconel X-750, Monel K-500 and Incoloy 901, are particularly susceptible. Alloys Incoloy 800 and 825 are the least likely to suffer hydrogen damage.

Preventive measures are pretty much limited to selecting the least susceptible alloys and reducing, as much as practical or possible, the temperatures to which the alloys are subjected.

Stress-Corrosion Cracking

Until recently, it was commonly believed that the nickel-base alloys were immune to stress-corrosion cracking. They were frequently used to replace austenitic stainless steels in applications where the steel had failed. Today, however—perhaps because of the increasing number of alloys available and their increasing usage in more severe environments—there is a heightening awareness of the susceptibility of nickel-base alloys to stress-corrosion cracking. As a practical matter, though, unless the alloy has been cold-worked or heat-treated to increase its strength, and unless it is immersed in a high-chloride medium at elevated temperatures, stress-corrosion cracking is not likely to be a problem. Further, while there is no hard and fast critical temperature limit, the consensus is that it has to be above 400°F (205°C). In any event, Alloys 625, C-276, and C-22 are at least a couple of orders of magnitude more resistant than Type 316 stainless steel.

Erosion and Cavitation

In general both the nickel-chromium and the nickel-copper alloys have excellent resistance to erosion and cavitation, hence their frequent use for propeller and pump shafts, impellers, and valve components. This is discussed in more detail under Propulsion Systems in chapter 17.

SUMMARY

Nickel-base alloys are truly superior metals for the marine environment, but there are performance differences among the different alloys. Equivalents to the proprietary grades mentioned above are available from a variety of other producers. These generally are referred to as *Alloy* 625 or *Alloy 825*, for example. The best way to be certain of the alloy you are considering is by reference to the UNS designation.

The most common and troublesome forms of corrosion in nickel-base alloys are localized (pitting and crevice corrosion) and galvanic corrosion. If alloys with less than 0.05 percent carbon content are used, and if proper welding procedures and appropriate welding consumables are employed, intergranular corrosion is unlikely. Also, if nickel-base alloys are not cold-worked, not coupled with mild steel, and not employed at very high temperatures (above 400°F), the probability of hydrogen embrittlement or stress-corrosion cracking failures is low.

These are relatively new superalloys primarily used in critical applications in industries where their high initial cost can be justified. They are excellent for exhaust system components, especially in diesel engine exhaust systems, where the combination of high temperatures, salt water, and sulfur constitutes an extremely harsh environment, but cost limits their use in the boating industry. Hopefully as volume usage builds in other industries, costs will come down, and nickel-base alloys will start showing up in our boat fittings.

CHAPTER 11

Copper and Copper Alloys

The copper-base alloys make up an impressive collection of marine metals. Known to mariners for their biofouling resistance, these alloys also offer a wide range of mechanical properties, ease of fabrication, versatility of application, and—usually—favorable economics. However, according to the Copper Development Association, 93 percent of all the copper consumed in the United States in 1998 was selected for its excellent electrical and thermal conductivity or for its corrosion resistance.

This is a very diverse group of metals that includes a number of different families with lots of members, each with special characteristics and unique capabilities. They all have names, nicknames (several have more than one), and numerical designations (also several). It can all be quite confusing. In this chapter we define the various families, the particular alloys that survive and thrive in the marine environment, and for what jobs they're suitable.

THE FAMILIES

Copper-base alloys are generally divided into several families according to their chemical compositions. Each family has a commonly accepted name, but it isn't always clear to which family a specific alloy belongs. This can, and does, lead to the improper use of certain alloys and to their subsequent failure in service. We'll try to sort all of this out.

Table 11-1 shows the major families and their UNS designations as currently allocated.

Originally, the U.S. copper industry established a three-digit system preceded by the letters "CA." The UNS systems absorbed the old CA designations by shortening the prefix to "C" and expanding the number to five digits, so the old numerical designations are included in the new ones and are clearly recognizable. Broadly, UNS numbers C10000 to C79999 are assigned to wrought forms, and C80000 to C99999 are assigned to cast forms.

COPPER ALLOYS

More than 50 different wrought copper alloys are used in hundreds of applications in at least 20 industries besides the marine industry. The same alloys used in electrical, electronic, and plumbing components ashore also find their way into our boats and yachts. The corrosion resistance of the copper alloys is very good in seawater and excellent in salt atmospheres.

Copper alloys are typically more than 99 percent copper with very small amounts of one or more of the following alloying elements—silver (Ag), arsenic (As), antimony (Sb), phosphorus

Table 11-1

Major Copper Alloy Families and Their UNS Designations

Unified Numbering System (UNS)

Major Family	Wrought Forms	Cast Forms
copper alloys	C10100–C15815	C80100–C81200
high-copper alloys	C16200–C19900	C81400–C82800
brasses	C21000–C48600	C83300–C89940
bronzes	C50100–C69710	C90200–C95900
copper-nickel alloys	C70100–C72950	C96200–C96950
nickel-silver alloys	C73500–C79830	C97300–C97800
leaded copper		C98200–C98840
special alloys		C99300–C99750

(P), and tellurium (Te). These elements are added to optimize particular mechanical properties for specific applications and have little or no effect on the corrosion resistance of the alloy.

Copper alloys have a proud history of useful marine service. Copper nails and rivets have long been used as fastenings in traditional wooden boats, with copper clinch nails and roves used in the construction of canoes and clinker-built boats. Copper sheathing has been (and to some extent still is) used on the bottoms of wooden vessels to confound the terrible wood-boring teredo and to inhibit marine growth.

Copper alloys are used in a wider variety of applications on modern boats, where they fulfill such essential functions as electrical wiring, switches, contacts and terminals, piping and tubing for hot and cold freshwater systems, gasoline, oil, and hydraulic lines, heat exchanger and radiator tubing, and many more.

There are really no practical alternatives to the use of copper alloys in our electrical systems, nor is there any compelling reason to seek any. The same cannot be said for the use of copper in plumbing and piping applications, an issue that gets our attention in chapter 19.

Corrosion resistance of the copper alloys in marine, industrial, and rural atmospheres is excellent. Corrosion rates in unpolluted air and waters, both fresh and salt, is essentially negligible—less than 0.055 mil/yr. (0.014 mm/yr.). In marine atmospheres a greenish patina is formed on the surface, which some people find attractive. This protective film is of little significance in terms of corrosive damage except in the case of electrical contacts, where it can interfere with the efficient functioning of the device. Electrical contacts should be kept in reasonably tight enclosures, inspected periodically, and cleaned if necessary.

Copper alloys are susceptible to erosion corrosion in high-velocity water flows. This shows up mainly in engine coolant piping, which we discuss in more detail in chapter 17. See table A7-18 (page 285) for the chemical and mechanical properties of the copper alloy types, along with their typical applications.

HIGH-COPPER ALLOYS

The high-copper alloys are more highly alloyed than the copper alloys. Typically, such elements as lead, cadmium, beryllium, tin, phosphorus, and nickel are added. In the wrought form, the high-copper alloys have copper contents less than 99.3 percent but more than 96 percent. The cast high-copper alloys have copper contents of more than 94 percent. Small amounts of silver may be added to optimize certain mechanical properties.

Typically, these alloys are used in similar but more demanding applications requiring enhanced mechanical properties, improved thermal or electrical conductivity, or performance in higher-temperature environments. Spring contacts, fuse clips, switch gear, valve components, and turnbuckle barrels are among the items frequently made of these alloys.

The additional elements in high-copper alloys are added to enhance mechanical properties such as machinability, hardness, and strength and have little or no effect on corrosion resistance. High-copper alloys have excellent resistance to seawater corrosion and biofouling, but, like the copper alloys, they are susceptible to erosion corrosion at high water velocities. Their increased strength does improve their resistance to this form of corrosion. See table A7-19 (page 286) for the chemical and mechanical properties of the high-copper alloys, along with some of their uses.

BRASSES

The brasses are copper alloys in which zinc is the principal alloying element. (Contrast this with the bronzes, which have tin as the principal alloying element.) The amount of zinc typically varies from 5 to 45 percent. Other alloying elements may also be present.

Brasses have a number of attractive features. They are aesthetically attractive, are easy to shape, drill, and join, and can be riveted, brazed, or silver soldered. However, they also have some character deficiencies that must be understood and kept in mind if we're going to use them on our boats with any success.

As with all metal alloys, the strengths and weaknesses of the brasses depend greatly on the chemical composition of the particular alloy. In the brasses, the amount of zinc is critical. When zinc is present in amounts greater than about 15 percent, the alloy is susceptible to both dezincification and stress-corrosion cracking. At levels below 15 percent, resistance to both these forms of corrosion increases greatly. Adding small amounts of tin, together with small amounts of arsenic or antimony, significantly reduces susceptibility to dezincification. The addition of these "inhibitors" results in some very useful brass alloys.

Other alloying elements such as beryllium, chromium, lead, manganese, phosphorus, and tellurium have very little or no effect on corrosion resistance, but they do affect strength and hardness. It is essential to know which brass alloy is being used for which purpose.

The brasses consist of some 75 wrought forms and 25 or more cast forms, each differing, sometimes only slightly, in the percentages of both major and minor alloying elements. Not all are suitable for use in marine environments. However, many, if not most, can find their way onto or into our boats, and there's little we can do about that. There's really no way to know what grades have been used in onboard equipment and hardware. We can, however, know what grades are suitable for marine use and their limitations. See table A7-20 (page 286) for the chemical and mechanical properties of the marine brasses, along with some of their typical applications.

Red Brass (C23000, C83300 to C83800)

Red brasses are 85-15 (copper-zinc) brasses. The wrought forms are used in heat exchanger tubing, plumbing fixtures and pipe, and radiator cores. Cast forms are frequently used in valves, pumps, plumbing fittings, and fixtures.

Corrosion resistance is excellent in all atmospheres—industrial, rural, and marine. Corrosion rates in the marine atmosphere range from 0.013 mil/yr. (0.0003 mm/yr.) to 0.022 mil/yr. (0.0006 mm/yr.) with no pitting or crevice attack. Red brasses are affected by atmospheric pollutants, and exposure to hydrogen sulfide will cause rapid tarnishing.

Self-corrosion resistance is also excellent in freshwater in the absence of excessive acidity or mineral content. If there is carbon dioxide available in the water, pitting can result. Also, if the water velocity is high, say greater than about 6 ft./sec. (1.8 m/sec.), erosion corrosion can occur.

In seawater, corrosion resistance is very good, affected by salt concentration, temperature, and pollutants. Erosion corrosion is also a problem, even at moderate flow velocities. The red brasses are resistant to both dezincification and to stress-corrosion cracking.

Cartridge Brass (C26000 to C26200)

The cartridge brasses, sometimes referred to as *alpha brasses*, are 70-30 brasses. These are the most ductile of the brasses and get their name from their use in cartridge shells, which must be very ductile to withstand the high stresses they undergo when fired. Cartridge brasses find application on boats in fasteners, plumbing accessories, locks, hinges, springs, and other hardware.

Corrosion rates in marine atmospheres are excellent—on the order of 0.006 to 0.008 mil/yr. (0.00015 to 0.00020 mm/yr.). In marine environments these brasses develop the familiar green protective patina. Immersed in either freshwater or seawater, they have reasonably good resistance to general or uniform corrosion, depending on the water's temperature, velocity, salt content, and pollutants. However, with more than 15 percent zinc, they are susceptible to both dezincification and stress-corrosion cracking. One exception is alloy C26130. Because it has a small amount of arsenic, this is an inhibited alloy and is more resistant to dezincification than other cartridge brasses.

Yellow Brass (C26800 to C27200 and C85200 to C85800)

Yellow brasses are 65/35 brasses. Their primary uses are automotive applications, such as radiator cores and tanks, and in plumbing systems as bathroom fixtures and accessories, sink strainers, and the like. Marine applications have been limited to the odd fastening.

Atmospheric corrosion resistance is pretty much the same as for the cartridge brasses, but yellow brasses have a greater susceptibility to dezincification when immersed in seawater unless inhibitors have been added. Inhibited versions are reported to enjoy much wider use in Europe and seem to be making limited gains in the United States.

Muntz Metal (C28000, C36500, C36800, C37000)

The Muntz metals are 60-40 brasses and are sometimes referred to as *alpha-beta brasses*. They are also classed as leaded brasses—copper-zinc alloys whose principal alloying element is lead. They are used in boat equipment as heat exchanger and condenser tubing and tube sheets.

These alloys are not greatly different in their resistance to atmospheric and immersion corrosion from the cartridge brasses. Their resistance to all clean atmospheres is very good. Corrosion resistance in both freshwater and seawater is reasonably good, but these alloys are susceptible to dezincification and stress-corrosion cracking under appropriate conditions, such as immersion in stagnant or slowly moving seawater.

Admiralty Brass (C44300, C44400, C44600)

Another prominent group of brass alloys is the tin brasses. These are basic copper-zinc alloys with a small amount of tin added to increase the alloy's corrosion resistance. Admiralty brasses are essentially 70-30 cartridge brass, with about 1 percent tin added, along with trace amounts of either arsenic, antimony, or phosphorus inhibitors. The principal marine use of the admiralty brasses is in condenser, evaporator, and heat exchanger tubing.

The admiralty brasses have excellent resistance to general and uniform corrosion in all clean atmospheres—typically in the range of 0.011 to 0.014 mil/yr. (0.00028 to 0.00036

mm/yr.). Like the other brasses, they are affected by pollutants and other environmental factors. Also, like the other brasses, they develop the typical greenish copper chloride protective film.

Corrosion resistance of the admiralty brasses when immersed in either freshwater or seawater is outstanding, always with the usual caveats concerning salt concentration, temperature, velocity, pollutants, and mineral content—all of which is to say that under some less than usual conditions, pitting or even dezincification can occur. These alloys, while superior to many of the other brasses, are not immune to these forms of corrosion and should not be used underwater without cathodic protection.

Naval Brass (C46200, C46400, C46500, C47000, C48200, C48500)

Naval brass is another tin brass. Sometimes referred to as *Tobin bronze*, it is not a bronze at all, but a 60-40 brass with about 1 percent tin added. Principal marine uses include decorative fittings, turnbuckles, fastenings, and prop shafts.

Here again, the addition of tin measurably improves corrosion resistance as does, in some cases (e.g., C46500), the addition of arsenic as an inhibitor. Atmospheric corrosion resistance is very good. Immersion corrosion is also quite good in both freshwater and seawater. Naval brasses are susceptible to erosion corrosion at moderate water velocities, say 3 to 6 ft./sec. (0.9 to 1.8 m/sec.). They are susceptible to dezincification in stagnant or slowly moving brackish water. Also, under certain conditions—sulfur dioxide or ammonia exposure—they are subject to stress-corrosion cracking. Naval brasses used underwater must have cathodic protection.

Aluminum Brass (C68700)

Aluminum brass is approximately 78 percent copper, 20 percent zinc, about 2 percent aluminum, and with a trace amount of arsenic. Its principal marine applications are condenser, evaporator, and heat exchanger tubing, and seawater piping.

This is probably the best of the brasses for marine use. Corrosion resistance in marine atmospheres and in both freshwater and salt water is excellent. It is highly resistant to dezincification and to erosion corrosion, even at water velocities as high as 10 ft./sec. (3 m/sec.). It is the aluminum oxide constituent of the protective film that provides this enhanced erosion-corrosion performance. Unfortunately, this film also makes aluminum brass difficult to join by soldering. Despite its improved corrosion resistance, this brass also requires cathodic protection when used underwater.

Manganese Bronze (C86100 to C86800)

Manganese bronze is not actually a bronze, but a (nominal) 60–40 cast brass. Copper content can range from 55 to 67 percent, while zinc content ranges from 21 to 41 percent. So it is really a high-zinc brass. Manganese is added to enhance strength. It is widely used for all sorts of marine castings for portlights, cleats, heavy-duty valve parts, and many other fittings.

The corrosion resistance of manganese bronze is similar to that of other 60–40 brasses (e.g., Muntz metal and naval brass) and not as good as that of aluminum brass. It is also susceptible to dezincification. Manganese bronze is widely used underwater in such applications as stuffing boxes, rudder blades, and props. It must have cathodic protection.

What are we to conclude from this litany about the use of brasses on boats? Many are functionally suitable for light-duty interior applications, although they may tarnish. As for exterior applications, most are subject to dezincification when exposed to salt spray. The addition of tin and inhibitors such as arsenic, antimony, and phosphorus help considerably, but these are "inhibitors," not "eliminators." Ideally, brasses should not be used below the waterline, and where they are, they must be protected.

BRONZES

Time was when bronze was simply an alloy of copper and tin. However, like just about everything else, bronze has gotten more complicated. Nowadays the bronzes are more commonly alloys of copper, phosphorus, tin, zinc, and sometimes small amounts of other elements. Bronze is harder than brass and more corrosion resistant. Many bronze alloys are as strong as the high-quality stainless steels but are more easily worked. Bronze is also more ductile, an important feature since this greater ductility provides a welcome margin of safety. You may begin to detect a little note of personal bias here; bronze is my favorite all-round marine metal. See table A7-21 (page 287) for the chemical and mechan-

Table 11-2

Bronze Family and UNS Designations

Type	UNS	Composition
Wrought Forms		
phosphor bronzes	C50100 to C52400	copper-tin-phosphorus
leaded phosphor bronzes	C53400 to C54400	copper-tin-lead-phosphorus
brazing alloys	C55180 to C55284	copper-phosphorus and copper-silver-phosphorus
aluminum bronzes	C60800 to C64210	copper-aluminum
silicon bronze	C64700 to C66100	copper-silicon
other alloys	C66400 to C69710	various
Cast Forms		
tin bronzes	C90200 to C91700	copper-tin
leaded tin bronzes	C92200 to C92900	copper-tin-lead
high-lead bronzes	C93100 to C94500	copper-tin-lead
nickel-tin bronzes	C94700 to C94900	copper-tin-nickel
aluminum bronzes	C95200 to C95500	copper-aluminum-iron and copper-aluminum-iron-nickel

ical properties of the marine bronzes, along with some of their typical applications. Table 11-2 gives the bronze family and their UNS designations.

Phosphor Bronzes

The principal alloying element in phosphor bronzes is tin, ranging from less than 1 percent to as much as 10 percent. Tin increases the alloy's strength and its corrosion resistance in the marine environment. The phosphorus, from which these alloys get their common name, functions as a deoxidizer. Lead and iron are also present in trace amounts, typically less than a tenth of a percent.

The wrought forms of phosphor bronze are used in applications requiring good electrical or thermal conductivity, corrosion resistance, and "springiness." Examples are fuse clips, electrical coil, and leaf spring contacts. Phosphor bronze is also used in bolts, marine shafting, wire rope, snap shackles, and other hardware items.

The phosphor bronze alloys are more often used in the cast form, and these are chemically more complicated in terms of alloying elements. This is because the casting alloys typically require greater fluidity, machinability, and resistance to galling. This last requirement is because phosphor bronze castings are frequently used in machined parts requiring bearing or frictional surfaces.

The atmospheric corrosion resistance of the phosphor bronzes is excellent—typically less than 0.091 mil/yr. (0.0025 mm/yr.) in marine atmospheres. When immersed, its corrosion resistance is excellent in freshwater and very good in seawater. Alloys with 8 to 10 percent tin content have outstanding resistance to erosion corrosion and stress-corrosion cracking and are strongly resistant to marine growth.

Tin is not produced domestically in the United States and must be imported. Alloys that use this element must reflect this in their cost.

Aluminum Bronzes

The aluminum bronzes are copper plus 3 to 15 percent aluminum and, in some cases, 2 to 5 percent nickel and 3 percent or less manganese.

They are used extensively in marine hardware of all kinds—fittings and fixtures, fastenings, tanks, pump and valve parts, props, and shafts.

These are truly fine marine metals, highly resistant to pitting and crevice corrosion, stress-corrosion cracking, erosion corrosion, and cavitation. The aluminum in the surface film greatly enhances their resistance to oxidation and impingement corrosion. They have excellent strength—stronger than the phosphor bronzes, even at temperatures up to 500°F (260°C). Typical corrosion rates for the aluminum bronzes, in terms of thickness loss, are on the order of 0.47 mil (0.012 mm) after 24 years! Alloy C61000 is typical of the aluminum bronzes.

They do, however, have a tendency toward intergranular corrosion, although this is seldom a problem in normal boating applications. More significant for us, aluminum bronze is susceptible to *dealuminification*, a form of dealloying that is similar to dezincification, only it is the aluminum that dissolves out. The result is the same, a seriously weakened fitting. When nickel is added in substantial amounts, say 4 percent or more, the problem is effectively overcome. The nickel also adds strength. These alloys are referred to as the *nickel-aluminum bronzes* (NAB).

Manganese also adds strength, and alloys with both nickel and manganese added are commonly called *nickel-aluminum-manganese bronzes* (e.g., C63000). Both nickel-aluminum bronzes and nickel-aluminum-manganese bronzes are frequently used for prop shafts and props and also for heavy-duty bolts. They are excellent in these applications.

Silicon Bronzes

The silicon bronzes are probably the most familiar of the bronze alloys in the boating community. These are basically copper plus 1 to 3 percent silicon and are well known for strength and excellent corrosion resistance. Silicon bronze is widely used in all sorts of marine hardware, in heat exchanger tubing, and even in boat shafting when of the appropriate temper. Everdur is the trade name of a popular and widely used family of silicon bronze fastenings—boat nails, screws, nuts, bolts, and other hardware.

They have excellent corrosion resistance, both to atmospheric exposures and when immersed in seawater.

Typical corrosion rates for silicon bronze in marine atmospheres is on the order of 0.054 mil/yr. (0.0014 mm/yr.), and in seawater, approximately 0.83 mil (0.021 mm) after 20 years of immersion. However, the silicon bronzes are what is called "hot-short." This is a tendency to crack when the part is subjected to mechanical stress in a critical temperature range. It is due to the presence of a low-melting-temperature constituent at the grain boundaries and can occur, for example, at temperatures of about 700°C to 800°C (1,290°F to 1,475°F)—the kind of elevated temperatures that might occur during welding or brazing. Minute cracking (microfissuring) occurs, which may be visible only under a magnifying glass but which can seriously weaken the fitting. Here's a place where the talents of a knowledgeable, experienced welder are indicated.

Gunmetal (Tin Bronze)

Before we had the Unified Numbering System, and before we had the large number of alloy types and grades we have today, widely used alloys were referred to by trade names or, frequently, by nicknames derived from the common usage. Some of these alloys are still "gainfully employed" in the marine industry. Gunmetal is one such type, a fine alloy still in current usage.

Basically, the gunmetals are 88 percent copper plus some 6 to 10 percent tin. Also referred to as G-bronze (C90300) and M-bronze (C92200), gunmetal is currently used in pumps, shafts, and valves (and, still, ordnance). A major use of gunmetal was as a marine fastener material, but this application has largely been taken over by the 91 to 98 percent copper, 1 to 4 percent silicon bronzes (C63700, C65100, C65500, C65520, C66100) popularly known by the trade name Everdur.

COPPER-NICKEL ALLOYS

The copper-nickel alloys, popularly called *cupronickels*, are a family of copper-base alloys that have nickel as the principal alloying element. The addition of nickel to copper improves its strength and also its resistance to corrosion erosion and cavitation in salt, brackish, fresh, and even polluted waters. Cupronickels have excellent resistance to stress-corrosion cracking and corrosion fatigue and also good resistance to biofouling. They are available in both wrought and cast forms.

Taken altogether—strength, durability, corrosion resistance, resistance to marine fouling, good weldability, and ease of fabrication—the characteristics of cupronickel make it the ideal material for hull plates. Why would anyone build a boat out of anything else? Cost! This stuff's not cheap.

Boats have been built with copper-nickel hulls, though. *Copper Mariner*, although not the first or the only copper-nickel vessel, is an excellent example. This 69-foot (20.4 m) shrimp trawler was built in 1971, a joint effort of the International Nickel Company and the Copper Development Association. The objective was to determine whether the characteristic resistance to corrosion and marine fouling of a 90–10 copper-nickel would result in sufficient savings in fuel and maintenance costs to justify the use of copper-nickel hulls. *Copper Mariner* produced a return on investment of 13 to 17 percent (after taxes) in fewer than 7 years. After 20 years of commercial operations the hull had required no maintenance, nor had it shown any significant signs of general or pitting corrosion.

A second shrimp trawler, *Copper Mariner II*, was built in 1976. Other boats soon followed. Fire boats, pilot boats, and even yachts have since been built of copper-nickel or a composite of a 90–10 copper-nickel clad on to carbon steel (a more cost-effective construction method). But a copper-nickel hull remains difficult to justify on the basis of cost-effectiveness for noncommercial boats and yachts and where the length of ownership is too short for the owner or builder to realize the benefits.

The two most popular copper-nickel alloys contain 10 percent nickel (C70600, C96200) and 30 percent nickel (C71500, C96400). Both contain small amounts of manganese, which increases corrosion resistance, and iron, which increases the alloy's resistance to erosion corrosion. Chromium can be used in partial replacement of some of the iron to add additional strength (C72200). Copper-nickel alloys are truly outstanding metals for the marine environment, but cost has prevented them from being used as extensively in boating and yachting equipment as one might expect (or hope). See table A7-22 (page 288) for the chemical and mechanical properties of the copper-nickels and their typical uses.

NICKEL SILVERS

The nickel silvers get their name from their color, which tends to be more whitish yellow than the other copper alloys. They are used primarily as base metals for flatware, musical instruments, costume jewelry, and other products. They are not used to any significant extent in the marine industry.

CORROSION OF THE COPPER-BASE ALLOYS

Like most other metals, copper and copper-base alloys get their characteristic corrosion resistance from the oxide films that form on their surfaces. This protective film—typically cuprous oxide—forms very quickly when clean alloys are first exposed to seawater. The film is approximately 50 percent complete within the first hour or so, 75 percent complete in a week, and very nearly fully complete in about three months. The film continues to build and corrosion rates continue to decrease over time.

Atmospheric Corrosion

Corrosion rates in marine atmospheres are extremely small, typically around 0.12 mil or less per year (<0.003 mm/yr.) initially, then decreasing to about 0.04 mil. (0.001 mm/yr.). There are some corrosion rate differences between alloys, but these are less significant than the differences caused by such environmental factors as humidity, temperature, the length of time that the surface remains wet, and the amount and

nature of any pollutants that may be present in the atmosphere.

The design of the part or structure can have a significant effect on the extent of corrosive damage it may suffer. Free drainage that prevents accumulations of rain or salt water helps to minimize atmospheric corrosion. So do smooth and polished surfaces.

Immersion Corrosion

Immersion corrosion rates are also extremely low and show the same tendency to decrease with time. The long-term corrosion rate of copper alloys is on the order of 1.0 mil/yr. (0.025 mm/yr.). The copper-nickels are even better at around 0.04 mil/yr. (0.001 mm/yr.).

Polluted waters have been found to be the major cause of early failures in condenser and heat exchanger tubing aboard vessels that spend significant amounts of time at their moorings. Harbor cleanup programs and the establishment of environmental pollution controls have diminished levels of pollution in many harbors, but this remains a problem in many locations. Particularly detrimental are sulfate-reducing bacteria in bottom mud and sediment and on the natural sulfates in seawater. Also, decaying plant and animal matter in seawater lie stagnant in raw-water piping systems on the boat.

Even the 90–10 copper-nickels (e.g., C70600) are susceptible to levels of sulfide concentrations as low as 0.01 milligrams per liter. There are chemical inhibitors that can be introduced into the cooling water to prevent this from happening, but this is cost prohibitive in a "once-through" cooling system. In a practical sense, preventive measures for the average boatowner are limited to the use of closed cooling systems or not allowing seawater to lie stagnant in the system.

Galvanic Corrosion

Generally speaking, the copper-base alloys are galvanically compatible with each other in seawater. There are, as you can see from the galvanic series, slight differences in the corrosion potentials of the various copper-base alloys. For example, the copper-nickels are slightly more noble (cathodic) than copper-base alloys that do not contain nickel. However, the differences are so slight—typically less than 0.16 V—as not to pose a problem unless the ratio of the area of the cathodic surface to that of the anodic surface is very large.

Erosion Corrosion

The corrosion resistance of the copper-base alloys depends on the growth and maintenance of a protective oxide layer that forms on the surface. Flowing seawater can erode this surface layer. The higher the flow velocity, the greater the erosion corrosion potential.

The presence of small amounts of iron and manganese in the alloy increases its resistance to erosion corrosion, and the addition of chromium further improves erosion-corrosion resistance. Alloy C72200, a copper-nickel with all three, offers the greatest resistance to erosion corrosion. Tests have shown that in water velocities up to 32 ft./sec. (9.75 m/sec.), C72200 showed no signs of attack while C71500 and C70600 both suffered damage at water velocities as low as 15 ft./sec. (4.57 m/sec.).

The message here is that it is highly desirable to pay attention to and control water velocities (pipe diameters, pump capacities, constrictions, obstructions, etc.), even with the best of the copper-base alloys.

Biofouling

All copper alloys have an inherent resistance to biofouling, which makes them attractive for applications in heat exchanger and condenser tubing, piping, and other parts of seawater cooling systems. By biofouling we refer to such biological fouling as barnacles, mussels, and other such marine invertebrates. As mentioned above, actual operational experience with trawlers and private yachts built with C70600 or C71500 hull plate has demonstrated excellent biofouling resistance and significant reduction in fuel and hull-maintenance costs.

However, some minimum amount of corrosion must be taking place for this biofouling prevention to occur. The exact process is complex and a bit esoteric for our purpose, but what is meaningful for us is that the resistance to fouling is a result of the corrosion process. If this is prevented, say by cathodic protection, fouling by marine organisms is likely to occur.

Dealloying

Brasses and nickel silvers that contain more than 15 percent zinc are susceptible to dealloying—dezincification, in this case. The higher the proportion of zinc, the greater the damage. With the advent of the inhibited grades, dealloying is not so frequently encountered nowadays, making many brasses perfectly suitable for use in light-duty interior applications aboard boats.

The aluminum bronzes are also susceptible to dealloying (dealuminification). Here the preventive is proper welding techniques and heat treatment. Unless you are especially skilled in the mystic arts of welding, it is well to engage the services of a professional when working with aluminum bronze.

SUMMARY

The copper alloys are an impressive family of marine metals. In terms of desirable properties for applications in the marine environment, these metals have it all—excellent corrosion resistance, resistance to marine fouling, weldability, ease of fabrication, a broad range of strengths, ductility, and more. The few shortcomings are all readily dealt with by proper alloy selection and proper joining and fabrication methods.

Although there may be little we can do to ensure that appropriate grades are used in the fixtures, fittings, and equipment we find on our boats, we can take pains to inquire as to the materials used, or we can buy only from manufacturers with a reputation for high quality. It may cost a little more initially, but, as the saying goes, you get what you pay for.

CHAPTER 12

Other Marine Metals

A number of other metallic materials can be found on boats performing useful and sometimes critical functions in vessel systems. They are, in most cases, susceptible to corrosion or participate in and contribute to galvanic couples, so we should discuss them briefly.

TIN

Tin is rarely used as a stand-alone material. It is soft and has low strength and a low melting point, not really desirable characteristics for a marine structural metal. Tin's primary use is as a coating on steel, commonly referred to as *tinplate*. The principal use of tinplate is in packaging and containers, such as "tin" cans (which really aren't tin—they're 99 percent steel). In this form the coating is extremely thin—0.004 to 0.08 mil (0.0001 to 2 mm)—and offers little corrosion protection except in the mildest of indoor environments.

Heavier tin coatings, up to 1.2 mils (0.03 mm), are used in the production of electrical and electronic components, such as connectors, wire, fastenings, and bus bars. Tin coatings have been studied extensively in all kinds of atmospheres, with the studies concluding that the protection offered by even a heavy coat of tin is not very high in outdoor environments. The significance of this for us is in the components and fittings that we use in our electrical systems, such as terminal strips, circuit blocks, ring and spade connectors, wire terminals, and lugs. It is logical that lower-quality components will have the thinner coatings, but even the best of these should be protected from the environment.

We have already seen tin used as an alloying element to enhance corrosion resistance. It is also use to create bearing alloys and in tin-base soft solders.

Bearings

We're talking here primarily about *plain bearings*—that is, bearings that provide a sliding contact between mating surfaces such as rotating shafts or journals. Plain bearings are used in electric motors and generators, as main and connecting rod bearings in gasoline and diesel engines, and in marine gear units. The bearing material is typically a thin coating cast most frequently on steel strip but sometimes on bronze or brass. Tin- and lead-base babbitt (also referred to as *white metal*) alloys are probably the best-known bearing materials.

The tin-base bearing alloys typically contain 87.5 to 89 percent tin, 6.75 to 7.5 percent antimony, and 3.5 to 5.75 percent copper. The lead-base alloys contain from 75 to 92 percent lead, 3.5 to 15 percent antimony, and 1 to 10 percent tin. Both are resistant to the corrosive effects of the acids sometimes formed in lubricating oils under operating conditions, but—as you might expect from the combination of metals used in them—they do not respond well to salt water, especially the tin-base alloys. These have been known to develop a hard, crusty oxidation product in marine use. The potential for galvanic action between tin-base bearing alloys and the steel backing makes them unsuitable for any use that might include exposure to seawater.

Solders

Soldering is a method of joining metals by the use lead- or tin-base alloys with melting points below 800°F (427°C). It is sometimes referred to as *soft* soldering. Brazing is similar but uses *hard* solders—sometimes called *silver solders* or *spelter (zinc) solders*—with melting points higher than 800°F.

Soldering is a convenient method of joining two metals primarily to achieve an efficient electrical connection or a tight seal. Soldered joints lack strength and should not be relied upon for the mechanical integrity of the joint.

The soft solders can contain anywhere from 1 to 95 percent tin and from 30 to 97.5 percent lead. Some also contain small amounts of antimony or silver. More than 20 types of soft solders are in common use. The most popular for general-purpose soldering are 60–40 (lead-tin), 50–50, and 35–65.

There are two factors that have a significant influence on the corrosion behavior of soldered joints: the use of fluxes and the area of the soldered joint with respect to the area of the metals being joined.

A good solder joint requires clean and oxide-free surfaces. Flux is applied to remove any oxide film and to keep it from reforming. Rosin flux is used for electrical soldering because the residue is noncorrosive and nonconducting. Rosin is effective in preventing the formation of oxide films but is not effective in removing oxide films already formed. Stronger fluxes such as zinc chloride and ammonium chloride (also called sal ammoniac) are very good at removing oxide films, but the residue from these fluxes is corrosive and must be removed.

With regard to the area effect, this is the same old cathode-to-anode-area ratio problem we have discussed before. Check the positions of the metals in the galvanic series. The most favorable condition is when the solder is more noble than the metals being joined. When the reverse is true, the solder will be attacked if it is immersed in seawater.

I have already mentioned the low mechanical strength of soldered joints. This is not just an issue with electrical wiring connections; fuel and gas lines and, perhaps less obvious, raw-water piping need other means of support for components joined in this way. I should also point out that all commonly used solders melt at approximately 361°F (592°C), so in the event of a fire

aboard, soldered joints may fail and release the fuel, gas, or water.

LEAD

Lead is soft, weak, and very heavy; it is a poor conductor of both heat and electricity and poses health risks under certain conditions. Despite these apparent character flaws, lead has features that make it a very useful metal, and even its seemingly unattractive traits make it the material of choice for some marine applications.

Lead and lead-base alloys are used in applications where an inexpensive corrosion-resistant metal is called for and where strength and hardness are not essential. In the marine industry, lead finds application primarily in solder, lead-acid batteries, and as ballast, where its heavy weight is a valuable feature. Lead is about 60 percent heavier than cast iron and more than four times heavier than cement or fire brick.

Lead is a fairly noble metal with a corrosion potential range of –0.19 to –0.23 volts. The protective films that form on lead and its alloys are very effective, and normal atmospheric corrosion is essentially negligible—less than 0.070 mil/yr. (0.0018 mm/yr.). Lead roofing has survived for hundreds of years. As a matter of fact, if the protective films are not damaged, the expected life of lead in normal atmospheres is unlimited.

In natural and domestic waters, corrosion rates depend on water hardness. In hard water—water with greater than 125 ppm calcium and magnesium salts—the protective films are reinforced. However, this can be countered by chloride ions, if also present in the water, which inhibit the formation of the protective film and may even penetrate it. This is the circumstance with seawater, but even in this environment, corrosion rates remain quite low—typically less than 0.60 mil/yr. (0.015 mm/yr.).

Oxide films are not as hard or as protective in soft water (<125 ppm), and corrosion rates depend more on the concentrations of dissolved carbon dioxide and oxygen in the water. Potable water frequently is soft and has considerable quantities of carbon dioxide and oxygen. Corrosion rates in normal domestic waters containing chlorine are on the order of 0.38 mil/yr. (0.0006 mm/yr.). This is sufficient to prohibit its use for containing potable waters, which are not permitted to have lead content exceeding 0.05 ppm.

The usual precautionary statements must be made concerning galvanic corrosion. When lead is in contact with other metals less noble than itself, it can suffer galvanic attack, depending on the difference in potentials and relative surface areas. Protective measures are required—either coating (painting) or cathodic protective systems. Lead is also susceptible to corrosive damage from stray currents.

Although it doesn't happen very often, I should mention (just so I can say I told you so) that lead is susceptible to bacterial corrosion when organic matter is present and aeration is poor, such as in mud. Further, the decomposition of hydrocarbons present in some coatings can produce acids that may attack lead.

A significant weakness of lead is its low "creep" strength. Creep is the tendency of a metal under stress to change its dimensions. For example, a lead pipe suspended at its ends will have a tendency to sag in the middle. When this occurs, it exposes new surfaces that are not as yet protected by protective films. In a corrosive environment these areas will suffer corrosive damage. Pure lead is especially susceptible. Lead alloys with small amounts of antimony or tin are less susceptible and are the ones that should be used for external lead ballast keels.

Lead castings can also be susceptible to intergranular corrosion along grain boundaries. This is not a frequent occurrence, but it can cause a significant loss in strength—so it's something to keep an eye on.

A final word of caution is in order. Lead can be hazardous to your health if proper precautions are not taken during casting, melting, pouring, shaping, and even cleaning. Even alloys containing as little as 5 percent lead can give off dangerous fumes. Lead is readily absorbed into the blood by inhaling fumes and by ingestion. The effects are cumulative, and continued exposure can result in lead poisoning. Children are especially susceptible. Proper precautions involve good ventilation and the use of a respirator designed for protection against metal fumes.

ZINC

Zinc is used in electric fuses, roofing and gutter materials, pharmaceutical compounds, plant food, and wide variety of other applications, but on a boat zinc is synonymous with sacrificial anodes. It also has important marine applications as an alloying element—as we've already seen—and as a protective coating.

Sacrificial Anodes

We know that when two metals in electrical contact are immersed in an electrolyte, the more anodic metal will corrode preferentially, thus protecting the more noble metal. Zinc, being more anodic than all other metals in the galvanic series except magnesium, is intentionally placed in close proximity to the metal fitting to be protected and electrically connected to it. The zinc then corrodes sacrificially, protecting the fitting.

A zinc anode must be more than 99 percent pure zinc if it is to function efficiently. Even minute amounts of iron or lead greatly degrade performance, so just any old piece of junkyard zinc won't do. Zinc anodes are commercially available in all manner of shapes and sizes for installation on shafts, rudders, outboard motor lower units, and inside engine cooling systems.

Galvanized Coatings

One of the simplest methods of preventing or at least retarding corrosion is to coat the metal surface to prevent moisture and oxygen from reaching it. Zinc is used extensively for this purpose. Not only is a zinc coating impermeable to moisture and oxygen, corrosion and abrasion resistant, and tightly bonded to the metal surface, but the zinc also forms an anodic coating that protects the metal substrate electrochemically. It functions as a cathodic protector even when there are small breaks in the coating.

The two basic methods of coating metal with zinc are electroplating and hot-dip galvanizing. Typically, electroplated coatings range from 0.2

to 1.0 mil (0.005 to 0.025 mm), depending on the service conditions. Hot-dip galvanizing produces thicker coatings that range from about 6.8 to 11.9 mils (0.172 to 0.32 mm). Since the life of a galvanized steel is directly related to the thickness of the coating, hot dipping is the preferred process for longer life.

In normal atmospheres, zinc has a high degree of resistance to corrosion, typically in the area of 0.005 to 0.5 mil/yr. (0.00013 to 0.013 mm/yr.), but it can suffer dramatically from industrial pollutants. Corrosion rates in hard waters are on the order of 0.6 mil/yr. (0.015 mm/yr.), and somewhat higher in soft waters due to lower concentrations of calcium and magnesium salts and higher concentrations of carbon dioxide and oxygen. The high chloride content of the seawater tends to inhibit the formation of protective films, resulting in a higher corrosion rate initially, but it levels off after a couple of years to about the same level as that in freshwater. In any case, zinc-coated steel should not be used in applications where it is exposed to seawater without protective coatings.

Castings

Zinc alloys are also used for small castings of such boat fittings as cleats, chocks, and strap eyes. Most of these castings are made from two zinc alloys, AG40A and AC41A, commonly referred to as *pot metal*. Zamak is one popular trade name for pot-metal fittings. Zinc alloys are popular with hardware makers because they are inexpensive, require low casting heat, and die-cast well. Most pot metal parts intended for marine use are chrome plated for appearance, but they lack the strength of fittings made from stainless steel or bronze. They also are susceptible to serious degradation of their mechanical properties, losing as much as 30 percent of their tensile strength and up to 70 percent of their impact strength, even in atmospheric exposures.

TITANIUM

Combining high strength with low weight and outstanding corrosion resistance, titanium alloys have long been a mainstay of the aircraft industry. It is an equally attractive marine metal, and titanium alloy pin and snap shackles, U-bolts, eye straps, swivels, backstay adjusters, and other fittings can be found on high-performance racing sailboats. The cost of titanium fittings remains sobering, but it is encouraging to note that the titanium producers consider the consumer marine market to be of great importance in terms of potential future demand for such items as propellers, shafts, collars, struts, stanchions, and a variety of deck and rigging fittings.

The atmospheric corrosion resistance of titanium alloys is excellent. They tend to form a highly adherent, protective oxide film that, if damaged, will instantaneously repair itself. Corrosion rates less than 1.5 mils/yr. (0.038 mm/yr.) are typical. Titanium is highly noble (−0.05 to +0.06 volts), but it is easily polarized, which tends to minimize its galvanic effect on other metals. It has a high affinity for hydrogen and oxygen and thus is susceptible to embrittlement in galvanic couples.

MAGNESIUM

At about two-thirds the weight of aluminum, magnesium alloys offer real advantages in a variety of industrial applications. However, magnesium is the most anodic of the metals in the galvanic series and is highly susceptible to galvanic corrosion. With the exception of its use in emergency flares, magnesium has little application in the marine industry.

URANIUM

In the 1970s and 1980s, there was a flurry of interest in depleted uranium for use as ballast keels in sailing yachts. Because of uranium's great density—more than twice that of cast iron and 25 percent more than lead—the keel could be very thin and compact, reducing drag and improving performance. This advantage was very attractive to racing sailors, and some racing sailboats were built with depleted uranium keels. However, the International Yacht Racing Union subsequently outlawed the use of this material in the 1980s.

There is credible evidence that the dust produced when depleted uranium is being worked is both radioactive and toxic. The material is also nasty stuff to machine, to cast, or to do just about anything else with. Given its cost, limited availability (at the consumer level), special handling requirements (machining, plating for corrosion and personnel protection), and the limited size of the community that is susceptible to its appeal (racing sailors with lots of money), depleted uranium has not achieved any appreciable use in the marine industry.

CARBON-FIBER COMPOSITES

Carbon-fiber composites consist of carbon fibers embedded in a polymer matrix—similar to fiberglass but with carbon fibers substituted for the glass fibers. The specific type and processing of the fibers as well as their orientation in the matrix are critical to the performance of the material. Fiber orientation can be unidirectional (parallel to each other), woven, or even three-dimensional. Carbon-fiber composites offer low weight, high strength, high abrasion resistance, and great workability, and they are easily formed into complex shapes.

Originally developed in the aerospace industry, carbon fiber found some limited use in the marine industry as far back as the 1970s. Today the material is widely used in masts, rudders, tiller and tiller extensions, propeller shaft sleeves, and even in sailboat hulls, all primarily in pursuit of improved boat performance. Carbon-fiber masts, for example, are stiffer and about half the weight of aluminum masts. Reducing weight aloft markedly improves performance. Using carbon fibers in hull construction provides greater stiffness for the same or less weight. This reduces hull deformation when the boat is being driven hard, which has a great effect on hull speed.

However, (and there's always a "however"), carbon fiber does have some unattractive features. Aside from the cost—a carbon fiber mast can cost twice as much as a comparable aluminum mast—carbon fiber has very high electrical conductivity. This is a potential problem in the event of a lightning strike, and it introduces potential problems of galvanic and electrolytic corrosion. We talk more about carbon fiber in chapter 21.

SUMMARY

Tin, lead, and zinc all have a proud legacy of going to sea, and these long-standing workhorses are still doing their jobs today. Uranium has come and gone. Two other relative newcomers, titanium and carbon-fiber composites, hold great promise as costs decline and familiarity rises.

CHAPTER 13

Cathodic Protection Systems

Cathodic protection has been around since the early 1800s when it was first used to control corrosion on British warships. It has been widely used in the United States for many years to protect pipelines carrying natural gas and petroleum and on offshore oil production platforms. And, as many of us can attest, it's been used for years on recreational and commercial boats. It's a tried-and-true method of corrosion prevention and protection when properly designed, installed, and maintained.

All cathodic protection schemes operate on the basis of the galvanic corrosion process, so like galvanic corrosion, cathodic protection systems require an anode, a cathode, an electrical connection between the two, and an electrolyte. *Cathodic protection cannot occur if any of these four things is missing.* Somehow this seems to be a difficult message to get across.

Every few years a marvelous new cathodic protection product appears on the market, promising to prevent corrosion in automobiles despite the absence of an electrolyte. Sales are brisk until word of their ineffectiveness spreads or until some member of the corrosion engineering fraternity, offended by the producer's claims to have overcome the fundamental laws of electrochemistry, challenges them. Usually, there follows a brief flurry of litigation (or mutual threats) and sharply falling sales, and the miraculous mechanism fades into obscurity—alas, only to rise again a few years or continents removed.

The fact is that air is a very poor electrolyte. It does not allow current to flow and complete the circuit. All four elements, at least at this stage of development of electrochemical science, are required.

When we discussed multimetal corrosion in chapter 6, we said that the difference in corrosion potentials of two metals immersed in the same electrolyte causes electrons to flow from the metal with the more negative potential (anode) to the metal with the less negative potential (cathode). Electrons arriving at the cathode increase its negative potential. Concurrently, the negative potential of the anode decreases. The flow of electrons continues until the two metals are at the same potential, that is, until there is no voltage difference between them. In the cathodic protection system, we purposely provide a source for the supply of electrons to the metal we want to protect. The larger the surface area of the cathode, the more electrons required.

TYPES OF CATHODIC PROTECTION SYSTEM

There are two basic types of cathodic protection systems. In a sacrificial anode system—called *passive protection*—we intentionally add a metal to the circuit to supply the electrons to the cathode. Sacrificial anode systems are simple, require little but regular maintenance (checking and replacement), and have low installation cost for smaller vessels. In impressed-current systems—known as *active protection*—we supply the electrons from a specially designed power supply system and controller. Impressed-current systems are more complex, more efficient, especially in large systems, and more costly. If they malfunction, they can cause serious problems.

Impressed Current Systems

The impressed-current type of cathodic protection system depends on an external source of direct current. Alternating current cannot be used since the protected metal would likewise be alternating—between anodic and cathodic. Basically, an anode immersed in the electrolyte (sea-water) is connected to one side of a DC power supply, and the metal to be protected is connected to the other side. The galvanic current flow (quantity of electrons) is detected and measured against a reference electrode. If unfavorable, current flow is adjusted automatically by the power supply control system to compensate.

We need to be careful here in discussing these connections in terms of positive and negative terminals. The sign conventions used in the United States are the opposite of those used in much of the scientific and international community. The important point to remember is that *the electrons must flow into the structure* to be protected.

Impressed-current systems are considerably more complex and more expensive than sacrificial anode systems, but they have some very attractive features. They can develop much higher voltages than sacrificial anode systems, so they can either "push" current through lower-conductivity electrolytes (e.g., soil, freshwater, concrete) or through longer distances (e.g., larger vessels, longer pipelines, offshore platforms). They function automatically and at precisely the appropriate levels to achieve their purpose. And, depending on the currents drawn and the size of the anode, they can last considerably longer than sacrificial anodes.

Disadvantages include the possibility of "overprotecting" certain metals. This can cause hydrogen embrittlement in high-strength steels. With aluminum it can result in accelerated corrosion of the very structure we're trying to protect.

Another potential problem is the debonding of organic protective coatings (paint). Small amounts of moisture migrate through the coating over time, and the impressed current generates hydrogen gas on the protected metal surface. The pressure developed by the gas causes the coating to blister and crack. This exposes more metal on the cathode, demanding more current—eventually, perhaps, more than the power supply can provide.

The current demanded from the impressed-current system power supply will vary depending on salinity, amount of pollution in the surrounding water, condition of the anodes, and speed of the boat. These systems require careful monitoring and maintenance, and the current flow must be maintained and controlled. Finally, impressed-current systems, if not properly installed and maintained, can cause stray-current corrosion.

The general consensus is that large vessels or structures, with full-time, skilled crew, may be better able to benefit from the better efficiency and lower maintenance costs of an impressed-current system. However, Mercury Marine has offered an impressed-current protection for its inboard-outboard engines for many years.

Sacrificial Anode Systems

We already know that when metals are in a galvanic couple, the difference in their corrosion potentials causes the anodic (least noble) metal to corrode and release metallic ions into the electrolyte. Since the least noble, or more negative, metal in the circuit always corrodes first, we can control the corrosion by simply adding to the circuit a metal that has two characteristics:

- It has a corrosion potential more negative than the metal we're trying to protect.
- It is expendable, that is, not essential to the operation of the system.

This added component is called a *sacrificial* anode.

A word about galvanic *couples*: the term *couples* does not refer to quantity, as in two, but rather to a joining together or coupling. There can be (and often are) more than two metals involved. It is better to think of these as galvanic *circuits*. The least noble of all of the metals in the "circuit" corrodes first, then the next least noble, and so on. If the boat has a bonding system, widely separated metal fittings may be part of this galvanic circuit. And, as we have already noted, if your boat has a shore power system, other boats in the marina may also be part of a galvanic circuit.

Typical onboard galvanic couples are props and prop shafts, metal rudders and rudderposts, stainless steel screws in an aluminum spar (wetted by spray), and dissimilar metals in raw-water cooling systems.

All right, we've decided we are going to sacrifice some poor, less noble (unfortunate choice of terms) metal as a sacrificial anode to protect our more noble fittings. So, which metal is to be our sacrificial lamb? Any metal less noble than the metal we want to protect will do the job, but some metals are both more efficient in this role and less costly. Typically, sacrificial anodes are one of three metals—aluminum, magnesium, or zinc.

Aluminum

Aluminum, at a corrosion potential of about −0.76 to −1.00 volts, is an excellent sacrificial anode material. It is used extensively in seawater applications in the offshore industries where its light weight is a significant advantage. Properly alloyed for this application (small amounts of tin or antimony), it does not passivate—develop a corrosion resistant protective film—in seawater.

Aluminum does have some shortcomings: it is susceptible to erosion in fast-moving water, it tends to suffer from pitting corrosion at elevated temperatures, and it is not as efficient as zinc. Also, often it is aluminum that we want to protect.

Aluminum alloy anodes are found in boat applications primarily on some outboard and inboard-outboard engines. They last longer than zinc but are not as rugged and must be used in places on the engines where they do not bear a load or serve a structural purpose.

Magnesium

Magnesium has a corrosion potential of between −1.60 and −1.63 volts and is therefore much more active than both aluminum and zinc. At first glance this would seem to make magnesium preferable even to zinc. The problem is that magnesium is too active. At these high corrosion potentials, the current generated can damage surrounding paint.

Magnesium anodes are regularly used for the protection of soil-buried structures such as pipelines. They were tried in the offshore industries, without much success. They do find use in some marine applications on outboard and inboard-outboard engines, but only in freshwater. Sometimes they are also used in onboard hot-water heaters. Magnesium anodes should *not* be used in salt water.

Zinc

At a corrosion potential between −0.98 and −1.03 volts, zinc is more active than aluminum and less active than magnesium. Zinc anodes are widely used in both freshwater and seawater for a wide variety of protection applications. They are also used extensively in the offshore oil and pipeline industries.

Zinc is particularly well suited to use on vessels that spend time both in harbor and estuarine waters and offshore. (Pollutants in harbors and estuaries tend to cause aluminum anodes to passivate.) Zinc anodes are used to protect metal hulls, tanks, engines, heat exchangers, oil coolers, props and shafts, rudders and rudderposts, trim tabs, and innumerable other fittings and fixtures.

It's critically important that the zinc anodes be extremely pure. The American Society for Testing and Materials (ASTM) standard B418 calls for 99.5 percent pure zinc for Type 1 and 99.99 percent for Type 2. The American Boat and Yacht Council recommends a minimum purity of 99.5 percent (standard E-2, Cathodic Protection of Boats). Zincs available from marine chandlers should satisfy these minimum requirements.

Anode Installation

Whichever type of sacrificial anode is used, it must have sufficient surface area to supply enough electrons to protect all of the exposed cathodic surfaces. It should have sufficient mass to last a reasonable length of time, and it must be electrically connected to the fitting or component you want to protect. Check sacrificial anodes a couple of times each season and replace any that are 50 percent depleted.

Sacrificial anodes must not be painted. This has been said so many times in boating books and magazines that I almost hesitate to add my voice to the chorus, but you'd be astonished at how often I see boats with zincs covered with bottom paint. *Zincs don't work when painted.*

That only leaves us with questions about how many zincs, how big they should be, and where we should put them. For information on designing a protective system for your boat, refer to appendix 3, Quantity, Size, and Placement of Zinc Anodes.

CHAPTER 14

Corrosion Avoidance

Cathodic protection is not, as you have probably guessed, the only method for dealing with corrosion problems on the boat. Corrosion avoidance begins in the design process. Although corrosion concerns may ultimately take a back seat to structural integrity, they should be a consideration. Good maintenance practices are another way of avoiding corrosion, things as simple as rinsing away salt accumulations and avoiding standing water.

Corrosion protection systems, for the most part, are designed to *control* corrosion, not necessarily *eliminate* it. The goal is to reduce the rate of corrosion to a level that will allow the part, fitting, or structure to perform its function satisfactorily, safely, and reliably over its expected lifetime. Aside from cathodic protection systems, the following methods are available to us:

- change the materials of construction
- alter structural design features
- change the environment
- apply coatings of various types

We look at coatings in the next chapter. For now, let's begin with what we can do during design and construction.

MATERIALS SELECTION

The use of high-quality materials appropriate for the specific application is our first line of defense. For applications below the waterline, this generally means bronze, cupronickels, and perhaps one of the superaustenitic or duplex stainless steels. Above the waterline it means stainless steels, marine-grade aluminum, and maybe certain of the inhibited brasses. It also means avoiding uninhibited brasses and unprotected carbon steel. The specific choice of materials will be determined by a number of factors—required

mechanical properties, expected lifetime, consequences of failure, aesthetics, personal preferences and, of course, budget.

Materials selection is not just the first step. It is also the simplest way to ensure satisfactory performance, from the perspective of corrosion resistance. We have two distinct concerns—the innate corrosion resistance of the metal itself and its behavior when coupled with other metals. We found earlier that the metals and alloys high (most noble) on the galvanic scale have the greatest inherent resistance to corrosion in seawater. That means we want to consult the galvanic series before we select any metal to use in the marine environment.

If the fitting is to be in contact with another metal, the galvanic series again serves us well. When selecting metals that will be in direct contact with each other in seawater, the goal is to choose metals as close in the series as possible. When the difference in their corrosion potentials is less than 0.20 volts (200 millivolts), galvanic corrosion will proceed at an extremely slow rate, and the metals will not normally need additional protection. If the difference is greater than 0.2 volts, the metals must be insulated from each other, or you will need to provide some form of protection.

Ideally, you want to avoid mixing metals underwater. Fasten bronze hardware with bronze fastenings, stainless steel hardware with stainless steel fastenings, and so on. This goes a long way toward preventing galvanic corrosion. Where this isn't possible, use fastenings as close as possible in the galvanic scale to the part being secured—and preferably more cathodic (noble). The metal lowest in the galvanic scale (most anodic) is the one that corrodes, so if that is the bigger, more massive part, it can better withstand a little corrosion. If it is the smaller, lighter, and often highly stressed fastening that is the least noble, the same amount of corrosion can result in a catastrophic failure. The use of stainless steel screws in aluminum fittings is an example of this strategy.

Keel cooler construction provides an instructive example of materials selection in a difficult and critical application. Functioning like a radiator to dissipate the heat from the engine coolant, keel coolers are mounted outside the hull, under water. They are subject to high-velocity salt water on the outside, turbulent, hot water inside, and hull vibration and flexing; of necessity, they are constructed of dissimilar metals. One popular brand consists of 70–30 cupronickel alloy tubes, solid bronze headers, and Monel fastenings. These metals are all very close to each other in the galvanic scale and all at the cathodic end of the scale; thus they are inherently corrosion resistant. The manufacturer of these coolers reports that some New England lobster fishermen are on their third and fourth boats with the same keel coolers, now 30 to 40 years old. Enough said.

DESIGN AND CONSTRUCTION

Many of us live with (or try to live with) persistent corrosion problems on our boats that have the potential for serious and expensive damage. They are an ever-present source of irritation and the subject of a perpetual search for the *permanent* solution. The conditions that are the root cause of many of these problems were designed or built into the boat by very competent designers and builders who were, alas, not corrosion engineers and for whom corrosion was not the primary concern.

Design decisions are seldom absolute, nor are those of the builder. The list of factors that must be considered includes structural integrity, seaworthiness, seakeeping ability, availability of materials, accommodation requirements, and cost. All necessitate compromises based on some system of priorities. One designer or builder, for example, may recognize a potential corrosion problem area and decide that "regular" maintenance is an acceptable solution. An-

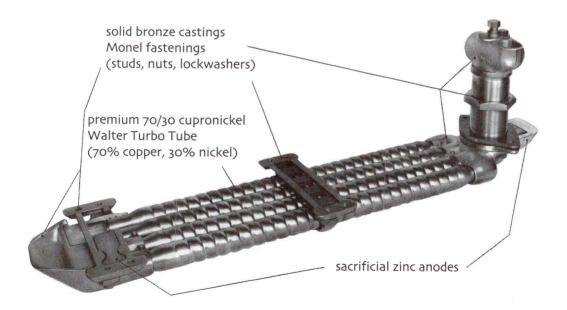

solid bronze castings
Monel fastenings
(studs, nuts, lockwashers)

premium 70/30 cupronickel
Walter Turbo Tube
(70% copper, 30% nickel)

sacrificial zinc anodes

Fig. 14-1. External keel cooler. The use of corrosion-resistant alloys and zinc anodes is shown here.
Walter Machine Company, Inc.

other may choose to "spare no expense" to eliminate the problem. Still others may decide in favor of periodic replacement of the problem component.

Not all of these approaches are optimum for all eventual owners. However, there are some typical situations where a proper choice at the design or build stage can reduce the potential for corrosion. The guiding principle for many of theses choices is the knowledge that corrosion flourishes in stagnant water or mud, where there is a lack of oxygen to establish or maintain the protection films that most metals form on their surfaces. Our assignment (should we choose to accept it) is to identify and eliminate those places in the boat's structure or in its support systems where water can accumulate. That's simple enough, right? Just to make sure, let's consider some examples.

Structures, Shapes, and Surfaces

What we're looking for here are places in the vessel's structure that can collect moisture and have no way for it to drain. The water stands longer in these areas, so the metal stays wet longer. This results in higher corrosion rates.

Remember, we're talking about accumulated moisture, not just rain, spray, or seawater. Relative humidity, the amount of water vapor in the air with respect to the air's saturation limit of air, is frequently a significant factor. For example, carbon steel exhibits very low corrosion rates at relative humidities below 50 percent. However, at relative humidities of 65 percent or more, there is a sharp increase in corrosion rate.

Because most metals readily give up heat, metals on a boat will often be cooler than the surrounding air at night, resulting in condensation on the metal surfaces. If the surface has hygroscopic (moisture-absorbing) dirt, dust, or salts on it—as most surfaces on a boat do—this further compounds the problem.

There are a number of actions we can take to keep moisture from collecting on our boats:

- avoid upturned angle brackets, channels, and the like
- eliminate pockets, dead ends, and the like
- keep surfaces clean and free of debris

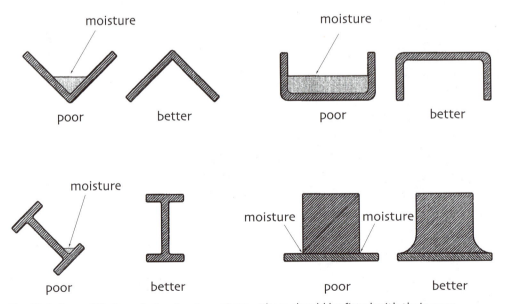

Fig. 14-2. L- and U-shaped structural members. These should be fitted with their open sides down to permit water to drain. Where necessary, fillers should be used to fill the spaces where moisture can collect.

- avoid cracks, crevices, and joints
- grind weld beads down flush with the surface
- eliminate weld splatter

Some of these suggestions are illustrated in figure 14-2.

Also avoid sharp corners and rough, uneven surfaces. Protective coatings on these kinds of surfaces tend to be thinner and more susceptible to wear or chipping damage, exposing unprotected metal (fig. 14-3).

Joints, Cracks, and Crevices

Joints, cracks, and crevices are all sites where dirt, dust, hygroscopic salts, and other debris can collect, become saturated with moisture, and cause accelerated corrosion. What's more, the corrosion loosens the joint, leading to vibration, wear, and fretting (fig. 14-4).

Getting joints "right" is really important. You wouldn't make them if you didn't need them, and they don't get any less important with time. They cannot be allowed to deteriorate without compromising the integrity of their intended function.

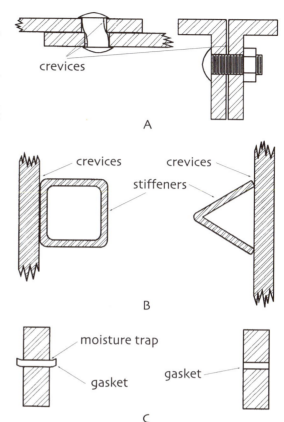

Fig. 14-4. Joints. A. Riveted and bolted joints should be snug, tight, and clean; sloppy or misaligned joints can create crevices. B. Welded joints must be joined with a continuous, smooth bead, leaving no crevices to trap moisture. C. Gaskets should be trimmed flush to prevent moisture traps.

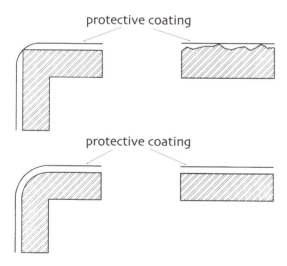

Fig. 14-3. Corners and surfaces. Sharp corners and rough, uneven surfaces should be avoided since protective coatings tend to be thinner in these areas and subject to chipping and abrasion.

Piping, Tubing, and Tanks

Piping and tubing—all plumbing fittings and fixtures, in fact—should be installed with a view to proper drainage. Tubing runs with low spots can leave pools of trapped water in the low places when the system is shut down, leading to unseen corrosion at an accelerated rate.

But with piping we get to worry not just about trapped water but also about high-velocity streams and entrained particles. Fast water can be as destructive as stagnant water, and if sediment (sand, dirt, etc.) is entrained in the stream, the corrosive effect is compounded.

This situation occurs most frequently in the vessel's engine-cooling system.

Constrictions and obstructions—any disturbance to the smooth flow of fluids—can cause damage (fig. 14.5). The damage can be especially severe if the fluid is carrying dirt or other solid particles. For example, a 90° tailpiece on a raw-water seacock is a bad idea. Such situations should be avoided wherever possible. Two 45° elbows would be better. In water and fuel tanks, internal baffles, deflectors, or doubler plates to reduce the effects of liquid movement or impingement streams should be fitted.

Air Circulation and Ventilation

Dirt, debris, paint cloths gone astray, one of my favorite pocket knives—all manner of things have an uncanny ability to find their way into tight spaces where they absorb moisture and cause corrosion problems. Figure 14-6 suggests a few such instances; you'll no doubt think of others.

One final word about mechanical and structural considerations: don't forget what we said about the area ratios of the anode and cathode surfaces. The surface area of the cathode (more noble) metal should be kept small with respect to the surface area of the anode (less noble) metal. Ideally, this is done by selecting appropriate metals. It can also be done by coating (painting) the surface of the cathode (see chapter 15).

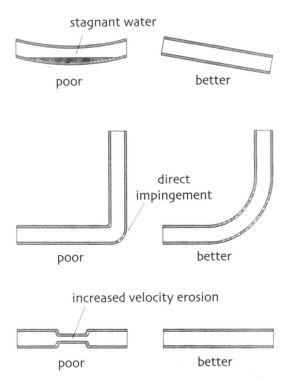

stagnant water

poor   better

direct impingement

poor   better

increased velocity erosion

poor   better

Fig. 14-5. Piping and tubing. Disturbances to flow in piping and tubing can create turbulence and cause impingement damage, so avoid obstructions and constrictions to flow streams. The greater the radius on bends and turns, the better.

INSULATION

We can avoid galvanic corrosion by breaking the electrical contact between dissimilar metals. We do this by inserting a substance between them that functions as an electrical insulator, precluding the possibility of electron flow between the metals. The materials used for these purposes are typically available in sheet or strip form—rubber, Mylar, or plastic electrical tape, respectively—or in squeeze tubes—silicones, polysulfides, or polyurethanes. Generally, sheet and strip materials are faster and easier to work with. With these materials, a gasket is simply cut to shape and inserted between the mating faces. With the products in squeeze tubes, a thin coat is applied to each face of the parts to be joined and is allowed to cure before joining them to avoid bonding the parts together.

In either case, fastenings such as screws and bolts present a separate problem. These are admittedly difficult to do, and several methods are used, with varying degrees of success depending on closeness of fit of the fastening. The fastening may be coated with a *thin* layer of the squeeze tube material and allowed to cure before assembling. Or, better yet, try one of the products discussed further on in the section on proprietary formulations. Another option is the use of *thin-wall* heat-shrink tubing. This tubing with adhesive lining on the inner surface is readily available in wall thicknesses as thin as 0.031 inches, and even less without the adhesive (which is not really necessary in this application), from marine

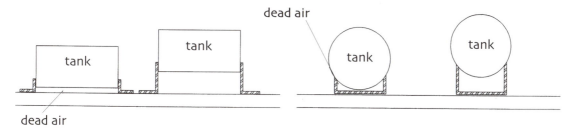

Fig. 14-6. Air circulation and ventilation. Avoid dead air space that can trap dirt and debris. Provide for a free flow of air around tanks and other structures.

supply stores. Thinner wall thicknesses are available from specialty industrial supply houses— 0.002 inches and even down to 0.00015 inches for special applications (and at special prices!). Shrink tubing approximately the same diameter as the fastening is slid over the thread and shank and shrunk with a heat gun, hair dryer or match. None of these methods are foolproof but all are beneficial.

Plastics

Plastics generally fall into two broad categories—thermoplastics and thermosetting plastics. Thermoplastics consist of long polymer chains that *are not* cross-linked (chemically connected to each other). These materials soften when heated and harden when cooled. Some of the more common thermoplastics are polyethylene, polypropylene, polystyrene, nylon, polyvinyl chloride (PVC), and certain polyurethanes.

Thermosetting plastics consist of long polymer chains that *are* cross-linked to each other during the curing process. Thermosetting materials can't be softened by heating. Some of the more common thermosetting plastics in the boating industry are epoxies, polyesters, silicones, and some polyurethanes and rubbers.

Plastics and elastomers (natural and synthetic rubbers, neoprene) are truly remarkable materials with many useful properties. Of interest to us are their excellent electrical insulation properties. They can be applied as thin-, medium- or high-build coatings by brush, roller, spray, dip, or even syringe. However, many plastics have relatively low temperature limits—150°F (66°C)

for polypropylene and 175°F (79°C) for PVC and polyethylene, which rules out their use in engine manifolds and exhaust systems. Above these temperatures the plastics may scorch, char, get brittle, crack, or even burn. Also, their properties may change with time as a result of moisture absorption and other aging factors.

Many plastics are hygroscopic and will absorb water, resulting in swelling and softening under conditions of elevated temperature and pressure. However, natural waters (fresh, brackish, and salt) have little effect on most plastics at normal ambient temperatures. PVC, chlorinated polyvinyl chloride (CPVC), polyethylene (PE), and polypropylene (PP) are excellent insulators in natural-water service and, along with nylon (with glass additives) and vinyl, also find extensive use in small-craft plumbing fittings.

The popular Marelon is actually a glass-reinforced nylon and is widely used in the boating industry for all kinds of plumbing and deck fittings. Nylon is also used for pipe and hose fittings. Fiberglass-reinforced plastics (FRP), either polyester or epoxy based, are used not only for just small-craft hull structures, but also for seawater piping and tanks in offshore and chemical-processing industries. Solid FRP is being used extensively by the energy industry in high-pressure (up to 3,000 psi) piping carrying high-salt-content fluids for considerable distances. According to corrosion specialists in these industries, the benefits are no corrosion, no cathodic protection required, and no bacterial problems. Plastic fittings offer the same advantages to the mariner.

Sealants

Sealants are the chemical compounds normally found at your local chandlery and intended to form watertight and airtight seals between two or more surfaces. Sealants can also be used to insulate one surface from another by applying a thin coat to each surface and allowing the sealant to cure before joining.

Sealants are normally packaged in squeeze tubes or cartridges and have various degrees of adhesive strength. They cure to a tough, flexible, rubbery consistency. The three principal classes are *polyurethanes*, *polysulfides*, and *silicones*.

Polyurethane

The polyurethane sealants are known for their outstanding adhesive strength. They will cure underwater and are used for joints that are intended to be permanent—hull-to-deck joints, portlight frames, and underwater through-hull fittings. They have excellent chemical and moisture resistance. The thing to keep in mind with polyurethane sealants is that *they are intended to be permanent*. If you ever have to remove a fitting bedded with this stuff, you'll not want to do it again—ever! Examples of polyurethane sealants are 3M-5200 and Sikaflex 420. Put on a thin coat, let it cure, and join the parts.

Polysulfide

Polysulfide sealants have similar physical properties to polyurethanes, without the enormous adhesive strength. They can be used both above and below the waterline. They come in two-part and single-part formulations. Physical and mechanical properties of both are essentially the same, except that the one-part type takes a little longer to cure. Examples of polysulfides are 3M 101 and BoatLIFE's Life Caulk. Polysulfide sealants should not be used in contact with ABS, PVC, acrylic or polycarbonate plastics, or other plastics (except Delrin and nylon), as it will chemically attack them.

Silicone

Silicone sealants are very elastic and have excellent chemical and moisture resistance. Silicone makes an excellent barrier film between dissimilar metals. It does not have the adhesive strength of either polysulfide or polyurethane, so this is the sealant to use on joints that will one day have to be separated.

Much of the advertising literature states that silicone sealants are suitable for use below the waterline. However, some experienced and authoritative people in the boating industry recommend against this. Their experience shows that silicones have a tendency to break down when used below the waterline in salt water, causing silicone-bedded fittings to leak.

Proprietary Formulations

There are a number of sealants specially designed for use as galvanic isolators and lubricants. These are used to prevent nuts, bolts, and screws from freezing, rusting, and galling. A common use for these sealants is on the threads of stainless steel machine screws installed in an aluminum mast, but these products can be used anywhere both lubrication and corrosive protection are required. Some examples are CRC Corrosion Inhibitor, Boeshield T-7, Corrosion Block, Corrosion X, and LanoCote, to name just a few. These are aerosol spray formulas designed to exclude or displace moisture and lubricate the parts.

SUMMARY

Much can be done during design and construction phrases to prevent future corrosion problems. Selecting appropriate materials, avoiding contact between dissimilar metals, and paying attention to anode-cathode-area ratios are all well worth the effort. Also recommended is eliminating or filling corners, crevices, and other potential water pockets in structural members. There should be adequate space around and under tables, fixtures, and deck furniture to permit thorough periodic cleaning and to allow fresh air to flow through these spaces. These few simple steps will pay off handsomely in the future.

CHAPTER 15

Coating to Prevent Corrosion

Coatings are the most widely used method to protect metals against atmospheric corrosion. Coating materials can be as simple as a film of oil (with or without the addition of solvents and tars) or as advanced as thermally sprayed coatings of barrier or sacrificial metals and high-purity silica, alumina, and silicon-nitride ceramics. Methods of application range from the trusty oil-soaked rag to sophisticated vapor deposition techniques. Not all materials and methods are suitable for marine applications.

In *all* cases, however, surface preparation is crucial. Typically, parts to be coated are cleaned by some sort of caustic bath, rinsed, acid-pickled or grit-blasted to remove oxides and to roughen the surface to enhance adhesion, rinsed again, and fluxed, and then the coating is applied. Surface preparation is probably the most important step in the coating process. Most coating failures can be traced back to inadequate surface preparation.

Coating systems can be divided into two broad groups—metallic and nonmetallic. Nonmetallic coatings refer primarily to organic materials, such as paints, but anodizing, ceramic, and a number of other coatings also fall under the nonmetallic heading. We take a look at metallic coatings first.

METALLIC COATINGS

Metallic coatings are just that—coatings of various metals and alloys applied to the surface of less costly and less corrosion-resistant substrate metals, most often mild steel. They can be separated into two groups—*barrier* coatings and *sacrificial* coatings—although, as you might expect, there is some overlapping.

Barrier coatings protect the substrate metal by preventing moisture from penetrating to the surface of the substrate metal. They also provide protection from abrasion and wear by their hardness and lubricity. This would, of course, assume that the coating metal is more corrosion resistant than the substrate metal. Some examples of barrier-coating metals are chromium, nickel, and tin.

Sacrificial coatings also provide some degree of barrier protection and corrosion resistance, but they combine that with cathodic protection. The coating functions as a sacrificial anode. Scratches or breaks in a sacrificial coating are self-healing when immersed (or wet) as long as the coating remains. Examples of sacrificial coatings for mild-steel substrate are zinc, aluminum, and cadmium. Zinc and aluminum are the metals most widely used in marine applications, but the relatively small differences in corrosion resistance of these three metals is not as significant as the thickness of the coating.

APPLICATION PROCESSES

There are a number of coating methods, some old and well established, some very new and not yet in common use in the boating community.

Hot-Dip Coatings

As the name implies, an item given a hot-dip coating has been immersed in a bath of molten metal. Hot-dip coating is used to apply coatings of zinc, aluminum, lead, tin, and some alloys of these metals. Marine hardware is usually coated with zinc (galvanizing) or, to a much lesser extent, aluminum (aluminizing).

The thickness of the coating is a function of the temperature of the molten bath, the length of time the part is immersed, and the rate at which it is withdrawn from the bath. Obviously, the longer an item remains in the hot bath, the higher the item's temperature. What may not be so obvious is that the cooler the bath or the cooler the part, the thicker the coating. An operator wanting to conserve on coating metal might run the bath a little hotter or leave the piece in a little longer. There is, however, a practical limit on how hot the bath can be. A zinc bath typically operates at 830°F to 870°F (443°C to 465°C), so there is a limit as to how thin the coating can be made. Unless zinc is purposely removed by wiping or centrifuging, the piece will normally have a coating thickness of between 3.0 and 3.75 mils (0.076 to 0.095 mm). They can, of course, be much thicker. For thinner coatings, a different process—electroplating or possibly thermospraying—must be used.

The hot-dip process begins with the removal of dirt, grease, rust, and scale, followed by prefluxing to dissolve surface oxides. Then comes immersion in the molten metal bath and, finally, quenching and removal of excess coating metal. Except for final cooling and cleaning, each of the steps consists of a series of baths (cleaning, rinsing, pickling, rinsing, fluxing, dipping). For small job shops, the process is mostly manual, but it is automated for production operations, with a conveyor carrying the parts through the various baths.

Sherardizing and Mechanical Coating

Sherardizing is a process of coating with a thin layer of zinc by heating the part in a mixture of sand (used to distribute the heat uniformly) and zinc powder. The coating thickness is limited to about 1.5 mils (0.038 mm).

Mechanical coating (mechanical galvanizing) is a similar process. Here, the parts are loaded into the galvanizing barrel—a plastic- or rubber-lined tumbler that resembles a cement mixer. The barrel also contains glass beads of various sizes, water, and some proprietary chemicals. As the barrel rotates, zinc dust is added from an overhead feed hopper. Peened by the impact from the glass beads, the fine zinc dust is cold-welded to the tumbling parts. By controlling the amount of zinc, the plating thickness can be varied from 0.1 to 5 mils (0.0025 to 0.127 mm).

Electroplating

The fundamental basis of electroplating is the same electrochemical process of electrolysis we discussed in chapter 6 when we talked about galvanic cells. We saw that when a cathode (negative electrode) and an anode (positive electrode) are immersed in an electrolyte, and a source of direct current is connected between them, there is a migration of ions (metallic particles) between them. In electroplating, the part to be coated is made the negative electrode, and the coating metal is supplied either in the form of a sacrificial positive electrode or as metallic salts added directly to the plating bath (electrolyte).

Electroplated coatings can be decorative, provide wear resistance, build up surface dimensions, and protect from corrosion. Lots of different metals are applied as electroplated coatings. Zinc, cadmium, and chrome are the ones of most interest to us since these are the most widely used in the marine environment.

Thermal Spray

Thermal spraying is like paint spraying except that the coating being applied is tiny molten particles. The coating material feedstock, which can be metallic or nonmetallic, is in either a wire or powder form. It is fed into a spray unit, called a *gun*, where it is heated to a molten state and propelled by a stream of compressed gas onto the substrate. The heat necessary to melt the feedstock is produced by the combustion of gases, usually oxyacetylene or high-velocity oxygen (flame spraying), electric arc (arc spraying), or a plasma (plasma spraying). Thermal spraying requires a skilled operator to achieve a smooth, even coating of appropriate thickness and to minimize porosity.

Zinc, aluminum, and zinc-aluminum alloys are the most widely used coating materials, although austenitic stainless steels, aluminum bronzes, and other materials are also used for special applications. Both flame-spraying and arc-spraying methods are portable, and thermal spray coatings are commonly applied on-site.

A thermal spray coating can be significantly

thicker than galvanizing, an important feature, but it cannot be too thick since very thick coatings can introduce a thermal expansion mismatch between the coating and the substrate that results in their separation. The coating also must not be too thin since thin coatings tend to be porous. Thermal-spray coatings are usually applied to a thickness of 3 to 7 mils (0.076 to 0.18 mm). Unfortunately, thickness monitoring while spraying is extremely difficult.

One of the most attractive features of thermal spraying is that it can be used on a wide variety of substrate materials, such as metals, glass, cloth, and, most interesting to us, wood and fiberglass. While the coating particles are exposed to high temperatures, the surface of the substrate material does not exceed 200°F (93.3°C) and in many cases will be lower. In fact, thermal spray coatings can even be applied to paper of the lowest quality, such as newsprint, and the paper doesn't even get hot. According to tests performed by the American Welding Society, thermally sprayed steel specimens have demonstrated as much as 20 years of complete substrate protection in seawater and in marine atmospheres. Current marine applications are primarily on ships—weather deck machinery, interior wet spaces, and the like—but this is a most attractive coating technology that we will surely see used more widely on both recreational and commercial vessels.

Clad Metals

Clad metals are composites of two or more metals bonded together. Perhaps the most familiar application is a thermostatic bimetal, in which a metal or alloy with a high coefficient of thermal expansion is bonded to one with a low coefficient of thermal expansion. When the resulting structure is heated, it bends sharply from its normal condition. Such bimetals are used in all sorts of control devices—thermostats, circuit breakers, overload protectors, and automotive chokes.

Our more immediate interest is corrosion prevention. Usually, a highly corrosion-resistant metal or alloy such as stainless steel, cupron-ickel, Monel, or Hastelloy is clad to a common mild steel. These metals are bonded together by cold-rolling, hot-rolling, hot-pressing, explosion and extrusion bonding, and weld overlaying. In all of these except weld overlaying, the bond is accomplished by forcing clean, oxide-free metal surfaces together under tremendous pressures. As many as 100 different combinations of metals and as many as 15 layers have been bonded to produce structures with some very unique and attractive properties.

Clad metals are widely used in the chemical, offshore oil, and automotive industries. High cost has limited their application in the marine industry, with the exception of weld overlay, which is quite frequently used in repairing and restoring worn shafts and other wear surfaces.

Vapor Deposition

Vapor deposition is a family of coating methods in which the coating material is transferred and deposited in the form of individual atoms or molecules. It was developed to improve the mechanical properties—wear, friction, or hardness—of metal surfaces but recently has begun to make inroads in corrosion resistance applications.

Sputtering

Sputtering is the principal method of *physical vapor deposition* (PVD). A source—called the *target*—is bombarded by gas ions accelerated by a high voltage. Atoms, or molecules, dislodged from the target are deposited on the substrate, forming the coating. Sputtering is gaining wide acceptance where high-quality coatings with good adhesion are required, such as on turbine blades, but the coating thickness is typically in the range of 0.004 mil (0.0001 mm).

Evaporation

The earliest of the PVD processes, evaporation was used primarily to aluminum-coat plastics and glass for decorative purposes. It has little application for corrosion protection applications and in any case has been pretty much supplanted by sputtering.

Ion Plating

Ion plating is another PVD process. It is performed under pressure and generates a plasma that greatly increases the deposition energy. The equipment required is complex, and the process is difficult to control, but it produces a coating with better adhesion and fewer imperfections. Use of the process is increasing.

Chemical Vapor Deposition

Chemical vapor deposition (CVD) is typically less costly than PVD. Widely used in the semiconductor and cutting tool industries, it is capable of depositing coatings that have superior structure, are very dense, and are up to 0.25 inches (6.4 mm) thick. However, the process involves extremely high temperatures that greatly limit the substrates that can be coated.

Vapor-deposited coatings, if thick enough, are for all intents and purposes pore-free—providing excellent barrier protection. Cost, however, limits its current corrosion protection role to high-end applications, primarily in aircraft and aerospace. New interest in these technologies by the automotive industry as an alternative to electroplating and hot-dipping could soon change that.

COATING METALS

Zinc Coatings

Zinc coating actually consists of several distinct layers. Those closest to the steel substrate are zinc-iron alloys, while the outer surface layer is essentially pure zinc. The surface zinc layer is relatively soft, but the intermediate layers are actually harder than the steel substrate. These layers provide the barrier protection against wear, abrasion, and impact.

The surface layer also offers protection. What happens is that a freshly galvanized coating, when exposed to the weather, quickly forms a thin zinc oxide film, which is then converted to zinc hydroxide in the presence of moisture and, finally, through reaction with carbon dioxide in the atmosphere, to zinc carbonates. This is the grayish-colored film characteristic of zinc coatings. It is quite insoluble and provides protection against corrosion.

Cathodic protection results from the fact that zinc is anodic to steel and corrodes preferentially, even where bare steel is exposed by scratches, drilled holes, or sheared edges. The service life of a galvanized component is directly dependent on the thickness of the coating. This is where hot-dip galvanizing is superior to other coating methods. The hot-dip process produces a much thicker coating than any other method except thermal spraying. A hot-dip coating can be up to 6 mils (0.152 mm) thick.

A couple of cautionary words are needed. The structure of the coating is greatly influenced by the chemistry of the steel substrate, and the coating structure is critically important to the impact resistance of the coating. If the wrong steel grade is used for the substrate, excessive bending, twisting, or impact will result in flaking off of the galvanized coating. The best steel grades are those containing less than 0.15 percent carbon. Cast iron parts can be galvanized, but the cast iron should be a grade that is low in silicon and phosphorus in order to avoid brittleness in the surface of the part.

For similar reasons, care must be taken in welding galvanized steel. When gas metal arc welding, also commonly known as MIG (metal inert gas) welding, is used, tiny cracks can be caused by the reaction of zinc with silicon in the electrode. Galvanized steel should be welded using an electrode with the lowest possible silicon content.

Many of us, especially the traditionalists among us, have occasion to take an old (or, for that matter, newly fabricated) chainplate, mast tang, or some other piece of equipment to our local galvanizing shop for coating or recoating. The fitting to be galvanized must be clean and free of oil, grease, and paint, so thorough cleaning, degreasing, and grit-blasting to white metal (or as near white as possible) is a *must*. The rough surface resulting from grit-blasting enhances the coating process and produces a thicker, more tightly adherent coating. The part must not have any closed chambers or voids—a sealed tube, for example. Rapidly expanding trapped air can cause such parts to explode when immersed in the bath of molten zinc— picture that!

Also, it is well not to leave the details of the galvanizing open to the interpretation of the shop unless you know from past experience that the job will be done to your satisfaction. Otherwise, specify that the galvanizing be done in accordance with an appropriate standard, such as ASTM A123/A123M or British Standard BS 729 Marine Grade. Fittings coated to these standards will give many years of satisfactory service.

Atmospheric Corrosion Resistance

When exposed to the atmosphere, zinc is 20 to 30 times more corrosion resistant than steel. Exactly how long a galvanized coating will last depends on a number of factors:

- how often and for how long it is exposed to moisture in any of its forms—rain, sleet, snow, or dew
- the number, type, and concentration of pollutants in the atmosphere
- exposure to sea spray or wind-borne abrasives

The worst conditions are found in heavily industrialized areas where factories, power stations, and the like discharge sulfurous gases and corrosive fumes into the atmosphere. These pollutants react with the zinc carbonate film to produce zinc sulfate, which is soluble and readily washed away. This exposes fresh zinc carbonate, and the cycle repeats itself. In this environment a galvanized deck fitting with a coating thickness of about 2 mils (0.051 mm) will last between 5 and 10 years before showing signs of rust. The same fitting in a rural environment should last 30 years.

When exposed to salt-laden air, the zinc surface layer forms zinc chloride, which is also highly soluble, and a similar kind of corrosion cycle as described above takes place. In marine use, the same hot-dipped (2 mils or 0.051 mm thick) fitting should last 20 to 25 years before showing signs of rust.

Freshwater Corrosion Resistance

Zinc has the happy faculty of being able to form corrosion-inhibiting magnesium and calcium deposits on its surface when these elements are present in the water. These deposits prevent access to the coating by the dissolved oxygen in the water and lower the rate of corrosion. Water containing high levels of magnesium and calcium salts is referred to as *hard*. Corrosion rates of 0.1 to 0.2 mil/yr. (0.0025 to 0.0051 mm/yr.) can be expected in hard waters. River waters are typically softer, containing lower concentrations of the salts, resulting in corrosion rates on the order of 0.8 mil/yr. (0.020 mm/yr.) per year. The critical nature of water hardness is demonstrated most graphically by the corrosion rate of zinc in distilled water—up to 6 mils/yr. (0.152 mm/yr.), or nearly eight times faster than in river water.

Temperature is also a factor. According to one study, yearly corrosion rates increase from about 0.78 mil at 68°F to 2.74 mils at 122°F, to 15.2 mils at 131°F, and then increase sharply to about 115.4 mils at 149°F (0.02 mm at 20°C to 0.070 mm at 50°C, 0.39 mm at 55°C, 2.9 mm at 65°C). This last temperature is very close to the settings of many hot-water systems.

Seawater Corrosion Resistance

Magnesium and calcium salts also play a part in the corrosion behavior of zinc in seawater, but here the dominant constituent is sodium chloride. Other factors are pollutants and sediments, the availability of dissolved oxygen (or the lack of it), and whether the water is stagnant, still, or moving—and how fast.

When the available oxygen is not sufficient to replace that which is consumed in the corrosion process (this happens in stagnant water), the zinc is attacked locally, resulting in localized pitting corrosion. If there is sufficient dissolved oxygen available—as in open water—the corrosion tends to occur uniformly over the entire surface, but at an increased rate.

What are the effects of the dissolved salts? The sodium chloride follows its normal aggressive tendency to increase the rate of corrosion, but magnesium and calcium salts inhibit the attack. The result of this contest of the elements is that the corrosion rate of zinc in seawater initially exceeds the corrosion rate in freshwater. However, after about two years, the seawater rate decreases to about the same as the freshwater rate, approximately 0.6 to 1.0 mil/yr. (0.015 to 0.025 mm/yr.).

In polluted estuarine or harbor waters, corrosion rates will be higher. The corrosion rate is also accelerated in moving water. Even at moderate velocities, such as those experienced at many tidal-water moorings (2 to 3 knots), corrosion rates can increase to 2 or 3 mils/yr. (0.051 to 0.076 mm/yr.).

Zinc coatings provide significant protection, but their finite thickness means they have a finite life. The corrosion rate of galvanized steel is distinctly superior to that of aluminum, cadmium, lead, or tin coatings. In one test, all the other coatings failed within two years, while the zinc-coated samples were just about expired, as far as their ability to protect their steel substrates was concerned, after six years.

Sealants and Coatings

Galvanizing doesn't necessarily obviate the need for paint. If we apply a proper coating over a properly cleaned, degreased, and prepared galvanized surface, we can greatly extend the service life of the steel substrate. Proper coatings consist of a conversion coating, such as a chromate or phosphate, followed by an organic coating, or alternatively, a zinc primer followed by an organic topcoat. The conversion coating is the superior method.

Zinc-Nickel Coatings

In search of a coating alloy with better corrosion resistance, zinc has been combined with cobalt and with iron, but alloys of about 90 percent zinc and 10 percent nickel electroplated on steel substrates have been found to produce optimum characteristics in terms of surface properties and corrosion resistance. These coatings provide excellent adhesion under stress, good barrier coating properties, better hardness and scratch resistance than cold-rolled steel, better performance at high temperatures, good weldability, sac-

rificial protection of the substrate steel, and considerably greater protection against corrosion than does zinc.

Zinc-nickel alloy plating has been in use in many applications in Europe and Japan for several years and is making rapid inroads in the United States. Precoated zinc-nickel sheet can be finished with smoother, unblemished surfaces than with electrocoated zinc coatings, making it attractive to the automotive and appliance industries. Zinc-nickel coating has also found wide use in brake, fuel, and exhaust lines that require bending and crimping after plating.

Thickness for thickness, zinc-nickel coatings provide 5 to 6 times better resistance to corrosion than electroplated zinc. In salt spray tests, a panel with a coating thickness of 0.12 mil (0.003 mm) survived 910 hours before showing any sign of red rust (corrosion of the steel substrate) while the panel with a pure zinc coating was 100 percent rusted at 300 hours. Panels with a zinc-nickel coating thickness of 0.40 mil (0.010 mm) and with a chromate treatment lasted some 3500 to 4000 hours before showing signs of red rust.

Zinc-nickel plating is not suitable for applications requiring immersion in salt water without supplemental protection, usually in the form of an organic overcoat.

Aluminum Coatings

Two basic types of aluminum-coated steels—referred to as Type 1 and Type 2 aluminized steels—are currently in wide commercial use. Type 1 coatings contain between 7 and 11 percent silicon and about 3.5 percent iron. The rest is aluminum. This makes an alloy that is very fluid and easy to cast. It forms a more ductile and uniform but thinner coating layer than Type 2.

Type 1 provides resistance to both heat and atmospheric corrosion. It has excellent heat reflectivity up to 900°F (482°C) and resists heat scaling up to 1,250°F (677°C). Coating thickness is about 1 mil (0.025 mm), and it produces an attractive, satin-like finish. It is used in heat-critical applications such as heat exchangers for residential furnaces, microwave ovens, automobile and truck muffler systems, and heat shields for catalytic converters.

Type 2 coatings are commercially pure aluminum (97.5 percent); they are thicker and not as ductile as Type 1. They will, however, withstand mild forming operations such as corrugating and roll forming. Coating thickness is approximately 1.5 mils (0.038 mm). Atmospheric corrosion resistance is superior to that of Type 1 coatings and is reported to outlast zinc-coated sheet steel in industrial environments by as much as 5 to 1. Typical applications are roofing and siding, enclosures for street lighting fixtures, and corrugated steel water pipe. Aluminized stainless steels in automotive exhaust systems deliver superior resistance to corrosion by hot exhaust products and road salts.

Atmospheric Corrosion Resistance

The protection mechanism for aluminum coatings is similar to that for solid aluminum; upon exposure to oxygen in the atmosphere, a tightly adherent protective aluminum oxide layer is formed on the surface. Thus, both Type 1 and Type 2 aluminum coatings offer excellent atmospheric protection for steel substrates. Type 2 coatings, however, are thicker, and the protective oxide layers have shown better atmospheric corrosion resistance.

The difference in corrosion potential between the silicon and the aluminum in Type 1 coatings can cause pitting corrosion, resulting in a rusty discoloration of the metal surface. The corrosion product itself, however, inhibits further corrosion, and aside from the unfavorable appearance, the coating continues to provide excellent protection to the substrate. According to one report, Type 1 panels have been exposed in mild industrial atmospheres for over 40 years with no evidence of base metal deterioration.

In five-year tests conducted at both industrial and marine sites, Type 2 coatings demonstrated corrosion rates of about 50 percent of those for the Type 1 coatings and approximately 10 percent of those for galvanized steels.

Freshwater Corrosion Resistance

There isn't much numerical data available on the corrosion behavior of immersed aluminum-coated steel because these products have not generally found a lot of use in aqueous environments. When was the last time you saw an aluminized pail? What we do know is that the protective oxide layer formed in air is dissolved when the aluminum is immersed in water. The oxides must be reformed with the dissolved oxygen in the water, and this must happen faster than the rate at which the aluminum surface is attacked by other ions such as chlorides, nitrates, or sulfates in the water. Soft waters are the least aggressive to the aluminum surface.

Seawater Corrosion Resistance

Aluminum-coated steels are not recommended for seawater use. Observed corrosion rates are on the order of 7.8 mils/yr. (0.20 mm/yr.) for Type 1 and 1.5 mils (0.038 mm) for Type 2.

Aluminum-Zinc Coatings

Zinc coatings offer no significant protection at high temperatures. Aluminum coatings provide good high-temperature protection but do not provide cathodic protection to exposed steel. Aluminum coatings are also susceptible to crevice corrosion in marine applications.

An aluminum-zinc alloy coating consisting of 55 percent aluminum, 43.4 percent zinc, and the rest silicon—called 55Al-Zn—provides both barrier and cathodic (sacrificial) protection. While this coating provides less cathodic protection than zinc, it gives a much longer service life. This is because the rate of corrosion is largely determined by the dominant aluminum content, which has a much lower corrosion rate than zinc. Steels coated with this alloy are used extensively in metal roofing, automotive components, appliances, and corrugated steel pipe.

Atmospheric Corrosion Resistance

In one 12-year study, 55Al-Zn coatings turned out to have from two to six times better atmospheric corrosion resistance than galvanizing. Typical thickness losses after 12 years in marine atmospheres were between 0.32 and 0.48 mil (0.008 to 0.012 mm).

Freshwater Corrosion Resistance

In comparative laboratory tests of freshwater corrosion performance, 55Al-Zn-coated panels outperformed galvanized panels quite decisively. Tests were made in distilled water (very soft) and in distilled water containing 85 mg/L of chloride ions to simulate more aggressive conditions. (Note that river water averages about 7.8 mg/L of chloride ions.) In distilled water the galvanized panels suffered thickness losses of about 0.042 mil (0.0011 mm), while the 55Al-Zn-coated steel panels lost only 0.0005 mil (0.000013 mm)—a very significant difference. In the more aggressive aqueous media, the galvanized panels lost 0.049 mil (0.0012 mm) versus 0.005 mil (0.00013 mm) for the 55Al-Zn-coated panels.

In industrial applications, 55Al-Zn coatings have shown greater durability than a galvanized coating three times as thick.

Seawater Corrosion Resistance

At the time of this writing, experiential data on the performance of 55Al-Zn coatings in seawater applications is sparse. According to the most informed and most authoritative sources, however, it is not likely that these coatings would be very different from either galvanized or aluminum coatings in seawater. Some form of additional protection (e.g., coatings, cathodic protection) for long-term applications is likely to be necessary.

Cadmium Coatings

Similar to zinc coatings, cadmium-electroplated coatings provide sacrificial protection to the substrate metal, including scratches, drilled holes, and sheared edges. Cadmium also has excellent corrosion resistance, good thermal and electrical conductivity, solderability, and a nice combination of surface hardness and self-lubrication that results in good wear properties. With the addition of a conversion coating, its corrosion resistance is greatly enhanced.

Atmospheric corrosion resistance is superior to that of zinc. Test panels, some with a 1 mil (0.025 mm) coating of zinc and others with the same thickness of cadmium exhibited the first sign of rusting in a coastal environment at 2 years and at 2 to 3 years, respectively. In rural atmospheres, the zinc panels survived for 5 years before rusting, whereas the cadmium coatings

showed rust after 8 to 15 years. Cadmium is (or was), along with zinc, the standard coating used to provide corrosion protection to steel fasteners in the marine environment, but its use is declining due to its toxicity. Cadmium electroplating is highly regulated. The Occupational Safety and Health Administration (OSHA) imposes stringent worker-exposure limitations. Wastewater discharges from cadmium plating baths must conform to regulations imposed by the Clean Water Act, and sludge from the process must be treated and handled as hazardous waste under the Resource Conservation and Recovery Act (RCRA). These requirements add significantly to the cost and complexities, often spurring a switch to aluminum and zinc alloys, particularly electroplated zinc-nickel coatings. Zinc-nickel offers a substantial improvement in corrosion resistance and is readily adaptable to existing equipment and processes.

Chromium Plating

Chrome plating is actually a fairly complex *system* of electroplated coatings—not alloys, but layers of different metals. It typically consists of a base coating of nickel, with or without a copper underlayer, and a surface layer of chromium. In components intended for industrial-grade applications, the nickel base layer is most often a double (sometimes even a triple) layer, 1 to 5 mils (0.025 to 0.127 mm) thick. The copper layer, if one is used, is typically from 0.32 to 0.5 mil (0.008 to 0.013 mm). The chromium surface layer may be from about 0.05 to 0.5 mil (0.00013 to 0.013 mm). Chromium layers of less than this thickness are generally considered to be purely decorative.

Chromium platings are barrier coatings and provide no sacrificial protection, but they do form a dense self-healing protective oxide layer that aids greatly in corrosion resistance. However, the corrosion resistance of chromium platings is not just a function of the electrochemical nature of the chromium plating but also of its thickness, the presence or absence of microcracks, and the density of the microcracks. A crack-free chromium surface layer would be ideal, but chrome platings have high internal stresses and thus do not remain crack-free in service. Since the plating constitutes a barrier to moisture penetration, the coatings must be thicker than the depth of the microcracks to provide protection.

In platings up to about 5 mils (0.127 mm) thick, microcracks are typically less than about 0.004 mil (0.0001 mm) wide and less than 0.3 mil (0.008 mm) deep. Salt spray tests have shown that corrosion resistance increases with coating thickness up to about 0.2 mil (0.0051 mm). As plating thickness is increased beyond this level, up to about 0.4 mil (0.010 mm), microcracking begins to occur, and corrosion resistance decreases. As plating thickness is increased above the 0.4 mil (0.010 mm) level, corrosion resistance increases sharply. This is because the initial cracks are covered with chromium, and although additional surface cracking may take place, there are fewer corrosion paths to the substrate.

These salt spray tests showed that for test panels with a coating thickness of 0.2 mil (0.0051 mm), a service life of some 500 hours may be expected before general rusting occurs. At twice this plating thickness, only about 150 hours may be expected. In other tests, conducted by the ASTM, various types of nickel-chromium and copper-nickel-chromium coatings on flat and contoured steel panels were evaluated in marine atmospheres for a period of three years. These tests indicated that the best performance was obtained by panels with a double layer of nickel 1 mil (0.025 mm) thick with a thin surface layer—0.01 mil (0.00025 mm)—of microcrack-free chromium. However, thin platings are susceptible to cracking in service, especially on deck fittings and fixtures.

Fortunately, microcracks are not as detrimental to corrosion resistance as one might expect. Microcracks are not empty spaces but rather areas of different composition and structure. Microcracks are also extremely narrow, typically less than 0.004 mil (0.0001 mm) wide, and since water does not wet chromium, water does not readily enter the microcracks.

The problem we face is that there is really no way to know what the plating structure is on any of the fittings we buy. My own experience runs the gamut, from chromium coatings that peel off after less than a year's service (for example, inexpensive cabin lighting fixtures) to those that show slight pitting after many years of service (deck cleats and bow eyes). So what it comes down to is what it always seems to come down to—buy good-quality products from a reputable manufacturer and hope for the best. Regular cleaning and waxing, where that is practical, will go a long way toward extending the life of chromed fittings.

Other Metal Coatings

There are some other metals that, although frequently used as coatings on steel in various applications, are not often encountered in marine work. However, since they may occasionally turn up in, on, or around the boat, we ought to discuss them briefly. All are barrier-type coatings, providing no sacrificial protection to the substrate, and all are cathodic to steel, so if scratched or penetrated down to the substrate, severe corrosion of the substrate (large cathode, small anode) will result.

Nickel

Nickel is most often used as an underlayer for other metals, but it is also used as a corrosion-resistant coating by itself in such applications as pump components and valves. Nickel, however, is not very corrosion resistant in chloride-containing atmospheres such as the marine environment, so while a coating of adequate thickness will provide protection to the substrate for many years, it will suffer the ravages of general surface corrosion. Nickel coatings for marine applications really don't make a lot of sense. Organically coated (painted) hot-dip galvanized coatings will give much better service in both atmospheric and immersion applications at about one-fifth the cost.

Nickel-Tungsten

Nickel-tungsten alloy electroplated on steel, a recent development, is claimed to outperform chrome and nickel coatings in wear and corrosion resistance. Coating efficiencies are said to be twice those of chromium electroplating, resulting in cost savings—hopefully of sufficient magnitude to make them available to commercial and recreational boating. Only time will tell.

Lead

Lead is highly resistant to corrosion in all types of atmospheric exposures, as demonstrated by lead roofing hundreds of years old that continues to provide satisfactory service. In marine exposures, chlorides contained in the salt air do affect corrosivity but not excessively. Typically, corrosion rates may start out in the first several years at about 0.050 to 0.075 mil/yr. (0.0013 to 0.002 mm/yr.) and average out to 0.020 to 0.023 mil/yr. (0.00051 to 0.00058 mm/yr.).

In freshwater, long-term average corrosion rates range from 0.08 to 0.38 mil/yr. (0.002 to 0.0096 mm/yr.). In seawater moving at less than one knot, corrosion rates on the order of 0.20 to 0.40 mil/yr. (0.0051 to 0.010 mm/yr.) per year have been observed.

Most applications of lead coatings on steel are in the form of *terneplate*—a lead-tin (typically, 3 to 8 percent tin) alloy coating, which provides greater protection than pure lead and is solderable. Terne-coated steel is used in roofing metals, gasoline tanks, and fuel and brake lines (it does not contaminate the gasoline). Lead coatings are seldom used in marine applications.

Tin

Tin is frequently used as a coating for steel and copper. Tin is easily soldered, and oxides of tin are electrically conductive, so it finds wide use in electrical applications such as conductors, connectors, and contacts. Tin is highly resistive to sulfur-induced corrosion, making it well suited for protection of copper wire and cable with insulation sheathings that contain sulfur. Also, since its corrosion products are not toxic, tinned steel is widely used in the food-packaging industry. Tin forms a barrier coating. It does not galvanically protect the substrate steel so, here again, if the coating is scratched, the exposed steel will suffer severe corrosion.

Although corrosion rates are on the order of 0.12 mil/yr. (0.003 mm/yr.) tin-plate is porous.

Tests have shown that with a coating thickness of 1 mil (0.025 mm), maximum service life to first signs of rusting was one year. As might be expected, tin coatings have not achieved any significant usage in the recreational and commercial boating industry.

Tin Alloys

Coatings of tin-cadmium, tin-copper, tin-nickel, tin-cobalt, tin-zinc, and various combinations of these materials have been the subject of considerable research and development. A number of proprietary alloy coatings have been developed and patented, mostly for special applications. Few, if any, of these have achieved any significant usage in the boating world for the same reasons we have discussed before—high cost and low-volume usage.

ORGANIC COATINGS

The term *organic coatings* refers to paint and other liquid coatings. Organic coatings are the major methods of atmospheric corrosion control. They consist primarily of a natural or synthetic binder, pigments, and solvents plus proprietary additions (plasticizers, extenders, etc.). Upon curing—drying, oxidizing, or polymerizing, depending on the particular type of binder—they form an adherent protective film.

Water (moisture) and oxygen must be present on the surface of steel for the corrosion process to take place, and you'll recall that the rate of corrosion is accelerated if chloride (or sulfate) salts are present in the moisture. The function of the paint film is to prevent one or more of these from reaching the metal surface.

So far so good. Now, you'll also recall that there are basically three methods of protection—barrier, passivation of the surface, and galvanic. Paint coatings are primarily barrier protective systems in which the paint film retards (but doesn't prevent) migration of water, oxygen, and entrained salts to the metal surface.

The binder is the most influential component in determining the properties of the coating, but the pigment also may contribute to reducing the rate at which water and oxygen can diffuse through the coatings. Flake-shaped pigment particles can overlap—like roof shingles—and lengthen the diffusion path. The pigment may passivate the surface, as with zinc chromate, making it less susceptible to corrosion. And zinc pigmentation may also provide galvanic protection, but the zinc content of the coating must be *very* high if it is to function in this way. For the most part, however, organic coatings provide barrier protection.

Traditionally, the boating and yachting community has demanded more than just barrier protection from their coatings. They must also be decorative and aesthetically pleasing, although this is not always obvious to the observer. I remember a steel tuna boat painted aqua all over, and I mean *all* over—hull, house, tower, pulpit, rails, ladders, everything. Protective? Probably. But aesthetically pleasing? As I write this I'm looking out the window at a beautiful new 42-foot sportfisherman with fuchsia topsides and a pale blue boot stripe. Beauty is most certainly in the eye of the beholder. Other communities—for example, workboats, commercial fishing vessels, barges, wharves, pilings, bridges, and other structures exposed to corrosive atmospheres—have other, perhaps more practical, priorities. Thus we focus our commentary on the protective properties of the various coatings available.

Acrylic Coatings

Acrylic coatings can be formulated as thermoplastic coatings, thermosetting coatings, or water-base coatings. In general, acrylic coatings provide high gloss, color retention, and good moisture, weathering, and ultraviolet resistance. Acrylics are commonly used as topcoats in atmospheric exposure. However, they typically are softer and more flexible than many other coatings and for this reason are considered more suitable for interior joinerwork than for hull or topside exteriors. Acrylics are not considered suitable for immersion service.

Thermoplastic

Thermoplastic acrylics are solvent based. Upon application the solvent evaporates and the coating hardens. These are the coatings one generally finds in aerosol cans. Thermoplastic acrylics are widely used for automotive finishes due to their ease of coloration and dispersion of metallic reflective pigments. Thermal reflow is another important feature of these coatings. After initial application, the coatings can be heated under lamps or in an oven to melt and reflow the finish coatings to remove sanding marks and small flaws. Thermoplastic acrylic coatings are used on some galley appliances.

Thermosetting

Thermosetting acrylics are formed by combining acrylate esters with nonacrylic polymers. These coatings are typically harder and more resistant to heat and solvents than the thermoplastic types. Thermosetting acrylic coatings find their application as finish coatings on household appliances such as refrigerators and some galley appliances.

Water-Base

Water-base acrylics are the acrylic emulsion paints commonly used for both interior and exterior house paints. The water-base acrylics have several advantages over the oil-base paints also popular with homeowners. They dry much faster—second coats can be applied in about an hour—and cleanup is easier. They also adhere better to damp wood and masonry and have much greater resistance to blistering, chalking, and yellowing. Oil-base paints, however, do have better penetration and adhesion on porous surfaces such as wood.

Certain additives in water-base acrylics are hydrophilic (they like water) and tend to attract water from the environment. Thus, when immersed in water for long periods of time, water-base acrylics tend to soften, swell, and lose adherence. They are not suitable for immersion service.

Alkyd Coatings

The term *alkyd* is a contraction of *alcohol* and *acids*, which are combined to produce the coating. Alkyds are oleo-resinous, meaning a combination of oils and resins. They have essentially replaced the old oil-base paints favored by traditionalists and earlier generations of boatbuilders and owners.

Coating properties depend to a large extent on the particular type of drying oils used in the formulation. Linseed, tung, castor, coconut, and fish oils are all used, and all have their advantages and disadvantages. However, soybean oil seems to have emerged as the oil of choice. Soybean alkyds have good drying properties and color retention. Linseed oils produce a faster drying rate but have a tendency to darken after prolonged exposure to light.

Alkyds have good resistance to atmospheric weathering and are widely used for structural steels such as water tanks and bridges. They are not chemically resistant and are not suitable for use on alkaline surfaces (such as concrete) or for immersion service. In general, they are superior to the original oil-base paints, having faster drying times and better hardness, water resistance, and durability. Also, their low cost, their ease of mixing and application, and the fact that they penetrate and adhere well to poorly prepared surfaces make them very popular. Alkyds are used for boat and ship surfaces above the waterline as well as for interior finishes.

Vinyls

Vinyl coatings are most commonly combinations of the two polymers—about 86 percent polyvinyl chloride (PVC) and about 14 percent polyvinyl acetate (PVA). These are true copolymers (the term *copolymer* is frequently used in the marine trades when referring to ablative bottom paints). Introduced in the late 1940s, vinyl paints rapidly gained wide acceptance and were probably the most widely used of all the corrosion-protection paint systems used on boats right up through the 1980s. They are typically low-solid, high-solvent coatings. They are insoluble in oils, greases, and alcohols; they have excellent resistance to both freshwater and salt water and good abrasion resistance. However, coating thickness is rather low, in the range of 1.5 to 2.0 mils (0.038 to 0.051 mm) per coat, and pinholes in the dried film are more prevalent than in other coating systems. This necessitates multiple coats. Examples of vinyl paints are Interlux Viny-Lux and Woolsey Vinelast.

By the mid-1980s considerable pressure was building to limit the amount of volatile organic compounds (VOC) of paints to 3.5 lb./gal. (420 g/L), far less than the solvent content of vinyl paints at that time, which was on the order of 75 to 90 percent of the total volume of the paint. Many states—not all—have enacted legislation restricting the solvent content of paints, so these coatings may not comply with VOC regulations in some regions. The enactment of uniform federal legislation on solvent content could impact formulations and availability of these coatings in the future.

Chlorinated Rubber Paints

Chlorinated rubber paints are a form of solvent-deposited coating that is used much more extensively in Europe than in the United States. These paints have very low water-vapor-transmission rates, on the order of one-tenth that of alkyd paints, and are used as swimming pool paints, highway marking paints, and masonry and marine coatings. These coatings have excellent adhesion to steel, concrete, and wood. They are widely used to protect steel in various chemical atmospheres as well as in both freshwater and saltwater immersion. Chlorinated rubber paints are used as a coating on steel hulls.

Bituminous Coatings

Bituminous coatings refer to *coal-tar pitches* and *asphalt*. Here again, these coatings are used more in Europe than in United States and are more common on large commercial work vessels and structures than on recreational craft. In appearance, both coal-tar pitch and asphalt are black thermoplastic tars, and both have excellent resistance to moisture penetration and corrosive atmospheres. However, they are chemically and physically different and should not be mixed or applied over each other.

Bituminous coatings are applied either as hot melted liquids called *hot melts*, as solvent-base liquids called *solvent cutbacks*, or as water-base emulsions. In hot-melt coatings the material is heated to an almost waterlike viscosity (350° to 475°F or 177° to 246°C) and usually applied with mops, although it is sometimes brushed, rolled, or sprayed. Solvent cutbacks and emulsions can be brushed, rolled, or sprayed and do not require heating.

Coal-Tar Enamels

Coal-tar enamels (pitches) have excellent salt and freshwater resistance—better, in fact, than all other types of coatings. Coal-tar pitches are susceptible to surface cracking from ultraviolet light and cold weather, but because the underlying thicknesses remain plastic, this cracking is not detrimental to corrosion resistance. Coal-tar pitches are widely used as moisture-resistant coatings on underground pipelines and in seawater immersion on barge bottoms and pilings. A principal advantage is relatively low cost. When used as roof coatings, coal-tar pitches are protected from ultraviolet exposure by additional coatings or by a layer of gravel or crushed stone.

Asphalt

Asphalt coatings have good water resistance, although not as good as the coal tars, but they are much less susceptible to ultraviolet degradation. They do not have good resistance to solvents or oils. These coating materials are frequently used in applications involving atmospheric exposures where coal tars would not be suitable.

Epoxy Coatings

Epoxy coatings are nearly always two-part systems. The first part consists of the epoxy resin, together with pigments and solvent. The second part is the copolymer curing agent. The two parts are mixed just prior to application. In general, epoxies have good adhesion and excellent resistance to acids, solvents, and water. They are widely used on swimming pools, on aquaculture structures, and as marine coatings.

The properties of the coatings depend to a large extent on the specific curing agent used.

The two most commonly used curing agents in marine protective coatings are polyamines and polyamides.

Polyamine-Cured Epoxies

Polyamine-cured epoxies have excellent resistance to most acids, alkalis (as in concrete), and both freshwater and salt water. They also have good resistance to solvents on short exposure. They are harder and less flexible than other epoxies and have a tendency to chalk when exposed to ultraviolet light. They require some care in application: they have limited pot-life; they must not be applied in damp or high-moisture environments; they will not cure at temperatures below 40°F (4°C); and second coats must be applied within 72 hours. Also, their full protective properties do not develop for about seven days. Amine-cured epoxies have excellent adhesion to concrete and steel and are commonly used in seawater applications.

Polyamide-Cured Epoxies

Polyamide-cured epoxies are superior to amine-cured epoxies in water immersion applications. They have excellent adhesion, have high gloss, and are harder and tougher than the amine-cured epoxies. Some amide-cured epoxy formulations can be applied to wet or even underwater surfaces. Otherwise, they have application characteristics and limitations similar to the amine-cured epoxies.

Coal-Tar Epoxies

Coal-tar epoxies are combinations of coal tar and an epoxy resin in one container and a curing agent—either an amine or an amide—in the other container. The coal tar functions as a filler in the epoxy matrix and produces coatings with the same adhesion and toughness as the other epoxies, plus extremely high moisture resistance. Amine-cured coal-tar epoxies are, however, more difficult to apply. Second coats should be applied within 48 hours, and the coating will not cure at temperatures below 50°F (10°C). Also, they tend to get brittle when exposed to ultraviolet light. However, coal-tar-epoxy coatings feature truly outstanding resistance to both freshwater and salt water, good resistance to acids, alkalis, and solvents, and a relatively low cost.

Polyurethane Coatings

Polyurethane coatings are the result of a reaction between an *isocyanate* and a *polyol*. The isocyanate is a reactive complex chemical group that contains nitrogen, carbon, and oxygen. It co-reacts with the polyol to form the polyurethane film. The two are packaged separately and mixed prior to application. The polyol contains the pigment, the solvent, and the additives used to control thickness, flow, and setting properties. A word of caution: isocyanates are quite hazardous as liquids and vapors, and exposure should be limited and controlled. Solid polyurethane films are not a problem except when being drilled, sawed, and sanded, which can create hazardous dust.

There are a number of different and often proprietary polyols (typically a polyester, polyether, epoxy, or acrylic), each tailored to emphasize or enhance some characteristic of the coating—resistance to specific chemicals, temperature tolerance, corrosion resistance, cost, and so forth. The two types of polyols most commonly used in the marine industry are acrylics and polyesters.

Acrylic Urethanes

Acrylic urethanes are probably the most widely used urethanes for corrosion protection in atmospheric exposure applications. They have excellent atmospheric resistance, high gloss, and good color retention. They accept tinting and pigmentation readily, thus making them available in a wide variety of colors. Acrylic urethanes are not, however, recommended for immersion service.

Polyester Urethanes

Polyester urethanes produce relatively hard films with less impact resistance than the acrylic urethanes. Chemical and moisture resistance of the polyester urethanes is superior to that of the acrylic urethanes, but they are likewise unsuitable for immersion service.

Zinc-Rich Coatings

The binder in a zinc-rich coating might be any of several of the coatings referred to above but be highly loaded with zinc dust pigment. Zinc-rich coatings are primarily used as primers, and they must be applied to a thoroughly cleaned steel surface. Upon curing, the zinc particles are held in contact with the steel and with each other. The zinc becomes the anode of a galvanic cell and sacrifices itself to protect the cathodic steel. This effectively eliminates corrosion at the surface of the metal, even at scratches, pinholes, and defects in the coating. However, the metal surface must be meticulously cleaned to near-white metal if the part is to be immersed.

These paints lay down a film of metallic zinc that has many of the properties of zinc coatings applied by hot-dipping, electroplating, thermal spraying, or mechanical plating. The zinc powder used as pigments in these coatings normally has a total zinc content greater than 99 percent. They must be applied over clean surfaces in order to provide the metal-to-metal contact necessary for the coating to perform successfully. White-metal grit blasting is preferred; however, near-white or commercial-grade blast cleaning is acceptable. These coatings are widely used in the marine industry in both marine atmospheric and seawater immersion applications such as offshore drilling platforms and ship holds.

Zinc chromate is a zinc-rich coating that is used on both ferrous and nonferrous metals. This is the familiar yellow—sometimes greenish—primer widely used on steel and aluminum hulls and as a protective coating on steel plate after pickling.

RUST PREVENTIVES

Of the many fascinating areas involved in building, repairing, owning, and maintaining boats, few start the creative juices flowing like the subject of rust-preventive solutions. Raise the subject down at the yard—especially around the old-timers—then sit back and take notes. You'll hear about some of the strangest and most interesting concoctions since you last read the Wizard of Id comic strip. Some of them even work—and quite well!

There are those who, with fondness, will recall Cosmoline, the trademark name of the industry and military standard for rust and corrosion prevention going back to the Civil War. Cosmoline, like most rust preventives of that period, was simply a grease-like compound of petrolatum (petroleum jelly) that was smeared on metal surfaces and provided only barrier protection. It was widely used by the military during World War II and the Korean War, and old vets bemoan its lack of availability.

Many turned to substitutions or their own mixtures. Wheel-bearing grease was favored by some for its high-temperature properties and anti-rust additives. It does have some beneficial effects, but, alas, it lacks the ability to penetrate the surface and displace moisture.

Others offer what has come to be known as "Ed's Red." This is a mixture of automatic transmission fluid (ATF), kerosene, acetone, and various other ingredients, depending on who's advocating it. Sometimes motor oil is substituted for the ATF—not a good idea since most contain detergents that are hygroscopic (absorb moisture). The kerosene is the penetrant, carrying the oil into the surface of the metal and, hopefully, displacing some moisture. Sure to follow is a discussion of kerosene versus turpentine versus paint thinner, each with its own advocates. Fact is, the principal difference is cost. Kerosene's big advantage is that it's cheaper.

"Yah, but," say the naysayers, "these coatings dry off fairly quickly and must be recoated within days or rust returns." At this point, someone is sure to suggest that you have to add some paraffin to the mix to give it longevity. There quickly follows a discussion of what type of wax should be used—floor wax, sealing wax, furniture wax, beeswax, or something else. Then we come to the critical question—how to dissolve the wax in the kerosene?

"Why," answers the old-timer, "you simply put the kerosene in a pan, put it on the stove, and raise its temperature above the melting point of the wax." This is where they lose me. Heating kerosene or paint thinner over direct heat in a shop full of combustible materials doesn't strike me as a particularly good idea. (The kitchen, of course, is out of the question!)

Perhaps more to the point, though, is why would you want to go through all of this when there are many fine, precisely formulated and optimized, proprietary formulations available at the local chandlery? These are available in convenient spray cans, quarts, 5-gallon pails, and even 55-gallon drums, and they can be applied by spraying, brushing, rolling, or dipping, depending on the size of both the job and your wallet. They provide long-term protection against acids, alkalis, salts, and all kinds of corrosion; displace moisture; absorb corrosion; form a moisture barrier; and have high penetration and lubrication. They can be used on sheaves, fittings, cables, hinges, switches, motors, electrical circuits, and electronics.

The number and variety of commercially available rust preventives on the market boggles the mind. Some of the more popular and proven brand names are LanoCote, Boeshield T-9, Corrosion Block, Corrosion X, and, for the old vets, Rust Veto 342, the modern version of Cosmoline by the same manufacturer who brought you the original.

Some of the do-it-yourself potions do work pretty well. My own favorite is a blend much favored by boatbuilder and guru of old tried-and-true methods Pete Culler. He called it *deck oil*; we call it *magic magoosallum*. It consists of a gallon of boiled linseed oil, a pint of turpentine, and a pint of pine tar. Pete used it for just about everything—unpainted decks, inside the skiff, as a starter coat for wooden spars, on an old rusty boat trailer, and on the mushroom mooring pulled up and stored outside for the winter. We've used it for most of those jobs and also for painting the hull of an old Eldredge-McGinnis *Samurai* sloop we had out of the water during restoration, to keep it from drying out.

RUST REMOVERS: CONVERTERS AND SURFACE-TOLERANT COATINGS

Rust converters are a relatively new, controversial, and still developing technology. Even the terminology is still in flux. Terms being used are *rust passivators*, *rust converters*, *rust neutralizers*, *surface-tolerant coatings*, and several others. Most are proprietary liquid coatings designed to treat corroded metal surfaces by removing, neutralizing, or converting the affected surfaces and to leave them ready for adding a topcoating without the necessity for other surface preparation. Topcoats that are tolerant of poorly prepared surfaces are also included in this group.

These coatings seem to be enjoying a more favorable reception in the European community than here in the United States. There is not a lot of experiential data available on them, and some experts hold to the opinion that nothing comes near to a proper surface preparation—grit-blasting to white or near-white metal. However, some very large and well-respected old firms are actively involved in the development of these products, and they have demonstrated some impressive, if limited, successful applications. This is a very promising area that we'll have to monitor carefully over the next several years.

SUMMARY

There is more to corrosion protection than zinc anodes. A vast assortment of metal coatings and claddings is available that can be used to advantage in critical applications. A wide and expanding variety of organic coatings and new paint formulations—properly applied—can add years of relatively maintenance-free service. A great number of proprietary products can prevent or remove corrosion and add lubricity in critical applications. And, finally, new areas of developing technologies hold considerable promise for corrosion minimization or elimination in the not-too-distant future.

CHAPTER 16

Hull Corrosion

Most small-craft hulls are constructed of one of four principal materials—wood, fiberglass, aluminum, or steel. A fifth, ferro-cement, is not used for production of boats, but a number of one-offs have been built by knowledgeable, well-qualified builders who favor this material. And, depending on whether your definition of the term *composite* includes fiberglass, there could be several more. In any case, in this chapter we consider the various hull construction types and the corrosion problems associated with each. First though, let's talk in general about fastenings.

FASTENINGS

The most common cause of corrosion problems suffered by hull structures can be traced to the deterioration of fastenings, whether they fasten wood to wood, metal to wood, or metal to metal.

We need to understand what makes these little devils sick. Obviously, the corrosion resistance of metal used in the fastener is of great importance. The specific environment is likewise of critical importance. For example, when joints are subjected to stress, such as the normal working of a boat underway, the load is transmitted through the fastening from one structural member to the other. These stresses can be very high. If the hull is wood, repeated cycling tends to deform the wood around the fastening, allowing the joint to move and open. Wood hulls, by the way, have more fastenings by far than any other hull type (more than 2,000 in a 28-foot sailboat).

Eventually, there is enough deformation to allow water to penetrate and cause the fastening to corrode. As the corrosion progresses, more movement of the members results, more water penetrates, and more corrosion takes place. All of which is to say that *all* joints are worthy of some care in the making. Surfaces should be well and properly mated, forming a tight, snug joint. Fastenings should be of an appropriate type and size for the job, carefully located, and driven in properly sized pilot holes to ensure maximum strength, rigidity, holding power, and resistance to moisture penetration.

Dissimilar metals should not be used—easy to say, but not always easy to do. We can fasten bronze fittings with bronze fastenings and galvanized fittings with galvanized (hot-dipped) fastenings, but the fasteners for Monel and aluminum fittings are likely to be stainless steel, preferably 316. The basic rule is the fastening should always be more noble than the material being fastened, never less noble. For example, *never* use copper alloy fasteners (brass or bronze) in aluminum, as this will result in severe pitting and corrosion of the aluminum. Unfortunately, some amount of galvanic corrosion still takes place in the aluminum even when we use stainless steel fasteners. The resultant enlargement of the fastener hole could allow the fastener to drop out.

However, what about a situation where you have a wooden hull fastened with galvanized fastenings and you want to install a bronze underwater through-hull? You will, of course, make every effort to be sure that the bronze fastenings for the through-hull don't come into contact with any galvanized fastenings. But what if they do? We have three of the four required elements for the deadly galvanic cell: an anode (the galvanized fastenings), the cathode (the bronze through-hull and its fastenings), and a path for electrons (the physical contact between the two). All we're missing is a path for ionic conduction, an electrolyte, such as seawater. But how does the seawater get to the hull fastenings? Easier than you might think—missing bungs or otherwise exposed fastenings, or just plain old wet wood. In this instance, a galvanic cell will exist, and galvanic corrosion will take place. The important point here is the critical nature of fastenings.

I strongly recommend coating all fasteners, even in cases where fastener and substrate metals are similar. Most common greases are not effective for this. The moisture wicks up between the grease and the metal surface and actually increases crevice attack. As we saw in previous chapters, there are some specially formulated greases and lubricants that adhere to and displace water from metallic surfaces. Do not use graphite or graphite-containing lubricants, packings, or gaskets. Graphite forms a galvanic couple with most metals in seawater and greatly accelerates corrosion of the less noble metal.

It is worth mentioning (again) here that some high-strength materials—typically those above about 140,000 psi (965 MPa) tensile strength or 100,000 psi (689 MPa) yield strength—are susceptible to hydrogen released at the cathodically protected surfaces in structures protected with sacrificial anodes or impressed current systems. Some bolt metals fall in his category and should be avoided. Also, under the heading of "it doesn't happen very often, but in case anybody should ask you," copper alloy fasteners have been known to fail from stress-corrosion cracking due to ammonia in seagull droppings. Then there is our old friend dezincification. High-zinc brasses should *never* be used as substitutes for copper, silicon bronze, or aluminum bronze below the waterline. Finally, the free-machining stainless steels, for example, Types 303 (UNS S30300), 303Se (UNS S30323), and 416 (UNS S41600), will corrode rapidly in marine service and should not be used.

One more thing about fastenings: there are basically two types of threads—rolled and cut. Cut threads are preferred. We have already said that fastenings must fit snugly in their holes. With rolled threads, the diameter of the unthreaded shank is smaller than the outside diameter of the threads, so the shank cannot possibly fit tightly in the hole. Rolled threaded bolts are quite common because they are less costly to manufacture, and these fastenings are perfectly adequate when, for example, the fastening is purely in tension. However, this is not the case in hull structures, especially in sailboats. Fastenings with rolled threads should not be used in hull structures.

Machine Bolts

Machine bolts are used for heavy joining jobs (e.g., pulling the more massive backbone and structural members together), where the fastening may need further tightening (as members shrink), and where removal and replacement are anticipated.

Machine bolts are readily available in just about any metal you could want or need, from mild steel through titanium and including 18-8, 316, 317 stainless steel, bronze, aluminum, and Monel. They can be purchased with a wide variety of head types, including the familiar hexagonal and square types commonly found in boat work. All should be used with a washer of the *same material* and of *appropriate size* to spread the load over a broader area. In most cases bolts should be well bedded with a carefully selected sealant. The holes should be the same diameter as the bolts. Nut and bolt assemblies, because of their inherent crevices and stresses, are susceptible to corrosive damage in marine service. Galvanized (hot-dipped) steel does pretty well in atmospheric conditions but may deteriorate fairly rapidly when immersed in salt water.

Machine Screws

Bolts of smaller diameter—say less than ¾ in. (1.9 cm)—are referred to as machine screws. These are the fasteners you'll find on such things as locker doors, electrical fixtures, and some deck hardware on smaller craft. Heads are more likely to be slotted than square.

Machine screws are readily available in mild steel, 18-8 stainless steel, and brass. You can also get galvanized machine screws, but because hot-dipping tends to clog the smaller threads (and slots), the zinc coating is typically electroplated.

Here again, proper pilot holes, washers (under the nut, of course), and bedding on weather deck hardware are highly recommended.

Drift Bolts

A drift bolt is more like a humongous nail than a bolt. It is made from a length of rod stock, one end of which is pounded to a sort of chisel point. The other end is peened over after a washer or clinch ring is placed under it. The pilot hole should be *slightly* shorter than the length of the bolt and *slightly* smaller in diameter—to ensure a snug drive fit. If the pilot hole is too short or too tight, the bolt may split the wood. Some care has to be taken in driving to be sure not to bend the bolt.

Drift bolts are used to fasten heavy structural members such as floors to frames, stringers to clamps, and deck beams to shelves. Drift bolts are sometimes used as through-fastenings, like huge rivets. In this case the hole is drilled all the way through, and the bolt is made about two diameters longer to leave room for another clinch ring and peening. Pairs (or a series of pairs) of drift bolts should be driven at opposing angles to lock the members together.

Drift bolts are most often galvanized steel, but both copper and silicon bronze are also used. Care should taken with galvanized drift bolts to be sure that they have been hot-dipped and that the coating is not damaged when driving, exposing bare steel.

Carriage Bolts

Carriage bolts are machine bolts with a round, smooth, unslotted head. They have a square shank just under the head that is drawn or driven into the wood to keep the bolt from turning during tightening. Carriage bolts are typically employed where the members are too small for drift bolts or where there is good chance of a drive fastener splitting the members. The hole should be the same diameter as the bolt, with the bolt about one-and-a-half diameters longer to allow for the nut and washer. Carriage bolts, like drift bolts, are usually galvanized steel but also are available in stainless (18-8) and silicon bronze.

Lag Bolts

Sometimes called lag screws, these are actually large screws with a square head to enable the use of a wrench in driving the fastening. Typically, they are used only where it is either not possible or extremely difficult to use a through-bolt. Lag bolts are not highly regarded by many builders because it is bothersome and time-consuming to set them properly. Lags are available in galvanized steel, 18-8 stainless steel, and silicon bronze.

Hanger Bolts

Hanger bolts are essentially lag screws with the upper end of the shank threaded for a nut. They are used mostly for fastening stern bearings and shaft stuffing boxes and for securing the engine mounts to the beds. These are fittings that must be removed occasionally for servicing or replacement, which hangar bolts permit without disturbing the screw in the wood. This is important since periodic removing and retightening screw fastenings in wood wears the thread in the wood and reduces the holding power of the screw. Hanger bolts are driven by running a nut down to the end of the threads and turning it in with a wrench. They are available in the same materials as are lag screws.

Screws

The wood screw is the workhorse of wooden boat construction and repair. Flathead screws are used for plank and deck fastening as well as a number of other less obvious but important joining jobs all over the boat. They are commercially available in just about any metal we might consider for boatbuilding (and in some we shouldn't). Local marine supply stores are likely to stock galvanized steel, silicon bronze, stainless steel, and brass screws. They can special-order Monel. The suitability of each of these metals depends on where the screw will be used.

Screws hold things together—planks to frames, for example—so they carry tensile loads. They also prevent the joined pieces from moving past each other, so they also carry shear or lateral loads. Both functions are of considerable importance to the boat owner since in the case of tensile stress they keep the planks from falling off , and in the case of shear stress they keep the planks from moving back and forth laterally when the boat is driven hard and the hull "works." Critical to both functions is the area of the fastener that bears against the wood. A thick fastening with sharp, clean thread surfaces bearing against the wood is better than a thin fastening with little thread surface. This will be significant when we talk about both galvanized screws and nails further on.

Another thing to keep in mind is that screws used below the waterline in wood, fiberglass, or ferro-cement receive no benefit from the boat's cathodic protection system (zinc anodes). Also, as we have already seen, metals buried in damp host materials and denied access to a fresh supply of oxygen are susceptible to severe crevice corrosion. Therefore, the service life of the fastener will depend on the inherent corrosion resistance of the metal.

Galvanized Screws

I remember reading some time back about a 43-foot (13 m) Alden-designed Malabar-type schooner yacht that was built in 1926 using galvanized fastenings. Life expectancy back then was about 20 years for a galvanized-fastened boat, but this one was still sailing and just about ready for some serious frame and backbone replacement in 1988. Now, this is surely the exception rather than the rule, and the yacht had had meticulous care, but it had had almost no alteration or rebuilding in all of those 62 years.

When this schooner was abuilding, galvanized screws were used extensively, even in fine yachts. Also, galvanized fastenings were of considerably better quality back then. The old-timers will tell you that a very high quality Swedish iron was used, that the threads were cut specifically to receive a very heavy hot-dip zinc coating, and that "you can't get them kind anymore." Most of what is commonly available nowadays is a much thinner electroplated zinc coating on mild steel and is really not suitable for immersion in salt water.

Hot-dipped galvanized fasteners are available—at a premium price—and are still being used, but the coatings are not of the quality of former years. Typically, especially on the smaller sizes, the slots are clogged and the threads are pretty rough. I must have a gross of such rejects somewhere in the shop that I kept "just in case." Aside from their being difficult to use, their holding power is greatly decreased. Also, once galvanized screws start to rust, they cause considerable damage to the wood around them, so this necessitates earlier refastening. The reason usually given for using galvanized screws is their lower cost, but if you consider the potential for earlier refastening, the greater difficulty in using them in terms of time and frustration, and the number of unusable screws you might find in a box, it strikes me as false economy.

Silicon Bronze

Popularly known as *Everdur*, silicon bronze is probably the most widely used of all types of fasteners for boat work. Nearly as strong as mild steel, silicon bronze screws not only provide good tensile and shear stress properties, but they also seldom twist off when being driven. Add excellent corrosion resistance in saltwater immersion, and you've got one pretty fine fastening. As I write this, I'm looking at a bunch of silicon bronze screws we took out of a 32-year-old Eldredge-McInnis *Samurai* sloop. We replaced them at the time since we had them out, but I kept them because they are still in pretty fine shape. There is some reddish copper oxide and greenish copper chloride discoloration, but the shanks show no loss of metal, and the threads are still fairly sharp. That's not bad after thirty-odd years in salt water.

Silicon bronze screws are generally of good quality with sharp, machine-cut threads. They are produced in a wide range of sizes, head types, and driving configurations (slotted, Phillips, Torx) suitable for manual or power driving. When you consider that it takes no more time to set a silicon bronze screw than any other type—less, actually, if you include the pick-and-choose process necessary with some galvanized screws—the difference in cost is not as great as the price of the screws alone might suggest. Truly, these are a most robust and versatile fastening.

Stainless Steel

Do not use stainless steel screws below the waterline! How's that for a provocative statement? We're talking here specifically about the so-called marine grades—18-8, 316, and 317—but the fact is, *no* stainless steel fastening should be used below the waterline. When moisture becomes trapped (stagnant) against the stainless steel, it quickly becomes deoxygenated, and the *passive* stainless steel turns *active* and is subject to severe crevice corrosion. This means that stainless steel screws should be used only where the wood will remain fairly dry. It also explains the importance of proper sealing and bedding of stainless steel deck hardware. In any place where the host wood is damp and the fastening is deprived of oxygen, stainless steel should not be used. This is a place for silicon bronze or hot-dipped galvanized screws.

Brass

Brass fastenings are unsuitable for saltwater immersion and should not be used anywhere they will be exposed to high levels of salt-laden moisture. Brasses containing more than about 16 percent zinc are highly susceptible to dezincification, which effectively destroys the metal's usefulness as a fastening. Most brass used in the manufacture of screws and bolts has high zinc content, as much as 30 percent. If you really feel the need to use brass fastenings, use them only on interior joiner work. And go gently; brass is not very strong, and it's fairly easy to twist off the heads if the screws are driven too hard.

Coated Screws

Recently, a new type of screw has shown up in hardware stores and building supply centers. They're referred to as "deck screws" and sold for use in porches, decks, and fences. They're completely ceramic coated and supposedly virtually immune to corrosion. They haven't been around long enough for there to be much long-term service-life data. I don't know of anyone who has used them in boat work, but they sound like they have potential. We'll have to keep an eye on them.

NAILS AND RIVETS

Nails come in lots of varieties—boat nails, wire nails, hatch nails, clench nails, clout nails, annular ring nails, and more. Some nails also can be used for riveting, as can plain rod stock and, of course, rivets—both solid and blind. Whether you use nail or rivet, which is more suitable in terms of corrosion, comes down to the type of metal, its coating (or the lack thereof), its size and mass, and where it is used on the boat.

Nails

Boat Nails

A boat nail is a robust forged and hot-dipped galvanized square-section fastening, driven by hammering, and traditionally used for fastening both bottom- and topside planking and planking in other places in the backbone structure of the vessel. It once was the fastener of choice wherever the thickness of the timber would permit. No less an authority than Howard Chapelle, naval architect and historian emeritus of the Smithsonian Institution, calls the lowly boat nail "unsurpassed" where strength and cost are prime considerations. Their sharp, square edges, large heads, and rough surfaces give them good holding power. The high-quality forged iron and thick, hot-dip zinc coatings give them excellent corrosion resistance and long life. Where thickness of the members permit, nails are driven all the way through in pilot holes slightly smaller than the shank of the nail and "clenched," that is, bent back into the wood on the inside to further increase their holding power. Boat nails are very difficult to withdraw; often the plank has to be cut away.

In the 1930s and 1940s, when boat nails were used extensively in both workboats and fine yachts, they were forged of high-quality iron and treated to the best possible hot-dip galvanizing. Much of what is available today is plain old mild steel with electroplated coatings. Where hot-dip coatings are available, they are not of the quality of those of yesteryear. This is due in part to changes in the galvanizing processes brought about by environmental and workplace health and safety requirements, which necessitated changes in bath temperatures and duration. In any case, the result is that we cannot expect the same service performance from today's galvanized nails as from those of the past.

Clench Nails and Rivets

Clench (some people say "clinch") nails are made of both galvanized iron and copper or copper alloy. They have round, straight, nontapered shanks brought to a point at the end—essentially the same as common nails. While these nails can be clenched and sometimes are, they are primarily used as rivets for fastening frames to planking, stringers to frames, and planking laps in lapstrake construction. A closely related member of the family is the "clout" nail, a small, square-sectioned copper nail used as a clench fastener in small craft of light construction, such as canoes and small lapstrake boats.

When used as a rivet, the nail is driven through a pilot slightly smaller than the shank (the same size in hardwoods) and then a *burr* or *rove* (like a tight-fitting washer) is forced over the point of the nail and driven tight against the wood with a special hollow-pointed rove iron. After the end of the nail is cut off, leaving about one and a half diameters above the rove, the cut end is headed, or shaped, by tapping it with *light* blows from a small ball-peen hammer while a helper holds a *holding* or *bucking* iron against the head.

Clenching is a littler trickier. The hole is drilled as for riveting, but as the nail is driven through the members, the end is turned over and formed into a hook by holding the face of a hammer against the side of the nail. When the hook is fully formed, the nail is driven home

against a heavy hammer held against the crown of the hook to force the point of the nail back into the wood.

With the exception of the brasses, copper or copper-alloy nails have excellent corrosion resistance and make for very long lasting fastenings. However, some copper nails and roves may deteriorate with age. The end of the nail or rivet turns a sort of bluish green, crumbles, and loses its rove. It is the headed-over part, not the shank, that tends to corrode—both from work hardening and saltwater exposure. Roves can be checked by slipping the point of an awl under the rove and exerting a little upward pressure. Paint coating on the fastening should be touched up, and needless to say, rivets with missing or faulty roves should be replaced promptly to head off leaky seams. The danger with galvanized nails lies in the coatings, which, if not of good quality, can be damaged and flake off from the bending and pounding.

Annular Ring Nails

Annular ring fasteners resemble common nails—flat head and round shank of uniform diameter to within a short distance of a sharp point. The shank of these fasteners, however, has a series of annular rings. As the nail is driven, the wood fibers are formed, or deformed, into wedges in the annular grooves, greatly increasing holding power. Some quite remarkable claims are made—65 percent more holding power than an unclenched galvanized nail, 30 percent more than a clenched nail, and 3 percent more than a wood screw. Builders who have used these nails report as much as 25 percent less planking labor with these fastenings, an impressive savings.

Probably the best-known annular ring fastener is the *Anchorfast*. Anchorfast nails, made by the Independent Nail Company of Taunton, Massachusetts, are made of Monel and have a unique rolled-thread pattern, technically known as a *fetter ring*. The same ring pattern in silicon bronze is known by the trade name *Stronghold*. Monel and silicon bronze both exhibit excellent corrosion resistance and long service life, but the Monel Anchorfast is the superior fastener because it is stiffer and less susceptible to bending when driven and thus is more tolerant of pilot hole dimensions. Pilot holes should be between 50 and 70 percent of the shank diameter, depending on the hardness of the wood. Hole depth should be about 80 percent of the nail's length.

Now for the bad news. The use and availability of boatbuilding nails has declined along with the decline in wooden boat building. At the time of this writing, Independent Nail Company no longer produces either Anchorfast or Stronghold nails as part of their regular production schedule. They will be happy to make up a batch of either on special order, but the minimum order size is 2,000 pounds. That would be about 2 million nails of average size—that's a lot of nails!

Rivets

There are basically two types of rivets that are of interest to us: solid rivets and blind rivets. Pop is a trade name for a particular brand of blind rivet.

Solid Rivets

The applicable standards for solid rivets in both the United States (ANSI B18.1.1) and the United Kingdom (BS 641) distinguish between large and small rivets. In both standards large rivets are those with shank diameters of $\frac{1}{2}$ inch (1.2 cm) or greater. We are interested in small rivets. These rivets are available in aluminum, steel, Monel, stainless steel, and many other metals.

Riveted aluminum small craft such as canoes, drift boats, skiffs, and runabouts in sizes up to about 24 feet (7.3 m) typically use 5052- or 5086-grade solid-aluminum rivets with a diameter of approximately 0.160 to 0.190 inches (0.4 to 0.48 cm). Rivet diameter should be 1.2 to 1.4 times the square root of the plate thickness. The hole size should be about $\frac{1}{16}$ inch (0.159 cm) larger than the diameter of the rivet. It is important that the hole be properly sized and cleanly made. The rivet, after forming, should fit the hole completely. If there is any irregularity or looseness, the next larger size of rivet should be used.

Two basic types of riveted joints are in common use: the *lap joint* and the *butt joint*. In the ordinary lap joint, the sheets to be joined overlap each other and are held together by one or more rows of rivets. Plates or sheets to be butt-jointed are brought together edge-to-edge with the seam covered by a *buttstrap* or *backing plate*. This assembly is then held together by one or more rows of rivets through the buttstrap and each plate.

The center of a rivet should be a minimum of $1\frac{1}{2}$ to 2 times the rivet diameter from the edge of the plate. The spacing between rivet centers in a row should be as close as practical but not less than 4 times the rivet diameter. Adjacent rows should be at least $1\frac{3}{4}$ rivet diameters apart. This is to avoid tearing of the holes under shearing stresses.

Aluminum is highly resistant to single-metal corrosion but highly susceptible to galvanic corrosion. Only rivets of marine-grade aluminum should be used in fastening aluminum boats. The use of any other rivet material will result in the loss of metal around the fastener and the loss of the rivet. It is a good practice to dip the rivets in zinc chromate before they are inserted into the hole. It is also a good idea to coat the overlapping surfaces with an epoxy base coating or sealant before joining to ensure a good seal.

A common problem with aluminum rivets is loosening from pounding, vibration, or plain old working of the hull. If discovered early enough—before the rivets get too loose and become misshapen—they are simply hammered up again with the dolly bar and ball-peen hammer. If a rivet is too far gone and cannot be tightened up, it must be drilled out with a drill slightly larger than the existing hole and replaced with the next larger size rivet. Incidentally, you will seldom find only one loose rivet, so check adjacent and nearby rivets while you're at it.

Blind Rivets

When you can't use a bucking iron (dolly iron) on the backside—on hollow aluminum spars, for example—you have to use blind rivets, commonly called *pop rivets*. Pop, however, is actually a trade name for a broad line of blind rivets manufactured by Emhart Industrial. Blind rivets are used for a variety of fastening jobs in both aluminum and fiberglass boats. Figure 16-1 shows a typical blind fastener before and after setting.

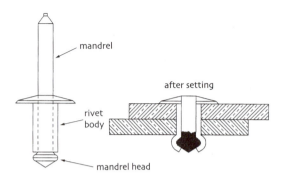

Fig. 16-1. Typical blind fastener, or pop fastener, before and after setting. Note the open end, which can permit water penetration.

Blind rivets consist of the *rivet body* and the *setting mandrel*. The rivet body is placed in the hole, and a special riveting tool (a pliers type of hand tool) is placed on the mandrel. When you squeeze the tool, it grips the mandrel and sets the rivet by pulling the mandrel head into the rivet body, expanding it. At a predetermined force, the mandrel breaks—with a pop—and the rivet is set.

Hole size is critical. Too small, and you risk tearing the edges of the hole; too large, and both shear and tensile strength of the joint are reduced, and the rivet will not set properly. The best guide is the manufacturer's recommendations. Spacing of rivet centers should be at least 3 times the rivet diameter and at least 2 rivet diameters from the edge of the plate.

This is a very versatile family of fasteners, available either open-ended or closed-ended (water- and vapor-tight) in a variety of rivet body and mandrel metals—5052, 5056, 300 series stainless steel, Monel, and even a PVC-insulated version for joining dissimilar metals. For most boat applications you will want the closed-end type with both the rivet body and a flush-break mandrel of 5052 aluminum. The mandrel is retained in the body, so steel mandrels, either plain or stainless steel, are not suitable.

Other Fasteners

Staples

Staples are very versatile—fast and simple to install and, in silicon bronze or Monel, a highly corrosion-resistant fastening. They are often used as fastenings in lighter construction such as canoes and kayaks. They are also great for laying laminated frames in place, securing successive epoxy-coated strips until the desired buildup is achieved.

There's a tendency to try to use the longest possible leg length. As a rule, however, if the staple does not penetrate completely, it means that the leg length is too long, so a shorter staple should be used. Also, it takes a little practice to get into the habit of snugging the head of the gun down to the work and not letting it bounce.

Threaded Inserts

One type of threaded insert fastener has a plastic body that encapsulates a threaded metal insert. The plastic body is inserted into a blind hole, much like a blind rivet. Tightening a conventional machine screw in the threaded insert causes the body to expand, fixing it securely in place. Typical of this type of fastening is the Well-Nut, manufactured by Emhart. Since the body of the bushing is plastic (or neoprene), there is no danger of galvanic corrosion. These are useful devices for mounting mast-top fixtures such as antennas and wind indicators.

Another type of insert is the Jack Nut (also manufactured by Emhart), designed for use in thin, soft, or brittle materials. A special installation tool collapses the body of the fastener against the mounting plate on the inside, leaving a permanent, reusable threaded insert. These are available in brass, plain steel, and steel with one of several different coatings. One of the available coatings is PVC, which insulates the fastener from the mounting plate.

THROUGH-HULLS

Through-hull fittings constitute probably the greatest potential threat to the watertight integrity of the hull. Many boats have sunk as a result of failed through-hulls. I remember reading, in W. D. Booth's excellent little book on refurbishing older fiberglass boats, how with very little pressure his engine intake seacock broke off in his hand right at the hull. That scares me!

It is critically important not just to properly maintain your through-hulls but to select the proper ones to begin with.

There are hundreds of types of valves, designed for a variety of applications in all kinds of industries and fabricated from all kinds of materials. Very few are suitable for marine service.

Industrial Valves

Most industrial and domestic valves you find at your local plumbing supply or hardware store are *gate* or *globe* valves. Gate valves have a wheel-type handle attached to one end of a threaded stem and a vertical disk, or *gate*, fastened to the other end. The disk slides up or down in a slot in the valve body as the stem is rotated. Most gate valves are designed to operate either in the fully open or fully closed position and tend to chatter (vibrate) if left in an intermediate position.

A globe valve is physically similar to a gate valve, but the disk is perpendicular to the stem and is screwed down against a seat to close the valve. Globe valves are designed to regulate the volume of flow as against merely preventing or allowing full flow.

Most industrial valves—gate or globe—are made of brass and will dezincify if exposed to salt water. Even valves with bronze bodies nearly always have brass or steel internal components. A tendency to jam, combined with corrosion of the stem, often results in a broken stem, leaving you with a closed valve when you want it open or, worse yet, an open valve when you need it closed. The *only* place on the boat where these types of valves should be used is as flow control faucets in the vessel's domestic freshwater system. They are not suitable for any other service on the boat.

Marine Seacocks and Through-Hulls

The term *sea-valve* refers to any positive closure device specifically designed for marine use. The term *seacock* refers to a sea-valve with a flanged base that allows the valve body to be fastened directly to the hull. A *through-hull* is a threaded pipe with a flange that is mounted through the hull and secured with a retaining nut. A sea-valve that is threaded onto a through-hull is called an *in-line sea-valve*. The distinction becomes significant because in-line sea-valves are more susceptible to accidental damage and aren't considered as safe as seacocks.

All Bronze, Tapered Plug

The traditional seacocks have a bronze body around a bronze tapered cylindrical plug with a hole through it. A lever attached to the plug rotates it just a quarter turn—90 degrees—to put the hole in line with the flow or at right angles to it. This type of seacock is simple, rugged, and highly corrosion resistant. It is, of course, susceptible to both galvanic and electrolytic (stray-current) corrosion, with the most probable cause of failure being dissimilar fastenings securing the fitting to the hull. This type of seacock is very reliable but *must* have regular maintenance.

All Bronze, Rubber Plug

This type of seacock substitutes a rubber cylinder—with a hole through it—for the bronze tapered one. A threaded T-handle opposite the operating lever pushes a metal plate against the rubber plug, "swelling" it against the sides of the valve body for a tight seal. These are very reliable and require less maintenance than the tapered plug type. However, the required two-step operation to open or close them was not very popular, and production has been discontinued. (Replacement parts are still available from Groco.)

All Bronze, Ball Type

This is by far the most popular type of seacock on the market today. The plug is a ball with a hole through it, rotating in Teflon, nylon, or hard plastic seats. Construction is simple and reliable, and the valve requires little if any lubrication, just regular use. The body of the valve is bronze, and the ball is either chrome-plated bronze or 316 stainless steel. The 316 stainless steel ball is superior for seawater applications. After prolonged exposure to seawater, the chrome plating has been known to lift and eventually peel off, and it may cause the valve to jam.

As to corrosion problems, except for the chrome plating that encapsulates the bronze ball, the dissimilar metals, that is, the ferrous ball and the nonferrous valve body, are isolated from each other by the plastic seals so there is little opportunity for internal galvanic corrosion.

Plastic Body, Ball Types

These seacocks are essentially the same in construction as the bronze ball type, except that the body is some form of reinforced plastic. The ball is usually plastic but may be either stainless steel or chrome-plated bronze; as before, it is seated on Teflon, nylon, or hard plastic seals. These seacocks are lightweight and impervious to galvanic, electrolytic, and single-metal corrosion (except for the metal ball, if one is used). They do require lubrication twice a year, and as with all valves, they should be operated on a regular basis (at least once every thirty days) to avoid "freezing."

The most popular of the plastic through-hull fittings are made of Marelon, the trademark of a glass-reinforced nylon material that has been optimized for marine use by the Forespar Products Company. Marelon fittings exceed all current U.S. and European Community (EC) standards for marine seacocks and through-hulls.

Incidentally, it is not a good idea to mix Marelon seacocks with bronze through-hulls, or vice versa—not from any corrosion considerations, but rather from a mechanical fit point of view. They do not seat well and will continually weep.

BALLAST SYSTEMS

Inside ballast is most often in the form of small units of lead or iron, called pigs, but the variety of other materials used is limited only by the imagination. They include beach stones and bags filled with sand, cast iron sash weights, scrap iron of all kinds, even concrete or resin with and without embedded scrap metal. In one of my first boats, a little 24-foot (7.3 m) carvel-planked centerboard sloop that carried a ton of sail, I used fire brick. I couldn't afford those nice, clean lead pigs. Outside ballast is usually cast lead or cast iron, either exposed or enclosed in fiberglass, but it may also be steel or even concrete with scrap iron mixed in.

The corrosion problems that concern us, with both inside and outside ballast, are those suffered by the ballast itself and those that may be caused by the ballast.

Inside Ballast

If inside ballast is lead, there is little to be concerned about as far as corrosion goes. However, if it is cast iron, we must take precautions, especially when the boat has copper alloy fittings and fastenings. If the cast iron and the copper alloy come into contact when immersed in bilge-water, galvanic corrosion will occur. Even if there is not contact, the cast iron will rust severely, producing a rusty soup sloshing around in the bilge. Possible solutions are the usual ones—a rust-preventive coating of paint, epoxy, or plastic, all of which will require periodic maintenance.

Cement is often found in sailboat bilges. If it is there for ballast, it will almost certainly have some form of low-cost metal scrap mixed in since cement alone weighs only around 193 lb./cu. ft. (3,100 kg/m^3), compared to 491 lb./cu. ft. (7,865 kg/m^3) for steel. The cement may only serve as a sealant over the top of other ballast, usually steel in the form of bars or scrap, or cast iron in a variety of forms. Some less expensive fiberglass boats and many ferro-cement boats are built this way. Or the cement might be there simply to ensure good fore and aft drainage to get accumulated water to the bilge pumps.

In any case, there should not be any cracks, chips, or crevices at the edges to let water penetrate into or down to the metal ballast. The resulting rust, because it occupies more volume than the metal that produced it, may widen the cracks and break down the cement structure. Indications of rust in cracks or at the edges of the cement are a pretty fair sign that moisture is getting to the metal below or within the cement. If this is happening in a wooden boat, there is likely to be damage in the form of rot or decay in the frames where they emerge from the cement.

Unfortunately, the only way to find out what's going on down there is to excavate—chip out the cement and expose what's in or under it. This is a time-consuming and therefore costly job.

Outside Ballast

Outside ballast is typically in the form of an iron or lead casting bolted to the backbone of the boat. The choice of lead or cast iron is largely one of cost. Lead weighs about 710 lb./cu. ft. (11,373 kg/m³), whereas cast iron is about 447 lb./cu. ft. (7,160 kg/m³). Cast iron is considerably less expensive and quite satisfactory for most cruising sailboats. Plate steel may also used for outside ballast in the form of fin keels.

In terms of corrosion, cast lead is to be preferred. Immersed iron and steel will, of course, rust, and such keels must be protected. A proper coating system, consisting of preparation of the base metal, primer, topcoat, and antifouling, is the recommended treatment.

Resin or concrete mixed with scrap iron or steel is sometimes encased in a steel form or a hollow keel, with a sealing layer at the top to keep out moisture. Water penetration will cause the embedded ferrous scrap metal to rust, and the rust, which occupies more space than metal, will push the sealing layer up and, ultimately, the sides out. This allows more water to enter, and the situation gets worse. Eventually, the ballast mass may become less securely held and start to shift within its encasement, constituting a hazard to the vessel in heavy weather sailing.

Ballast keels are typically bolted in place. In cast iron keels, holes for the keel bolts are usually recessed at the bottom of the keel to accept the washer and nut and some sort of sealant to keep water out. Ballast keels are sometimes *galleried*, meaning access to the bottom nut is via a hole in the side of the casting (fig. 16-2).

Keel bolts for cast iron keels may be of mild steel, galvanized mild steel, or a chrome-nickel-molybdenum stainless steel such as 316. If stainless steel bolts are used, it is essential to maintain proper sealing at both the top and bottom of the

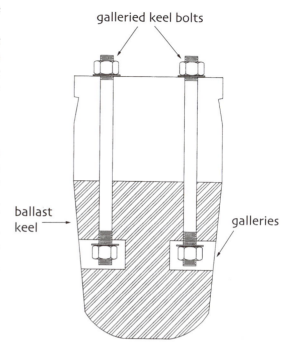

Fig. 16-2. Galleried ballast keel. Access to the bottom nuts is through slots cast into the ballast keel, which are filled after the bolts have been tightened.

bolt and at the ballast keel-backbone joint. Passive stainless steel can become active and susceptible to severe corrosion when immersed in stagnant seawater. Silicon bronze, aluminum bronze, nickel-aluminum bronze, and Monel keel bolts have been used, but these alloys are not galvanically compatible with the ballast iron and should be electrically insulated from it.

For cast lead ballast keels, the keel bolt may be cast into the lead or through-bolted as with iron ballast keels. Keel bolts may be of silicon bronze, aluminum bronze, nickel aluminum bronze, or Monel. The same precautions regarding the bedding/sealing of ends and joints should be taken.

Keel Bolts

Under the best of conditions, the environment surrounding keel bolts is harsh. Outside ballast is under considerable stress and "works" as the boat is sailed, especially so in heavy weather, and there is the occasional grounding—all of which constitutes some very heavy dynamic loading. The top of the bolt, together with its nut and washer, is constantly exposed to oxygen-depleted salt water. If the sealant under the washer fails, or the bolt head encapsulation, if any, leaks and water seeps into the bolt hole, the stagnant seawater will just sit there—ideal conditions for crevice corrosion to occur. A failure of the seal between the top of the ballast keel and the bottom of the boat is another potential cause of accelerated corrosion. This is, in fact, the area where most corrosion damage takes place. It results in extreme thinning of the bolt—called *waisting*. I can illustrate the consequences with an incident from my own sordid past.

We had hauled the boat over the road some 25 miles and had just put it in the water. There followed a brief but spirited discussion between my son and me concerning the bilge plug. I thought he had tightened it; he thought I had. We hastily put the slings back under it, thinking we'd raise it just long enough for me to check it. The slings wound up just forward and just aft of the ballast iron. I ducked under and hastily checked the plug. I was about to turn away when I noticed a large gap between the top of the ballast iron and keel up forward. Subsequent checking revealed that the most forward keel bolt had broken. When we replaced the keel bolts, we found that several of the nominal 1-inch diameter bolts had lost more than 25 percent of their diameter in the area of this joint. The lesson, of course, is that keel bolts should be checked periodically.

Look for weeping around the tops of the bolts while the boat is in the water. When it is up on the stands, check for weeping from the bottom of the keel bolts or from the joint between the ballast keel and the hull. Other signs are blackened wood, peeling paint, and rusting washers or bolt heads. (Incidentally, you might want to check the heads of other below-the-waterline through-hull fastenings such as those in the stem, floors, and deadwood.)

If there are any trouble signs, you may want to enlist the aid of a surveyor. He or she will probably do just as you've already done, inspect the ends and the joint carefully, but will do so from a much broader experience base. A surveyor may also bang on the bolts with a hammer, listening for the clear, sharp ring of healthy metal or the dull, dead thud of a corroded bolt. It sounds easy, but it takes a practiced ear.

Withdrawing one or two bolts for inspection may be the next step. This is a job for the yard (trust me on this one). Keel bolt removal under the best of conditions is a tough, lousy job. Incidentally, don't withdraw the easiest ones. These are probably the ones pulled in past inspections and are more likely to be in good shape. The rule of thumb (there are more rules of thumb in marine work than there are thumbs) is that if the removed keel bolts show more than 10 percent loss of thickness, it's a good idea to replace them all. It's less costly and safer than replacing them one or two at a time.

You must drop the keel to inspect bolts cast in place. Having them X-rayed is an alternative, but the process is fairly expensive. To my way of thinking, nothing is as conclusive as looking at the real thing. Cutting off the old bolts and redrilling for new ones is a fairly straightforward job when the keel is lead, less so when it is concrete. Casting a new keel may make more sense.

If there are no signs of weeping, it's still a good idea to back off the nuts inside the boat, clean up the threads, and inspect the washer and the sealant—one bolt at a time. If the washer is deformed, replace it with as large and heavy a washer as is practical—after renewing the sealant. It is a good idea to coat the top threads of the keel bolt with a nickel-base anti-seize lubricant before putting the nut back on and tightening down.

As for protective coatings on mild steel keel bolts prior to insertion, galvanizing, red lead, zinc-rich paints, bituminous paints, oils, and greases have all been used, and all will provide some measure of protection. However, keel bolts are pretty snug fitting and require driving, so coatings inevitably will be scraped off to one extent or another. Thus, sealing the tops and bottoms to prevent water penetration is of equal importance.

Centerboards

Centerboards are typically of plate steel, wood, or wood with lead or steel attached to the bottom for weight. Generally a wire cable passing through a sheave to a winch completes the system. Most if not all of these components, except the winch, reside within the centerboard trunk, where oxygen-depleted water and salt-laden moist air create ideal conditions for corrosion. The steel must, of course, be protectively coated, but more important in terms of catastrophic failure are the wire rope, the sheave, the winch, and their fastenings. These critical elements are subject to considerable wear and stress, and paint is not a practical solution. This is the place for one of those proprietary formulations we talked about in the last chapter, possibly a spray lubricant and rust preventive with moisture displacement properties applied during your annual wear and corrosion inspection at haulout time.

A word of caution here: think of the centerboard as your own personal guillotine. Before you crawl under the boat and look up in the slot, take some carefully thought-out precautions. Place blocks strategically, lock the winch, and do as much as you can from above.

Keel Bands

Certain types of powerboats, primarily older, traditional wooden vessels, have a steel strip along the keel shoe to protect the wooden keel in groundings. The keel band is difficult and costly to repair since the boat has to be supported in such a way that the bottom of the keel is accessible for its whole length. It is really worthwhile to keep protective coatings on the keel band and to check the fastenings as part of annual maintenance, replacing any that are questionable.

STEERING SYSTEMS

Outboard Rudders

In the simplest of steering systems, the rudder swings on pairs of hinge-like fittings known as gudgeons and pintles. On the many traditional sailboats that incorporate this type of steering, the rudder itself is usually wood, perhaps strengthened with metal rudder straps. The rudder straps, gudgeons, and pintles and their fastenings are frequently of a ferrous metal (stainless steel or chrome-plated mild steel) or of bronze. Corrosion problems are pretty much limited to self-corrosion of the ferrous metals, assuming we have been wise enough not to mix dissimilar metals. Gudgeons and pintles must be checked regularly for signs of rust and crevice corrosion.

Inboard Rudders

Inboard rudders are attached to a round bar or tube—called the post or the stock—that rotates inside a tube through the hull forward of the waterline. The rudder may be supported only by the post and called a *spade rudder*, or it might also be hinged to the keel or a skeg. A turning force applied to the top of the post turns the blade attached to the bottom. Inboard rudders are likely to be metal or a composite.

Metal Rudders

Metal rudders are most frequently employed on powerboats. They may be galvanized sheet steel, plain mild steel, stainless steel, or bronze—usually manganese bronze. The rudder stock may be stainless steel, Tobin bronze (naval brass), or Monel. The blade is joined to the post by riveting, through-bolting, or welding. Rudder bearings can be bronze or plastic, and the rudderhead fitting is perhaps a ferrous metal. With this mix of metals we must be concerned about several different forms of corrosion.

Where stainless steel is used, it is likely to be Type 304 or 316. If the blade is welded to the post, we must be concerned whether the low-carbon (304L and 316L) grades were used or, alternatively, if the assembly was heat-treated. Otherwise failure due to weld decay is a potential hazard when the assembly is under stress.

You will recall that stainless steels are susceptible to corrosion fatigue and to stress-corrosion cracking. Rudder assemblies are frequently under severe stress and may experience moderately high frequency vibration, a cyclic stress that can lead to fatigue. Rudder assemblies should be regularly examined for such tell-tale signs as hairline cracking, especially at the joining of the blade and the post. Stainless steel is also susceptible to crevice corrosion, not so much on the blade, which is exposed to well-oxygenated moving seawater, but on the post where it enters the rudder tube.

Mild steel rudders should be inspected for simple wastage of the metal from self-corrosion or, if dissimilar metals are involved, galvanic corrosion. Cathodic protection in the form of zinc anodes should be installed and maintained on all metal rudders.

Fiberglass Rudders

Fiberglass rudders are not—not just fiberglass, that is. In most cases, they consist of a metal rudderpost with a metal web-like fin welded (sometimes bolted) to the post (see fig. 16-3). Foam, balsa, or wood forms the core and gives the rudder its shape. The fiberglass skin seals and protects the core.

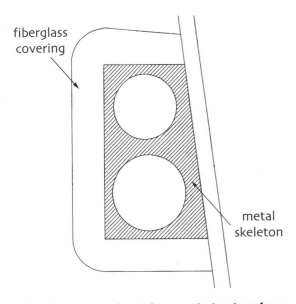

Fig. 16-3. Internal metal support structure for a fiberglass rudder. If the fiberglass covering develops a crack that would allow seawater to penetrate to the internal web structure, rust and weakening can result.

This type of rudder lives in fear of holes, rips, punctures—anything that permits water to penetrate the core. Waterlogging, rotting of the core materials, and expansion followed by cracking or delaminating are all possibilities, but of specific interest to us are problems of stainless steel that finds itself in stagnant, oxygen-depleted seawater. This can seriously weaken the structure and set the stage for serious problems at very inopportune times. This kind of deterioration can usually be detected before catastrophic failure (but probably not before it causes some sloppy and embarrassing docking incidents). Close inspection during haulouts looking for signs of rust weeping from breaches in the fiberglass skin should warn you of impending trouble.

If you suspect trouble, or perhaps even if you don't, it is a good idea to tie off the wheel or tiller so it can't move and then put your weight against the rudder. Any movement of the rudder not exactly followed by the rudderstock is an indication of serious problems requiring, in all probability, reconstruction or replacement of the rudder.

Hydraulic Systems

Hydraulic steering systems, while they can get a bit complex, are quite reliable and trouble-free. If the system is properly installed and maintained, the principal corrosive threat is usually from water in the hydraulic fluid, which may cause rusting of critical elements in the system. Even if the system is meticulously maintained, water can still be present in the system as a result of condensation in fluid reservoirs. Preventive measures consist of keeping the fluid reservoirs topped off and periodically checking for the presence of water in the fluid. If moisture is found, you will need to drain the contaminated fluid to remove the water, refill the reservoirs with a proper hydraulic fluid, and bleed the system.

Mechanical Systems

Mechanical systems (excluding cable systems) are based on some sort of gear systems. If kept properly aligned and lubricated, they are not especially susceptible to problems of corrosion, any more so, that is, than the basic metals involved. Wear is the more common failure mode.

Cable Systems

For all of its simplicity, a cable steering system is very demanding of its components and its installation if it is to function reliably. The angle of entry (the lead) of the wire cable into quadrants, sheaves, and other bearing and turning surfaces is critical. If the lead is not optimum, not only is there the possibility of the cable coming off, but more specifically for us, there is certain to be excessive wear of both the cable and the sheave or quadrant. Where there is wear and exposure to salt water, corrosion will be accelerated.

Nothing but 7 × 19 Type 316 stainless steel wire rope should be used in the steering system. This is the most flexible of the three commonly available types. The others are too stiff. The cable must be kept lubricated, not only to reduce wear but also to keep moisture from penetrating into the strands, where it becomes stagnant and depleted of oxygen—the worst possible condition for stainless steel. Soak a rag in oil and rub it along the entire length of the wire rope, working the oil into the strands while watching closely for signs of rust. This will also reveal broken strands. If *any* broken strands are found, the cable must be replaced. Evidence of rust suggests that the cable is probably old and that moisture has at some time penetrated the cable. Wire rope is not all that expensive, and replacement sure beats the alternative of catastrophic failure.

Some steering cable is plastic covered to protect the wire strands both from wear and moisture penetration. If the plastic sheathing is damaged, the probability is high that moisture has penetrated the strands. Since accurate and reliable assessment of the damage to the cable's integrity is not possible, the cable should be replaced. Also take the time to determine how the plastic covering became damaged and correct the cause.

Sheaves used in steering systems frequently contain dissimilar metals—bronze bushings, stainless steel shafts, carbon steel bearings—ideal conditions for galvanic corrosion if suffi-

cient moisture is present. Keeping sheaves clean and well lubricated forestalls this problem. Plastic sheaves typically use plastic bearings and do not require lubrication, but they do require regular cleaning.

WOOD HULLS

Wood hulls are susceptible to damage and deterioration primarily from several different types of microorganisms that cause various kinds of wood rot; from corrosion of the various metal fastenings, fittings, and fixtures that hold them together and service their needs; and, of course, from the frailties of the humans that design, build, maintain, and sail them. Discussion of the various kinds of bugs that like to eat the boat, while undoubtedly fascinating, is, as writers like to say, "beyond the scope of this text." As to those of us who are the designers, builders, repairers, and operators of these vessels, that too is beyond the scope of this book, except insofar as corrosion of the metals and the conditions that support it are concerned. The principal metals of concern in the wood hull are the fastenings, the various through-hull fittings, and such sometimes metallic fixtures as floors. In this section we discuss these and some of the things we can do to protect them.

Fastenings above the Waterline

Some metals not suitable for immersion service could be satisfactory in topside applications. Fasteners above the waterline are not generally subjected to conditions as hostile as those at or below the waterline. Also, monitoring of their condition and accessibility for repair or replacement is much easier.

Silicon bronze and 316 stainless are preferred. Type 304 stainless steel, galvanized steel, and inhibited low-zinc (less than 15 percent) brasses are acceptable. Mild steel, the free-machining grades (303, 303Se), and 400 series stainless steels should not be used. No stainless steel should be used where the wood may become saturated, such as in hull planking.

Galvanic effects will be concentrated in the immediate area of contact, not spread over the entire wetted surface as it is below the waterline. Localized attack can be severe, though, as stainless steel fastenings in aluminum sometimes demonstrate. However, the corrosive damage is pretty much confined to an area within about $\frac{1}{2}$ inch (1.27 cm) of the contact between the two metals. Filling screw or bolt holes with a water-displacing lubricant, one that does not contain graphite, will provide a measure of protection against galvanic corrosion.

Fastenings below the Waterline

Conditions at splash zone or below the waterline are, as you would expect, considerably more hostile than they are topside. Constant immersion in seawater or contact with seawater-soaked wood—or both—is highly conducive to crevice corrosion. Underwater fastenings get no protection from cathodic protection systems, so whether they survive, how well, and for how long depends on the fastener's own corrosion resistance—and whatever else we might be able to do to make their lives a little more bearable.

Immersion is particularly damaging to the stainless steels, including Type 316, and these fastenings should not be used at or below the waterline. An exception might be made for some of the superalloys such as the 6 percent molybdenum stainless steels and nickel-chromium-molybdenum alloys, which, indeed, are finding increased usage in marine applications, but it is hard to justify them for boat fastenings on the basis of cost. We poor boaters must find more practical means of holding our boats together.

That means is silicon bronze and galvanized steel. Silicon bronze is to be preferred, but galvanized steel has been and is still being used successfully, even in the most demanding and critical of the below-the-waterline applications—bilge fastenings, floor bolts, keel bolts, and so on. This is another case of "the shin bone's connected to the . . . ." The ballast casting is *hung* from the keel timber, the keel timber is *hung* from the floors, and the floors are *hung* from the framing. I use the term *hung* here to stress the demands placed on these fastenings. Given the critical role of these fastenings and the difficulties involved in replacing them, great care

in their selection, installation, and maintenance is more than justified.

Galvanized bolts and drifts are commonly found in these applications. The point at which most corrosive damage occurs to the fastening is at the joint between the members—the joint between ballast iron and the keel, between the keel and the floor timber, and between the floor timber and the frame (and, incidentally, between planking and frames). These joints are where most metal is lost, causing the fastenings to become "wasp-waisted" (see fig. 16-4). Fasteners should not be threaded in this area.

In regard to what we can do to make life easier for these fastenings, at the top of the list is the application and maintenance of a good sealant at the joints and under washers at the fastener ends. This goes a long way toward extending the life of these fastenings. We can also coat them, even the plank fastenings. It's messy but worthwhile. One choice for a wooden hull is old: thick, or thickened, red lead. Some of the newer epoxy-base coatings will also work. The coating provides lubrication while driving and protection

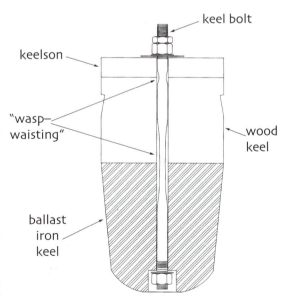

Fig. 16-4. *Wasp-waisting*, **or narrowing, of a typical bilge fastening.** The most severe corrosion occurs at the joint between the ballast keel and the keel.

for the fastening, and it fills voids in the joint. Everyone seems to have their own recipe for such coatings, so feel free to experiment.

Through-Hulls

Through-hull fittings have perhaps the worst working conditions of all. On the outside of the hull they are exposed to constant immersion in seawater; on the inside, they are sometimes immersed and sometimes not; and in between, there is constant exposure to seawater-saturated, oxygen-depleted wood. In addition, they may be subjected to impact and shear stresses, and they are at risk of decapitation from heavy gear (or crew members) coming adrift. Through-hulls must be fabricated from a material that is inherently corrosion resistant and has great, or at least adequate, mechanical strength. This rules out the ferrous metals and the common brasses, and it suggests that we must be selective in the use of the plastic fittings.

Most of the copper-alloy sea-valves, seacocks, and through-hulls are made of cast phosphor, a leaded-tin bronze with a minimum yield strength of 20,000 psi (957 kPa). This type of bronze corrodes extremely slowly in seawater and even more slowly in wet wood. Those bronze fittings in my wooden sailboat showed no visible effects of corrosive wastage even after 30 years in salt water.

A coat of paint can extend the life of bronze fittings, but they hardly need any corrosion protection at all. As a matter of fact, providing them with cathodic protection may do more harm than good due to "overprotection." The result is overproduction of hydroxyl ions and the formation of sodium hydroxide in the saturated wood around the fitting. This phenomenon is at the root of the controversy concerning bonding (see chapter 18).

Needless to say, bronze through-hulls should be fastened with bronze fastenings. Of course, the entire matter is moot if you've installed Marelon (glass-reinforced nylon) fittings.

Floor Timbers

Floor timbers in wooden boats are sometimes made of metal—either wrought iron (not so much anymore), mild steel, or bronze. Corrosion concerns are pretty much the same as those for through-hulls. Ferrous metal floors require protective organic coatings (paint) or cathodic protection—or both. Copper-base alloy floors require little or no protection, but they will benefit from organic coating and are subject to the same questions concerning bonding.

Corrosion Prevention

The major metallic fittings and fastenings that require protection in a wooden hull are the fastenings, the prop and shaft, and the rudder assemblies. It is, of course, not possible to provide cathodic protection to the fastenings since this would require each to be electrically connected to a zinc anode. Organic coatings are the best protection we can provide. Hopefully the fastening was coated before it was driven, it was properly sealed and bunged, and the bungs have been maintained. This, followed by a good paint system, is all that stands between our poor fasteners and the ravages of the cruel ocean. In this I would choose a reputable paint manufacturer, get some of their instruction pamphlets (they're often helpful), and *follow their instructions to the letter*. Through-hull fittings on the outside of the hull are normally covered by the coating system.

The prop, shaft, and rudder assemblies can be protected with zinc anodes. A zinc anode on a metal rudder also provides protection for the rudderpost, at least that part that is immersed. For the propeller and shaft, the anode is usually in the form of a collar clamped to the shaft, but a prop nut zinc is sometimes used. Zinc anodes may also be attached to the struts, although these will protect only the strut, not the prop and shaft.

Alternatively, we could mount a zinc (one or more) anode on the outside of the hull in close proximity to and in line-of-sight of the shaft and prop and then connect it (or them) electrically to the prop and shaft. This is done by connecting a wire between the zinc-mounting bolts on the inside of the hull and the electrical system's common ground on the engine block (frequently an engine mounting bolt). This method has a couple of attractive advantages over mounting the zinc on the fitting to be protected. It provides a broader distribution of the ion exchange field and more uniform protection over the surface of the fitting. Also, by electrically connecting other underwater fittings to the common ground point, they too receive cathodic protection from the zinc (or zincs).

These systems depend for their effectiveness on extremely low-resistance electrical paths. Practically, this means fat conductors—not smaller than #8 AWG—and low-resistance contacts. The electrical path between the engine block and the propeller shaft normally fails to meet these low-resistance requirements. Lubricating oils in the engine and reduction gears introduce resistance in the electrical path, as do shaft couplings. A flexible coupling will sever the electrical path entirely. A shaft brush-grounding assembly bypasses these resistances to provide a low-resistance connection between the engine ground and the prop shaft. If the rudder and rudderstock are to be included in the protection system, the rudderstock must also be electrically connected.

The methods of determining the optimum quantity and placement of remote zinc anodes are equally applicable to other hull materials, so these methods are covered in appendix 3, Quantity, Size, and Placement of Zinc Anodes.

FIBERGLASS/COMPOSITE HULLS

Fiberglass is often used to describe materials reinforced with something other than glass fibers, but *composite* is the proper generic term. We distinguish those composites based on glass fibers as *fiberglass-reinforced plastic* (FRP).

Fastenings

The fastenings most commonly used in FRP construction are bolts, self-tapping screws, and blind (pop) rivets. All of the usual caveats apply—use compatible metals; silicon bronze is preferred over galvanized; stainless steel should not be used where it does not have access to a fresh supply of oxygen; and fasteners below the waterline will receive no benefit from cathodic pro-

tection systems. However, there are some situations that are peculiar to fiberglass hulls.

Through-bolts are preferable, but where you don't have access to both sides, you'll have to use blind rivets or screws. Due to the hardness and incompressibility of fiberglass laminate, wood screws are not suitable: self-tapping (sheet metal) screws must be used. Screws are satisfactory *only* for lightly loaded fittings, and *only if* they are of a suitable alloy, properly sized and properly installed. Moisture trapped in the hole against the screw can cause crevice corrosion in stainless steel fastenings, so you should use a sealant.

Blind or pop rivets are frequently used for deck-to-hull joints and where backside access is not available. Here, the principal concerns are for the metals used in the fastening, but the specific type of blind fastener can also be important. Closed-end types (to prevent moisture penetration) in which both the body and the mandrel are of 316 stainless steel and/or coated (plated or painted) should be used.

A word of caution is in order concerning composites using carbon (graphite) fibers. Carbon fibers are both electrically conductive and highly noble. This has several implications for us. First, less noble metals, such as fastenings, in contact with carbon fibers and immersed in seawater will corrode. Also, two dissimilar metals in contact with the same carbon fiber structure are in electrical contact with each other, and if immersed in the same body of water, the least noble metal will suffer accelerated corrosion. Through-bolts, or other fastenings, should be insulated from contact with the carbon fiber. Electrical shrink tubing works well in such applications.

Wood-Epoxy Composite

The foremost member of this family is the cold-molded form of construction. Essentially, the hull consists of thin layers of wood laid up such that the grain of each successive layer is at 90 degrees to the previous one. The layers are bonded together with epoxy. Properly designed and built cold-molded hulls are without seams, joints, and local fastenings, and there is no transverse framing and no stringers to trap water. Because the hull is totally encapsulated in epoxy, it is virtually immune to rot, but protection concerns for through-hulls, keel bolts, prop, shaft and struts, and the rudder assembly still apply, particularly in regard to cathodic overprotection.

Although this construction form evolved from the Ashcroft method, it is not to be confused with that earlier form. The Ashcroft method was similar in construction but predated modern epoxies and depended on many small fastenings to hold its successive diagonal planking layers together and thus does not enjoy the advantages discussed above.

STEEL HULLS

Steel hull boats will inevitably corrode in either freshwater or salt water. To compensate, they are generally built with heavier gauge steel than is necessary for structural strength in their intended application. (Also, it is just extremely difficult to weld steel plate that is thinner than 1/8 inch, or 3 mm). However, a carefully applied and maintained epoxy paint system combined with an equally well planned and maintained cathodic protection system can pretty well protect a steel hull, both above and below the waterline. Modern epoxy primers and linear polyurethane coatings have gone a long way toward, if not eliminating, then at least greatly reducing the need for frequent chipping, scraping, and painting. Done properly, this not a trivial process, but it is critical that it be done properly. The best advice here is to select a top-quality paint system and follow the manufacturer's instructions to the letter. The manufacturer best knows what is required to apply a successful, long-lasting coating system, and they have a significant stake in the outcome.

The problem areas are the external hull at and above the waterline and the entire inside of the boat. You may want to apply extra coatings on these areas. If the interior was properly coated, it becomes a question of keeping it clean and promptly touching up scratches and scrapes.

In a properly designed and built steel hull, frames, beams, and stringers are fitted in such a way that water coming aboard will drain freely to the bilges without getting trapped in low spots, corners, or crevices. Passages and limber holes must be kept clear of dirt, debris, and blockages. The following are other places where dirt can accumulate:

- welded seams
- floors
- stringers and stringer-frame intersections
- engine bearers
- flanges, brackets, and deck fittings
- lower ends of frames
- wood-metal joints (under wooden decks)

I'm sure you can think of others. Just look in places where you'd rather not find it.

It is worthwhile to take some care in selecting the contractor to do your grit-blasting. I remember hearing of an incident in which a contractor had grit-blasted a steel structure with an abrasive grit that was probably contaminated with beach sand. When the coating failed, the grit was analyzed and found to contain some 500 ppm chlorides and 150 ppm sulfates. The coating had to be stripped and cleaned and recoated—at considerable expense. Get recommendations from others around the yard.

An organic coating system is the first line of defense against rust and corrosion on steel hulls, but these hulls also need cathodic protection. It is essential to have the right number and mass of zinc anodes properly placed (see appendix 3) and properly monitored and maintained. Once you've figured out how much zinc you need and where it should go, it's a good idea to weld bolts to the hull to hold the anodes. This makes replacement faster and easier, even with the boat in the water, so you'll be more likely to replace them when necessary. There is no need to wire the anode to the common ground point. The metal hull provides this connection.

ALUMINUM HULLS

Aluminum of the appropriate marine grade (5000 series) is highly resistant to corrosion in both freshwater and salt water. Boatbuilders who have worked exclusively in aluminum for many years claim that a properly designed and built hull of unpainted marine-grade aluminum will last indefinitely in salt water—despite aluminum's reputation to the contrary. This reputation appears to derive from a number of small craft that were built from surplus aircraft aluminum (2000 series) after World War II—and failed decidedly. Unfortunately, that reputation persists in some quarters to this day.

It isn't necessary to paint aluminum boats above the waterline—and many workboat owners don't—but they must be painted below the waterline to prevent fouling. As with steel hulls, putting on a proper coating system is not a trivial task, but it is critically important. The process consists of gritblasting, chemical cleaning, primer coat, two or more barrier coats, and then the antifouling coat.

Antifouling paints containing tributyltin-oxide (TBTO) and tributyltin (TBT) have been prohibited from sale to the public, except for 16-oz. (454 g) spray cans for outboard and outdrive lower units. Tin-base coatings can still be used on aluminum boats, but they can be purchased and applied only by EPA- and state-licensed operators, who must pay a fee and carry liability insurance. That means that, for most of us, this is a job for the yard. The alternative—not recommended—is to use a copper-oxide bottom paint over a thick and carefully applied epoxy-base barrier coat. The barrier coat is critically important to prevent galvanic interaction between the aluminum and the copper.

The interior surfaces of an aluminum hull, especially below the waterline, should be painted to provide protection from galvanic corrosion caused by dissimilar metal objects falling into the bilge. As far as the topsides are concerned, most noncommercial owners prefer to paint them, not just for aesthetic reasons but also to reduce glare and heating effects.

Aluminum, even marine grade, is a highly active metal, less noble than any of the other metals commonly used in, on, and around boats—which means that the major concern (aside from hot deck surfaces and bare feet) is galvanic and electrolytic (stray-current) corrosion. Great care must be taken in the use of any other metals on the boat. This includes the obvious things such as fastenings, deck hardware and fittings, and weld filler metals, but even minute amounts of dissimilar metals such as the copper in antifouling paints or metal particles trapped in a grinding wheel or hand file, or even a copper penny dropped into the bilge, can cause serious corrosive damage. Any copper-bearing alloy—brass, bronze, even Monel—will cause severe corrosive damage unless appropriate precautions are taken.

If dissimilar metals must be used, they must be insulated from the aluminum hull with pads of neoprene, wood, or some other nonconductive material. Fasteners should be coated with a polysulfide sealant or perhaps a zinc-rich primer before installing them to reduce, if not eliminate, galvanic action between the fastening and the aluminum.

Underwater fittings—through-hulls (with proper backing blocks or built-up hull sections, and properly insulated), prop and shaft, rudder and rudderpost—require cathodic protection. Aluminum hulls in freshwater use magnesium anodes because of the lower conductivity of the water. Zinc is used in salt water. Number and placement depend on the size and displacement of the boat (see appendix 3).

Not so incidentally, bird droppings can cause accelerated corrosion of aluminum—which will come as no surprise for those of you who have aluminum boats. Bird excrement is highly alkaline and can cause severe corrosive damage to aluminum (and to steel). Marine stores sell molded plastic, actual-sized reproductions of owls that are designed to scare the daylights out of careless or otherwise out-of-control seagulls. I'm not all that sure how well they work, but they are quite attractive, beautifully painted, and quite realistic. It might be worthwhile keeping your eye out for any bird-dropping-bedecked decoys on aluminum boats in the mooring field.

FERRO-CEMENT HULLS

Ferro-cement as boat construction material burst onto the scene in the 1960s. Touted as a strong and inexpensive hull material requiring few special skills, it attracted an instant following. Called *stone* boats by our British, Australian, and New Zealand cousins, ferro-cement found even greater acceptance in those countries, and many more ferro-cement boats were built there.

Hulls consist of a mild steel and wire mesh (chicken wire) armature plastered with Portland cement. Early ferro-cement boats were (and are) especially susceptible to serious corrosion problems. Salt water and oxygen migrating through the cement to the armature cause extensive rusting. Since the rust occupies more volume, it causes the cement to crack, which further exacerbates the problem.

Sophisticated concrete additives—plasticizers, pH control, cure-modifying agents—along with better plastering techniques, more attention to galvanizing, and even epoxy-coated frame and mesh, have gone a long way toward overcoming early problems. However, the touted advantages of low cost, simplicity of building, and low level of required skills are all lost. We are left with a boat that costs pretty nearly the same as boats of other more familiar and, to many, more attractive materials. Add to this the notoriously poor resale value of ferro-cement boats, and the result is few being built today. Still, there are a substantial number of stone boats and enthusiastic owners out there, so a few words on corrosion and corrosion prevention are warranted.

If you think about it, we are dealing with what is essentially a steel-hull boat, albeit encased in a thin shell of cement. Ferro-cement has many of the same problems as steel, and many of the same preventive methods are applicable. First is the need for a robust organic coating system to prevent moisture penetration to the steel armature (and to prevent marine growth). The new epoxy-base coating systems have proved useful here. They bond and last well, especially when applied over an epoxy-tar-base primer. But coating system technology is constantly advancing, and you should be guided here by the coating manufacturer.

Fastenings and through-hull fittings made of metals or alloys—especially copper alloys—galvanically incompatible with the steel armature must be electrically isolated from it. If not, those exposed to seawater will quickly form galvanic cells, and rapid corrosion and possibly progressive deterioration of the armature will occur. The process takes a little longer above the splash zone. Line the holes with epoxy or a plastic sealant. If space allows, encase through-bolts in heat-shrink tubing. For fastenings below the waterline, 316 stainless steel is the preferred alloy.

COPPER SHEATHING

Copper sheathing was once quite common on wooden boats venturing into the tropics, protecting the planking from marine borers (teredo worms). Today our scientific friends in the coating industry have concocted all sorts of toxic tasties for the nasty little critters, and sheathing has given way to more convenient toxic antifouling coatings. Thus, you may be surprised to learn that copper sheathing is still being done, not only in restorations of classic vessels but also in special applications—such as for ice protection at the waterline in frigid latitudes.

From the little factual data available it seems that something between 30 and 40 years of useful life can be expected from $1/8$ inch (3 mm) sheathing. As for the fastenings under the sheathing, I am aware of one situation in which the copper sheathing was removed for recoppering after some 40 years, and both the wood planking and the bronze fastenings were reported to be as good as new. This is not really a scientific observation, but it does testify to the protection offered by a copper bottom properly done.

Obviously, there is serious potential for galvanic corrosion. In fact, it was the severe damage to iron fastenings from copper sheathing that caused the 18th century British navy (which started this copper bottom stuff) to go to all non-iron fastenings. Through-hulls, through-bolts, and other skin fittings must be of bronze or else isolated from contact with the copper sheathing.

WOOD VENEER SHEATHING

What we're talking about here is commonly referred to as *cold-molded sheathing* or perhaps *cold-molded overlay*, and it has been the subject of some controversy. Basically, the skin fittings are removed, the hull is taken down to bare wood, the seams reefed and filled with epoxy, and the hull faired off. Then successive layers, usually three, of thin veneer (Douglas fir, mahogany, cedar, or some similar wood) are laid up diagonally, each epoxied and stapled to the hull and the layer below. The staples are bronze or aluminum but in any event are protected from exposure to seawater by the epoxy coatings.

The method came on the scene in the early 1980s when it was used to restore the 45-year-old, 36-foot (11 m) Alden yawl *Isla Trothe*. The poster-child project of this method is probably *Curlew*, a 28-foot (8.5 m), 90-year-old Falmouth Quay punt that was brought back from the edge of the grave in 1985 by Tim and Pauline Carr. A survey in 1997 showed *Isla Trothe* (now *Shibumi*) was still in sound condition. The Carrs, living aboard and cruising in high southern latitudes, report that *Curlew* is in excellent condition, with no signs of rot or deterioration.

The controversy surrounding this method of restoration has to do with questions of structural integrity, failing bond between the old and new hulls from wet-dry cycling, rotting encapsulated wood, and aesthetic offense. Fortunately, our concern is only the impact of sheathing on corrosion, and about this there are basically three points to be made:

1. Inasmuch as the outer skins effectively prevent the inner fastenings from exposure to seawater—just as we attempt to do in conventional construction through bungs, sealants, and paint coatings, only more effectively—the plight of the inner fastenings is no worse than it would be in a conventional wood hull.
2. There is typically less water inside a sheathed hull, meaning less moisture vapor to be picked up by the wood interior. If, as is recommended, the ventilation of the interior of the hull is increased or enhanced, interior conditions are, if anything, more favorable.
3. The burden of maintaining structural integrity of the vessel is now largely assumed by the cold-molded outer shell, and the role of fastenings in the old wooden hull is greatly reduced.

So, without taking sides in the "whether to use wood veneer sheathing" discussion, we can conclude that this form of construction (repair, if you prefer) poses no new or unique problems from a corrosion point of view. All of the precautions that one would take with a wooden boat are appropriate and sufficient.

CHAPTER 17

Propulsion Systems

We have seen that corrosion thrives in conditions where metals high in the galvanic series are exposed to moisture, especially salt-laden moist air. We know that corrosion is also a consequence of electrical contact between dissimilar metals immersed in the same body of water, especially salt water. We have also seen that the presence of acids can cause corrosive damage, and that elevated temperatures can exacerbate the situation and accelerate the damage. All of these conditions exist simultaneously in internal combustion engines installed in boats, so it should be no surprise that engines can and do suffer corrosive damage.

ENGINES

The basic unit of every engine is the block, a cored casting, typically of cast iron but in some cases aluminum. Large holes are provided in the casting for the cylinders, and smaller holes are provided as passageways for lubricating oils and coolant fluids. All other essential engine components are either built into the engine block or fastened onto it. To the untutored eye an engine block can appear to be a pretty rough casting not requiring a great deal in the way of precision. However, critical measurements of internal surfaces are, in fact, very precise, machined in some cases to a few ten-thousandths of an inch.

In the perpetual pursuit of higher horsepower-to-weight ratios, considerable effort has been made to reduce the weight of the engine. One result is thinner "walls" within the engine that not only decrease the weight but also increase the rate of heat transfer to the coolant. Another is the use of cylinder liners made of steel. There are basically two types of liners: wet and dry. All of the outer surface of a dry liner lies against the inner surface of the cylinder hole in the block, while the outer surface of a wet liner is directly exposed to the coolant fluid (as shown in fig. 17-1). Wet liners are by far the more common in modern engines.

Lubricating oil is splashed up onto the highly polished inner surfaces of the cylinder liner walls to lubricate piston travel. The piston ring in the bottom groove, called the oil ring, prevents excess oil from reaching the combustion chamber. The other rings are compression rings, containing the combustion. Combustion is a highly complex chemical process that produces extreme heat, thermal expansion, mechanical stresses, and some nasty by-products, including sulfuric acid from residual sulfur in the fuel. As rings wear, some blowby of the combustion gases occurs, resulting in acid contamination of

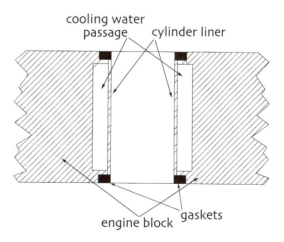

Fig. 17-1. The wet cylinder liner. This liner is a polished steel tube that functions as the engine cylinder. It is set into the engine block with watertight gaskets as shown (circular gasket around the top and bottom so that cooling water can circulate against it).

the oil in the oil pan. This leads to pitting of cylinder liners and bearing surfaces, resulting in progressively increasing friction and, ultimately, to component failure.

Cylinder wall pitting can also result from cavitation erosion. This type of pitting occurs on the outer surface of the cylinder liner when combustion-caused vibration of the cylinder wall (liner) creates vapor bubbles in the coolant fluid. The collapse of these bubbles removes the metal's protective oxide layer, leaving it vulnerable to corrosion and pitting. In the extreme case, pitting breaches the liner, allowing coolant to leak into the cylinder and contaminate the lubricating oil.

These problems all have to do with internal corrosive damage to operating engines, either from the fuel or from the cooling fluid. Engine manufacturers as well as fuel and oil producers are well aware of these problems, and it would be hard to find an industry that has expended more time, effort, and money in search of solutions. We'll talk more about fuels, lubricating oils, and cooling systems further on.

Another corrosion concern has to do with *not* operating the engine. There are many pleasure boats and not a few commercial fishing boats that sit idle for considerable periods of time without running their engines. While this does suspend engine wear, it exposes internal components to corrosion. Protective lubricating oil that normally coats all susceptible metal surfaces gradually drains down, exposing these surfaces to moist, salt-laden air. Corrosion begins to occur. This is more likely with diesel engines since the residual amounts of sulfur are likely to be greater in diesel fuel than in gasoline, especially in parts of the world where pollution controls are not so stringent. A diesel engine should be started on a regular basis—say once a week—and allowed to run at fast idle until it warms up to normal operating temperature to ensure that not only has oil reached all the places it should, but that all moist air inside the engine has been discharged. It should be put in gear—both forward and reverse (make sure the boat is well secured)—for short periods to distribute the oil in the transmission as well.

Finally, all electrical components should be mounted as high as practical to avoid getting splashed by water sloshing around in the bilge. Alternators are particularly susceptible to corrosion from moist salt air on terminals and brush springs. Another common source of engine problems is corroded terminals and wire connections in the ignition system. It's a good idea to spray these occasionally with a moisture-displacing lubricant designed for this purpose. One of the big advantages of the diesel engine for marine use is that the fuel ignites by compression rather than spark ignition.

OUTBOARDS AND OUTDRIVES

The blocks in outboard engines are generally of die-cast aluminum, a process that produces very smooth and precise parts requiring little finish machining. Some engine blocks are manufactured from high-silicon-content aluminum alloys with sufficient surface hardness and smoothness of finish to make cylinder liners unnecessary. Others use cylinder liners. Outdrives mostly use marinized automotive engine blocks that are typically of cast iron with cylinder liners.

Nowadays most outboard motor housings are high-impact plastics, but older housings are likely to be aluminum. Paint provides the primary corrosion protection. The paint schedule is typically some form of aluminum primer, an epoxy undercoat, the decorative paint—usually an epoxy—and finally a clear coating over that. Anywhere this coating is compromised—chips, scratches, and so forth—will be subject to rapid and intense corrosive attack. Thus you'll want to touch-up breaches promptly.

Despite the ability of aluminum to form a protective oxide coating in the atmosphere, it is very vulnerable to corrosion when immersed in salt water. The motor should be raised up out of the water whenever it is not in use. This is one of the principle disadvantages of outboards mounted in motor wells unless provision is made for raising the motor.

Outboard and outdrive lower units that remain in the water must be coated with a tin-based antifouling paint. Copper-based paints cannot be used on aluminum lower units without a barrier coat between the aluminum and the paint. Otherwise the aluminum will suffer corrosive attack from the galvanically incompatible copper.

Although you probably don't want to hear this, the key to putting on a successful protective coating—or any coating, for that matter—is surface preparation. Get the surface down to bare metal, scrub it clean with soap and water, rinse it thoroughly with fresh clean water, and allow it to dry. Go to the chandlery and buy a good-quality paint system including primer, undercoat, and topcoat. The next step is also very important. The surface must be completely dry when the primer goes on. Either do the job inside in a dry environment or wait for a good dry day. Then follow the manufacturer's direction to the letter.

The lower unit is usually protected by one or more sacrificial anodes located below the waterline. These come in various sizes and shapes, some unique to individual brands and models of motors. Anodes may be combined with a trim tab, attached to the cavitation plate or, in the case of OMC, built into the bearing carrier that mounts over the prop shaft.

Sacrificial anodes are normally zinc with small amounts (less than 0.5 percent) of cadmium and aluminum to prevent the formation of surface oxides. Magnesium anodes are also available for motors used in freshwater. Sacrificial anodes must be monitored closely and replaced when they are significantly used up. I replace mine when they're no more than 50 percent depleted. They're not that expensive, and renewing them is excellent insurance.

Mercury Marine has an impressed current protection system called MerCathode that is available as an option. This is an electronically controlled system that senses the need for protection of the immersed aluminum parts and generates a compensating electric current that it feeds to the exposed parts (see chapter 13).

Outboard and outdrive cooling systems function on the same principle and in the same manner as those of inboard engines. The water surrounding the boat (raw water) is picked up by scoops on the lower unit, pumped through the cooling passages in the engine, and then discharged through the exhaust (for cooling). Like inboards, outboard engines suffer from faulty pumps, defective or corroded thermostats, scale buildup, and, especially, plugged cooling passages. Flushing is a nagging chore that no one looks forward to and many simply do not do. The fact is, flushing after every use is still the best practice, frequent flushing is highly recommended, and thorough flushing before storing for the winter is a must. Flushing is particularly beneficial for an engine operating in salt water, as it dissolves salt deposits before they can harden and restrict the flow of cooling water. However, even freshwater rivers and lakes can have suspended mud, sand, debris, and pollutants that can clog cooling passages, and the effects are cumulative and corrosive. A thorough flushing requires a run of at least 15 minutes with a good flow of clean fresh water. Heat exchangers are available as options on some outboard motors to permit freshwater cooling. This is a costly but worthwhile expenditure.

As with inboard engines, lubricating oils for outboard and outdrive engines perform other valuable functions, such as neutralizing acids, suspending contaminants, and inhibiting rust and corrosion. They do this through additives that are part of the oil's formulation. The oil does not "wear out"—the additives do. The proper choice and use of lubricating oils is one of the most important things you can do to ensure a full, reliable, and satisfactory life for your engine. Lubricating oils are our next subject.

LUBRICATING OILS

The primary purpose of engine oils is to reduce friction and wear by providing a high-viscosity fluid film between moving metal surfaces. Engine oils are combined with a variety of additives whose specific nature depends on the type of engine for which the oil formulation was designed. Some additives enhance lubricating properties. These are called *viscosity index improvers*. Others are *detergent/dispersant* additives that hold particulates in suspension so they

DEALING WITH A SUBMERGED ENGINE

Outboard motors have been known to exhibit suicidal tendencies, suddenly leaping off the transom and diving to the bottom for no apparent reason. Even boats with inboard engines have been known to sink (much to my chagrin). Thus, a few words about sunk engines—inboard, outboard, and outdrive—may be in order.

My first advice is that unless you're a professional marine mechanic or a highly skilled amateur, the safest course of action is to get the engine to a professional as soon as possible. Depending on how long the motor was submerged and whether it was in freshwater or salt water, there may be internal damage (bearings, cylinder walls, etc.), but there is really no way to know without disassembly and inspection. And if the engine was running when it took its dive, there is the real possibility that rods or wrist pins may have been bent if water, which is incompressible, was inducted into the cylinders. If you decide to let a mechanic sort all of this out, make all the necessary arrangements *before* raising the engine and then get it to the workshop as quickly as possible after getting it out of the water.

Employing a mechanic is not always convenient or even possible. In such circumstances, the following procedure may be followed.

1. Most important, leave the motor submerged until you're ready to work on it, but don't leave it under water any longer than you absolutely have to. This applies to inboards as well. If the motor is exposed to air for any significant length of time—say 24 to 48 hours—while it is still saturated with salt water, rusting and corrosion will occur very quickly. Cylinder walls, crankshaft, and bearing journals will suffer rapid corrosive attack, and engine overhaul will probably be necessary.

2. Once you've raised the engine and exposed it to the air, start your work immediately and carry it out expeditiously. The objective is to get all the water, salt, sand, silt, and other debris out of the engine as quickly as possible. Uncover all possible engine openings— spark plugs, filters, caps, filler plugs, drain valves, and so forth—and position the engine so that the water can drain out of these openings. Crank the engine by hand to force the water out of the cylinders. The engine should turn freely, smoothly, and evenly. Tight spots or binding may indicate damaged rods or wrist pins, so don't start the engine before you've verified and corrected this.

3. When you've removed all the water, flush the engine thoroughly with fresh water. Fill the engine—crankcase, cylinders, fuel tanks if integral— to overflowing with kerosene, diesel fuel, or, better still, one of the fluid thin-film moisture-displacing anticorrosion lubricants, such as Corrosion X or Corrosion Block. Allow this to sit for a short while, say half an hour, then drain the engine. Close drain valves, replace plugs and caps, install new filters, and fill the crankcase and/or injection tank with fresh engine oil.

4. Start the engine and let it run long enough to heat up and dry off internally. Check the oil for any signs of water—gooey, frothy, cream-colored emulsification. If water is present, change the oil and filters and run the engine again. Repeat this until there is no sign of water in the oil, and then run the engine at low speeds with no load to dry it out thoroughly and ensure complete distribution of the oil. If this is an outboard engine with fuel injection, run it with about twice the usual amount of oil in the mixture—until you see blue smoke in the exhaust. Thereafter, run it easy until you think it is thoroughly dried out and the engine performs normally.

will flow to the filters and be trapped. There are also *antioxidant* and *stabilizer* additives that retard the breakdown of the oil during operation, *alkalis* that neutralize acids resulting from blowby of combustion gases, *antifoaming agents*, and *corrosion inhibitors*. These additives are, in many cases, developed by third-party manufacturers and sold to a wide range of oil producers. The oil companies then "do their proprietary thing" to arrive at the combination of additives and lubricating properties they want to offer in their products.

It is the additives that are "used up" during operation, hence the need for regular oil changes. Also, the oil eventually becomes loaded with particulates too fine for the filters to trap and loses its ability to function as required. We can avoid this destructive condition by maintaining a schedule of frequent oil changes.

Most outboard engines are two-stroke and require oil to be mixed with the gasoline in some designated proportion, usually 50:1 (gasoline: oil). Too much oil makes the engine difficult to start and results in blue smoke exhaust; too little oil provides insufficient lubrication, and the engine will overheat and possibly seize.

There are two common American Petroleum Institute (API) designations for two-stroke gasoline-engine oil: TC and TC-W3, where the *TC* stands for "two-cycle" and the *W* for "water-cooled." Most, but not all, outboard engine manufacturers specify the use of TC-W3 oils. It is best to follow the manufacturer's recommendations to ensure your engine will benefit from proper lubrication and necessary additives.

The API designation for oil intended for four-stroke gasoline engines is *S*, which stands for "spark ignition." For diesel engines—two- or four-stroke—the API designation is *C*, which refers to "compression ignition." The letter or letters following the *S* or *C* indicate the nature of the additive package, with letters in the early part of the alphabet denoting generally more comprehensive and superior additive compositions. The API grades these oils according to the following service categories:

four-stroke gasoline engines	API SJ
four-stroke diesel engines	API CF, CF–4, and CF-G
two-stroke diesel engines	API CF–2

The manufacturer of the engine will specify the appropriate grade(s).

The prudent owner or operator might consider having engine oil analyzed on a regular basis. As mentioned above, in the normal course of engine operation, all of the products of combustion, wear, corrosion, and contamination wind up in the oil. Spectrographic analysis of a used oil sample can determine what elements are present and their quantities. In the hands of a trained analyst, this can reveal a tremendous amount of information concerning just what is taking place inside the engine. The cost for oil analysis is quite modest—less than $25 at the time of this writing—and the information gained is invaluable.

Engine oil is critical, not only for lubrication and corrosion protection, but also for preventing the buildup of carbon sludge that can clog the oil passages, restrict oil flow, and result in serious damage to the engine. The use of the proper grade of oil is crucial for the performance and protection of the engine, but frequent oil changes, especially in diesel engines, is no less so.

COOLING SYSTEMS

The objective of an internal combustion engine is to convert 100 percent of the potential energy contained in the fuel into usable power at the shaft. However, engines are not 100 percent efficient; something on the order of 20 to 40 percent of the fuel's energy is "lost" as heat. A certain amount of heat is necessary since these engines typically are designed to operate at about 200°F (93°C). A thermostat usually sets the minimum operating temperature. If the temperature is too low, the engine is less efficient, and fuel is wasted. Incomplete combustion results in soot and sludge, the engine becomes unresponsive, and its performance suffers. Also, moisture, a by-product of the combustion process, condenses and contaminates the lube oil.

An operating temperature that is too high can be even more serious. Consequences may include inadequate engine lubrication and subsequent wear, and the formation of carbon and varnish and possible damage to the engine. If the cooling system is operating as it should, that is, carrying off excess heat, the engine will run in the range of the temperature set by the thermostat. Water is the universal cooling fluid, and since water is corrosive to most alloys, this poses problems that must be dealt with. Also, mineral and organic matter in the water can contribute to the formation of insulating films (scale) on the heat transfer surfaces.

Much of the heat that must be removed is in the engine block, and cooling passages—referred to as the water jacket—are provided for this purpose. However, temperatures at the exhaust manifolds can get extremely high—around 1,200°F (650°C) for diesel engines and 1,380°F (750°C) for gasoline engines. The cooling system must also provide cooling to the exhaust system.

There are two basic types of cooling systems in common use in marine engines: *once-through systems* and *closed recirculating systems*. The cooling water in a once-through system passes through the engine only once and is then discharged. Considerable volumes of water are used, usually taken from the water in which the boat operates—river, lake, or ocean. This type of cooling is commonly referred to as *direct cooling* or *raw-water cooling*. It does not lend itself to the use of corrosion inhibitors.

Closed recirculating systems are charged with a cooling fluid that continuously recirculates. Heat transferred to the recirculating coolant is subsequently transferred to a second and separate cooling medium through some form of heat exchanger. Corrosion inhibitors can be part of the fluid circulating through the engine. These systems are commonly referred to as *indirect* or *freshwater cooling systems*.

As we have already learned, whenever dissimilar metals are present and immersed in water, especially salt water, galvanic corrosion is a serious potential problem. High temperatures only make the problem worse. Engine manufacturers try to mitigate this problem by avoiding the use of metals that are widely separated in the galvanic series and by taking advantage of favorable area relationships so that small components, such as core plugs and pipe plugs, are made of materials that are cathodic to other alloys used in the system.

Manufacturers also make provision for the insertion of sacrificial zinc anodes into the circulating cooling system. From the outside, it looks like a pipe plug that threads into the block. A replaceable "pencil" zinc threads into the internal end of the pipe plug. Most engines have two or more internal zincs. These should be checked on a regular basis—at least a couple of times a year. Unfortunately, this is one of the most commonly neglected chores around a boat.

Raw-Water Cooling Systems

Raw-water cooling is simple and inexpensive. Many raw-water-cooled engines have delivered years of trouble-free performance in lobster and fishing boats operating in the salt water virtually every day of the year, most without the benefit of regular (or even irregular) freshwater flushing. However, these engines were designed and built for raw-water cooling, having heavier castings, larger cooling water passages, and thicker wall sections.

The "raw" water is picked up by a through-hull scoop on the underbody, flows through a seacock to a filter, and from there flows to the raw-water pump. The pump pushes it through the cooling water passages in the engine block, around the cylinders, the valves, the head, and the exhaust manifold. Finally, the water is injected into the exhaust and discharged through the exhaust pipe, where it cools the pipe (or hose) and contributes greatly to muffling exhaust noise (see fig. 17-2). It is a good idea to have a check valve on the intake to prevent draining when the engine is not in operation and one on the discharge side to prevent water from entering the system in following seas or when backing down. These must be checked regularly to make sure that they operate freely.

Raw-water systems do have disadvantages. First of all, antifreeze, with its corrosion-inhibiting additives, cannot be employed. Aside from the loss of corrosion protection, this means that the system must be drained after every use in winter operations to prevent damage from freezing, and that piping runs have to be laid out without any low spots to trap water.

Raw-water systems are also susceptible to clogging and blockage from silt, sand, marine growth, rust, and scale. Both silt and sand, if allowed to settle for significant periods of time, can result in poultice corrosion. Sand can also cause impingement erosion at elbows or sharp

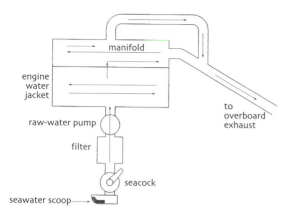

Fig. 17-2. Raw-water cooling system. Raw water is picked up by the forward-facing scoop, with a screen on the scoop keeping seaweed and debris from entering. The seacock allows the raw-water inlet to be shut off for engine service or safety. The raw-water pump forces the water through the engine block water jacket to the exhaust manifold and to the exhaust pipe for discharge overboard.

turns in the piping. Any kind of debris can deprive the engine of cooling water and result in serious overheating and engine damage. Scale is crystallized salts of magnesium and calcium that tend to form on the internal surfaces of the cooling passages. It acts as a very effective insulator, greatly reducing the efficiency of heat transfer from the engine to the cooling water. Scale forms more rapidly at higher temperatures, so to retard scale formation, raw-water-cooled engines typically run cooler—at around 140°F (60°C)—but this makes the engine significantly less efficient.

What this boils down to is that raw-water systems require more regular maintenance: cooling water passages must be kept open; pumps must be inspected for impingement erosion; impellers must be replaced regularly; filters must be kept clean; thermostats must be checked periodically; and the prudent skipper will always keep a watchful eye on the temperature gauge.

Cleaning a raw-water system is normally done by flushing the system with freshwater supplied by a garden hose. The objective is to force a good volume of water at pressure through the cooling system to carry silt, sand, mud, and other loose debris out of the system. Scale, however, is essentially unaffected by flushing. It must be removed chemically.

Commercial products are available from automotive or marine supply stores that will remove scale when used according to the instructions, but these are typically acid-based compounds, and care should be taken to be sure that they are compatible with the metals in the engine block and cooling system. There are also some do-it-yourself formulations based on oxalic or phosphoric acid, but if you're not knowledgeable and experienced with these, serious damage to the engine can result, particularly if the block or the head is aluminum. My recommendation is to stick with an established and proven commercial solution, *formulated for your engine*, and to follow the instructions for use and for proper disposal of the effluent. Or, perhaps better yet, let the yard do it.

Freshwater Cooling Systems

The principal advantages of a raw-water cooling system are simplicity and low initial cash outlay, but these features come at the cost of reduced operating efficiency, greater maintenance cost, and shorter engine life. Freshwater cooling is far superior. It enables the engine to operate at a steady and more efficient temperature. It keeps the problems associated with silt, sand, and salt out of the engine. It allows the use of antifreeze with its corrosion-inhibiting additives. And it makes year-round use of the boat practical (not necessarily comfortable) if the skipper is up to the rigors of winter boating.

The freshwater cooling system is really not all that much more complicated. To create two physically separate water circuits requires only a few additional components—a second pump, a heat exchanger, a header tank, and some plumbing. In the freshwater circuit, coolant moves from the header tank through external piping to the cooling water passageways and then through one side of the heat exchanger and back to the tank, circulating around and around as long as the engine is running. The header tank, also called an expansion or surge tank, provides space for the water to expand as it is heated. This also enables us to pressurize the system, thus raising the boiling point of the coolant and allowing the engine to operate at higher and more efficient temperatures. See figure 17-3.

Water flow in the raw-water circuit is much the same as I have already described. Seawater picked up at the intake scoop flows through the strainer to the pump, only instead of going to the engine it is pumped through the raw-water side of the heat exchanger. Then, as before, it passes through the oil cooler (if one is fitted) and out the exhaust.

A word about the coolant fluid is in order here. There are basically three types of antifreeze: one for potable water systems, one solely for engine winter storage, and one for operating en-

gine winterizing. The differences have to do with the chemicals and additives in the formulation. Potable water antifreeze formulations contain no toxic or severe chemicals and provide protection only against freeze-ups. Those for winter engine layup do have corrosion inhibitors and rust preventives but do not have the chemical additives required for high-temperature operation. Antifreeze formulations designed for use at operating temperatures are perfectly suitable for both engines in winter storage and for operating engines. Obviously, the two engine antifreeze types *must never be used in drinking water systems.*

Antifreeze products may be based on either *ethylene glycol* or *propylene glycol*. Ethylene glycol is highly toxic and, if not properly dis-

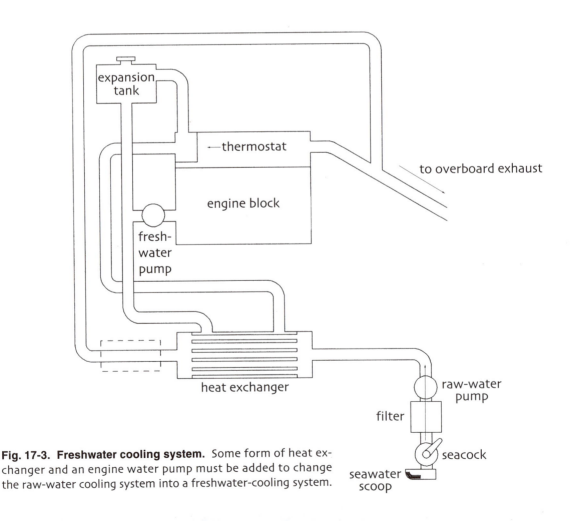

Fig. 17-3. Freshwater cooling system. Some form of heat exchanger and an engine water pump must be added to change the raw-water cooling system into a freshwater-cooling system.

posed of, can be fatal to pets and domestic animals. Propylene glycol is every bit as effective but has the advantage of being nontoxic and biodegradable. It is slightly more expensive.

The coolant fluid as used in the engine consists of a mixture of antifreeze—typically 50 to 70 percent, depending on the particular antifreeze used—and freshwater. Freshwater contains considerable quantities of free oxygen, and as we've seen, oxygen is a principal and necessary element in the corrosion process. As the coolant is circulated around the closed, pressurized system, repeatedly heated and cooled, the oxygen content is reduced to negligible levels. This is one of the not-so-obvious advantages of the closed freshwater system. For this reason, it is not a good idea to change the cooling fluid any more often than necessary, say once a year at winter layup.

Heat Exchangers

The heat exchanger is a very simple device. Typically it consists of a group of tubes passing through a closed tank or shell. Figure 17-4 shows a simplified diagram of the heat exchanger.

The seawater flows in at one end, *through* the tubes (tubeside flow), and out through the outlet port. The freshwater from the engine water jacket flows in one end of the shell, circulates *around* the tubes (shellside flow), and flows out the other end, and returns to the header tank. All problems of silt, sand, and debris are removed from the engine and transferred to the heat exchanger. If allowed to accumulate, silt, sand, and other debris small enough to get through the raw-water filter will eventually block the tubes. The reduced volume of water flow through the tubes will result in steadily increasing temperature over time. The temperature gauge can provide an indication that this is taking place.

Heat exchangers are susceptible to several forms of corrosive damage. One of the most common is poultice corrosion under sediment (mud, silt) deposits. Larger debris—sticks, stones, and so on—lodged in the tubes can also cause turbulence downstream that can result in pinholes in the tubes. One bronze heat exchanger that we took out of a boat after 30 years in service showed little visible evidence of corrosion on the outside. However, the copper tubes were perforated from corrosion that had occurred on the inside surfaces.

Velocity of the water flow can also cause

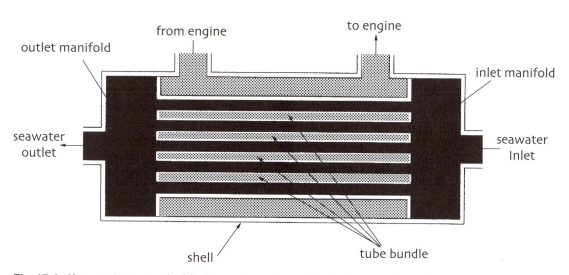

Fig. 17-4. Heat exchanger. The black area shows the path of the seawater as it flows through the raw-water side of the heat exchanger. The gray area shows the path of the engine coolant as it flows through the freshwater side of the exchanger.

problems. Velocities less than 3 ft./sec. (0.9 m/sec.) are not sufficient to prevent sediment buildup, biological fouling, or clogging from small bits of debris collecting in the tubes. Excessive velocities, however, can cause erosion and impingement damage. What is "excessive" depends on the alloy used in the tubes. Velocities of 5 to 6 ft./sec. (1.5 to 1.8 m/sec.) is excessive for copper in seawater applications, but most other commonly used alloys perform well up to 9 ft./sec. (2.7 m/sec.). Stainless steels, either 304 or 316, are not really suitable for heat exchangers used in seawater. The alloy of choice for heat exchanger tube applications is 70-30 cupronickel.

Not all heat exchangers can be opened up for cleaning, but those that can should be periodically flushed out, opened up, and cleaned to remove sediment and debris. The frequency of cleaning depends on the water in which the boat operates. In brackish, inshore estuarial waters where there is a lot of silt, mud, and sand, monthly flushings may not be too often. In clean waters, flushing, disassembly, and brushing at the annual layup is likely to be sufficient.

Leaving the heat exchanger full, or even wet, for any significant period of time is highly conducive to corrosion. The water becomes stagnant, and bacteria colonies form, paving the way for microbiologically induced corrosion. Also, corrosion will take place under sediment deposits—another reason for running the engine up to normal engine temperatures at least once a week.

Just a word about disassembly and brushing to remove sediment. Ideally, this will be done using a stiff, nonmetallic brush. Sediment deposits, however, can be quite obstinate, and it may be necessary to speak more harshly to them. In such instances, some people resort to the use of a wooden dowel. However, if you find this necessary, go gently, dear reader. It is not all that difficult to do real damage to soft tubes. When heat exchangers—including oil and transmission fluid coolers—fail, they can cause serious damage to the engine. It will be well worth your effort to keep them in good shape and drained or protected during winter storage.

Keel Coolers

The type of heat exchanger we've been discussing is typically fitted inside the boat. There is another type that mounts outside the boat—on the side of the keel or on the underbody. This type, called a *keel cooler*, differs from conventional heat exchangers in that it has no *shell* or housing. The heat exchanger tubes are simply exposed to the water in which the boat is afloat.

The primary advantage of a keel cooler is that there is no second raw-water circuit. Coolant is circulated through the keel cooler tubes, transferring engine heat directly to the surrounding water. The problems of silt, mud, sand, and debris getting into the exchanger are eliminated. However, if the boat will have a wet exhaust system, cooling water for the exhaust is still necessary, so a raw-water pump and hoses must still be fitted, along with screens and filters. Exchangers for oil or transmission fluid cooling can be installed in this circuit.

The vulnerability with keel coolers is the obvious one of exposure to damage from floating debris or from grounding. When the manifold castings are of bronze and the tubes are of 70-30 cupronickel, a keel cooler does not require much in the way of maintenance—just keep it clean and replace the sacrificial zinc anodes. According to the Walters Machine Company, a keel cooler builder, the most common problem is some well-meaning but inexperienced yard worker painting the cooler. This usually shows up when the owner comes back to the yard with an overheating problem. When the boat operates in waters with a lot of floating debris and the cooler is not properly guarded, bent tubes can also be a problem. The tubes are separately replaceable, but the boat has to be hauled, and the owner experiences both inconvenience and cost. In general, keel coolers are sufficiently rugged, and some have been functioning without problems for more than 30 years.

EXHAUST SYSTEMS

We want an exhaust system to safely carry exhaust gases away from the crew and out of the boat, and hopefully to perform this function quietly. Components in the system must be able to withstand extreme heat, the acidic by-products of combustion, and, in the case of wet exhaust, the corrosive nature of hot seawater. Piping must be large enough and straight enough to provide unrestricted gas flow. Also, it is of the utmost importance that the system not allow even the smallest amount of water to get back into the engine. Water is not compressible, and severe damage to pistons, connecting rods, or wrist pins can result.

Dry Exhaust System

In a dry system, the exhaust leaves the engine manifold and runs vertically up through the deck and the house to a stack with the outlet high enough to carry away the noxious fumes. The outlet is capped or flapped to prevent rain water from getting into the system (see fig. 17-5).

Dry exhaust systems are used primarily on commercial and high-performance craft. Since the entire run from the manifold to the outlet is extremely hot, it must be well shielded to pre-

vent burns—both to the boat and the crew. When wood is periodically exposed to very hot surfaces (250°F or 121°C) over a long period of time and without a significant flow of air, a form of carbon—called *pyrophoric*—can develop. Pyrophoric carbon can ignite from the heat, setting the boat on fire. Wood surfaces in the area of a dry stack exhaust must be well shielded, ventilated, and monitored regularly.

Wet Exhaust System

Figure 17-6 shows a typical wet exhaust system you might find in a power cruiser where the engine is mounted above the waterline. Raw cooling water is injected into the exhaust gas flow after it leaves the manifold. The water spray greatly reduces the temperature of the exhaust gases and of the exhaust system hardware. Typically, the exhaust stream is then carried through a silencer (or muffler) to the exhaust outlet at the transom and discharged. The dry section of the system, before the cooling water is injected, gets dangerously hot and must be *lagged* or insulated (shown by the dotted lines in the illus-

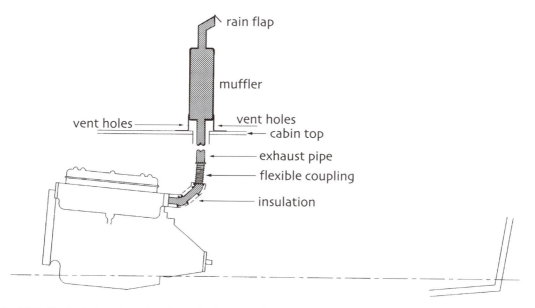

Fig. 17-5. Typical dry exhaust system. In the dry exhaust system, no cooling water is injected. The exhaust comes off the engine manifold and is taken vertically up through the deck and the cabin top to discharge the exhaust gases through an aft-facing capped elbow. This type of system must be well ventilated and heat shielded.

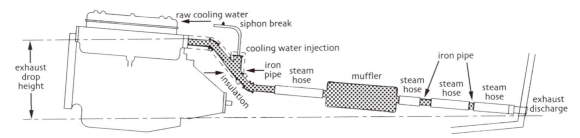

Fig. 17-6. Traditional wet exhaust system. The traditional wet exhaust system is built up of black iron pipe and pipe fittings. Raw cooling water is injected into the system to cool down the exhaust gases and the exhaust system components. Mufflers are of metal, and the system is highly susceptible to corrosion. The hot or "dry" section between the engine manifold and the cooling water injection point must be "lagged" or insulated.

tration). This was once done with asbestos, but nowadays risers are thickly wrapped with fiberglass tape.

If the position of the engine is not sufficient to ensure that the highest point in the exhaust line is above the waterline at all angles of heel, as is often the case with sailboats, a *riser* must be added to the system, as illustrated in figure 17-7. Dimensions and relative placement of exhaust system components are critical. Follow the engine manufacturer's instructions.

Of the important things that the exhaust system must *not* do, it must not increase unduly or excessively the back pressure on the engine. For this reason, and to minimize opportunities for erosion corrosion damage, sharp and abrupt turns in the system are to be avoided, especially after the cooling water is injected into the system. The use of 45° elbows is to be preferred, but limited use of 90° ells in the dry section is quite common to conserve space.

From the point of view of corrosive damage, it all comes down to the materials used in the system. The best systems use the least amount of metal.

Exhaust Riser

It is still necessary, due to the temperatures involved and galvanic compatibility, to use metallic piping—threaded nipples, 45° and 90° ells

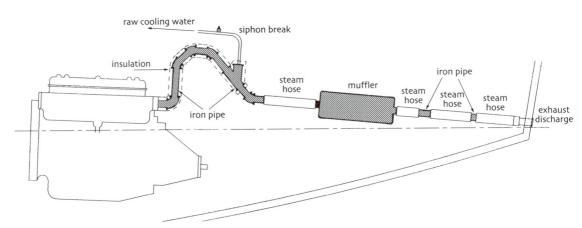

Fig. 17-7. Traditional sailboat wet exhaust system. An exhaust riser was added after the manifold because the engine is mounted below the waterline.

and injection elbows, or, in some cases, a water-jacketed riser (fig. 17-8)—in the dry section between the manifold and the cooling water injection point. Traditionally, these components have been schedule 80 cast iron, a robust material that is galvanically compatible with the commonly used cast iron manifolds. However, cast iron is susceptible to rusting and scaling that can break loose and clog the cooling water injection orifices, resulting in overheating.

It would be nice to have an equally robust, galvanically compatible, and corrosion-resistant metal, but the alloys that come immediately to mind all have shortcomings. Aluminum, while compatible with engines having aluminum manifolds, is not as hard or as strong as cast iron and poses galvanic compatibility problems with other fittings. Bronze has compatibility problems with both iron and aluminum, is relatively soft, and has a higher susceptibility to erosion and impingement corrosion. Also, it is aggressively attacked by the sulfuric acid from residual sulfur in diesel fuels. Most of the common

grades of stainless steel—18-8, 302, and 304—will corrode if used in wet exhaust systems. Although 316L is sometimes used, its performance is marginal. Some of the more exotic nickel-base alloys such as Hastelloy C, Inconel 625, and Incoloy 825 are excellent. However, exhaust system components of these alloys are not readily found, and if they are found, they are costly.

Metal exhaust components are, of course, susceptible to corrosion. Injection elbows eventually leak due to erosion corrosion. The tip-off—unless you spend a lot of time in the engine room and witness the water spurting and spraying from the elbow—will be the smell of exhaust fumes in the living spaces. In the case of the water-jacketed riser, perforation of the inner jacket can let water into the exhaust system whenever the engine is shut down. It may then drain into the manifold and from there into the engine. The water-jacketed riser is an excellent device, but the prudent operator will keep a close eye on its condition. Commercial fishermen often favor the dry stack because it eliminates any possibility of flooding the engine through the exhaust system.

Siphon Break

A siphon break, also called a *vented loop*, is a necessary part of any below-the-waterline installation. Typically, this consists of a loop of hose or tubing connected between the raw-water outlet on the engine and the raw-water injection point for the exhaust. An air-admitting valve is installed at the top of the loop and as close to the boat's centerline as possible. The loop must be high enough to ensure that the valve will be above the waterline at all angles of heel. Generally, the valve is the failure point. Corrosion and/or clogging (by salt crystals or other debris) causes the valve to fail to operate, sticking on either the open or closed position. In the open position, the valve will dribble, spurt, or spray seawater onto the engine and its wiring. In the closed position, seawater will be siphoned up into the exhaust riser and could find its way back into the engine. In any case, there are no acceptable consequences of a failed or malfunctioning siphon break. That leaves pe-

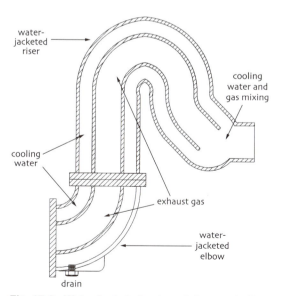

Fig. 17-8. Water-jacketed exhaust riser and elbow. This system is essentially a heat exchanger in which the raw cooling water flows in the space between the inner and outer pipes, and exhaust gases flow through the inner pipe.

riodic inspection and regular maintenance as our only alternative.

Also, the critical role of the lowly raw-water pump must be emphasized. Failure of the raw-water pump could result in rapid overheating and serious damage to a wet exhaust system (not to mention the engine).

Piping

Downstream of the point of cooling-water injection, wire-reinforced marine exhaust hose is not only suitable but preferable. The hose should be designed for exhaust applications and should meet the standards recommended by ABYC and SAE J006 or UL 1129. Exhaust lines should run on the centerline of the boat or as close to that as possible, and slope down from the engine a minimum of $1/4$ in./ft. More is better. Fire-retardant and heat-resistant fiberglass connectors are available (in place of iron pipe fittings) to connect sections of exhaust hose, and rubber exhaust elbows are available for the tight turns. Both are essentially impervious to corrosion, but they must be kept several inches downstream of the cooling water injection point. Exhaust line runs should have no droops or sags that can trap water, and all hose joints should be double-clamped with *all-stainless steel* hose clamps.

Some measure should be taken to prevent following seas from driving water up the exhaust when the engine is not running. This is often accomplished by looping the exhaust hose well above the waterline, but care must be taken that this doesn't increase back pressure excessively. Check valves and seacocks (always recommended on through-hulls close to the waterline) also may be used.

Mufflers and Silencers

In the marine industry, the terms *muffler* and *silencer* are frequently used interchangeably. There are those, however, who distinguish between the two. For these people, silencers are vertical cylindrical tanks with the inlet typically high on the side and the outlet taken from the bottom of the tank through a pipe exiting the top. They are recommended in applications where the engine exhaust manifold may be below the waterline at any angle of heel. As exhaust gas and water from the exhaust riser enter the tank, the water collects in the tank. When it covers the bottom of the outlet pipe, pressure forces the water up the pipe and out the exhaust. This popular "waterlift silencer" system is widely used on auxiliary sailboats (fig. 17-9). Silencers should include a drain plug.

Mufflers, according to those who distinguish between the two, are typically similar in shape to the familiar automotive mufflers—that is, oval or cylindrical in cross section. They are usually mounted horizontally and always *above the waterline*. Mufflers are commonly available in fiberglass, synthetic rubber, neoprene, and cross-linked polyethylene—all essentially impervious to corrosion.

Mufflers are frequently omitted in dry exhaust systems. For commercial fishing vessels,

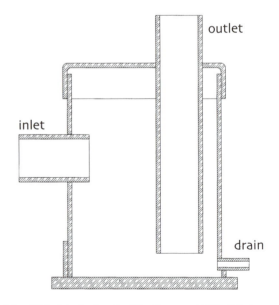

Fig. 17-9. Typical waterlift silencer. With this type of muffler, used when the engine is mounted below the waterline, exhaust gases and cooling water from the exhaust riser enter the tank. The gases are forced out the outlet, and the water collects in the bottom. Once the water covers the bottom of the outlet pipe, the pressure forces the water up the pipe and out the exhaust.

maximum time for fishing and minimum yard time for maintenance or repairs are considerably higher on their list of priorities than noise reduction. For the owners and operators of high-performance power craft, power and noise are one and the same, and the more of both the better. Since there is no cooling water in a dry exhaust system to bring the temperature down within the range of the nonmetallic materials, stainless steel and hard aluminum are frequently the materials of choice when mufflers are installed.

A couple of final thoughts concerning the exhaust system. We have far better materials to work with nowadays than we did back in the days of black iron pipe and steam hose. It is possible to put together a system that, with the possible exception of the exhaust riser or dry section, eliminates corrosion as a significant problem. However, keep in mind that the exhaust system is a critical element in the safety of the boat and its crew. The system must be gas-tight; any leakage of exhaust fumes into the boat's interior is extremely dangerous.

PROPELLERS AND SHAFTS

Most propellers in everyday use are manganese bronze. At 58 percent copper and 39 percent zinc, manganese bronze is really a brass and as such is subject to dezincification. Higher-quality props may be manufactured from Nibral, an alloy of nickel, aluminum, and bronze. Nibral is an excellent but expensive prop material.

Shafts are typically Aquamet, stainless steel, or Tobin (naval) bronze. Aquamet is a trade name for a proprietary stainless steel formulation. Tobin bronze is roughly 60 percent copper and 39 percent zinc. Like manganese bronze, it is really a brass and subject to dezincification.

Bronze props are often mounted on Aquamet or stainless steel shafts. Whatever the combination of prop and shaft, all of these materials require cathodic protection.

It is perhaps more common for the anode to be clamped to the shaft. These are roughly spherical in shape to minimize turbulence. A thin, square section collar of zinc is intended for situations where the clearance between the prop and the stern or strut is limited. Zinc collars should be located on the shaft where they will offer the least amount of interference to the flow of water into the strut bearing or into the prop. Be sure to fit the zinc to a clean shaft—no bottom paint or grease. It must make good electrical contact with the shaft. Also available is a prop-nut zinc anode, which is screwed onto the end of the shaft and secured with a locking pin.

Zinc anodes work best when they are directly attached to the metal they are protecting. However, the prop and shaft can be protected by a remotely located zinc fastened to the boat's underbody. There is a case to be made for a single, remotely located zinc (or group of zincs). With separate zincs on each fitting, some could be overprotected while others are not receiving enough protection. Connecting all fittings to the same zinc means that they will be held at the same potential and that protection will be more uniform. Also, you have only the one zinc or group of zincs to worry about.

Avoid anodes that simply have a couple of through-holes in them for fastening. As the zinc corrodes, the holes open up, and the anode comes loose. The zinc should have a cast-in plate and fasteners, typically of stainless steel, to prevent this.

Ideally, a zinc anode and its through-bolts should be insulated from a wooden hull to reduce the possibility of alkali damage to the wood. The mounting bolts can be insulated with heat-shrink tubing whose length is equal to the thickness of the hull plus any fairing block. Insulate the zinc from the fairing block with plastic, epoxy, or silicone. Mount it reasonably close to the metals it is protecting and where it will be immersed at all times. A teardrop-shaped zinc will cause less turbulence.

In this case, since the zinc anode is not in direct contact with the metals it is to protect, there is no path for the electrons. The circuit must be completed by means of a wire—minimum #8 AWG stranded with green sheathing—from the zinc's through-bolt inside the hull *to the shaft*. Connecting the wire to the engine block and relying on the conductivity of the block, transmission housing, and shaft coupling is not a good idea. The electrical conductivity of this path will be lower than desirable and, in any case, not reliable. (A flexible shaft coupling completely insulates the shaft from the engine.) The connection should be directly to the shaft through a spring-loaded phosphor bronze shaft brush. If the contact must be made to the engine block or forward of the shaft coupling, the coupling must be electrically bridged with a jumper wire from one side of the coupling to the other.

Remember also that the zincs have to be in electrical contact with the water. *Do not paint them!*

SUMMARY

With the materials that are available to us today, with regular attention to the use of proper coatings and galvanic protection methods, and with conscientious adherence to regular maintenance tasks and winter layup procedures, propulsion systems can give many years of trouble-free service.

For the engine, frequent oil changes will ensure fresh additives and corrosion inhibitors to fortify protective oil films on cylinder walls and bearing surfaces. An occasional treatment of engine wiring with a moisture-displacing anticorrosive spray formulated for this purpose should be a regular part of your maintenance schedule. These measures apply equally to outboards and outdrives.

The cooling system, with its high temperatures, fast-moving water—salt, fresh, or both—and its mild steel and cast iron components, is particularly susceptible to corrosive damage. Regular and frequent freshwater flushing of raw-water circuits and maintenance of proper levels of the appropriate type of antifreeze—preferably propylene glycol—are essential. Engine zincs should be inspected at least a couple of times each season and replaced if fifty percent or more depleted.

Corrosion protection for props and shafts boils down to sacrificial anodes properly installed and maintained. Sacrificial anodes are also required on outboard and outdrive lower units, and these, too, must be inspected regularly and replaced timely.

We are talking here about the vessel's propulsion system. It's not as much fun as the topside stuff, but it's really very useful and not something you want to be without.

CHAPTER 18

Electrical and Electronic Systems

Unless your boat is oar-powered, its operation is almost certain to depend on some kind of electrical system. When that system fails, you may lose the ability to start the engine, navigate with GPS, loran, or radar, communicate with others or call for assistance, or even show navigation lights. All of these functions require a steady, dependable supply of electricity, usually at 12 volts. If electrical devices see significantly less voltage than this, they begin to show their displeasure. They may get noisy or erratic, or their speech may get blurred. Transmitters won't transmit as far, receivers won't receive as well, and lamps won't emit as much light. Many electrical devices will simply refuse to function at all.

There is also the question of safety. Dave Gerr, in one of his many informative and entertaining magazine articles, reports that more than 25 percent of all boat fires are caused by electrical failures. It is quite possible for electrical shorts in the 12-volt DC electrical system to generate sufficient heat to ignite wood and fiberglass. When you're 10 miles off and the only thing there is to stand on is aflame under your feet, it's not the time to be wishing you'd paid more attention to proper care and maintenance of this critical system.

To make matters worse, alas, no other systems on the boat are as susceptible to performance-degrading corrosive damage as the electrical and electronic systems and equipment. Just think about all of the different metals and alloys involved—copper and copper alloys in wire, contacts, and printed circuit boards; steels and stainless steels in connectors, switches, relays, and terminal strips; tin and lead and their alloys in wire and solder; and gold, palladium, and silver on contacts and connectors. The situation is not improved by operating atmospheres that range from total immersion in the bilge, through the high humidity and high temperature of the engine room, to the salt-laden, spray-soaked flybridge of a tuna tower.

And there is more bad news. The situation is even more problematical with modern-day electronic equipment. Because of increased complexity and the closer spacing of circuitry and components, extremely low levels of corrosive contaminants can cause degradation or complete failure.

It is helpful to think about the electrical system in terms of its separate functions—power generation and storage, control and distribution, and the devices (loads) that are the reason for putting up with this useful and, perhaps, necessary but troublesome servant.

POWER GENERATION AND STORAGE

Most boats have some combination of components and devices aboard whose job it is to generate, store, deliver, and replenish electrical power. The principal elements for these functions are the batteries, which store the power, a charging source—normally an engine-driven alternator—that replenishes and maintains the supply, and a battery-isolator/selection switch that provides a measure of confidence-building redundancy into the system. There can be additional elements, but our interest is electrical system corrosion, not electrical system design.

Before we go any further, let's review some basics. When an electric current (I) flows through a resistance (R), an amount of voltage (V) equal to the current multiplied by the resistance (I × R) is "dropped." This voltage is lost; that is, it isn't available to the other components or loads that may need it. Voltage drops occur

167

wherever the current encounters resistance in the circuit.

Keep in mind that we start out with only about 12.5 volts on a fully charged battery, and that a battery is considered to be discharged at 11.5 volts or so. Since most loads perform best when they have a full 12.5 volts at their terminals, we can't afford to lose much of this before the performance of our electrical equipment is degraded or the device ceases to function at all.

Consider an example based on a simple engine-starting circuit. There are two principal resistances that concern us: the intrinsic resistance of the wire or cables and the contact resistance between mating surfaces. Let's trace the current flow path and take a rough count of the number of resistances in the simplified starting circuit of figure 18-1.

We can trace the flow of the current along the following path:

1. the contact surface between the positive battery post and the battery cable clamp

2. the contact surface between the cable clamp and the battery cable

3. the battery cable itself to the ring terminal at the input post on the battery selection switch

4. the contact surface between the cable and the ring terminal

5. the contact surface between the ring terminal and the post

6. the contact surface between the contacts in the switch

7. the contact surface between the output post and the ring terminal on the starter cable

8. the contact surface between the ring terminal and the starter cable

9. the starter cable itself from this terminal to the ring terminal at the starting motor

10. the contact surface between the cable and the ring terminal at the starter

11. the contact surface between the ring terminal and the post on the starter

12. the starting motor windings to the starting motor housing

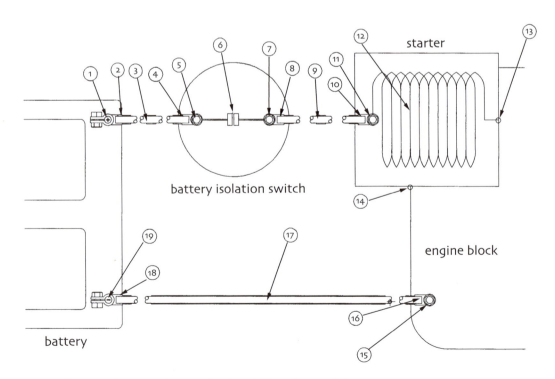

Fig. 18-1. Circuit resistances. See text for description of current flow.

13. the contact surface between the starter housing and the engine block
14 the contact surface between the engine block and the common ground stud
15. the contact surface between the common ground stud and the ring terminal on the negative battery cable
16. The contact surface between the ring terminal and the cable
17. the negative return cable itself to the battery clamp at the battery
18. the contact surface between the cable and the negative battery clamp
19. the contact surface between the negative battery clamp and the negative post on the battery

We have identified 19 resistances in this circuit. Let's ignore those of the cables and windings for the moment. That leaves 15 contact resistances. A reasonable estimate of the resistance of a large-area contact between high-conductivity materials is about 0.001 ohms, so the approximate resistance in this circuit due to contact surfaces is 15 × 0.001 ohms, or 0.015 ohms. If we assume a modest 75 amperes for the starting motor current for a small gasoline engine, the voltage drop due to contact resistances alone would be 1.1 volts. When we subtract the 1.1 volt drop from the nominal 12.5 volts at the battery, that leaves us 11.4 volts at the starting motor. Were we considering a large diesel engine, starting current might run to 200 amps or more. In this case the voltage drop would be 0.015 × 200, or 3.0 volts, leaving us just 9.5 volts at the starter—barely enough to spin the motor at the rpm necessary for starting.

Keep in mind that our resistance estimates are based on clean, tight, full-surface contacts. Loose, dirty or partial-surface contacts, or—more to the point for us—corrosion can increase contact resistances by up to several orders of magnitude. When that happens, we begin to experience problems. This is why the terminals and lugs on battery and starter cables must be closed-end at the terminal end and sealed at the cable end.

Excessive resistance is also a safety concern.

Resistance (R) multiplied by the square of the current flowing through it (I × I) is equal to the amount of heat dissipated in the resistance. For example, a 10-amp current flowing through a 1-ohm resistance will dissipate 100 watts—more heat than the soldering iron in your toolbox. To give you a comparative marker, a 50-watt soldering iron can generate temperatures up to about 600°F (316°C)! Think about that. Metal heated to 600°F (316°C) in close proximity to or contact with wood, cloth, oily rags, cleaning solvents, or any number of combustible materials can, and often does, result in flames.

What we have said here in regard to the battery and starting circuit applies directly to all of the electrical circuitry on the boat. The magnitude of the current flows may be lower—typically less than 10 amps—but resistance is likely to be substantially higher due to the smaller contact areas. It is of critical importance in all circuits to make good, clean, tight, full-surface contacts (this is where soldering comes in) and to protect them from corrosion.

Maintaining good, tight contacts is just good craftsmanship—"a proper job properly done," as my mentors used to say (endlessly). To protect the contacts from corrosion, there are any number of methods and materials—some are old, such as cup, wheel-bearing, and silicone greases and petroleum jellies; and some are new, such as corrosion-resistant sprays. All will keep corrosion from degrading the contact if the coating is maintained.

With regard to the protective sprays, these can be divided into two types: those that deposit a thin, wax-like protective layer and those that deposit an equally thin but moisture-displacing film of a proprietary composition. I prefer the moisture-displacing type.

High-quality marine battery cables are not cheap. AWG Type 2 cable is recommended and can be as much as three or four times more costly than economy alternatives. Making up your own cables using automotive or welding cable and clamp-on or solder-on battery clamps is not a good idea. Both the wire and the contact surfaces are susceptible to corrosion, which increases resistance and results in cable deterioration and a safety hazard. Preassembled marine cables feature tinned fine-strand copper wire and heavy-duty tinned copper terminal ends. The ends are molded in an extra thick coating of plastic to prevent water from wicking up into the cable. The coating on the wire itself is thicker than that of automotive or welding cable to prevent moisture from penetrating into the strands through abrasions or punctures. This is not a place to cut corners or to try to save money.

DISTRIBUTION AND CONTROL

Power from the battery is distributed to the various loads through the distribution panel. This typically consists of an aluminum or plastic panel with circuit-protection devices mounted to it. The protection devices may be either fuses and toggle switches or circuit breakers. A panel may also contain various types of circuit and device monitoring instruments.

Distribution panels can be simple 2-circuit fuse and toggle panels, or they can be sophisticated control centers with 30 or more DC circuit breakers and illuminated digital voltage and current monitoring on one side and a similar number of AC circuit breakers on the other, also with monitoring instrumentation.

To facilitate wire routing and connections, the back of the panel will contain common-feed bus blocks as well as individual branch terminals for each circuit. When you consider the number of connectors, contacts, and electrical mating surfaces, you can see that what we said above concerning the importance of clean, tight, full-surface contacts, well protected with a moisture-displacing corrosion protection spray, is directly applicable here. Distribution panels do introduce a lot of contacts and connections, but when properly done, they work reliably and well with a minimal amount of maintenance—cleaning and protective coating.

Now look at figure 18-2, the back panel wiring for a 36-foot inshore commercial fishing boat skippered by a hardworking fisherman who didn't have time for the electrical niceties. This is the alternative to a proper, Bristol fashion distribution system. Ask yourself how in the

devil you would provide the maintenance that such a system would—and did—require. This boat had a severe stray-current corrosion problem, resulting from exposed wires in the bilge.

Moisture is the great enemy of electrical and electronic equipment. It penetrates into all the cracks and crevices where you really don't want it—wire splices, butt connectors, screw contacts, fuse blocks, and even non-marine-grade circuit breakers. Contacts and mating surfaces oxidize, resistance increases, voltage is lost, heat is generated, and, at best, performance deteriorates or equipment fails. At worst, a fire results. It behooves us to take all possible and practical measures to prevent moisture from getting to all electric items aboard.

The distribution panel itself should be in a dry location, typically in the main cabin, and as high in the boat as possible. Provision should be made in the enclosure for drainage at the bottom and ventilation at the top. Cables and wires should enter and exit from the sides and should lead down and away from the enclosure, forming drip loops. Rags, paper, and other hygroscopic materials should not be placed on, in, or around the enclosure. Finally, *after* you are

Fig. 18-2. Wiring in a 36-foot commercial fishing boat without a distribution panel. This is an excellent example of what not to do. This boat had no distribution panel, no wiring plan or diagram, and severe stray-current corrosion problems.

sure that all contacts, connections, and metal surfaces are clean and properly made up, a moisture-displacing corrosion-preventive spray should be used *according to the manufacturer's directions.*

Incidentally, when you are faced with the necessity of cleaning up a dirty or corroded contact strip, fuse holder, or bus bar, don't be tempted to use steel or bronze wool. They both leave tiny fragments of metal. The steel rusts, and the bronze can cause leakage paths or shorts. Use instead a nonmetallic sandpaper or even a plastic scrubbing pad from the galley.

Wiring

The only wire that should be used in a boat's electrical system is *marine-grade* multistrand tinned copper wire with a heavy protective sheathing. Solid conductor wire is widely used in home construction, but it should never be used on a boat. The hull and all of its systems are subjected to considerable vibration and sometimes severe dynamic shock, and solid conductor wire simply does not stand up well under these conditions, especially in a corrosive environment. It tends to work-harden and fracture. This can cause all sorts of mysterious, hard-to-find faults before it fails completely. Marine-grade multistrand wire is far more flexible and better able to withstand shock and vibration. And wire with heavier sheathing and in which each individual strand is tinned is also better able to withstand the corrosive atmosphere.

Think about it. All of the boat's electrical systems—engine starting and running, bilge pumps and alarms, navigation and accommodation lighting, and electronics—depend on these wires. This is really not a good place to cut corners. Prorated over the life of the boat, the one-time cost of using marine-grade multistrand tinned copper wire is very small, especially when you consider the downside risks.

The sheathing should be heavy thermoplastic to provide moisture and abrasion resistance or, better yet, a cross-linked polymer to provide moisture, abrasion, and heat resistance. Some types recommended by ABYC (E-9 Direct Current Electrical Systems on Boats) are TW, THW,

and THWN (thermoplastic sheathing) for general wiring applications, XHHW (cross-linked polymer sheathing) for high-heat areas, and MTW, which is also oil resistant, for engine room applications.

The ABYC standard also recommends that these wires be Type 2 or Type 3. Type 3 has more and finer strands than Type 2 and is therefore more flexible. Type 1 includes solid wire and stranded wire that has fewer strands than Type 2 and is *not* recommended. The Code of Federal Regulations (CFR Title 33, Section 183.425) prohibits the use of solid conductor wire in small craft and requires that in systems under 50 volts DC, the wire meets the standards of—*and be marked*—SAE J378 and SAE 1127 or 1128. In systems over 50 volts DC, the conductor must also meet Article 310 of the National Fire Protection Association (NFPA), No. 70 of the National Electrical Code for moisture absorbency, and flame-retarding requirements. However, it should be kept in mind that automotive wire (SAE) is not designed for marine applications and is not typically as resistant to moisture penetration from spray, dripping, or immersion. Though stranded, it is rarely tinned and consists of coarser, stiffer strands. SAE wire can be up to 12 percent smaller than AWG boat cable; thus, in many applications, larger-gauge wire must be used to stay within the recommended voltage drops. All of this may not be at the top of your list of critical features, but insurance companies do seem to place considerable importance on it in the event of what the Coast Guard refers to as an "incident."

Solder Splices

Soldering is another subject about which there is considerable controversy. There are those who swear by soldered splices, while others insist that crimped connectors are better. The fact is that a properly made soldered splice—wires twisted together, soldered, encapsulated in electrician's putty or some other moisture-excluding plastic encapsulation, and then covered with either heat-shrink tube or high-dielectric plastic tape, or both—makes an excellent electrical connection. Soldered splices have been used successfully since long before today's crimp connectors became available.

Soldering has become controversial because a high percentage of soldered connections are not properly made. The twist connection is poorly made. The wire surfaces are not clean. A proper solder flux was not used. Insufficient heat resulted in a poor ("cold") solder joint. The consequence of these failings is a high-resistance connection. Excessive heat results, the solder softens or melts, and the splice comes apart. Soldering also has the effect of transforming the flexible stranded conductor into a solid conductor with its susceptibility to fatigue failure.

ABYC standards do not allow solder to be used as the *sole* means of mechanical connection. Even if one is sure that he or she can and will make proper, reliable solder joints, there is the insurance aspect to consider.

Crimp Connectors

Crimp connectors and terminals are universally accepted and widely used in the marine industry and are now the preferred means of making electrical connections. All manner of crimp-type terminals and connectors are available. Crimp connectors must be matched in size to both the wire and the stud to which it is to be fitted. They use a standard color code for this purpose—red for 22–18 AWG wire, blue for 16–14 AWG, and yellow for 12–10 AWG.

Not all crimp connectors are suitable for marine applications. Those found in automotive supply stores are not made for marine applications and should not be used. A good-quality marine-grade crimp connector or terminal will have, as a minimum, the following characteristics:

- annealed, tin-plated, copper terminal ends
- seamless tin-plated brass or bronze sleeve for crimping to wire conductors
- nylon (not PVC) insulating sleeve, long enough to extend over the wire sheathing

Annealing softens the metal and facilitates a higher conductivity contact. The tin plating improves corrosion resistance. The seamless barrel should be serrated and funnel-shaped to guide the wires into the crimp area. Also, a seamless barrel permits crimping from any position and makes for superior mating surfaces. The nylon requirement is important since nylon will not crack or rupture when crimped and is resistant to ultraviolet (UV) light, diesel, and oil. PVC is used on the less expensive and automotive-type terminals.

Marine-grade connectors and terminals are more expensive than lesser types, but when you consider that the most common problems on boats are electrical system failures that inevitably result in costly repairs, replacements, fires, or even sinkings, I have to conclude that this is money very well spent indeed. Some marine-grade terminals have an extra tinned brass sleeve within the insulating sleeve that goes over the wire's insulating jacket. This allows double crimping—one on the terminal barrel to crimp it to the wire conductor, and the second on the brass sleeve to crimp the terminal's insulation to the wire's sheathing. This provides a beneficial strain relief.

The importance of the tool used to cut and strip the wiring and to crimp these fittings cannot be overemphasized. It should be of good quality and, equally important in my opinion, should be the one made or recommended by the manufacturer of the terminals and connectors you are using. Such tools are of very moderate cost and should be a part of your onboard toolbox.

There are basically two ways to make a completely airtight and waterproof crimped connection, either on a crimp terminal or an in-line connector. The first way is to use a terminal or connector with an adhesive-lined, heat-shrink sleeve. The sleeve should overlap the terminal end so that, when heated, the shrink tube covers the ends of the terminal, making a waterproof fitting. The other way is to cover regular nylon insulated terminals or connectors with adhesive-lined heat-shrink tubing.

A word of caution is in order here. There are basically three types of heat-shrink sleeving generally available. The thin-wall type typically found in electronic supply stores does not form a watertight seal and offers little protection from abrasive damage. The other two types are both adhesive lined and do form waterproof seals. One has a thin wall, the other a thicker wall. The thicker-walled, adhesive-lined type is recommended.

Wire nuts like those commonly used in household wiring should never be used in marine wiring. Typically, the threaded metal insert in these devices is of mild steel and is subject to rusting and all of the horrid consequences that this invites.

ELECTRONIC EQUIPMENT

Recent and ongoing studies show that corrosion is becoming a more significant factor in the reliability of electronic equipment. This is because of equipment designs requiring greater component densities and the trend toward faster digital signal processing that results in smaller components, closer spacings, and thinner metallic sections. Electronic equipment can include a wide variety of metals and alloys. Printed circuit boards alone may contain copper, copper alloys, copper-clad materials, electroplating, solder, tin, and lead. Electrical contacts may consist of copper alloys, clad steels, gold, palladium, silver, and tin. Connectors may use beryllium copper, stainless steels, gold, palladium, silver, and tin. Switches and relays include copper alloys, steels, stainless steels, electroplating, and various contact surface materials.

All of this means that electronic equipment is highly susceptible to both single-metal (atmospheric) and galvanic corrosion. Many electronics manufacturers have found it necessary to use sealed enclosures to prevent corrosion. Even so, moisture intrusion continues to be a problem. Elastomer (rubber compound) gaskets and O-rings are the usual methods of sealing an enclosure's covers, lids, access panels, and cable entries. However, water vapor does eventually migrate through any elastomeric sealant and eventually increases the level of humidity inside the cabinet. One study using butyl rubber gaskets to seal the enclosure showed that, starting at an internal relative humidity of zero percent and external relative humidity of 90 percent, the internal humidity would reach a level of 50 per-

cent in approximately 7 years. Under the same conditions but if ethylene propylene rubber gaskets were used, the time would only be nearly 2 years. If silicone rubber gaskets were used, the time to reach 50 percent relative humidity inside would be 3 weeks! These studies also revealed that the relative humidity inside the box must remain below 40 percent to ensure that corrosion problems would not occur.

One obvious conclusion is that electronic equipment that uses forced ventilation (fans) from the ambient atmosphere for cooling should be avoided in marine atmospheres. This type of cooling will greatly accelerate corrosion as a result of the moist salt air circulating in intimate contact with internal circuitry.

Another conclusion that may be drawn from this is that electronic equipment to be used on a boat should be designed for marine applications. Such designs will include encapsulated components and protective *conformal coatings* on printed circuit boards. The printed circuit boards should be mounted vertically above the bottom of the enclosure to prevent moisture accumulation. Cable entries should be on the sides of the box (not the bottom), and cabling should lead down and away from their connectors and should be arranged to form drip loops in the cable runs.

Contacts and Connectors

Contacts and connectors are especially susceptible to corrosive damage in today's electronic equipment. A major reason for this is the extremely low connector contact forces and the very low voltages involved, which result in greater sensitivity to tiny amounts of corrosion products and contaminants. Contact surfaces are typically plated with tin, gold, or silver. Tin plating is susceptible to oxide formation that gradually increases the contact resistance. Most frequently failure of this type of contact is due to fretting corrosion, that is, repeated oxidation of the contact surfaces due to vibration and minute movement of the contact surfaces. Gold is not subject to atmospheric corrosion, but due to economic and mechanical considerations, gold plating is often very thin and has pores at which galvanic corrosion can occur in marine atmospheres. This can seriously degrade the contact surfaces and result in poor or intermittent contact. Silver has, at times, been used as an underplating for the gold. However, it was found that if there were any sulfides in the environment, the contacts deteriorated rapidly. Nickel underplating of contacts has proved effective in reducing these effects. Preventive methods are pretty much limited to preventing moisture penetration, providing good mechanical support with strain relief at the connectors, and ensuring that connectors are properly made up and sealed. Adhesive-lined heat-shrink tubing works well at sealing contacts and connectors. There are also a number of moldable plastic sealants that are designed for this application.

Printed Circuit Boards

Printed circuit boards are also susceptible to corrosive damage from moisture in the marine atmosphere. Some high-end products have printed circuit boards with a protective *conformal coating*—a sprayed plastic type of film that forms a physical barrier against moisture and contaminants. However, beyond excluding moisture from the interior of electronic equipment, there is little that we, as users of the equipment, can do to protect internal printed circuit boards.

Some manufacturers of corrosion-inhibiting sprays recommend their use inside the equipment enclosure. I have some reservations about this. I am familiar with the successful use of certain of these sprays on and inside electronic equipment, including on the circuitry, but this was in relatively low-frequency telecommunications equipment. My concern is with the use of sprays in high-frequency or digital-processing circuitry. The closer spacings and higher densities of these circuits are carefully designed and controlled and have a direct relationship to the frequencies or speeds at which the equipment operates. Changing the nature of the dielectric constant between them—and sprays may do just that—could possibly affect their operation.

From time to time we hear of small sealed packages of desiccant that can be placed inside enclosures to absorb moisture. I don't think this

a good idea. The desiccant is typically a salt (lithium chloride) that eventually becomes saturated and can absorb no more. That leaves us with a soggy bag of salt inside the equipment. All in all, I believe it best to restrict our preventive efforts to the outside of the enclosure as discussed above.

Soaked Electronics

I would be remiss if I didn't address the question of salvaging electronic equipment that has been immersed. This is another controversial subject, or perhaps it is more confusing than controversial. In any event, it is a recurring and largely unresolved question: Can drenched electronic equipment be salvaged, and if so, how? There is no easy, clear-cut answer. It depends upon many factors. Was it just splashed or totally immersed? How deep? How long? Salt water or freshwater? What kind of equipment? How old? And, on a practical level, is it insured? For how much?

There are all sorts of stories about people who have salvaged an expensive piece of electronic equipment at little or no cost, and it performed satisfactorily for many years afterward—although, come to think of it, I haven't heard any recently. The fact is, the older the equipment, the better its chances for survival, for all of the reasons mentioned above.

If the equipment was totally immersed for more than a few hours, the probability of a successful restoration is extremely low. Most shops are reluctant to even attempt to salvage equipment that has been submerged for any length of time, even as few as 24 hours. The chances of success are small, and the liability is considerable since most onboard electronics are directly related to vessel safety. If the salt water has penetrated into tiny cracks and crevices, it is highly unlikely that flushing will get it all out; inevitably, it will eventually cause trouble. Recent indications are that it may take six months or a year, but eventually the equipment will fail from the effects of the immersion.

Should you even try to save soaked electronics? For yacht owners with full coverage on the boat and its equipment, the decision is not difficult—scrap the gear and replace it. For a commercial fisherman with a high-deductible policy and for recreational boaters on limited budgets, it becomes a cost-benefit issue. The shop cost to make the attempt might be several days of bench time—at up to $80 per hour (at this writing)—and you should also consider the potential cost of an untimely failure, perhaps offshore. High-cost equipment—radar, autopilots, satcoms, large-scale plotters—may be worth trying to save. Less expensive gear—lorans, VHF radios, CBs—probably is not. My feeling is that the best course usually will be to cut your losses—replace the gear and resolve to be more careful in the future.

Should you decide to try to salvage a piece of gear—understanding that success, if any, may be short-lived—fast action is critical. Get the equipment up as quickly as possible and begin rescue operations immediately. Rinse it completely and thoroughly in clean freshwater. Follow this with an alcohol rinse to absorb moisture and hasten the drying process. Allow the alcohol to vaporize completely. Put the equipment into the oven at about 120°F (49°C). If an oven is not available, use a heat gun or hair dryer. Duration of the drying process depends upon the mass and complexity of the equipment, so this is a judgment call on your part. Be sure the heat level is low enough not to melt anything. Finish with a light moisture-displacing, corrosion-inhibiting spray, keeping in mind what we said above.

This is the best you can do. My advice—when in doubt, don't. The doubtful outcome and the downside risks are just not worth it.

BONDING, GROUNDING, AND LIGHTNING PROTECTION

Bonding is one of the more controversial subjects associated with marine electrical systems in general and marine corrosion in particular. A number of experts and knowledgeable professionals, both individuals and organizations, have taken positions and expressed their opinions on the subject of electrical system bonding. Lightning protection, while not so controversial, is a com-

plicating factor. Both bonding and lightning-protection systems impose specific requirements on the boat's grounds and its grounding systems that, in turn, have implications for corrosion processes. Therein lies the conflict.

Bonding

Bonding is the practice of electrically connecting the *exposed, metallic, non-current-carrying* components on the boat to the common ground point of the boat's DC electrical system. This includes engines, tanks, metal cabinets, and housings—all large metal objects. Physically, you run a heavy copper bus bar—a flattened-out length of ¾- or 1-inch copper tubing, for example—right down the center (ideally) of the boat. This is called the *common bonding conductor*. Flattened copper tubing works well because it can be drilled and tapped or through-bolted for jumper connections, but the common conductor also could be bare, stranded, tinned copper, or insulated stranded wire, but not braided copper. Be careful to keep it up out of the bilgewater.

Next, you attach jumper wires, called *bonding conductors*, to each of the metal components to be bonded and connect them to the common bonding conductor. These jumper wires are separate from and in addition to any DC (and AC, if any) grounding conductors. They should be *at least* #8 AWG, green-covered, stranded copper wire. The key to a good bonding system is its high conductivity or low electrical resistance, so the jumpers should follow as short and straight a route to the common bonding conductor as possible.

Finally, connect the common bonding conductor, or bus bar, to the boat's common grounding point. This is the only point at which the DC electrical system grounding circuit and the electrical bonding system are connected. The bonding system is not to be used as a negative return for the boat's DC system. *The bonding system never intentionally carries current.*

Equipment that should be connected to the bonding system includes

- engines and transmissions
- propellers and shafts

- metal cases of motors, generators, and pumps
- metal cabinets and control boxes
- electronic equipment cases
- metal fuel and water tanks, fuel fittings, and electrical fuel pumps and valves
- metal battery boxes or trays
- metal conduit or armoring
- large nonelectrical metal objects as required for lightning protection
- underwater metal fittings in contact with bilge-water

There are basically three reasons for bonding:

- electrical system grounding
- lightning protection
- corrosion protection

Electrical System Grounding

If a piece of electrical equipment should develop a short circuit from the power supply side (+12 V in the case of DC appliances, 120 V for AC equipment) to the equipment's metal case, the case would then be "hot" and would be a potentially dangerous source of electrical shock or ignition. Connecting the equipment's metal case to the AC or DC green grounding conductor provides a low-resistance path to ground, holding the equipment case at ground potential, eliminating the danger of shock and ignition and reducing the possibility of corrosion due to stray electrical currents. Also, grounding the metal case will prevent electronic emissions from inside the case, as well as absorption of such emissions from outside the case, both of which can interfere with electronic equipment performance. A grounded case can also provide a measure of protection from induced currents resulting from *nearby* lightning strikes.

Lightning Protection

According to the National Lightning Safety Institute, studies by the National Weather Service (1992) and by the Air Force Safety Center (1996) revealed that

- Annually, lightning kills more people than tornadoes and hurricanes combined.
- Lightning kills some 163 Americans per year and injures many more.

- Property loss is estimated in the hundreds of millions of dollars per year.
- It is estimated that at any given moment nearly 2,000 thunderstorms are in progress over the earth's surface.
- Lightning strikes the earth 100 times each second.

Charlie Wing cites another interesting statistic in his *Boatowner's Illustrated Handbook of Wiring*. He says that 13 percent of lightning deaths occur to people in boats. Now, if that doesn't make you think a little bit about lightning protection, you must have some pretty interesting other stuff to think about.

Basically, the lightning protection system consists of another network of heavy wires, the main one running from an *air terminal* (what most people think of as a lightning rod)—either the traditional type or the static dissipater type—to an underwater groundplate. This "down" wire should be minimum #6, preferably #4 AWG.

A grounded air terminal forms a *zone of protection* around the boat. This zone of protection has a base radius that is equal to the height of the air terminal above the water. It must be high enough so that a line drawn from the top of the air terminal down to the water surface at a 45 degree angle does not intersect any part of the hull. For the 36-foot fishing boat shown in figure 18-3, that means the tip of the air terminal must be 16 feet above the wheelhouse roof. The higher the air terminal, the greater the area of protection. Such a lightning protection system is not a guarantee that lightning will not strike the boat. In the event lightning does strike, the idea is to capture the energy from the lightning and conduct it to ground safely and without damage to the vessel, its equipment, or its personnel.

Typically, the air terminal is mounted at the top of a mast. A metal mast connected to the groundplate at the bottom can be used to conduct the lightning to ground. If the mast is nonconductive, the terminal must be connected directly to the groundplate with a #4 AWG grounding conductor. It is possible to use antennas or outriggers for lightning protection, but

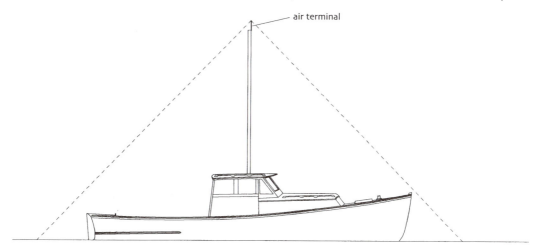

air terminal

Fig. 18-3. Zone of protection for a 32-foot Jonesport. The zone of protection has a base radius equal to the height of the air terminal above the water. It should be high enough that a line drawn from the top of the air terminal down to the water at a point on the circumference of the radius does not intersect any part of the hull.
Plans by Royal Lowell in *Boatbuilding Down East* with permission of William W. Lowell, Lisbon, ME.

they have to be metallic, have a minimum electrical conductivity equal to that of #6 AWG copper wire, and connect directly to ground. In all cases, the path to ground must be as short and straight as possible.

The ideal location for the groundplate is directly under the mast. Any metal surface that is submerged in the water and has an area of at least one square foot can serve as a groundplate. The objective is to maximize the surface area from which the lightning-induced energy can be dissipated into the surrounding water. However, current thinking is that it is not surface area that is critical, but rather edge length. Groundplates, as well as air terminals and mounting bases, are available from all major marine supply houses.

In the event of a lightning strike, if there are any large metal objects—tanks, winches, engines, handrails, and so on—in close proximity, say within six feet, of the grounding conductor, there will be a strong tendency for side flashes between the metal object and the grounding conductor. Connecting these metal objects to the grounding conductor with a #6 AWG (at least) wire reduces the risk of side flashes, which are extremely dangerous to anyone in their path.

To minimize the flow of lightning discharge current through engine bearings, it is better to connect the engine block directly to the groundplate rather than to an intermediate point on the grounding conductor.

If an air terminal system is properly implemented and the groundplate is in the water, anyone or anything within the zone receives some degree of protection. There are, of course, no guarantees with lightning, but history and lightning statistics are clearly on your side.

Corrosion Protection

What, you may rightly wonder, does lightning protection have to do with corrosion? Maybe nothing. But if our boat has more than one immersed metal component and these are electrically connected, what we have is a galvanic cell. In other words, we have met all the conditions required for galvanic corrosion to occur.

That is, in fact, just what we have done. When we connect the engine block (cast iron) to the bonding system, the prop (bronze) and prop shaft (stainless steel) are connected also. We also bonded the through-hulls (assuming they're bronze), so they, too, are connected to the steel shaft and require protection, as does the ground-plate. We can attach a sacrificial zinc anode to the bonding system, and if it's big enough, it will protect all these metals by slowly (we hope) sacrificing itself. Greater love hath no metal. So we have solved all our problems, and the world is now a kinder, gentler, and friendlier place for our faithful old boat.

Not so fast. First, the bonding system may be providing protection to many components (bronze fittings) that don't need it, at the cost of rapidly consuming zincs and possibly depriving other components (iron) of full protection. Secondly, the increased electrochemical activity results in an increase in the production of those nasty hydroxyl ions at the cathode (bronze fittings). If these hydroxyl ions don't combine with metal ions at the anode—because it's too far away—and don't get flushed away by moving water, they will combine with free hydrogen ions (H^+) and/or sodium ions (Na^+) in the seawater to form hydrogen peroxide (H_2O_2) and sodium hydroxide (NaOH), respectively. Although both of these compounds attack wood—a serious concern when the hull is wood or fiberglass with a wood core or when there are wood through-hull backing blocks—sodium hydroxide, also known as caustic soda or lye, is used commercially in the pulping process to remove lignin, the chief constituent that gives wood its hardness and strength. Sodium hydroxide destroys the wood around the fitting and can seriously compromise the safety of the vessel.

Bonding can also have an effect on stray-current or electrolytic corrosion. This is the most serious type of corrosion because currents involved can be many times greater than those of galvanic corrosion, and because the cause can be difficult to find and correct. There are some situations in which bonding prevents stray-current corrosion and others where bonding can actually be the cause of stray-current corrosion.

Consider a situation in which a bilge pump, immersed in bilgewater, develops an internal short from the positive 12-volt side to the metallic pump housing. If the pump housing is connected to the bonding system, the current is conducted straight to ground. Thus, bonding of immersed metal components will prevent corrosion due to stray currents originating inside the boat. Now let us consider a situation in which an electric field exists in the water surrounding the boat. There is a voltage gradient (difference) from one end of the boat to the other. Such fields can be caused by nearby boats with improper AC wiring, for example. Since there is a voltage difference between, say, a through-hull up forward and the prop back aft, a current will flow through the path of least resistance. If the through-hull, prop, shaft, and engine are all connected to the bonding system, this will constitute the lowest resistance path. If the electric field is such that the through-hull is positive with respect to the prop, the prop will corrode. Here we see a situation in which the bonding system actually caused the stray current corrosion. Thankfully, the sacrificial zinc on the shaft will protect the prop and shaft. See chapter 7 for a discussion of stray-current corrosion and methods for troubleshooting stray-current corrosion problems.

There appears to be a common belief that bonding *all* immersed non-current-carrying fittings in the boat is advocated by standards-setting groups such as the American Boat and Yacht Council. Actually, this is not the case. ABYC Standard E-1, Bonding of Direct Current Electrical Systems, has been dropped from the *Standards Manual*. The subject of bonding is covered in E-9, DC Electrical Systems, section 9.21, DC Grounding and Bonding, which does recommend bonding all exposed, electrically conductive non-current-carrying parts of fixed DC electrical equipment and appliances that may normally be in contact with bilge or seawater. Typically, these are not the fittings that cause the formation of caustic soda problems because the bilgewater provides the flushing action necessary to prevent the formation of caustic hydroxides. It is the fittings between the bilgewater level and the waterline—where the wood is saturated with salt water and there is no flushing action—that will be most susceptible to the formation of caustic soda. If these fittings are electrically isolated, ABYC does not require them to be bonded.

So should you bond or not? I can only tell you where I come down. My boats have not been bonded. The through-hulls in my last boat had been in the boat (double diagonal planked in mahogany and bronze fastened) for more than 30 years. They showed no sign of deterioration, and there was no significant softening of the wood around them. The engine was protected with engine zincs, and I had zincs on the stainless steel shaft and manganese bronze prop. The electrical system was carefully thought out, properly installed, and meticulously maintained, and I have had no stray-current problems.

Having said all that, the advantages discussed above for bonded electrical systems are real and beneficial, especially those provided by the light-ning protection system. I haven't bonded my boat because I haven't felt the need, and frankly, I've just never gotten around to it; perhaps I'm too lazy, too busy, or too cheap (or all of the above); but my next boat will be bonded and lightning-protected. Also, keep in mind that you can comply with ABYC recommendations and not jeopardize the wood around those fittings that are vulnerable to damage by delignification. These are the fittings that do not come into contact with the bilgewater and need not be bonded.

With a bonded system you will probably consume zincs faster. You should check them often, a couple of times a season or more frequently if convenient. To be safe, they should be replaced when they are 50 percent consumed.

CHAPTER 19

Plumbing Systems

We are concerned here with the corrosion susceptibility of two (we hope) separate systems—the freshwater (potable water) system and the wastewater system. Both are primary vessel systems and, if not critical, then very important to the creature comforts of the crew, whether on a cruise, a weekend sail, or even a day sail. Yet I can think of no system on the boat that receives less attention, not to say affection.

Basic boat plumbing is typically very simple. What complicates it, as you might have guessed, is the materials used in assembling the systems. In older boats it was common practice to use steel (carbon or stainless), aluminum, or copper tanks, copper or iron piping and fittings, and brass or iron valves. Today a wide variety of advanced plastic materials have supplanted these corrosion-susceptible metals in the most susceptible functions. Thus, what you can expect in the way of corrosion problems on your boat depends in large measure on the age of the boat and that of its plumbing.

FRESHWATER SYSTEMS

A typical pressurized freshwater system is shown in figure 19-1. The system consists of one or more water storage tanks and a pump—activated by an integral pressure switch—that draws water from the tanks when an opened tap drops the pressure. A filter ahead of the pump protects the pump from debris that may clog it; it does nothing for water quality (bacteria, algae, etc.). An accumulator tank is not always part of a "basic" system but should be. It improves the smooth, steady flow of water and virtually adds years to the life of the pressure switch, the Achilles' heel of the water pump. Whether a hot water heater is a basic component may depend on just how much you enjoy

cold showers. From my point of view, the hot water heater is basic.

Freshwater Tanks

Of the various metals used to construct potable water tanks—carbon steel, stainless steel, aluminum, and copper—none is without definite limitations and shortcomings. All are susceptible to some form of corrosion to some extent.

Carbon Steel

Carbon steel in damp atmospheres is highly susceptible to corrosion, that is, rusting, and requires some sort of specially formulated coating to ensure long-term satisfactory performance. To do this job properly, the steel should be grit-blasted and coated with a 20 to 30 mil (0.5 to 0.76 mm) 100 percent solid polyurethane lining that is listed by the National Science Foundation (NSF) for this application. The coating should be tested for "holidays" to be sure it is free of pinholes. There are other industrial coatings (paints) that are approved by NSF or the Food and Drug Administration (FDA) for use with potable water. These are commercially available through industrial supply houses, and surface preparation for them is pretty much the same. Note that coatings in applications that are subject to dynamic stresses are susceptible to cracking that will allow water penetration, which will result in rusting and further coating separation.

Stainless Steel

Stainless steel also has its drawbacks as a water tank material. Stainless steel depends for its corrosion-resistance properties on the availability of a fresh supply of oxygen to sustain the chromium oxide protective film. When it finds itself held against a moist or damp material, the necessary supply of oxygen is denied, and the

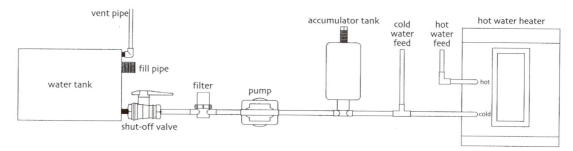

Fig. 19-1. Basic pressurized water system. The basic components in a typical pressurized freshwater system. After plans by Royal Lowell in *Boatbuilding Down East* with permission of William W. Lowell, Lisbon, ME.

metal is subject to corrosive damage in that area. (Aluminum suffers from this same dependency.) Also, potable water by definition is freshwater in which the chloride content is less than 250 ppm by U.S. standards and less than 350 ppm by World Health Organization (WHO) standards. However, city water may contain chloride levels of 1500 ppm or even higher, depending on the source. This can cause pitting or crevice attack in stainless steels.

We also have to be concerned about traces of bacteria in the water supply since stainless steel is susceptible to microbiologically induced corrosion. Well water, for example, can contain high counts of the iron bacteria *Gallionella* and the iron-manganese bacteria *Siderocapsa*. There are cases in the literature where ⅛-inch (3 mm) wall thickness 316L piping containing such well water corroded through in the area adjacent to the welds in two to four months. Many such failures have been reported when untreated well or river water was allowed to remain standing in stainless steel containers. The lessons here are two: you must consider carefully the source of the water you take (many marinas provide well water), and regular flushing of the system, say a couple of times each season, is a good idea.

Galvanized

Galvanized tanks have also been used in the past, although their use has been pretty much discontinued. Given all of the health concerns surrounding heavy metals, the use of galvanized tanks is to be discouraged. The allowable level of zinc in potable water nowadays is 0.00018 oz./qt. (5 mg/L). That's not a whole lot! There are too many attractive and economical alternatives to warrant the use of galvanized steel.

Copper

Copper is used extensively in freshwater systems. Probably the largest single application of copper tubing is for hot and cold water piping in homes and other buildings and in radiant hot water heating systems. Copper was also used quite frequently in older boats for water tanks. Minerals (dissolved salts of calcium or magnesium) in the water combine with dissolved carbon dioxide and oxygen and react with the copper to form a protective film on the surface of the copper. This is the reason for the low corrosion rate—something on the order of 0.2 to 1.0 mil (0.005 to 0.25 mm) per year. However, in soft waters—water with little or no mineral content—these protective films are not able to form, and corrosion rates can be significantly greater.

There is another, and perhaps greater, concern with the use of copper tanks, and that is the solder used in their fabrication. This can result in dangerously high concentrations of lead in the water, which, as we have more recently come to understand, can represent a serious health hazard. Here again, usage has fallen quite sharply in recent years, and more attractive alternatives make the use of copper tanks difficult to justify.

Aluminum

Aluminum is a popular choice for water tanks. Aluminum and its alloys are lightweight, are easy to fabricate, have a moderate cost (especially when compared to stainless steel and Monel), and have good corrosion resistance (except for the copper-bearing grades, the A92000 and A0200 series) to freshwater. However, much depends on the specific water chemistry. Aluminum is very susceptible to attack by certain heavy metal ions, particularly iron, copper, and lead. Very slight concentrations of even a few parts per million will cause severe pitting. Copper tubing upstream of aluminum tanks can easily contain such concentrations (see chapter 9).

Also, aluminum is highly susceptible to severe pitting resulting from poultice corrosion. This happens when there are damp organic materials, such as insulation under restraining straps, wood blocking (especially oak), and accumulations of dirt and debris. The conclusion—if you can afford to have your water tanks made of stainless steel, or better yet Monel, it will be well worth the expense in terms of tank life and taste.

Monel

Monel is the premium material from which to fabricate water tanks. It is considerably more expensive than the other materials mentioned above, but it is stronger, is far less susceptible to corrosion, and does not impart strange flavors to the water. This is the material of construction for such heavy-duty industrial applications as water meter parts, pumps, valves, strainers, and hot-water tanks and is widely used for long-term freshwater and seawater storage service.

Fiberglass

Built-in fiberglass water tanks are frequently used in fiberglass boats. They can be shaped to take advantage of otherwise unusable space in the hull, and, of course, they are for all intents and purposes immune to corrosion. Epoxy is the recommended resin for use in this application (as opposed to polyester or vinyl ester resins), and interior surfaces should have two or more coats of an epoxy potable-water-tank coating—available from a number of paint manufacturers.

Polyethylene

From this writer's perspective, having suffered the frustrations of mild steel tanks (leaky seams, cleaning corners, susceptibility to corrosion), the material of choice for water tanks is thick-wall high-density polyethylene plastic. These tanks are relatively lightweight when compared with metal tanks. They are seamless, one-piece constructions and are extremely tough. They are not susceptible to stress fractures or weak corners, and they can be built in any shape desired to take advantage of otherwise unusable space in the hull. They are easy to clean and are immune to corrosion and corrosive damage. In short, they can provide satisfactory, trouble-free service for many, many years.

Piping

The material used for water piping depends to a large extent on the age of the boat. In older boats you may find iron, stainless steel, rubber, clear plastic, or copper. And yes, as in some boats I've seen, "all of the above." In more recent years, some type of plastic piping is more likely. As we got older, we got smarter. It almost goes without saying that iron pipe and vintage rubber hose are not suitable and should be replaced. Iron pipe is highly susceptible to corrosive damage, and rubber hose is prone to deterioration and tends to lend a certain distinctive flavor to the water. Stainless steel's susceptibility to corrosion also makes it a poor choice. As for the other materials, let's talk about them. One point to keep in mind: any tubing to be used for potable water systems must be approved by the FDA for that purpose.

Copper

All of the things we have already said about copper tanks applies equally to copper tubing. Copper tubing is also very susceptible to impingement corrosion, the erosion that occurs in fast-flowing turbulent water. The water flow removes the protective oxide film, leaving the metal vulnerable to erosion corrosion. In copper piping, water flow rates should not be greater than about 3 feet per second (1 meter per second). The flow rate is a function of the diameter of the tubing and the capacity of the freshwater pump as shown in the equation

$$V = \frac{GPM}{2.45 \times D^2}$$

where GPM is flow in gallons per minute, D is the internal diameter of the pipe in inches, and V is the velocity in feet per second.

In a typical system with a 3.8 GPM (0.24 L/sec.) pump and ¾- to 1-inch (19.0 to 25.4 mm) internal diameter (ID) tube, the flow rate would be about 2.8 ft./sec. (0.85 m/sec.), just barely within the nominal limit of 3 ft./sec. However, flow rates are accelerated at bends, turns, and constrictions, so with the same pump on ½-inch (12.7 mm) tubing, the flow rate would be about 6.2 ft./sec. (1.9 m/sec.). You will be well over the limit and can expect to get erosion corrosion, especially at elbows, tees, and other constrictions.

Within these limitations—and properly installed with short lengths of flexible hose at couplings to pumps, tanks, and other rigidly mounted components to isolate the tubing from vibration and shock—copper can perform, and has performed, quite satisfactorily for many years. But it is still copper and still subject to corrosion—atmospheric, galvanic, and stray current. There are attractive alternatives.

Clear Vinyl Hose

Clear vinyl hose is *not* one of those attractive alternatives, despite the fact that it has been used extensively for quite some time. Clear hose admits light, and this fosters the growth of mold, fungi, and bacteria. This results in black particles adrift in the water and oddly flavored drinking water. Clear plastic vinyl hose is really not suitable for potable water systems.

Polybutylene

Polybutylene, a plastic resin popularly referred to as PB, was used extensively in the production of water piping from about 1979 until about 1995. PB was a low-cost material, infinitely easier to install than copper piping, and it gained rapid acceptance as a revolutionary new pipe of the future. PB was used in millions of homes throughout the United States and Canada. Its

use in marine systems was, of course, considerably less, but nonetheless appreciable. Unfortunately, polybutylene piping experienced an extraordinary number of failures causing millions of dollars in damages and massive litigation that continues to this day. Although conclusive scientific evidence is sparse, the consensus is that oxidants, such as chlorine, react with the polybutylene, causing it to become brittle and develop tiny cracks. The strength of the pipe is seriously diminished and subject to sudden failure. In any event, PB has been abandoned, and if you have any on your boat, it would be a good idea to change it for one of the newer plastic pipe systems.

Rigid Opaque Plastic

Rigid opaque plastic tubing makes excellent water piping. This is the popular PVC and CPVC plastic tubing and fittings, which are increasingly familiar to both homeowners and the boating community. Because it is opaque, we don't have to worry about the little organic critters that are a problem with clear hose. Because it's plastic, it's virtually immune to corrosion, and it's even easier to work with than copper tubing. No solder (or lead) is involved; joints are glued. It does require isolation from shock and vibration, as does any rigid piping, but all in all, PVC is a very attractive alternative to copper.

Flexible Opaque Plastic

Flexible opaque plastic tubing suitable for potable water systems is a more recent development. One such hose is referred to as PEX hose, which stands for "polyethylene, cross-linked." Cross-linking refers to the molecular structure of the material and results in considerably increased strength. This is a very attractive alternative to the older materials discussed above. It's strong, flexible, and easy to lay out and install. It won't corrode and it's opaque, so there are no light-loving little bugs.

A similar polyethylene tubing, although not cross-linked, is also available commercially. Although perhaps not quite as strong as PEX, its strength is more than adequate for our application, and it is more flexible. These are excellent piping materials for marine use in both hot and cold water systems. They are available in colors, typically red for hot water, blue for cold water, and green for raw water—a nice touch that makes troubleshooting a lot easier. A wide variety of fittings for polyethylene tubing are available, including valves and adapters. Plumbing with this system is generally a bit more costly than with other materials, but simplicity, lower weight, and faster assembly, disassembly, and modification more than offset the additional cost.

Pumps

The pump most commonly used in freshwater systems is the diaphragm pump. This is an excellent pump for this service—simple, reliable, relatively quiet, and, perhaps most important, capable of being run dry without damage. In older designs, the pump is belt driven. Newer designs utilize all sorts of gears and linkages to conserve space and achieve greater efficiencies. A modern multichamber, multidiaphragm pump can deliver greater pumping capacity in a considerably smaller package, but the basic operating principle remains essentially the same. On the suction stroke, an activating mechanism pulls the diaphragm back, creating suction that opens the intake check valve and draws water into the chamber. On the reverse stroke, the advancing diaphragm creates pressure on the volume of water in the chamber, forcing the intake check valve closed and the output check valve open, and expelling water through the output port.

In terms of corrosion problems, there are surprisingly few. These are primarily limited to the housings, which are typically aluminum, and to the fastenings, which are typically stainless steel. As you might expect, this often results in seized fastenings that make the pump difficult to disassemble for simple repairs and cleaning. Also, as with all electrical devices, performance of the pump is dependent upon supplied voltage. If wires, contacts, or connections are corroded, voltage at the pump will be lower than it should be, and the pump will run slow and may overheat. If a pump motor is running hot, check the wiring for excessive voltage drop and the connections and splices for corrosion. Clean up the wires, remake the connections, and protect them with adhesive shrink tubing.

In older pumps, the pressure switch was not sealed from the atmosphere, and pitting and corrosion of the contacts was a common problem. More recently, these switches are sealed units, and corrosion usually does not take place. More often than not, problems that arise are caused by old age or excessive operation (short-cycling) due to the lack of an accumulator tank.

Pump diaphragms usually consist of several layers of some sort of impregnated fabric and are not subject to corrosion in the usual sense. They are, however, subject to damage from harsh chemicals. Rubber check valves are at similar risk. Care must be taken in the use of chemicals to clean or disinfect the system. Household bleach (chlorine) is a commonly used flushing agent in pressurized water systems, but the amount of bleach used and the flushing procedure can be critical to avoiding pump damage. Mineral deposits and debris can also cause pump failure. A filter (strainer) in the line before the pump is always a good idea.

Accumulator Tank

An accumulator tank is simply an empty chamber with an entry port at the bottom. It is plumbed into the system after the pump (fig. 19-1). Water doesn't compress, but air does. The compressed air in the top of the accumulator makes water flow smoother and reduces damaging short-cycling. Accumulator tanks may be made of stainless or coated steel, nylon, or ABS plastic. Corrosion considerations are essentially the same as for water tanks.

Hot Water Tanks

In a typical marine water heater, the inner tank, with an inlet fitting at the bottom and an outlet at the top, is surrounded by a layer of insulation, all enclosed within a protective shell. An AC electric heating element is mounted through an access panel on the side of the heater shell. A DC element may be substituted. The heat exchanger coil is fitted with engine cooling water from the manifold brought in at the top and returned at the bottom. Ancillary (but essential) appurtenances, such as the pressure relief valve, thermostat, drain, and, in some cases, mixing valves and proprietary devices whose purpose is to keep the water warmer longer (not essential, but nice) are omitted to avoid confusion (the writer's, not the reader's). They're not really necessary to our discussion of corrosion susceptibilities.

One such hot water heater, the Raritan Model 1700, uses a glass-lined steel tank, polyethylene foam insulation, and a polymer outside shell. It has a 75 psi temperature and pressure relief valve and an adjustable thermostat. Hot water heaters are typically available in 6-, 12-, and 20-gallon models, for 120- or 240-volt operation, and with or without a heat exchanger.

Protective outer shells may be made of stainless steel, coated carbon steel, or polyurethane with a hardened finish coat. Since hot water heaters are usually installed in relatively protected areas—engine rooms, lockers, or lazarettes—we are concerned here with only atmospheric corrosion. Coated steel will rust—eventually. Plastic shells are immune to rust and generally cheaper. If the physical appearance of your hot water heater is important to you, the polished stainless steel shells will certainly make you proud.

Insulating materials are mostly polyurethane foam, although fiberglass is sometimes used. Neither is susceptible to corrosion. Heaters with polyurethane foam insulation seem to maintain heat significantly better.

The tank itself is most often made of stainless steel or "glass-lined" carbon steel, although marine-grade aluminum is sometimes used. Glass-lined tanks are carbon steel with a porcelain coating. Tiny glass beads are fused at high temperatures (800°F or 425°C) to form a coating on the metal substrate. As with all barrier coatings, it must be free from defects, discontinuities, and porosity. Typically two separate coatings are applied for a total coating thickness of between 6 and 9 mils (0.152 to 0.229 mm). Porcelain is very brittle, and its coefficient of thermal expansion is different than that of carbon steel. This results in cracking and crazing over time, and water inevitably finds its way to

the steel substrate. For this reason, glass-lined hot water heaters are usually fitted with a replaceable magnesium sacrificial anode, which is frequently an integral part of the hot water discharge fitting. Depleted anodes can cause discoloration, an unusual smell or taste in the water, and, ultimately, the lack of corrosion protection and failure of the tank. The anode should be checked at least once a year by removing it; if it is significantly depleted, it should be replaced. Be sure to shut off the power and drain the tank before checking the anode—and follow the manufacturer's instructions.

Stainless steel tanks are not without their susceptibilities. Aside from galvanic corrosion, stainless steels are susceptible to four basic types of corrosion that are significant in this application: pitting, crevice, intergranular, and stress-corrosion cracking. Pitting usually results from minor imperfections—inclusions, surface damage, or a tiny flaw in the protective film that forms on the surface of stainless steels. The localized chemical environment in the pit is substantially more aggressive than it is throughout the tank as a whole. A high flow rate over the surface tends to discourage the formation of pits and the concentration of corrosion constituents. Chloride is the most common agent for initiation of pitting. It is not possible to establish for each grade of stainless steel a specific chloride level at which the pitting attack becomes critical. However, freshwater can contain chloride levels as high as 600 ppm, sufficient to cause concern, especially if the water is treated with additional chlorine for purification or flushing.

Crevice corrosion can be thought of as a severe form of pitting corrosion. Any crevice inside the tank—metal-to-metal joints, gaskets, washers, through-wall fittings—will restrict oxygen access and result in corrosive attack. It is not possible to avoid or eliminate all such crevices, but a well-designed tank will keep them to a minimum.

Intergranular corrosion, you will remember, is what is commonly called weld decay. It results from the sensitization developed in the heat-affected zone during welding. These areas are deficient in the chromium that is necessary for the formation of the protective films on stainless steels. An improperly welded tank and the use of improper filler metals or grade of stainless steel can result in susceptibility to this form of corrosion.

Stress-corrosion cracking requires residual or applied surface tensile stresses, chlorides, and an electrolyte (water). Most mill products— sheet, plate, pipe, and tubing—contain enough residual tensile stresses from processing to be susceptible without the presence of any external stresses. Cold-forming and welding add additional stresses. With regard to the chlorine concentration, laboratory studies have shown that stress-corrosion cracking can occur with chloride concentrations of less than 10 ppm.

Aluminum is sometimes used for both the heating tank and the heat exchanger. The aluminum is a corrosion-resistant marine grade and reportedly not as susceptible as stainless steel to leaks at welded seams. Experiential data are lacking, but this is not the material of choice for the top-of-the-line hot water heaters.

The conclusion for us, unless we fabricate our own stainless steel tanks, is to purchase a quality product from a reputable manufacturer, keep the tanks clean, avoid excessive amounts of chlorine, and use the system regularly to keep the water in the tank from stagnating.

If the heat exchanger coil is not cupronickel, it should be. The exchanger is a key element in the system, and if it fails, coolant water and *toxic ethylene glycol* (antifreeze) coolant could leak into the tank. Any peculiar flavor or smell in the water should be considered a warning sign, and the system should be carefully checked for leaks.

Copper fittings are corrosion resistant and are to be preferred over galvanized fittings. Copper tubing is frequently used in the hot water circuit and will give good service, but keep in mind what we said about water velocity and erosion corrosion. Electrical heating elements specifically designed for this application are of tin-plated copper and stand up well. Most die of old age, although some are victims of negligent homicide when they are activated in a dry tank. Death under these circumstances is mercifully

quick. Be sure not to activate the heating element when the tank is dry.

Also, it is worth keeping mind that this is, at least in part, an electrical device. It has electrical connections, and care must be taken to keep contacts, connectors, and splices clean and free of corrosion. Remember that when shore power is used, we're dealing with 120 volts AC that can be lethal. A proper ground connection is critical.

WASTEWATER SYSTEMS

Federal marine sanitation laws require that all boats with *installed* toilet facilities must also have a *marine sanitation device* (MSD) that treats *and/or* stores the waste. MSDs are Coast Guard–certified Types 1, 2 (macerators), and 3 (holding tanks). We combine the toilet and the chosen MSD with piping, valves, and perhaps pumps to assemble a sanitation system that satisfies our needs and complies with discharge regulations. Some of these components are susceptible to corrosion.

Toilets

There is little to go wrong with a manual marine toilet, as long as it's operated correctly (it seldom is), cared for regularly (it seldom is), and given a periodic rebuild (again, it seldom is). As far as corrosion is concerned, the preventive requirement is regular care. Other than thoroughly flushing the head (toilet) after each use, this primarily consists of lubricating the piston O-rings or leathers (for the traditionalists) and the chamber walls. I put a few drops of light machine oil in the pump cylinder two or three times a season, but pouring mineral oil, baby oil, or a proprietary toilet lubricant into the bowl also works. Basically, the idea is to keep the pump works lubricated and thus protected from wear and corrosion.

Also important is a regular check for leaking seals. Any metals in the base of the toilet, such as fastenings, are subject to rapid and aggressive corrosion when exposed to leaking bowl contents (urine). This usually goes unnoticed until serious rot in the sole under the head has taken place. Avoiding this type of corrosive damage is basically a question of maintaining the seals. A rebuild every year or two is the best thing you can do to avoid this. It's really a simple by-the-numbers kind of job with the manufacturer's rebuild kit. It makes a nice (well, tolerable) off-season project. Take the head out in the fall at winter layup, bring it home, and on one of those long, cold weekends, get out in the shop, turn on the ball game, and enjoy yourself. Something to look forward to—rebuilding the head.

Electric macerating heads are really not much more complex than simple manual heads. They typically have an impeller pump instead of a piston pump and a macerator that chops up the bowl contents much like a kitchen sink disposal. Salt water and bowl contents can be damaging to rubber and neoprene seals and impellers. If allowed to stand in the pump for any extended shutdown period, they can cause corrosion of the pump shafts and impeller housings. The resulting scoring and roughening of these surfaces cause them to chew up impeller and shaft seals. They are, of course, quickly damaged if the pump is allowed to run dry. Dry running can also damage shaft seals, allowing bowl contents to get into motor bearings and causing corrosion. At this point, replacement of the housing or the pump is the only option.

Prevention consists of frequent, thorough freshwater rinses, especially before any shutdown period, even one as short as two or three days. A freshwater rinse at the end of the day before leaving the boat is an excellent practice. Diaphragm pumps are sometimes used in this application and are superior to impeller pumps. Diaphragm pumps are more expensive than impeller pumps but can outlast them by as much as five times without the need for constant maintenance.

The electrical circuitry and the electronic controls associated with these toilets are susceptible to corrosion when exposed to salt water or leakage from the toilet. In the better-quality products, the connectors are gold plated for lower resistance, higher conductivity, and corrosion resistance. It is important to keep in mind that these are electrical devices, and that corroded contacts, connections, and splices can cause voltage drops resulting in lowered, and perhaps inadequate, voltage where it's needed. Visual inspection and a "heat check" at wire connections, terminals, and splices will reveal corroded or deteriorated contact areas.

The question of head pump lubrication is an area rife with folklore, old sailor's tales, and creative concoctions. People have been know to use and vigorously defend mineral oil, olive oil, vegetable oil, corn oil, any old cooking oil, lithium grease . . . and I'm sure I've left out someone's favorite lubricant. Others take the position that these pumps don't need lubrication so much as a good dose of vinegar to dissolve and clean out calcareous deposits (calcium and magnesium carbonate). Some even advocate a periodic dose of bleach. The fact is, some lubrication is a good idea, not only for efficient pump operation, but also as a corrosion inhibitor. None of these lubricants are likely to do any harm (beyond creating an oil slick around the boat that may cause your neighbors in the mooring field some concern), but they should be used sparingly. I incline toward a good commercial product from an established manufacturer of marine or swimming pool products.

The vinegar will help with the calcareous deposits to some extent if the problem is not too far advanced. If you're thinking about using bleach, *don't*. Bleach should never be put down a marine head; it attacks and degrades rubber and neoprene gaskets, seals, and impellers. It really doesn't do much in the way of cleaning, anyway, other than to make the dirt whiter. Stick with commercially proven products from reputable suppliers.

Some toilets eliminate the inlet pump and valves altogether, using a vacuum pump to pull waste out of the bowl and clean water in. Though not as common and a bit pricey, this design has the advantage of simplicity. There is very little to go wrong, and this head requires little or no preventive maintenance. It uses very little freshwater per flush—about a pint—which is good for holding tank capacity. It can be set up to use seawater for flushing, but this greatly increases the requirement for maintenance.

Type 1 and 2 MSDs

Where treated discharge is legal, vessels 65 feet and under may use either Type 1 or 2 MSDs. Larger vessels must use a Type 2. Both macerate and chemically treat bowl contents, but to different standards, with the standard for Type 2 being the more stringent. Both types must be Coast Guard certified.

Aside from pump impellers, the principal corrosion concern is shaft seals and gaskets damaged by exposure to harsh chemicals. Although a relatively infrequent occurrence, this allows sewage to get to places where it shouldn't go, such as bearings and shafts. Housings and structural members are typically made of highly corrosion-resistant polymer plastics. Again, the best preventive procedure is frequent freshwater flushes.

Holding Tanks

A Type 3 MSD is a holding tank. This includes all forms of sewage storage devices, even the holding tank in a Porta Potti. Both aluminum and stainless steel have been used for holding tanks. This is not a suitable application for these metals—or for any of the common metals, for that matter. Urine is extremely corrosive. It rapidly and aggressively attacks seams, weld laps, and crevices. Typically, metal tanks will begin leaking at the seams and fittings in a year or two. Coatings are not very effective, and repairs are frequent and expensive. Frequent freshwater flushes are helpful, but it is extremely difficult to flush well enough and often enough to significantly postpone the inevitable. The most cost-effective solution for metal holding tank problems is to change them for a more suitable material.

Seamless, thick-walled, molded polyethylene is the material of choice. However, wall thickness is critical. Corrosion is not a problem, but wall thickness is critical to the satisfactory performance of the tank. If the wall is too thin, odors will be apparent in the vicinity of the tank. A top-quality, thick-walled—at least $1/4$ inch (6.35 mm) for a small tank—seamless, molded polyethylene tank will last for many, many years with no leakage or odor problems.

Vented Loops

When a toilet is installed below the waterline, as it is on most sailboats and in many powerboats, there is the risk that water will siphon back into the toilet, perhaps flooding the boat. To prevent this, discharge (and sometimes inlet) hoses lead to and from a U-shaped tube mounted above the waterline at all angles of heel. The tube has a simple valve at the top that opens to admit air and break the siphon. These devices, called vented loops or siphon breaks, are available in bronze, Marelon, and plastics. The valve is susceptible to clogging by salt crystals, corrosion products, dirt, and debris. Periodic inspection, disassembly, and cleaning are essential.

SUMMARY

Let's clean up a few loose ends and add some useful points that weren't mentioned above. Double-clamp every hose connection using *all-stainless steel* (screw and barrel, too) hose clamps. Replace any clamps that show a significant amount of corrosion. They might have another season in them, but then, they might not.

Y-valves and seacocks enjoy frequent use and regular doses of lubrication. This should be a regular part of those maintenance chores that give you so much pleasure.

As for the toilet system, it's a good idea to avoid the use of metals whenever possible. There is an abundance of attractive, simple, nonmetallic alternatives for nearly all of the components in these systems. Never put—or allow anyone else to put—anything into the toilet that isn't specifically made and marketed for that purpose. No detergents, bleach, household cleaners containing pine oil, alcohol, vegetable oils, or drain cleaners.

Make it a practice to pump the head sufficiently to completely flush the discharge hose at every use. An occasional freshwater rinse is beneficial, especially if the boat is not going to be used for a week or two. And that biannual, off-season rebuild will go a long way toward ensuring trouble-free, enjoyable cruising.

CHAPTER 20

Deck Gear

Deck gear is the exterior fittings, fixtures, and structures used in operating or securing the vessel—such things as cleats, mooring bitts, fairleads, pad eyes, lifeline stanchions, pulpits, towers, and ground tackle. In this gear we're concerned with two types of corrosive damage: damage that is obvious, is primarily cosmetic, and proceeds so slowly that sudden catastrophic failure is not likely; and damage that can proceed undetected, fail suddenly, and present a safety hazard to the vessel or its crew. We can illustrate this distinction by observing that although failure of a cleat, bitt, or davit can represent a serious hazard to the vessel or the crew, catastrophic failure due to corrosion of such fixtures is not common.

Unless yours is a very traditional boat, the majority of the deck and cockpit hardware is likely to be made of stainless steel or anodized aluminum. Let's consider the suitability of these metals—and others—for deck-gear service.

STAINLESS STEELS

Stainless steels, both 304 and 316, are used extensively in cleats, chocks, samson posts, handrails, davits, and a broad range of other deck hardware and furniture. They are so resistant to atmospheric corrosion that weight loss and corrosion rates are not considered meaningful. Their greatest susceptibility is to pitting and crevice corrosion. Pitting, the reader will recall, results from conditions on the surface that create tiny sites (anodes) that differ in potential from the surrounding surface. Since the surrounding area constitutes a very large cathode, corrosion in the pits can be very intense, and the result is actual penetration of the surface and the formation of tiny pinholes. These anodic sites can be caused by surface flaws or anomalies, dirt or salt crystal concentrations, dings, dents, and scratches. Preventive measures consist of the avoidance of dings, dents, and scratches—which may be difficult in this instance—and freshwater rinsing and flushing at the end of the day. Also, periodic polishing of these surfaces will go a long way to prevent pitting.

The stainless steels are also susceptible to crevice corrosion. Likely places are at welds, lap joints, and under bolt heads. Welds, if not properly done—wrong filler metal or excessive heat—are particularly susceptible to intergranular corrosion (weld decay) and degradation of the strength of the joint. With purchased fittings there's not much you can do about the welds, other than thoughtful selection of manufacturers and frequent flushing with fresh water.

ALUMINUM

Marine-grade aluminum alloys (5XXX and 6XXX series) have excellent resistance to atmospheric corrosion due to their tendency—like the stainless steels—to form a protective oxide film when exposed to oxygen. I'm not a big fan of painting marine-grade aluminum whose exposure is limited to the marine atmosphere. If the aluminum is kept clean and not abused—scratched, scraped, or chafed—paint shouldn't be necessary and is just another maintenance chore on an already long list.

Most larger aluminum structures—towers, arches, davits, rub rails, and handrails, to name a few—are bright anodized these days and do not require much in the way of maintenance. Anodizing is *not* a coating. As we learned in chapter 9, it is an electrochemical process that actually changes the outer surface layers of the metal. The surface oxide (Al_2O_3, or *alumina*), while quite hard, can be scratched or rubbed off, initially exposing the porous alumina beneath and eventually exposing bare aluminum that is then subject to pitting corrosion. Here again, frequent washing with freshwater, occasional waxing (with one of the commercial preparations designed for this application), and some care to avoid scratching or damaging the coating are your best defenses.

Stainless steel fastenings are used with aluminum fittings. Since the fastening is cathodic to the larger aluminum structure, this is consistent with the large-anode small-cathode principle.

GALVANIZED STEEL

It is not often nowadays that one finds galvanized mild steel deck and cockpit fittings in the local chandlery, although they are still available and are not uncommon on workboats and traditional craft. They are not generally thought of as attractive by the boating public, although the traditionalists find that they lend character to the vessel. Commercial fishermen find them practical, affordable, and serviceable. The fact of the matter is that they are a very sensible, useful, and functional option. They have the mechanical properties of the steel substrate metal and the corrosion protection offered by the zinc coating.

Since the life of a galvanized steel fitting is a direct function of the thickness of the coating, hot-dip galvanizing is the strong favorite. Studies have shown that a fitting with a hot-dip coating thickness of 3 mils (0.076 mm) may have a useful service life of between 30 and 35 years in a mild marine environment. This drops to between 10 and 15 years in a heavy industrial environment. So a boat moored in a harbor in close proximity to industrial areas can expect a service life somewhere between these two. That's not all that bad. Since it is pollutants in the atmosphere, such as acid rain, that cause the reduced life expectancy, a generous squirt with a freshwater hose at the end of the day is good practice.

BRONZE

For a large and dedicated group of traditionalists in our community, bronze is still the preferred material for all sorts of deck and cockpit hardware. The bronzes get their excellent atmospheric corrosion resistance in the same way as other marine metals—they form protective oxide films (cuprous oxide). This film forms very quickly on exposure to oxygen. What's even better, the film continues to build over time, and as it does, the corrosion rate continues to decline. Initial corrosion rates in the marine atmosphere typically are on the order of some 0.12 mil/yr. (0.003 mm/yr.), decreasing to about 0.04 mil/yr. (0.001 mm/yr.). Think about that. Even at the initial rate, it would take 260 years to lose $1/32$ inch (0.79 mm) of surface! Bronze gear hardly needs any help, but a freshwater rinse at the end of the day won't do any harm.

For those who prefer the more contemporary look of chrome, there is the happy compromise of chrome-plated bronze. Remember though, you'll still need the end-of-the-day rinse and a periodic polishing.

BRASS

The brasses are basically copper alloys in which zinc is the major alloying element. When the zinc content is greater than 15 percent, the alloy is susceptible to both dezincification and stress-corrosion cracking. However, when zinc content is below 15 percent, or when small amounts of tin and arsenic or antimony are added, resistance to both these forms of corrosion increases greatly.

The brasses are economical and easy to work or cast. Exposed brass, however, tarnishes rapidly, quickly developing that familiar greenish patina. It must be polished frequently to maintain its characteristic bright, attractive finish. Plain, uncoated brass deck hardware is not very common. When brass is used nowadays, usually in light-duty cleats, chocks, vents, and housings, it is almost always chrome plated.

Typically, a chrome plating will consist of a base coating of nickel, with or without a copper underlayer, and a surface layer of chromium. High-quality, industrial-grade chrome plating will have a double, or even a triple, thickness base layer of nickel—perhaps as much as 5 mils (0.127 mm) thick—a copper underlayer of 0.5 mil (0.013 mm), and a chrome surface layer of about 0.5 mil (0.013 mm). But there are lower-quality chrome platings as well. Inexpensive items, with purely decorative chrome plating intended for benign interior environments, may have thinner layer thicknesses, may not have any copper layer, and possibly may even have the chrome plating applied directly to the primary metal substrate. Poor chrome plating may have pinholes in the coating, admitting moisture and exposing the substrate metals to atmospheric corrosion. You are left with whatever corrosion resistance the substrate metal can provide.

I have a 30A AC shore power inlet that was in service for over 20 years. It was installed in an open cockpit, fully exposed to salt air, spray, and an occasional saltwater soaking. It received little care (I'm ashamed to say), and it looks pretty good. With some soap and water and a little chrome cleaner and polish, it would look like new. It's still perfectly serviceable; we changed it in order to go to a 50A service. This is a top-quality product. It's chrome-plated brass, and the chrome is a full three-layer, heavy-duty plating.

ZAMAK

Some chrome-plated deck fittings, particularly rail caps, flagstaff sockets, light-duty cleats, and chocks, are not brass. The substrate metal is either zinc (pot metal) or Zamak (a zinc-aluminum alloy). These metals are used because they are inexpensive, are cast at low heat, and lend themselves well to die casting, producing parts with fine, sharp detailing. However, they have only moderate strength, hardness, and corrosion resistance, and if the chrome plating should fail, they are susceptible to serious degradation of their mechanical properties in atmospheric exposures. In my opinion, they should be used only in light-duty or decorative items in freshwater applications.

WINCHES

As far as atmospheric corrosive damage to the exterior surfaces of winches is concerned, the above comments are directly applicable, as are the preventive measures. However, we must concern ourselves also with the susceptibility of the internals of these infernal machines. Winches are complex assemblies of multiple gear sets, ratcheting pawls, and roller bearings precisely fitted and assembled. These components should be—but are not—Monel, titanium, and the super-austenitic stainless steels. They are, of economic necessity, bronze, stainless steel, and, in some cases, anodized aluminum. This is not a very compatible group, galvanically speaking.

Winches are not sealed. They are susceptible to penetration by salt air and seawater that can and does find its way under the drum and into the drivetrain and bearing areas. When the moisture evaporates, it leaves behind the solids—salt crystals, dirt, and sand. Without proper maintenance, the cycle repeats and the concentration of contaminants builds up. This can seriously degrade the performance of the winch. The inevitable result is corrosion and abrasive wear of critical parts.

What can we do about it? Well, we're not going to get off with just an end-of-the-day freshwater rinse. While that is a good thing to do—and we should do it—it will not eliminate the possibility of internal corrosive damage. The details of the servicing procedure are peculiar to the specific make and model winch, but all consist of a few basic steps:

- *carefully* disassemble the winch
- thoroughly clean and scrub with the manufacturer's recommended solvent, being careful not to use a solvent that will attack the plastic parts
- check carefully for physical wear and corrosive damage and replace worn or corroded parts
- relubricate with light oil or grease
- reassemble

This is not a difficult job, although it can be a little tricky. Some parts are spring loaded and, given the opportunity, may try to escape. As to the frequency with which you should service your winch, that depends on how you use the boat. If you do only light cruising in freshwater, most likely every two years would be fine. The same kind of cruising in salt water would require an annual overhaul. If the boat is raced in salt water, two or three times each season is more likely. Hey, that's not so bad—America's Cup boats have to do it after every race!

A winch cover is a good idea when the winch is not in use. Not only does it keep out dirt, dust, and spray, but it also keeps the winch cool and the gear-lubricating grease from melting and draining off.

BACKING PLATES

Backing plates should be used with most of the fittings and structures we're discussing here. Backing plates are required on any fitting that is subject to large or sudden stresses. They are especially important when the fitting is mounted on a relatively thin section such as a fiberglass deck, cabin top, or coaming.

Typically, backing plates are made of stainless steel, aluminum (marine grade), or plywood. Thickness depends on the nature of the fitting. Aluminum backing plates are seldom less than $\frac{3}{8}$ inch (0.95 cm), although $\frac{1}{4}$ inch (0.64 cm) is sometimes used. Stainless steel backing plates are seldom less than $\frac{1}{4}$ inch (0.64 cm). For installation, see figure 20-1.

In selecting materials for backing plates, we should always keep in mind their susceptibilities to corrosion and the galvanic consequences of our choices. The first concern is the rule of cathode-anode area ratios—the area of the cathodic metal must be small compared to that of the anodic metal. This is because the cathodic metal, in effect, draws current (electron and ion flow) from the anodic metal in an effort to equalize their electrical potentials, thus causing the deterioration of the anodic metal. The smaller the area

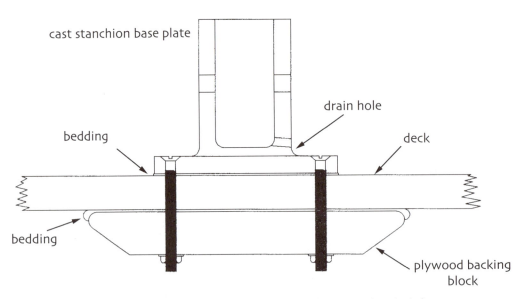

Fig. 20-1. Backing plate installation. A properly installed stanchion or other deck fitting likely to be called upon to bear significant loads should have a rugged backing plate under the deck. The backing block in the above drawing is made from ⅝-inch marine-grade plywood, although some prefer a heavy stainless steel plate. Some prudent sailors will use a similar backing arrangement between the stanchion base and the deck on the topside. Any backing plate or block must be well bedded to prevent moisture penetration.

of the cathodic metal, the smaller the current draw, and the smaller the corrosive damage to the anodic metal. This is why we use stainless steel (cathodic) fasteners in aluminum (anodic) structures. How much smaller does the cathode have to be? There is no specific quantitative answer. The best I can tell you is the smaller the better. When in doubt, isolate the two parts with a nylon or other insulator.

Note that I said deterioration of the anodic metal will be *smaller*, not *eliminated*. If moisture is allowed to occupy (or penetrate) the space between the threads of a stainless steel fastener and the aluminum structure, there may still be localized corrosion, pretty much confined to the contact surfaces. This results in "frozen" fastenings. Thus, even though the cathode-anode ratio is favorable, it's a good idea to dip the fastening in some conformable substance such as silicone or paint before driving the fastener.

Another thing to keep in mind is that stainless steel depends on an environment in which a fresh supply of oxygen is available to maintain the protective chromium oxide layer. If it is exposed to moisture and that moisture is oxygen depleted (stagnant), there is no oxygen to maintain its protective film. In this circumstance, stainless steel fasteners will suffer corrosive damage just as would an ordinary mild steel fastener. (Also, if the fastener holes are allowed to leak, there is a high probability of water damage to balsa core or plywood decks.) What does this mean in terms of backing plates? Bed them well to keep moisture out and maintain them snug. This applies to all backing plates, not just those for winches and cleats.

For my part, I've always used good-quality, thick (⅝- or ¾-inch) marine-grade plywood—edges broken, corners rounded, sanded, well coated, and sealed with epoxy. They are things of beauty!

LIFELINE SUPPORTS

In chapter 21 we talk about rigging wire, including that used as lifelines. Our focus here is on the critically important deck hardware that supports the lifelines. Lifelines serve one primary purpose—to keep people from falling overboard. If your boat doesn't have them, it should! If it does have them, and you're depending on them for your safety, you shouldn't—at least not until you have carefully and thoroughly inspected stanchions, stanchion bases, bow and stern pulpits, and wire and terminals. These should be inspected not only for structural integrity but also for corrosive damage or susceptibility.

The bronze-stepped stanchion base shown in figure 20-2 is cast manganese bronze and was removed from a 30-foot sailboat after some 30 years of faithful service. If you look closely, you can see the crack running across the bottom flange at the base of the socket. Actually, the baseplate was completely broken off; we brazed the broken parts together to make a pattern from which a new part was cast. All it took to cause this failure was a *gentle* nudge from a powerboat with about a foot more freeboard and a little flare in the sides. The contact was so gentle that the damage wasn't even noticed until several hours later—and we were standing right there! It doesn't take all that much force

Fig. 20-2. Bronze-stepped stanchion baseplate. The base of the bronze stanchion was broken off at the base flange following just a gentle nudge from another boat.

to cause this kind of damage. The stanchion, if you think about, is a great lever; any force applied at the top is *multiplied* by the height of the stanchion.

Although this particular failure was not caused by corrosion, there is something of value to be leaned from it concerning lifeline systems. On the inboard side the baseplate was bolted through the deck and through a hefty ⁵/₈-inch marine-grade plywood backing block. On the outboard side there wasn't sufficient room on the underside of the deck for through-bolts and a backing plate, so the baseplate was fastened with a pair of 12 × 3 bronze wood screws into the toerail, as shown in figure 20-3. This arrangement worked fine for many years, and it had been tested several times in heavy seas. However, the first time it was subjected to a significant thrust *from outboard*, the screws tore loose, the through-bolts held, and the baseplate cracked. It makes one wonder what would have happened if the boat had heeled sharply, and suddenly a crew member had grabbed onto a stanchion on the upper side. We'll never know. What it does suggest is that this type of stan-

chion base may be fine for forces applied from inboard to outboard but is not as dependable for forces applied from outboard to inboard, especially if it has been weakened by corrosive damage.

Common sense will tell us to be sure that all pulpits and stanchions are properly secured to a solid, strong base that is itself solidly through-bolted to a substantial baseplate. The lifeline cable and its terminals must also be in good condition (see chapter 21). Your inspection should—must—include physical testing. Some people say to just give things a good strong pull. Others, advocating a more true-to-life test, suggest that you throw your full weight against the lifeline or stanchion—a bit risky, but more realistic. Both say we should not worry about breaking anything (easy for them to say). Better now, they point out, than 30 miles off when the seas are running 5 to 10 feet and breaking at the tops. If you should decide on the full-body-weight test, it would be a good idea to bring the boat up to the beach and be prepared for a swim. A less dramatic but safer and fairly realistic alternative, depending on the audacity of the one conducting the test, would be to sit solidly and securely on the cabin top and administer a good solid boot thrust to the top of the stanchion.

Lifeline stanchions are usually stainless steel or bright anodized aluminum. To maintain their appearance, keep them clean and hosed down with freshwater and try not to whack them with sharp metal objects. An occasional coat of wax or polish also helps and will protect them from pitting corrosion.

Stanchions are typically inserted into a presumably substantial cast metal base and pinned with a machine screw or cotter pin. Bases, for the most part, are stainless steel, chrome-plated bronze, or chrome-plated Zamak. There are several potential corrosion problems in this arrangement. Since moisture can and does collect in the socket of the base, there is the potential for galvanic corrosion between the stanchion and the base, and between the machine screw or cotter pin and both the stanchion and the base. It is important to be sure that these components are galvanically compatible.

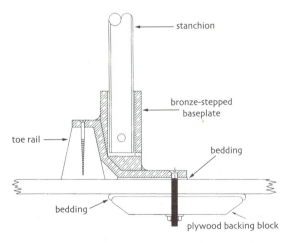

stanchion

bronze-stepped baseplate

toe rail

bedding

bedding

plywood backing block

Fig. 20-3. Stepped stanchion baseplate installation. This shows the installation of the stanchion base in figure 20-2. A heavy backing block was used on the underside of the deck. Space did not permit through-fastening on the outboard edge of the base.

There is also the problem of water collecting in the base socket if no provision is made for drainage. This water may become oxygen depleted and fail to maintain the protective film on stainless steel parts. This problem can be exacerbated by wear between the socket and the base as the stanchion works in the socket. Since the chrome plating on the stanchion is just a flash coating, it is not very thick. Although it is quite hard, it can be abraded, exposing the nickel layer and ultimately the base metal. An annual inspection of the stanchion ends for corrosive damage—and replacement if indicated—is in order.

If the base is not cast but welded, regular inspection of the welds is called for. Look for excessive rusting or hairline cracks. A dye penetrant or a magnifying glass is helpful. Sending the base out to a testing and inspection lab is another option. Tool and die shops do this all the time, and the cost is not all that high.

Keep in mind that we're talking here not just about lifeline stanchions but about bow and stern pulpits as well. There is a growing tendency to attach all kinds of gear to the stern pulpit. Radar antennas, solar panels, and wind generators are all mounted on poles braced to the pulpit. Similarly configured dinghy davits add weight and wind resistance up and outboard. All of these place great static loads on the entire lifeline system. Check them carefully, and if you have doubts about anything, have a qualified rigger or marine surveyor look at it—or go ahead and replace it. It's just not worth the risk.

ANCHOR SYSTEMS

The critical elements of the anchoring system are—from the top down—anchor windlass, bow roller and accessories, chain, end fittings (shackles and thimbles), and the anchor itself. Let's take them in order.

Windlass

If there's a worse place on the boat than the windlass to put an electrically (or hydraulically) operated, complex, mechanical contrivance made up of a number of dissimilar metals, I'd be hard put to tell you where it is. A typical anchor windlass may have parts made of aluminum, bronze, and both carbon and stainless steels. Then, just to make things worse, we have to mount the thing right up in the eyes of the boat, where it gets soaked and sprayed constantly with salt water.

Many windlasses have anodized or epoxy-coated aluminum above-deck housings, which pose a couple of problems as far as corrosive damage is concerned. The first is damage to the housing itself—paint lifting on painted housings, and chafing and abrasion on both painted and anodized finishes. Abrasion, mostly by the anchor rode, is the more serious. It wears away the protective coating, exposing fresh, unprotected aluminum that forms a new layer of aluminum oxide, which is then worn away. The process repeats itself, and the eventual result is significant physical wear.

The second problem area is the one we spoke of earlier when we talked about aluminum deck gear, stainless steel backing plates, and stainless steel fastenings—you certainly wouldn't use mild steel, would you? The unfortunate, but inevitable, outcome is localized corrosion and seized fastenings. What can we do about this? First, keep the windlass covered when you're not using it. Second, give it frequent washdowns with freshwater. Third, coat the through-deck fastenings with heavy water-resistant grease or a corrosion inhibitor—not foolproof but a definite help. Fourth, consider the use of a heavy marine-grade plywood backing block if space permits.

Some above-deck housings are chrome-plated bronze. Here our concerns are with the quality of the chrome plating, and for that we must trust the manufacturer.

More serious than cosmetic and fastener problems are those that can result from corrosive damage to the internals of the windlass. Internal corrosion leads to increasingly degraded performance and, ultimately, to seizure of the windlass. Windlass seizure is not only awfully inconvenient, but if the windlass is electric, it can be downright dangerous. A seized windlass acts essentially as a dead short. Extremely high current can flow, resulting in overheating of the motor and the wires, and—if not properly fused—can lead to fire.

The internals of top-quality windlasses are sealed (although not necessarily *hermetically* sealed) and waterproofed. When properly installed, the control box and solenoid switches will be located in a dry, protected location. Connection terminals will have a coating of silicone or other grease and will be covered with protective boots.

Windlasses, like all mechanical equipment, depend upon lubrication for protection not only from physical wear but also from corrosion. If left unused for long periods of time, these lubricants drain off metal surfaces, exposing them to the moist internal atmospheres created by condensation. The eventual result is corrosion. Such damage can be expensive and time-consuming to repair. Be sure to keep your windlass properly oiled and lubricated and to operate it on a regular basis to keep these lubricants well distributed throughout the internals of the gearbox and motor.

One major windlass manufacturer recommends disassembly of the above-deck unit, freshwater washing, and oiling of the seal, shaft, cone clutch, and spline with light oil (SAE 10) every six months—or every season for those of us in the northern climates. That's also a good time to check, clean, and, if indicated, remake the electrical connections. In any case, you should follow the instructions that came with your windlass.

Bow Rollers and Deck Accessories

Other devices found on the foredeck and also exposed to constant saltwater soaking are bow rollers, anchor chocks and brackets, and chain stoppers. These items should be of noncorrosive materials—stainless steels and Delrin—and require very little maintenance. The bow roller should be checked periodically for wear and corrosion of the roller shaft, and all through-deck fastenings should be inspected periodically for corrosion or loose nuts. Keep in mind what we said earlier about avoiding dings, dents, and scratches on stainless surfaces. Otherwise, regular washdowns with freshwater are essentially all that's necessary.

Chain

Chain may be made of low-carbon steel, high-carbon steel, or stainless steel. The low-carbon steels are available as Proof Coil or BBB, the difference being in the length of the links. Proof Coil is used for general marine applications. BBB chain has slightly shorter links and is designed for use with windlasses that specify BBB chain. Hightest, high-carbon steel chain has slightly longer links than BBB and is designed for use with windlasses that specify this chain. These chains may be either galvanized or plastic (vinyl or polymer) coated. Stainless steel chain, typically but not necessarily of Type 316, is commonly available in either Proof Coil or BBB lengths. Chain is rated according to its *working load limit* (WLL), which is a conservative rating—generally some 25 to 30 percent of the breaking strength.

Of greatest significance for us in this discussion of chain is the basic type of steel used and, if of carbon steel, whether it is galvanized. In the carbon steel chains, first and most important is whether the chain is hot-dip galvanized or electroplated. The service life of the chain is directly related to the thickness of the galvanized coating. Hot-dip galvanized coatings are considerably thicker than those applied by the electroplating process and thus are much preferred. The actual service life of a hot-dipped galvanized chain is very dependent on the local conditions, but it is typically between three and five years *excluding considerations of damage to the coating from wear and abrasion*, which can greatly shorten the useful life of the chain.

Stainless steel has a much superior corrosion resistance and is some 10 to 20 percent stronger than low-carbon steel chains but not as strong as high-test chain. Corrosive damage to the stainless steel is minimal under normal conditions of immersion in free-flowing seawater. The problem comes about when marine growth is allowed to accumulate on the chain, denying the chain access to the fresh supply of oxygen it needs to form its protective coating. This permits the initiation of pitting and crevice corrosion.

Of the plastic coatings, vinyl is preferred over polymer. Vinyl coatings are thicker and provide greater resistance to abrasion—at the cost of some flexibility in the chain. Both coatings offer some corrosion protection *as long as the coating is not pierced or chafed away*, which, unfortunately, happens rather quickly and frequently. Probably the greatest benefit of a plastic coating is the protection it offers to the topsides and foredeck.

The greatest damage to the chain in anchoring or mooring systems results from the wear and abrasion that take place at the bottom end of the mooring or anchor rode. As currents and tides change direction and the boat swings on its anchor, the links at the bottom of the chain—and the end fittings—can suffer considerable wear and accelerated corrosion rates. Reversing the chain end for end each year, to even out the wear, can significantly extend its useful life.

I recently came across some interesting information concerning corrosive damage on a chain mooring system that had been in place for nearly 20 years. The chain was used to hold some floating pontoons at a naval installation in Japan. Divers sent down to inspect the moorings found that sections of the chain that had been buried in 12 to 18 inches (30 to 46 cm) of bottom sediment did not show the anticipated characteristics—rust, flaking, and so on. Instead they found extreme brittleness, and when given a solid tap, the links crumbled into pieces. Results of analyses of the sediment and the chain metal are not complete, but the damage exhibits all the characteristics of some form of microbiologically corrosive damage. I'm not exactly sure what lessons we can learn from this, but one thing's for sure—20 years is too long a period between ground tackle inspections.

Thimbles and Shackles

Anchor rode end fittings—thimbles, shackles, and swivels—are where the greatest wear takes place, and these are the most common failure points in the system. Depending on where you keep your boat, conditions can vary from benign—small freshwater lakes and ponds—to downright hostile. The thimble and shackle in figure 20-4 are from a mooring in the narrows at the outlet of a river that also carried all the runoff from a large marshy area. The river normally ran at about 3 to 4 knots, but after a heavy rain or storm it could get considerably faster. The thimble was of galvanized carbon steel and had been down less than six months. This is anything but a benign environment; in fact, one of our earlier boats sank in this mooring field during a summer storm. The point is that physical wear, accelerated by corrosion, can be severely damaging in a relatively short period of time.

The physical wear removes the galvanizing pretty quickly, exposing bare unprotected metal, which quickly forms a soft layer of rust. This is rapidly worn away, and so on. There is really not much you can be do to prevent this. Coatings are quickly worn off, as are greases, oils, and inhibitors. All that really leaves us with is the careful choice of materials and periodic inspection of the tackle. It is a good idea, where possible, to use end fittings one size larger than what the chain calls for. The more robust fitting will give a longer service life.

Thimbles and shackles are commonly available in both galvanized carbon steel and stainless (18-8 or 316) steel. Recently, a number of rope manufacturers have begun offering anchor

Fig. 20-4. Mooring line thimble. Notice that the thimble is almost completely worn away at the bottom in just one season from May to September.

rodes with nylon thimbles, even on rodes up to ¾ inch (1.9 cm). I must admit that I am not favorably disposed toward nylon thimbles and have yet to find anyone who has had success with them. Their only virtue seems to be that they are not susceptible to corrosion. However, I've heard a lot of complaints about cracking, deformation, popping out of splice eyes, and even breaking completely in two. I'm sure that there are light-duty applications in which they would be satisfactory, but I would be wary of deterioration from UV exposure.

The question arises frequently about mixing metals in ground tackle applications—stainless steel end fittings with galvanized chain and anchors, and vice versa. Here we must fall back on the cathode-to-anode area ratio, which we want to be very low. Let's say, for example, that we wanted to use a $^5/_{16}$-inch (8 mm) stainless steel shackle on a 50-foot (15 m), $^5/_{16}$-inch galvanized chain. The ratio of the cathode (stainless shackle) area to anode (galvanized chain) is roughly estimated at 1 to 77. Thus, while there may be some localized corrosion at the point of contact, neither the chain nor the shackle will suffer severe corrosive damage, and reasonable service life can be expected. In the opposite case—stainless chain and galvanized shackle—the cathode-to-anode ratio would be 77 to 1, and the shackle would suffer severe corrosion and short service life. Having said all that, it is preferable to use compatible metals throughout. Also, it is worth repeating concerning galvanized fittings that hot-dipped galvanizing is greatly preferred over electroplated galvanizing.

Anchors

Anchors are commonly available in galvanized steel, stainless steel, aluminum, and even titanium. Aluminum and titanium offer light weight and corrosion resistance, but they tend to be more expensive, especially titanium (which also offers great strength). Stainless steel also offers corrosion resistance and strength but does not offer much advantage in terms of weight. Galvanized steel anchors are by far the most common, and only hot-dipped galvanized should be considered.

Anchors are truly low-maintenance items, requiring little upkeep. Painting is of little benefit since it is rapidly worn off the first time the anchor is set in a sand or gravel bottom. Even galvanized anchors gradually lose their zinc coatings, and after a time they begin to bleed rust on your topsides and pretty, clean foredeck. Then it's time to consider regalvanizing or replacement. That's simply a cost-benefit consideration. If allowed to go on rusting, eventually the weight loss will become significant, the normally sharp fluke ends will become blunt. and the attachment ring will deteriorate to a dangerous point.

Our discussion above concerning end fittings and galvanic compatibility with chain also applies with respect to anchors. The cathode-to-anode ratio rule should be considered if mixed metals are to be used.

SUMMARY

Most deck fittings are essential to the operation of the vessel or the safety of both vessel and crew. Corrosion of some of these items results in merely cosmetic damage, whereas corrosion on others can place the vessel and crew in jeopardy. It is not possible to eliminate corrosion entirely, but there are definite—and essential—actions we can take to extend the safe and reliable service life of the fitting or system. These generally consist of not much more than careful selection of the fittings and fixtures in the first place, followed by regular inspections and routine maintenance. This is little enough to ensure both vessel and crew safety and the pleasurable or profitable use of the boat.

CHAPTER 21

Masts, Spars, and Rigging

The mast and its support components—spreaders, stays, shrouds, terminals, toggles, turnbuckles, and chainplates—comprise a tightly integrated, interdependent system that is highly stressed under static conditions and subject to even greater dynamic stresses when sailing. Failure can occur at a number of points in the system, many—or possibly any—of which could bring down the entire rig. The principal components are all susceptible to stress, fatigue, corrosion, or rot, and detection of these conditions requires close and regular inspection.

MASTS

Masts today can be wood, metal, or composite. Each of these materials presents unique corrosion concerns.

Aluminum

Aluminum spars are generally extruded sections of 6061-T6 (A06061) or 6063-T6 (A06063) grade aluminum. These are excellent corrosion-resistant grades, and aluminum masts, when properly done, are relatively low-maintenance systems. In general, problems with aluminum spars are with the fittings rather than the mast extrusion. However, aluminum masts are of relatively thin section, typically on the order of 0.10- to 0.35-inch (2.5 to 9 mm) wall thickness and cannot afford to lose much wall thickness without suffering significant strength reduction. They are susceptible to galvanic corrosion, especially with copper, so all copper and copper-bearing metals must be isolated from contact with an aluminum mast.

Both A06061 and A06063 are marine-grade alloys with good resistance to atmospheric corrosion. When exposed in the marine atmosphere, they quickly develop a protective barrier oxide film such that the corrosion rate actually declines with time. For the most part, the result is a mild roughening of the surface but no significant thinning of the mast section. The consequences of atmospheric corrosion usually have more to do with appearance than serious corrosive damage—as long as the protective film remains intact. If the film is chafed or abraded away, it loses its protection—and a little surface metal. If this process is repeated often enough, significant loss of metal can occur. The oxide also soils your nice white sails and makes them unsightly.

Some aluminum spars are anodized, an electrochemical bath process done before any fittings are installed (fig. 21-1). These spars are highly resistant to corrosion and tend to maintain their finish well. However, even anodized spars eventually get dull and lose their bright attractive surface, and they are not immune to damage from chafing and abrasion. Freshwater flushing helps, but, practically speaking, there's only so much you can do—and reach. There are some fine aluminum spray touch-up paints on the market for scratches and abrasions. For improving appearance and providing a measure of protection, an automotive or boat spray wax works quite well. You simply spray it on a clean surface, let it dry, and rub it up to a shine. You'll have to do it at least once a season, but it's not difficult—it's a lot easier than painting. A good paint coating can be very attractive, protective, and long lasting if done properly, but painting aluminum requires special care and preparation.

There are some places where corrosion, both atmospheric and galvanic, can be quite serious. Welds are the first places to look on an aluminum spar. Poorly done welds will have rough, sharp edges and crevices where water can collect and cause corrosion. Corroded welds should be

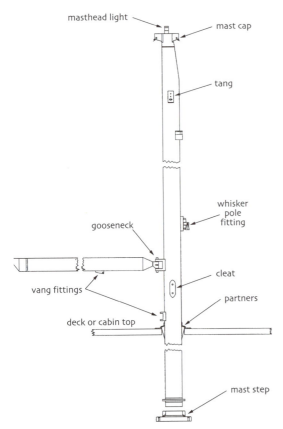

Fig. 21-1. Typical aluminum mast system. Areas of susceptibility to corrosive damage are welds, section joints, mountings of dissimilar metal fittings and accessories, pockets, crevices, and areas where water can collect and chlorides can concentrate, such as at the partners and in the mast step.

Fig. 21-2. Corroded mast heels. The heel of the mast at the mast step is highly susceptible to corrosive damage, especially if no provision is made in the mast step for drainage of accumulated water. Drain holes should be provided and checked regularly to see that they are clear.

redone immediately. Rivets are another place that should be checked regularly. Look for looseness and corrosion. Faulty rivets should be drilled out and replaced with the next larger size.

Anywhere water is allowed to collect and stand against the mast, pitting corrosion can be severe. Examples are at the mast coat, where a keel-stepped mast goes through the deck or cabin top, at the heel of the mast at the mast step, and at the spreader fittings (fig. 21-2).

Where corrosion has occurred on a painted mast, the paint will have bubbled. The more extensive the bubbling, the more serious the corrosion. On an unpainted mast you will see a gritty, white, powdery deposit. Scraping or brushing away this deposit with a stiff brush will reveal the extent of the corrosive damage. Compare the depth of the corrosion pits with the thickness of the mast at normal openings in the mast. If the corrosive penetration approaches 25 percent of the wall thickness, or if the damage forms a continuous ring around the mast, serious weakening has occurred, and repair or replacement is essential. If there is any doubt, have a rigger or surveyor look at it.

Wood

Most wooden masts nowadays are of hollow-section construction with solid reinforcing blocks where spreaders, tangs, and other components are attached. Sitka spruce is the preferred wood due to its great strength-to-weight ratio. However, it is not particularly resistant to rot, especially when it does not have good ventilation, as in the bilge. A well-made mast will have holes drilled down through the reinforcing blocks to allow condensation and accumulated moisture to drain down to the mast step. There should also be drain holes at the step to let water out (fig. 21-3).

Ideally, the mast would be treated internally with a rot preventive when it was built and reg-

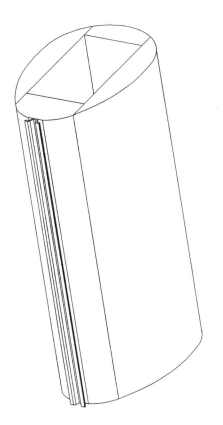

Fig. 21-3. Hollow-section wood mast. Most wood masts are made of Sitka spruce, which is not especially rot resistant. Proper construction provides holes drilled down through the internal solid reinforcing blocks to allow moisture to drain down to the mast step. An annual treatment with a wood preservative is recommended.

ularly thereafter. Cuprinol, or a similar product, is the popular treatment of choice, although the traditionalists swear by a linseed oil, turpentine, and pine tar concoction that Pete Culler used to call *deck oil* (see appendix 8). Whatever your choice, it's a good idea to give a wood mast a dose of one of these potions annually during winter layup. It's not a big job. When you've got the mast put up on the horses, simply raise one end, pour in enough of the treatment to flood the inside cavity, slosh it around, turn it over

periodically to make sure the mast is thoroughly saturated, and let it sit.

Fastenings in a wooden mast should be of silicon bronze. Mild steel should be avoided because of rusting and deterioration of the wood surrounding the fastening, resulting in a weak and unreliable fastening. Even when galvanized, it is just a matter of time before rusting will occur. If bronze cannot be used because of galvanic compatibility, stainless steel, preferably Type 316, should be used.

Steel

Steel masts are sometimes used in very large sailing vessels, but weight makes steel impractical for most sailboat applications. However, many small commercial boats use steel spars for general lifting or for handling fishing gear. Typically, these are of cold-rolled steel. Almost any low-carbon steel may be used.

With steel spars, any place where water can accumulate is a potential problem area—gaps between adjoining surfaces, pockets, troughs, and corners (see chapter 14). All fittings attached to the mast should be continuously welded along their perimeters and the welds ground smooth to avoid water traps and to facilitate painting. It is best if the mast is made air- and watertight; that is, all seams should be continuously welded, and the mast should be fitted with external halyards and sheaves so that there need be no entry or exit boxes to allow water to get inside. If openings exist through which water can get into the mast, water traps and drains must be provided, and the mast should be painted internally to inhibit corrosion. If electrical wiring is run internally (in PVC tubing), waterproof plugs and connectors or cable-gripping wire seals must be used at the entry and exit points.

The external surface of the mast must, of course, be painted (see chapter 15). Remember, with mild steel, surfaces subject to wear or abrasion corrode quickly. When the paint, galvanizing, or whatever you've used is worn away, rust quickly forms, which is in turn worn away, and the destructive process repeats. The speed with which this takes place is truly surprising. In terms of standing rigging fittings and trawl gear, this can be downright dangerous.

Carbon Fiber

Carbon occurs in its natural state as graphite, a highly noble *metal* with a corrosion potential on the order of +0.23 to +0.30 volts—at the most noble or cathodic end of the galvanic series. Thus it is highly resistant to atmospheric corrosion. That's the good news. The bad news is that the metals typically used in fittings and fastenings—aluminum, at –0.76 to –1.00 volts; steel, at –0.60 to –0.71 volts; and even bronze, at –0.4 to –0.31 volts—are all quite anodic with respect to carbon fiber. Given the necessary electrolyte—salt water or spray—the inevitable result is accelerated corrosion of the less noble metal. Titanium, at –0.05 to –0.06 volts, and Type 316 stainless steel, at 0.00 to –0.10 volts, are marginally acceptable. Stainless fastenings are sometimes used. However, with galvanic separations in the 200-millivolt range and an unfavorable cathode-to-anode area ratio, it comes down to the *relative size and duration of localized wetted surfaces*. It's possible that these fastenings can provide satisfactory service life, but they should be inspected annually. Alternatively, a fiberglass or epoxy plug for the fastening can be used. Such plugs are often installed by the manufacturer, but since the producer can't always anticipate exactly what fittings the boatowner will want to add or where to add them, they can be added by the owner or the yard.

Some corrosion concerns can be avoided by fabricating such fittings as masthead boxes, mast steps, and spreader sockets of carbon fiber, but cost considerations make this economically questionable. In practice, aluminum or stainless steel is used for these parts. Manufacturers of carbon fiber spars are, of course, aware of the corrosion implications of this practice, and some will insulate such fixtures from the mast with a fiberglass pad under the fitting and fiberglass plugs fabricated into the mast for fasteners. You should also keep this in mind if you want to install such fittings and fastenings into your mast. Make sure there is no direct contact between the fitting and its fastenings and the carbon fiber spar. Insulating pads can be of Delrin, Teflon, nylon, Mylar, or polyethylene. Also, it's a good idea to seal the edges between the carbon fiber spar and the fitting with a silicone sealant to prevent water from getting in.

BOOMS AND SPREADERS

Booms may be made of any of the materials of which masts are made, and the problems, solutions, and maintenance are essentially the same as those discussed above for masts. The differences are in the end fittings.

Booms normally have an outhaul sheave at the after end and a gooseneck fitting at the mast. These are, of course, made of metal—bronze or stainless steel in the case of a wood boom, stainless steel or aluminum in the case of aluminum. Don't even think about using bronze—or any copper-base alloy—on an aluminum spar.

If the boom is the roller-reefing type, the end caps at the after end and at the gooseneck must be configured to rotate. This necessitates mechanical assemblies that typically consist of closely fitted gears, bearings, and housing of *dissimilar* metals. They are exposed to moist, salt-laden air, salt spray, wear, stress, and corrosion. If not given regular maintenance, they will perform sluggishly—or jam—when you need them most. Maintenance consists of annual disassembly, thorough cleaning, and lubrication with a moisture-displacing anticorrosion lubricant. Any worn or corroded parts must be replaced.

Spreaders do not get the maintenance attention they deserve. If a spreader fails, the mast has lost the support of the shrouds on that side. If the boat is under sail, the mast, and consequently the boat and crew, are significantly endangered. When a boat is hauled for the winter, the mast and its rigging are put up in the shed and typically not given another thought until spring. Then, when the weather gets nice, we can't wait to get the covers off and the boat in the water. Some who keep up with this sort of thing warn that damage or corrosion at the spreaders is second only to faulty swage fittings as the primary cause of mast failures. Spreaders should be a priority item on your annual checklist of maintenance items.

Varnished wood spreaders are the most vulnerable. They are notorious for rapid deterioration on the top surface. Varnish, even the most expensive exterior varnish with UV absorbers, stabilizers, antioxidants, and so on, does not offer the degree of protection against sunlight deterioration that paint does. In tropical climates, cracking and peeling can occur in just a few months. This allows moisture to penetrate and cause rapid rotting of the wood and corrosion of the fastenings at the "spreader roots," where the spreader is attached to the mast. Painting the top surface of the spreader will greatly reduce this problem.

Fastenings at the spreader roots commonly consist of a stainless steel or bronze plate on the top surface and a matching one on the bottom surface with through-bolts or clevis pins. These should be thoroughly bedded to prevent moisture intrusion. If there has been deterioration of the wood in this area, drilling out *all* the rotted wood, plugging the holes with a thickened epoxy filler, and redrilling for the bolts or pins will usually solve the problem.

Concerns about aluminum spreaders are essentially the same as those for aluminum masts—welds, rivets, screws, and through-bolts should show no signs of corrosion. While you're inspecting fastenings, look for cracks around the holes.

Wire rope shrouds typically run through a groove in the end of the spreader and are secured with wire seizing. The end of the spreader is then covered with a boot or taped to prevent chafing of overlapping jibs. Here we can experience corrosion due to moisture that seeps under the covering or galvanic corrosion between the dissimilar metals present there. Taking the time at the end of the season to remove the boot or tape and closely inspect this area will pay dividends in the avoidance of future rigging failure. Before replacing the covering boots, give the spreader tips a generous squirt of a moisture-displacing anti-corrosion spray.

MAST STEP

The heel of the mast and the mast step, whether on deck or on the keel, are highly susceptible to corrosion. In the case of wood masts, anticipate rot, deterioration, and corrosion of fastenings in this area. Water tends to seep down both the outside and the inside of the mast and collect in the mast step. Where the step is on the keel, air circulation around it is likely to be poor. To further complicate matters, the heel of the mast works when sailing, so there are also the problems of abrasion and wear to exacerbate deterioration caused by moisture penetration (fig. 21-4).

In the case of aluminum, steel, and carbon fiber masts stepped on the keel, there is also the potential for galvanic corrosion of bronze or steel keel bolts and floor fastenings, should they come in contact with the mast. Avoiding or insulating such contacts and keeping the bilge dry will go a long way toward eliminating this source of corrosive damage. For dissimilar metal fasteners in the mast and step, we must turn to isolation and insulation—that is, moving the fastenings or insulating them from contact. This is easier said than done, but doable. Mast steps deserve a place on your maintenance schedule. Inspect them regularly to be sure that water traps and drain holes are clear. If there aren't any drain holes, make some. Effective drainage and good ventilation are essential, and these can often be bolstered with protective paint coatings and corrosion-inhibiting lubricants.

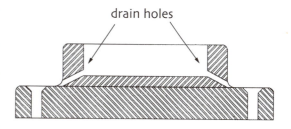

drain holes

Fig. 21-4. Mast step. Water allowed to stand in the mast step can result in accelerated corrosion and structural weakening of the mast heel.

MAST PARTNERS

If the mast is stepped on the keel, the place in the deck where the mast passes through is referred to as the *partners* (fig. 21-5). Typically, this opening is greater in diameter than the mast to allow for some adjustment. The mast is fixed in place by driving wedges of wood, plastic, or some other compliant material into the space between mast and deck; then the opening is covered with a *mast boot* or *coat* to keep water out.

The almost inevitable moisture penetration—seepage past the boot or down the sail track—and a lack of air circulation make this area vulnerable to corrosion. The area of the mast under the wedges is particularly susceptible. Recently, a new product has become available that appears to represent a significant advance. Replacing traditional mast wedges, this two-part polymer is poured into the space between the mast and the partners. It takes some three days to set up and comes as a kit with all the components necessary to form a mold in the space between the mast and the partners. However, it does shrink 0.0002 inch for each inch of polymer

(0.005 mm per 25.4 mm) when curing, and water can still invade this space. A carefully applied bead of a polysulfide sealant should prevent this.

Often an aluminum mast will be internally reinforced in the area of the partners and provided with drain holes above the boot. Maintenance and prevention consists of keeping drain holes clear and removing the boot periodically for examination of the mast. If corrosion is a problem here and moisture penetration cannot be stopped, a protective paint coating in this area, properly applied (see chapter 15), may be necessary. It doesn't have to be pretty, just protective.

MAST CAP

The mast cap, also called the masthead box, is one of the more important of the mast fittings (fig. 21-6). Much of the rigging is attached to it, making it the point at which most of the

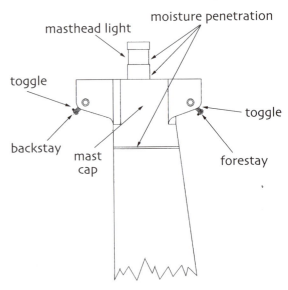

Fig. 21-6. Masthead caps, boxes, and equipment. With wooden masts, the problems are largely moisture penetration and wood softening. With aluminum masts, it's moisture penetration and localized corrosion of fittings and fastenings. In all materials, it's the masthead equipment—lights, antennas, instruments—and corrosion of electrical contacts and connections.

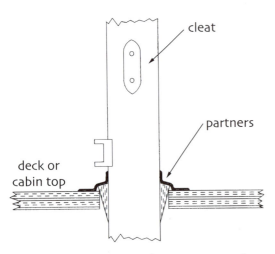

Fig. 21-5. Mast partners. The mast partners is another common area for corrosive damage. Chloride concentration at the wedge-mast interface can result in severe circumferential pitting or rot around the mast, seriously weakening the spar. Moisture must be prevented from penetrating this area.

strain is applied. Mast caps are often cast aluminum alloy on smaller boats, and sometimes galvanized steel on older boats, but most are fabricated from stainless steel. Concerns are mostly with galvanic corrosion between the cap and its fastenings and the mast. We don't really have many options here; structural requirements dictate the use of a high-strength metal and, for the most part, corrosion is localized and limited to the interface between the two dissimilar metals. Careful and thorough examination is a must at the beginning and end of the season when the stick is out of the boat.

SAIL TRACK

The extruded sail track or luff track in aluminum masts doesn't normally cause serious problems as long as nylon slides or bolt ropes are used. However, dirt, grease, and salt will accumulate in the luff groove, and corrosion of the track can occur (fig. 21-7). It's a good idea during the winter

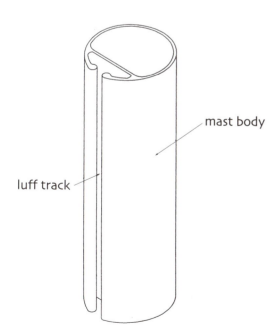

Fig. 21-7. Luff or sail track. The luff track is more a source of corrosion-induced frustration than serious corrosive structural damage. If corrosion products are allowed to build up, slides—even nylon slides—may jam.

mast body

luff track

layup, while you've got the mast out of the boat and horizontal, to wash the track with fresh water, dry it thoroughly, and rub it smoothly and evenly with automotive or boat wax.

On wooden masts there are basically two types of sail track commonly used: the luff groove, which is a slot routed into the after side of the mast, and the metal slide track. The luff groove has the virtue of simplicity, immunity to corrosion, and virtual trouble-free service since it only sees the luff rope. The metal slide track is another story. Brass, aluminum, and stainless steel are all susceptible to corrosion that can create friction and jam the slides. Nylon slides help a great deal, but lubricating the slides and track with a moisture-displacing corrosion inhibitor also goes a long way toward ensuring a trouble-free season. You just lower the sail, piling up the slides at the bottom of the track, spray them all together, and raise the sail, thus distributing the lubricant throughout the length of the track. It's easier than going aloft.

On a steel mast a well-bedded wood spacer is mounted on the after face of the mast and the sail track fastened to this spacer. Since we cannot get to the backside of the fasteners (inside the mast), machine screws tapped into the mast are the obvious choice. But we must be conscious of the potential for galvanic corrosion between the mild steel mast and the track fasteners. Ensuring that no moisture gets between the mast and the wood spacer will greatly minimize this potential.

FITTINGS AND FASTENINGS

Some spar fittings are cast aluminum—either 356 (A0356.0) for end caps and other light duties, or 535 (A0535.0) for cleats and other load-bearing fittings. Others, particularly tangs, pad eyes, and the like are of stainless steel. Even bronze fittings, usually in the form of halyard winches, are sometimes attached to aluminum masts. Here again, all metal fittings that are not aluminum must be insulated from the mast by the use of pads of neoprene, PVC, Delrin, wood, or some other nonconductive material.

Fastenings are normally stainless steel screws or rivets. Galvanic corrosion will inevitably take place but will be limited to the interface between the fastening and the mast. Look for tell-tale white powdery residue around the fastening. Eventually the fastening will freeze in place, and removal will be, for all practical purposes, impossible. Preventive maintenance for threaded fastenings consists of annual withdrawal, cleaning of the mating surfaces, coating with a moisture-displacing anti-corrosion lubricant or a proprietary product like Tefgel or Loctite (blue), and replacement. With rivets, eventually the white powdery deposit falls away, the hole is enlarged, and the rivet becomes loose. The fix consists of drilling out the old rivet and replacing it with the next larger size. Be sure to use a closed-end (water- and vapor-tight) rivet with both the rivet body and mandrel metals of aluminum (5052 or 5056), stainless steel, or Monel, depending on the stress the fitting will undergo. If you do find a loose rivet in a fitting, it's a good idea to change all the rivets at the same time. This has the advantage of allowing you to remove the fitting entirely so you can rebed it with a sealant. Don't use an adhesive sealant such as 3M-5200; it isn't necessary, and later removal will be a bear!

Keep an eye out for cracks and pitting corrosion in mast tangs, chainplates, and other fittings subject to stress and vibration. Conditions here are conducive to corrosion fatigue in these critical fittings. Use a magnifying glass or one of the commercially available dye-penetrant kits. If any cracks are found, the part should be replaced.

The same stress and vibration makes metal fastenings in wooden masts prone to water penetration, corrosion of the fastening, and rotting of the wood. The result is loose and potentially failed fittings. In such cases, drill out the fastener hole a couple of sizes larger and fill it with an epoxy or filler mixture. Before driving the new fastening, it is be a good idea to dip it in paint, epoxy, or a silicone or polysulfide coating. It's messy, but it works.

MASTHEAD EQUIPMENT

More often than not, failures of masthead electronics are the result of faulty connections, usu-

ally at the bottom of the mast. However, the connections at the masthead, even when properly made, are also vulnerable to moisture penetration followed by corrosion, signal degradation, poor performance, and, ultimately, failure. Everything we said back in chapter 18 concerning wire connections applies here. It is especially important for masthead and spreader connections—unless you enjoy the prospect of going aloft while at sea a whole lot more than I do.

For the electronics, the point of greatest susceptibility is the coaxial cable connector, such as the PL-259 type or BNC types (fig. 21-8). These connectors are fine examples of mechanical design and manufacturing, but they were not originally intended for outside application in the marine environment. Tolerances are loose enough to permit water entry, and the materials are susceptible to corrosion. Also, the coaxial cable itself, by virtue of its construction, has a tendency to wick moisture between the sheath and the tinned-copper braided shield (fig. 21-9).

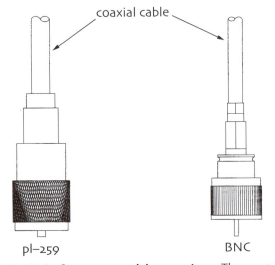

coaxial cable

pl–259   BNC

Fig. 21-8. Common coaxial connectors. There are basically two types of connectors in common use: PL-259 and BNC. These are a common source of corrosion-induced communication problems. For the most part, they are not marine-designed components. If not properly installed and if moisture is allowed to penetrate, corrosion will degrade the electrical equipment, and performance will suffer.

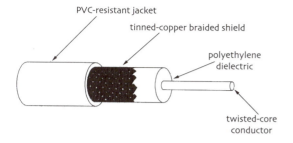

Fig. 21-9. Coaxial cable. Coaxial cable, due to the nature of its construction, tends to wick up moisture between the PVC sheath and the tinned-copper braided shield, resulting in deterioration of the braided shield and degradation of equipment performance. The entire connector, and the coaxial cable for several inches on either side, should be enclosed in a length of adhesive-lined shrink tube.

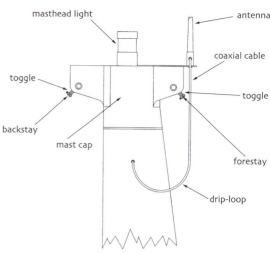

Fig. 21-10. Cable drip-loops. A loop in the coaxial cable permits water to collect on the cable, run down to the bottom of the loop, and drip off without getting into the mast.

The result is that these connectors have a useful (trouble-free) life, if properly made up, of about three years. The best thing you can do to ensure that you get peak performance and failure-free operation is first to make up the connector following the manufacturer's directions to the letter. Before screwing the coupling ring to the plug assembly, put a dollop of silicone sealant or a commercially prepared product intended for this purpose inside the coupling ring to seal the gap between the cable and the connector. Before making up the final connection, cut a piece of adhesive-lined shrink tube long enough to cover the combined connectors (male and female) and slide it over the cable. Screw the two connectors together, then slide the heat-shrink tubing over them and heat it gently to seal the entire connection. Don't forget to put a drip-loop in the cable (fig. 21-10).

STANDING RIGGING

There are basically three types of standing rigging in common use: galvanized wire rope, stainless steel wire rope, and rod rigging. Galvanized wire rope is used mostly on commercial vessels for reasons of cost-effectiveness and by traditionalists for authenticity. Stainless wire rope, by far the most popular, is just about the

de facto standard for recreational yachts. It provides a better appearance and lower maintenance, and it doesn't get nice white sails dirty. Rod rigging is used almost exclusively by high-tech, high-performance sailboats.

Wire Rope

Wire rope is made up of multiple strands of thinner wire twisted together into a specific configuration. Various types of wire rope exhibit different strength and flexibility characteristics (fig. 21-11). The most common type for standing rigging is 1 × 19—a central strand with eighteen strands of the same gauge wire wound around it. Because it is too inflexible to wrap around a thimble or a rigging eye, 1 × 19 wire requires rigging terminals of one type or another.

Both galvanized and stainless steel wire rope are susceptible to several forms of corrosive damage—rusting, pitting, and crevice corrosion. Rod rigging is less susceptible because of the alloy normally used—Nitronic 50—and because rod has a smoother surface and fewer crevices. Both wire and rod are also susceptible to corrosion fatigue and, according to some, to stress-corrosion cracking, although the last is open to question.

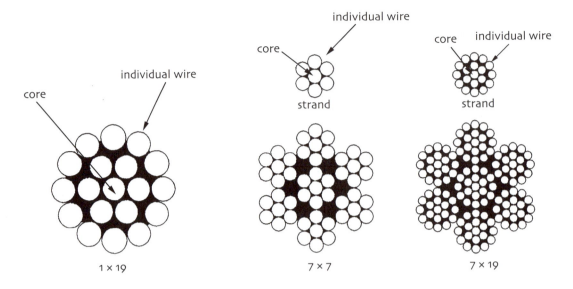

Fig. 21-11. Common types of wire rope. There are three types of wire rope in common marine use: 1 × 19, 7 × 7, and 7 × 19. The designations refer to the number and size of the wires in the core and in the strands. 1 × 19 contains 1 strand of 19 wires, is the least flexible, and is commonly used for standing rigging. 7 × 7 consists of 7 strands of 7 wires each, has intermediate breaking strength and flexibility, and is sometimes used for standing rigging in small craft. 7 × 19 has 7 strands of 19 wires each, has the lowest breaking strength, is the most flexible, and is commonly used for running rigging.

Salt spray and salt-laden moist air saturates the wire rope, seeps down into the lay of the strands, and wicks down to the core, where it becomes oxygen depleted. The moisture evaporates, causing the salt crystals to build up, or it drains down and accumulates in the lower terminal fittings, where it stagnates and evaporates. The strands at the center of the cable tend to corrode first and most rapidly because of oxygen depletion. The difference in oxygen concentration at the core and at the outside strands also constitutes a galvanic couple, leading to corrosion and, eventually, broken strands. The most likely failure point is at the end terminals, but rust and broken strands do occur along the length of the wire rope, especially low down on the shrouds and stays. The telltale warning signs are broken strands or *gashers*.

Corrosion fatigue is the failure of a metal component due to the combination of cyclic stress and a corrosive environment. Cracking is the result. Either the cyclic loading or the corrosive environment alone could eventually have the same outcome, but when the two occur simultaneously the damage is accelerated and intensified. In the case of yacht rigging, the cyclic stress is due to vibration in the shrouds and stays. The corrosive environment is the salt spray and salt-laden moist air. Corrosion fatigue can affect not just the shrouds and stays but also the rigging fittings, especially tangs and chainplates (more about this later).

Stress-corrosion cracking also involves the failure of a metal part in a corrosive environment while under stress, only in this case, the stress is tensile and static rather than cyclical and dynamic. The portion of the metal component under stress becomes anodic with respect to the adjacent material. This results in a large cathode–small anode galvanic couple and rapid deterioration of the anodic area. The structural deterioration in the presence of tensile stress tends to separate the surfaces, causing rapid crack propagation and eventual failure of the part. There is very little visible evidence of corrosive damage. The crack is believed to initiate at surface defects—pits, crevices, or flaws. Stress-corrosion cracking is extremely difficult to detect, sometimes turning up as a sudden failure even after several years of trouble-free service.

Stress-corrosion cracking as a rigging concern is a bit controversial. Postmortem examinations of failed rigging are not conclusive, and some controlled experiments on austenitic stainless steel specimens have been unable to replicate stress-corrosion cracking in marine atmospheres. Critical conditions that must exist simultaneously for stress-corrosion cracking to occur are the level of tensile stress, the concentration of chlorides in an aqueous form, and the temperature. The stress must be tensile in nature and can be either applied or residual. The level required is actually very small—as little as 10 percent of the yield strength of the alloy. The chloride level necessary is also very small, well below the levels normally found in seawater. It is generally believed that stress-corrosion cracking does not occur below a threshold temperature of approximately 140°F (60°C), but more recent studies indicate that this threshold decreases significantly with increasing chloride concentration. Given the cumulative concentrations of salt crystals referred to above and the temperatures that can occur on metal surfaces under a blazing summer sun, especially in the tropics, this writer comes down on the side of those who feel that stress-corrosion cracking is a possible, even likely, explanation for some otherwise unexplained rig failures.

To prevent stress-corrosion cracking, select a metal alloy that is resistant to this form of corrosion, such as the superaustenitic or "6 Mo" (6 percent molybdenum) alloys—254 SMO, 20Mo-6, or AL-6XN. Or alleviate the conditions that cause it by reducing residual stress levels through heat treating, eliminating places where aqueous chlorides can collect or concentrate, lowering the ambient temperature, and applying some form of cathodic protection. All of these may be difficult to do in the case of

yacht rigging, although we can, and should, take measures to avoid or eliminate chloride accumulation in the lower shrouds, stays, and fittings.

A single broken strand is probably no big deal, depending on what kind of sailing you do. However, when you find one broken strand, the chances are good that there are others—probably many others. That's why many knowledgeable and experienced authorities say that there is no acceptable number of broken strands. If you find any broken strands, the time for replacement has arrived.

Careful inspection is called for here. Run a soft rag or a thick pad of tissue paper up and down the cable. Broken strands will snag the fibers. Mark each broken strand with a short length of masking tape. For a more detailed examination in questionable areas, bend the cable in a short curve—gently here, you don't want to kink it. If the wire rope is beginning to deteriorate, the rust and broken strands will be evident down in the lay of strands.

When galvanized wire rope begins to corrode, it rusts, typically in the strands at the core. The rust increases as the deterioration progresses, giving early warning of impending failures. When the rust is very slight, many people turn the wire rope end for end and get another season or two out of it. It's a judgment call.

Chafe from sheets and sails can rapidly wear away the galvanizing on the wire, and once the protective galvanized coating is gone, rusting begins. The most susceptible places are low down on the shrouds from jib sheets, on the forestay from the jib hanks, and up near the spreaders from the main sail. Preventive measures include "baggy wrinkle" up near the spreaders and flexible PVC hose down low on the shrouds and stays.

Galvanized wire rope is normally lubricated as part of the manufacturing process. A happy consequence is reduced friction between strands when the wire is tensioned and eased in use. Maintaining this lubrication is a matter of simply rubbing the wire down once a year with an oil-soaked rag. You can use light machine oil, one of the newer semi-synthetic oils, or a moisture-displacing anti-corrosion spray. Galvanized wire rope also can be wormed, parceled, and served, and history tells us that if so cared for, it can have an almost indefinite service life. On smaller boats, tar-saturated friction tape can be used under the serving. Never ever use plastic tape; it will trap moisture, causing corrosion, and it will ultimately stiffen and unwrap. In any case, if serving and parceling are used, it's a good idea to strip off some of the serving once a year at various places to be sure that no moisture has gotten in and caused corrosion.

Stainless steel wire rope for yacht rigging is normally laid up dry in the manufacturing process. This leaves the rope vulnerable to friction along the wires as tension on the shrouds and stays increases and decreases, and there is no lubricant to resist penetration by salt water and dirt. Corrosion is to be expected.

When stainless steel wire rope begins to corrode, it develops pitting and crevice corrosion in the strands at the core. Unfortunately, this is not visible in the early stages. Occasionally, you may notice some brownish staining on a strand or two. Mark these areas with a dab of white paint and make a note in the maintenance log to check these areas regularly. Pitting and crevice corrosion in stainless steel wire rope is extremely serious. These form the initiation sites for stress-corrosion cracking.

I wouldn't be too quick to write off the use of a lubricant on stainless wire rope. The chemical industry, aware of our concerns with oil staining of clothing, both in the yachting and in the skiing communities, has been at work and has developed some clear, semi-synthetic, biodegradable lubricants that are readily washed out of clothing—and presumably sails. Talk with your sailmaker.

Stainless steel grades most commonly used in wire rope are the 18-8's, primarily Types 302 and 304. However, Type 316 is the standard high-corrosion-resistance grade. It is the recommended grade of the Offshore Racing Council—and the only way to go if you have a choice.

Wire rope intended for lifelines and steering cables is frequently coated (sheathed) with nylon or vinyl in order to extend its life by protecting it from abrasion, sealing in cable lubricants, and keeping out dirt and moisture. However, if the sheathing becomes cracked or cut, moisture can penetrate and wick up under the sheathing, resulting in pitting, crevice corrosion, and broken strands. This can be a serious failing since the damage is not visible. The Offshore Racing Regulations do not permit the use of sheathed wire in lifelines.

Rod Rigging

The alloy of choice for rod rigging is a special grade of stainless steel called Nitronic 50. We discussed this back in chapter 8. This alloy may be familiar to you as Aquamet 22, commonly used in prop shafts. These are essentially the same alloy except that the Aquamet 22 is hardened. Both are 22 percent chromium, 12 percent nickel, and 2 percent molybdenum and are thus highly corrosion-resistant.

Comparative tests of Aquamet 22 and 316 in quiet seawater for a period of nine months show that after cleaning off barnacles and other marine growth, the Aquamet 22 was completely unaffected, whereas the 316 suffered significant pitting and crevice corrosion. Also, when one considers that the rod is smooth, with no crevices to trap and hold water and concentrate salt crystals, Nitronic 50 rod rigging is highly resistant to atmospheric corrosion.

Insofar as pitting and crevice corrosion may constitute initiation sites for stress-corrosion cracking, and since there are no places for chlorides to accumulate and concentrate, we can expect that rod rigging will also be more resistant to this form of corrosive damage. However, it is not unaffected by corrosion fatigue. When it is subjected to many stress cycles, minute cracking begins to occur at the stress concentration point, typically at the rod terminals and at the spreaders if the rod is made to bend around the spreader tip. Manufacturers of rod rigging are aware of this and have taken steps to deal with it. Special stress-relieving tapered sleeves are used at the terminal ends and "spreader bends" at the spreader tips. These fittings are designed to prevent stress concentration by distributing the stresses along the rod. Proper toggling, the avoidance of areas where water can accumulate, and regular inspection and examination for microcracks are essential precautions against sudden failure.

TERMINALS, TURNBUCKLES, AND CHAINPLATES

We've talked about masts, spars, shrouds, and stays and about their susceptibilities to corrosion-induced failure. However, these are not the most likely causes of failure in rigging systems. More often than not, a terminal fitting, turnbuckle, chainplate, or their fastenings are at fault in a rigging system failure.

Terminal Fittings

One of the oldest methods still in common use is the clamped eye splice. It's simple, quick, and inexpensive, and it holds well. It has the advantage of being open to air circulation and to view—

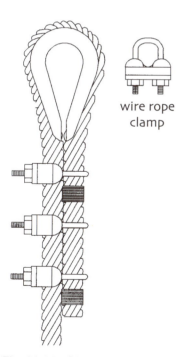

wire rope clamp

Fig. 21-12. Clamped eye splice. This terminal is open to both air circulation and visual inspection, but it does have corners and crevices where moisture can collect and chlorides can concentrate. Regular inspections and freshwater flushing when you hose down the boat are a good idea.

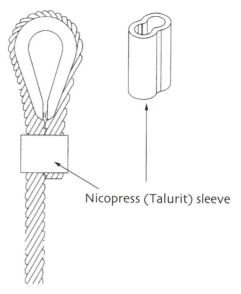

Nicopress (Talurit) sleeve

Fig. 21-13. Nicopress or Talurit terminal fittings. This popular terminal method is simple and quick and holds well. Moisture penetration into the spaces between the sleeve and the wire strands can cause pitting and broken strands. Regular inspection and flushing are recommended.

and the disadvantage of having lots of cracks and crevices to accumulate and concentrate salt deposits. When seized or covered, pitting and crevice corrosion are highly likely, resulting in weakened or broken strands and eventual corrosion fatigue and failure. Any covering should be removed annually and the wires carefully inspected (fig. 21-12).

A more popular current option is the Nicopress or, in the United Kingdom, Talurit fitting. With this type of fitting, a terminal eye is formed by sliding a double-barreled metal sleeve or ferrule over the standing wire rope, bending the rope around the thimble, passing its bitter end through the other side of the sleeve, and then crimping the sleeve with a special tool. Sleeves are available in copper, tin-plated copper, zinc-plated copper, and aluminum (fig. 21-13).

These terminal fittings are fast and easy to use, hold well, and make a neat-looking termination. However, they too have many cracks and crevices where moisture and salt can concentrate and can cause pitting and crevice cor-

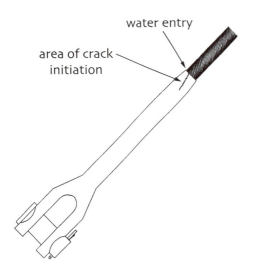

water entry

area of crack
initiation

Fig. 21-14. Swage terminal fittings. The swage ter-minal is probably the most commonly used of all terminal fittings. Like the Nicopress and Talurit fit-tings, moisture intrusion in the spaces between the wire strands and the top of the swage can cause pit-ting and broken wire strands. In addition, conditions here also favor stress-corrosion cracking, especially in the tropics.

rosion—especially at and under the sleeve. The sleeve should be as tightly fitting as possible to preclude moisture entry. Coating with a dollop of sealant after crimping will also help keep out moisture. Ideally, the sleeve metal should be as close as possible to that of the wire rope in the galvanic series (table 4-1); for example, alu-minum sleeves on galvanized wire and copper sleeves on stainless steel wire.

Swage terminals are probably the most widely used of all wire-terminal fittings. The swage terminal is a stainless steel fitting consist-ing of an eye, fork (or clevis), or threaded stud on one end and a sleeve on the other. The sleeve is precisely sized to be a tight-fitting covering for the wire rope. The wire is inserted into the sleeve to the full depth, and then the sleeve is put through a set of hydraulic rollers and subjected to tremendous pressure. This results in a cold-worked bond between the sleeve and the rope. These fittings have far fewer places for moisture and salt to concentrate, but the stresses intro-duced by cold-working the sleeve, together with

the salt-laden atmosphere, set up conditions fa-vorable for stress-corrosion cracking failures.

Swage terminals must be properly done, preferably by a professional rigging shop using a hydraulic machine designed for the purpose and operated by a skilled operator. The use of ex-cessive pressure or repeated rolling will result in a brittle terminal highly susceptible to crack-ing. The use of less than optimum pressure re-sults in a weak terminal susceptible to moisture penetration, corrosion, and failure. Not all swaging machines are hydraulic; some are based on mechanically forcing the fitting through a set of dies, usually two or more times; this often results in a banana-shaped terminal that is com-pletely unacceptable! Improper swaging is, in my opinion, the major reason for the poor rep-utation these terminal fittings have, especially in the tropics. According to one manufacturer of these fittings, the expected service life of a swaged terminal of "proper quality" is unlim-ited in normal coastal cruising. However, I have heard of actual lifetimes ranging from less than 2 years to more than 15 years. Obviously, then, not all swages are created equal!

People do attempt to seal the opening at the top of the swage with all sorts of things: Life Caulk (a polysulfide), two-part epoxy adhesives, 3M-5200 (a polyurethane), and so on. The prob-lem is that unless the sealant is applied when the terminal is new and in a dry atmosphere, the moisture is sealed in under the sealant. One of the better methods is to thoroughly rinse and flush the fitting and allow it to dry thoroughly; then apply only enough heat to melt beeswax or some-thing similar down into the opening. This is not foolproof but is a worthwhile procedure.

When inspecting the rig, the things to look for are, first of all, the dreaded bent or banana-shaped fitting; these should be replaced. Also, look for cracks in the body of the terminal; these, too, are not reliable and should be re-placed. Rusting or broken strands where the cable enters the fitting should be questioned; if in doubt, have a rigger check it. Although the upper shroud fittings are not immune to these problems, it is the lower terminals that are most susceptible to corrosive damage (fig. 21-14).

Another class of terminal fitting is a mechanical assembly that relies on compressive forces applied by the assembly process to hold the wire rope in the fitting. Mechanical terminal fittings are quite common on yachts today, second only to swage fittings. Proper assembly of these terminals is not difficult but requires some care. A threaded nut is slid up over the wire rope, and then the wire rope is partially unlaid. A cone or wedge slides over the core strands and is caged by the exterior strands. The interior of the end fitting is given a small dollop of a polymer sealant (not an adhesive) to seal the wire entry, and then the threaded end fitting and the threaded nut are assembled, firmly clamping the individual wires between the cone or wedge and the interior of the terminal fitting.

When properly assembled, mechanical terminals have an excellent reputation for durability and reliability. They are not susceptible to stress-corrosion cracking and are highly resistant to moisture penetration and salt concentration. This type of terminal is often referred to by the trade name of one of the best-known manufacturers of it: Norseman or Sta-Lok (fig. 21-15).

There is one more wire terminal end fitting that we should discuss. The *spelter* fitting gets its name from the Dutch word for zinc. In this case it refers to the molten zinc that is used to hold the end of the wire rope in the terminal fitting. The end wires of the cable are unlaid, spread apart, cleaned, tinned, and inserted into the socket end of the fitting. The fitting is then heated, and molten zinc is poured into the socket. These simple fittings are easily made up, have a nice finished appearance, and are just about impervious to moisture penetration or concentration. The modern version of the spel-

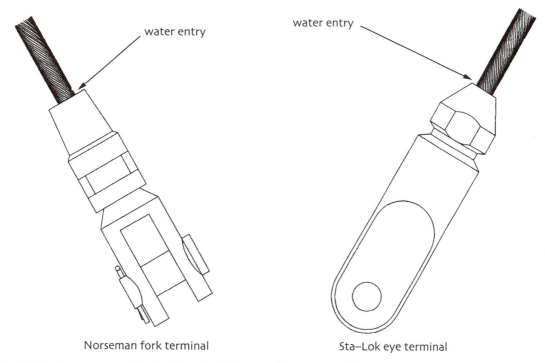

water entry

water entry

Norseman fork terminal

Sta–Lok eye terminal

Fig. 21-15. Norseman and Sta-Lok terminal fittings. These terminals have an excellent reputation for durability and reliability. Moisture penetration—the ever-present threat—is prevented in the properly assembled terminal by the polymer sealant inserted in the top of the fitting during assembly.

ter fitting uses fast-setting epoxy in place of the molten zinc.

All of these fittings are continuously exposed to salt-laden moist air and salt spray, and they undergo an occasional drenching in salt water. The moisture penetrates cracks and crevices and collects in pockets. When it evaporates, it leaves deposits of salt crystals that accumulate and concentrate, creating the conditions in which pitting and crevice corrosion and stress-corrosion cracking can flourish. It is a good idea to seal all openings and crevices on *all* lower fittings—of any type—with a sealant. However, if the fittings are already in use and have been exposed to salt-laden moisture, you'll just be sealing in the moisture and salt crystals, and the damage can still occur. *Thorough flushing and drying before sealing is a must.*

Terminal fittings should be uncovered or opened up and examined at least once a year. It takes only a few hours and is well worth the time. Clean up the fitting, and use a good light source and a magnifying glass—or better yet, use a dye-penetrant kit. You're looking for cracks, broken strands, serious pitting, and crevice corrosion. If there's any doubt, have a rigger look at it or replace it.

Turnbuckles

Turnbuckles are used to take up slack in the standing rigging. They come in two basic types: open body and closed body (fig. 21-16). In the open-body type, the main body of the turnbuckle—the barrel—has a large open slot on either side, exposing the ends of the threaded studs. The closed-body type is just that—the barrel is closed, concealing the threaded studs.

Advocates of closed-body turnbuckles prefer them because they have a tendency to exclude water and because a grease fitting can be fitted in the barrel. The cavity can be pumped full of grease periodically, which keeps the threads lubricated, prevents them from seizing, and inhibits corrosion. The opposing view says that closed-body turnbuckles have a greater tendency to collect, accumulate, and concentrate water and salt, and there's no way to know what's

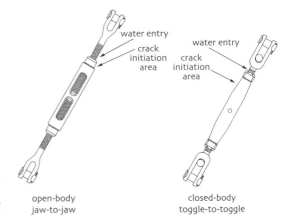

Fig. 21-16. Turnbuckles. Closed-body turnbuckles have the advantage of superior resistance (*not* immunity) to water intrusion if they are kept filled with grease. If not, they have a greater tendency to accumulate and concentrate water and salt under conditions favorable for stress-corrosion cracking. Also, aside from disassembly, there's no way of knowing what's going on inside them. Open-body turnbuckles are more open to penetration by salt-laden moisture and have greater susceptibility to pitting and crevice corrosion, but their better visibility makes inspection and flushing easier.

going on inside. For my part, I prefer the open-body type; I like to see what's going on in there.

Open-body advocates say that this type of turnbuckle doesn't retain water and therefore is less likely to corrode. They are also easier to inspect. The first claim, concerning moisture retention, is open to question. Open-body turnbuckles are more open to penetration by moist salt-laden air and to drenchings when sailing hard and the rail goes under. While the free flow of air through them will hasten drying, the salt deposits are left and will absorb moisture from the air, resulting in pitting and crevice corrosion and the possibility of stress-corrosion cracking. However, this overlooks the ease with which they can be flushed with a hose. For this reason, on commercial boats, it is customary to fill the open-body cavity with waterproof grease, wrap the turnbuckle with canvas, and then cover it with a sewn canvas sleeve.

Marine turnbuckles come in four basic materials: galvanized steel, stainless steel, bronze, and a combination of bronze and steel. Galvanized turnbuckles are the most susceptible to corrosion, especially on the threads. The galvanizing on the threads is soon worn off when the turnbuckles are adjusted, and unless they are treated as above or given regular sprays with a moisture-displacing anticorrosion lubricant, the turnbuckles are subject to rapid rusting and eventual weakening.

Stainless steel does corrode when it is made to stand in oxygen-depleted moisture, which is just what happens inside the turnbuckle and around the threads and clevis pins. These are the places where salt crystals concentrate, and given normal loading and some temperature elevation from a tropical sun, we have the conditions necessary for stress-corrosion cracking.

Stainless steel is also susceptible to *galling*, which takes place on metal-to-metal surfaces under frictional pressure. Tiny metal particles are torn from one or both surfaces and bond between the surfaces, effectively "cold-welding" the surfaces together. The presence of dirt, abrasive particles, or corrosion products facilitates the process. This happens frequently in stainless-to-stainless threaded fasteners and is a too-common failure mode in turnbuckles. The solution is to keep the thread surfaces clean and well-lubricated with a moisture-displacing, anticorrosion lubricant.

Bronze turnbuckles are resistant to corrosion and to galling. There are also turnbuckles with stainless steel bodies and bronze threaded inserts and with chrome-plated bronze bodies and stainless screws. Experience has shown that initial concerns about galvanic reactions between the bronze and the stainless steel were unfounded. The reason is that the extent of galvanic corrosive damage is a function of both the galvanic separation of the metals in the galvanic series and the duration of wetness in the electrolyte (seawater). Galvanic separations of 200 mV or less are generally considered to be acceptable in mild to moderate exposure. The galvanic separation in this case is approximately 190 mV, and the duration of immersion is short. This type of turnbuckle has been in wide use for many years with no notable problems.

Turnbuckles should receive periodic inspection throughout the sailing season and a thorough examination at least once a year. Look for cracks, pitting, and crevice corrosion on the barrel, threads, clevis pins, and toggle ends. Flush turnbuckles thoroughly and then dry and spray them with anticorrosion lubricant.

CHAINPLATES

Chainplates are the attachment points on the hull for the shrouds and stays. They typically are made up of steel plate and are shaped, formed, or welded to the correct angle of alignment with the shroud or stay. Chainplates are under considerable strain, and if they are misaligned, the result is severe working of the fitting and its fastenings. This sets up the conditions for moisture penetration and several forms of corrosive damage (fig. 21-17). Chainplate fastenings are a common place for moisture penetration and, ultimately, wood rot, delamination, and crevice corrosion of the fastener. Watch for signs of moisture penetration, such as rust stains, looseness, and damage to the gelcoat. It's a good idea to withdraw a couple of fastenings every year to see what's going on. With chainplates that pierce the deck, most of the corrosive damage occurs where the chainplate goes through the deck. In this case the chainplate itself must be withdrawn.

In the case of metal hulls, chainplates are sometimes simply welded to the outside of the hull. These are traps for water collection and the corrosion that inevitably follows. It is preferable that chainplates be fabricated separately, bolted on to doubler plates, and properly and thoroughly bedded.

The more serious failure modes for chainplates are corrosion fatigue and intergranular corrosion (weld decay). Corrosion fatigue occurs when the chainplate is subjected to cyclical stress—for example, from variable loads and vibration. The effect is accelerated by pitting and

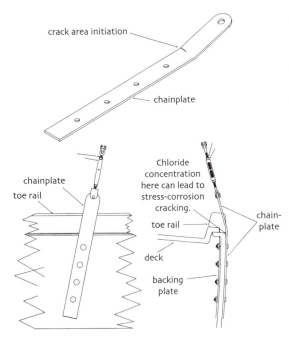

Fig. 21-17. Chainplates. Aside from plain old uniform atmospheric corrosion, which is more unsightly than threatening, the problems encountered by chainplates are from stress, sensitization, chloride concentration, and the resulting susceptibility to corrosion fatigue, intergranular corrosion (in the case of welds), and stress-corrosion cracking.

crevice corrosion, usually at the bend or weld in the chainplate. This is exactly the case when the chainplate is not in perfect alignment with the stay or shroud. Failure can occur, usually at the bend or the weld, even though the maximum stress is considerably less than the yield strength. Look for pitting, crevice corrosion, and tiny cracks in these areas. Lifting or bubbling of paint coatings is another indication of pending trouble.

RUNNING RIGGING

The running rigging consists of the various lines that control sails and spars—such as halyards, sheets, downhauls, outhauls, and topping lifts. These lines are natural fiber, synthetic fiber, wire, or some combination of these. Natural fibers need to be checked regularly for rot and

deterioration;, even when they are tarred or chemically treated, they cannot come close to the longevity or ease of handling of the synthetics. The traditional synthetic fibers for rope are nylon, polyester (Dacron and Terylene), and polypropylene, but a number of newer high-tech synthetics are widely available—Kevlar, Technora, Spectra, and Vectran—and more are coming out every day.

Our concern here is wire rope. The wire rope used in running-rigging applications is typically 7×19. This type is very flexible, which allows it to run through blocks and over sheaves without damage. It may be galvanized or stainless steel. Sometimes a rope-to-wire splice is used on halyards to provide a fiber "tail" for ease of handling on the hauling end. Splices, connections, and terminations are the same as those for standing rigging, except that Nicopress and Talurit are the most popular.

Like standing rigging, wire running rigging is vulnerable to salt air and spray penetration into the core, resulting in the same corrosion problems and making the same precautionary measures appropriate. But running rigging suffers the added insult of being constantly pulled and hauled and run through blocks. Chafed and broken strands are the likely consequences. Halyards are most susceptible. Look for signs of rust and broken strands.

The strands in 7×19 wire rope are considerably smaller than those in the 1×19 standing rigging, and there are many more of them to break. One or two broken strands are not as critical here as they are for the standing rigging, except to your hands and the bloodstains on the deck. However, where there is one broken strand, there is a good chance that there are, or will soon be, more. Frequent inspections are recommended—at the beginning, in the middle, and again at the end of the season. Be sure to examine the whole length of the halyard. If one or two broken strands are found, cut them off flush and tuck the ends back into the lay. Dab some white paint on the spot, down into the lay where it will not wear off, and keep an eye on it. Just don't wait till the halyard looks like a Dalmatian puppy before replacing it.

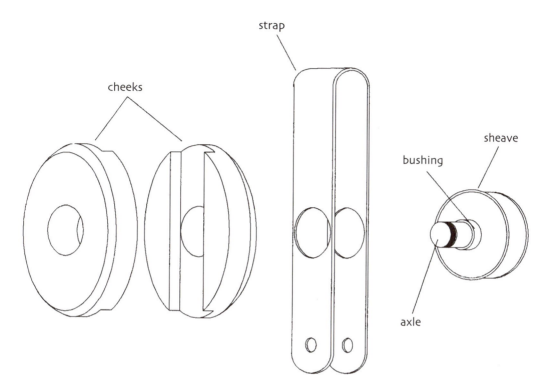

Fig. 21-18. Wooden cheek blocks. Not seen much anymore, these old beauties are immune to the usual problems of atmospheric corrosion of the body of the block, but they have the same susceptibilities to corrosive damage to the axle, bearings, and sheaves as their more modern counterparts.

BLOCKS AND SHEAVES

The block is a mechanical assembly whose essential elements consist of the cheeks, straps, sheave(s), axles, bushings, or bearings (fig. 21-18). Old-fashioned wooden cheek blocks are not used much anymore except by traditionalists. Modern blocks are lighter and more efficient.

Aside from aesthetics and efficiencies, our concerns are with the critical functional elements and their susceptibilities to corrosive damage. Modern blocks have aluminum, stainless steel, plastic, or composite cheeks. The straps are almost invariably stainless, although titanium is sometimes used in blocks intended for competitive racing. Corrosive damage to the cheeks and straps may be unsightly but is seldom the cause of block failure (fig. 21-19).

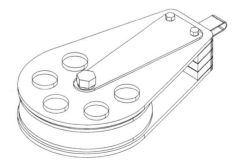

Fig. 21-19. Typical modern block assembly. Cheeks on the modern blocks may be of aluminum, stainless steel, plastics, or composites. Atmospheric corrosion of the cheek plates is unsightly but usually not structurally serious. In most cases, the load is carried by the straps, not the cheeks. The most vulnerable parts of the block assembly are the sheaves, bearings, and axles.

The sheave is the grooved wheel in the center of the block that carries the line. Sheaves are most commonly made of plastic for natural or synthetic rope and aluminum for wire rope. There's no problem with corrosion in plastic sheaves and only the normal moderately accelerated corrosion due to the physical wear on the contact surface of aluminum sheaves.

The part of the block that is most vulnerable to corrosion problems is the bushing or bearing-axle assembly (fig. 21-20). In a typical block, the center of the sheave is fitted with a bushing (essentially a press-fit sleeve, also called a *plain bearing*) or a roller bearing that spins on the axle. Bushings might be oil-impregnated bronze, plastic (usually Delrin), or a combination of Nomex and Teflon reinforced with carbon fiber, commonly referred to as *NTE*. NTE bushings are found in the more expensive blocks. They are rugged and durable, and they get better (less friction) with age. Delrin, an acetal resin, is tough, slick, and an excellent bearing material. It is less expensive than NTE. Nylon is another slick, tough bearing material, but it does absorb a small amount of moisture, causing it to swell

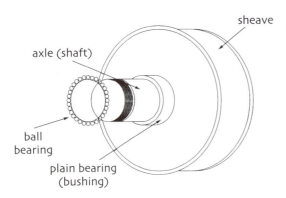

Fig. 21-20. Sheave assembly. This is the part of the block that is most vulnerable to corrosive damage. Corrosive damage results from saltwater, dirt, and grit intrusion into the shaft or bearing assembly. Abrasion-enhanced corrosion and, because of the dissimilar metals used, galvanic corrosion can occur. Regular thorough rinsing in fresh water and lubrication are the recommended preventive measures.

and increase friction. None of these materials is susceptible to corrosion. Roller bearings may be of bronze (in bronze sheaves), stainless steel, or, in some cases, an advanced plastic. Ball bearings are sometimes used on either side of the sheave to reduce side-load friction.

Corrosion damage in blocks results from the saltwater, dirt, and grit intrusion into the axle or bearing assembly. It may manifest itself as crevice corrosion on the bearing surface, or as galvanic corrosion of dissimilar metals. Also, abrasive damage may result from salt crystals left behind and built up from repeated saltwater soakings. Galvanic corrosion typically occurs at aluminum-stainless steel interfaces, such as exist when the cheeks are aluminum and the straps and fastenings are stainless steel.

Sheaves should be inspected at least once a year for surface corrosion and wear and to be sure that the sheave spins freely and smoothly with no screeching or squealing. Check for lateral play in the axle. If significant movement or sloppiness of fit is found, disassembly and replacement of worn parts is in order. Screeching and squealing may call for only a generous squirt of a moisture-displacing spray lubricant. Thorough rinsing in freshwater to flush out salt crystals, dirt, and grit will go a long way toward maintaining top performance from your blocks and avoiding failures. Stubborn salt crystal deposits will usually yield to aggressive flushing with hot freshwater. Salt encrustations also may be dissolved by rinsing with regular white household vinegar. Go carefully and rinse thoroughly; vinegar is an acetic acid and may attack metals if left on the surface.

SUMMARY

The root causes of rig failures and dismastings are not, in most cases, the mast, stays, or shrouds but rather the associated terminals, turnbuckles, fittings, and fastenings. These components typically do not fail without some sign of impending failure. The warning signs are rust, corrosion, distortion, and cracks—tiny microcracks at first, almost undetectable. When cracks are large enough to be obvious to the casual observer, they are very advanced and dangerous. The same is true for rust, corrosion, and distorted or misshapen fittings.

On chainplates, look for cracks on the inside of the bend. Damage to the gelcoat around the chainplate is often another early warning sign. On turnbuckles, check for rust on the threads inside the body and cracks in the body itself. Signs of trouble on terminal fittings are rust, broken strands where the wire cable enters the fitting, and cracks in the body. Pay particular attention to the fittings at the lower ends of shrouds and stays—these are the most vulnerable. On metal masts and booms, watch out where cleats, tangs, pad eyes, and winches of dissimilar metals are installed. Also keep an eye on welds and the areas around rivets and fastenings. Be aware of how blocks and masthead sheaves are working. Feel for lack of smoothness; listen for strange noises, screeches, and squeals.

This kind of checking is something that should be ongoing. When you're hanging out at the mooring or doing chores around the boat, just take a look around. If you're reluctant to go up the mast, consider hiring a rigger. It will be well worth the cost.

If you lay your boat up for the winter, wash everything thoroughly with freshwater—inside the mast and out, the mast heel, and the mast cap. Be conscious of flushing out all the salt crystal deposits in the corners and crevices. Let everything dry thoroughly, get a coat of protective wax (boat or auto) on the spars, and don't store the rig with stainless rigging laying against the aluminum spars.

Abbreviations and Symbols

Ω	Ohms (unit of electrical resistance)
⇔, ⇒, ⇐	direction of a chemical reaction
°C	degrees Celsius (centigrade)
°F	degrees Fahrenheit
μm	micron (micrometer)
<	less than
>	greater than
°C	degrees Celsius (centigrade)
°F	degrees Fahrenheit
μA	microampere
μm/yr.	microns per year
A	ampere
A/m²	ampere per square meter
ABS	acrylonitrile-butadiene-styrene
ABS	American Bureau of Shipping
ABYC	American Boat and Yacht Council
AC	alternating current
Ag	silver
Ag/AgCl	silver–silver chloride reference electrode
Ah	amp-hour
AISI	American Iron and Steel Institute
Al	aluminum
Al_2O_3	aluminum oxide (alumina)
ANSI	American National Standards Institute
AOD	argon-oxygen decarburization
API	American Petroleum Institute
Ar	argon
ASM	ASM International (formerly the American Society for Metals)
ASME	American Society of Mechanical Engineers
ASTM	American Society for Testing and Materials
at.%	atomic percent
atm	atmospheres (pressure)
avdp	avoirdupois
AWG	American Wire Gauge
AWS	American Welding Society
Be	beryllium
C	carbon
Ca	calcium
Cd	cadmium
CDA	Copper Development Association
CE	CE mark (European Community, a European standards group akin to UL in the U.S.)
CF	corrosion fatigue
Cl	chlorine
cm	centimeter
Cor-Ten	a weathering steel developed by the U.S. Steel Group of USX Corp.
CP	cathodic protection
cpm	cycles per minute
cps	cycles per second

CPVC	chlorinated polyvinyl chloride
Cr	chromium
Cu	copper
CuO	copper oxide
DC	direct current
E	exponential; together with the positive or negative member that follows, indicates the number and direction of decimal places to move the decimal point
e^-	electron
EC	European Community
EPA	Environmental Protection Agency
F	fluorine
Fe	iron
Fe_2O_3	ferric oxide (rust)
Fe_3O_4	magnetite
FRP	fiber-reinforced plastic
ft.	foot
g	gram
g/m²/d	grams per square meter per day
gal.	gallon
GMAW	gas metal arc welding
GPM	gallons per minute
GRP	glass-reinforced plastic (fiberglass)
GTAW	gas tungsten arc welding
H	hydrogen
HAZ	heat-affected zone
He	helium
HEC	hydrogen embrittlement cracking
H_2O_2	hydrogen peroxide
H_2O	water
HSLA	high-strength, low-alloy (steel)
Hz	hertz, a unit of frequency
I or i	current
ICCP	impressed current cathodic protection
ID	inside diameter
IGA	intergranular attack
in.	inch
ISO	International Organization for Standardization
K	potassium
kg	kilogram
kPa	kilopascal
kpsi	1000 lb. per square inch
kW	kilowatt
L	liter
lb.	pound
lb.-f	pounds-force
Li	lithium
LMC	liquid metal cracking
m	meter
m²	square meter

m/s	meters per second
mA	milliampere
max.	maximum
mg	milligram
Mg	magnesium
mi.	mile
mi./h	miles per hour
MIC	microbiologically influenced corrosion
MIL	military
mil	1/1000 of an inch
mils/yr.	mils per year
MIL-STD	military standard
min	minimum or minute
mL	milliliter
mm	millimeter (10^{-3} meter)
mm/yr.	millimeters per year
Mn	manganese
Mo	molybdenum
MPa	megapascal
MSD	marine sanitation device
MTI	Materials Technology Institute (of the Chemical Process Industry)
mV	millivolt
MW	megawatt
N	newton or nitrogen
Na	sodium
NACE	National Association of Corrosion Engineers
NaCl	sodium chloride
NaOH	sodium hydroxide
Ne	neon
Ni	nickel
NiDI	Nickel Development Institute
No.	number
O_2	oxygen
O/B	outboard
OD	outside diameter
OSHA	Occupational Safety and Health Administration
oz.	ounce
P	phosphorus
Pa	pascal
PB	polybutylene
Pb	lead
PE	polyethylene
PEEK	polyetherether-ketone
PET	polyethylene-terephthalate
PEX	polyethylene, cross-linked
pH	negative logarithm of hydrogen ion activity (measure of acidity)

PP	polypropylene
ppb	parts per billion
ppm	parts per million
ppt	parts per thousand
psi	pounds per square inch
pt.	pint
PTFE	polytetrafluoroethylene
PU	polyurethane
PVC	polyvinyl chloride
PVD	physical vapor deposition
PVDC	polyvinylidene chloride
PVDF	polyvinylidene fluoride
R	electrical resistance
RF	radio frequency
RH	relative humidity
rms	root mean square
s	second
S	sulfur
SAE	Society of Automotive Engineers
SAW	submerged arc welding
SCC	stress-corrosion cracking
SCE	saturated calomel electrode
SHE	standard hydrogen electrode
SI	Système International d'Unités (International System of Units)
SiO_2	silica
SMAW	shielded metal arc welding
Sn	tin
SNAME	Society of Naval Architects and Marine Engineers
SRB	sulfate-reducing bacteria
SSB	single side band
t	time
TBT	tributyl tin
TBTO	tributyl tin-oxide
Ti	titanium
UHF	ultrahigh frequency
UHMWPE	ultrahigh molecular weight (polyethylene)
UL	Underwriter Laboratories
UNS	Unified Numbering System
UTS	ultimate tensile strength
UV	ultraviolet
V	voltage
VHF	very high frequency
W	watt
yd.	yard
yr.	year
Z	electrical impedance
Zn	zinc

APPENDIX 2

Conversion Factors

Scientific notation is used for the numbers in the tables.

E −0X = move the decimal point X places to the left

E +0X = move the decimal point X places to the right

E +00 = retain the decimal point as is

To convert from	To	Multiply by	Conversely by
Area			
Square centimeters (cm²)	circular mils	1.974 E +05	5.067 E −06
	circular mm	1.273 E +02	7.854 E −03
	ft.²	1.076 E −03	9.290 E +02
	in.²	1.550 E −01	6.452 E +00
	m²	1.000 E −04	1.000 E +04
	mils²	1.550 E +05	6.452 E −06
	mm²	1.000 E +02	1.000 E −02
Square feet (ft.²)	cm²	9.290 E +02	1.076 E −03
	in.²	1.440 E +02	6.944 E −03
	m²	9.290 E −02	1.076 E +01
	mm²	9.290 E +04	1.076 E −05
	cm²	9.290 E +02	1.076 E −03
	in.²	1.440 E +02	6.944 E −03
	m²	9.290 E −02	1.076 E +01
	mm²	9.290 E +04	1.076 E −05
Square inches (in.²)	circular mils	1.273 E +06	7.854 E −07
	cm²	6.452 E +00	1.550 E −01
	dm²	6.452 E −02	1.550 E +01
	ft.²	6.940 E −03	1.441 E +02
	m²	6.450 E −04	1.550 E +03
	mils²	1.000 E +06	1.000 E −06
	mm²	6.452 E +02	1.550 E −03
Square meters (m²)	cm²	1.000 E +04	1.000 E −04
	ft.²	1.076 E +01	9.290 E −02
	in.²	1.550 E +03	6.452 E −04
	mm²	1.000 E +06	1.000 E −06
Square millimeters (mm²)	circular mils	1.974 E +03	5.067 E −04
	circular mm	1.273 E +00	7.854 E −01
	cm²	1.000 E −02	1.000 E +02
	in.²	1.550 E −03	6.452 E +02
	m²	1.000 E −06	1.000 E +06
Square mils (mils²)	circular mils	1.273 E +00	7.855 E −01
	cm²	6.452 E −06	1.550 E +05
	in.²	1.000 E −06	1.000 E +06
	mm²	6.450 E −04	1.550 E +03
Corrosion Rate*			
Grams per square meter per day (g/m²/d)	μm/yr.	3.650 E +02/d	2.740 E −03d
	in./yr.	1.440 E −02/d	6.944 E +01d
	mdd	1.000 E +01	1.000 E −01
	mils/yr.	1.440 E +01/d	6.944 E −02d
	mm/yr.	3.650 E −01/d	2.740 E +00d

To convert from	To	Multiply by	Conversely by
Inches per year (in./yr.)	µm/yr	2.540 E +04	3.937 E −05
	g/m²/d	6.960 E +01*d*	1.440 E −02/*d*
	mdd	6.960 E +02*d*	1.437 E−03/*d*
	mils/yr.	1.000 E +03	1.000 E −03
	mm/yr.	2.540 E +01	3.937 E −02
Micrometers (microns) per year (µm/yr.)	g/m²/d	2.740 E −03*d*	3.650 E +02/*d*
	in./yr.	3.940 E −05	2.538 E +04
	mdd	2.740 E −02*d*	3.650 E +01/*d*
	mils/yr.	3.940 E −02	2.540 E +01
	mm/yr.	1.000 E −03	1.000 E +03
Milligrams per square decimeter per day (mdd)	µm/yr.	3.650 E +01/*d*	2.740 E −02*d*
	g/m²/d	1.000 E −01	1.000 E +01
	in./yr.	1.440 E −03/*d*	6.960 E +02*d*
	mils/yr.	1.440 E +00*d*	6.960 E −01*d*
	mm/yr.	3.650 E −02/*d*	2.740 E +01*d*
Millimeters per year (mm/yr.)	µm/yr.	1.000 E +03	1.000 E −03
	g/m²/d	2.740 E +00*d*	3.650 E −01/*d*
	in./yr.	3.940 E −02	2.540 E +01
	mdd	2.740 E +01*d*	3.650 E −02/*d*
	mils/yr.	3.940 E +01	2.540 E −02
Mils per year (mils/yr.)	µm/yr.	2.540 E +01	3.940 E −02
	mdd	6.960 E −01*d*	1.440 E +00/*d*
	mm/yr.	2.540 E −02	3.973 E +01
	g/m²/d	6.960 E −02*d*	1.440 E +01/*d*
	in./yr.	1.000 E −03	1.000 E +03

*d = metal density in grams per cubic centimeter

Electrical

To convert from	To	Multiply by	Conversely by
Amperes (A)	µA	1.000 E +06	1.000 E −06
	mA	1.000 E +03	1.000 E −03
Amperes per square foot (A/ft.²)	A/m²	1.076 E +01	9.294 E −02
Amperes per square inch (A/in.²)	A/cm²	1.550 E −01	6.452 E +00
	A/m²	1.550 E +03	6.452 E −04
	A/mm²	1.550 E −03	6.452 E +02
Amperes per square meter (A/m²)	A/cm²	1.000 E −04	1.000 E +04
	A/in.²	6.452 E −04	1.550 E +03
Microamperes (µA)	A	1.000 E −06	1.000 E +06
	mA	1.000 E −03	1.000 E +03
Microfarads (µF)	F	1.000 E −06	1.000 E +06
Milliamperes (mA)	µA	1.000 E +03	1.000 E −03
	A	1.000 E −03	1.000 E +03
Millivolts (mV)	V	1.000 E −03	1.000 E +03
Ohms	kilohms	1.000 E −03	1.000 E +03
	megohms	1.000 E −06	1.000 E +06
	microhms	1.000 E +06	1.000 E −06
Volts (V)	µV	1.000 E +06	1.000 E −06
	mV	1.000 E +03	1.000 E −03

Flow Rate

To convert from	To	Multiply by	Conversely by
Cubic feet per hour (ft.³/h)	L/min	4.719 E −01	2.119 E +00
	cm³/s	7.866 E +00	1.271 E −01
	ft.³/min	1.670 E −02	5.988 E +01
	gal. (US)/h	7.481 E +00	1.337 E −01
	L/h	2.832 E +01	3.531 E −02
Cubic feet per minute (ft.³/min)	L/min	2.831 E +01	3.532 E −02
	cm³/s	4.720 E +02	2.119 E −03
	ft³/h	6.000 E +01	1.667 E −02
	gal. (US)/min	7.481 E +00	1.337 E −01
	gal. (US)/s	1.247 E −01	8.019 E +00
	L/s	4.720 E −01	2.119 E +00
	m³/s	4.720 E −04	2.119 E +03

To convert from	To	Multiply by	Conversely by
Cubic feet per second (ft.³/s)	cm³/s	2.832 E +04	3.537 E −05
	gal. (US)/min	4.488 E +02	2.228 E −03
	L/min	1.699 E +03	5.886 E −04
	L/s	2.832 E +01	3.531 E −02
	m³/s	2.832 E −02	3.581 E +01
Cubic inches per minute (in.³/min)	m³/s	2.731 E −07	3.668 E +06
	gal. (US)/min	2.642 E +02	3.785 E −03
	gal. (Brit)/min	2.200 E +02	4.546 E −03
	L/min	1.000 E +03	1.000 E −03
Gallons (British) per hour (gal. (Brit)/h)	m³/min	7.577 E −05	1.320 E +04
Gallons (British) per second (gal. (Brit)/s)	cm³/s	4.546 E +03	2.200 E −04
Gallons (US) per hour (gal. (US)/h)	ft.³/h	1.337 E −01	7.481 E +00
	L/h	3.785 E +00	2.642 E −01
	m³/min	6.309 E −05	1.585 E +04
Gallons (US) per minute (gal. (US)/min)	ft.³/hr	8.021 E +00	1.247 E −01
	ft.³/s	2.228 E −03	4.488 E +02
	L/s	6.309 E −02	1.585 E +01
Gallons (US) per second (gal. (US)/s)	cm³/s	3.785 E +03	2.642 E −04
	ft.³/min	8.021 E +00	1.247 E −01
	L/min	2.271 E +02	4.403 E −03
Gallons per hour (gal./h)	L/min	6.309 E −02	1.585 E +01
Gallons per minute (gal./min)	L/min	3.785 E +00	2.642 E −01
Liters per minute (L/min)	ft.³/min	3.532 E −02	2.831 E +01
	ft.³/s	5.886 E −04	1.699 E +03
	gal. (US)/min	2.642 E −01	3.785 E +00
	gal. (US)/s	4.403 E −03	2.271 E +02
Liters per second (L/s)	ft.³/min	2.119 E +00	4.719 E −01
	ft.³/s	3.530 E −02	2.833 E +01
	gal. (Brit)/min	1.320 E +02	7.576 E −03
	gal. (Brit)/s	2.200 E −01	4.454 E +00
	gal. (US)/min	1.585 E +01	6.309 E −02
	gal. (US)/s	2.642 E −01	3.785 E +00
Length			
Angstroms (Å)	μm	1.000 E −04	1.000 E +04
	cm	1.000 E −08	1.000 E +08
	in.	3.937 E −09	2.540 E +08
	mm	1.000 E −07	1.000 E +07
Centimeters (cm)	in	3.937 E −01	2.540 E +00
	μm	1.000 E +04	1.000 E −04
	Å	1.000 E +08	1.000 E −08
	ft.	3.281 E −02	3.048 E +01
	m	1.000 E −02	1.000 E +02
	mil	3.937 E +02	2.540 E −03
	mm	1.000 E +01	1.000 E −01
Feet (ft.)	cm	3.048 E +01	3.281 E −02
	in.	1.200 E +01	8.333 E −02
	m	3.048 E −01	3.281 E +00
	mm	3.048 E +02	3.281 E −03
Inches (in.)	Å	2.540 E +08	3.937 E −09
	cm	2.540 E +00	3.937 E −01
	ft.	8.333 E −02	1.200 E +01
	m	2.540 E −02	3.937 E +01
	mils	1.000 E +03	1.000 E −03
	mm	2.540 E +01	3.937 E −02
Meters (m)	cm	1.000 E +02	1.000 E −02
	ft.	3.281 E +00	3.048 E −01
	in.	3.937 E +01	2.540 E −02

To convert from	To	Multiply by	Conversely by
	mil	3.937 E +04	2.540 E −05
	mm	1.000 E +03	1.000 E −03
Micrometers *also Microns* (μm)	Å	1.000 E +04	1.000 E −04
	cm	1.000 E −04	1.000 E +04
	in.	3.937 E −05	2.538 E +04
	mils	3.937 E −02	2.540 E +01
	mm	1.000 E −03	1.000 E +03
Millimeters (mm)	μm	1.000 E +03	1.000 E −03
	Å	1.000 E +07	1.000 E −07
	cm	1.000 E −01	1.000 E +01
	ft.	3.281 E −03	3.048 E +02
	in.	3.937 E −02	2.540 E +01
	m	1.000 E −03	1.000 E +03
	mils	3.937 E +01	2.540 E −02
Mils (mil)	μm	2.540 E +01	3.937 E −02
	ft.	8.333 E −05	1.200 E +04
	in.	1.000 E −03	1.000 E +03
	mm	2.540 E −02	3.937 E +01
Mass			
Grams (g)	grains	1.543 E +01	6.480 E −02
	kg	1.000 E −03	1.000 E +03
	lb. (avdp)	2.205 E −03	4.535 E +02
	oz. (avdp)	3.527 E −02	2.835 E +01
Kilograms (kg)	g	1.000 E +03	1.000 E −03
	grains	1.542 E +04	6.485 E −05
	lb. (avdp)	2.205 E +00	4.536 E −01
	oz.(avdp)	3.527 E +01	2.835 E −02
Pounds (avdp) (lb.)	g	4.536 E +02	2.205 E −03
	grain	7.000 E +03	1.429 E −04
	kg	4.536 E −01	2.205 E +00
	oz. (avdp)	1.600 E +01	6.250 E −02
	kg	4.536 E −01	2.205 E +00
Milligrams (mg)	g	1.000 E −03	1.000 E +03
	grains	1.543 E −02	6.481 E +01
	kg	1.000 E −06	1.000 E +06
	lb. (avdp)	2.205 E −06	4.535 E +05
	oz. (avdp)	3.527 E −05	2.835 E +04
Ounces (avdp) (oz.)	g	2.835 E +01	3.527 E −02
	grains	4.375 E +02	2.286 E −03
	lb. (avdp)	6.250 E −02	1.600 E +01
Parts per Million (ppm)			
ppm	g/L	1.000 E −03	1.000 E +03
	grains/gal. (Brit)	7.016 E −02	1.425 E +01
	grains/gal. (US)	5.842 E −02	1.712 E +01
	lb./million gal.	8.345 E +00	1.198 E −01
	percent	1.000 E −04	1.000 E +04
Temperature			
°Fahrenheit (°F)	°C	5/9 (°F − 32)	9/5 °C + 32
°Celsius (°C)	°F	9/5 °C + 32	5/9 (°F − 32)
Volume			
Ounces, British fluid (oz., Brit flu)	cm³	2.841 E +01	3.521 E −02
	gal. (Brit flu)	6.250 E −03	1.600 E +02
	in.³	1.734 E +00	5.767 E − 01
	oz. (US flu)	9.610 E −01	1.041 E +00
Ounces, U.S. fluid (oz., US flu)	cm³	2.957 E +01	3.381 E −02
	cup	1.250 E −01	8.000 E +00

To convert from	To	Multiply by	Conversely by
	gal. (US flu)	7.810 E −03	1.280 E +02
	in.^{3}	1.805 E +00	5.541 E −01
	L	2.957 E −02	3.382 E +01
	m^3	2.957 E −05	3.381 E +04
	oz. (Brit flu)	1.041 E +00	9.608 E −01
	pt. (US flu)	6.250 E −02	1.600 E +01
	qt.(US flu)	3.120 E −02	3.205 E +01
	tablespoon	2.000 E +00	5.000 E −01
	teaspoon	6.000 E +00	1.667 E −01
Pints, British fluid (pt., Brit flu)	cm^3	5.683 E +02	1.760 E −03
	gal. (Brit)	1.250 E −01	8.000 E +00
	L	5.683 E −01	1.760 E +00
	oz. (Brit, flu)	2.000 E +01	5.000 E −02
	pt. (US, flu)	1.201 E +00	8.327 E −01
	qt. (Brit)	5.000 E −01	2.000 E +00
Pints, US fluid (pt., US flu)	cm^3	4.732 E +03	2.113 E −04
	ft.^{3}	1.671 E −02	5.984 E +01
	in.^{3}	2.888 E +01	3.463 E −02
	m^3	4.732 E −04	2.113 E +03
	cup	2.000 E +00	5.000 E −01
	gal. (US, liq.)	1.250 E −01	8.000 E +00
	L	4.732 E −01	2.113 E +00
	oz. (US, flu)	1.600 E +01	6.250 E −02
	pt. (Brit)	8.327 E −01	1.201 E +00
Quarts, British (qt., Brit)	cm^3	1.137 E +03	8.799 E −04
	in.^{3}	6.936 E +01	1.442 E −02
	gal. (Brit)	2.500 E −01	4.000 E +00
	gal. (US)	3.002 E −01	3.331 E +00
	L	1.137 E +00	8.799 E −01
	qt. (US, liq)	1.201 E +00	8.327 E −01
Quarts, US flu (qt., US flu)	cm^3	9.464 E +02	1.057 E −03
	ft.^{3}	3.340 E −02	2.994 E +01
	in.	5.775 E +01	1.732 E −02
	m^3	9.464 E −04	1.057 E +03
	gal. (US)	2.500 E −01	4.000 E +00
	L	9.464 E −01	1.057 E +00
	oz. (US, flu)	3.200 E +01	3.125 E −02
	pt. (US, liq)	2.000 E +00	5.000 E −01
	qt. (Brit)	8.327 E −01	1.207 E +00
Gallons, British (gal., Brit)	cm^3	4.546 E +03	2.200 E −04
	ft.^{3}	1.065 E −01	6.231 E +00
	in.^{3}	2.774 E +02	3.605 E −03
	gal. (US, liq)	1.201 E +00	8.327 E −01
	L	4.456 E +00	2.244 E −01
	oz. (Brit, flu)	1.600 E +02	6.250 E −03
	oz. (US, flu)	1.537 E +02	6.505 E −03
Gallons, US fluid (gal., US flu)	cm^3	3.785 E +03	2.642 E −04
	ft.^{3}	1.337 E −01	7.481 E +00
	m^3	3.785 E −03	2.642 E +02
	gal. (Brit)	8.327 E −01	1.207 E +00
	L	3.785 E +00	2.642 E −01
	oz. (US, flu)	1.280 E +02	7.873 E −03
	pt. (US, liq)	8.000 E +00	1.250 E −01
	qt. (US, liq)	4.000 E +00	2.500 E −01

Quantity, Size, and Placement of Zinc Anodes

Method 1. *Using a Silver/Silver-Chloride (Ag/AgCl) Reference Electrode*

This is the procedure recommended by the American Boat and Yacht Council in Standard E-2. It is an empirical method and is based on a trial-and-adjust procedure. It is the simplest and most appropriate for smaller craft on which a single zinc anode is adequate. A DC voltmeter—preferably a high impedance digital multimeter (DMM) capable of measuring voltages in the 300 millivolt range—and a silver/silver-chloride reference electrode are required. Typically, the reference electrode is on one end of a long test lead and is hung over the side of the boat in close proximity to the fitting to be tested. The other end of the test lead consists of a terminal and is retained inside the boat. The procedure is as follows:

1. Place the reference electrode (silver/silver chloride) in the water near the fitting or component that you want to protect; for example, the prop and shaft.
2. Measure the voltage by placing the negative test lead from the DMM to the reference electrode terminal and the positive (red) test lead from the meter to the fitting or component to be protected (i.e., the prop shaft) inside the boat. It may be necessary to extend the leads. Make sure you've got good contact with the metal.
3. Take note of the meter reading. For example, the reading should be in the range of −270 to −340 millivolts for a manganese prop on a naval bronze shaft. *(The actual readings are effected by such factors as salinity, temperature, and degree of pollution, so expect some variation.)*
4. Now place the sacrificial zinc anode in the water and electrically connect it to the metal fitting that is to be protected (the prop shaft). Allow some time for the metals to polarize, 12 to 24 hours.
5. Take note of the meter reading. If the zinc anode is large enough to protect the prop and shaft, the meter will read approximately 200 millivolts more negative than the previous reading, which in this case would be −470 to −540 millivolts.

If the anode is adequate, install it permanently and wire it up. Periodic measurements will tell you when you need to replace the anode. Keep in mind, though, that unless you have painted or otherwise covered the mounting surface of the trial zinc, you will have more zinc exposed than will be exposed when the zinc is mounted, so some allowance must be made for this.

In general, a meter reading for a protected fitting should be between 200 to 400 millivolts more negative than the potential listed in the galvanic series (table 4-1, page 21). Less than 200 millivolts indicates that the fitting is not protected and is corroding. Greater than 400 millivolts indicates that the fitting is overprotected.

Method 2. *Wood and Fiberglass Hulls*

This method is based on the fact that the principle factors in determining the amount of zinc required are the propeller, propeller shaft, rudder, and rudder post. It is recommended by Dave Gerr in his book, *The Elements of Boat Strength,* published by International Marine.

Vessels are divided into four basic cases according to the length of prop shaft exposed and the materials from which the rudder and rudder post are made. Figure A3-1 indicates the weight in pounds of the required zinc anodes for any propeller diameter from 10 to 24 inches (254 to 610 mm). Figure A3-2 covers propeller diameters from 24 to 60 inches (610 mm to 1.52 m).

The four cases of vessels are as follows:

- Case 1. Single prop vessel, centerline propeller, no exposed shaft, wood, or fiberglass rudder assembly.
- Case 2. Same as Case 1 except: bronze or stainless rudder, rudder post, and fittings.
- Case 3. Long exposed shaft and strut assembly, wood or fiberglass rudder assembly.
- Case 4. Same as Case 3 except: bronze or stainless rudder, rudder post, and fittings.

By referring to the appropriate graph, you can select the correct weight of anode for the boat. Let's assume your boat is a 38-foot (11.6 m) fiberglass boat with a 28-inch-diameter (710 mm) prop, no exposed shaft, and a stainless rudder, rudder post, and fittings. This would be a Case 2 boat. Now look at figure A3-2 and find the 28-inch prop diameter on the vertical axis. Follow this

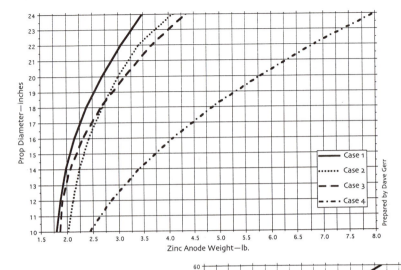

Fig A3-1. Anode Weight vs. Prop Diameter—10–24 inches—Bronze and/or Stainless Shaft Assemblies on Nonmetal Hulls

Prepared by Dave Gerr

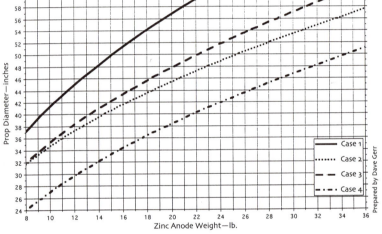

Fig A3-2. Anode Weight vs. Prop Diameter—24–60 Inches—Bronze and/or Stainless Shaft Assemblies on Nonmetal Hulls

Prepared by Dave Gerr

line across the graph to the point where it intersects the Case 2 line, then drop straight down to the horizontal axis and read the weight of the zinc anode required—13 pounds (5.9 kg). Since zinc weighs about 4 ounces per cubic inch, this would be equivalent to a plate zinc measuring about 12 by 6 by 0.75 inches (305 by 152 by 20 mm). A good installation would be two zincs, each half this size, on either side of the underbody midway between the stern bearing and the rudder post.

Method 3. Metal Hulls

On wood and fiberglass boats, the zincs are there to protect the fittings from each other. They must be *bonded* (electrically connected) to each other and to the fittings they are protecting. On metal boats, the zincs are there to protect the hull *from the fittings* (and from itself). Here, zincs mounted directly on the hull are bonded to each other and to the hull, which they are protecting from the

hull itself. However, if the fittings are made of a metal that is dissimilar to the metal of the hull, they must be isolated from the hull. Therefore, *the fittings are not being protected by the hull zincs*. If the fittings are to be protected, they must be connected to each other and to a completely separate and isolated zinc of their own.

Steel

The amount of zinc required to protect a steel hull depends on the amount of wetted surface on the hull. To compute the amount of wetted surface, the popularly accepted method is the one used by M. G. Duff, a British corrosion company. The formula is

wetted surface of hull (sq. ft.) = waterline length (ft.) x [waterline beam (ft.) + draft (ft.)] x hull-shape factor

The specific hull-shape factor depends on the type of vessel. I like the breakdown Dave Gerr uses for the multiplication factor, as excerpted from *The Elements of Boat Strength*.

- Cargo vessels, tankers, dredges, and very heavy, full-bodied craft—1.2.
- Tugs, trawlers, ferries, heavy motor cruisers, full-bodied sailboats—1.0
- Medium displacement, medium and light lobster boats, average sailboats—0.75
- Very light craft without external keels—0.50

To determine the amount of zinc required in pounds, calculate the total wetted surface in square feet, multiply it by the appropriate factor (i.e., 0.75 for an average sailboat), and then divide this number by 16.75. See figure A3-3. This should be distributed about the underbody of the hull, both fore and aft and on both sides.

The zincs are bonded directly to the hull. They can be welded on or through-bolted, but the best way to mount zincs to a steel hull is to weld bolts of the appropriate size to the hull, slip a zinc over each bolt, *put on a lockwasher* and nut, and turn it down—easy installation and easy replacement. You can even do a replacement while the boat's in the water.

Aluminum

For aluminum hulls the method for determining the required amount of zinc is essentially the same as for steel. That is, you first determine the wetted surface area of the hull, but then you divide this number by 220. This gives you the total *surface area* of zinc required. See figure A3-4.

Here again, a system of mounting that makes installation and replacement easier suggests a bolt-on arrangement. However, with an aluminum hull, some reinforcement of the hull, such as a backing plate, is recommended. This can be welded to the hull and drilled and tapped for the anode mounting bolts. Fasteners should be passivated stainless steel (304 or 316) bolts.

Anode Placement

The zinc anodes are placed as follows:

- Two zincs: One each port and starboard about 33 percent of the waterline forward of the transom.
- Four zincs: Two each port and starboard—two about 20 percent of the waterline forward of the transom, two about 53 percent forward of the transom.
- Six zincs: Three each port and starboard—two about 16 percent of waterline forward of the transom, two about 42 percent forward of the transom, and two about 66 percent forward of the transom.
- Eight zincs: Four each port and starboard—two about 14 percent of waterline forward of the transom, two about 16 percent forward of the transom and on or near the keel, two about 42 percent forward of the transom, and two about 66 percent forward of the transom.

In general, the zincs should be placed approximately midway between the keel and the waterline at the turn of the bilge, except as noted above.

Fig A3-3. Steel Hull Zinc Anode Weight

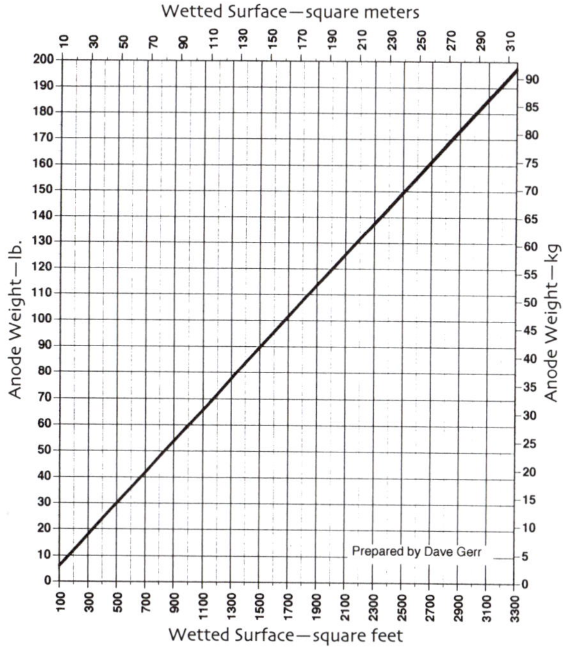

Fig A3-4. Aluminum-Hull Zinc Anode Surface Area

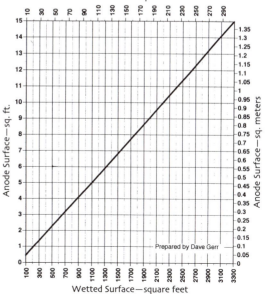

 APPENDIX 4

UNS Equivalent Grades

Note: There is frequently more than one equivalent designation and/or specification for a given UNS. We have attempted to select those most appropriate for use in boats and boating. This list is not exhaustive; other grades and specifications may exist whose compositions are sufficiently similar to be useful in a given application. Military specifications exist for many of these grades but have not been included here.

UNS	Country	Designation	Description	Specifications
Carbon Steel				
G10080	Australia	K1008, R1008, S1008	Bar	AS 1442, AS 1443
		C1008, R1008	Plate	AS 1446
	France	XC6, XC6FF, XC10		AFNOR, AFNOR NF A35-551
	Germany	1.0318, 1.0322, 1.0331, 1.0337		DIN
		1.0320, 1.0332, 1.0359, RRSt23	Plate, Sheet	DIN, DIN 1614 Part 1
		1.0347, RRSt13	Sheet	DIN 1623 Part 1
	International	HR3	Sheet, Hot-Rolled, 3 mm	ISO 3573
		CR3	Sheet, Hot-Rolled	ISO 3574
	Italy	3CD8		UNI 5598
		CB10FU		UNI 7356-74
	Japan	STKM11A (11A)		JIS G3445
		S9CK	Bar, Wire, Rod	JIS G40541
	Sweden	1142-42	Plate, Cold-Rolled, 3 mm	SIS 141142
		1146-32, 1146-42	Sheet, Cold-Rolled, 3 mm	SIS 141146
		1147-32, 1147-42	Sheet, Cold-Rolled, 3 mm	SIS 141147
		1311-00	Bar, Plate, As Rolled, 40 mm	SIS 141311E
	UK	3CR	Sheet, Strip, Cold-Rolled	BS 1449
		3CS	Sheet, Strip	BS 1449
		3HR	Sheet. Strip, Hot-Rolled	BS 1449
		3HS	Sheet, Strip	BS 1449
	USA	1008	Bar	ASTM A29
		1008	Sheet, Cold-Rolled	ASTM A619, ASTM A620
		1008	Sheet, Strip, Hot-Rolled	ASTM A621, ASTM A622
		1008	Plate	ASTM A830
G10120	Australia	K1012, S1012		AS 1442, AS 1443
	Canada	C1012		DEF STAN 95-1/1
	France	AF37C12		AFNOR NF A33-101
		XC12		AFNOR NF A35-551
	Germany	1.0439, RSD13		DIN
	Japan	S12C	Bar, Wire, Rod	JIS G4051
	Sweden	1332		SS 14
	UK	12CS, 12HS	Sheet, Strip	BS 1449
		141-360	Plate	BS 1501
	USA	1012	Bar	ASTM A29

230

UNS	Country	Designation	Description	Specifications
	USA	1012 1012	Sheet, Strip, Hot-Rolled Plate	ASTM A635 ASTM A830
G10150	Australia	S1015 S1015	Bar Plate	AS 1443 AS 1446
	France	XC15 XC18	Bar	AFNOR AFNOR NF A35-552
	Germany	1.1135, 1.1148, 1.0401, C15 1.1140, 1.1141	Bar, Cold-Drawn	DIN DIN 1652 DIN 17210
	International	C15, C15e, C15ea	Bar	ISO 683-XVIII
	Italy	C16 CB15 C15		UNI 5331, 7065 UNI 7356 UNI 7846
	Japan	F15Ck, S15c, S15Ck		JIS G4051
	Sweden	1370		SS 14
	USA	1015 1015 1015	Bar Multiple Forms Plate	ASTM A29 ASTM A659 ASTM A830
G10160	Australia	K1016, S1016 K1016, S1016	Bar Bar	AS 1442, AS 1443 AS 1443
	Canada	C1016		DEF STAN 95-1/1
	Germany	1.0419, 1.142, GS-Ck16 1.0467, 1.0468		DIN DIN 17115
	Japan	S17C	Bar	JIS G4051
	Sweden	1370, 2101		SS 14
	UK	080M15, 170H15, 173H16		BS 970
	USA	1016 1016 1016	Sheet, Strip, Hot-Rolled Multiple Forms Plate	ASTM A635 ASTM A659 ASTM A830
G10170	France	XC15 XC18 XC18S	Bar, As Rolled, 16 mm Plate, Hot-Rolled, 16 mm	AFNOR AFNOR NF A35-552 AFNOR NF A35-554
	Germany	1.1141		DIN 17210
	Japan	S15C		JIS
	Sweden	1370-00		SIS 141370
	UK	17CS, 17HS 17	Plate, Sheet, Cold-Rolled/ Annealed	BS 1449 BS 1449 Part 1
	USA	1017 1017 1017	Bar Sheet, Hot-Rolled Plate	ASTM A29 ASTM A635, A659 ASTM A830
G10180	Australia	K1018		AS 1442, 1443
	France	AF42C20		AFNOR NF A33-101
	Germany	1.0453, C16.8		DIN
	UK	080A17		BS 970
	USA	1018 1018 1018	Bar Sheet, Hot-Rolled Plate	ASTM A29 ASTM A635, A659 ASTM A830
G10190	France	XC18S	Plate, Hot-Rolled, 16 mm	AFNOR NF A35-554
	USA	1019 1019 1019	Bar Sheet, Hot-Rolled Plate	ASTM A29 ASTM A635 ASTM A830
G10200	Australia	CS1020, K1020, S1020 CS1020, S1020	Bar Plate	AS 1442 AS 1446
	France	CC20 XC18		AFNOR AFNOR NF A35-551,

UNS	Country	Designation	Description	Specifications
	France			AFNOR NF A35-552, AFNOR NF NF A35-566
		C20, XC18S		AFNOR NF A35-553, AFNOR NF A35-554
	Germany	1.0427, 1.0460, C22.3, C22.8		DIN
		1.0402, 1.1149, 1.1151, C22		DIN 17200
	International	C20, C20e, C20ea, C20eb		ISO 683-XVIII
	Italy	3CD20, ICD20		UNI 5598
		C20		UNI 5949-67
		C21		UNI 6922
		CB20FF		UNI 7356
	Japan	S20C, S20CK		JIS G4051
	Sweden	1450-00, 1450-01		SIS 141450
	UK	040A20, 060A20		BS 970
	USA	1020		ASTM A29
		1020	Sheet, Hot-Rolled	ASTM A635, A659
G10210	Australia	S1021		AS1442, 1443
	France	21B3		AFNOR NF A35-551, 552, 553, 557, 566
	Italy	C20		UNI 5332, 7065
	Japan	S22C		JIS G4051
	UK	070M20, 080M20		BS 970
	USA	1021	Bar	ASTM A29
		1021	Sheet, Strip, Hot-Rolled	ASTM A635, A659
G10220	Australia	K1022	Bar	AS 1442, 1443
			Plate	AS 1446
	Canada	A	Pipe	CSA B193
	France	20MB4		AFNOR
		20MB5		AFNOR NF A35-551, 556, 557, 566
		20MB5	Bar	AFNOR NF A35-552, 553
	Germany	1.0432, 1.1133, 1.1138		DIN
	Italy	20Mn4		UNI 5771
	Japan	SMnC21	Bar, Rod	JIS G4106
	UK	9		BS 3111
		170H20		BS 970
		120M19	Bar, Rod	BS 970 Part 1
	USA	1022	Bar	ASTM A29
		1022	Sheet, Cold-Rolled	ASTM A568
		1022	Sheet, Hot-Rolled	ASTM A635
		1022	Plate	ASTM A830
G10230	Europe	C22BKD		EURONORM 119/IV
	France	XC25	Bar, Quenched/Tempered	AFNOR NF A35-552
	Germany	1.1150, CK22.8		DIN
		1.1152, Cq22		DIN 1654
		1.1151, CK22		DIN 17200
	Italy	C20		UNI 5332, UNI 7065
	Japan	S20C, S20CK		JIS G4051
	UK	22	Sheet, Plate, Cold-Rolled/Annealed	BS 1449 Part 1
		050A22, 060A22, 080A22	Bar, Rod	BS 970
	USA	1023	Bar	ASTM A29
		1023	Sheet, Hot-Rolled & Cold-Rolled	ASTM A568
		M1023	Bar	ASTM A575
		1023	Sheet, Hot-Rolled	ASTM A659

UNS	Country	Designation	Description	Specifications
	USA	1023	Plate	ASTM A830
		1023	Bar	SAE J1397
G10250	Australia	S1025	Bar	AS 1442, AS1443
		CS1025	Plate	AS 1446
	Canada	C1025		DEF STAN 95-1/1
	France	XC25	Bar, Quenched/Tempered	AFNOR A35-552, 566
	Germany	1.1160, 22MN6		DIN
		1.0415, D25-2		DIN 17140
		1.0406, 1.1158, C25, Ck25		DIN 17200
	International	C25	Bar, Forged, Quenched/ Tempered	ISO 683-I
		C25	Bar, Forged, Quenched/ Tempered, Cold-Rolled	ISO 683-I
		C25, C25e, C25ea, C25eb	Bar, Wire, Normalized	ISO 683/18
	Italy	1CD25, 3CD25		UNI 5598
	Japan	S25C, S28C	Bar, Wire, Rod	JIS G4051
	UK	CEW-103	Tube, Annealed or Normalized	BS 1717
		CEW-104	Tube, As Drawn, As Drawn/Tempered	BS 1717
		C1025	Bar	DEF STAN 95-1-1
	USA	1025	Bar	ASTM A29
		1025	Wire, Rod	ASTM A510
		1025	Sheet, Hot or Cold-Rolled	ASTM A568
		M1025	Bar	ASTM A575
		1025	Plate	ASTM A830
G10260	Australia	K1026	Bar	AS 1442, AS 1443
	Germany	1.1155, 1.1156, GS-CK24, GS-CK25		DIN
	Italy	C25		UNI 7845, 7847
	UK	CDS-103	Tube, Annealed or Normalized	BS 1717
		070M26, 080A25, 080A27		BS 970
	USA	1026	Multiple Forms	ASTM A273
		1026	Bar	ASTM A29
		1026	Wire, Rod	ASTM A510
		1026	Tube, Cold-Drawn	ASTM A512
		1026	Tube	ASTM A519
		1026	Sheet, Hot or Cold-Rolled	ASTM A568
		1026	Plate	ASTM A83D
G10290	Australia	230R, 230S, 410C	Bar, As Rolled	AS 1302
	Canada	X46, X52		CSA B193
	France	CC28		AFNOR
		AF50C30		AFNOR NF A33-101
	Germany	1.056, 28Mn4		DIN
	Japan	STKM15A(15A)		JIS G3445
		STKM15C(15C)	Tube	JIS G3445
		S28C	Bar, Wire, Rod	JIS G4051
	UK	060A27	Bar, Rod	BS 970 Part 1
		080a27		BS 970 Part 1
	USA	1029	Bar	ASTM A29
		1029	Wire, Rod	ASTM A510
		1029	Multiple Forms	SAE J412
G10300	Australia	CS1030, K1030, S1030	Bar	AS 1442
		CS1030, K1030, S1030	Bar	AS 1443
	Europe	C30BKD		EURONORM 119/IV
	France	XC32		AFNOR NF A35-552, 553
	Germany	1.1811, G-31Mn4		DIN

UNS	Country	Designation	Description	Specifications
	Germany	1.1172, Cq35 1.0530, D30-2, 1.0528, 1.1178, 1.1179, C30, Ck30, Cm30	Rod	DIN 1654 DIN 17200

	International	C30, C30e, C30ea, C30eb
		C30
		
		C30ea
		
		C30eb
			Bar, Wire—Normalized
			Bar Forged Quenched/
			    Tempered
			Bar, Rod Quenched/
			    Tempered
			Bar, Rod Quenched/
			    Tempered 16 mm diam.
				ISO 683/18
				ISO R683-1
				
				ISO R683-III
				
				ISO R683-III

	Italy	CB35 C30 3CD30 C30 Fe50-3 C30, C31 C30		UNI UNI 5332 UNI 5598 UNI 6403 UNI 6783 UNI 7065 UNI 7845, 7847
	Japan	S30C	Bar, Wire, Rod	JIS G4051

	UK	30CS, 30HS
		060A30, 080A30(En5B),
		    080M30(En5),
		    080M30(En5),
		    080M30(En5)
			Bar, Rod, Forged	BS 1449
				BS 970

	USA	1030 1030 1030 1030 1030 1030 1030 1030 1030	Bar Wire, Rod Tube Cold-Drawn Tube Sheet, Hot or Cold-Rolled Bar, Hot-Worked Plate Bar Multiple Forms	ASTM A29 ASTM A510 ASTM A512 ASTM A513, A519 ASTM A568 ASTM A576 ASTM A830 SAE J1397 SAE J412
G10350	Australia	K1035, S1035 K1035, S1035 S1035	Bar Bar Plate	AS 1442 AS 1443 AS 1446
	Europe	C35BKD, C35KD		EURONORM 119/IV
	France	XC35, XC38TS AF55C35 XC38	 Plate, Hot-Rolled, Normalized, 16 mm diam.	AFNOR AFNOR NF A33-101 AFNOR NF A35-554
	Germany	1.1173, Ck34 1.1172, Cq35 1.0516, D35-2 1.0501, 1.1180, 1.1181, C35, Ck35, Cm35	 Wire, Rod	DIN DIN 1654 DIN 17140 DIN 17200
	International	C35 2 C35, C35E C35 C35E C35EA, C35EB	Tube—Hot-Finished Bar, Wire—Normalized Bar—Forged Quenched/ Tempered	ISO 2937 ISO 2938 ISO 683/18 ISO 683/I ISO 683/I ISO 683/III
	Italy	C33 1CD35, 3CD35 C35, C36 CB35 C36		UNI 5333 UNI 5598 UNI 7065 UNI 7356 UNI 7847
	Japan	S35C	Bar, Wire, Rod	JIS G4051
	Sweden	1550-00 1550-06	Bar, Plate, Sheet, Tube Bar, Cold-Worked	SIS 141550 SIS 141550

UNS	Country	Designation	Description	Specifications
	Sweden		40 mm diam.	
		1572-00, 1572-03, 1572-04, 1572-05, 1572-08	Bar, Forged, Plate, Sheet	SIS 141572
	UK	CDS105/106	Tube—Annealed	BS 1717
		060A35, 080A32(En5C), 080A35(En8A)		BS 970
		080A37, 080M36	Bar, Rod, Forged	BS 970 Part 1
	USA	1035	Multiple Forms	AMS 5080, 5082
		1035	Bar	ASTM A29, A576
		1035	Wire, Rod	ASTM A510
		1035	Tube	ASTM A513, A519
		1035	Sheet—Hot or Cold-Rolled	ASTM A568
		1035	Plate	ASTM A827, A830
G10370	Australia	K1037	Bar	AS 1442, AS 1443
	Canada	X46, X52		CSA B193
	Germany	1.0520, 1.0561, 31Mn4, 36Mn4		DIN
	Japan	S35C	Bar, Wire, Rod	JIS G4051
	UK	10		BS 3111
		170H36		BS 970
		080M36	Bar, Rod, Forged	BS 970
	USA	1037	Bar	ASTM A29
		1037	Wire, Rod	ASTM A 510
		1037	Sheet—Hot or Cold-Rolled	ASTM A568
		1037	Bar—Hot-Worked	ASTM A 576
		1037	Plate	ASTM A830
		1037	Bar	SAE J1397
		1037	Multiple Forms	SAE J412
G10380	Australia	K1038, XK1038	Bar	AS 1442, AS 1443
	France	XC38TS		AFNOR
		XC38Hi	Bar, Rod, Wire	AFNOR NF A335-552
	Germany	1.1176, Ck38		DIIN
	USA	1038	Bar	ASTM A29
		1038	Bar, Rod, Forged	ASTM A304. SAE J1268
		1038	Wire, Rod	ASTM A510
		1038	Sheet—Hot or Cold-Rolled	ASTM A568
		1038	Bar—Hot-Worked	ASTM A 576
		1038	Plate	ASTM A830
		1038	Multiple Forms	SAE J412
G10390	Australia	K10390	Bar	AS 1442, AS 1443
	France	40M5		AFNOR
		XC38H2		AFNOR NF A35-552
		38MB5		AFNOR NF A35-553, 556
		35M5, 38MB5,XC38H2, XC42,XC42TS		AFNOR NF A35-557
	Germany	1.1157, 1.1190, 40Mn4, Ck42Al		DIN
	UK	150M36		BS
		CDS 105/106		BS
		40G		BS 4543
		060A40, 080A40(En8C), 080M40(En8), 170HA1		BS 970
		120M36		BS 970 Part 1
	USA	1039	Bar	ASTM A29. SAE J1397
		1039	Wire, Rod	ASTM A510
		1039	Sheet—Hot or Cold-Rolled	ASTM A568
		1039	Bar, Hot-Worked	ASTM A576
		1039	Plate	ASTM A830
		1039	Multiple Forms	SAE J412
G10400	Australia	CS1040, K1040, S1040	Bar	AS 1442, As 1443
		K1040, S1040	Plate	AS 1446

UNS	Country	Designation	Description	Specifications
	France	AF60C40		AFNOT NF A33-101
		F60	Forging	AFNOR NF A36-612
	Germany	1.0541, D40-2		DIN 17140
		1.0511, 1.1186, 1.1189, C40, Ck40, Cm40		DIN 17200
	International	C40, C40e, C40ea, C40eb 3	Bar, Wire—Normalized	ISO 683-XVIII
			Bar, Rod	ISO 683/III
		C40, C40e	Bar—Quenched/Tempered	ISO R683-1
		C40, C40e	Forging—Quenched/Tempered, Cold-Rolled	ISO R683-1
		C40ea, C40eb	Bar—Quenched/Tempered 16 mm diam.	ISO R683-III
	Italy	3CD40, ICD40		UNI 5598
		Fe60-3		UNI 6783
		C40		UNI 6923, 7065
		C41		UNI 7065
	Japan	S40C	Bar, Wire, Rod	JIS G4051
	UK	1287, 25.93		BS
		40CS, 40Hs		BS 1449
		Class 1 Grade C, Class 8		BS3146
		060A40, 080A40(En8C)	Bar, Rod, Forging	BS 970
		080M40(En8)		BS 970
	USA	1040	Bar—Cold-Formed	ASTM A108
		1040	Bar	ASTM A29
		1040		ASTM A449
		1040	Wire, Rod	ASTM A510
		1040	Tube	ASTM A519
		1040	Sheet—Hot-Rolled, Cold-Rolled	ASTM A568
		1040	Plate	ASTM A827, A830
		1040	Bar	SAE J1397
		1040		SAE J412
G10420	Australia	K1042, K6, S6		AS 1442, AS 1443
		K1042, S1042		AS 1446
	France	CC45, XC42, XC42TS		AFNOR
		XC42H1		AFNOR NF A35-552
		C40, XC45		AFNOR NF A35-553
		XC48		AFNOR NF A35-554
	Germany	GS-Ck45		DIN
		1.0517, D45-2		DIN 17140
		1.1191, Ck45		DIN 17200
	Japan	S43C, S45C	Bar, Wire, Rod	JIS G4051
	Sweden	1672		SS 14
	UK	060A42, 080A42(En8D)	Bar, Rod, Forging	BS 970
	USA	1042	Bar	ASTM A29
		1042	Wire, Rod	ASTM A510
		1042	Sheet—Hot-Rolled, Cold-Rolled	ASTM A568
		1042	Bar—Hot-Rolled, Cold-Rolled	ASTM A576
		1042	Plate	ASTM A830
		1042	Bar	SAE J1397
		1042		SAE J412
G10430	France	CC45		AFNOR
		XC42H2		AFNOR NF A35-552
	Germany	C45		DIN
		1.0558, GS-60.3		DIN 1681
		1.0503		DIN 17200
	Italy	C45		UNI 3545
		C43		UNI 7847

UNS	Country	Designation	Description	Specifications
	Japan	S43C, S45C		JIS G 4051
	Sweden	1650-00, 1650-01, 1650-06		SIS 141650
	UK	060A42, 080A42(En8D), 080M46		BS 970
		060A47, 080H46, 080M40		BS 970 Part 1
	USA	1043	Bar	ASTM A29, SAE J1397
		1043	Wire, Rod	ASTM A510
		1043	Sheet—Hot-Rolled, Cold-Rolled	ASTM A568
		1043	Bar—Hot-Worked	ASTM A576
		1043	Plate	ASTM A830
		1043		SAE J412
G10440	Germany	1.0517, D45-2		DIN 17140
	USA	1044	Bar	ASTM A29, SAE J1397
		1044	Rod, Wire	ASTM A510
		M1040	Bar	ASTM A575
		1044	Bar—Hot-Worked	ASTM A576
		1044		SAE J412
G10450	Australia	K1045, S1045	Bar	AS 1442, AS 1443
		K1045, S1045	Plate	AS 1446
	Europe	C45KD		EURONORM 119/IV
	France	XC42, XC42TS, XC48TS		AFNOR
		AF65C45		AFNOR NF A35-101
		XC48H1		AFNOR NF A35-552
		XC45		AFNOR NF A35-553
		XC48		AFNOR NF A35-554
	Germany	1.1192, Cq45		DIN 1654
		1.0503, 1.1191, 1.1201, C45		DIN 17200
		Ck45, Cm45, GS-Ck45, 1.1193, Cf45		DIN 17212
		Cq45		DIN LW
		1.1184, CK46		DIN WW
	International	C45ea	Bar, Rod—Quenched/ Tempered 16 mm	ISO 683-III
		C45, C45e, C45ea, C45eb 3	Bar, Wire—Normalized	ISO 683-XVIII ISO 683/XII
		C45, C45e, C45ea, C45eb	Bar, Forging—Quenched/ Tempered	ISO R683-1
	Italy	C45		UNI 3545, 5332, 7065, 7845, 7874
		3cd45, icd45		UNI 7065, 7847
		C46		UNI 7065, 7847
	Japan	S45C, S48C	Bar, Rod, Wire	JIS G 4051
		SCC5		JIS G5111
	Sweden	1664, 1672-01	Bar, Plate, Sheet, Forging— As Rolled	SIS 141672
		1672-03, 1672-04	Bar, Plate, Sheet, Forging—Quenched/ Tempered	SIS 141672
		1672	Bar, Plate, Sheet, Forging	SIS 141672, SS 14
	UK	060A47, 080A47, 080M46		BS 970 Part 1
		080M46	Bar, Rod, Forging—Cold- Drawn from Hot-Rolled	BS 970 Part 1
		080M46	Bar, Rod, Forging—Hard Tempered 4 in.	BS 970 Part 1
		080M46	Bar, Rod, Forging— Normalized 2.5 in.	BS 970 Part 1
	USA	1045	Bar—Cold-Formed	ASTM A108
		1045 Class 3	Forging	ASTM A266
		1045	Bar	ASTM A29

UNS	Country	Designation	Description	Specifications
	USA	1045M	Bar	ASTM A304, SAE J1268, J1397
		1045	Bar—Stress Relieved, Cold-Drawn 20-30 mm	ASTM A311
		1045	Wire, Rod	ASTM A510
		1045	Tube	ASTM A519
		1045	Sheet—Hot-Rolled, Cold-Rolled	ASTM A568
		1045	Bar—Hot-Worked	ASTM A576
		1045	Strip—Cold-Rolled	ASTM A662
		1045	Plate	ASTM A827, A830
G10460	Australia	K1046	Bar	AS 1442, AS 1443
	France	45MATS		AFNOR
		XC48H2, XC48H1, XC48TS		AFNOT NF A35-552
	Germany	1.0519, 1.1159, 45Mn41, GS-46Mn4, 1.0503, C45		DIN DIN 17200
	UK	AWS		BS 3100
		080M46	Bar, Rod, Forging—Cold-Drawn from Hot-Rolled	BS 970 Part 1
		080M46	Bar, Rod, Forging—Hard Tempering	BS 970 Part 1
		080M46	Bar, Rod, Forging—Normalized 2.5 in.	BS 970 Part 1
	USA	1046	Bar	ASTM A29
		1046	Wire, Rod	ASTM A510
		1046	Sheet—Hot-Rolled, Cold-Rolled	ASTM A568
		1046	Bar—Hot-Worked	ASTM A576
		1046	Plate	ASTM A830
		1046	Bar	SAE J1397
		1046		SAE J412
G10490	France	XC48TS		AFNOR
		XC48H1		AFNOR NF A35-552
		XC48		AFNOR NF A35-554
	Italy	C48	Bar	UNI 6403
		C48		UNI 7847
	Japan	S50CM	Strip—Cold-Rolled	JIS G3311
		STKM17A (17A), STKM17C(17C)		JIS G3445
	UK	060A47, 080A47, 080M46		BS 970
	USA	1049	Bar	ASTM A29, SAE J1397
		1049	Wire, Rod	ASTM A510
		1049	Sheet—Hot-Rolled, Cold-Rolled	ASTM A568
		1049	Bar—Hot-Worked	ASTM A576
		1049	Plate	ASTM A830
		1049		SAE J412
G10500	Australia	K1050, S1050	Bar	AS 1442, AS 1443
	France	XC50	Strip—Cold-Rolled	AFNOR NF A35-553
		F70	Forging	AFNOR NF A35-612
	Germany	Ck53, D53-3		DIN
		1.0540, 1.1206, 1.1210, 1.1241, C50, Ck50, Cm50		DIN 17200
		1.1213	Multiple Forms—Quenched/Tempered 16 mm	DIN 17212
		Cl53	Multiple Forms—Quenched/Tempered 16 mm	DIN 17212
		1.1219, Cf54		DIN 17230

UNS	Country	Designation	Description	Specifications
	International	C50, C50e, C50ea, C50eb	Bar, Wire—Normalized	ISO 683-XVIII
		C50, C50e	Bar, Forging—Quenched/ Tempered	ISO R683-1
		C50, C50e	Bar, Forging—Quenched/ Tempered, Cold-Rolled	ISO R683-1
		C50ea, C50eb	Bar, Rod—Quenched/ Tempered 16 mm diam.	ISO R683-III
	Italy	C50		UNI 5332
		3CD50, ICD50		UNI 5598
		Fe70-3		UNI 6783
		C50, C51		UNI 7065
		C50		UNI 7845, 7847
		C53		UNI 7847
	Japan	S50CM	Bar, Wire, Rod	JIS G4051
		S53C, S55C		JIS G4051
	Sweden	1674-00	Bar, Forging, Plate, Sheet	SIS 141674
		1674-01	Bar, Forging, Plate, Sheet—Normalized	SIS 141674
		1674-03, 1674-04, 1674-05	Bar, Forging, Plate, Sheet— Quenched/ Tempered	SIS 141674
		1674-08	Bar, Forging, Plate, Sheet— As Rolled, As Forged	SIS 141674
		1674		SS 14
	UK	50CS, 50HS		BS 1549
		060A47, 060A52, 080A52(En43C)	Bar, Rod, Forging	BS 970 Part 1
		080M50(En43A)	Bar, Rod, Forging—Cold-Drawn from Normalized	BS 970 Part 1
		080M50(En43A)	Bar, Rod, Forging—Hard Tempered 4 in.	BS 970 Part 1
		080M50(En43A)	Bar, Rod, Forging— Normalized 6 in. diam.	BS 970 Part 1
	USA	1050	Bar, Rod, Plate, Sheet, Forging	AMS 5085
		1050	Bar—Cold-Formed	ASTM A108
		1050	Bar	ASTM A29, SAE J1397
		1050	Bar—Cold-Drawn, Stress Relieved 20—30 mm	ASTM A311
		1050	Wire, Rod	ASTM A510
		1050	Tube	ASTM A519
		1050	Sheet—Hot-Rolled, Cold-Rolled	ASTM A568
		1050	Bar—Hot-Worked	ASTM A576
		1050	Strip—Cold-Rolled	ASTM A682
		1050	Plate	ASTM A827, A830
		1050		SAE J412
G10530	Australia	K1050, S1050	Bar	AS 1442, AS 1443
	France	52M4TS		AFNOR
		XC54	Strip—Cold-Rolled	AFNOR NF A35-553
	Germany	1.1210, Ck53		DIN
		1.1213, Cf53		DIN 17230
		1.1219. Cf54		DIN 17230
	Italy	C53		UNI 7847
	Japan	S53C		JIS G4051
	Sweden	1674		SS 14

UNS	Country	Designation	Description	Specifications
	UK	080A52(En43C)		BS 970
		080A52	Bar, Rod, Forgings	BS 970 Part 1
		080A52	Bar, Forgings	BS 970 Part 1
	USA	1053	Bar	ASTM A29
		1053	Wire, Rod	ASTM A510
		1053	Bar—Hot-Worked	ASTM A576
		1053	Forgings, Bar—Hot-Rolled, Cold-Rolled	SAE J403
		1053		SAE J412
G10550	Australia	K1055	Bar	AS 1442, AS 1443
	France	XC55		AFNOR
		AF70C55		AFNOR NF A33-101
		XC55H1	Bar, Rod, Wire	AFNOR NF A35-552
		XC55H2	Bar, Rod, Wire	AFNOR NF A35-552
		XC54	Strip—Cold-Rolled	AFNOR NF A35-553
	Germany	1.1202		DIN
		1.121	Strip—Quenched/Tempered	DIN
		1.121	Strip—Solution Annealed	DIN
		1.1220, 1.1820, C55W		DIN
		Ck53, D53-3	Strip	DIN
		D53-3		DIN
		1.0518, D55-2		DIN 17140
		1.0535, 1.1203	Multiple Forms—Quenched/Tempered 16 mm	DIN 17200
		1.1209	Multiple Forms—Normalized 16/100 mm diam.	DIN 17200
		C55	Multiple Forms—Normalized 16/40 mm diam.	DIN 17200
		CM55		DIN 17200
		1.1213, Cf53	Multiple Forms—Quenched/Tempered 16 mm diam.	DIN 17212
		1.1219, Cf54		DIN 17230
	International	C55, C55e, C55ea, C55eb	Bar, Wire—Normalized	ISO 683 XVIII
		C55, C55e, C55ea, C55eb	Bar, Forging—Quenched/Tempered	ISO R683-I
		C55, C55e, C55ea, C55eb	Bar, Forging—Quenched/Tempered, Cold-Rolled	ISO R683-I
		C55ea, C55eb	Bar, Rod—Quenched/Tempered—16 mm diam.	ISO R683-III
	Italy	3CD55		UNI 5598
		C55, C56		UNI 7065
		C55		UNI 7845
		C53, C55		UNI 7847
	Japan	S53C	Bar, Wire , Rod	JIS G4051
	Sweden	1655-00	Bar, Forging, Plate, Sheet, Tube—As Rolled	SIS 141655
		1655-01	Bar, Forging, Plate, Sheet, Tube—Normalized	SIS 141655
		1655		SS 14
	UK	En45	Wire, Rod	BS 1429
		AWS		BS 3100
		060A57	Bar, Rod, Forging	BS 970 Part 1
		070M55	Bar, Rod, Forging—Cold-Drawn from Normalized	BS 970 Part 1
		070M55	Bar, Rod, Forging—	BS 970 Part 1

UNS	Country	Designation	Description	Specifications
	UK		Hardened, Tempered 4 in.	
		070M55	Bar, Rod, Forging—Normalized 2.5 in.	BS 970 Part 1
		080A52(En43C)	Bar, Rod, Forging	BS 970 Part 1
		080A57	Bar, Rod, Forging	BS 970 Part 1
	USA	1055	Bar	ASTM A29, SAE J1397
		1055	Wire, Rod	ASTM A510
		1055	Sheet—Hot-Rolled, Cold-Rolled	ASTM A568
		1055	Bar—Hot-Worked	ASTM A576
		1055	Strip—Cold-Rolled	ASTM A682
		1055	Plate	ASTM A830
		1055	Various	SAE J403
G10600	Australia	K1060	Bar	AS 1442, AS 1443
	France	CC55		AFNOR
		XC60		AFNOR NF A35-553
	Germany	1.0642, 60Mn3		DIN
		1.0601, C60		DIN 1652
		1.1221, 1.1223	Multiple Forms—Quenched/Tempered 16 mm	DIN 17200
		Ck60	Normalized 16/40 mm diam.	DIN 17200
		Cm60	Normalized 16/100 mm diam.	DIN 17200
		1.174		DIN 17350
		C60W		DIN 17350
	International	C60, C60e, C60ea, C60eb	Bar, Wire—Normalized	ISO 683 XVIII
		C60, C60e	Bar, Forging—Quenched/Tempered	ISO R683-I
		C60, C60e	Bar, Forging—Quenched/Tempered, Cold-Rolled	ISO R683-I
		C60ea, C60eb	Bar, Rod—Quenched/Tempered 16 mm	ISO R683-III
	Italy	C60		UNI 3545, 7064, 7065, 7845, 7874
		3CD60		UNI 5598
		C61		UNI 7065
	Japan	S60CM	Strip	AS 1442
		S58C	Plate	AS 1446
	Sweden	1678		SS 14
	UK	En45A	Wire, Rod	BS 1429
		60CS, 60HS		BS 1449
		050A57, 080A57	Bar, Rod, Forging	BS 970 Part 1
	USA	1060	Bar	ASTM A29, SAE J1397
		1060	Wire, Rod	ASTM A510
		1060	Sheet—Hot-Rolled, Cold-Rolled	ASTM A568
		1060	Bar—Hot-Worked	ASTM A576
		1060	Strip—Cold-Rolled	ASTM A682
		1060	Plate	ASTM A830
		1060		SAE J412
G10700	Australia	K1070, S1070	Bar	AS 1442
		S1070	Plate	AS 1446
	France	XC70		AFNOR
		XC68		AFNOR NF A35-553
	Germany	1.0643, 70Mn3		DIN
		1.0603, 1.1231, C67, Ck67		DIN 17222
	Italy	C70		UNI 3545, 7064, 7065, 7845, 7874

UNS	Country	Designation	Description	Specifications
	Japan	S70CM	Strip	JIS G3311
	Sweden	1770-00	Bar, Strip, Wire	SIS 141770
		1770-02	Bar, Strip, Wire	SIS 141770
		1770-03	Bar, Wire—Quenched/ Tempered 2.5 mm	SIS 141770
		1770, 1778		SS 14
	UK	70CS, 70HS		BS 1449
		080A72, 060A72	Bar, Rod, Forging	BS 970 Part 1
		070A72(En42)	Bar, Forging	BS 970 Part 5
	USA	1070	Bar	ASTM A29, SAE J1397
		1070	Rod, Wire	ASTM A510
		1070	Sheet—Hot-Rolled, Cold-Rolled	ASTM A568
		1070	Bar—Hot-Worked	ASTM A576
		1070	Strip—Cold-Rolled	ASTM A682
		1070	Plate	ASTM A830
G10780	France	XC80		AFNOR
		XC75		AFNOR NF A35-553
	Germany	1.1252, 1.1253, 1.1255, 1.1262, D75-3, D78-3, D80-3, D83-3		DIN
		1.0620, 1.0622, 1.0626, D78-2, D80-2, D83-2		DIN 17140
		1.1248, Ck75		DIN 17222
		1.1525, C80W1		DIN 17350
	Italy	3CD80		UNI 5598
	Japan	SUP3	Bar, Wire, Rod—Quenched/ Tempered	JIS G4801
	Sweden	1774	SS 14	
	UK	060A78	Bar, Rod, Forging	BS 970 Part 1
	USA	1078	Bar	ASTM A29, SAE J1397
		1078	Wire, Rod	ASTM A510
		1078	Sheet—Hot-Rolled, Cold-Rolled	ASTM A586
		1078	Bar—Hot-Worked	ASTM A576
		1078	Plate	ASTM A830
		1078	Various	SAE J403
G10800	Australia	K1082	Bar	AS 1442
	France	XC80		AFNOR
	Germany	1.1259, 1.1265, 80Mn4, D85-3		DIN
	Italy	3CD80, 3CD85		UNI 14778
	Sweden	1778-02	Strip—Annealed 2 mm	SIS 14778
		1778-04	Strip—Quenched 0.125 mm diam.	SIS 14778
	UK	80CS, 80HS		BS 1449
		060A78	Bar, Rod, Forging	BS 970 Part 1
	USA	1080	Bar	ASTM A29, SAE J1397
		1080	Wire, Rod	ASTM A510
		1080	Sheet—Hot-Rolled, Cold-Rolled	ASTM A568
		1080	Bar—Hot-Worked	ASTM A576
		1080	Strip—Cold-Rolled	ASTM A682
		1080	Plate	ASTM A830
		1080		SAE J412
G10840	Australia	K1084		AS 1446
	Germany	1.0647, 85Mn3		DIN
		1.1830, C85W		DIN 17350
	UK	En42D		BS 1429
		060A86		BS 970 Part 1
	USA	1084	Bar	ASTM A29, SAE J1397

UNS	Country	Designation	Description	Specifications
	USA	1084	Wire, Rod	ASTM A510
		1084	Sheet—Hot-Rolled, Cold-Rolled	ASTM A568
		1084	Bar—Hot-Worked	ASTM A576
		1084	Plate	ASTM A830
G10900	France	XC90	Strip	AFNOR NF A35-553
	Germany	1.1273, 1.1819		DIN
		90Mn4		DIN
	Italy	C90		UNI 3545, 7064, 7065, 7845, 7874
		3CD95		UNI 5598
	UK	95CS, 95HS		BS 1449
		060A96	Bar, Rod, Forging	BS 970 Part 1
		060A96	Bar, Forging	BS 970 Part 5
	USA	1090	Bar	ASTM A29, SAE J1397
		1090	Wire, Rod	ASTM A510
		1090	Sheet—Hot-Rolled, Cold-Rolled	ASTM A568
		1090	Bar—Hot-Worked	ASTM A576
		1090	Plate	ASTM A830
G10950	Australia	K1095	Bar	AS 1442
	Canada	C1095		DEF STAN 95-1/1
	France	XC100	Strip	AFNOR NF A35-553
	Germany	1.1275, 1.1282, 1.1291, 1.1645, C105W2, Ck100, D95S3, MK97		DIN
		1.0618, D95-2	Wire, Rod	DIN 17140
		1.1274, Ck101		DIN 17222
		1.1545, C105W1		DIN 17350
	Italy	C100		UNI 3545
		C100		UNI 7064
	Japan	SUP4	Bar, Wire, Rod—Quenched/Tempered	JIS G4801
	Sweden	1870-02	Strip—Annealed 2 mm diam.	SIS 141870
		1870-04	Strip—Quenched	SIS 141870
		1870		SS 14
	UK	En44B	Wire, Rod	BS 1429
		95CS, 95HS		BS 1449
		060A96, 060A99	Bar, Rod, Forging	BS 970 Part 1
		060A96	Bar, Forging	BS 970 Part 5
	USA	1095	Bar—Cold-Formed	ASTM A108
		1095	Bar	ASTM A29, SAE J1397
		1095	Wire, Rod	ASTM A510
		1095	Sheet—Hot-Rolled, Cold-Rolled	ASTM A568
		1095	Bar—Hot-Worked	ASTM A576
		1095	Strip—Cold-Rolled	ASTM A682
		1095	Plate	ASTM A830
		1095		SAE J412
Weathering Steels				
K11510	Germany	1.8962, 9CrNiCuP324		DIN
	USA	1	Plate, Sheet	ASTM A242, SAE 950D, SAE J410C
K11430	Germany	1.8962, 9CrNiCuP324		DIN
		1.8963, WTSt52; WTSt510-3		DIN 17119
	USA	3A		ASTM A502
		A	Bar, Plate, Sheet	ASTM A588
K12043	Germany	1.8962, 9CrNiCuP324		DIN
		1.8963, WTSt52; WTSt510-3		DIN 17119

UNS	Country	Designation	Description	Specifications
	USA	B	Bar, Plate, Sheet	ASTM A588
K11538	Germany	1.8962, 9CrNiCuP324		DIN
		1.8963, WTSt52; WTSt510-3		DIN 17119
	USA	C	Bar, Plate, Sheet	ASTM A588, SAE 950A, SAE J410c
K11552	Germany	1.8962, 9CrNiCuP324		DIN
		1.8963, WTSt52; WTSt510-3		DIN 17119
	USA	D		ASTM A588
Stainless Steel—Austenitic				
S20200	Canada	202	Sheet, Strip, Plate, Bar	CSA G110.3
		202	Sheet, Strip, Plate, Bar—Hot-Rolled, Annealed	CSA G110.6
	France	Z8CNM19.8	Sheet, Strip, Plate, Bar	AFNOR NF A35-583
	Germany	X12CrNiMn19.9	Sheet, Strip, Plate, bar	TGL 39672
	International	13	Sheet, Strip, Plate, Bar	COMECOM PC4-70
		A-3	Sheet, Strip, Bar—Solution Treated	ISO 683/13
	Japan	SUS202	Bar—Solution Annealed 180 mm diam.	JIS G4303
		SUS202	Plate Sheet—Hot-Rolled, Solution Annealed	JIS G4304
		SUS202	Plate Sheet—Cold-Rolled, Solution Annealed	JIS G4305
		SUS202	Strip—Hot-Rolled, Solution Annealed	JIS G4306
		SUS202	Strip—Cold-Rolled, Solution Annealed	JIS G4307
	UK	284516	Sheet, Strip, Plate	BS 1449
	USA	202	Plate, Sheet, Strip	ASTM A412
		202	Forging	ASTM A473
		202	Sheet, Strip, Plate, Bar	ASTM A666
		30202	Sheet, Strip, Plate, Bar	SAE J405
S30100	Australia	301	Sheet, Strip, Plate—Annealed 1.2 mm diam.	AS 1449
	Canada	301	Sheet, Strip, Plate—Hot-Rolled, Annealed	CSA G110.6
	France	Z12CN17.07	Bar 25 mm diam.	NF A35-572
		Z12CN17.07	Sheet, Strip, Plate	NF A35-573
		Z12CN17.07	Wire, Rod	NF A35-575
		Z12CN17.07	Plate	NF A35-209
	Germany	1.4310, X12CrNi177	Strip, Wire	DIN
	International	14	Sheet, Strip, Plate, Bar, Forging	ISO 683/13
	Italy	X12CrNi1707	Bar, Wire	UNI 6901-71
		X12CrNi1707	Sheet, Strip, Plate	UNI 8317-81
	Japan	SUS 301	Bar—Solution Annealed	JIS G4303
		SUS 301	Sheet, Plate—Hot-Rolled	JIS G4304
		SUS 301	Sheet, Plate—Hardened 0.4 mm	JIS G4305
		SUS 301	Sheet, Plate—Cold-Rolled, Solution Annealed	JIS G4305
		SUS 301	Strip—Hot-Rolled, Solution Annealed	JIS G4306
		SUS 301	Strip—Cold-Rolled, Solution Annealed	JIS G4307
		SUS 301-CSP	Strip—Cold-Rolled	JIS G4313
	Sweden	1331-02	Sheet, Strip, Bar, Wire,	SIS 142331

UNS	Country	Designation	Description	Specifications
	Sweden		Forging—Solution Annealed	
		2331-06	Wire—Cold-Drawn 8 mm	SIS 142331
		2331-11	Strip—Cold-Worked 2.5 mm diam.	SIS 142331
		2331-12	Strip—Cold-Worked 2 mm diam.	SIS 142331
		2331-14	Strip—Cold-Worked 2 mm diam.	SIS 142331
		2331-16	Strip	SIS 142331
		2331-17	Strip—Cold-Worked 2 mm diam.	SIS 142331
		2331-18	Strip—Cold-Worked 1.5 mm diam.	SIS 142331
		2331-19	Strip—Cold-Worked 1.4 mm diam.	SIS 142331
	UK	301S21	Sheet, Strip—Half-Hard	BS 1449
		301S21	Sheet, Strip—Solution Annealed 0.5/1 mm diam.	BS 1449
	USA	301	Plate, Sheet, Strip	ASTM A167
		301	Sheet, Strip, Plate, Bar	ASTM A177
		301	Tube	ASTM A554
		301	Sheet, Strip, Plate, Bar	ASTM A666
		30301	Sheet, Strip, Plate, Bar	SAE J405
S30200	Australia	302	Bar	AS 1449
		302	Sheet, Strip, Plate— Annealed 1.2 mm diam.	AS 1449
	Canada	302	Bar	CSA G110.3
		302	Sheet, Strip, Plate—Hot- Rolled, Annealed or Hot-Rolled, Quenched/ Tempered	CSA G110.6
		302	Sheet, Strip, Plate—Hot- Rolled, Cold-Rolled, Annealed, Quenched/ Tempered	CSA G110.9
	France	Z10CN18.09	Plate	AFNOR NF A35-209
		Z10CN18.09	Bar	AFNOR NF A35-572
		Z10CN18.09	Sheet, Strip, Plate—Cold- Rolled 5 mm diam.	AFNOR NF A35-573
		Z10CN18.09	Wire, Rod 60% Hard	AFNOR NF A35-575
	Germany	1.43	Sheet, Strip, Plate, Bar, Wire, Forging	DIN
		X10CrNi18.8	Sheet, Strip, Plate, Bar, Wire, Forging	DIN
		x10CrNi18.9	Sheet, Strip, Plate, Bar, Wire, Forging, Tube	TGL 7143
	International	14	Sheet, Strip, Plate, Bar, Tube, Forging	COMECOM PC4-70
		X10CrNi189E	Cold Head Ext.	ISO 4954
		12	Solution Treated	ISO 683/13
		X10CrNi188	Spring	ISO 6931
	Italy	X10CrNi1809	Bar, Wire	UNI 6901-71
		X10CrNi1809	Sheet, Strip, Plate	UNI 8317-81
	Japan	SUS302	Bar, Forging—Solution Annealed 180 mm diam.	JIS G4303
		SUS302	Sheet, Plate—Hot-Rolled, Solution Annealed	JIS G4304
		SUS302	Sheet, Plate—Cold-Rolled, Solution Annealed	JIS G4305
		SUS302	Strip—Hot-Rolled Solution	JIS G4306

UNS	Country	Designation	Description	Specifications
	Japan		Annealed	
		SUS302	Strip—Cold-Rolled Solution Annealed	JIS G4307
		SUS302	Wire, Rod	JIS G4308
	Sweden	2332-02	Sheet, Strip, Plate, Bar, Wire, Tube, Forging—Solution Annealed	SIS 142332
	UK	302S25	Sheet, Strip—Annealed	BS 1449
		302S31	Bar, Wire, Forging	BS 970
	USA	302		ASME SA240, SA479
		302	Plate, Sheet, Strip	ASTM A167, A240
		302	Bar, Shapes	ASTM A276
		302	Wire	ASTM A313, A368, A478, A492
		302	Bar	ASTM A314
		302	Forging	ASTM A473
		302	Wire, Bar, Shapes	ASTM A479
		302	Bar, Wire	ASTM A493
		302	Tube	ASTM A511
		302	Sheet, Strip, Plate, Bar	ASTM A666
S30215	Canada	302B	Bar	CSA G110.3
	Japan	SUS302B	Plate, Sheet—Hot-Rolled	JIS G 4304
		SUS302B	Plate, Sheet—Cold-Rolled	JIS G4305
		SUS302B	Strip, Hot-Rolled	JIS G4306
		SUS302B	Strip—Cold-Rolled	JIS G4307
	USA	302B	Plate, Sheet, Strip	ASTM A167
		302B	Bar, Shapes	ASTM A276
		302B	Bar for Forging	ASTM A314
		302B	Forging	ASTM A473
		302B	Wire	ASTM A580
		302B	Sheet, Plate, Bar	SAE J405
S30300	Australia	303	Bar	AS 1444
	Canada	303	Bar	CSA G110.3
	Germany	1.4305, X10CrNiS189	Bar	DIN
	International	17	Solution Treated	ISO 683/13
	Italy	X10CrNiS1809	Bar	UNI 6901-71
	Japan	SUS303	Bar—Solution Annealed 180 mm diam.	JIS G4303
		SUS303	Wire, Rod	JIS G4308
	Sweden	2346-02	Bar, Wire—Solution Annealed	SIS 142346
	UK	303S31	Bar	BS 970
		303S22	Bar, Rod	BS 1506
	USA	303		ASME SA194, SA 320
		303	Nuts	ASTM A194
		303	Bolting	ASTM A320
		303	Forging	ASTM A473
		303	Wire	ASTM A581
		303	Bar—Hot-Rolled, Cold-Formed	ASTM A582
		30303	Bar	SAE J405
S30323	Canada	303Se	Bar	CSA G110.3
	International	17a	Solution Treated	ISO 683/13
	Japan	SUS303Se	Bar—Solution Annealed 180 mm diam.	JIS G4303
		SUS303Se	Wire, Rod	JIS G4308
	UK	303S42	Wire	BS 1554
		303S42	Bar, Rod	BS 970
	USA	303Se		ASME SA194, SA320, SA340
		303Se	Nuts	ASTM A194

UNS	Country	Designation	Description	Specifications
	USA	303Se	Bar for Forging	ASTM A314
		303Se	Bolting	ASTM A320
		303Se	Forging	ASTM A473
		303Se	Wire	ASTM A581
		303Se	Bar—Hot-Rolled, Cold-Formed	ASTM A582
		30303Se	Bar, Wire	SAE J405
S30400	Australia	304	Bar	AS 1444
		304	Sheet, Plate, Strip	AS1449
	Canada	304	Bar	CSA G110.3
		304	Sheet, Strip, Plate	CSA G110.6
		304	Plate—Hot-Rolled, Annealed/Quenched/Tempered	CSA G110.9
	Europe	X6CrNi1810KD	Multiple Forms—Solution Annealed 15/63 mm diam.	EURONORM
	France	Z6CN18.09	Sheet, Strip, Plate	AFNOR NF A35-573
		Z6CN18.09	Bar	AFNOR NF A35-574
		Z6CN18.09	Bar, Wire, Rod	AFNOR NF A35-577
		Z6CN18.09	Sheet, Strip, Plate	AFNOR NF A36-206
		Z6CN18.09	Forging	AFNOR NF A36-607
	Germany	1.4301, X5CrNi1810	Sheet, Strip, Plate, Bar, Wire, Tube, Forging	DIN
		X5CrNi19.9	Sheet, Strip, Plate, Bar, Wire, Tube, Forging	TGL 39672
	International	15	Sheet, Strip, Plate, Bar, Wire, Tube, Forging	COMECOM PC4-70
		X5CRNi1810	Cold Head Ext.	ISO 4954
		11	Sheet, Plate, Bar—Solution Treated	ISO 683/13
	Italy	X5CrNi1810	Sheet, Strip, Plate, Bar, Wire, Forging	UNI 6901-71
	Japan	SUS304	Bar—Solution Annealed 18 mm diam.	JIS G4303
		SUS304	Plate, Sheet—Hot-Rolled—Solution Annealed	JIS G4304
		SUS304	Plate, Sheet—Cold-Rolled—Solution Annealed	JIS G4305
		SUS304	Strip—Hot-Rolled, Solution Annealed	JIS G4306
		SUS304	Strip—Cold-Rolled, Solution Annealed	JIS G4307
		SUS304	Wire, Rod	JIS G4308
		SUS304—CSP	Strip—Cold-Rolled	JIS G4313
	Sweden	2332	Sheet, Strip, Plate, Wire, Tube	SS14 2332
		2333	Sheet, Strip, Plate, Bar, Wire, Tube	SS14 2333
	UK	304S15	Sheet, Strip, Plate, Bar, Forging	BS 1449
		304S16	Sheet, Strip	BS 1449
		304S31	Sheet, Strip, Plate, Bar, Wire, Forging	BS 1449
		304S31	Sheet, Strip, Plate, Bar, Wire, Forging	BS 1502
		304S31	Sheet, Strip, Plate, Bar, Wire, Forging	BS 1503
		304S31	Sheet, Strip, Plate, Bar, Wire, Forging	BS 1506
		304S18	Tube, Pipe	BS 3605
		304S25	Tube, Pipe—Solution	BS 3605

UNS	Country	Designation	Description	Specifications
	UK		Annealed	
		304S15	Sheet, Strip, Plate, Bar, Forging	BS 970
		304S31	Sheet, Strip, Plate, Bar, Forging	BS 970
	USA	304		ASME SA182, SA194, SA213, SA240, SA249, SA312, SA 320, SA 359, SA376, SA403, SA 409, SA 430, SA 479, SA688
		304	Plate, Sheet, Strip	ASTM A167
		304	Bar, Forging	ASTM A182
		304	Bolting	ASTM A193
		304	Nuts	ASTM A194
		304	Tube	ASTM A213
		304	Sheet, Strip, Plate	ASTM A240
		304	Tube, Welded	ASTM A249
		304	Tube, Seamless Welded	ASTM A269, A270, A271
		304	Bar, Shapes	ASTM A276
S30430	Australia	302HQ	Wire, Rod	AS 1449
	France	Z6CNU1810	Wire, Rod	NF A35-575
	Germany	1.4567, X3CrNiCu189	Wire, Rod	DIN
	International	X3CrNiCu1893E	Cold Head Ext.	ISO 4954
	Japan	SUSXM7	Wire, Rod	JIS G4315
	UK	394S17	Wire	BS 3111
	USA	304Cu		AISI
		XM-7		ASTM A493
S30409	International	F48	Forging	ISO 2604-1
	Italy	X8CrNi1910	Bar	UNI 6901-71
		X8CrNi1910	Tube	UNI 6904-71
		X8CrNi1910	Sheet, Strip, Plate	UNI 8317-81
	Japan	SUSF304H	Forging—Solution Annealed 130 mm diam.	JIS G3214
		SUSF304HTP	Pipe—Solution Annealed 8 mm diam.	JIS G3459
		SUSF304HTB	Tube—Solution Annealed 8 mm diam.	JIS G3463
	UK	304S49		BS 1501
		304S551	Bar	BS 1502
		304S50		BS 1503
		304S59	Tube, Pipe	BS 5059
	USA	304H		ASME SA182, SA213, SA240, SA249, SA312, SA376, SA403, SA430, SA479
		304H	Bar, Forging	ASTM A182
		304H	Tube	ASTM A213
		304H	Sheet, Strip, Plate	ASTM A240
		304H	Tube, Welded	ASTM A249
		304H	Tube, Seamless	ASTM 271
		304H	Tube, Seamless Welded	ASTM A312
		304H	Pipe	ASTM A358, A403, A430
		304H	Pipe, Seamless	ASTM A376
		304H	Wire, Bar, Shapes	ASTM A479
S30403	Australia	304L	Bar	AS 1444
		304L	Sheet, Strip, Plate—Annealed 1.2 mm	AS 1449
	Canada	304L	Bar	CSA G110.3
		304L	Sheet, Strip, Plate—Hot-Rolled, Annealed or Hot-	CSA G110.6

UNS	Country	Designation	Description	Specifications
	Canada		Rolled, Quenched/ Tempered	
		304L	Sheet, Strip, Plate—Hot-Rolled, Cold-Rolled, Annealed, Quenched/ Tempered	CSA G110.9
	Europe	X2CrNi1810KD, X3CrNi1810KD	Wire, Rod—Solution Annealed 15/63 mm diam.	EURONORM 119-74V
	France	Z2CN18.10	Bar 25 mm diam.	AFNOR NF A35-572
		Z2CN18.10	Sheet, Strip, Plate—Cold-Rolled 5 mm diam.	AFNOR NF A35-573
		Z2CN18.10	Wire, Rod—60% Hard	AFNOR NF A35-575
	Germany	1.4306, X2CrNi1911	Sheet, Strip, Wire, Tube	DIN
	International	16	Sheet, Strip, Plate, Bar, Wire	COMECOM PC4-70
		X2CrNi1810E	Cold Head Ext.	ISO 4954
		10	Sheet, Plate, Bar,—Solution Treated	ISO 683/13
	Italy	X2CrNi1811	Bar	UNI 6901-71
		X2CrNi1811	Tube	UNI 6904-71
		X2CrNi1811	Bar, Rod	UNI 7500-75
		X2CrNi1811	Sheet, Strip, Plate	UNI 8317-81
	Japan	SUS304L	Tube	JIS G3447, G3463
		SUS304L	Pipe	JIS G3459
		SUS304L	Bar—Solution Annealed 180 mm diam.	JIS G4303
		SUS304L	Sheet, Plate—Hot-Rolled, Solution Annealed	JIS G4304
		SUS304L	Sheet, Plate Cold-Rolled, Solution Annealed	JIS G4305
		SUS304L	Strip—Hot-Rolled, Solution Annealed	JIS G4306
		SUS304L	Strip—Cold-Rolled, Solution Annealed	JIS G4307
		SUS304L	Wire, Rod	JIS G 4308
	UK	304S11	Sheet, Strip, Plate, Bar, Rod	BS 1449, 970
		304S12	Bar, Rod	BS 1501
		304S12	Cast	BS 1504
		304S22	Tubes, Pipe	BS 3605
	USA	304L	Sheet, Strip, Plate, Bar, Wire	AMS 5511, 5647
		304L		ASME SA182, SA213, SA240, SA249, SA312, SA403, SA479, SA688
		304L	Plate, Sheet, Strip	ASTM A167, A240
		304L	Bar, Forging	ASTM A182
		304L	Tube	ASTM A213, SA511, SA554
		304L	Tube, Welded	ASTM A249, A688
		304L	Tube, Seamless/Welded	ASTM A269, A312, A632
		304L	Bar	ASTM A276, A479
		304L	Pipe	ASTM A403
		304L	Forging	ASTM A473
		304L	Wire	ASTM A478, A580
S30453	Europe	X2CrNiN1810KW	Bar	EURONORM 114-74V
	France	Z2CN18.10AZ	Plate, Bar	NF A35-582
		Z2CN18.10AZ		NF A36-209
	Germany	1.4311	Plate, Bar	DIN
		X2CrNiN1810KW	Plate, Bar	DIN 17400
	International	10N	Solution Treated	ISO 683/13
	Italy	X2CrNiN1811	Plate, Bar	UNI 7500-75

UNS	Country	Designation	Description	Specifications
	Japan	SUS304LN	Bar	JIS G4303
		SUS304LN	Plate, Sheet—Hot-Rolled	JIS G4304
		SUS304LN	Plate, Sheet—Cold-Rolled	JIS G4305
		SUS304LN	Strip—Hot-Rolled	JIS G4306
		SUS304LN	Strip— Cold-Rolled	JIS G4307
	Sweden	2371	Plate, Bar	SS14 2371
	UK	304S62		BS 1501
		304S61		BS 1502
	USA	304LN	Bar, Shapes	ASTM A276
S30453	Europe	X3CrNiN1810KKW	Bar	EURONORM 114-74V
	France	Z2CN18.10AZ	Plate, Bar	NF A35-582
		Z2CN18.10AZ		NF A36-209
	Germany	1.4311	Plate, Bar	DIN
		X2CrNiN1810	Plate, Bar	DIN 17400
	International	10N	Solution Treated	ISO 683/13
	Italy	X2CrNiN1811	Plate, Bar	UNI 7500-75
	Japan	SUS304LN	Bar	JIS G4303
		SUS304LN	Plate, Sheet—Hot-Rolled	JIS G4304
		SUS304LN	Plate, Sheet—Cold-Rolled	JIS G4305
		SUS304LN	Strip—Hot-Rolled	JIS G4306
		SUS304LN	Strip—Cold-Rolled	JIS G4307
	Sweden	2371	Plate, Bar	SS14 2371
	UK	304S62		BS 1501
		304S61	Bar	BS 1502
	USA	304LN	Bar	ASTM A276
S30451	France	Z5CN18.09Az		NF A36-209
	Germany	X5CrNiN19.7	Sheet, Strip, Plate, Bar	TGL 7143
	Italy	X5CrNiN1810	Sheet, Strip, Plate, Bar	UNI 7500-75
	Japan	SUS304N1	Bar	JIS G4303
		SUS304N1	Plate, Sheet—Hot-Rolled	JIS G4304
		SUS304N1	Plate, Sheet—Cold-Rolled	JIS G4305
		SUS304N1	Strip—Hot-Rolled	JIS G4306
		SUS304N1	Strip—Cold-Rolled	JIS G4307
		SUS304N1	Wire, Rod	JIS G4308
	UK	304S65		BS 1501
		304S71	Bar	BS 1502
	USA	304N	Sheet, Strip, Plate, Bar	AMS 5511, 5647
		304N		ASME SA182, SA213, SA240, SA249, SA312, SA358, SA376, SA430, SA479
		304N	Bar, Forging	ASTM A182
		304N	Tube	ASTM A213
		304N	Sheet, Strip, Plate	ASTM A240
		304N	Tube, Welded	ASTM A249
		304N	Tube, Seamless/Welded	ASTM A312
		304N	Pipe	ASTM A358, A403, A430
		304N	Pipe, Seamless	ASTM A376
		304N	Wire, Bar, Shapes	ASTM A479
S30500	Canada	305	Bar	CAS G110.3
		305	Sheet, Strip, Plate—Hot-Rolled, Annealed or Hot-Rolled, Quenched/Tempered	CSA G110.6
		305	Sheet, Strip, Plate—Hot-Rolled, Cold-Rolled Annealed, Quenched/Tempered	CSA G110.9

UNS	Country	Designation	Description	Specifications
	Europe	XCRNi1812KD	Sheet, Strip, Plate, Bar, Rod—Solution Annealed	EURONORM 119-74V
	France	Z8CN1812E	Wire, Rod—60% Hard	NF A35-575
		Z8CN1812E	Wire, Rod	NF A35-575
		Z8CN1812E	Bar, Wire, Rod	NF A35-577
		Z8CN1812E	Plate	NF A36-209
	International	X5CrNi1712E	Cold Head Ext.	ISO 4954
		13	Solution Treated	ISO 683/13
	Italy	X8CrNi1910	Sheet, Strip, Plate	UNI 8317-81
	Japan	SUS305	Bar—Solution Annealed 180 mm diam.	JIS G4303
		SUS305	Sheet, Plate—Hot-Rolled, Solution Annealed	JIS G4304
		SUS305	Sheet, Plate—Cold-Rolled, Solution Annealed	JIS G4305
		SUS305	Strip—Hot-Rolled, Solution Annealed	JIS G4306
		SUS305	Strip—Cold-Rolled, Solution Annealed	JIS G4307
		SUS305	Wire, Rod	JIS G4308
	UK	305S19	Sheet, Strip—Solution Annealed 3 mm diam.	BS 14449
	USA	305	Sheet, Strip, Plate, Bar, Wire	AMS 5514, 5685, 5686
		305		ASME SA193, SA194, SA240
		305	Plate, Sheet, Strip	ASTM A167, A240
		305	Tube, Welded	ASTM A249
		305	Bar	ASTM A276
		305	Wire	ASTM A368, A313, A478, A492, A493, A580
		305	Forging	ASTM A473
		305	Tube	ASTM A511, A554
		30305	Sheet, Strip, Plate, Bar, Wire	SAE J405
S30800	Canada	308	Bar	CSA G110.3
		308	Sheet, Strip, Plate—Hot-Rolled, Annealed or Hot-Rolled, Quenched/Tempered	CSA G110.6
	Germany	X5CrNi1812	Sheet, Strip, Plate, Bar, Wire, Rod	DIN 14303
		1.4303	Sheet, Strip, Plate, Bar, Wire, Rod	DIN
	Japan	SUS308	Bar—Solution Annealed 180 mm diam.	JIS G4303
	USA	308	Plate, Sheet, Strip	ASTM A169
		308	Bar	ASTM A276
		308	Forgings	ASTM A473
		308	Wire	ASTM A580
		30308	Bar, Wire	SAE J405
S30900	Canada	309	Bar	CSA G110.3
		309	Sheet, Strip, Plate—Hot-Rolled, Annealed or Hot-Rolled, Quenched/Tempered	CSA G110.6
	France	Z15CN24.13	Sheet, Strip, Plate, Bar, Tube, Forging	NF A35-586
	Italy	X16CrNi2314	Bar, Wire, Rod	UNI 6901-71
		X16CrNi2314	Tube	UNI 6904-71

UNS	Country	Designation	Description	Specifications
	Italy	X16CrNi2314	Sheet, Strip, Plate	UNI 8317-81
	UK	309S24	Sheet, Strip, Plate—Solution Annealed 3 mm	BS 1449
		309S24	Wire, Rod	BS 2901
	USA	309		ASME SA249, SA312, SA358, SA403, SA409
		309	Plate, Sheet, Strip	ASTM A167
		309	Tube, Welded	ASTM A249
		309	Pipe, Seamless Welded	ASTM A312
		309	Pipe	ASTM A358, A403
		309	Pipe, Welded	ASTM A409
		309	Forgings	ASTM A473
		309	Tube	ASTM A511, A554
		309	Wire	ASTM A580
		30309	Sheet, Strip, Plate, Bar, Wire	SAE J405
S30908	Canada	309S	Bar	CSA G110.3
		309S	Sheet, Strip, Plate—Hot-Rolled, Annealed or Hot-Rolled, Quenched/Tempered	CSA G110.6
		309S	Sheet, Strip, Plate—Hot-Rolled, Annealed, Quenched/Tempered or Cold-Rolled	CSA G110.9
	France	Z10CN24.13	Wire, Rod	NF A35-583
	Germany	1.4833	Sheet, Strip, Plate, Bar, Wire	DIN
		X7CrNi2314	Sheet, Strip, Plate, Bar, Wire	DIN
	Italy	X6CrNi2314	Bar, Wire, Rod	UNI 6901-71
		X6CrNi2314	Tube	UNI 6904-71
		X6CrNi2314	Forging	UNI 7500-75
		X6CrNi2314	Sheet, Strip, Plate	UNI 8317-81
	Japan	SUS309S	Bar—Solution Annealed 180 mm	JIS G4303
		SUS309S	Sheet, Plate—Hot-Rolled, Solution Annealed	JIS G4304
		SUS309S	Sheet, Plate—Cold-Rolled, Solution Annealed	JIS G4305
		SUS309S	Strip—Hot-Rolled, Solution Annealed	JIS G4306
		SUS309S	Strip—Cold-Rolled, Solution Annealed	JIS G4307
		SUS309S	Wire	JIS G4308
	USA	309S	Sheet, Strip, Plate, Bar, Wire	AMS 5523, 5574, 5650, 7490
		309S		ASME SA240, SA479
		309S	Plate, Sheet, Strip	ASTM A167, A240
		309S	Bar	ASTM A276
		309S	Forging	ASTM A473
		309S	Tube	ASTM A511, A554
		309S	Wire	ASTM A580
		30309S	Sheet, Strip, Plate, Bar	SAE J405
S31000	Australia	310	Bar	AS 1444
		310	Sheet, Strip, Plate—Annealed 1.2 mm	AS 1449
	Canada	310	Bar	CSA G110.3
		310	Sheet, Strip, Plate—Hot-Rolled, Annealed or Hot-Rolled, Quenched/Tempered	CSA G110.6

UNS	Country	Designation	Description	Specifications
	Canada	310	Sheet, Strip, Plate, Bar	CSN 172556
	France	Z12CN25.20	Sheet, Strip, Plate, Bar	NF A35-578
		Z12CN25.20	Wire, Rod	NF A35-583
	Germany	1.4845	Sheet, Strip, Plate, Bar	DIN
		X12CrNi25.21	Sheet, Strip, Plate, Bar	DIN
	International	F68	Forging	ISO 2604-1
	Italy	X22CrNi2520	Tube	UNI 6904-71
		X22CrNi2520	Sheet, Strip, Plate	UNI 8317-81
	Japan	SUH310	Bar—Solution Annealed 18 mm diam.	JIS G4311
		SUH310	Sheet, Plate—Solution Annelaed	JIS G4312
		SUH310	Wire	JIS G4316
	UK	310S24	Sheet, Strip, Plate—Solution Annealed 30 mm diam.	BS 1449
		310S24	Forging—Annealed	BS 970
	USA	310		ASME SA182, SA213, SA249, SA312, SA358, SA403, SA409
		310	Plate, Sheet, Strip	ASTM A167
		310	Bar, Forging	ASTM A182
		310	Tube	ASTM A213, A511, A554
		310	Tube, Welded	ASTM A249
		310	Bar	ASTM A276
		310	Tubeless, Seamless Welded	ASTM A312, A632
		310	Pipe	ASTM A358, A403
		310	Pipe, Welded	ASTM A409
		310	Forging	ASTM A437
		310	Bar, Wire	SAE J405
S31008	Canada	310S	Bar	CSA G110.3
		310S	Sheet, Strip, Plate—Hot-Rolled, Annealed or Hot-Rolled, Quenched/ Tempered	CSA G110.6
		310S	Sheet, Strip, Plate—Hot-Rolled, Annealed, Quenched/Tempered	CSA G110.9
	Italy	X6CrNi2520	Tube	UNI 6904-71
		X6CrNi2520	Bar	UNI 7500-75
		X6CrNi2520	Sheet, Strip, Plate	UNI 8317-81
	Japan	SUS310S	Bar—Solution Annealed 180 mm diam.	JIS G4303
		SUS310S	Sheet, Plate—Hot-Rolled, Solution Annealed	JIS G4304
		SUS310S	Sheet, Plate—Cold-Rolled, Solution Annealed	JIS G4305
		SUS310S	Strip—Hot-Rolled, Solution Annealed	JIS G4306
		SUS310S	Strip—Cold-Rolled, Solution Annealed	JIS G4307
		SUS310S	Wire, Rod	JIS G4308
	USA	310S	Sheet, Strip, Plate, Bar, Wire	AMS 5521, 5572, 5577, 5651, 7490
		310S		ASME SA240, SA479
		310S	Plate, Sheet, Strip	ASTM A167, A240
		310S	Bar	ASTM A276, A479
		310S	Forging	ASTM A473
		310S	Tube	ASTM A511, A554
		310S	Wire	ASTM A580
		310S	Plate, Bar, Wire	SAE J405

UNS	Country	Designation	Description	Specifications
S31400	Canada	314	Bar	CSA G110.3
	France	Z12CNS2520	Plate, Bar	NF A35-578
	Germany	1.4841	Sheet, Plate, Bar, Wire	DIN
		X15CrNiSi2520	Sheet, Plate, Bar, Wire	DIN
	International	34	Sheet, Plate, Bar, Wire	COMECON PC4-70
	Italy	X16CrNiSi2520	Bar	UNI 6901-71
	USA	314	Sheet, Plate, Bar, Wire	AMS 5522, 5652, 7490
		314	Bar, Shapes	ASTM A276
		314	Forging	ASTM A473
		314	Wire	ASTM A580
		30314	Plate, Bar	SAE J405
S31600	Australia	316	Bar	AS 1444
		316	Sheet, Strip, Plate—Annealed 1.2 mm diam.	AS 1449
	Canada	316	Bar	CSA G110.3
		316	Sheet, Strip, Plate—Hot-Rolled, Annealed or Hot-Rolled, Quenched/Tempered	CSA G110.6
		316	Sheet, Strip, Plate—Hot-Rolled/Cold-Rolled, Annealed	CSA G110.9
	Europe	X6CrNiMo1722KD	Wire, Rod—Solution Annealed 16/63 mm diam.	EURONORM 119-74V
	France	Z6CND17.11	Bar 25 mm diam.	NF A35-572
		Z6CND17.11	Sheet, Strip, Plate—Cold-Rolled 5 mm diam.	NF A35-573
		Z6CND17.11	Bar, Rod	NF A35-574
		Z6CND17.11	Wire, Rod 60% Hard	NF A35-575
		Z6CND17.11	Bar, Wire	NF A35-577
		Z6CND17.11	Plate	NF A36-209
		Z6CND17.11	Forging	NF A36-607
	Germany	1.4401	Wire—Hard Drawn 0.2 mm diam.	DIN
		X5CrNiMo17122	Sheet, Strip, Plate, Bar, Wire, Tube, Forging	DIN
		X5CrNiMo1911	Sheet, Strip, Plate, Bar, Wire, Tube, Forging	TGL 39672
		X5CrNiMo1811	Sheet, Strip, Plate, Bar, Wire, Tube, Forging	TGL 7143
	International	F62	Forging	ISO 2604-1
		TS60	Tube	ISO 2604-2
		TS61	Tube	ISO 2604-2
		P60	Plate	ISO 2604-4
		P61	Plate	ISO 2604-4
		X5CrNiMo17122E	Cold Head Ext.	ISO 4954
		20	Sheet, Plate, Bar—Solution Treated	ISO 683/13
		20a	Sheet, Plate, Bar—Solution Treated	ISO 683/13
		X5CrNiMo17122	Spring	ISO 6931
	Italy	X5CrNiMo1712	Bar	UNI 6901-71
		X5CrNiMo1712	Tube	UNI 6904-71
		X5CrNiMo1712	Sheet, Strip, Plate	UNI 8317-81
	Japan	SUS316TP	Pipe	JIS G3459
		SUS316	Bar—Solution Annealed 180 mm diam.	JIS G4303
		SUS316	Sheet, Plate—Hot-Rolled, Solution Annealed	JIS G4304

UNS	Country	Designation	Description	Specifications
	Japan	SUS316	Sheet, Plate—Cold-Rolled Solution Annealed	JIS G4305
		SUS316	Strip—Hot-Rolled, Solution Annealed	JIS G4306
		SUS316	Strip—Cold-Rolled, Solution Annealed	JIS G4307
		SUS316	Wire, Rod	JIS G4308
	Sweden	2343	Sheet, Strip, Plate, Wire, Tube, Forging	SS14 2343
		2347	Sheet, Strip, Plate, Wire, Tube, Forging	SIS14 2347
	UK	316S31	Sheet, Strip, Plate	BS 1449
		316S33	Sheet, Strip, Plate	BS 1449
		316S16	Plate	BS 1501
		316S31	Bar, Wire, Forging	BS 1502
		316S32	Bar, Wire, Forging	BS 1502
		316S17	Wire	BS 3111
		316S18	Tube, Pipe—Solution Annealed	BS 3605
		316S26	Tube, Pipe—Solution Annealed	BS 3605
		316S24	Tube	BS 3606
		316S31	Bar	BS 970
		316S33	Bar	BS 970
	USA	316	Sheet, Strip, Plate, Bar, Wire	AMS 5524, 5573, 5648, 5690, 5696, 7490
		316		ASME SA182, SA193, SA194, SA213, SA240, SA249, SA312, SA320, SA358, SA376, SA403, SA409, SA430, SA479, SA688
		316	Plate, Sheet, Strip	ASTM A167, A240
		316	Bar, Forging	ASTM A182
		316	Bolting	ASTM A193, A320
		316	Nuts	ASTM A194
		316	Tube	ASTM A213, A511, A554
		316	Tube, Welded	ASTM A249
		316	Tube, Seamless Welded	ASTM A269, A312, A632
		316	Bar	ASTM A276, A479
		316	Pipe, Seamless Welded	ASTM A312
		316	Wire	ASTM A313, A368, A478
		316	Pipe	ASTM A358, A403, A430
		316	Pipe, Seamless	ASTM A376
		316	Pipe, Welded	ASTM A409
		316	Forging	ASTM A473
		30316	Sheet, Strip, Plate, Bar, Wire	SAE J405
S31640	France	Z6CND17.12	Sheet, Strip, Plate—Cold-Rolled 5 mm diam.	NF A35-573
		Z6CND17.12	Bar, Rod	NF A35-574
		Z6CND17.12	Wire, Rod	NF A35-583
	Germany	X6CrNiMoNb17122	Sheet, Strip, Plate, Bar, Wire, Tube	DIN 17440
		1.458	Sheet, Strip, Plate, Bar, Wire, Tube	DIN
		X5CrNiMoNb17.11	Sheet, Strip, Plate, Bar, Wire	TGL 39672
	International	23	Sheet, Strip, Bar—Solution Treated	ISO 683/13
	Italy	X6CrNiMoNb1712	Bar, Wire	UNI 6901-71
		X6CrNiMoNb1713	Bar, Wire	UNI 6901-71

UNS	Country	Designation	Description	Specifications
	Italy	X6CrNiMoNb1712	Tube	UNI 6904-71
		X6CrNiMoNb1713	Tube	UNI 6904-71
		X6CrNiMoNb1712	Bar, Forging	UNI 7500-75
		X6CrNiMoNb1712	Sheet, Strip, Plate	UNI 8317-81
		X6CrNiMoNb1713	Sheet, Strip, Plate	UNI 8317-81
	UK	318S96	Wire, Rod	BS 2901
	USA	316Cb	Wire	ASTM A313
S31603	Australia	316L	Bar	AS 1444
		316L	Sheet, Strip, Plate, Annealed 1.2 mm diam.	AS 1449
	Canada	316L	Bar	CSA G110.3
		316L	Sheet, Strip, Plate—Hot-Rolled, Annealed or Hot-Rolled, Quenched/Tempered	CSA G110.6
		316L	Sheet, Strip, Plate Hot-Rolled, Cold-Rolled, Annealed	CSA G110.9
	Europe	X2CrNiMo18133KD	Wire, Rod—Solution Annealed 15/63 mm diam.	EURONORM 119-74V
	France	Z2CND17.12	Sheet, Strip, Plate—Cold-Rolled 5 mm diam.	NF A35-573
		Z2CND17.12	Bar, Rod	NF A35-574
		Z2CND17.12	Wire, Rod 60% Hard	NF A35-575
		Z2CND17.12	Bar, Wire, Rod	NF A35-577
		Z2CND17.12	Plate	NF A36-209
		Z2CND17.12	Forging	NF A36-607
	Germany	1.4404	Sheet, Strip, Plate, Wire, Tube, Forging	DIN
		X2CrNiMo17132	Sheet, Strip, Plate, Wire, Tube, Forging	DIN
	International	22	Sheet, Strip, Plate, Bar, Wire, Tube, Forging	COMECON PC4-70
		F59	Forging	ISO 2604-1
		P57	Plate	ISO 2604-4
		P58	Plate	ISO 2604-4
		X2CrNiMo17133E	Cold Head Ext.	ISO 4954
		19	Solution Treated	ISO 683/13
		19a	Solution Treated	ISO 683/13
	Italy	X2CrNiMo1712	Bar, Rod	UNI 6901-71
		X2CrNiMo1712	Tube	UNI 6904-71
		X2CrNiMo1712	Forging	UNI 7500-75
		X2CrNiMo1712	Sheet, Strip, Plate	UNI 8317-81
	Japan	SUS316LTBS	Tube	JIS G3447
		SUS316LTP	Pipe	JIS G3459
		SUS316L	Bar—Solution Annealed 180 mm diam.	JIS G4303
		SUS316L	Sheet, Plate—Hot-Rolled, Solution Annealed	JIS G4304
		SUS316L	Sheet, Plate—Cold-Rolled, Solution Annealed	JIS G4305
		SUS316L	Strip—Hot-Rolled, Solution Annealed	JIS G4306
		SUS316L	Strip—Cold-Rolled, Solution Annealed	JIS G4307
		SUS316L	Wire, Rod	JIS G4308
	Sweden	2348	Sheet, Strip, Plate, Bar, Tube	SS14 2348
		2353	Sheet, Strip, Plate, Bar, Tube	SS14 2353

UNS	Country	Designation	Description	Specifications
	UK	316S11	Sheet, Strip, Plate	BS 1449
		316S13	Sheet, Strip, Plate	BS 1449
		316S12	Plate	BS 1501
		316S37	Plate	BS 1501
		316S82	Plate	BS 1501
		316S14	Tube, Pipe—Solution Annealed	BS 3605
		316S22	Tube, Pipe—Solution Annealed	BS 3605
		316S24	Tube	BS 3606
		316S29	Tube	BS 3606
		316S11	Bar, Rod	BS 970
	USA	316L	Sheet, Strip, Plate, Bar, Wire	AMS 5507, 5653
		316L		ASME SA182, SA213, SA240, SA249, SA312, SA403, SA479, SA688
		316L	Plate, Sheet, Strip	ASTM A167, A240
		316L	Bar, Forging	ASTM A182
		316L	Tube	ASTM A213, A511, A554
		316L	Tube, Welded	ASTM A249, A688
		316L	Tube, Seamless, Welded	ASTM A269, A632
		316L	Bar	ASTM A276
		316L	Pipe, Seamless, Welded	ASTM A312
		316L	Pipe	ASTM A403
		316L	Forging	ASTM A473
		316L	Wire	ASTM A478, A580
		316L	Wire, Bar, Shapes	ASTM A479
		30316L	Shape, Plate, Bar, Wire	SAE J405
S31653	France	Z2CND17.12Az	Sheet, Strip, Plate, Bar	NF A35-582
		Z2CND17.13Az	Sheet, Strip, Plate, Bar	NF A35-582
	Germany	1.4406, 1.4429	Strip, Plate, Bar	DIN
		X2CrNiMoN17122	Strip, Plate, Bar	DIN 17440
		X2CrNiMoN17133	Strip, Plate, Bar	DIN 17440
		X2CrNiMoN18.12	Sheet, Strip, Plate, Bar	TGL 7143
	International	X2CrNiMoN17133E	Cold Head Ext.	ISO 4954
		19aN	Solution Treated	ISO 683/13
		19N	Solution Treated	ISO 683/13
	Italy	Z2CN1712, Z2CN1713	Bar	UNI 7500-75
		Z2CN1712, Z2CN1713	Sheet, Strip, Plate	UNI 8317.81
	Japan	SUS316LN	Bar	JIS G4303
		SUS316LN	Sheet, Plate—Hot-Rolled	JIS G4304
		SUS316LN	Sheet, Plate—Cold-Rolled	JIS G4305
		SUS316LN	Strip—Hot-Rolled	JIS G4306
		SUS316LN	Strip—Cold-Rolled	JIS G4307
	Sweden	2375	Sheet, Strip, Plate, Bar	SS14 2375
	UK	316S62	Plate	BS 1501
		316S61	Bar	BS 1502
		316S63	Bar	BS 1506
	USA	316LN	Bar, Shapes	ASTM A276
S31651	Germany	1.3952, X5CrNiMoN1814	Sheet, Strip, Plate, Bar	DIN
	Japan	SUS316N	Bar	JIS G4303
		SUS316N	Sheet, Plate—Hot-Rolled	JIS G4304
		SUS316N	Sheet, Plate—Cold-Rolled	JIS G4305
		SUS316N	Strip—Hot-Rolled	JIS G4306
		SUS316N	Strip—Cold-Rolled	JIS G4307
	UK	3016S66		BS 1501
		3016S65, 316S67	Bar	BS 1502
	USA	316N		ASME SA182, SA213, SA240,

UNS	Country	Designation	Description	Specifications
	USA			SA249, SA312, SA358, SA376, SA403, SA430, SA479
		316N	Bar, Forging	ASTM A182
		316N	Tube	ASTM A213
		316N	Sheet, Strip, Plate	ASTM A240
		316N	Tube, Welded	ASTM A249
		316N	Bar	ASTM A276, A479
		316N	Pipe, Seamless, Welded	ASTM A312
		316N	Pipe	ASTM A358, A403, A430
		316N	Pipe, Seamless	ASTM A376
S31635	Australia	316Ti	Sheet, Strip, Plate— Annealed 1.2 mm diam.	AS 1449
	France	Z6CNDT1712	Sheet, Strip, Plate	NF A35-573
		Z6CNDT1712	Bar	NF A35-574
		Z6CNDT1712	Wire, Rod	NF A35-575
		Z6CNDT1712	Plate	NF A36-209
		Z6CNDT1712	Forging	NF A36-607
	Germany	1.44571	Sheet, Strip, Plate, Bar, Wire, Tube, Forging	DIN
		X6CrNiMoTi17122	Sheet, Strip, Plate, Bar, Wire, Tube, Forging	DIN 17440
		X8CrNiMoTi1811	Sheet, Strip, Plate, Bar, Wire, Tube	DIN 7143
	International	21	Sheet, Strip, Plate, Bar, Wire	COMECON PC4-70
		X6CrNiMoTi122E	Cold Head Ext.	ISO 4954
		21	Sheet, Plate, Bar—Solution Treated	ISO 683/13
	Italy	X6CrNiMoTi17122	Bar	UNI 6901-71
		X6CrNiMoTi17122	Tube	UNI 6904-71
		X6CrNiMoTi17122	Forging	UNI 7500-75
		X6CrNiMoTi17122	Sheet, Strip, Plate	UNI 8317-81
	Sweden	2350	Sheet, Strip, Plate, Bar, Wire	SS14 2350
	UK	320S31	Sheet, Strip, Plate	BS 1449
		320S17	Plate	BS 1501
		320S33	Forging	BS 1503
		320S31	Bar, Forging	BS 970
	USA	316Ti	Wire	ASTM A313
S31700	Australia	317	Bar	AS 1444
		317	Sheet, Strip, Plate— Annealed 1.2 mm diam.	AS 1449
	Canada	317	Bar	CSA G110.3
		317	Sheet, Strip, Plate—Hot-Rolled, Annealed or Hot-Rolled, Quenched/ Tempered	CSA G110.6
		317	Sheet, Strip, Plate—Hot-Rolled, Cold-Rolled, Annealed, Quenched/ Tempered	CSA G110.9
	Germany	1.4449, X5CrNiMo1713	Sheet, Plate, Bar	DIN
	Italy	X5CrNiMo1815	Sheet, Plate, Bar	UNI 7500-75
	Japan	SUS317	Bar—Solution Annealed 180 mm diam.	JIS G4303
		SUS317	Sheet, Plate—Hot-Rolled, Solution Annealed	JIS G4304
		SUS317	Sheet, Plate—Cold-Rolled, Solution Annealed	JIS G4305

UNS	Country	Designation	Description	Specifications
	Japan	SUS317	Pipe	JIS G4359
	Sweden	2366	Sheet, Plate, Bar	SS14 2366
	UK	317S16	Sheet, Strip, Plate—Solution Annealed 3 mm diam.	BS 1449
		317S96	Wire, Rod	BS 2901
	USA	317		ASME SA240, SA249, SA312, SA403, SA409
		317	Plate, Sheet, Strip	ASTM A167, A240
		317	Tube, Welded	ASTM A249
		317	Tube, Seamless Welded	ASTM A269, A632
		317	Bar	ASTM A276
		317	Pipe, Seamless Welded	ASTM A312
		317	Pipe	ASTM A403
		317	Pipe, Welded	ASTM A409
		317	Forging	ASTM A473
		317	Wire	ASTM A478, A580
		317	Tube	ASTM A511, A554
		30317	Sheet, Strip, Plate, Bar, Wire	SAE J405
S31703	Australia	317L	Bar	AS 1444
	Canada	317L	Sheet, Strip, Plate—Hot-Rolled Annealed or Hot-Rolled, Quenched/Tempered	CSA G110.6
		317L	Plate—Hot-Rolled, Cold-Rolled Annealed, Quenched/Tempered	CSA G110.9
	France	Z2CND19.15	Sheet, Strip, Plate—Cold-Rolled, 5 mm diam.	NF A35-573
		Z2CND19.15	Bar	NF A35-574
		Z2CND19.14	Wire, Rod	NF A35-583
		Z2CND19.15	Plate	NF A36-209
	Germany	1.4438	Sheet, Strip, Plate, Bar, Wire, Tube, Forging	DIN
		X2CrNiMo18164	Sheet, Strip, Plate, Bar, Wire, Tube, Forging	DIN 17440
	International	24	Sheet, Plate, Bar—Solution Treated	ISO 683/13
	Italy	X2CrNiMo1816	Bar, Rod	UNI 6901-71
		X2CrNiMo1815	Bar, Forging	UNI 7500-75
		X2CrNiMo1816	Sheet, Strip, Plate	UNI 8317-81
	Japan	SUS317LTP	Pipe	JIS G3459
		SUS317L	Bar—Solution Annealed, 180 mm diam.	JIS G4303
		SUS317L	Plate, Sheet—Hot-Rolled, Solution Annealed	JIS G4304
		SUS317L	Plate, Sheet—Cold-Rolled, Solution Annealed	JIS G4305
	Sweden		Sheet, Plate, Strip, Bar, Tube	SS14 2367
	UK	317S12	Sheet, Strip, Plate—Solution Annealed 3 mm diam.	BS 1449
	USA	317L		ASME SA240
		317L	Sheet, Strip, Plate	ASTM A167, A240
S34700	Canada	347	Bar	CSA G110.3
		347	Sheet, Strip, Plate—Hot-Rolled Annealed or Hot-Rolled, Quenched/Tempered	CSA G110.6
		347	Sheet, Strip, Plate—Hot-	CSA G110.9

UNS	Country	Designation	Description	Specifications
	Canada		Rolled, Cold-Rolled Annealed	
	France	Z6CNNb18.10	Sheet, Strip, Plate—Cold-Rolled, 5 mm diam.	NF A35-573
		Z6CNNb18.10	Bar, Wire	NF A35-574
		Z6CNNb18.10	Plate	NF A36-209
		Z6CNNb18.10	Forging	NF A36-607
	Germany	1.455	Sheet, Strip, Plate, Bar, Wire, Tube	DIN
		X6CrNiNb1810	Sheet, Strip, Plate, Bar, Wire, Tube	DIN 1740
		X5CrNiNb2010	Sheet, Strip, Plate, Bar, Wire, Tube	TGL 39672
	International	20	Sheet, Strip, Plate, Bar, Wire, Tube	COMECON PC4-70
		16	Sheet, Strip, Plate, Bar, Wire, Tube	ISO 683/13
	Italy	X6CrNiNb1811	Bar, Wire	UNI 6901-71
		X6CrNiNb1811	Tube	UNI 6904-71
		X6CrNiNb1811	Plate	UNI 7500-75
		X6CrNiNb1811KG; KW		UNI 7660-71
		X6CrNiNb1811		UNI 7660-71
		X6CrNiNb1811	Sheet, Strip, Plate	UNI 8317-81
	Japan	SUS347TK	Tube	JIS G3446
		SUS347TP	Pipe	JIS G3459
		SUS347TB	Tube	JIS G3463
		SUS347	Bar—Solution Annealed, 180 mm diam.	JIS G4303
		SUS347	Sheet, Plate—Hot-Rolled, Solution Annealed	JIS G4304
		SUS347	Sheet, Plate—Cold-Rolled, Solution Annealed	JIS G4305
		SUS347	Strip—Hot-Rolled, Solution Annealed	JIS G4306
		SUS347	Strip—Cold-Rolled, Solution Annealed	JIS G4307
		SUS347	Wire, Rod	JIS G4308
	Sweden	2338	Sheet, Strip, Plate, Bar, Wire, Tube	SS14 2338
	UK	347S31	Sheet, Strip, Plate	BS 1449
		347S17	Plate	BS 1501
		347S31	Bar	BS 1502
		347S17	Tube—Solution Annealed	BS 3605
		347S18	Tube—Solution Annealed	BS 3605
		347S31	Bar, Wire	BS 970
	USA	347		AMS 5512, 5556, 5571, 5575, 5654, 5674, 7229, 7490
		347		ASME SA182, SA193, SA194, SA213, SA240, SA249, SA312, SA320, SA358, SA376, SA403, SA409, SA430, SA479
		347	Plate, Sheet, Strip	ASTM A167
		347	Bar, Forging	ASTM A182
		347	Bolting	ASTM A193, A320
		347	Nuts	ASTM A194
		347	Tube	ASTM A213, A511, A554
		347	Tube, Welded	ASTM A249
		347	Tube, Seamless Welded	ASTM A269, A632
		347	Tube, Seamless	ASTM A271
		347	Bar	ASTM A276, A479

UNS	Country	Designation	Description	Specifications
	USA	347	Pipe, Seamless Welded	ASTM A312
		347	Pipe	ASTM A358, A403, A430
		347	Pipe, Seamless	ASTM A376
		347	Pipe, Welded	ASTM A409
		347	Forging	ASTM A473
		347	Wire, Rod	ASTM A493, A580
		30347	Sheet, Strip, Plate, Bar, Wire	SAE J405
S38400	Canada	348	Bar	CSA G110.3
		348	Sheet, Strip, Plate—Hot-Rolled, Annealed or Hot-Rolled, Quenched/Tempered	CSA G110.6
		348	Sheet, Strip, Plate—Hot-Rolled, Cold-Rolled, Annealed	CSA G110.9
	USA	348		ASME SA182, SA213, SA240, SA249, SA312, SA358, SA376, SA403, SA409, SA479
		348	Plate, Sheet, Strip	ASTM A167
		348	Bar, Forging	ASTM A182
		348	Tube	ASTM A213
		348	Sheet, Strip, Plate	ASTM A240
		348	Tube, Welded	ASTM A249
		348	Tube, Seamless Welded	ASTM A269, A632
		348	Bar	ASTM A276, A479
		348	Pipe, Seamless Welded	ASTM A312
		348	Pipe	ASTM A358, A403
		348	Pipe, Seamless	ASTM A376
		348	Wire	ASTM A409
		348	Sheet, Strip, Plate, Bar, Wire	SAE J405
		30348		
S38400	France	26NC18.16	Wire, Rod, 60% Hard	NF A35-575
		26NC18.16	Wire, Rod	NF A35-575
		26NC18.16	Bar, Wire	NF A35-577
	Germany	1.4321; X2NiCr1816	Bar, Wire	DIN
	International	X6NiCr1816E	Cold Head Ext.	ISO 4954
	Japan	SUS384	Wire	JIS G4315
	USA	384	Bar, Wire	ASTM A493
		30384	Bar, Wire	SAE J405
Stainless Steels—Ferritic				
S42900	Japan	SUS429	Bar—Annealed, 75 mm diam.	JIS G4303
		SUS429	Sheet, Plate—Hot-Rolled, Annealed	JIS G4304
		SUS429	Sheet, Plate—Cold-Rolled, Annealed	JIS G4305
	USA	429		ASME SA182, SA240, SA268
		429	Sheet, Strip, Plate	ASTM A176, A240
		429	Forging	ASTM A182, A473
		429	Tube	ASTM A268, A511, A554
		429	Bar	ASTM A276
		429	Wire	ASTM A493
		51429	Bar, Wire	SAE J405
S43000	Australia	430	Bar—Annealed	AS 1444
		430	Sheet, Strip, Plate—Annealed, 1.2 mm diam.	AS 1449
	Canada	430	Bar—Annealed	CSA G110.3

UNS	Country	Designation	Description	Specifications
	Canada	430	Sheet—Hot-Rolled, Annealed, Quenched/ Tempered	CSA G110.5
		430	Strip—Cold-Rolled, Annealed, 1.2 mm diam.	CSA G110.5
		430B	Sheet, Strip, Plate	CSA G110.9
	Europe	X8Cr17KD	Sheet, Strip, Plate, Bar— Quenched/Tempered	EURONORM 117-74V
	France	Z8C17	Sheet, Strip, Plate, Bar	AFNOR NF A35-586
	Germany	1.4016; X8Cr17	Sheet, Strip, Bar, Wire, Tube, Forging—Annealed	DIN 17440
		1.4016; X8Cr17	Sheet, Strip, Bar, Wire, Tube	TGL
	International	7	Sheet, Strip, Plate, Bar	COMECON PC4-70
		8	Annealed	ISO 683/13
	Italy	X8Cr17	Sheet, Strip, Plate, Bar, Wire, Tube—Annealed	IUNI 6904-71
	Japan	SUS430	Bar—Annealed, 75 mm diam.	JIS G4303
		SUS430	Sheet, Plate—Hot-Rolled, Annealed	JIS G4304
		SUS430	Sheet, Plate—Cold-Rolled, Annealed	JIS G4305
		SUS430	Strip—Hot-Rolled, Annealed	JIS G4306
		SUS430	Strip—Cold-Rolled, Solution Annealed	JIS G4307
		SUS430	Wire, Rod	JIS G4308
	Sweden	2320	Sheet, Strip, Plate, Bar, Tube—Annealed	SIS 142320
	UK	430S15	Sheet, Strip, Plate, Bar, Wire	BS 1554
	USA	430	Bar, Wire	AMS 5503, 5627
		430		ASME SA182, SA240, SA268, SA479
		430	Sheet, Strip, Plate	ASTM A176, A240
		430	Bar	ASTM A182, A276, A479
		430	Tube	ASTM A268, A511, A554
		430	Forging	ASTM A473
		430	Wire	ASTM A493, A580
		51430	Bar, Wire	SAE J405
Stainless Steel—Martensitic				
S41000	Australia	410	Sheet, Strip, Plate— Annealed, 1.2 mm diam.	AS 1449
		410	Bar, Wire	AS 2837
		En56A	Bar	AS G18
	Canada	410	Bar	CSA G110.3
		410	Sheet, Strip, Plate—Cold- Rolled, Annealed, 1 mm diam.	CSA G110.5
		410	Sheet, Strip, Plate	CSA G110.9
	Europe	C12Cr13KD	Wire, Rod	EURONORM 117-74V
	France	Z12C13	Sheet, Strip, Plate, Bar, Wire, Rod—Quenched/ Tempered	AFNOR NF A35-572
	Germany	1.4006	Sheet, Strip, Bar, Wire, Tube, Forging—Annealed	DIN 17440
		X10Cr13	Sheet, Strip, Bar, Wire, Tube, Forging—	DIN 17440

UNS	Country	Designation	Description	Specifications
	Germany		Quenched/Tempered	
	International	3	Sheet, Strip, Plate, Bar, Wire	COMECON PC4-70
		3	Annealed, Quenched/Tempered	ISO 683/13
	Italy	X12Cr13	Sheet, Strip, Plate, Bar, Wire	UNI 6904-71
	Japan	SUS410	Bar—Quenched/Tempered, 75 mm diam.	JIS G4303
		SUS410	Sheet, Plate—Hot-Rolled, Annealed	JIS G4304
		SUS410	Sheet, Plate—Cold-Rolled, Annelaed	JIS G4305
		SUS410	Strip—Hot-Rolled, Annealed	JIS G4306
		SUS410	Strip—Cold-Rolled, Annealed, Quenched/Tempered	JIS G4307
		SUS410	Sheet, Strip, Plate, Bar, Wire, Rod	JIS G4308
	Sweden	2302	Sheet, Strip, Plate, Bar, Wire—Quenched/Tempered	SIS 142302
	UK	410S21	Sheet, Strip, Plate	BS 1449 Part 2
		AR	Bar—Oil-Hardened, Air-Hardened	BS 1506-713
		AX	Bar	BS 1506-713
		BX	Bar	BS 1506-713
		151A	Bar, Wire	BS DTD
		97B	Tube	BS DTD
	USA	410	Sheet, Strip, Plate, Bar, Wire	AMS 5504, 5505, 5591, 5613, 5776, 5821, 7493
		410		ASME SA194, SA196, SA240, SA268, SA479
		410	Sheet, Strip, Plate, Bar, Wire, Forging	ASTM A176, A194
		410	Sheet, Strip, Plate—Annealed	ASTM A240
		410	Bar—Annealed	ASTM A276
		410	Forging—Annealed	ASTM A473
		410	Bar—Annealed	ASTM A479
		410	Bar—Heat Treated (2)	ASTM A479
		410	Bar—Heat Treated (3)	ASTM A479
		410	Wire	ASTM A493, A580
		410	Tube	ASTM A511
		51410	Bar, Wire	SAE J405, J412
S42000	Australia	420	Bar	AS 1444
		420	Sheet, Strip, Plate—Annealed, 1.2 mm diam.	AS 1449
	Canada	420	Bar	CSA G110.3
	France	Z20C13	Sheet, Strip, Plate, Bar, Wire—Quenched/Tempered	AFNOR NF A35-572
	Germany	1.4021; X20Cr13	Sheet, Strip, Bar, Wire, Tube, Forging—Quenched/Tempered	DIN 17440
		1.4021; X20Cr13	Sheet, Strip, Plate, Bar, Wire	TGL
	International	4	Sheet, Strip, Plate, Bar,	COMECON PC4-70

UNS	Country	Designation	Description	Specifications
	International		Wire	
		4	Annealed, Quenched/Tempered	ISO 683/13
		5	Annealed, Quenched/Tempered	ISO 683/13
	Italy	X20Cr13	Sheet, Strip, Plate, Bar, Wire, Tube—Quenched/Tempered	UNI 6901-71
	Japan	SUS420J1	Bar—Quenched/Tempered, 75 mm diam.	JIS G4303
		SUS420J1	Plate, Sheet—Hot-Rolled, Annealed	JIS G4304
		SUS420J1	Plate, Sheet—Cold-Rolled, Annealed	JIS G4305
		SUS420J1	Strip—Hot-Rolled, Annealed	JIS G4306
		SUS420J1	Strip—Cold-Rolled	JIS G4307
		SUS420J1	Wire, Rod	JIS G4308
		SUS420J1	Wire	JIS G4309
	Sweden	2303	Sheet, Strip, Plate, Bar, Wire, Forging—Quenched/Tempered	SIS 142302
	UK	420S29; 420S37	Bar, Forging—Hard-Tempered, 150 mm	BS 970 Part 4
	USA	420	Bar, Wire	AMS 5506, 5621, 7207
		420	Bar	ASTM A276
		420	Forging	ASTM A473
		420	Wire	ASTM A580
Aluminum-Base Alloys				
A0443	USA	443	Cast	ASTM B108, B26, B618
A0514	Japan	AC7A	Cast	JIS H5202
	International	Al-Mg3	Cast	ISO R164
	Russia	AL13	Cast	GOST 2685
	USA	514	Cast	ASTM B26, B618
A0520	Germany	3.3591/G-AlMg10	Cast	DIN 1725 Part 2
	International	Al-Mg10	Cast	ISO R164
	Russia	AL27-1	Cast	GOST 2685
		AL27-2	Cast	
		AL8	Cast	GOST 2685
	South Africa	Al-Mg10A	Cast	SABS 989, 990, 991
	UK	LM10	Cast	BS 1490
	USA	520	Cast	ASTM B26 B618
A94032	Canada	0.4032	Wrought	CSA HA.8
	Czech Republic	AlSi12Ni1Mg	Wrought	CSN 424237
	Japan	4032	Wrought	JIS H4140
	UK	38S	Wrought	
	USA	4032	Wrought	
A95052	Australia	5052	Sheet, Plate	AS 1734
	Austria	AlMg2.5	Wrought	ONORM—M3430
		Al99.85Mg2.5	Wrought	ONORM—M3430
	Belgium	5052	Wrought	NBN P21-001
	Canada	0.5052	Sheet, Plate	CSA HA.4
		0.5052	Bar, Rod, Wire	CSA HA.5
		0.5052	Tube, Pipe	CSA HA.7
		0.5052	Tube, Pipe	CSA HA.7.1
		0.5052	Rod, Wire	CSA HA.6

UNS	Country	Designation	Description	Specifications
	France	5052	Bar	NF A50411
		5052	Sheet, Plate	NF A50451
	Finland	AlMg2.5	Wrought	SFS 2587
	Germany	3.3523/AlMg2	Wrought	DIN 1725 pt1
	India	HG30	Wire	IS 739
		HT20	Tube	IS 738
	Japan	5052	Sheet, Plate	JIS H4000
		5052	Bar	JIS H4040
		5052	Tube	JIS H4080
		5052	Pipe	JIS H4090
		5052	Wrought	JIS H4100
		5052	Wire	JIS H4120
	International	Al-Mg2.5	Wrought	ISO R827, R209
		Al-Mg2.5	Sheet, Plate	ISO TR2136
		Al-Mg2.5	Tube	ISO 6363
		Al-Cu2Mg	Wrought	ISO 209
		Al-Si1Mg	Wrought	ISO R827
		Al-Si1Mg	Forgings	ISO R829
		Al-Si1Mg	Tube	ISO 6363
	Norway	NS17210/AlMg2.5	Plate, Shapes, Strip	NS 17201
	Pan America	5052	Wrought	COPANT 862
	Sweden	4120-00	Plate, Sheet	SIS 144120
		4120-02	Plate, Sheet, Strip	SIS 144120
		4120-14	Plate, Sheet	SIS 144120
		4120-18	Sheet, Strip	SIS 144120
		4120-24	Sheet, Strip	SIS 144120
		4120-40	Sheet, Strip	SIS 144120
		4120-44	Sheet, Strip	SIS 144120
		4120	Sheet	MNC 40E
	Russia	Amg	Wrought	
		1520	Wrought	GOST 4784
		AMg2	Wrought	GOST 4784
	UK	2L55	Wrought	
	USA	5052	Bar, Rod, Wire, Sheet, Tube, Extrusions	AMS 4004, 4015, 4016, 4017, 4069, 4070, 4071, 4114
		5052	Bar, Rod, Wire, Sheet, Tube, Extrusions	ASTM B209, B210, B211, B221, B234, B241, B313, B316, B404, B483, SAE J454
A95083	Australia	5083	Plate, Sheet	AS 1734
		5083	Rod, Bar	AS 1866
	Austria	AlMg4.5Mn	Wrought	ONORM M3430
	Belgium	5083	Wrought	NBN P21-001
	Canada	5083	Bar, Rod, Wire, Plate, Sheet, Tube, Pipe, Extrusions	CSA GM41
		0.5083	Plate, Sheet	CSA HA.4
		0.5083	Bar, Rod, Wire	CSA HA.5
	Finland	AlMg3	Sheet, Rod, Tube	SFS 2588
	France	AG4.5MC	Wrought	NF A50-411, 451
		5083	Plate, Sheet	NF A50451
		5083	Bar, Tube	NF A50-411
	Germany	3.3547/AlMg4	Wrought	DIN 1725 Part 1
	India	54300	Bar, Rod	IS 733
		54300	Plate	IS 736
	International	Al-Mg4.5Mn	Tube	ISO R827
		Al-Mg4.5Mn	Sheet, Plate	ISO TR2136
		Al-Mg4.5Mn	Tube	ISO 6363
	Japan	5083	Plate, Sheet	JIS H4000

UNS	Country	Designation	Description	Specifications
	Japan	5083	Bar	JIS H4040
		5083	Tube	JIS H4080
		5083	Wrought	JIS H4100
		5n02	Wire	JIS H4120
	Norway	NS17215/AlMg4.5Mn	Plate, Sheet, Strip	NS 17215
	Pan America	X7007	Wrought	COPANT 862
	Sweden	4040-00	Sheet, Strip	SIS 144140
		4040-00	Plate	SIS 144140
		4040-02	Sheet, Plate, Strip	SIS 144140
		4040-12	Plate	SIS 144140
		4040-22	Sheet, Strip	SIS 144140
		4040-24	Sheet, Strip	SIS 144140
		4140	Sheet	MNC 40E
	UK	NT8	Tube	BS 1471
		5083	Bar, Rod, Wire, Plate, Sheet, Strip	BS N8
	USA	5083	Bar, Rod, Wire, Plate, Sheet, Strip, Tube, Pipe, Extrusions	AMS 4056, 4057, 4058, 4059, ASTM, B209, B210, B221, B241, B247, B547; SAE J454
A95086	Australia	5086	Sheet, Plate	AS 1734
	Belgium	5086	Wrought	NBN P221-001
	Canada	0.5086	Sheet, Plate	CSA HA.4
	France	5086	Bar, Rod, Wire, Plate, Sheet, Strip, Tube, Pipe, Extrusions	NF A-G4MC
		5086(AG4MC)	Wrought	NF A50-411,701
		5086(AG4MC)	Bar, Wire, Tube	NF A50-411
		5086(AG4MC)	Sheet, Plate	NF A50-451
		AG4MC (5086)	Sheet, Bar	AIR 9051-A
	Germany	Al-Mg4	Bar, Rod, Wire, Plate, Sheet, Strip, Tube, Pipe, Extrusions	DIN 1725 PT1
		3.3545/AlMg4Mn	Wrought	DIN 1725 PT1
	International	Al-Mg4	Sheet, Plate	ISO TR2136
		Al-Mg4	Tube	ISO 6363
		Al-Mg4	Wrought	ISO R827
	Norway	NS 17213/AlMg4	Plate, Sheet, Strip	NS 17213
	Pan America	X5854	Wrought	COPANT 862
		5086	Wrought	COPANT 862
	Russia	AMg4	Wrought	GOST 4784
		1540	Wrought	GOST 4784
	UK	NS4	Plate, Sheet, Strip	BS 1470
		NT4	Tube	BS 1471
		NG4	Wire	BS 1475
	USA	5086	Bar, Rod, Wire, Plate, Sheet, Strip, Tube, Pipe, Extrusions	ASTM B209, B210, B221, B241, B313, B345, B547; SAE J454
A95456	India	HT14	Tube	IS 738
	Russia	AMg6	Wrought	GOST 4784
		45Mg2	Wrought	
		AMg61N	Wrought	
	UK	NG61	Wire	BS 1475
	USA	5456	Bar, Rod, Wire, Plate, Sheet, Strip, Tube, Pipe, Extrusions	ASTM B209, B210, B221, B241; SAE J454
A96061	Australia	6061	Sheet, Plate	AS 1734
		6061	Wire, Rod, Bar, Strip	AS 1865

UNS	Country	Designation	Description	Specifications
	Australia	6061	Bar, Rod	AS 1866
		6061	Tube	AS 1867
	Canada	0.6061	Plate, Sheet	CSA HA.4
		0.6061	Bar, Rod, Wire	CSA HA.5
		0.6061	Rod, Wire	CSA HA.6
		0.6061	Tube, Pipe	CSA HA.7
		0.6061	Tube	HA.7.1
		0.6061	Forgings	HA.8
	France	6061	Bar, Wire, Tube	NF A50411
		6061	Sheet, Plate	NF A50451
	International	Al-Mg1SiCu	Wrought	ISO R827
		Al-Mg1SiCu	Forgings	ISO R829
		Al-Mg1SiCu	Tube	ISO 6363
		Al-Mg1SiCu	Sheet, Plate	ISO TR2136
	Japan	6061	Sheet, Plate, Strip	JIS H4000
		6061	Bar	JIS H4040
		6061	Tube	JIS H4080
		6061	Wrought	JIS H4100
		6061	Wire	JIS H4120
		6061	Wrought	JIS H4140
		6061	Plate	JIS H4180
	Pan America	6061	Wrought	COPANT 862
	Russia	1330	Wrought	GOST 4784
		AD33	Wrought	GOST 4784
	UK	HB20	Wrought	BS 1473
		HE20	Bar, Tube	BS 1474
		HG20	Wire	BS 1475
		L117	Wrought	
	USA	6061	Bar, Rod, Wire, Plate. Sheet, Tube, Pipe, Forgings, Extrusions	AMS 4025, 4026, 4027, 4043, 4053, 4115, 4116, 4117, ASTM B209, B211, B308, B632
	Yugoslavia	AlMg1SiCu	Wrought	JUS CC2.100
A97075	Australia	7075	Wire, Rod, Bar, Strip	AS 1865
	Austria	AlZnMgCu1.5	Wrought	ONORM M3429
	Canada	0.7075 Alclad	Plate, Sheet	CSA HA.4
		0.7075	Plate, Sheet	CSA HA.4
		0.7075	Bar, Rod, Wire	CSA HA.5
		0.7075	Tube, Pipe	CSA HA.7
		0.7075	Forgings	CSA HA.8
	Czech Republic	AlZn6Mg2Cu	Wrought	CSN 424222
	Europe	7075	Sheet	AECMA prEN2092
		7075	Sheet	AECMA prEN2162
	France	AZ5GU(7075)	Sheet, Bar	AIR 9051-A
		7075(AZ5GU)	Tube	NF A50411
		7075(AZ5GU)	Bar	NF A50411
		7075(AZ5GU)	Sheet, Plate	NF A50451
		7075(AZ5GU)	Wrought	NF A50506
	Germany	3.4365/AlZnMgCu1.5	Wrought	DIN 1725 pt1
	International	Al-Zn6MgCu	Sheet, Plate	ISO TR2136
		Al-Zn6MgCu	Tube	ISO 6363
		Al-Zn6MgCu	Wrought	ISO R827
	Japan	7075	Sheet, Plate, Strip	JIS H4000
		7075	Bar	JIS H4040
		7075	Tube	JIS H4080
		7075	Wrought	JIS H4100
	Norway	NS17411/ALZn6MgCu	Bar, Plate, Sheet, Strip, Tube, Forgings	NS 17411

UNS	Country	Designation	Description	Specifications
	Norway	NS17412/ALZn6MgCu	Bar, Forgings	NS 17412
	Pan America	7075	Wrought	COPANT 862
	Russia	V95	Wrought	GOST 4784
	UK	C77S	Wrought	
		M75S	Wrought	
	USA	7050	Plate, Forgings, Extrusions	AMS 4050, 4108
		AlZn5.5MgCu	Wrought	

Nickel Base Alloys

UNS	Country	Designation	Description	Specifications
N04400(1)	Czech Republic	Ni70Cu30	Wrought	CSN 423431
	Germany	2.4360/NiCu30Fe	Wrought	DIN 17743
	Japan	NiCuW	Wire	JIS H4554
		NiCuB	Bar, Rod	JIS H4553
		NiCuR	Strip (currently obsolete)	JIS H4555
	UK	NA13	Bar	BS 3076
		NA13	Sheet	BS 3072
		NA13	Strip	BS 3073
		NA13	Tube	BS 3074
		NA13	Wire	BS 3075
	USA	N04400	Wire	AMS 4731
		N04400	Plate, Sheet, Strip	AMS 4544C
		N04400	Tube	AMS 4574B
		N04400	Tube	AMS 4574A
		N04400	Bar, Forgings	AMS 4675A, 4674D
		N04400	Wire	AMS 4730D
		N04400	Wrought	ASTM F96, F467, F468
		N04400	Rod, Bar	ASTM B164
		N04400	Tube	ASTM B163
		N04400	Plate, Sheet, Strip	ASTM B127
		N04400	Pipe	ASTM B165
		Monel 400 (1)		
N05500(2)	Germany	2.4375/NiCu30Al		DIN 17743
		2.4374		DIN 17743
	UK	NA18	Bar	BS 3076
		NA18	Sheet	BS 3072
		NA18	Strip	BS 3073
		NA18	Tube	BS 3074
		NA18	Wire	BS 3075
		4	Tube	BS 3127
	USA	N05500	Bar, Forging	AMS 4676A
		N05500	Bar, Rod, Wire, Sheet, Strip	QQ N-286D
		N05500	Wrought	ASTM F467, F468
		Monel K-500 (1)		
N06002(3)	UK	NA40		BS 2901 Part 5
	USA	ERNiCrMo-2	Bare Welding Rod	AWS A5.14-89
		N06002	Pipe	ASTM B619
		N06002	Plate, Sheet, Strip	ASTM B435
		N06002	Rod	ASTM B572
		N06002	Tube	ASTM B626
		N06002	Tube, Pipe	ASTM B366
		N06002	Tube, Pipe	ASTM B622
		N06002		ASTM B567
		Hastelloy X (3)		
N06022(4)	USA	ERNiCrMo-10	Bare Weld Electrode	AWS A5.14-89
		Hastelloy C-22 (3)		
N06600	Germany	2.464		
	USA	N06600	Bar, Rod	ASTM B166
		N06600	Forgings	ASTM B564

UNS	Country	Designation	Description	Specifications
		No6600	Pipe	ASTM B517
		No6600	Plate, Sheet, Strip	ASTM B168
		No6600	Strip	ASTM B516
		No6600	Tube	ASTM B163
		No6600	Tube, Pipe	ASTM B167, B366
		Inconel 600(3)	Solid Solution Stengthened	
No6625	UK	NA43		BS 2901 pt 5
	USA	ERNiCrMo-3	Bare Weld Electrode	AWS A5.14-89
		No6625	Bar, Rod	ASTM B446
		No6625	Plate, Sheet, Strip	ASTM B443
		No6625	Tube, Pipe	ASTM B366, B444
		Inconel 625 (3)	Solid Solution Stengthened	
No6635(5)	USA	Hastelloy S (2)		
No7750 (6)	USA	Inconel X-750 (3)		
No8800(7)	USA	Incolloy 800 (4)		
No8825 (8)	USA	Incolloy 825 (4)	Solid Solution Stengthened	
No9901(9)	USA	Incolloy 901 (4)	Hardenable	
N10001(10)	France	Ni-Mo28	Bar, Sheet	NF A54-401
	Germany	2.46		DIN
	USA	ERNiMo-1	Bare Weld Electrode	AWS A5.14-89
		Hastelloy B (2)	Solid Solution Stengthened	
N10002 (11)	France	NiMo16Cr15	Bar, Sheet	NF A54-401
	Germany	2.4602		DIN
	UK	ANC16	Investment Cast	
	USA	Hastelloy C (2)	Solid Solution Stengthened	
N10004 (12)	USA	ERNiMo-3	Bare Weld Electrode	AWS A5.14-89
		Hastelloy W (2)	Solid Solution Stengthened	
N10276	Germany	2.4520/NiFe16CuMo		DIN 17745
		2.4537		DIN 17745
		NiMo16Cr		DIN 17742
	UK	DTD328	Sheet	DTD328
		ANC9	Investment Cast	BS 3146
	USA	ERNiCrMo-4	Bare Weld Electrode	AWS A5.14-89
		Hastelloy C-276 (2)	Solid Solution Stengthened	
Copper-Base Alloys				
C10100	Australia	101	Bar, Rod	AS 1567
	Japan	C1011	Sheet, Plate, Strip, Pipe, Tube, Rod	JIS H3510
	USA	C10100	Rod, Sheet, Tube, Pipe—Oxygen-Free	ASTM B133, B152, B187, B188, B2, B272, B280, B3, B372, B42, B432, B48, B49, B68, B75, F68
		OFE	Oxygen-Free Electronic	CDA
C11000	Australia	110	Bar, Rod	AS 1567
	Canada	Cu-ETP(110)	Sheet, Strip, Plate, Bar	CSA HC.4.1
	Finland	Cu-ETP	Sheet, Strip, Rod, Bar, Wire	SFS 2908
		Cu-FRHC	Sheet, Strip, Rod, Bar, Wire	SFS 2908
	France	Cu/a2	Bar, Shapes	NF A51118
		Cu/al	Bar	NF A51118
	India	ETP Copper	Wrought, Forged—Annealed	is 6912
	International	CuETP	Wrought, Plate, Sheet,	ISO R1337

UNS	Country	Designation	Description	Specifications
	International		Strip, Rod, Bar, Tube, Wire	
	Japan	C1100	Wrought, Sheet, Plate	JIS H3100
		C1100	Bar	JIS H3140
		C1100	Rod	JIS H3250, H3260
		C1100	Pipe	JIS H3300
	UK	C101	Wrought	BS 1036
		C102	Wrought	BS 1037
	USA	ETP 99.5Cu-040	Wrought Bar, Rod, Wire, Plate, Sheet, Strip, Tube, Forgings, Cast	AMS 4500, AMS 4701, ASME SB11, ASME SB12, ASTM B101, ASTM B152, ASTM B212, ASTM B248, ASTM B451, SAE j463
		ETP	Electrolytic Tough Pitch	CDA
C12000	Canada	Cu-DLP(120)		CSA
	Finland	Cu-DLP	Sheet	SFS 2906
	France	Cu/b	Bar, Shapes	NF A53301
	International	Cu-DLP	Wrought	ISO 1637
		Cu-DLP	Plate, Sheet, Strip, Rod, Bar, Tube	ISO 1337
	Japan	C1201	Sheet, Plate	JIS H3100
		C1201	Rod	JIS H3260
		C1201	Pipe	JIS H3300
	Mexico	DHP	Tube	DGN W-23
	USA	DLP	Pipe—Deoxidized, Low Residual Phosphor	CDA
C12200	Australia	122	Rod, Bar	AS 1567
		122	Tube	AS 1572
	Canada	Cu-DHP(122)	Sheet, Strip, Bar, Sheet	CSA HC.4.1
	Czech Republic	Cu99.85		CSN 423003
		Cu99.75		CSN 423004
	Denmark	5015	Wrought	DS 3003
	Finland	Cu-DHP	Tube	SFS 2907
	France	Cu/a3		NF A51118
	International	Cu-DHP	Plate, Sheet, Strip	ISO 1634
		Cu-DHP	Tube	ISO 1635, 1637
		Cu-DHP	Plate, Sheet, Strip, Rod, Bar, Tube	ISO R1337
	Japan	C1220	Sheet, Plate	JIS H3100
		C1220	Rod, Bar	JIS H3250, H3260
		C1220	Pipe	JIS H3300
		C1221	Pipe	JIS H3300
	Mexico	RR	Tube	NOM W-17
	South Africa	Cu-FRHC	Tube	SABS 460
		804	Bar	SABS 804-807
		805	Bar	SABS 804-807
		806	Bar	SABS 804-807
		807	Bar	SABS 804-807
	USA	DHP	Tube—Deoxidized, Low Residual Phosphor	CDA
C16200	Czech Republic	CuCd1		CSN 423058
	International	CuCd1	Wrought	ISO 1637, 1638
		CuCd1	Bar	ISO R1336
	UK	C108	Wire	BS 2873
		C108	Plate	BS 2875

UNS	Country	Designation	Description	Specifications
	USA	99Cu-1Cd (Cadmium Copper)	Rod, Wire, Plate, Sheet, Strip	ASTM B105, B9; SAE J463
C17200	International	CuBe2CoNi	Plate, Sheet, Strip, Rod, Bar, Tube Wire, Forgings	ISO R1187
	Japan	C1720 C1720	Sheet, Plate Rod, Bar	JIS H3130 JIS H3270
	Norway	CuBe2CoNi		NS 16355
	USA	Alloy 25 (Beryllium Copper)	Rod, Bar, Plate, Strip, Tube Billets, Forgings	AMS 4530, 4532, 4650, 4725, ASTM B194, B196, B197 B570
C18200	International	CuCr1 CuCr1 CuCr1	Wrought Forgings Plate, Sheet, Rod, Bar, Tube	ISO 1637 ISO 1640 ISO R1336
	USA	99CU-1Cr (Chromium Copper)	Plate, Sheet, Rod, Tube, Forgings	ASTM F9
C21000	Czech Republic	CuZn4		CSN 423200
	International	CuZn5 CuZn5 CuZn5	Plate, Sheet, Strip Tube Plate, Sheet, Strip, Tube, Wire	ISO 1634 ISO 1638 ISO 4261
	Japan	C2100 C2100	Sheet, Plate Rod	JIS H3100 JIS H3260
	Mexico	TU-95	Sheet, Plate	DGN W-27
	USA	95Cu-5Zn (Gilding Metal)	Bar, Wire, Plate, Sheet, Strip	ASTM B134, B36
C22000	Australia	220	Plate, Bar, Sheet, Strip	AS 1566
	Canada	HC.4.Z10 (220)	Sheet, Bar, Strip, Plate, Spring	CSA HC.4.2
	Czech Republic	CuZn10		CSN 423201
	Finland	CuZn10	Sheet	SF 2915
	France	CuZn10 CuZn10 CuZn10	Sheet Tube Bar, Wire	NF A51101 NF A51103 NF A51104
	International	CuZn10 CuZn10 CuZn10	Plate, Sheet, Strip Tube Plate, Sheet, Strip, Rod, Bar	ISO 1634 ISO 1638 ISO 4261
	Japan	C2200 C2200 C2200	Sheet, Plate Rod Pipe	JIS H3100 JIS H3260 JIS H3300
	Mexico	TU-90	Sheet	DGN W-27
	Norway	CuZn10	Sheet, Strip, Plate, Bar, Tube	NS 16106
	UK	CZ101 CZ101	Sheet, Strip Wire	BS 2870 BS 2873
	USA	90Cu-10Zn (Commercial Bronze)	Bar, Wire, Plate, Sheet, Strip, Tube	ASTM B130, B131, B134, B135, B36, B372, SAE J463
C22600	Mexico	TU-87	Sheet	DGN W-27
	USA	C22600	Jewelry Bronze	
C23000	Australia	230	Plate, Bar, Sheet, Strip	AS 1566
	Canada	HC.4.Z15 (230)	Sheet, Plate, Bar, Strip, Spring	CSA HC.4.2
	Czech Republic	CuZn15		CSN 423202
	Denmark	5112	Wrought	DS 3003
	Finland	CuZn15	Sheet, Strip, Bar, Wire,	

UNS	Country	Designation	Description	Specifications
	Finland		Rod, Tube	SFS 2916
	France	CuZn15	Bar, Wire	NF A51104
	International	CuZn15	Plate, Sheet, Strip	ISO 1634
		CuZn15	Tube	ISO 1635
		CuZn15	Wrought	ISO 1637, 1638
		CuZn15	Plate, Sheet, Strip, Rod, Bar, Tube, Wire	ISO 4261
	Japan	C2300	Sheet, Plate	JIS H3100
		C2300	Rod	JIS H3260
		C2300	Pipe	JIS H3300
	Mexico	TU-85	Sheet	DGN W-27
	Sweden	5112-02	Rod, Wire, Strip, Sheet, Plate	SIS 145112
		5112-4	Sheet, Strip, Wire, Rod, Plate	SIS 145112
		5112-5	Sheet, Plate, Strip	SIS 145112
	UK	CZ102	Sheet, Strip	BS 2870
		CZ102	Wire	BS 2873
	USA	85Cu-15Zn (Red Brass)	Wire, Sheet, Tube, Pipe	ASME SB111, SB359, SB43, ASTM B111, B134, B135, B359, B36, B395, B43
C26000	Australia	260	Plate, Bar, Sheet, Strip	AS 1566
	Canada	HC.4.Z30(260)	Sheet, Strip. Bar, Plate, Spring	CSA HC.4.2
	Czech Republic	CuZn30	Wrought	CSN 423210
	Finland	CuZn30	Sheet	SFS 2918
	France	CuZn30	Sheet	NF A51101
		CuZn30	Tube	NF A51103
		CuZn30	Bar, Wire	NF A51104
	India	CuZn30	Plate, Sheet, Strip	IS 410
		CuZn30	Rod	IS 4170
		CuZn30	Wire	IS 4413
	International	CuZn30	Plate, Sheet, Strip	ISO 1634
		CuZn30	Tube	ISO 1635
		CuZn30	Wrought	ISO 1638
		CuZn30	Plate, Sheet, Strip, Rod, Bar, Tube, Wire	ISO 4261
	Japan	C2600	Rod	JIS H3100, H3250, H3260
		C2600	Pipe	JIS H3300, H3320
	Mexico	LA-70	Sheet, Spring	DGN W-25
	Norway	CuZn30	Sheet, Strip, Plate	NS 16115
	Sweden	5122-02	Plate, Sheet, Strip	SIS 145112
		5122-03	Plate, Sheet, Strip	SIS 145112
		5122-04	Plate, Sheet, Strip	SIS 145112
		5122-05	Plate, Sheet, Strip	SIS 145112
	UK	CZ106	Sheet, Strip	BS 2870
		CZ106	Wire	BS 2873
		CZ106	Rod	BS 2874
		CZ106	Plate	BS 2875
	USA	70Cu-30Zn (Cartridge Brass)	Rod, Wire, Sheet, Tube	AMS 4505, 4555, ASTM B129, B134, B135, B19, B36, B569, B587
C26200	USA	C26200 (Cartridge Brass)		
	Czech Republic	CuZn32		CSN 423212
C26800	Canada	HC.4Z34(268)	Bar, Strip, Plate	CSA HC.4.2
	France	CuZn33	Sheet	NF A51101
		CuZn33	Bar, Wire	NF A51104

UNS	Country	Designation	Description	Specifications
	India	CuZn33	Strip	IS 3168
	International	CuZn33	Plate, Sheet, Strip	ISO 1634
		CuZn33	Wrought	ISO 1638
		CuZn33	Plate, Sheet, Strip, Rod, Bar	ISO 4261
	Japan	C2680	Pipe	JIS H3320
	UK	C107	Sheet, Strip	BS 2870
		CZ107	Sheet, Strip	BS 2870
		CZ107	Wire	BS 2873
		C107	Plate	BS 2875
	USA	C26800 (Yellow Brass)		
C27000	Japan	C2700	Rod	JIS H3250, H3260
		C2700	Pipe	JIS H3300
	Sweden	5150-07	Sheet, Strip, Wire, Rod	SIS 145150
	USA	65Cu-35Zn (Yellow Brass)	Rod	ASTM B134, B135, B587
C27200	Australia	272	Plate, Bar, Sheet, Strip	AS 1566
	Czech Republic	CuZn37		CSN 423213
	Denmark	5150	Wrought	DS 3003
	Finland	CuZn37	Sheet, Strip, Bar, Rod, Wire, Tube	SFS 2919
	France	CuZn36	Sheet	NF A51101
		CuZn36	Tube	NF A51103
	Japan	C2720	Sheet, Plate	JIS H3100
	Norway	CuZn37	Sheet, Strip, Plate, Bar, Rod, Wire, Tube	NS 16120
	South Africa	Cu-Zn37	Tube	SABS 460
	Sweden	5150-02	Sheet, Strip, Plate, Bar, Rod, Wire, Tube	SIS 145150
		5150-03	Sheet, Strip, Plate, Bar, Rod, Wire	SIS 145150
		5150-04	Sheet, Strip, Plate, Bar, Rod, Wire, Tube	SIS 145150
		5150-05	Sheet, Strip, Plate	SIS 145150
		5150-10	Strip, Wire, Tube	SIS 145150
		5150-11	Sheet, Strip, Plate	SIS 145150
	UK	CZ108	Sheet, Strip	BS 2870
		CZ108	Tube	BS 2871
		CZ108	Wire	BS 2873
	USA	C27200 (Brass)		
C28000	Australia	280	Rod, Bar	AS 1567
	Canada	HC.9.ZF391-SC		CSA
	Czech Republic	CuZn40		CSN 423220
	France	CuZn40	Sheet	NF A51101
		CuZn40	Tube	NF A51103
		CuZn40	Bar, Wire	NF A51104
	India	CuZn40	Plate, Sheet, Strip	IS 410
		Lead Free Brass	Forgings	IS 6912
	International	CuZn40	Plate, Sheet, Strip	ISO 1634
		CuZn40	Tube	ISO 1635
		CuZn40	Wrought	ISO 1637, 1639
		CuZn40	Sheet, Strip, Plate, Bar, Rod, Wire, Tube	ISO 4261
	Japan	C2801	Sheet, Plate	JIS H3100
		C2800	Rod	JIS H3250, H3260
		C2800	Pipe	JIS H3300
	UK	CZ109	Forgings	BS 2872
		CZ109	Rod	BS 2874
	USA	60Cu-40Zn (Muntz Metal)	Rod, Plate, Tube, Forgings	ASME SB111, B111, B135

UNS	Country	Designation	Description	Specifications
C31400	USA	Leaded Commercial Bronze		
C31600	USA	Leaded Commercial Bronze, Nickel Bearing		ASTM B140
C36500	Australia	365	Rod, Bar	AS 1567
		365	Forgings	AS 1568
	Finland	CuZn40Pb	Sheet	SFS 2925
	India	CuZn40	Rod, Bar	IS 4170
		60/40 Brass	Forgings	IS 6912
	International	CuZn40Pb	Plate, Sheet, Strip	ISO 1634
		CuZn40Pb	Wrought	ISO 1637, 1638
		CuZn40Pb	Plate, Sheet, Strip, Rod, Bar	IS 426-2
	Sweden	5163-00	Plate, Sheet	SIS 145163
		5163-04	Plate, Sheet	SIS 145163
	UK	CZ123	Sheet, Strip	BS 2870
		CZ123	Forgings	BS 2872
		CZ123	Rod	BS 2874
		CZ123	Plate	BS 2875
	USA	Leaded Muntz Metal	Plate, Sheet, Tube	ASME SB171; ASTM B171, B432
C37000	Australia	370	Plate, Bar, Sheet, Strip	AS 1566
	Canada	HC.9.ZP361-SC		CSA
	Czech Republic	CuZn39Pb1		CSN 423222
	Norway	CuZn40Pb	Sheet, Strip, Plate	NS 16140
	Sweden	5165-00	Bar, Tube	SIS 145165
		5165-02	Strip, Bar	SIS 145165
		5165-04	Strip, Bar, Wire, Tube	SIS 145165
		5165-10	Wire	SIS 145165
	USA	60Cu-39Zn-1Pb (Free Cutting Muntz Metal)	Bar, Rod, Plate, Sheet, Strip, Forgings	ASTM B135
C38000	Czech Republic	CuZn40Pb2		CSN 423223
	Denmark	5186	Wrought	DS 3003
	USA	Architectural Bronze		
C38500	Denmark	5170	Wrought	DS 3003
	France	CuZn40Pb3	Bar, Wire, Extrusions	NF A51105
	International	CuZn39Pb3	Wrought	ISO 1637
		CuZn39Pb3	Rod, Bar, Tube	ISO 426-2
	UK	CZ121	Rod	BS 2874
	USA	Architectural Bronze		
C44300	Canada	HC.4.ZT281V (443)		CSA
	India	CuZn29Sn1As	Tube	IS 1545
	International	CuZn28Sn1	Plate, Sheet, Strip	ISO 1634
		CuZn28Sn1	Tube	ISO 1635
		CuZn28Sn1	Plate, Sheet, Tube	ISO 426-1
	Japan	C4430	Pipe	JIS H3300
	South Africa	Cu-Zn28Sn1	Tube	SABS 460
	Sweden	5220-12	Tube	SIS 145220
	Switzerland	CuZn28Sn1	Tube	VSM 11557
	UK	CZ111	Tube	BS 2871
	USA	70Cu-28Zn-1Sn (Admiralty Brass, Arsenical)	Plate, Tube	ASME SB111, SB359, SB395, SB543; ASTM B111, B171, B3559, B395, B543
C44400	USA	Admiralty Brass, Antimonial		
C46200	Japan	C4621	Sheet, Plate	JIS H3100
	USA	Naval Brass		
C46400	Canada	HC.4.ZT391(464)	Bar, Plate, Sheet, Strip	CSA HC.4.9

UNS	Country	Designation	Description	Specifications
	Czech Republic	CuZn38Sn1		CSN 423237
	International	CuZn38Sn1	Plate, Sheet, Strip	ISO 1634
		CuZn38Sn1	Plate, Sheet, Rod, Bar, Tube, Forgings	ISO 426-1
	Norway	CuZn38Sn1		NS 16220
	UK	CZ112	Sheet, Strip	BS 2870
		CZ112	Forgings	BS 2872
		CZ112	Rod	BS 2874
		CZ112	Plate	BS 2875
	USA	60Cu-39.2Zn-.8Sn (Naval Brass)	Bar, Rod, Sheet, Tube	AMS 4611; ASME SB171; ASTM B124, B171, B21, B283, B432; SAE J461, J463
C46500	USA	Leaded Naval Brass, Arsenical		
C48200	USA	60.5Cu-38Zn-.8Sn.7Pb (Naval Brass)	Bar, Rod, Wire, Plate, Forgings	ASTM B124, B21
C48500	USA	60Cu-37.5Zn1.8Pb.7Sn (Leaded Naval Brass)	Bar, Rod, Wire, Plate, Sheet, Forgings, Strip	ASTM B124, B21, B283
C61000	India	CuAl7	Tube	IS 1545
	International	CuAl8	Plate, Sheet, Strip	ISO 1634
		CuAl8	Plate, Sheet, Strip, Bar	ISO 428
	USA	ERCUaL-a1	Bare Weld Rod Electrode (Aluminum Bronze)	AWS A5.7-91R
C63000	Canada	HC.5.AN105F(630)		CSA
	Czech Republic	CuAl10Fe4Ni		CSN 423047
	UK	C105	Sheet, Strip	BS 2870
		CA105	Plate	BS 2875
	USA	82CU-10AL-5nI-3Fe (Aluminum Bronze)	Bar, Rod, Tube, Forgings	AMS 4640; ASME SB150, SB171; ASTM B124, B150, B171, B283; SAE J463
C64700	Czech Republic	CuNi2Si		CSN 423054
	International	CuNi2Si	Plate, Sheet, Strip	ISO 1634, 1637
		CuNi2Si	Strip, Rod, Bar, Wire	ISO R1187
	USA	Silicon Bronze		
C65500	Australia	655	Plate, Bar, Sheet, Strip	AS 1566
		655	Rod, Bar	AS 1567
		655	Forgings	AS 1568
	Canada	HC.4.S3(655)	Bar, Sheet, Strip, Plate	CSA HC.4.7
	International	CuSi3Mn1	Plate, Sheet, Strip	ISO 1634
		CuSi3Mn1	Wrought	ISO 1637
		CuSi3Mn1	Plate, Sheet, Strip, Rod, Bar, Tubing, Wire, Forgings	ISO R1187
	UK	CS101	Sheet, Strip	BS 2870
		CS101	Forgings	BS 2872
		CS101	Wire	BS 2873
		CS101	Rod	BS 2874
		CS101	Plate	BS 2875
	USA	97CU-3Si (Silicon Bronze)	Rod, Wire, Sheet, Tube	AMS 4615, 4665; ASME SB315, SB96, SB98; ASTM B100, B124, B263, B315, B96, B97, B98, B99; SAE J463
C66100	USA	Silicon Bronze		
C68700	Australia	687	Tube	AS 1572
	Denmark	5217	Wrought	DS 3003
	Finland	CuZn20Al2	Tube	SFS 2928
	France	CuZn22Al2		NF

UNS	Country	Designation	Description	Specifications
	India	CuZn21Al2As	Tube	IS 1545
	International	CuZn20Al2	Plate, Sheet, Strip	ISO 1634
		CuZn20Al2	Tube	ISO 1635
		CuZn20Al2	Plate, Tube	ISO 426-1
	Japan	C6870	Pipe	JIS H3300
	Norway	CuZn20Al2	Tube	NS 16210
	South Africa	Cu-Zn21Al2	Tube	SABS 460
	Sweden	5217-02	Tube	SIS 145217
	Switzerland	Cu-Zn21Al2	Tube	VSM 11557
	UK	CZ110	Sheet, Strip	BS 2870
		CZ110	Tube	BS 2871
		CZ110	Plate	BS 2875
	USA	Aluminum Brass, Arsenical		
C69710	USA	Copper Zinc Alloy		
C70600	Denmark	5667	Wrought	DS 3003
	Finland	CuNi10Fe1Mn	Tube	SFS 2938
	France	CuNi10Fe1Mn		NF
	International	CuNi10Fe1Mn	Plate, Sheet, Strip	ISO 1634
		CuNi10Fe1Mn	Tube	ISO 1635
		CuNi10Fe1Mn	Plate, Sheet, Strip, Rod, Bar, Tube	ISO 429
	Japan	C7060	Sheet, Plate	JIS H3100
		C7060	Pipe	JIS H3300
	Norway	CuNi10Fe1Mn	Tube	NS 16410
	Sweden	5667	Tube	SIS 145667
	Switzerland	CuNi10Fe1Mn	Tube	VSM 1557
	USA	90Cu-10Ni (Copper Nickel 90/10)	Wire, Plate, Sheet, Tube, Pipe	ASME SB111, SB171, SB359, SB395, SB402, SB466, SB467; ASTM B111, B122, B141, B171, B359, B395, B402, B432, B466, B467, B543, B552
C71500	Canada	HC.4.NF30(715)		CSA
	Czech Republic	CuNi30FeMn		CSN 423063
	France	CuNi30Mn1Fe		NF
	International	CuNi30Mn1Fe	Plate, Sheet, Strip	ISO 1634
		CuNi30Mn1Fe	Tube	ISO 1635
		CuNi30Mn1Fe	Wrought	ISO 1637
		CuNi30Mn1Fe	Plate, Sheet, Strip, Rod, Bar, Tube	ISO 429
	Japan	C7150	Sheet, Plate	JIS H3100
		C7150	Pipe	JIS H3300
	Norway	CuNi30Mn1Fe	Tube	NS 16415
	Sweden	5682	Tube	SIS 145682
	Switzerland	CuNi30FeMn	Tube	VSM 11557
	UK	CN107	Sheet, Strip, Strip	BS 2870
		NS107	Sheet, Strip	BS 2870
		CN107	Tube	BS 2871
		CN107	Plate	BS 2875
	USA	Copper Nickel 30%	Weld Applications	
C72200	USA	Copper Nickel Alloy	Weld Applications	
C83300	USA	Red Brass, Cast		
C83400	USA	C83400	Red Brass, Continuous Cast	
	Japan	YBsCln1, Cast		JIS H2202
C83800	Canada	ZP66-SC	Cast	CSA HC.9

UNS	Country	Designation	Description	Specifications
	Pan America	C83800	Bar, Continuous Cast	COPANT 801
	USA	C83800 Hydraulic Bronze	Leaded Red Brass, Cast	ASTM B271, B30, B505, B584; SAE J462
C85200	Canada	ZP243-SC	Cast	CSA HC.9
	USA	C85200	Leaded Yellow Brass, Cast	ASTM B271, B30, B584; SAE J462
C85800	Canada	ZF391P-SC	Cast	CSA HC.9
	Czech Republic	CuZn40	Cast	CSN 423319
	Germany	2.0342/GB-CuZn37Pb	Cast Ingot	DIN 17656
		2.0383/GB-CuZn39Pb	Cast	
	Norway	CuZn39Pb2Al	Die Cast	NS 16554
	Sweden	5253.06	Cast	SIS 145253
		5253-10	Cast	SIS 145253
	USA	C85800	Leaded Yellow Brass, Cast	
C86100	Germany	2.0608/GB-CuZn25Al5	Cast	DIN
	USA	C86100	Manganese Bronze, Cast	SAE J462
C86800	Germany	2.0606/GB-CuZn34Al2		
	USA	C86800	Leaded Manganese Bronze, Cast	
C87200	Canada	SC-SC	Cast	CSA HC.9
	USA	C87200	Silicon Bronze, Cast	ASTM B271, B30, B584; SAE J462
C87400	USA	C87400	Silicon Bronze/Brass, Cast	
C87600	USA	C87600	Silicon Bronze/Brass, Cast	
C87800	USA	C87800	Silicon Bronze/Brass, Cast	
C90200	USA	C90200	Tin Bronze, Continuous Cast	
C90300	USA	C90300	Tin Bronze, Continuous Cast	ASTM B271, B30, B505, B584
C91700	Germany	2.1063/GB-CuSn12Ni	Cast	
	International	CuSn12Ni2	Cast	ISO 1338
	USA	C91700	Nickel Gear Bronze	ASTM B427, B30
C92200	Canada	TZ64P-SC	Cast	CSA HC.9
	Pan America	C92200	Bar, Continuous Cast	COPANT 801
	USA	C92200	Naval Bronze, Cast	ASTM B271, B30, B505, B584, B61; SAE J462
C92900	USA	C92900	Leaded Tin Bronze, Cast	
C93100	Australia	931D	Cast	AS 1565
	International	CuSn8Pb2	Cast	ISO 1338
	USA	C93100	High-Leaded Tin Bronze, Cast	
C94700	Canada	TN55-SC	Cast	CSA H.9
	Pan America	C94700(HT)	Bar, Continuous Cast	COPANT 801
	USA	C94700	Nickel Tin Bronze, Cast	
C94900	USA	C94900	Nickel Tin Bronze, Cast	
C95200	Canada	AF93-SC	Cast	CSA HC.9
	Czech Republic	CuA9Fe3	Cast	CSN 423145
	France	U-A9Fe3Y200	Cast	NF A53-709
	Germany	2.0941/GB-CuAl10Fe	Cast	DIN 17656
	International	CuAl10Fe3	Cast	ISO 1338
	Japan	AlBCln1	Cast	JIS H2206
		AlBC1	Cast	JIS H5114
	Norway	CuAl10Fe3	Cast, Ingot	NS 16575
	Pan America	C95200	Bar, Continuous Cast	COPANT 801

UNS	Country	Designation	Description	Specifications
	Sweden	5710-03	Cast	SIS 145710
		5710-06	Cast	SIS 145710
	USA	C95200	Aluminum Bronze	
C95500	Canada	AF114N-SC	Cast	CSA HC.9
	Czech Republic	CuAl10Fe4Ni		CSN 423147
	Germany	2.0981/GB-CuAl1Ni		
	International	CuAl10Fe5Ni	Cast	ISO 1338
	Pan America	C95500(HT)		COPANT 801
	USA	C95500	Aluminum Bronze	
C95800	Denmark	5716	Cast	DS 3001
	France	U-A9N5FeY200	Cast	NF A53-709
	Germany	2.0976/GB-CuAl10Ni	Cast Ingot	DIN 17656
	Japan	AlBCln3	Cast	JIS H2206
		AlBC3	Cast	JIS H5114
	Norway	CuAl10Fe5Ni5	Cast Ingot	NS 16570
	South Africa	CuAl10Ni6Fe4	Cast	SABS 200
	Sweden	5716-03	Cast	SIS 145716
		5716-06	Cast	SIS 145716
		5716-15	Cast	SIS 145716
	USA	C95800	Aluminum Bronze, Cast	
C96200	Australia		Cast	AS 1565
	Germany	2.0815.01/GB-CuNi10	Cast	DIN 17658
	USA	C96200	Copper Nickel, Cast	
C96400	Australia		Cast	AS 1565
	Germany	2.0835.01/GB-CuNi30	Cast	DIN 17658
	Pan America	C96400	Bar, Continuous Cast	COPANT 801
	USA	C96400	Copper Nickel, Cast	ASTM B30, B369, B505

Source: Paul M. Unterweiser, ed., (1987), *Worldwide Guide to Equivalent Irons and Steels,* ASM International, Materials Park, OH 44073-0002

 APPENDIX 5

Weights of Common Materials

Material	Weight	
	lb./ft³	kg/m³
acetal, copolymer	98.3	1575.0
acrylonitrile-butadiene-styrene (ABS)	65.5	1049.0
aluminum (6000 series)	165	2643.1
brass, naval	534	8553.9

Material	Weight	
	lb./ft³	kg/m³
brick, common red	120	1922.2
brick, fire	150	2402.8
bronze	509	8153.4
cedar, red	24	384.4
cement, portland (as mixed)	197	3155.6

Material	Weight	
	lb./ft³	kg/m³
concrete, gravel	150	2402.8
copper, rolled	556	8906.3
cpvc	95.8	1534.6
diesel fuel	52.1	834.6
epoxy	78.3	1254.3
ethylene glycol	69.5	1113.3
fir, douglas	33	528.6
gasoline	45.9	735.2
glass, window	161	2578.9
hydraulic fluid	53.9	863.4
iron, cast	450	7208.3
iron, wrought	485	7768.9
kerosene	49.9	799.3
lead	709	1135.7
mahogany, honduras, dry	34	544.6
mahogany, spanish, dry	53	848.9
maple, dry	44	704.8
mortar, sand & cement, set	135	2162.5
mortar, sand & cement, wet	150	2402.8
oak, white	59	945.1
oak, red	44	704.8
oil, linseed	58.8	941.9
oil, lubricating	56.8	909.8
pine, white, dry	26	416.5
pine, yellow, southern, dry	45	720.8

Material	Weight	
	lb./ft³	kg/m³
plywood	38.4	615.1
polycarbonate (pcp)	74.9	1199.8
polyester, cast	78.0	1249.4
polyetheretherketone (peek)	81.8	1310.3
polyethylene, low density (pe)	57.7	924.3
polypropylene (pp)	56.5	905.0
polystyrene (ps)	65.5	1049.2
polyvinyl chloride (pvc)	81.2	1300.7
polyvinylidene fluoride (pvdf)	110.8	1774.8
rubber	95	1521.8
sand, dry	100	1601.8
sand, wet	120	1922.2
sewage, sludge	45	720.8
silicone epoxy	94.9	1520.2
steel, rolled	495	7929.1
steel, cast	490	7849.0
stone, crushed	100	1601.8
tin	459	7352.5
titanium	272.3	4361.8
tungsten	1224	1960.7
turpentine	54	864.9
uranium	1185	1898.2
water, pure	62.4	999.6
water, sea	64.08	1026.8
zinc, cast	440	7048.1

Clark, George L., and Gessner G. Hawley. *The Encyclopedia of Chemistry*. New York: Rheinhold, 1957.

Glover, Thomas J. *Pocket Reference*. 2d ed. Littleton CO: Sequoia Publishing, 1996.

Green, Robert E. *Machinery's Handbook*. 25th ed. New York: Industrial Press, 1996.

Korb, Lawrence J., and David L. Olson. *ASM Handbook*. Vol. 13, *Corrosion*. Materials Park OH: ASM International, 1987.

 APPENDIX 6

Wire Table: Standard Annealed Copper Wire (AWG)

Scientific notation is used for the numbers in the tables.

E –0X = move the decimal point X places to the left

E +0X = move the decimal point X places to the right

E +00 = retain the decimal point as is

AWG No.	Diameter (mils)	Cross Section Area (circular-mils)	Cross Section Area (inches)	Ohms per 1000 ft.
0000	4.600 E +02	2.116 E +05	1.662 E −01	4.901 E −02
000	4.096 E +02	1.678 E +05	1.318 E −01	6.180 E −02
00	3.648 E +02	1.331 E +05	1.045 E −01	7.793 E −02
0	3.249 E +02	1.050 E +05	8.289 E −02	9.827 E −02

AWG No.	Diameter (mils)	Cross Section Area (circular-mils)	Cross Section Area (inches)	Ohms per 1000 ft.
1	2.893 E +02	8.369 E +04	6.573 E −02	1.239 E −01
2	2.576 E +02	6.637 E +04	5.213 E −02	1.563 E −01
3	2.294 E +02	5.264 E +04	4.134 E −02	1.970 E −01
4	2.043 E +02	4.174 E +04	3.278 E −02	2.485 E −01
5	1.819 E +02	3.310 E +04	2.600 E −02	3.133 E −01
6	1.620 E +02	2.625 E +04	2.062 E −02	3.951 E −01
7	1.443 E +02	2.082 E +04	1.635 E −02	4.982 E −01
8	1.285 E +02	1.651 E +04	1.297 E −02	6.282 E −01
9	1.144 E +02	1.309 E +04	1.028 E −02	7.921 E −01
10	1.019 E +02	1.038 E +04	8.155 E −03	9.989 E −01
11	9.074 E +01	8.234 E +03	6.467 E −03	1.260 E +00
12	8.081 E +01	6.530 E +03	5.129 E −03	1.588 E +00
13	7.196 E +01	5.178 E +03	4.067 E −03	2.003 E +00
14	6.408 E +01	4.107 E +03	3.225 E −03	2.525 E +00
15	5.707 E +01	3.257 E +03	2.558 E −03	3.184 E +00
16	5.082 E +01	2.583 E +03	2.028 E −03	4.016 E +00
17	4.526 E +01	2.048 E +03	1.609 E −03	5.064 E +00
18	4.030 E +01	1.624 E +03	1.276 E −03	6.385 E +00
19	3.589 E +01	1.288 E +03	1.012 E −03	8.051 E +00
20	3.196 E +01	1.022 E +03	8.023 E −04	1.015 E +01
21	2.846 E +01	8.101 E +02	6.363 E −04	1.280 E +01
22	2.535 E +01	6.424 E +02	5.046 E −04	1.614 E +01

Note: Measurements at 68°F (20°C)

Source: H. P. Westman and J. E. Schlaikjer, *Reference Data for Radio Engineers*, 4th ed. (New York: International Telephone and Telegraph Corp., 1963).

 APPENDIX 7

Properties of Metals

Gray Cast Irons

The gray irons are generally divided into two groups. The first group ranges from 20,000 to 35,000 pounds per square inch (psi) in tensile strength and includes irons that are easily cast and machined. The second group ranges from 40,000 to 60,000 psi in tensile strength and includes irons that are typically more difficult to manufacture and machine. They are identified by letter-number combinations such as 20A, 25B, and 35C, where the prefix number indicates the minimum tensile strength in thousand pounds per square inch.

Typical applications of the gray cast irons include machine tools, automotive cylinder blocks, exhaust system components (such as elbows, Y's), cast iron pipe and fittings, and agricultural equipment.

Malleable Cast Iron

Typical properties for standard malleable cast iron are tensile strength of about 52,000 psi (359 MPa), yield strength of about 34,000 psi (234 MPa), and elongation (a measure of ductility) of 10 to 18 percent.

Two other types of malleable cast irons—cupola and pearlitic—can be produced by varying the heat-treating process. Cupola has a minimum tensile strength of 40,000 psi (276 MPa), minimum yield strength of 30,000 psi (221 MPa), and elongation of 5 percent. Cupola cast iron is used in special pipe fittings and valve components.

Pearlitic cast irons exhibit a broad range of properties. Tensile strengths range from 60,000 to 105,000 psi (414 to 724 MPa), yield strengths vary from 40,000 to 90,000 psi (276 to 621 MPa), and elongations range from 10 percent at the lowest tensile and yield strengths to 1 percent at the highest strengths. Pearlitic cast irons are used in place of steel castings or forgings or to replace standard malleable iron when greater strength or wear resistance is called for. They are also used in such engine applications as camshafts, crankshafts, water-cooled exhaust components, and transmission housings, and for various other components around the boat such as tiller arms, engine leveling shims, and oarlocks.

Ductile Cast Irons

Various grades are available ranging from 60,000 psi tensile strength, 40,000 psi (276 MPa) yield strength, and 18 percent elongation to 120,000 psi (827 MPa) tensile strength, 90,000 psi (621 MPa) yield strength, and 2 percent elongation.

Alloy Cast Irons

Alloy cast irons are used in automotive cylinders, pistons, piston rings, crankcases, brake drums, and various applications such as machine tools and special purpose uses where the casting must provide a higher degree of resistance to scaling at high temperatures.

There are four basic categories of alloy cast irons: Low and Moderately Alloyed Irons, High-Nickel Austenitic Cast Irons, High-Chromium Cast Irons, and High-Silicon Cast Irons. These alloys exhibit good strength, up to 70,000 psi (483 MPa), and are easily machined. They find automotive applications in engine cylinders and cylinder liners, in pistons and piston rings, and also in machine tools and dies and in high wear and abrasion uses. They are typically more costly than the unalloyed cast irons and find their principal application in the chemical- and petroleum-processing industries.

Low and Moderately Alloyed Cast Irons

In addition to the usual iron and silicon of the unalloyed cast irons, irons in this group also contain up to 5 percent nickel, 35 percent chromium, 4 percent molybdenum, and 3 percent copper. Corrosion resistance is substantially better than that of the unalloyed cast irons.

High-Nickel Cast Irons

These alloys contain large nickel and copper content. They are resistant to several common acids (sulfuric, phosphoric, hydrogen chloride) and caustics and are primarily designed for applications in the chemical-processing industries.

High-Chromium Cast Irons

Alloys in this group are essentially white cast iron with 12 to 30 percent chromium. They may contain other alloying elements to optimize their performance in specific applications. They are designed for application in marine and industrial atmospheres and have superior abrasion resistance.

Carbon Steel

Carbon steels are commonly used in many of the products we encounter every day, including all kinds of machines, automobile bodies and frames, and structural steel for buildings.

Low-Carbon Steels

AISI-SAE grades 1005 through 1030 constitute the low-carbon group. These are steels typically used in such applications as automobile bodies, fenders, hoods, and similar products.

Table A7-1

Chemical Properties of Low-Carbon Grades

Grade AISI/SAE	Grade UNS	Carbon, %	Manganese, %	Phosphorus, % max.	Sulfur, % max.
1005	G10050	0.06 max.	0.35 max.	0.040	0.050
1006	G10060	0.08 max.	0.25–0.40	0.040	0.050
1008	G10080	0.10 max.	0.30–0.50	0.040	0.050
1010	G10100	0.08–0.13	0.30–0.60	0.040	0.050
1012	G10120	0.10–0.15	0.30–0.60	0.040	0.050
1015	G10150	0.13–0.18	0.30–0.60	0.040	0.050
1016	G10160	0.13–0.18	0.60–0.90	0.040	0.050
1017	G10170	0.15–0.20	0.30–0.60	0.040	0.050
1018	G10180	0.15–0.20	0.60–0.90	0.040	0.050

Grade AISI/SAE	Grade UNS	Carbon, %	Manganese, %	Phosphorus, % max.	Sulfur, % max.
1019	G10190	0.15–0.20	0.70–1.00	0.040	0.050
1020	G10200	0.18–0.23	0.30–0.60	0.040	0.050
1021	G10210	0.18–0.23	0.60–0.90	0.040	0.050
1022	G10220	0.18–0.23	0.70–1.00	0.040	0.050
1023	G10230	0.20–0.25	0.30–0.60	0.040	0.050

Source: Erik Oberg, Franklin D. Jones, Horton L. Holbrook, and Henry H. Ryffel, *Machinery's Handbook,* 25th ed. Robert E. Green and Christopher J. McCauley, eds. (New York: Industrial Press, 1996), pp. 457–58.

Table A7-2

Mechanical Properties of Plain Carbon Steels

	Tensile Strength, psi (MPa)	Yield Strength, psi (MPa)	Hardness (Brinell)	Impact Strength, ft.lb. (kgf)
Average	96,889 (668)	61,500 (424)	206	38 (17.4)
Maximum	140,000 (965)	85,000 (586)	293	81.5 (37)
Minimum	61,000 (421)	44,300 (305)	126	3.0 (1.4)

Source: Based on a representative sample taken from Oberg et al., *Machinery's Handbook,* 25th ed., pp. 434–39 (plain carbon steel group).

Table A7-3 shows the approximate values for the standard mechanical properties of the low-alloy steels in the annealed condition for purposes of comparison with those for plain carbon steels.

Table A7-3

Mechanical Properties of Standard Alloy Steels (Annealed)

	Tensile Strength, psi (MPa)	Yield Strength, psi (MPa)	Hardness (Brinell)	Impact Strength, ft.lb. (kgf)
Average	92,733 (639)	56,421 (389)	183	45 (20.4)
Maximum	108,000 (745)	68,500 (472)	217	82.8 (37.6)
Minimum	74,250 (512)	40,000 (276)	149	7.4 (3.4)

Source: Based on a representative sample taken from Oberg et al., *Machinery's Handbook,* 25th ed., p. 434 (low-alloy steels group).

Table A7-4

Mechanical Properties of Standard Alloy Steels (Normalized)

	Tensile Strength, psi (MPa)	Yield Strength, psi (MPa)	Hardness (Brinell)	Impact Strength, ft.lb. (kgf)
Average	124,267 (857)	78,292 (540)	249	43 (19.5)
Maximum	185,500 (1,279)	125,000 (862)	363	98 (44.5)
Minimum	82,250 (567)	51,750 (357)	174	8.0 (3.6)

Source: Based on a representative sample taken from Oberg et al., *Machinery's Handbook,* 25th ed., p. 434 (low-alloy steels group).

Table A7-5

Composition of Martensitic Stainless Steels (percentage by weight)

Alloy	UNS	Chromium	Nickel	Molybdenum	Carbon	Manganese
410	S41000	11.5–13.5	0.75		0.15	1.0
420	S42000	12.0–14.0			0.15 min	1.0

Note: These grades also contain small amounts of silicon, phosphor, and sulfur. Some martensitic grades contain small amounts of molybdenum.
Source: Based on a representative sample taken from Oberg et al., *Machinery's Handbook,* 25th ed., p. 411–12.

Table A7-6

Composition of Ferritic Stainless Steels (percentage by weight)

Alloy	UNS	Chromium	Nickel	Molybdenum	Carbon	Manganese
430	S43000	16.0–18.0			0.12	1.0
429	S42900	14.0–16.0			0.12	1.0

Note: These grades also contain small amounts of silicon, phosphor, and sulfur. Some ferritic grades contain small amounts of nickel.
Source: Based on a representative sample taken from Oberg et al., *Machinery's Handbook,* 25th ed., p. 411–12.

Table A7-7

Composition of 18-8 Austenitic Stainless Steels (percentage by weight)

Alloy	UNS	Chromium	Nickel	Molybdenum	Carbon	Manganese
301	S30100	16.0–18.0	6.0–8.0		0.15	2.0
302	S30200	17.0–19.0	8.0–10.0		0.15	2.0
303	S30300	17.0–19.0	8.0–10.0	0.60	0.15	2.0
304	S30400	18.0–20.0	8.0–10.5		0.08	2.0
304L	S30403	18.0–20.0	8.0–12.0		0.03	2.0

Note: These grades also contain small amounts of silicon, phosphor, and sulfur. Some 18-8 grades contain small amounts of nitrogen.

Key Grades and Compositions of Austenitic Stainless Steels

Table A7-8 lists the standard austenitic stainless steel grades commonly considered marine grades with their chemical compositions.

Table A7-8

Common Marine Grades of Austenitic Stainless Steels and Their Chemical Compositions (percentage by weight)

Alloy	UNS	Chromium	Nickel	Molybdenum	Carbon	Other
302	S30200	17.0–19.0	8.0–10.0		0.15	
304	S30400	18.0–20.0	8.0–10.5		0.08	
304L	S30403	18.0–20.0	8.0–12.0		0.03	
316	S31600	16.0–18.0	10.0–14.0	2.0–3.0	0.08	
316L	S31603	16.0–18.0	10.0–14.0	2.0–3.0	0.03	
317	S31700	18.0–20.0	11.0–15.0	3.0–4.0	0.08	
317L	S31703	18.0–20.0	11.0–15.0	3.0–4.0	0.03	
321	S32100	17.0–19.0	9.0–12.0		0.08	0.40 Titanium

Note: All of these grades also have 2.0 percent manganese, 1.0 percent silicon, 0.045 percent phosphor, and 0.03 percent sulfur.
Source: Based on a representative sample taken from Oberg et al., *Machinery's Handbook,* 25th ed., p. 411–12.

Table A7-9

Common Marine Grades of Austenitic Stainless Steels and Their Mechanical Properties

Alloy	UNS	Tensile Strength, 1,000 psi (MPa)	Yield Strength, 1,000 psi (MPa)	Elongation (in 2") %	Hardness Rb (Bhn)
302	S30200	85 (586)	35 (241)	60	85 (150)
304	S30400	85 (586)	35 (241)	60	80 (149)
304L	S30403	75 (517)[*]	33 (228)	60	79 (143)
316	S31600	80 (552)	30 (207)	60	79 (149)
316L	S31603	75 (517)[*]	34 (234)	55	79 (149)
317	S31700	85 (586)	40 (276)	50	85 (160)
317L	S31703	85 (586)	35 (241)	55	80 (160)
321	S32100	85 (586)	35 (241)	55	80 (160)

[*]Plate form   *Source:* Based on a representative sample taken from Oberg et al., *Machinery's Handbook,* 25th ed., p. 411–12.

Table A7-10

Composition of High-Performance Austenitic Stainless Steels (percentage by weight)

Alloy	UNS	Chromium	Nickel	Molybdenum	Carbon	Manganese
22-13-5	S20910	22.0	12.5	2.3	0.02	5.0
Nitronic 50	S21910	22.0	12.5	2.25	0.04	5.0
Aquamet 22		22.0	12.5	2.25	0.04	5.0

Note: These grades also contain small amounts of silicon, phosphor, sulfur, and other residual elements.
Source: C. P. Dillon, *Corrosion Control in the Chemical Processing Industries*, 2nd ed. (NACE Internation Nitronic—1986 Armco Specialty Steel Division Product Data Bulletin 26-266 and Aquamet—1984, Bulletin 5-26).

Table A7-11

Mechanical Properties of High-Performance Austenitic Stainless Steels

	Yield strength, 2% psi (MPa)	Tensile strength, psi (MPa)	Elongation % in 2"
Alloy 22-13-5	65,000 (448)	120,000 (827)	45
Nitronic 50	111,000 (896)	130,000 (758)	15
Aquamet 22	105,000 (724)	135,000 (931)	20
316	36,000 (248)	82,000 (565)	69

Source: C. P. Dillon, *Corrosion Control in the Chemical Processing Industries*, 2nd ed. (NACE Internation Nitronic—1986 Armco Specialty Steel Division Product Data Bulletin 26-266 and Aquamet—1984, Bulletin 5-26).

Table A7-12

Composition of High-Performance Duplex Stainless Steels (percentage by weight)

Alloy	UNS	Chromium	Nickel	Molybdenum	Carbon	Nitrogen
2205	S31803	22	5.5	3.0	0.03	0.18
Ferralium 255	S32550	26	6.0	3.0	0.04	0.15

Source: NiDi Nickel Development Institute, NiDi Technical Series No. 10 044.

Table A7-13

Mechanical Properties of High-Performance Duplex Stainless Steels

	Yield strength, 2% psi (MPa)	Tensile strength, psi (MPa)	Elongation % in 2 inches
Alloy 2205	65,000 (448)	90,000 (620)	25
Ferralium 255	80,000 (550)	110,000 (760)	15
316	36,000 (248)	82,000 (565)	69

Source: 1990 NiDi Nickel Development Institute NiDi Technical Series No. 10 044.

Table A7-14

Nominal Composition of 6% Molybdenum Superaustenitic Alloys (percentage by weight)

Alloy	UNS	Chromium	Nickel	Molybdenum	Copper	Carbon
254 SMO	S31254	20	18	6.1	0.07	0.02 max.
AL-6XN	N08367	20	24	6.0	—	0.02 max.
Alloy 926[1]	N08926	20	25	6.2	1.0	0.03 max.
Alloy 25-6MO[2]	N08031	27	31	6.5	1.0	0.02 max.
654 SMO	S32654	24	22	7.3	0.5	0.02 max.

All grades have 0.20 nitrogen.   1. Also called Alloy 1925hMo   2. Also called Alloy 31

Table A7-15

Mechanical Properties for 1000, 2000, and 3000 Series Wrought Alloys

Alloy	Ultimate (Tensile) Strength, ksi (kPa)		Yield Strength, ksi (kPa)	
	min.	max.	min.	max.
1000 Series	10 (69)	27 (186)	4 (28)	24 (165)
2000 Series	25 (172)	72 (496)	10 (69)	66 (455)
3000 Series	16 (110)	41 (282)	6 (42)	36 (248)

Table A7-16

Mechanical Properties for Popular Marine Alloys

Alloy	Ultimate (Tensile) Strength, ksi (MPa)	Yield Strength, ksi (MPa)	Elongation, % in 2 in.
5052-H32	33 (227)	28 (193)	18
5086-H32	42 (290)	30 (207)	12
5083-H32	46 (317)	33 (228)	16

Table A7-17

Nominal Chemical* and Mechanical Properties of Marine Nickel-Base Alloys

Alloy	Ni	Cr	Mo	Cu	Fe	C max.	Tensile Strength, ksi	Yield Strength, ksi	Elongation, % in 2 in.
Monel 400	65	—	—	32	2	0.15	79	30	48
Monel K-500++	64	—	—	30	2	0.25	160	111	24
Hastelloy C-276	57	15	16	—	4	0.01	116	52	60
Hastelloy C-4	61	16	16	—	3	0.01	112	49	62
Hastelloy C-22	56	22	13	—	3	0.01	116	59	57
Inconel 600	75	15	—	—	10	0.08	90	36	47
Inconel 625	61	21	9	—	2	0.10	142	86	42
Inconel X-750++	73	16	—	—	7	0.8	185	130	20
Incoloy 8002	21	—	—	46	0.10	87	42	44	
Incoloy 825	42	22	—	—	30	0.05	91	35	50
Incoloy 901++	43	12	6	—	36	0.10	175	130	14
Type 316 Stainless	12	17	3	—	66	0.03	85	35	55

*Does not include small amounts of other alloying elements.   ++ Age-hardened.

Table A7-18

Nominal Chemical and Mechanical Properties of Representative Copper Alloy Types

UNS Number	Type	Chemical Composition, %	Tensile Strength, ksi		Yield Strength, ksi		Elongation, %	Typical Applications
			min.	max.	min.	max.		
C10100	OFE	Copper 99.99	32	66	10	53	55	buss bar, bus conductor, coaxial cable
		Arsenic 0.0005						
		Antimony 0.00004						
		Phosphorus 0.0003						
		Tellurium 0.0002						
C11000	ETP	Copper 99.90	32	66	10	53	55	Roofing, gutters, radiators, nails, rivets
		Oxygen 0.04						

UNS Number	Type	Chemical Composition, %	Tensile Strength, ksi		Yield Strength, ksi		Elongation, %	Typical Applications
			min.	max.	min.	max.		
C12200	DHP	Copper 99.9	32	55	10	53	55	Plumbing pipe and tubing, heat exchanger tubing, water, air, gasoline, hydraulic lines
		Phosphorus 0.008						

Table A7-19

Nominal Chemical and Mechanical Properties of Representative High-Copper Alloy Types

UNS Number	Type	Chemical Composition, %	Tensile Strength, ksi		Yield Strength, ksi		Elongation, %	Typical Applications
			min.	max.	min.	max.		
C16200	Cadmium Copper	Copper 98.78	35	100	7	69	57	Spring contacts, switch gear parts
		Cadmium 1.2						
		Iron 0.02						
C17200	Beryllium Copper	Copper 97.58	68	212	25	195	48	Fuse clips, springs, switch parts, valves
		Beryllium 2.0						
		Silicon 0.20						
		Aluminum 0.2						
		Lead 0.02						
C18200	Chromium Copper	Copper 98.5	34	86	14	77	40	Fuse clips, springs, switch and relay parts
		Chromium 1.2						
		Iron 0.10						
		Silicon 0.10						
		Lead 0.05						

Table A7-20

Chemical and Mechanical Properties of the Marine Brasses

UNS Number	Type	Chemical Composition, %	Tensile Strength, ksi		Yield Strength, ksi		Elongation, %	Typical Applications
			min.	max.	min.	max.		
Wrought Forms								
C23000	Red Brass	Copper 85	39	105	10	63	55	Heat exchanger tubing
		Zinc 15						
C26000	Cartridge Brass	Copper 70	44	130	11	65	66	Fastenings
		Zinc 30						Radiator cores and tanks
C27000	Yellow Brass	Copper 65	46	128	14	62	65	Fastenings
		Zinc 35						Radiator cores and tanks
C28000	Muntz Metal	Copper 60	54	74	21	55	52	Condenser tube plates
		Zinc 40						

UNS Number	Type	Chemical Composition, %	Tensile Strength, ksi		Yield Strength, ksi		Elonga-tion, %	Typical Applications
			min.	max.	min.	max.		
C44300	Admiralty Brass	Copper 70	48	55	18	22	65	Condenser, evaporator, and heat exchanger tubing
		Zinc 30						
C46200	Naval Brass	Copper 60	55	88	25	66	50	Marine hardware
		Zinc 40						Propeller shafts
C68700	Aluminum Brass	Copper 67	60 (nom.)		27 (nom.)		55	Condenser, evaporator, and heat exchanger tubing
		Zinc 20						
		Aluminum 2						
		Arsenic (trace)						
Cast Forms								
C83400	Red Brass	Copper 90	35 (nom.)		10 (nom.)		30	Valves, plumbing goods, pump castings, impellers
		Zinc 10						
C85200	Yellow Brass	Copper 72	38 (nom.)		13 (nom.)		35	Plumbing fittings and fixtures
		Zinc 24						
C86100	Manganese Bronze	Copper 67	85 (nom.)		50 (nom.)		20	Marine castings, propellers
		Zinc 21						
		Manganese 4						
		Aluminum 5						

Table A7-21

Chemical and Mechanical Properties of the Marine Bronzes

UNS Number	Type	Chemical Composition, %	Tensile Strength, ksi		Yield Strength, ksi		Elonga-tion, %	Typical Applications
			min.	max.	min.	max.		
Wrought Forms								
C51000	Phosphor Bronze	Copper—94.4	47	140	19	80	64	Fastenings, pump diaphragms
		Tin—5.0						
		Phosphorus—trace						
C61000	Aluminum Bronze	Copper—91.9	52	60	17	27	45	Marine hardware, piping, sheathing
		Aluminum—7.3						
C63000	Nickel-Aluminum-Manganese Bronze	Copper—80.0	90	118	50	75	20	Fastenings, propellers, pump and valve parts
		Aluminum—10.0						
		Nickel—4.8						
		Manganese—1.5						
C65500	Silicon Bronze	Copper—92.9	56	145	21	70	63	Marine hardware, propeller shafts

UNS Number	Type	Chemical Composition, %	Tensile Strength, ksi		Yield Strength, ksi		Elonga-tion, %	Typical Applications
			min.	max.	min.	max.		
		Silicon—3.3						
Cast Forms								
C90300	Tin Bronze (gunmetal)	Copper—87.5	45	21	30			Pump and valve parts, naval ordnance
		Tin—8.25						
		Zinc—4.0						
C95800	Aluminum Bronze	Copper—79.0	95	38	25			Propeller hubs and blades
		Aluminum—9.0						
		Nickel—4.5						

Table A7-22

Chemical and Mechanical Properties of the Copper-Nickel Alloys

UNS Number	Type	Chemical Composition, %	Tensile Strength, ksi		Yield Strength, ksi		Elonga-tion, %	Typical Applications
			min.	max.	min.	max.		
Wrought Forms								
C70600		Copper—88.6	44	60	16	57	42	Heat exchanger tubing
		Nickel—10.0						Seawater piping
		Iron—1.4						Ship/boat hull plating
C71500		Copper—69.5	49	95	13	85	40	Heat exchanger tubing
		Nickel—30.0						Seawater piping
		Iron—0.5						Seawater pumps and valves
C72200		Copper—82.2	46	70	18	66	46	Heat exchanger tubing
		Nickel—16.5						Seawater piping systems
		Iron—0.8						
		Chromium—0.5						
Cast Forms								
C96200		Copper—88.6	45 min.		25 min.		20 min.	Seawater plumbing fittings, elbows, impellers, valve parts, pump bodies
		Nickel—10.0						
		Iron—1.4						
C96400		Copper—69.1	68		37		28	Same as C96200
		Nickel—30						
		Iron—0.9						

APPENDIX 8

Glossary

acetal An engineering thermoplastic having good strength, wear resistance, and greater dimensional stability than nylon under wet and humid conditions.

acid A substance having a pH below 7.0. Acidic aqueous solutions turn blue litmus indicators red. Acids will react with certain metals, dissolving them to form salts.

acid rain Atmospheric precipitation with a pH range of 3.6 to 5.7. Burning of fossil fuels for heat and power is the major factor in the generation of oxides of nitrogen and sulfur, which are converted into nitric and sulfuric acids washed down in the rain.

acrylic Polymers used in the manufacture of synthetic textile fabrics such as Orlon and Acrilan.

acrylic resins Any of numerous thermoplastic or thermosetting polymers or copolymers of acrylic acid, methacrylic acid, esters of these acids, or acrylonitrile, used to produce paints, synthetic rubbers, and lightweight plastics. Acrylic plastics are clear, transparent, and resistant to fractures, weathering, and chemicals.

acrylonitrile-butadiene styrene (ABS) A rigid thermoplastic—low in cost, easily machined, and thermoformed.

active A state or condition in which a metal tends to corrode; the term also refers to the negative direction of electrode potential (opposite of passive or noble).

additive A chemical or a combination of chemicals added to fuel or to lubricating oil to enhance or achieve specific properties, such as contaminant particle entrapment and corrosion inhibition.

admiralty brass (C44300, C44400, C44600) Copper-zinc alloys that are 71 percent copper, 28 percent zinc, 1 percent tin. The addition of tin increases the corrosion resistance of the alloy. Also includes small amounts of arsenic, antimony, or phosphorus inhibitors. Excellent resistance to general and uniform corrosion in clean atmospheres. Should not be used underwater without cathodic protection.

Airex A PVC foam used in sandwich-core construction.

alkaline A substance having a pH greater than 7.0. The higher the pH, the more alkaline the solution.

alkyd A resin used in all types of organic coatings such as paints, enamels, lacquers, and varnishes to enhance high gloss, good adhesion, resistance to weathering, and long life. Alkyd resins have largely replaced oil-base paints as the most commonly used paint coating.

allotrope An alternative form of certain elements. Allotropes have different molecular structures and physical properties. Common examples are diamond and graphite, which are allotropes of carbon.

alloy A metallic substance that consists of more than one metal or, in some cases, a metal and one or more nonmetals. Alloys generally have chemical, mechanical, and metallurgical properties that are different from those of its constituents. Cast iron and steel are common alloys of iron and carbon; brass and bronze are examples of copper alloys.

Almag 35 (UNS AO535) An aluminum casting alloy used for fittings such as cleats, end caps, and plugs.

aluminum (Al) A silvery white, ductile metallic element. Aluminum has good conductive and thermal properties and is used to form many hard, lightweight alloys. Although very reactive chemically, aluminum resists corrosion by forming a protective oxide coating (alumina). Aluminum and its compounds are used in paints, foil, jewelry, and welding. Aluminum alloys of the 5000 series are used in boat hulls and structures, whereas those of the 6000 series are typically used in marine extrusions such as masts, spars, rails, and tubing. See also *amphoteric*.

ammeter An instrument used to measure, in amperes, the magnitude of an electric current. An ammeter is usually combined with a voltmeter and an ohmmeter in a multipurpose instrument. Older ammeters are based on the D'Arsonval galvanometer and are of the analog type, but digital ammeters are increasingly common.

ammonia (NH_3) Household ammonia, typically 3 to 5 percent NH_3, is a useful cleaning solution when diluted with water. The strength of the mixture will depend on the difficulty of the cleaning task. *Be careful not to mix or store ammonia with or near any solution containing chlorine. These two chemicals, if allowed to mix, will form a toxic gas.*

ampere The unit of measure for the flow of electric current. Commonly referred to as *amp* or *amps*. When one volt is applied across a resistance of one ohm, a current of one amp in magnitude will flow in the circuit. Fractions of an ampere are typically expressed in *milliamperes*—one-tenth of an ampere (0.1 A) is expressed as 100 milliamperes.

ampere-hour The mathematical product of the current flowing in a circuit in amperes multiplied by the length of time it flows in hours. Frequently used as a measure of the capacity of storage batteries.

amphoteric Chemically reactive with both acid and alkaline substances. Aluminum is amphoteric and highly susceptible to corrosion when overprotected.

annealing The process of heating a substance to a specific temperature and then slowly cooling it, frequently done during or after machining processes or after welding to relieve internal stresses and thus improve resistance to stress-corrosion cracking and corrosion fatigue. Typically, annealing does not result in significant changes in mechanical properties of the substance.

anode The electrode of an electrochemical cell with the more negative or less noble potential. The less noble metal of an electrolytic cell that tends to corrode.

anode reaction The chemical reaction that takes place at the anode of a galvanic cell. Anode reactions are those types of reactions that result in oxidation, such as

$$M(s) \rightarrow M(aq)^{2+} + 2e^-$$

anodizing An electrochemical process that alters the outer surface layers of the aluminum substrate metal. The object to be anodized is immersed in an acid electrolyte and becomes the anode. A direct current is passed through the electrolyte and the object (anode). A relatively thick layer of hard, porous aluminum oxide is formed on the surface. The object is then immersed in boiling water to seal the oxide film and make it impermeable. The oxide film may be colored before sealing with penetrating dyes or during the anodizing process through the use of a colored electrolyte.

argon-oxygen decarburization (AOD) A production process that produces steel of very low carbon content.

asphalt A bituminous coating. A black thermoplastic tar material used as coatings in paints and varnishes. Asphalt coatings are applied either hot as a melted liquid or cold when thinned with solvents.

atmosphere A measure of pressure. The air pressure at sea level is equal to 14.6592 pounds per square inch (psi), or 1.0332 kilograms per square centimeter (kg/cm^2), or 101,323 newtons per square meter (N/m^2).

atom The smallest unit of a chemical *element* having the properties of that element. Its central core, the nucleus, consists of positively charged particles, called *protons*, and uncharged particles, called *neutrons*. Surrounding the nucleus and orbiting it are negatively charged particles called *electrons*. Each atom has an equal number of protons and electrons. Electrons in the outermost orbits determine the atom's chemical and electrical properties. The number of protons in an atom's nucleus is called the *atomic number*. The total number of protons and neutrons combined is the atom's *mass number*. Atoms containing the same number of protons but different numbers of neutrons are different forms, or *isotopes,* of the same element. The entire structure has an approximate diameter of 10^{-8} centimeter and characteristically remains undivided in chemical reactions ex-

cept for limited removal, transfer, or exchange of certain electrons.

atomic number The number of protons in the nucleus of an atom. All atoms of an element have the same atomic number and differ in atomic number from atoms of other elements. The elements are arranged in the periodic table in the order of their atomic numbers.

austenite One of three common forms of crystalline structure for steel. Also referred to as the *gamma* structure; it is a face-centered cubic form. Austenitic steels are nonmagnetic and have greater corrosion resistance.

Bakelite A synthetic thermosetting phenol-formaldehyde resin. It is used in a wide variety of applications, most commonly as an electrical insulator.

base A substance that has a pH below 7.0 and that causes litmus indicators to turn blue. A large class of compounds, including the hydroxides and oxides of metals.

battery, electric Two or more electrolytic cells connected together to function as a source of direct current. The electrolyte may be either a liquid (wet cell) or a solid (dry cell). The term is also commonly used in referring to a single cell such as those used in flashlights, cameras, and other portable electronic equipment. The term *storage battery* refers to an assembly of wet cells, consisting of alternate plates of lead (negative) and lead dioxide (positive) immersed in a sulfuric acid electrolyte. Such batteries may be recharged a large but finite number of times.

binder The resin constituent of a plastic compound that holds the other components together; the substance applied to glass mat or preforms to bond the fibers prior to laminating or molding.

bond, chemical A force between two atoms or groups of atoms due to the attraction between electrons (−) and nuclei (+). *Covalent bonds* are formed by the sharing of one or more electrons between atoms. An *ionic bond* is a bond between two ions of opposite charge. Ionic bonds are also referred to as *polar covalent bonds*. The H_2O molecule is an example of polar covalent bonding. In this type of bonding, the molecule has a curved shape that permits one end to be relatively positive and the other end to be relatively negative.

bonding, electrical The practice of electrically connecting the exposed, metallic, non-current-carrying components—such as engine, transmission, prop and shaft, metal tanks, and motor housing—on the boat to the common ground of the boat's DC electrical system.

brackish water Water having salinity values ranging from approximately 0.5 to 17 parts per thousand. Water having a lower salt content than seawater but undrinkable.

brass An alloy having copper (55 to 90 percent) and zinc (10 to 45 percent) as its major constituents, and in some cases small amounts of other elements. Its properties vary with the proportion of copper and zinc and with the addition of other elements. See specific types.

brine Seawater containing higher concentrations of dissolved salts than that of the ordinary ocean.

bronze An alloy of copper having phosphorus, tin, zinc, and, sometimes, small amounts of other elements as its principal constituents. It is harder than *brass*, and its properties depend on the proportions of its components. See specific types.

casting The forming of a metal object by melting and pouring the components into a mold of a specific shape and form. Most castings are made in sand molds.

cathode The more noble metal of a galvanic couple; the protected metal or the metal with the greater tendency to resist corrosion.

cathode-to-anode ratio The ratio of the surface area of the cathode to that of the anode. The anodic surface must supply a quantity of electrons sufficient to shift the potential of the cathodic metal to a safer, more negative level and to maintain it at that level. The greater the cathodic area, the greater the current demand, and the greater the rate of galvanic corrosion. A high ratio is unfavorable; a low ratio is favorable.

cathodic disbondment The deterioration of adhesion between a protective coating and its protected substrate by products of the chemical reaction that takes place at a cathode.

cathodic protection A method for reducing or preventing the corrosion of a metal by making it more cathodic than the other metals immersed in the same electrolyte. This is accomplished by introducing into the electrolyte a source of electrons (current), which may be either a sacrificial anode, usually zinc, or an impressed current. See also *cathode-to-anode ratio*.

cavitation The rapid formation and collapse of large numbers of minute voids or cavities (bubbles) in a liquid subjected to intense, high-speed changes in pressure. Frequently, but not exclusively, occurring on the back face (low-pressure surface) of propeller blades and resulting in a pock-marked deterioration of the metal in this area. Cavitation damage can seriously impair the performance of the propeller.

CE mark The mark agreed upon and accepted by the member countries of the European Community indicating that the product has met the standards established by the group. Similar to the UL (Underwriters Laboratories) mark in the United States.

cell An anode and a cathode immersed in the same electrolyte and connected electrically by contact or an electrically conductive external path for electron flow. The anode and cathode may be separate metals or dissimilar areas on the same metal.

charge, electrical The property of matter that constitutes the basis of all electrical phenomena. The basic unit of charge, e, is the electron (−) or the proton (+). Charged particles are surrounded by electric fields of the same polarity as that of the particle itself. Oppositely charged particles attract while like charged fields repel.

chlorinated polyvinyl chloride (CPVC) A thermoplastic having properties similar to those of PVC but capable of functioning at a 40°F to 60°F (4.4°C to 15.6°C) higher temperature.

chlorine bleaches A chlorine solution that is highly corrosive and gives off fumes that are also corrosive. The higher the ambient temperature, the more corrosive the fumes. Great care must be taken in the use and storage of these solutions to avoid serious corrosive damage to electronic or other sensitive electromechanical devices.

cladding A metal coated or bonded onto another metal. The bonding may have been accomplished by rolling, extrusion, welding, diffusion bonding, casting, chemical deposition, or electroplating. Commonly referred to as bi-metals or clad-metals.

clout nail A small, square-cut nail, most commonly of copper, used in fastening the seams of small craft such as canoes and lapstrake boats. The nail is driven in tight-fitting pilot holes against a heavy backing iron that turns the point back into the plank being joined.

composites Any material that is composed of at least two distinctly different substances. Typically, composites consist of a layer or layers of laminar materials or of fibers, flakes, or particulates dispersed in a binder. Examples are fiberglass-reinforced plastics, carbon-fiber reinforced plastics, and foam-cored matrices. The term has come to include fiberglass-sheathed wood hulls where the sheathing is an integral structural member of the assembly.

compound A homogeneous substance consisting of atoms or ions of two or more elements in *specific* proportions and typically having properties different from those of its constituent elements. Compounds are differentiated from mixtures in which two or more elements may be present in any proportions.

conductivity The property of a material that enables it to conduct or transmit heat, electricity, or sound.

copper nails Nails made of copper in the same shape and form as common flathead wire nails and used for fastening planking and structural members in lightweight small craft construction. They are driven through tight pilot holes all the way through the members to be fastened, pulling them tightly together. A *burr* or *rove*, a tight-fitting washer, is forced over the point of the nail and driven tightly against the wood by using a special hollow-pointed *rove iron*. The end of the nail is cut off about one-and-a-half diameters from the burr. A heavy bucking iron is held against the head, and the end of the nail is peened over to form a rivet.

corrosion Commonly defined as *the deterioration of a metal or alloy by chemical or electrochemical reaction with its environment*. This definition is the subject of some discussion within the corrosion sciences community. Some favor a broader definition, and it appears that support for this position is growing. This group would prefer to define corrosion as *the deterioration of a material of construction or of its properties as a result of its exposure to an environment*. In this book we have elected to follow the later definition.

corrosion controller An automatic (typically electronic) or manually operated device in a cathodic protection system that regulates the flow of electric current.

corrosion fatigue A corrosion-induced failure mode in which a metal fractures prematurely under simultaneous conditions of a corrosive environment and repeated cyclic loading. The failure occurs at lower levels of stress or fewer cycles than it would in the absence of the corrosive environment.

corrosion monitor A voltmeter capable of measuring voltages in the low millivolt range, connected to read the difference in potential between a reference electrode, usually silver/silver-chloride (Ag/AgCl) and a metal hull or the boat's bonding system when they are immersed in the same electrolyte.

corrosion reactions Corrosion involves the conversion of a metal from the atomic to ionic state. This anodic reaction produces a positively charged metal ion and free electrons, as shown in the following reaction. Note that the exponent indicates the magnitude and polarity of the charge

$$M^0 \Rightarrow M^{N+} + ne^{N-}$$

for example, in the case of iron,

$$Fe^0 \Rightarrow Fe^{2+} + 2e$$

Corrosion is basically the anodic reaction (i.e., the loss of metal) and is an *oxidizing process* because it involves the loss of electrons. The anodic reaction cannot occur without a corresponding *cathode reaction*, which is the *reduction process*. The electrons released at the anode travel through the external circuit and react with some species at the surface of the cathode. In aqueous solutions, this reaction is the reduction of hydrogen ions to atomic hydrogen

$$H^+ + \tfrac{1}{2}O^2 + e \Rightarrow H^0$$

or the reduction of both water and dissolved oxygen to hydroxyl ions

$$H_2O + \tfrac{1}{2}O_2 + 2e \Rightarrow 2OH^-$$

couple, galvanic See *cell*

crevice corrosion A form of localized corrosion of a metal surface at or in close proximity to an area that is shielded from full exposure to the environment due to an adjoining metal surface. Crevice corrosion occurs as a result of a difference in ion or oxygen concentration between the metal and its immediate environment.

cross-linking A process used in the manufacture of poly-

mer plastics in which chemical links are established between the molecular chains for the purpose of enhancing the performance properties of the polymer.

current density The magnitude of current per unit area of an anode or cathode expressed in milliamperes per square inch.

Dacron A synthetic polyester fiber made from terephthalic acid and ethylene glycol and produced by DuPont. Known in the United Kingdom as Terylene. Commonly used in various fabric applications and in synthetic rope.

dealloying The selective corrosion of one or more components of an alloy. Specific examples are *decarburization*, *decobaltification*, *denickelification*, *dezincification*, and *graphitic corrosion*. See also *demetalization*.

deck oil A mixture of ingredients commonly found around a boat shop and highly favored by renown boatbuilder and writer Pete Culler. It consists of a gallon of boiled linseed oil, a pint of turpentine, and a pint of pine tar, mixed preferably when the oil is warm. Recommended for unpainted decks of working craft and the unpainted insides of skiff and bateau bottoms. The same mix is also used as a starter coat for wooden spars and other woodwork that will not be painted for a while. According to Culler, wooden cleats, pins, ships blocks, and any other small wooden items soaked for a month in this stuff become extremely hard and nearly weatherproof. It is also recommended for use on boat trailers and other rusty metal items to arrest and prevent further rusting.

Delrin A homo-polymer made by DuPont that can be machined, drilled, and cut. Delrin has high strength and wear-resistant properties and is not significantly hygroscopic. Arrange good ventilation, as the material smells unpleasant while it is being worked. There are some 37 formulations for different applications. An acetal plastic; acetals display good impact resistance, dimensional stability, and outstanding surface hardness due to their high degree of crystallinity. They have high dielectric strength, are resistant to many solvents, and exhibit negligible water absorption. Typical applications include roller bearings, gears, reels, counters, control cams, valves, and pump parts.

demetalization The removal of one of the alloying elements in an alloy by the electrolyte. This results in a "spongy" metal. A typical example is the removal of zinc from brass in chloride water—referred to as *dezincification*.

dielectric barrier An electrically nonconductive material, such as a coating or plastic sheet, that is placed between an anode and a cathode to prevent current flow.

Divinycell A family of structural cellular PVC foam used as core material in sandwich construction and made by Divinycell Polimex AB. Divinycell offers high strength-to-weight ratio, great dynamic strength, low water absorption, and excellent insulating properties.

It has an operating temperature range of –330°F to +250°F (–200°C to +120°C).

drying oil An organic oil, such as linseed oil, used as a binder in paints and varnishes. It dries into a tough elastic layer when applied in a thin film and exposed to air.

ductility The ability of a material to deform plastically without fracturing.

duplex stainless steel Stainless steel grades containing molybdenum and having a structure consisting of approximately 50 percent ferrite and 50 percent austenite, resulting in improved resistance to pitting, crevice corrosion, and stress-corrosion cracking in saltwater environments. Examples are alloy 2205 (UNS S31803) and alloy 255 (UNS S32550).

E-glass A borosilicate glass; the type most used for glass fibers for reinforced plastics. Suitable for electrical laminates because of its high resistivity. (Also called *electric glass*.)

earth ground A point that is at the same potential or voltage as the local earth.

electrochemistry That body of science devoted to those processes in which chemical and electrical phenomena interact.

electrode A conductive material through which an electrical current is injected into or withdrawn from an electrolyte.

electrode, reference A metal and metallic-salt mixture in solution (silver-silver chloride, for example) will develop and maintain an accurate reference potential to which the potential of other metals immersed in the same electrolyte may be compared.

electrolysis The process that takes place in a conducting solution when an electric current is passed through it. When a negative electrode (cathode) and a positive electrode (anode) are immersed in a conducting solution (electrolyte), and an external direct current source is connected to the electrodes, the positive ions (*cations*) migrate to the negative electrode, where they each gain an electron and become neutral. At the same time, the negative ions (*anions*) migrate to the positive electrode, where they each give up an electron and become neutral. These changes in the conductive solution—the electrolyte—constitute the process of electrolysis. Note that this process is something that happens *to the electrolyte*—the term is improperly used as a synonym for corrosion.

electrolyte An electrical conductor in which current is carried by ions rather than free electrons (as in a metal). Electrolytes include water solutions of acids, bases, or salts and certain pure liquids.

electron An elementary particle that carries a unit charge of negative electricity. Atoms consist of a dense, positively charged nucleus surrounded by electrons that orbit around the nucleus, forming a charged cloud of sufficient negative charge to balance the positive charge of the nucleus. The gain or loss of electrons results in a net charge (negative or positive, respectively), and the atom is said to be *ionized*.

electron, valence An electron in an outer shell of an atom that can participate in forming chemical bonds with other atoms.

electroplating A method of coating a metal with a thin layer of another metal or alloy by electrodeposition. The process is based on electrolysis in which a metal or alloy is ionized and plated on an object serving as a cathode.

electropolishing A technique in which a high polish is produced by making the specimen the anode in an electrolytic cell, where preferential dissolution at high points smoothes the surface. Electropolishing is sometimes used as a finishing process to reduce susceptibility to localized corrosion.

element The simplest form of homogeneous matter, which cannot be further reduced by chemical means. Hydrogen (H), carbon (C), oxygen (O), and iron (Fe) are examples of common elements. Chemists recognize some 110 elements, which are listed in the Periodic Table of Elements. All of the matter of the universe, whether simple or complex, is made up of these elements. The chemical properties of an element are determined by the distribution of electrons around the nucleus, especially the outer, or *valence*, electrons, which are the ones involved in chemical reactions.

elongation A measure of the ductility of a material. Elongation is expressed as the amount a material will stretch, due to applied stress over some defined unit length, before breaking under a tensile load.

epoxy resin A thermosetting resin used in the construction of fiberglass boats to encapsulate and bind the fiberglass reinforcing material. Other thermosetting resins used for this purpose are polyester and vinylester resins. Epoxy resins have higher bonding strength, superior abrasion resistance, less water absorption, and much lower shrinkage than the polyester or vinylester resins. They are, however, considerably more expensive and thus are not as commonly used.

erosion corrosion The removal of metal by the movement of fluids against the surface. The combination of erosion and corrosion can produce a severe rate of corrosion.

exfoliation Corrosion that progresses laterally from the initiation site along planes parallel to the surface, generally at grain boundaries. The formation of corrosion products along these lateral planes forces the metal apart and results in a layered appearance.

fatigue The failure or degradation of mechanical properties after repeated applications of stress.

fatigue life The number of cycles of deformation as a result of repeated applications of stress required to cause failure of the component.

fatigue strength The maximum cyclic stress a material can withstand for a given number of cycles before failure occurs.

ferritic A specific crystalline form (body-centered cubic) of carbon in iron.

fiberglass A thermosetting composite that has a high strength-to-weight ratio and excellent dielectric properties and is essentially unaffected by corrosion.

fiberglass cloth A open-weave fabric used extensively in small boat construction for surfacing hulls and deck structures and for repairing laminate defects. Cloth provides an improved appearance, but it is too expensive and requires too many layers in order to build up an adequate thickness; thus it is not cost-effective for general construction.

filiform corrosion Appears as a network of randomly distributed threadlike filaments, a wormlike structure; occurs particularly beneath thin organic coatings. Salts containing chlorides, which have been left on the surface prior to coating, are thought to be causal factors.

forging A cast ingot that has been hammered or pressed into shape under intense heat. Forgings are used for components in which a more homogeneous structure is needed than can be obtained by casting alone.

formula A symbolic representation of the composition or of the composition and structure of a compound.

fretting corrosion Occurs when two or more parts rub against each other. The rubbing action removes the corrosion products and exposes new metal to the electrolyte.

FRP Fiberglass-Reinforced Plastic. A general term covering any type of plastic-reinforced cloth, mat, strands, or any other form of fibrous glass.

galvanic (or bimetallic) corrosion Corrosion taking place between two different metals that are joined together in the presence of an electrolyte. Each metal has a potential different from any other metal when placed in an electrolyte. These potentials are shown in the *galvanic series of metals*. The metals at the top of the table are more anodic than those below them and, when in electrical contact in an electrolyte, will corrode in preference to the metal below them in the table. The further apart the metals, the faster will be the corrosion rate.

galvanic series A list of metals and alloys arranged in order of their potential as measured in relation to a reference electrode when immersed in seawater. The table of potentials is arranged with the anodic or least noble metals at one end and the cathodic or most noble metals at the other.

galvanizing Coating a metal surface with zinc using any of various processes, including *hot-dip galvanizing* and *electroplating*.

gelcoat A resin applied to the surface of a mold and gelled prior to layup. The gelcoat becomes an integral part of the finished laminate and is usually used to improve surface appearance and protect the laminate from the environment.

general (uniform) corrosion Corrosion that occurs more or less evenly over the surface. Differences in electri-cal potential occur on the surface of a piece of metal due to small differences in chemical composition, phase differences, amount of cold-work, and so on. These differences set up small corrosion cells, each with an anode and cathode. Corrosion continues until the metal is consumed or the film of rust formed on the surface sets up a barrier to the electrolyte.

gram-atomic weight (gram-atom) One mole of atoms of an element.

gray water Galley, bath, and shower water.

ground An object that makes an electrical connection with the earth. The vessel's ground is established by a conducting connection (intentional or accidental) with the earth, including any conductive part of the wetted surface of the hull.

gypsy The drum on an anchor windlass that takes the rope, as compared to the *wildcat*, which is the wheel that hauls the chain.

half-cell See *electrode, reference*.

hand layup The process of placing (and working) successive plies of reinforcing material or resin-impregnated reinforcement in position by hand.

hard water Water that contains certain salts, such as those of calcium or magnesium, which form insoluble deposits in boilers and form precipitates with soap.

heat treatment A process of hardening steel by heating it to a temperature at which austenite is formed, typically 1400°F to 1800°F (760°C to 870°C) and then cooling it rapidly (quenching) in water or oil. This results in a martensite form and sets up great internal strains that must be relieved by tempering or annealing.

helium (He) A noncombustible, inert, and unreactive gaseous element. Helium is used in arc welding.

hot-short cracking Microcracking along grain boundaries as a result of stress or deformations at temperatures near the melting temperature of the metal. It sometimes occurs during hot-working or welding on parts that are clamped or tightly held. Hot-shortness is caused by the presence of low-melting-point constituents along the grain boundaries.

hull potential The composite electrical potential (voltage) of the hull cathodic surfaces in an electrolyte as measured against a referenced electrode, most commonly silver/silver chloride.

hydrated A solid compound containing water molecules combined in a definite ratio as an integral part of the crystal.

hydrogen (H) A colorless, odorless, tasteless gaseous element. Hydrogen is slightly soluble in water and highly explosive. The hot flame produced by a mixture of oxygen and hydrogen is used in welding and in melting quartz and glass.

hydrogen embrittlement (HE) A process that results in a loss of ductility due to the absorption of atomic hydrogen by the metal. This may occur during the manufacturing process if hydrogen is allowed to enter the metal while in the molten phase. It may also occur when the metal is in the solid state, during electroplating operations, corrosion reactions, and cathodic protection. This may show up as blistering, internal cracking, and reduced ductility. If tensile stresses exceeding a critical level are present, crack growth leading to fracture may occur. If no corrosion is taking place, this is referred to as *hydrogen-assisted cracking* (HAC). If active corrosion is taking place—pitting or crevice corrosion—the cracking may be classified as *stress-corrosion cracking* but is actually *hydrogen-assisted stress-corrosion cracking*.

hygroscopic Capable of absorbing and retaining atmospheric moisture.

impact strength The ability of a material to withstand dynamic shock loading.

impressed current system A cathodic protection system that utilizes a direct current source (usually a battery) to attain the required millivolt shift in the metallic parts to be protected.

inert gas A gas that is not readily reactive with other elements; also referred to as *noble gas*. Helium, neon, argon, krypton, xenon, and radon are inert gases. They are sometimes called the rare gases. Inert gases are colorless, odorless, and tasteless and have very low chemical activity because their outermost, or valence, electron shell is complete, containing two electrons in the case of helium and eight in the remaining cases.

inhibitor A chemical substance or combination of substances that, when present in the environment, prevents or reduces corrosion without significant reaction with the components of the environment.

intergranular attack (IGA) Preferential attack at the grain boundaries of a metallic structure. The attack may be general, if an item is improperly heat-treated, or localized in heat-affected zones (HAZ) of welds—for example, the so-called weld decay of certain austenitic stainless steels.

ion Atom or group of atoms having a net electric charge as a result of the gain or loss of one or more electrons or protons. Atoms that lose electrons or gain protons have a net positive charge and are called *cations*. Atoms that gain electrons or lose protons have a net negative charge and are called *anions*.

ionization The formation of or separation into ions by heat, electrical discharge, radiation, or chemical reaction.

intergranular corrosion Corrosion that occurs at the grain boundaries due to a difference in potential between the anodic grain boundaries and the cathodic grains. *Sensitized* stainless steels—where carbides have been precipitated in the grain boundaries during improper heat treatment or in the heat-affected zone of a weld—are particularly susceptible to intergranular corrosion.

isolation, electrical The condition of being electrically separated from other metallic structures; not connected to the vessel's bonding system.

isolator A device installed in series with the (AC) grounding (green) conductor of the shore-power cable to effectively block low-voltage DC galvanic current flow but permit the passage of alternating current (AC).

Kapton Polyimide film. Polyimides are classified as specialty polymers because of their unique combination of chemical, electrical, and high-temperature physical properties. Kapton was used as an insulating layer between the aluminum and carbon fiber materials on the space shuttle orbiter to prevent galvanic coupling between the two dissimilar metals.

Kevlar A family of para-aramid fiber products made by DuPont. Kevlar has high tensile strength at low weight, high chemical resistance and toughness, low electrical conductivity, and good thermal stability. It is flame-resistant and self-extinguishing. It is used in bullet-proof vests and body armor, ropes and cables, composites, sporting goods, and other applications requiring high strength and low weight.

Klegecell Klegecell is produced by Divinycell Polimex AB. See *Divinycell*.

laminate To unite sheets of material, such as fiberglass mat or woven fabric, by a bonding material, usually with pressure and heat (normally used with reference to flat sheets); a product made by so bonding.

LanoCote A proprietary moisture-displacing corrosion-preventive lubricant made by Lanocote. Formulated to withstand saltwater marine conditions, LanoCote is useful in preventing thread seizure due to all types of corrosion on boats and machinery. Applied during assembly, LanoCote is recommended for use where dissimilar metals are fastened together, such as stainless steel fittings on alloy masts.

Law of Conservation of Energy *Energy can neither be created nor destroyed but may be converted from one form to another.*

Law of Conservation of Matter *Matter may neither be created nor destroyed in a chemical change.* In a closed system—one in which none of the products of change is lost—the total mass (measured by its weight) of matter remains constant. Thus when a sample of matter burns, the total weight of the products equals the weight of the sample plus the weight of oxygen consumed.

Law of Constant Composition Same as the Law of Definite Proportions.

Law of Definite Proportions *Elements unite to form compounds in definite proportions by weight.* Also called *The Law of Constant Composition*. Since only specific weights of elements are present in compounds, every compound must have a definite and constant composition.

Lewis structures Lewis dot diagrams show the valence electrons of a given atom (both bonded electrons and unbonded electrons). Therefore, each structure shows the electrons of an atom available for bonding. Generally, atoms prefer to be in a state with 8 electrons in the outer shell. These 8 electrons are represented by 8 places around the chemical symbol of the element. Since atoms prefer to have a filled-outer shell, Lewis structures can help predict the bonding behavior of electrons.

Lexan Hard, practically unbreakable polycarbonate resin used for shatterproof windows and the like, and produced by GE. Polycarbonates exhibit extremely high-impact strength over a range of temperatures from –60°F to 270°F (–51°C to 132°C). It is fine for precision parts, or where transparency is desired. Its water-clear transmittance (89 percent) makes it excellent for visors or guards. It shows good creep resistance and has a temperature-independent dielectric constant, as well as good insulating properties.

liquid metal cracking (LMC) The catastrophic brittle failure of a normally ductile metal when in contact with a liquid metal and subsequently stressed in tension.

lithium (Li) A highly reactive metallic element. A soft, silvery white corrosive alkali metal, lithium is the least dense of the metals. Lithium compounds are used in lubricating greases, special glasses, and ceramic glazes, as brazing and welding fluxes, and in the preparation of plastics and synthetic rubber.

localized corrosion Corrosion in which all or most of the attack occurs at discrete areas. Examples are crevice corrosion, pitting, and stress-corrosion cracking.

macerator An electrically operated device in which sanitary waste products are chopped into fine particles to produce a liquefied suspension prior to either overboard discharge or further treatment.

manganese bronze (C86100 to C86800) Manganese bronze is not actually a bronze, but a (nominal) 60/40 cast brass. Copper content can range from 55 to 67 percent, while zinc content ranges from 21 to 41 percent. Manganese is added to enhance strength. It is widely used for all sorts of marine castings, portlights, cleats, heavy-duty valve parts, marine fixtures and fittings, propellers, and more. Its corrosion resistance is similar to that of other 60/40 brasses, such as Muntz metal and naval brass, and not as good as that of aluminum brass. It is also susceptible to dezincification. Manganese bronze is widely used underwater in such applications as rudder stuffing boxes, rudder blades, and props. It must have cathodic protection.

Marelon A formulation of Zytel (DuPont), which is a high-temperature glass-reinforced nylon resin. Produced by Forespar Company, Marelon is noncorrosive, nonconductive, UV resistant, fire resistant; it has a temperature range from 40°F to 250°F (4.4°C to 121°C).

martensitic stainless steel One of three basic types of stainless steel. The martensitic grades are magnetic and are hardenable to the highest levels of any of the stainless steels; thus they are used largely in tool steel applications. They are not very resistant to severely corrosive environments such as salt water and atmospheres.

mass The amount of matter in a body regardless of its volume or of any forces acting on it. Unlike *weight*, mass is not dependent on gravity.

matter Something that has mass and exists as a solid, liquid, or gas.

melting point Pure elements have melting points, but most engineering materials have a melting range rather than a distinct melting point. Material with a narrow melting range is more difficult to weld with a structurally sound weldment.

metal An element having metallic luster, the capacity to lose electrons and form a positive ion, and the ability to conduct heat and electricity. The metals comprise about two-thirds of the known elements. Chemically, the metals differ from the nonmetals in that they form positive ions and basic oxides and hydroxides. Upon exposure to moist air, a great many metals undergo corrosion—that is, they enter into a chemical reaction; the oxygen of the atmosphere reacts with the metal to form the oxide of the metal, such as rust on exposed iron. Most of the metals used are in the form of alloys of two or more constituents.

micrometer A unit of length equal to one-thousandth (10^{-3}) of a millimeter, or one-millionth (10^{-6}) of a meter. Also referred to as a *micron*.

mill scale A heavy oxide layer formed during hot fabrication or heat treatment of metals.

mixture A sample of matter consisting of two or more different substances in varying proportions. Unlike a compound, which has a single set of properties, a mixture retains the properties of each of its components. Thus a mixture of powdered sulfur and powdered iron has a yellow color like sulfur when the percentage of sulfur is high; portions of the mixture are attracted to a magnet just as pure iron is. Such a mixture is an example of heterogeneous matter. The properties of a given mixture depend on the proportion of substances in the mixture. For example, the proper hardness in a cement mixture is obtained by varying the proportion of limestone to clay. Solutions, such as salt dissolved in water or sugar dissolved in water, are examples of homogeneous mixtures. Volumes of the same sample have the same properties, such as taste, density, and boiling and freezing points.

modulus of elasticity The ratio of the stress or load applied to the strain or deformation produced in a material that is elastically deformed. If a tensile strength of 2,000 pounds per square inch results in an elongation of 1 percent, the modulus of elasticity is 2,000 divided by 0.01, or 200,000 pounds per square inch (Young's modulus).

mole A quantity, 6.02×10^{23}.

molecule The smallest particle of a compound that has all the chemical properties of that compound. Molecules are made up of two or more atoms of the same or different elements. Ionic compounds, such as sodium chloride, are made up not of molecules but of ions arranged in a crystalline structure. Unlike ions, molecules carry no electrical charge.

monatomic Occurring as single atoms: helium is a monatomic gas.

monomer A simple molecule that is capable of reacting with like or unlike molecules to form a polymer.

MSD Marine sanitation device. Any equipment for installation onboard a vessel that is designed to receive, retain, treat, or discharge sewage, and any process to treat such sewage. As such, both the head (toilet), and the U.S. Coast Guard Type 1, 2, or 3 MSDs (which are separate devices from the head) are MSDs. Type 1 MSDs include a macerator, must have a bacteria count less than 1000 per 100 milliliters (3.4 oz.), produce no visible solids, and must have a USCG Certification label. Type 2 MSDs include a macerator, must have a bacteria count of less than 200 per 100 milliliters (3.4 oz.), must have less than 1,000 parts suspended particulate matter—in other words be almost absolutely clear (though not necessarily colorless). Type 3 MSDs are simply holding tanks—any holding tank, including one in a portable toilet.

multimeter A portable multifunctional electrical test instrument capable of measuring voltage, current, and resistance. Multimeters may be either analog or digital and are used for troubleshooting electrical circuit or corrosion problems.

Muntz metals (C28000) 60/40 brasses; sometimes referred to as *Alpha-Beta brasses*. They are also classed as *leaded brasses*—that is, copper-zinc alloys whose principal alloying element is lead. They are used in architectural applications and as large nuts and bolts. They are used in boat equipment as heat exchanger and condenser tubing and tube sheets. They are not greatly different from the cartridge brasses in their resistance to atmospheric and immersion corrosion. Their resistance to all clean atmospheres is very good. Their resistance in both freshwater and seawater is reasonably good, but they are susceptible to dezincification and stress-corrosion cracking under appropriate conditions, such as stagnant or slowly moving seawater.

muriatic acid The basis for some commercial products formulated for the removal of rust and scale from boiler tubes and other machinery. These products typically include chemical inhibitors designed to protect metal surfaces from the acid by forming a magnetic barrier that repels the acid ions and prevents them from attacking the metal. The rust and scale, which are not magnetic, are not protected and are consumed by the acid. Muriatic (hydrochloric) acid is a *fuming* acid; its fumes are not inhibited and are highly corrosive to electrical or electronic devices that are exposed to them. Great care must be exercised in the use of these products.

Mylar A brand of strong thin polyester film produced by DuPont and used in photography, in recording tape, and as insulation. It is available in thicknesses from 0.0005 to 0.02 inch (0.012 to 0.5 mm). It has high tensile, tear, and impact resistance and remains tough and flexible at temperatures from –94°F to 302°F (–70°C to 150°C). It is used as an electrical barrier in motors, transformers, wires and cables, and electronic equipment.

natural waters Refers to freshwater, brackish water, seawater, and brines. Freshwater will normally contain less than 1,000 ppm chlorides. Freshwater may be further classified as soft, moderately hard, or hard, depending on its calcium carbonate ($CaCO_3$) content. Soft water has less than 75 ppm, moderately hard water has 75 to 150 ppm, and hard water has more than 150 ppm. Brackish water contains more chlorides than freshwater but less than seawater, typically in the range of 1,000 to 10,000 ppm. Seawater may contain from 2.3 to 3.5 percent (25,000 to 35,000 ppm), depending on its geographical location. Brines have still greater concentrations of chlorides.

naval brass (46200, C46400, C46500, C47000, C48200, C48500) 60–40 tin brasses; also sometimes referred to as *Tobin bronze*. Their principal marine use is in hardware items such as decorative fittings, turnbuckles, fastenings, and prop shafts. Here again, the addition of about 1 percent tin does measurably improve corrosion resistance, as does, in some cases (C46500), the addition of arsenic as an inhibitor. Atmospheric corrosion resistance is very good, similar to that of Muntz metal, another 60–40 brass. Immersion corrosion is also quite good in both freshwater and seawater. It is susceptible to erosion corrosion at moderate water velocities—say 3 to 6 ft./s (0.9 to 1.8 m/s) and susceptible to dezincification in stagnant or slowly moving brackish water. Also, under certain conditions (sulfur dioxide, ammonia), the naval brasses are subject to stress-corrosion cracking. Naval brasses are used underwater but must have cathodic protection.

neutral A particle, an object, or a system that has neither positive nor negative electric charge.

noble The positive direction of electrode potential, thus resembling noble metals such as gold and platinum.

noble gas A gas such as helium, neon, argon, krypton, xenon, and radon, which is monatomic and, with limited exceptions, chemically inert. Also called *inert gas*.

noble metal A metal whose potential is highly positive relative to a common reference electrode; a metal with a marked resistance to chemical reaction, particularly to oxidation and to corrosion.

Nomex A paper-type material produced by DuPont and used as an electrical insulator in electrical motors, generators, alternators, and both dry and liquid filled transformers. Nomex is also used in electrical and electronic cables. It exhibits high heat and flame resistance, high UV resistance, low thermal conductivity, high chemical resistance, and excellent abrasion and wear resistance.

notch sensitivity The extent to which the sensitivity of a material to fracture is increased by the presence of a surface inhomogeneity such as a notch, a sudden change in section, a crack, or a scratch. Low notch sensitivity is usually associated with ductile materials and high notch sensitivity with brittle materials.

nylon A thermoplastic with excellent impact resistance; ideal for wear applications such as bearings and gears; self-lubricating under some circumstances; a complex polyamide. Nylon has good resistance to abrasion, heat, and most chemicals. It is almost non-flammable and is not affected by mildew. Resistance to oils and hydrocarbon solvents is also good. Almost all formulations are also self-extinguishing and retain stable mechanical properties at temperatures from −75°F to above 225°F (−59.4°C to 107.2°C). Nylon and Tufnol are hygroscopic and swell when saturated with water.

oxidation The combination of a substance with oxygen; a reaction in which the atoms in an element lose electrons and the valence of the element is correspondingly increased.

oxidation and reduction Complementary chemical reactions involving the loss (oxidation) or gain (reduction) of electrons by an atom or a molecule. These two reactions occur simultaneously, and the number of electrons lost by one substance is the same as the number of electrons gained by the other substance. The substance that loses electrons is said to be a *reductant* and is undergoing *oxidation*. The substance that gains electrons is said to be an *oxidant* and is undergoing *reduction*.

pascals (Pa) A unit of pressure in the meter-kilogram-second (SI) system. A pascal is a pressure of one newton per square meter. The kilopascal (kPa) equal to 1000 newtons per square meter is more commonly used in engineering work (one pound per square inch equals 6.895 kPa, likewise, 1000 psi equals 6.98 MPa, or MegaPascals).

passivation A reduction of the anodic reaction rate of a metal involved in corrosion. A process in metal corrosion by which metals become passive.

patina The coating, usually green, that forms on the surface of metals such as copper and copper alloys exposed to the atmosphere. Also used to describe the appearance of a weathered surface of any metal.

penny The term *penny* is an expression of length. The following are the standard penny lengths and inch equivalents:

Two penny equals one inch
Three penny equals 1¼ inches
Four penny equals 1½ inches
Five penny equals 1¾ inches
Six penny equals 2 inches
Seven penny equals 2¼ inches

Eight penny equals 2½ inches
Nine penny equals 2¾ inches
Ten penny equals 3 inches
Twelve penny equals 3¼ inches
Sixteen penny equals 3½ inches
Twenty penny equals 4 inches
Twenty-five penny equals 4¼ inches
Thirty penny equals 4½ inches
Forty penny equals 5 inches
Fifty penny equals 5½ inches
Sixty penny equals 6 inches

polyethylene terephthalate (PET) A dimensionally stable thermoplastic with superior machining characteristics compared to acetal.

petrolatum A colorless to amber-colored semisolid mixture of hydrocarbons obtained from petroleum. Also called *petroleum jelly*.

phenolic A thermosetting family of plastics with very low thermal expansion, high compressive strength, excellent wear and abrasion resistance, and a low coefficient of friction. Used for bearing applications and molded parts.

pine tar A thick, sticky brownish-black substance produced by the distillation of pine wood. Used in roofing compositions; formerly was used extensively in boatbuilding and maintaining. Pine tar was widely used in all sorts of coating applications and as a corrosion inhibitor on mooring and anchor shackles, turnbuckles, and all manner of screw threads. No longer commonly available.

pitting corrosion A form of localized corrosion in which the surface of the metal is attacked in small localized areas, sometimes resulting in very deep cavities.

plastics A broad class of synthetic organic materials that are readily molded and shaped under heat and pressure; the shape is retained upon removal of the heat and pressure. Plastics are made up of long chainlike molecules (polymers) that may be natural materials, such as *cellulose*, or synthetic resins. The two principal classes of plastics are *thermoplastic* types, which can be resoftened and reshaped repeatedly with the application of heat and pressure, and *thermosetting* plastics, which due to cross-linking of the molecular chains, cannot be resoftened and reshaped after they are formed.

polar bonds Covalent bonds with a large electronegativity difference but not large enough for the formation of an ionic bond. Since the electronegativity difference is unequal, the electrons spend more time around the more electronegative atom. As a result, the molecule has a slight polarity, which causes polar bonds to resemble weak ionic bonds.

polarization The change in potential of a metal as a result of current flow. The potential of an anodic metal becomes more noble and that of a cathodic metal becomes more active than their normal open circuit potentials.

polycarbonate A transparent thermoplastic with high-impact strength, excellent chemical resistance and electrical properties, and good dimensional stability.

polyester resin A thermosetting resin. Cure is effected through catalysts and promoters, or heat, to accelerate the reaction. These are the most commonly used resins in fiberglass boat production. Polyester resins are economical, easy to use, and provide good mold release; they do not present the health hazards associated with the epoxy resins.

polymer A chemical compound consisting of a number of monomers linked together by covalent bonds. Examples of natural polymers are cellulose, natural rubber, and silk. Synthetic polymers are the basis for plastics, synthetic fibers, and synthetic rubber.

polypropylene (PP) A lightweight thermoplastic, a polymer of propylene. It is less dense than water, has excellent electrical properties, and has good resistance to water absorption, oils, and solvents. It is used to make a wide variety of products, including packaging materials, textiles, luggage, and ropes that float.

polysulfide (PS) A popular adhesive sealant. It bonds well to most surfaces but will chemically attack plastics and should not be used on them. Teak must be primed before this sealant is applied. Both one-part and two-part sulfides are available, and the properties after curing are essentially the same. One-part polysulfides are easier to use but slower to cure.

polysulfone A durable thermoplastic having good electrical properties and temperature capabilities over the range –150°F to 300°F (–101.1°C to 148.9°C).

polyurethane (PU) A thermoplastic polymer used for padding and insulation in furniture, clothing, and packaging and in the manufacture of resins for adhesives, elastomers, and fillers. Polyurethanes have excellent impact and abrasion resistance and good resistance to sunlight and weathering. These adhesives are recommended for *permanent* bonding, such as hull-to-deck joints, because of their enormous adhesive strength. Polyurethanes will attack ABS and Lexan plastic.

poultice corrosion Corrosion that occurs where dirt, debris, insulation, and other matter are continuously kept moist and in contact with metal. The term is used in the automotive industry to describe the corrosion of vehicle body parts due to the collection of road salts and debris on ledges and in pockets that are kept moist by weather and washing.

polytetrafluoroethylene (PTFE) A thermoplastic that has an extremely low coefficient of friction, withstands temperatures up to 500°F (260°C), is inert to chemicals and solvents, is self-lubricating, and has a low thermal-expansion rate. PTFE has excellent impact and abrasion resistance and resists sunlight and weathering. It is lightweight, tough, flexible, and unaffected by acids and alkalis except if highly concentrated. It is an electrical insulator. It has low load capacity and is used mostly for light load applications. Teflon is a PTFE plastic.

polyvinyl chloride (PVC) A thermoplastic. PVC has good resistance to corrosive solutions and is used in a variety of plumbing applications, such as hose, pipe, and rigid fittings. It also has good electrical insulation properties.

proton A subatomic particle having a single positive electrical charge. Every atomic nucleus contains one or more protons. The mass of the proton is about 1,840 times the mass of the *electron* and slightly less than the mass of the neutron.

polyvinylidenefluoride (PVDF) A thermoplastic; outstanding chemical resistance; excellent substitute for PVC or polypropylene. PVDFs have good mechanical strength and dielectric properties.

raw water The water in which the boat is being operated, whether fresh, salt, or brackish.

reactant A substance involved in a chemical reaction, especially a directly reacting substance present at the initiation of the reaction.

reaction A change or transformation in which a substance decomposes, combines with other substances, or interchanges constituents with other substances.

reduction The addition of electrons to an atom or group of atoms, resulting in a decrease of valence.

resin A broad family of synthetic polymers, certain of which are commonly used in boatbuilding as the binder that encapsulates the fiber-reinforcing material. Typically these are polyester, vinylester, and epoxy, all of which are thermosetting resins. Polyesters and vinylesters require a catalyst, whereas the epoxy resins require a hardener to facilitate the curing process at normal ambient temperatures.

resin content The amount of resin in laminate expressed as either a percent of total weight or total volume.

RMS value Literally *root mean square;* also called the *effective value.* It is equal to 0.707213 times the peak value of the current or voltage.

rosin A translucent yellowish to dark brown resin derived from the sap of various pine trees and used to increase sliding friction, as on the bows of certain stringed instruments, and to manufacture a wide variety of products, including soldering fluxes.

roving A term used to designate a collection of bundles of continuous filaments, either as untwisted strands or as twisted yarns. Roving may be lightly twisted, but for filament winding the strands are generally wound as bands or tapes with as little twist as possible. Glass rovings are predominantly used in filament winding.

salt A chemical compound formed by replacing all or part of the hydrogen ions of an acid with metal ions or electropositive radicals.

seacock A sea-valve with a flanged base that allows the valve body to be mounted directly to the hull.

sea-valve Any positive closure device specifically designed for marine use.

sea-valve, in-line A sea-valve mounted on a through-hull.

seawater A complex mixture of inorganic salts (mainly sodium chloride), dissolved gases (mainly oxygen), various suspended solids, organic matter, and living marine organisms. However, the term also includes a number of different types, including open-ocean water, coastal waters, brackish estuarial waters, and bottom-sediment waters. Largely because of the presence of living organisms that influence the corrosion process, testing of the corrosion susceptibility of materials in simulated seawater has proven unreliable.

sensitization The increased susceptibility to intergranular corrosion in the area immediately adjacent to a weld (heat-affected zone). It occurs primarily in the austenitic stainless steels at the grain boundaries when the metal is heated to temperatures in the range of 1,000°F to 1,550°F (550°C to 850°C). Chromium combines with carbon and precipitates as chromium carbides, leaving the grain boundaries depleted of chromium and thus susceptible to corrosive attack in this area.

sewage Defined, in terms of marine sanitation, as *human body wastes and waste from toilet and other receptacles intended to receive or retain body waste.* Thus, sewage does not include garbage, trash, bath water, food, oil, gasoline, or any other waste.

sheave A wheel or disk with a grooved rim, used as a pulley.

sherardize A process for the coating of steel with a thin cladding of zinc by heating them in a mixture of sand and powdered zinc.

silica The oxidized form of silicon, SiO_2. Silica is generally used in the form of its prepared white powder, primarily in the manufacture of various types of glass, ceramics, and abrasives. It is also called *silicon dioxide.*

silicone A family of polymers containing alternate silicon and oxygen atoms as (Si-O-Si-O). They are used as adhesives, lubricants, and hydraulic oils and in electrical insulation. Silicones are very elastic, are highly chemical resistant, and make good insulation barriers between dissimilar metals. They are not as strong in adhesive strength as polysulfide or polyurethane but are compatible with plastics.

sodium chloride (NaCl) Common salt; a chemical compound containing equal numbers of positively charged sodium and negatively charged chlorine ions. When dissolved in water, the ions move about freely and conduct electricity. Salt makes up nearly 80 percent of the dissolved material in seawater.

sodium hydroxide (NaOH) A strong alkaline compound used in the manufacture of soaps and oven and drain cleaners; also called *caustic soda* and *lye.*

soft water Water that contains little or no dissolved salts of calcium or magnesium, especially water containing less than 85.5 parts per million of calcium carbonate.

spelter Zinc; the term is more commonly used in the Scandinavian countries.

spray-up A production technique in which a spray gun is used as the processing tool. In reinforced plastics, for example, fibrous glass and resin can be simultaneously sprayed into a mold. In essence, roving is fed through a chopper and injected into a resin stream that is directed at the mold by the spray system. In foamed plastics, very fast-reacting urethane foams or epoxy foams are fed in liquid streams to the gun and sprayed on the surface.

steel An alloy of iron and carbon with small quantities of other elements. Steelmaking involves the removal of iron's impurities and the addition of desirable alloying elements. Steel is often classified by its carbon content: *high-carbon steel* is hard and brittle; *low-* or *medium-carbon steel* can be welded and tooled. *Alloy steels,* the most widely used, contain one or more elements that give them special properties. *Aluminum steel* is smooth and has a high tensile strength. *Chromium steel* is used in automobile and airplane parts because of its hardness, strength, and elasticity. *Stainless steel* has a high tensile strength and resists abrasion and corrosion because of its high chromium content.

stray-current corrosion Corrosion that results when a current from a battery or other external electrical DC source causes a metal in contact with an electrolyte to become anodic with respect to another metal in contact with the same electrolyte.

stress-corrosion cracking (SCC) A corrosion-induced failure mode resulting from the simultaneous influence of static tensile stresses and a corrosive environment. The stresses may be internal, such as those caused by cold-work, welding, and heat treatment, or may be external forces caused by mechanical stresses set up by assembly practices.

sulfate-reducing bacteria (SRB) corrosion A form of anaerobic (oxygen-deficient) corrosion; the corrosive action of the sulfate-reducing bacteria in anaerobic environments. The shape and form of the attack is almost always localized and often looks much like pitting. Because anaerobic microenvironments can exist under barnacles, marine growth, crevices, and flaws in the coating system, anaerobic corrosion by SRB can take place in nominally aerated environments. Anaerobic corrosion of iron and steel has been encountered in waterlogged soils and bottom mud of rivers, lakes, marshes, and estuaries, especially when they contain decaying organic material.

superaustenitic alloys A relatively new group of alloys with approximately 6 percent or more molybdenum (Mo) content and having significantly improved resistance to chloride-pitting corrosion and stress-corrosion cracking. These alloys have very low carbon content and significant percentages of both nickel (Ni) and chromium (Cr). Some of these alloys have "S" type UNS designations, such as 254-SMO (UNS S31254) and 654-SMO (UNS S32654), and some have "N" type designations, such as AL-6XN (UNS N08367) and alloy 926 (UNS N08926).

surfacing mat A very thin mat, usually 7 to 20 mils thick, of highly filamentized fiberglass used primarily to produce a smooth surface on a reinforced plastic laminate.

tabernacle A hinged deck-mounted mast step that allows the raising and lowering of the mast; typically used on boats of less than 30 feet.

Tedlar A polyvinyl fluoride film (PVF); a family of films produced by DuPont and having excellent resistance to weathering, excellent electrical characteristics, low moisture absorption (less than 0.5 percent), excellent resistance to chemicals and solvents. It has been used on some Dacron sails as a UV protective film for the border of roller-furling sails. However, there have been reports that these applications have not been entirely successful, that the Tedlar tape has pulled away from the sail cloth due to UV embrittlement, leaving the sail unprotected. Better success is experienced on relatively light sails, weighing five ounces or less.

Tefgel A proprietary anticorrosion and antiseizing lubricant recommended for use on screw-type fastenings to prevent "freezing."

Teflon See *polytetrafluoroethylene (PTFE)*. Teflon is produced by DuPont.

tensile strength A measure of the load a material can sustain more or less indefinitely. This property can be changed radically by cold-work, heat treatment, or both, depending upon the nature of the material. It is expressed as psi.

Terylene A polyester fiber made from terephthalic acid and ethylene glycol. Terylene was first developed in 1941 in the United Kingdom, where it was marketed by the Imperial Chemical Industries under this trade name. The product is marketed in the United States by DuPont under the trade name Dacron.

thermal conductivity A measure of the capacity of a material to conduct or transfer heat. It is of importance primarily in heat exchanger design. Thermal conductivity is greater in pure metals than in their alloys.

thermal expansion Expressed as a decimal part of an inch per inch (or millimeter per millimeter) per unit of temperature. The practical significance of thermal expansion lies in the stresses caused by the difference in expansion between different components of equipment or between a substrate and its coating.

thermal spray coatings A group of coating or welding processes in which finely divided metallic or nonmetallic materials are deposited in a molten or semimolten condition to form a coating. The coating material may be in the form of powder, ceramic, rod, wire, or molten materials.

thermoplastic A plastic capable of being repeatedly softened by an increase of temperature and hardened by

a decrease in temperature. Thermoplastic polymers consist of long polymer chains that are not joined to each other (*cross-linked*). Polyethylene, polypropylene, polystyrene, polyester, polyvinyl chloride, acrylics, nylons, spandex-type polyurethanes, polyamides, polycarbonates, fluorocarbons, and cellulosics are common types of thermoplastics.

thermoset A plastic that can not be softened on heating. In a thermosetting plastic, the long polymer chains are joined to each other (*cross-linked*) during fabrication through the use of chemicals, heat, or radiation; this process is called *curing* or *vulcanization*. Alkyds, phenolics, ureas, melamines, epoxies, polyesters, silicones, rubbers, and polyurethanes are examples of thermoset plastics.

thixotropy The property of materials to be gel-like at rest but fluid when agitated; having high static shear strength and low dynamic shear strength at the same time.

Tobin bronze 60–40 brasses; also called the *naval brasses*. Their principal marine use is in hardware items such decorative fittings, turnbuckles, fastenings, and prop shafts.

toughness The ability to withstand impact; related in a general way to ductility.

Tufnol A thermoplastic. Tufnol and nylon are hygroscopic and swell when saturated with water.

tung oil A yellow or brownish oil extracted from the seeds of the tung tree and used as a drying agent in varnishes and paints and for waterproofing; also called *Chinawood oil*.

ultrahigh molecular weight polyethylene (UHMWPE) A specially formulated thermoplastic with zero water absorption, a very low coefficient of friction, and high compressive strength. It is an excellent material for bearing applications.

uniform corrosion See *general corrosion*.

ultimate tensile strength The ultimate or final stress sustained by a specimen in a tension test; the stress at the moment of rupture.

urine Waste matter that is 95 percent water, in which urea, uric acid, mineral salts, toxins, and other waste products are dissolved. It is highly corrosive to metals.

valence The combining capacity of an atom, represented by a positive or negative integer. Valence is determined by the number of electrons that the atom will lose, add, or share when it reacts with other atoms.

vented loop A U-shaped tube with a simple valve at the top that admits air, thus preventing the formation of a vacuum and the resulting siphon.

vinyl Chemical compounds containing the vinyl radical (CH_2CH), derived from ethylene and typically highly reactive, easily polymerized, and used as basic materials for plastics. Vinyls are tough, flexible plastics.

vinylester resin A thermosetting resin used in the construction of fiberglass boats to encapsulate and bind the fiberglass-reinforcing material. Other resins used for this purpose are polyester resin and epoxy resins; both are thermosetting resins. Vinylester resins have better mold release than the epoxies and are less expensive. Also, they do not present the health hazards associated with the epoxies. Vinylester resins have less water absorption and lower density than the polyesters but are somewhat more expensive.

viscosity   The resistance of a fluid to flow.

weight   A measure of the force of gravity on a body in pounds or grams. Unlike *mass*, the weight of a body depends on its location in the gravitational field of Earth or of some other astronomical body. Weight is a measure of the force with which a body is attracted to Earth. Weight is equal to the product of the body's mass and the acceleration due to gravity.

weld decay   More properly called *intergranular corrosion*; occurs as the result of *sensitization* in the heat-affected zone (HAZ), principally in stainless steels and certain nickel-base alloys during welding.

wildcat   The drum on an anchor windlass that takes the chain, as compared to the *gypsy*, which is the wheel that hauls the rope.

worming   Refers to a procedure with wire rope. After a splice has been made in wire rope, strands of spun yarn are laid in the grooves (*worming*), going with the lay of the wire rope. The splice is then spirally wrapped (*parceled*) with a strip of burlap or tarred canvas. After the worming and parceling have been completed, the entire splice is then *served* over the parceling with spun yarn or three-strand tarred nylon. Worming is done to facilitate handling and prevent water ingress.

wrought   Something that has been produced through the effort or activity of a person or a thing. It is essentially the same as *worked*, as in rolled, drawn, extruded, machined, forged, and so on.

yield strength   The stress at which a material exhibits a specified limiting deviation from the proportionality of stress to strain; the lowest strain at which a material undergoes plastic deformation. Below this stress, the material is elastic; above it, viscous.

Zamak   A zinc-aluminum alloy, consisting of 95 to 96 percent zinc, 3.5 to 4.3 percent aluminum, and trace amounts of copper, magnesium, and other metals. It has moderate strength and hardness and is an excellent, economical die-casting metal. Zamak fittings have a highly polished look when new but only a modest amount of corrosion resistance. They are only suitable for freshwater applications.

Bibliography

Ahrens, David. "Engine Advice: What Causes Pitting in Cylinder Liners?" *Marine Performance and Fisheries Products News* (spring 1998): 27.

Akashi, Massy. "Stress-Corrosion Cracking of Stainless Steels." *www.big.or.jp/massy/CorrFun/ssscc/intro.html* (1 March 1998).

Allenbach, Christian P. (*allenbach@surface.mat.ethz.ch*). Carbonitridation. *corros-l@listserv.rl.ac.uk* (21 Aug. 1997).

Ament, Peter. "Corrosion Fatigue of Structural Steel in Seawater." *http://dutsm.tudelft.nl/tmc/people/ament/project.html* (1999).

American Boat and Yacht Council. "Installation of Exhaust Systems For Propulsion and Auxiliary Engines." *Standards and Recommended Practices for Small Craft.* Edgewater MD: American Boat and Yacht Council, 1998, P-1.

American Boat and Yacht Council. *Standards and Recommended Practices for Small Craft.* E-9 Direct Current (DC) Electrical Systems on Boats, 1998; E-4 Lightning Protection, 1996. Edgewater MD: American Boat and Yacht Council, 1998.

American Bureau of Ships. *Rule Requirements for Materials and Welding 1996.* Part 2, *ABS Grade A Steel.* Houston: American Bureau of Ships (April 1997).

American Society for Testing and Materials. *Standard Specification for Carbon Structural Steel: Designation: A 36/ A 36M–96.* West Conshohocken PA: American Society for Testing and Materials, 1997.

Armco Advanced Materials. "Armco AQUAMET Boat Shafting," Product Data Bulletin no. S-26. Middletown OH: Armco Advanced Materials, 1985.

Armco Advanced Materials. *Development of the Stainless Steels.* Butler PA: Armco Advanced Materials, Dec. 1988.

ASM Handbook. vol. 13, *Corrosion,* by Lawrence J. Korb and David L. Olson. Materials Park OH: ASM International, 1987.

Asphahani, Aziz I., Juri Kolts, and Donald R. Muzyka. *Innovations in High Performance Alloys and Their Applications to the Offshore and Marine Industries.* Technical Information H-1059. Kokomo IN: Haynes International.

Baboian, Robert. "Corrosion of Clad Metals." In *ASM Handbook,* vol. 13, *Corrosion,* 887–90.

Benford, Harry. *Naval Architecture for Non-Naval Architects.* Jersey City NJ: Society of Naval Architects and Marine Engineers, 1991.

Biewenga, Bill. 1999. "It's the End of the Line." *Cruising World* (April 1999): 77.

Blevins, Steve. "Carbon Fiber Performance." Electronic bulletin board *www.tivanet.com* (1997). Available from *http:/home/prindle/messages/225.html.*

Booth, W. D. *Upgrading and Refurbishing the Older Fiberglass Boat.* Centerville MD: Cornell Maritime Press, 1985.

Brown, David G. "Don't Let Corrosion Steal Your Radio Voice." *Offshore* (March 1997): 75.

Brunswick Corporation. *Quicksilver: Everything You Need to Know about Marine Corrosion,* publication no. 90-809844-95. Fond du Lac WI: 1995.

Bryson, James H. "Corrosion of Carbon Steels." In *ASM Handbook,* vol. 13, *Corrosion,* 509–15.

Buchanan, George. *The Boat Repair Manual.* New York: Arco, 1985.

Buehler, George. 1991. "Thoughts on the Inexpensive Rig." *Boatbuilder* (July–Aug. 1991): 32.

Burkstrand, Beth. "Titanium Metals Boom Has the Company Flying High: As Aerospace Industry Gains, Timet Pursues More Down-to-Earth Lines." *Wall Street Journal* (20 Aug. 1997): B4.

Cadwalader, George. "A Cautionary Tale." *WoodenBoat,* no. 41 (July–Aug. 1981): 85.

Cadwalader, George. "A Cautionary Tale Continued." *WoodenBoat,* no. 70 (May–June 1986): 23.

"Cadmium Plating Alternatives." 1994. National Defense Center for Environmental Excellence. Technology Abstract. *www.ndcee.ctc.com/Core/ ab_cdplt.htm* (May 1998).

Calder, Nigel. *Boatowner's Mechanical and Electrical Manual: How to Maintain, Repair, and Improve Your Boat's Essential Systems.* 2nd ed. Camden ME: International Marine, 1996.

Calder, Nigel. "Building with Composites." *Ocean Navigator* (Jan.–Feb. 1996): 56–65.

Calder, Nigel. "Lightning and Composites." *Ocean Navigator* (Jan.–Feb. 1996): 73.

Calder, Nigel. *Marine Diesel Engines.* 2nd ed. Camden ME: International Marine, 1987.

Calder, Nigel. "Pressure Water." *Ocean Voyager Annual Handbook of Offshore Sailing.* Portland ME: Navigator Publishing, 1995, 49.

Calder, Nigel. *Repairs at Sea.* Camden ME: International Marine, 1988.

Calder, Nigel. "Repowering With a Diesel, Part II." *WoodenBoat* (Sept.–Oct. 1991): 92.

303

Calder, Nigel. "Wiring Plans: Tools and Techniques for Ensuring a Reliable Electrical System." *Ocean Navigator* (Nov.–Dec. 1995): 83.

Callahan, Steve. "STAR Systems." *Cruising World* (Feb. 1997): 44.

Carbon and (Low-) Alloy Steels. http://www. METALogic.be/reading/material/m_fe.htm (27 April 1997).

Carbon and Low-alloy Steels: Corrosion Hazards Overview. http://www.METALogic.be/reading/matcor/fe_ccc.htm (27 April 1997).

Carr, Michael. "Strong Direction: Composite Rudders Are Tough, Light and Designed for Performance." *Ocean Navigator* (Jan.–Feb. 1996): 73–75.

"Casting Magnesium." Newsgroup *rec.crafts.metalworking* (March 1998).

Champ, Jim. "Building Carbon Masts." Sailing Source. *www.sailingsource.com/cherub/masts.html* (16 April 1998).

Chapelle, Howard. 1941. *Boatbuilding.* New York: W. W. Norton, 1941.

Charp, P. "Depleted Uranium." Newsgroup *sci.environment* (July 1997).

Chen, Der-Tau. "Corrosion by Alternating Current." *Proceedings of the 9th Annual Congress on Metallic Corrosion.* Toronto, 1984.

Clemans, John. "Plumb-It-Yourself." *Motor Boating and Sailing* (March 1999): 97.

Code of Federal Regulations, Title 33, Vol. 2, Part 183, Section 425 Conductors, General; Section 430, Conductors in Circuits of Less Than 50 Volts; Section 435, Conductors in Circuits of 50 Volts or More (July 1999).

Colvin, Thomas E. *Steel Boat Building: From Plans to Bare Hull* (vol. 1). Camden ME: International Marine.

Colvin, Thomas E. *Steel Boat Building: From Bare Hull to Launching* (vol. 2). Camden ME: International Marine, 1986.

Committee of Stainless Steel Products. Review of the Wear and Galling Characteristics of Stainless Steels. Washington DC: American Iron and Steel Institute, 1978.

Crum, J. R. "Major Applications and Corrosion Performance of Nickel Alloys." In *ASM Handbook,* vol. 13, *Corrosion,* 653–56.

D'Antonio, Steve. "Your Marine Exhaust System." *Cruising World* (May 1998): 89.

Davison, Ralph M., and James D. Redmond. *Practical Guide to Using 6Mo Austenitic Stainless Steel.* NiDI Technical Series no. 10 032. Toronto: Nickel Development Institute. Reprinted from *Materials Performance* (Dec. 1988).

Davison, Ralph M., and James D. Redmond. *Practical Guide to Duplex Stainless Steel.* Technical Series no. 10 044. Toronto: Nickel Development Institute, 1990.

Davison, Ralph M., Terry DeBold, and Mark J. Johnson. "Corrosion of Stainless Steels." In *ASM Handbook,* vol. 13, *Corrosion,* 547–65.

Dawson, Ian Peter. "Carbon Fiber Tillers." Newsgroup *www.laser.org* (1998). Available from */archives/1995/msg00923.html.*

Dexter, Stephen. "Localized Biological Corrosion." *ASM Handbook,* vol. 13, *Corrosion:* 117–18.

Dillon, C. P. *Corrosion Control in the Chemical Process Industries.* 2nd ed. MTI Publication no. 45. St. Louis: Materials Technology Institute of the Chemical Process Industries, NACE International, 1994.

Dillon, C. P. "Corrosion of Aluminum in Water." *corros-l @listserv.rl.ac.uk* (19 Sept. 1997).

Dillon, C. P. 1990. "Imponderables in Chloride Stress Corrosion Cracking of Stainless Steels." *Materials Performance* (Dec. 1990): 66–67.

Dillon, Paul. "Potable Water Carrier." Newsgroup *nace@ nacecorrosionnetwork.com* (1 May 1998).

DuraPlane Marine Systems. "DuraPlane Trim Tabs." *http://proto.yachtworld.com.* (March 1998). Available from */pmy_online/jun97/hotp/gear/trimtabs.htm.*

"Electroplating: Barrier Coatings." *http://206.65.86.232/ plating.htm* (April 1998).

Elliott, Peter. "Design Details to Minimize Corrosion." In *ASM Handbook,* vol. 13, *Corrosion,* 338–43.

Experience Survey: Stress-Corrosion Cracking of Austenitic Stainless Steels in Water. 1987. MTI Publication no. 27. Houston TX: Materials Technology Institute of the Chemical Processing Industries.

Fales, Dan. "Tips from a Pro: Zinc or Swim." *Motor Boating and Sailing* (May 1997).

"Flair-It Online Catalog." *http://www.falir-it.com/pex* (Feb. 1999).

Fraser, Dave. 1997. "Marine Metals: Depleted Uranium." Newsgroup *sci. Materials* (March 1998).

Froats, Alan, and William Unsworth. 1987. "Corrosion of Magnesium and Magnesium Alloys." In *ASM Handbook,* vol. 13, *Corrosion,* 740–54.

"Galvanizing Process." MetalPlate. *http://www. metalplate.com/galvanizing/TIS1.htm* (May 1998).

Gedge, Graham. "Titanium as a Roof Material." Newsgroup *corros-l@listserv.rl.ac.uk* (1997).

Gerr, Dave. *The Elements of Boat Strength: For Builders, Designers, and Owners.* Camden ME: International Marine, 2000.

Gerr, Dave. "Exhaust Installations for Powerboats." *Boatbuilder* (Sept.–Oct. 1993): 6.

Gerr, Dave. "Galvanic Corrosion," *National Fisherman* (July 1991): 49.

Gerr, Dave. "Galvanic Corrosion: Part Two," *National Fisherman* (Aug. 1991): 57.

Gerr, Dave. *The Nature of Boats: Insights and Esoterica for the Nautically Obsessed.* Camden ME: International Marine, 1995.

Gerr, Dave. "Serious Hardware." *Offshore Magazine* (Aug. 1995): 35–43.

Getchell, David, R. *Outboard Boater's Handbook: Advanced Seamanship and Practical Skills.* Camden ME: International Marine, 1994.

Gladstone, Bernard. "Boatkeeper's Guide to Ropes and Lines." *Motor Boating and Sailing* (July 1991).

Glover, Thomas J. *Pocket Ref.* 2nd ed. Littleton CO: Sequoia Publishing, 1996.

Gnanamoorthy, J. B. "Stress Corrosion Cracking of Unsensitized Stainless Steels in Ambient-Temperature Coastal Atmosphere." *Materials Performance* (Dec. 1990): 63–65.

Goodchild, David. "Water Tanks." Newsgroup *rec.boats.building* (30 June 1998).

Gougeon, Meade. "Golden Dazy: Revolution in Wood." *WoodenBoat*, no. 16 (May–June 1997): 33.

Green, Robert E. *Machinery's Handbook*. 25th ed. New York: Industrial Press, 1996.

Guttenplan, Jack D. "Corrosion in the Electronics Industry." In *ASM Handbook*, vol. 13, *Corrosion*, 1107–13.

Hall, Peggie. "Fresh Water Maintenance." Newsgroup *rec.boats.cruising* (29 May 1998).

Hall, Peggie. Personal e-mail correspondence on toilet systems. (7 March 1999).

Hall, Spars. "Carbon Fiber Is . . ." *http://www.hallspars.com/carbon.html* (May 1999).

Harris, Jerry A. "Failure of Electronic Boards." Newsgroup *corros-l@listserv.rl.ac.uk* (17 Oct. 1997).

Haynes International. "Corrosion Resistant Hastelloy Alloy at a Glance: Hastelloy C-2000." Preliminary data sheet no. H-2105. Kokomo IN: Haynes International, 1995.

Haynes International. "Hastelloy Alloy C-4." Product brochure no. H-20007. Kokomo IN: Haynes International, 1988.

Haynes International. "Hastelloy C-22 Alloy." Product brochure no. H-20190. Kokomo IN: Haynes International, 1996.

Haynes International. "Haynes International." Product brochure no. H-1064E. Kokomo IN: Haynes International, 1993.

Heidersbach, Robert H. "Cathodic Protection." In *ASM Handbook,* vol. 13, *Corrosion*, 466–77.

Hollingsworth, E. H., and H. Y. Hunsicker. "Corrosion of Aluminum and Aluminum Alloys." In *ASM Handbook*, vol. 13, *Corrosion*, 583–609.

Holman, Betsy. "Check Your Rig." *Cruising World* (April 1989): 121.

Holtz, Chris. "Castlok Rigging Terminals." Newsgroup *rec.boats.building* (22 Sept. 1995).

Hugger, Ted. "Warp Speed: Sailing ADRENALIN on the Edge." *WoodenBoat*, no. 87 (March–April 1989): 67–79.

"Index of /Mat Web/reading/material/," *Iron and Steels: Corrosion Hazards Overview. http://www.METALogic.be/reading/mat-cor/fi_ccc.htm* (27 April 1997).

"Index of /Mat Web/reading/material/," *Iron and Steels in the Atmosphere: Materials Performance. http://www.METALogic.be/reading/air/fiatm.htm* (27 April 1997).

"Index of /Mat Web/reading/material/," *Plain Carbon Steels. http://www.METALogic.be/reading/material/m_f_carb.htm* (27 April 1997).

"Index of /Mat Web/reading/material/," *Steel: Performance in Various Corrosives. www.METALogic.be/reading/mat-envs/feeee.htm* (Sept. 1997).

InterCorr International. "Corrosion Resistant Alloys and the Influence of Alloy Elements: Aluminum and Aluminum Alloys." *www.clihouston.com/intercorr/asm/asm2.htm* (29 Jan. 1997).

InterCorr International. "Materials and Corrosion Information Resource." *www.intercorr.com/* (May 1997).

International Nickel. *Corrosion Resistance of the Austenitic Chromium-Nickel Stainless Steels in Atmospheric Environments.* Suffern NY: (April 1970).

International Nickel. *Fabrication of Chromium-Nickel Stainless Steel 300 Series.* Suffern NY: International Nickel (Sept. 1983).

International Nickel. *Standard Wrought Austenitic Stainless Steels, Manual 252.* Suffern NY: International Nickel (April 1975)

JCM Co. "BNC Connectors." Product literature. Johnson Components, Waseca MN 56093.

Johnson, Jim. "Potable Water Carrier." Newsgroup *nace@nacecorrosionnetwork.com* (7 May 1998).

Johnson, Steve. "Know Your Engine Lubricants." *Boat and Motor Dealer* (May 1998): 38.

Jones, Allen R. "Corrosion of Electroplated Hard Chromium." In *ASM Handbook*, vol. 13, *Corrosion*, 871–75.

Jones, R. H. "Stress-Corrosion Cracking." In *ASM Handbook*, vol. 13, *Corrosion*, 145–62.

Joseph, George. "Metals: Aluminum." *http://ugweb.cs.ualberta.ca/~gjoseph/alum.html* (17 Dec. 1997).

Kain, Robert M. "Marine Atmospheric Stress Corrosion Cracking of Austenitic Stainless Steels." *Materials Performance* (Dec. 1990): 60–62.

Kasten, Michael. "To Thine Own Chines Be True." *Cruising World* (Sept. 1997).

Kelly, Robert G. "Pitting." Chapter 18 in *InterCorr: Materials and Corrosion Resources*. Newsgroup *nace@nacecorrosionnetwork.com* (Oct. 1997).

Kennedy, Howard. "Potable Water Carrier." Newsgroup *nace@nacecorrosionnetwork.com* (1 May 1998).

Kirschenbaum, Jerry. "Electrolysis and Corrosion: Part 1." *WoodenBoat*, no. 23 (July–Aug. 1978): 30.

Kirschenbaum, Jerry, "Electrolysis and Corrosion: Part 2." *WoodenBoat*, no. 24 (Sept.–Oct. 1978): 78.

Kiser, Samuel Dwight. "Fabrication and Weldability of Nickel Alloys." In *ASM Handbook*, vol. 13, *Corrosion*, 652–53.

Klarstrom, D. L. "Characteristics of Nickel and Nickel-Base Alloys." In *ASM Handbook*, vol. 13, *Corrosion*, 641–43.

Klingel, Gilbert C. *Boatbuilding with Steel*. Camden ME: International Marine, 1973.

Klopman, Jonathan. "Depleted Uranium." Newsgroup *rec.boats.building* (March 1998).

Klopman, Jonathan. "Stainless Steel." *Professional Boatbuilder* (Aug.–Sept. 1998): 70.

Kocher, Robert L. "Another Vessel Can Eat the Hide Off Your Pride and Joy." *National Fisherman* (Feb. 1979): 78.

Kocher, Robert L. "Corrosion Process Shows Why Bonded Fittings Are a Bad Idea." *National Fisherman* (Sept. 1979): 80.

Kocher, Robert L. "A Look at Metal's Atomic Structure Sheds Light on Galvanic Corrosion." *National Fisherman* (Aug. 1979): 78.

Kocher, Robert L. "Stainless Will Corrode—As Will Most Metals." *National Fisherman* (Oct. 1978).

Kolts, Juri. "Environmental Embrittlement of Nickel-Base Alloys." In *ASM Handbook* vol. 13, *Corrosion*, 647–52.

Krause, Harry. "Zinc Hardware?" Newsgroup *rec.boats* (Aug. 1997).

Lawrence, Anne. 1984. "Shearwater." *WoodenBoat*, no. 59 (July–Aug. 1984):48-54.

Lawson, H. H. "Protection of Steel from Corrosion." In *ASM Handbook*, vol. 13, *Corrosion*, 521–30.

Leeco Steel Products. "Steel Plate and Sheet Categories." *www.leecosteel.com/products/category.htm* (30 March 1997).

Leidheiser, Henry, Jr. "Fundamentals of Corrosion Protection in Aqueous Solutions." In *ASM Handbook*, vol. 13, *Corrosion*, 377–79.

Lemoi, Warren. "Tungsten vs. Depleted Uranium." Newsgroup *rec.crafts.metalworking* (March 1998).

Lenard, Derek. "Denickelification of Cu-Ni." *corros-l @listserv.rl.ac.uk* (Dec. 1997).

Lewmar Marine. "Owner's Service Manual. Concept/Ocean/Capstan 1, 2, and 3 Windlass Range." Guilford CT: Lewmar Marine (Aug. 1998).

Lewmar Marine. "Owner's Service Manual." Vol. 8, "Winches." Issue no. 2. Guilford CT: Lewmar Marine, 1998.

Lewmar Winch Service Seminar. Annapolis MD (25 March 1999).

Lisk, Ian. "Corrosion and Cathodic Protection in Underground Piping Systems." *http://www.wateronline.com* (June 1997). Available from */times/features-articles*.

Lubenow, Andy. "Marine Metals." Newsgroup *rec.boats.building* (July 1997).

Manzolillo, J. L., E. W. Thiele, and A. H. Tuthill. "CA-706 Copper-Nickel Hulls: The *Copper Mariner*'s Experience and Economics." Paper presented at the annual meeting of the Society of Naval Architects and Marine Engineers, New York (11–13 Nov. 1976).

Marsden, George. "Marine Metals." Newsgroup *rec.boats.building* (1997).

Massimo, Cornago. Newsgroup *nace@nacecorrosionnetwork.com* (5 July 1998).

Maté, Ferenc. *From a Bare Hull*. Rev. ed. New York: Albatross, 1998.

Maykuth, Daniel, and William B. Hampshire. "Corrosion of Tin and Tin Alloys." In *ASM Handbook*, vol. 13, *Corrosion*, 770–83.

Mazia, Joseph, and David S. Lashmore. "Electroplated Coatings." In *ASM Handbook*, vol. 13, *Corrosion*, 419–31.

McClave, Ed. "Corrosion-Related Problems," *WoodenBoat*, no. 93 (March–April 1990): 94.

McClave, Ed. *Understanding Marine Corrosion*. Noank CT: McClave Marine.

Miles, Charles. "Titanium as a Roof Material." Newsgroup *corros-l@listserv.rl.ac.uk* (March 1998).

Money, K. L. "Stress-Corrosion Cracking Behavior of Wrought Fe-Cr-Ni Alloys in Marine Atmospheres." *Materials Performance*. Houston: National Association of Corrosion Engineers, 1978.

Montemarano, Jean A., and Barbara A. Shaw. "Metallic Coatings." In *ASM Handbook*, vol. 13, *Corrosion*, 906.

Mooney, Ted. "Protective Coatings." Surface discussion group. Newsgroup *sci.chem* (May 1997).

Naranjo, Ralph. "Between the Deck and a Wet Place." *Cruising World* (July 1998): 69.

Nautical Engineering. "Super Strong Anchor." *Motor Boating and Sailing* (March 1997): 147.

Neale, Tom. "Windlasses: The Gut Issues." *Cruising World* (April 1997): 43.

Nevison, Dale C. H. "Corrosion of Zinc." In *ASM Handbook*, vol. 13, *Corrosion*, 755–69.

Nicholson, Ian. *Surveying Small Craft*. Camden ME: International Marine, 1974.

"Nickel and Nickel Alloys." In Metalogic. *http://www.clihouston.com/intercorr/asm/asm2.htm* (Jan. 1998).

Nickel Development Institute. *Copper-Nickel Alloys: Properties and Applications*. TN30. Toronto: Nickel Development Institute, 1974.

Nickel Development Institute. *Corrosion Resistance of the Austenitic Chromium-Nickel Stainless Steels in Chemical Environments*. Publication no. 2828. Toronto: 1997.

Nickel Development Institute. *Mechanical and Physical Properties of Austenitic Chromium-Nickel Stainless Steels at Ambient Temperatures*. Publication no. 2978. Toronto: Nickel Development Institute, 1963.

Nickel Development Institute. *Resistance of Stainless Steel to Corrosion in Naturally Occurring Waters*. Publication no. 1262. Toronto: Nickel Development Institute.

Noah, Michael. U.S. Navy, COMFLEACT Yokosuka, Japan. "Subsurface Anchor Chain Corrosion." Newsgroup *marine-l@cgc.ns.ca* (24 July 1996).

"Non-Ferrous Alloys: Nickel and Nickel Alloys." In *Machinery's Handbook*, 25th ed., ed. Robert E. Green, 575–77.

Oldfield, John W., and Brian Todd. "Ambient-Temperature Stress Corrosion Cracking of Austenitic Stainless Steel in Swimming Pools." *Materials Performance* (Dec. 1990): 57–58.

Parker, Reuel. "Interior Furnishings and Fitting Out, Part I." *Boatbuilding* (May–June 1990): 30.

Paulis, Bob. Newsgroup *nace@nacecorrosionnetwork. com* (22 Nov. 1997).

Performance Yacht Systems. "Navtec Norseman Gibb: Nitronic 50 Solid Rod Rigging and Accessories." Product literature. Annapolis MD: Performance Yacht Systems, March 1998.

Peters, D. T. *A Review of Copper-Nickel Alloy Sheathing of Ship Hulls and Offshore Structures.* New York: Copper Development Association, 1991.

Phull, Bopinder S. LaQue Corrosion Institute. "AC versus DC Stray Current." Newsgroup *nace@ nacecorrosionnetwork.com* (2 Jan. 1998).

Pierson, Hugh O. "4987: CVD/PVD Coatings." In *ASM Handbook,* vol. 13, *Corrosion,* 456–58.

Pilling, John. "Carbon Fibers, Carbon-Polymer Composites and Carbon-Carbon Composites." *www.vii. com* (1998). Available from */~comp-sol/Carbon %20Fibers%20Composites.htm.*

Plumbing Express, Phoenix Construction. "What Is Polybutylene?" *http://www.plumbing911.com/poly/poly. html* (May 1998).

Pohlman, Steven L. "Stray-Current Corrosion." In *ASM Handbook,* vol. 13, *Corrosion,* 87.

Polan, Ned W. "Corrosion of Copper and Copper Alloys." In *ASM Handbook,* vol. 13, *Corrosion,* 610–41.

Pullizzi, Tom. Newsgroup *www.uk.finishing.org.uk/IMF/ BOOKS/html* (June 1998).

Putz, George, "Forging." *The Mariner's Catalog.* Vol. 1. Camden ME: National Fisherman and International Marine, 74.

Reiser, David B. (*reiserdb@ttown.apci.com*) "Corrosion of Aluminum in Water." *corros-l@listserv.rl.ac.uk* (19 Sept. 1997).

Remsen, Richard T. "Casting Bronze." *WoodenBoat,* no. 130 (May–June 1996): 80–87.

Roderiguez, Rafael. "Potable Water Carrier." Newsgroup *nace@nacecorrosionnetwork.com* (2 May 1998).

Ross, Ralph W., et al. *Practical Guide to Using Marine Fasteners.* NiDI Technical Series no. 10 045. Toronto: Nickel Development Institute, 1990. Reprinted from *Materials Performance* (April 1990).

Schaffer, Dennis. "The Design and Construction of Steel Masts." *Boatbuilder* (Sept.–Oct. 1993): 22.

Schutz, Ronald W., and David E. Thomas. "Corrosion of Titanium and Titanium Alloys." In *ASM Handbook,* vol. 13, *Corrosion,* 740–54.

Shaw, Peter. "Carbon Fiber Masts." *Sail* (July 1994): 81.

Slater, John E. "Corrosion in Structures." In *ASM Handbook,* vol. 13, *Corrosion,* 1,299–310.

Smith, Jerome F. "Corrosion of Lead and Lead Alloys." In *ASM Handbook,* vol. 13, *Corrosion,* 784–92.

Smith, L. M. *Engineering with Clad Steel.* NiDI Technical Series no. 10 064. Toronto: Nickel Development Institute, 1992. Originally presented at the Offshore Technology Conference, Houston (4–7 May 1992).

South Atlantic Galvanizing. "Mechanical Galvanizing." *http://www.galvanizers.com/mechanical.htm* (May 1997).

Spartite. "Spartite." Product literature. *www.spartite. com* (April 1999).

Sridhar, Narasi. "Behavior of Nickel-Base Alloys in Corrosive Environments." In *ASM Handbook,* vol. 13, *Corrosion,* 643–47.

Stavros, A. J. "Continuous Hot-Dip Coatings." In *ASM Handbook,* vol. 13, *Corrosion,* 423–36.

Stephenson, N. *Welding Status of Duplex Stainless Steels for Offshore Applications.* NiDI Technical Series No. 10 014. Toronto: Nickel Development Institute. Reprinted from *Welding and Metal Fabrication Journal 55* (May–June and July–Aug. 1987): 55, nos. 4 and 5.

Steward, Robert M. *Boatbuilding Manual.* Camden ME: International Marine, 1994.

Sweet, Beryl. "Corrosion Data on Aluminized Steel." Personal e-mail correspondence (17 May 1998).

Swenson, Erik. "Wet and Wired: How You Can Revive Drenched Electronic Equipment—And Would You Even Want To?" *National Fisherman* (July 1997): 40.

Todd, B. *Nickel-Containing Materials in Marine and Related Environments.* NiDI Technical Series no. 10 011. Toronto: Nickel Development Institute, 1986. Reprinted from *Proceedings, Nickel Metallurgy,* vol. 2, *Industrial Applications of Nickel,* a symposium sponsored by the Metallurgical Society of the Canadian Institute of Mining and Metallurgy and the Nickel Development Institute (17–20 Aug. 1986).

Toghill, Jeff. *The Boat Owner's Maintenance Manual.* Clifton Corners NY: John De Graff, 1979.

Toss, Brion. "A Guide to Block Selection." *WoodenBoat* (July–Aug. 1988): 93.

Truesdel, Scott. "Marine Metals." Newsgroup *rec. boats.building* (July 1998).

Tudor, Carl, and Robert Rick. "Metalizing: Current State of Art." Paper presented at the Shipbuilding Conference, Tyson's Corner VA, 1997.

Tuthill, Arthur H. *Fabrication and Post-Fabrication Cleanup of Stainless Steels.* NiDI Technical Series no. 10 004. Toronto: Nickel Development Institute (Nov. 1989).

Tuthill, Arthur H. "Guidelines for the Use of Copper Alloys in Seawater." *Materials Performance* 26, no. 9 (Sept. 1987): 12–22.

Tuthill, Arthur H. *The Right Metal for Heat Exchanger Tubes.* NiDI Technical Series no. 10 040. Toronto: Nickel Development Institute (1990). Reprinted from *Chemical Engineering* 97, no. 1 (Jan. 1990).

USCG Marine Safety Office, Portland, ME. "Safety Alert:

Pyrophoric Carbon Build-up Dangerous." *Maine Coastal News* (1–15 May 1997): 6.

Vanguard Metal Technologies. "New Zinc-Nickel Alloy Plating Process." 1988. *http://forsee.com/vanguard/plating/htm*.

Vanguard Piping Systems. "CRIMPSERT Insert Fittings and Crimp Rings for Vanex PLUS+SDR9 Cross-Linked Polyethylene (PEX)." *http://www.vanguardpipe.com/fittings.html* (Feb. 1999).

Verney, Michael. *Boat Repairs and Conversions.* Camden ME: International Marine, 1977.

Vitelec Electronics. "Coaxial Connectors." Product literature. Hampshire England.

Walker, Matthew. "Black Magic: Carbon Fiber Comes to Wooden Boats." *WoodenBoat* (Nov.–Dec. 1978): 76.

Warren, Nigel. *Metal Corrosion in Boats.* Camden ME: International Marine, 1980.

Watson, S. A. *Why Zinc-Nickel Coated Steels?* NiDI Reprint Series no. 14 002. Toronto: Nickel Development Institute, 1988. Reprinted from its magazine, *Nickel,* vol. 4, 1988.

Weaver, Rob. "Marine Metals." Newsgroup *rec.boats.building* (July 1997).

West, Gordon. "Electronics Know-How: Ask *Sail.*" *Sail* (March 1997): 57.

West, Gordon. 1998. "Your Electronics Quandaries." *Sail* (June 1998).

Whale Marine Products. "Semi-Rigid Pipework Systems." *http://www.whale-usa.com/marpro/tubes.htm* (March 1998).

Wichard. "Marine Hardware." *http://www.wichard.com* (March 1998). Available from */eng.htm*.

Willman, Vic (Raritan Engineering). Personal communications (March 1999).

Wilner, Eric. "High Mass Density Materials Thoughts." Newsgroup *rec.crafts.metalworking* (June 1997).

Wing, Charlie. *Boatowner's Illustrated Handbook of Wiring.* Camden ME: International Marine, 1993.

Wood, R. A. "The Titanium Industry in the Mid-1970s." Report MCIG-75-26, Columbus OH: Battelle Memorial Laboratories, 1975. *http://www.ul.cx.cmu.edu* (March 1998). Available from */books/titanium/titan119.htm*.

Wood, Tom. "Spring Rig Rundown." *Sail* (April 1999): 28.

Zadig, Ernest A. *The Complete Book of Pleasure Boat Engines.* Englewood Cliffs NJ: Prentice-Hall, 1980.

Zaki, Nabil. "Zinc-Alloy Plating." *http://www.gumm-chem.com/zna-art.htm* (1997).

Index